McGraw-Hill Education

1715 ACT
Practice Questions

Anaxos, Inc.

New York   Chicago   San Francisco   Athens   London   Madrid
Mexico City   Milan   New Delhi   Singapore   Sydney   Toronto

1 2 3 4 5 6 7 8 9 10   QVS/QVS   1 2 0 9 8 7 6 5 4

ISBN 978-0-07-183505-3
MHID 0-07-183505-9

e-ISBN 978-0-07-183506-0
e-MHID 0-07-183506-7

Library of Congress Control Number: 2014935813

McGraw-Hill Education products are available at special quantity discounts to use as premiums and sales promotions or for use in corporate training programs. To contact a representative, please visit the Contact Us pages at www.mhprofessional.com.

ACT is a registered trademark of ACT, Inc., which was not involved in the production of, and does not endorse, this product.

CONTENTS

INTRODUCTION

Congratulations! You've taken a big step toward ACT success by purchasing *McGraw-Hill Education: 1,715 ACT Practice Questions*. We are here to help you take the next step and score high on your ACT exam so you can get into the college or university of your choice!

This book gives you 1,500 ACT-style multiple-choice math, reading and writing, and science questions that cover all the most essential ACT material. In addition, 215 ACT-style questions in Part V are set as a full-length practice exam so you can test your knowledge of the material in a traditional ACT format.

Each answer is clearly explained in the Answer Key. The questions will give you valuable independent practice to supplement your regular textbooks and the ground you have already covered in your related school classes.

This book was written by expert teachers who know the ACT inside and out and can identify crucial information as well as the kinds of questions that are most likely to appear on the exam.

You might be the kind of student who needs to study extra a few weeks before the exam for a final review. Or you might be the kind of student who puts off preparing until the last minute before the exam. No matter what your preparation style, you will benefit from reviewing these 1,715 questions, which closely parallel the content, format, and degree of difficulty of the questions on the actual ACT exam.

If you practice with all the questions and answers in this book, we are certain you will build the skills and confidence needed to excel on the ACT. Good luck!

—*The Editors of McGraw-Hill Education*

PART I

MATH

CHAPTER 1
NUMBERS

QUESTIONS 1–71

1. What is the greatest common factor of 30, 90, and 130?
   - A. 2
   - B. 3
   - C. 5
   - D. 10
   - E. 30

2. Which of the following is an irrational number?
   - A. $\sqrt{\dfrac{100}{169}}$
   - B. $\sqrt{\dfrac{1}{4}}$
   - C. $\sqrt{16}$
   - D. $\sqrt{81}$
   - E. $\sqrt{99}$

3. Which of the following must be true whenever a, b, and c are integers such that $a < 0$ and $b > c > 0$?
   - A. $a - c > 0$
   - B. $c - b < 0$
   - C. $a + c > 0$
   - D. $-a - c < 0$
   - E. $a + b > 0$

4. If $3^0 = (1 - n)^{-3}$, then $n =$
   - A. -3
   - B. -1
   - C. 0
   - D. 1
   - E. 2

5. What is the largest integer smaller than $\sqrt{50}$?
   - A. 4
   - B. 6
   - C. 7
   - D. 9
   - E. 12

6. If m and n are integers, which of the following must be an even integer?
   - A. $2mn$
   - B. mn
   - C. $mn + 2$
   - D. $mn - 2$
   - E. $3mn$

7. If the equation $|x - a| = |y - a|$ is true, then which of the following must be true?
   - A. $|x| = |y|$
   - B. $x > a$
   - C. $|x + y| \neq 0$
   - D. $y < a$
   - E. $|-a + y| = |-a + x|$

8. If P is the set of multiples of 2, Q is the set of multiples of 3, and R is the set of multiples of 7, which of the following integers will be in P and Q but not in R?
   - A. -54
   - B. -50
   - C. 42
   - D. 100
   - E. 252

9. $1 + \sqrt{-(-5)^2} =$
   - A. -4
   - B. 6
   - C. 26
   - D. $1 + 5i$
   - E. $1 + 25i$

10. If $\left(2^{-\frac{1}{2}}\right)^{4y} = \dfrac{1}{8}$, then $y =$
    - A. -4
    - B. $-\dfrac{1}{8}$
    - C. $\dfrac{7}{8}$
    - D. $\dfrac{3}{2}$
    - E. $\dfrac{21}{16}$

11. Which of the following numbers is an imaginary number?
    - A. -3^2
    - B. $(-5)^2$
    - C. $\sqrt{5}$
    - D. $\sqrt{-49}$
    - E. $-\sqrt{36}$

12. Using the following number line, which pairs of points satisfy the equation $|x - y| < \frac{1}{2}$?

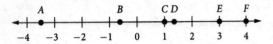

A. $x = A, y = B$

B. $x = B, y = C$

C. $x = C, y = D$

D. $x = D, y = E$

E. $x = E, y = F$

13. If $m^{-3} = 64$, then $8m =$

A. -192

B. -24

C. $\frac{1}{4}$

D. 2

E. 32

14. If $3(m + n)$ is even, then which of the following must also be even?

A. $m + n$

B. m

C. n

D. $3m$

E. $3n + 1$

15. A number is a multiple of both 4 and 9. Which of the following is NOT a possible value of the number?

A. -540

B. -324

C. 126

D. 144

E. 360

16. There are 45 students signed up for the performance band, while 30 are signed up for the jazz band. If 19 students are signed up for both bands, how many students are signed up for only one of the bands?

A. 11

B. 16

C. 37

D. 56

E. 75

17. Define $a \odot b = 2a - 3b$ for all integers a and b. What is the value of $-2 \odot 1$?

A. -7

B. -4

C. -1

D. 1

E. 8

18. Which of the following inequalities represents the same set as the set graphed on the number line shown?

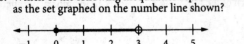

A. $0 < x < 3$

B. $0 \leq x \leq 3$

C. $-1 < x < 5$

D. $-1 \leq x < 3$

E. $0 \leq x < 3$

19. If the following numbers were ordered from smallest to largest, which would be in the third position?

$$\left(\frac{1}{2}\right)^{-2}, \frac{1}{3}, \sqrt{17}, \pi, \sqrt{3}$$

A. $\left(\frac{1}{2}\right)^{-2}$

B. $\frac{1}{3}$

C. $\sqrt{17}$

D. π

E. $\sqrt{3}$

20. If p and q are real numbers such that $(pq)^2 = 4$, then which of the following statements must also be true?

A. $pq > 0$

B. $pq = 2$

C. $p > 1$ and $q > 1$

D. If $p < 0$, then $q > 0$

E. If $p > 2$, then $q < 2$

21. For a real number m, $(2m^3)^4 =$

A. $2m^7$

B. $2m^{12}$

C. $8m^7$

D. $16m^7$

E. $16m^{12}$

22. What is the value of $|-2x - 5| - |-4 + 8|$ when $x = 7$?

A. -12

B. -4

C. 7

D. 15

E. 23

23. For positive integers x and y, $x + y = 21$. What is the smallest possible value of xy?

A. 10

B. 20

C. 38

D. 54

E. 110

Use the following table to answer questions 24 and 25. It shows the class level of the 500 students at Greenville High School.

Class	Number of Students
Freshmen	125
Sophomores	80
Juniors	175
Seniors	120

24. What percentage of students at Greenville High School are seniors?
    A. 12%
    B. 14%
    C. 24%
    D. 40%
    E. 75%

25. If the fraction of students who are freshmen is represented using a circle graph (pie chart), what should be the measure (in degrees) of the central angle of that portion of the graph?
    A. 12
    B. 25
    C. 40
    D. 65
    E. 90

26. For any real numbers a and b, $(10a^2)(5ab)(2ab^4)$ is equivalent to
    A. $100a^4b^5$
    B. $100a^2b^4$
    C. $17a^4b^5$
    D. $17a^2b^4$
    E. $17a^9b^9$

27. Let $x \triangle y = \dfrac{x+1}{y}$ for positive integers x and y. What is the value of $7\triangle(-2)$?
    A. -4
    B. -1
    C. 3
    D. 8
    E. 14

28. For a real number x, the expression $\dfrac{\sqrt{x}}{5}$ is an integer. Each of the following expressions must also be integers EXCEPT
    A. $\left(\dfrac{\sqrt{x}}{5}\right)^2$
    B. $10\sqrt{x}$
    C. $\dfrac{\sqrt{x}}{25}$
    D. $\dfrac{6\sqrt{x}}{5}$
    E. $-\sqrt{x}$

29. The following chart represents the final course grades for students in two math classes. What fraction of students in the courses received a final course grade of A or B?

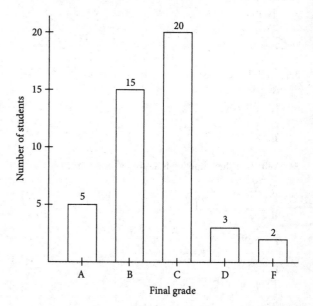

A. $\dfrac{1}{9}$

B. $\dfrac{2}{9}$

C. $\dfrac{3}{9}$

D. $\dfrac{4}{9}$

E. $\dfrac{5}{9}$

30. What is the value of $\sqrt{48} - \sqrt{27}$?
    A. 0
    B. $\sqrt{2}$
    C. $\sqrt{3}$
    D. $\sqrt{11}$
    E. $\sqrt{21}$

31. Which of the following is equivalent to i^2, where i is the imaginary number?
    A. -1
    B. 0
    C. 1
    D. $\sqrt{-1}$
    E. $\sqrt{-1^2}$

32. Which of the following values of x satisfies the inequality $\sqrt{26} < x < \sqrt{5}$?
    A. 3
    B. 5
    C. 6
    D. 9
    E. 10

33. $-2|-1 + 5| =$
    A. -8
    B. -6
    C. 2
    D. 6
    E. 8

34. Which of the following is a rational number?
    A. $\dfrac{\sqrt{2}}{2}$
    B. $\left(\sqrt{2} - 2\right)^2$
    C. $\dfrac{\sqrt{100}}{5}$
    D. $\sqrt{3}$
    E. $\left(3 + \sqrt{3}\right)^2$

35. If x and y are real numbers such that $0 < x < y^2$, then which of the following inequalities must be true?
    A. $x < y$
    B. $y > 0$
    C. $3x > y^2$
    D. $x < 1$
    E. $x < 3y^2$

36. What is the value of $\sqrt{x + (-x)^2}$ when $x = -1$?
    A. -1
    B. 0
    C. 1
    D. $\sqrt{2}$
    E. $\sqrt{3}$

37. What is the smallest integer larger than $\dfrac{\sqrt{26}}{5}$?
    A. 1
    B. 2
    C. 4
    D. 5
    E. 6

38. If $2^{-m} = \dfrac{1}{8}$, what is the value of m?
    A. -4
    B. -3
    C. 1
    D. 3
    E. 4

39. Using the following number line, which point satisfies the inequality $|-x + 1| > 4$?

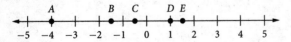

    A. A
    B. B
    C. C
    D. D
    E. E

40. Suppose that m is an even integer and n is an odd integer. Which of the following expressions must be an odd integer?
    A. $2(m + n)$
    B. $2(m + n) + 1$
    C. mn
    D. $2(mn)$
    E. $3(mn)$

41. Which of the following is equivalent to $\left(\dfrac{1}{4m^3}\right)^{-2}$ for any real number m?
    A. $\dfrac{1}{8m}$
    B. $\dfrac{1}{8m^5}$
    C. $\dfrac{1}{16m^6}$
    D. $8m^6$
    E. $16m^6$

42. The following circle graph represents the distribution of students in a local high school. If there are 1000 total students in the high school, how many more are 9th graders than 11th graders?

Distribution of students by grade level

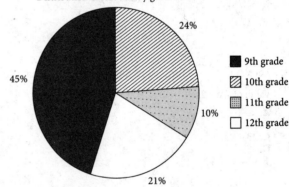

    ■ 9th grade
    ▨ 10th grade
    ▦ 11th grade
    ☐ 12th grade

    A. 500
    B. 450
    C. 350
    D. 120
    E. 100

43. Let a represent any positive integer. Which of the following is NOT larger than $\left(\dfrac{1}{a}\right)^2$?
    A. a
    B. a^2
    C. $\dfrac{1}{a}$
    D. $\left(\dfrac{2}{a}\right)^2$
    E. $\left(\dfrac{1}{2a}\right)^2$

44. If $0 < x < 16^{\frac{1}{2}}$ and $x = 2^m$ for some positive integer m, what is the value of x?
    A. 1
    B. 2
    C. 4
    D. 6
    E. 8

45. Let P represent the set of numbers with a factor of 5, and let Q represent the set of numbers that are less than 10 but larger than 0. Which of the following numbers is in both sets?

A. -10
B. -5
C. 2
D. 5
E. 8

46. Let $a \, \Xi \, b = b^2 - a^2 + 1$ for any real numbers a and b. What is the value of $(-2) \, \Xi \, (-3)$?

A. -12
B. -4
C. 3
D. 6
E. 14

47. What is the least common multiple of 12, 20, and 40?

A. 60
B. 120
C. 480
D. 800
E. 9600

48. If $2^m = 41$, which of the following inequalities must be true?

A. $1 < m < 2$
B. $2 < m < 3$
C. $3 < m < 4$
D. $4 < m < 5$
E. $5 < m < 6$

49. If p and q are real numbers such that $p > 5$ and $q > 4$, what is the smallest integer larger than the product pq?

A. 9
B. 10
C. 19
D. 20
E. 21

50. A number has three prime factors: 2, 3, and 7. Which of the following is a possible value of the number?

A. 12
B. 14
C. 49
D. 81
E. 84

51. If $\dfrac{3^p}{3^q} = 81$, which of the following statements must be true?

A. The sum of p and q must be 81.
B. The difference of p and q must be 4.
C. Both p and q must be integers.
D. Both p and q must be positive.
E. Either p or q must be positive.

52. For what values of a is the inequality $a^2 \le a$ always true?

A. $a < 0$
B. $a > 0$
C. $-1 \le a \le 1$
D. $a > 1$ and $a < -1$
E. The inequality is not true for any value of a.

53. There are 53 people signed up for a race on an upcoming Saturday, and there are 21 people signed up for a race on an upcoming Sunday. If 12 people signed up for both races, how many people are signed up for only one race?

A. 9
B. 41
C. 50
D. 62
E. 74

54. The value of $\dfrac{x+y}{y}$ is an integer when $y = 4$. Which of the following is a possible value of x?

A. -16
B. 2
C. 9
D. 15
E. 26

55. If a set is defined as all numbers satisfying a given inequality, then which of the following sets would NOT share any values with the set of values for x satisfying $-1 \le x < 5$?

A. $-5 \le x < -1$
B. $-5 < x \le -1$
C. $0 < x < 5$
D. $0 < x \le 5$
E. $0 \le x \le 5$

56. Let $x \rhd y = \dfrac{y}{x}$ for real numbers x and y. For what values of x is the value of $x \rhd (-1)$ always positive?

A. $x > 0$
B. $x < 0$
C. $x > -1$
D. $x < 1$
E. $x > 1$

57. If m is the number of distinct prime factors of 100, what is the value of $3m$?

A. 3
B. 6
C. 9
D. 12
E. 15

58. For any real number a, $(6a^5)^2 =$

A. $12a^7$
B. $36a^7$
C. $12a^{10}$
D. $36a^{10}$
E. $8a^3$

59. Using the following number line, which of the following statements must be true?

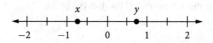

A. $|x - y| < 1$
B. $|x - y| = 1$
C. $|x - y| > 1$
D. $|x - y| < \dfrac{1}{2}$
E. $|x - y| = \dfrac{1}{2}$

60. The following table represents the number of town residents who live in each district. If the total number of residents in the town is 650, how many residents live in district 2?

District	Number of Residents
1	147
2	?
3	335
4	98

A. 42
B. 70
C. 315
D. 503
E. 552

61. Which of the following values of x satisfies the inequality $\frac{3}{2} < x < \frac{5}{2}$?

A. $\frac{\sqrt{9}}{2}$

B. $\frac{\sqrt{20}}{2}$

C. $\frac{\sqrt{25}}{2}$

D. $\frac{\sqrt{29}}{2}$

E. $\frac{\sqrt{31}}{2}$

62. If $xy^2 < 0$, then which of the following statements MUST be true?

A. The value of x is negative, while the value of y is positive or negative.
B. The value of y is negative, while the value of x is positive or negative.
C. The sign of x must be the same as the sign of y.
D. The sign of x must be different from the sign of y.
E. The values of x and y must be the same.

63. If $3^m = 1$, which of the following is a possible value of m?

A. -1
B. 0
C. 1
D. 2
E. 3

64. Which of the following is equivalent to $\frac{|x|}{x}$ when $x > 1$?

A. x
B. x^{-1}
C. -1
D. 0
E. 1

65. The remainder when an integer m is divided by 2 is 1. What is the remainder when $(m + 1)$ is divided by 2?

A. 0
B. 1
C. 2
D. 3
E. 4

66. What is the value of $\left(\frac{1}{3}\right)^x - \left(\frac{1}{2}\right)^y$ when $x = 2$ and $y = -1$?

A. $-\frac{17}{9}$

B. $-\frac{7}{4}$

C. $-\frac{1}{9}$

D. $\frac{1}{8}$

E. $\frac{2}{3}$

67. If the fraction $\frac{a}{25}$ is in simplified terms, which of the following CANNOT be a factor of a?

A. 1
B. 3
C. 5
D. 9
E. 14

68. If the value of $\frac{4^m}{4^n}$ is smaller than 1, which of the following MUST be true?

A. $m = 1$
B. $n = 1$
C. $m = n$
D. $m < n$
E. $m > n$

69. What is the value of $(-x)^2 - (-x)$ when $x = -2$?

A. -4
B. -2
C. 0
D. 2
E. 4

70. Which of the following expressions is equivalent to $\left(\frac{1}{2}x^2 y\right)^5$ for all x and y?

A. $\frac{1}{10}x^{10}y^5$

B. $\frac{1}{10}x^7 y^5$

C. $\frac{1}{32}x^{10}y^5$

D. $\frac{1}{32}x^7 y^5$

E. $\frac{5}{32}x^{10}y^5$

71. If 3 and 2 are factors of a, which of the following MUST be a factor of $14a$?

A. 4
B. 5
C. 8
D. 11
E. 19

CHAPTER 2

ALGEBRA

72. A cellular phone service contract requires customers to pay $45.00 a month for basic service in addition to $0.15 for each text message. If a customer's bill is $61.50, how many text messages did the customer send?

    A. 10
    B. 110
    C. 410
    D. 510
    E. 710

73. What is the value of x when $3x - 5 = 4x + 9$?

    A. -14
    B. -5
    C. 0
    D. 1
    E. 2

74. Which of the following is equivalent to $\frac{1}{a} + \frac{1}{b}$ for all non-zero values of a and b?

    A. $\frac{2}{a+b}$
    B. $\frac{1}{a+b}$
    C. 1
    D. $\frac{1}{ab}$
    E. $\frac{a+b}{ab}$

75. For what values of x is $x^2 - 3x - 10 = 0$?

    A. $x = 3$
    B. $x = 10$
    C. $x = 5$
    D. $x = 3$ and $x = 10$
    E. $x = 5$ and $x = -2$

76. If $\frac{m}{4} = \frac{m-1}{3}$, then $m =$

    A. -5
    B. -1
    C. 3
    D. 4
    E. 9

77. If $x - y = -5$ and $x + y = 1$, then $xy =$

    A. -6
    B. -2
    C. 1
    D. 3
    E. 12

78. In the matrix product shown, what is the value of x?
    $$\begin{bmatrix} -1 & 2 \\ 4 & 8 \end{bmatrix} \begin{bmatrix} 6 & 3 \\ 7 & -6 \end{bmatrix} = \begin{bmatrix} x & y \\ z & w \end{bmatrix}$$

    A. -6
    B. 5
    C. 8
    D. 14
    E. 20

79. Which of the following is a root of $-5x + x^2$?

    A. -5
    B. -3
    C. 1
    D. 3
    E. 5

80. For what values of m is $m^2 - 8m + 15 < 0$?

    A. $m < 3$
    B. $m > 3$
    C. $m < 5$
    D. $m > 5$
    E. $3 < m < 5$

81. The sum of two consecutive odd integers is 256. What is the value of the larger integer?

    A. 103
    B. 127
    C. 129
    D. 153
    E. 155

82. If $\frac{2p + q}{p} > 5$ and $p > 2$, which of the following inequalities MUST be true?

    A. $q > 0$
    B. $q > 2$
    C. $q > 6$
    D. $q > 10$
    E. $q > 12$

83. When $x \neq 0$, $\frac{x^2 - 4x^2 + x^2}{x} =$

    A. $-2x^6$
    B. $-2x^5$
    C. $-2x^4$
    D. $-2x^2$
    E. $-2x$

84. For what values of m and n would the following system of equations have infinite solutions?

$-3x + y = 2$

$mx + ny = -6$

A. $m = -3, n = -4$
B. $m = -3, n = 1$
C. $m = 9, n = 1$
D. $m = 9, n = -3$
E. $m = 3, n = -1$

85. What is the smallest integer for which the inequality $\frac{x}{4} - \frac{1}{4} \geq 1$ is true?

A. 4
B. 5
C. 6
D. 7
E. 8

86. Which of the following equations will always have the same solution or solutions as the equation $4xy - 1 = \frac{x}{2} + \frac{y}{3}$?

A. $4xy + 4 = 3x + 2y$
B. $8xy - 1 = 3x + 2y$
C. $12xy - 3 = 3x + 2y$
D. $20xy - 5 = 3x + 2y$
E. $24xy - 6 = 3x + 2y$

87. Which of the following inequalities represents the set of all values of x that satisfy the inequality $-3x + 4 > 6$?

A. $x < -\frac{2}{3}$

B. $x > -\frac{2}{3}$

C. $x > -\frac{10}{3}$

D. $x > -\frac{10}{3}$

E. $-\frac{10}{3} < x < -\frac{2}{3}$

88. What value of a is a solution to the inequality $a - x \geq c$ but is NOT a solution to the inequality $a - x > c$?

A. $a = -c$
B. $a = c$
C. $a = cx$
D. $a = c + x$
E. $a = c - x$

89. If $3^{xy} = \frac{1}{9}$, $2x + y = 0$, and x is positive, then $x + y =$

A. -3
B. -1
C. 2
D. 6
E. 9

90. If $k = -1$, then $\left(\frac{x+y}{k}\right)^2 =$

A. $-(x^2 + y^2)$
B. $x^2 + y^2$
C. $x^2 + 2xy + y^2$
D. $-(x^2 + 2xy + y^2)$
E. $x^2 - 2xy - y^2$

91. If $\log_2 x = 3$, what is the value of x?

A. 1
B. 2
C. 6
D. 8
E. 9

92. The expression $(x - a)(x + a) =$

A. $x^2 - 2a$
B. $x^2 - a^2$
C. $x^2 - 2a - a^2$
D. $x^2 - 2a + a^2$
E. $x^2 + 2a - a^2$

93. If $3x^2 - \frac{1}{2}x = 0$ and $x > 0$, what is the value of x?

A. $\frac{1}{6}$

B. $\frac{1}{2}$

C. $\frac{3}{2}$

D. 3
E. 6

94. For what values of b and c would the following system of equations have no solutions?

$2x + 8y = 2$

$x + by = c$

A. $b = 4, c = 1$
B. $b = 4, c = 3$
C. $b = 8, c = 4$
D. $b = 8, c = -2$
E. $b = 8, c = 2$

95. If $3m - 4 = 6n - 8$, which of the following expressions is equivalent to $3m - 8$?

A. $6n$
B. $6n - 12$
C. $6n - 8$
D. $6n - 4$
E. $6n + 4$

96. For all nonzero values of x and y, $a = \frac{x}{y}$. If $b = 2a - a^2$, which of the following expressions defines b in terms of x and y?

A. $\frac{x - x^2}{y}$

B. $\frac{2x - x^2}{y}$

C. $\frac{2x - x^2}{2y^2}$

D. $\frac{2xy - x^2}{y^2}$

E. $\frac{xy - x^2}{y^2}$

97. If $A = \begin{bmatrix} -1 & 2 \\ 4 & 9 \end{bmatrix}$ and $B = \begin{bmatrix} 0 & -8 \\ 1 & 1 \end{bmatrix}$ such that $A - B = \begin{bmatrix} x & y \\ z & w \end{bmatrix}$, what is the value of z?

   A. −1
   B. 0
   C. 3
   D. 4
   E. 5

98. The expression $\dfrac{6x - 4}{2}$ is equivalent to which of the following?

   A. $3x - 2$
   B. $3x - 4$
   C. $6x - 2$
   D. $6x - 4$
   E. $12x - 8$

99. If $4(x - 1) = 8(x - 2)$, then $x =$

   A. −2
   B. −1
   C. 1
   D. 3
   E. 4

100. How many positive integers satisfy the inequality $-5 \geq -7x$?

   A. None
   B. One
   C. Two
   D. Three
   E. Infinitely many

101. The sum of the terms $3x$, $4x - 1$, and $-2x$ is 9. What is the value of x?

   A. 1
   B. 2
   C. 5
   D. 10
   E. Cannot be determined from the given information

102. Which of the following values of a makes the equation $\dfrac{1}{2a} + \dfrac{1}{a} = 14$ true?

   A. $\dfrac{3}{28}$
   B. $\dfrac{1}{14}$
   C. $\dfrac{14}{3}$
   D. 14
   E. 16

103. Last week, a student began collecting rare coins. Since then, he has doubled his collection by obtaining 36 more coins than he started with. How many coins are currently in his collection?

   A. 18
   B. 36
   C. 72
   D. 84
   E. 116

104. Each of the following integers satisfies the inequality $-\dfrac{1}{2} \leq 5x \leq \dfrac{33}{2}$ EXCEPT

   A. 0
   B. 1
   C. 2
   D. 3
   E. 4

105. If the smallest of three consecutive integers is x, which of the following expressions represents their sum?

   A. $3x$
   B. $x + 3$
   C. $3x + 1$
   D. $3x + 3$
   E. $3x + 6$

106. Which of the following expressions is equivalent to $5x - \dfrac{15}{2}$?

   A. $-10x$
   B. $-5x$
   C. $5\left(x - \dfrac{1}{2}\right)$
   D. $5\left(x - \dfrac{3}{2}\right)$
   E. $5\left(x - \dfrac{15}{2}\right)$

107. If $a - b = 7$ and $2a + b = -1$, then $b =$

   A. −5
   B. −3
   C. 2
   D. 4
   E. 8

108. A company that sells two types of paper keeps twice as much of Type 1 in stock as it keeps of Type 2. Currently, the company has a total of 21,000 pounds of paper in stock. How many pounds of Type 2 paper does the company currently have in stock?

   A. 7000
   B. 10,500
   C. 14,000
   D. 18,500
   E. 42,000

109. What is the value of a when $6a - 1 = 2(a + 1)$?

   A. $\dfrac{3}{8}$
   B. $\dfrac{3}{4}$
   C. $\dfrac{1}{2}$
   D. 0
   E. $\dfrac{5}{2}$

110. For what positive value of x is $3x^2 - 19x = 14$?

   A. 2
   B. 3
   C. 7
   D. 14
   E. 19

111. If $mn = 4$, then $6(m^2n^2 - 1) =$
    A. 15
    B. 23
    C. 42
    D. 90
    E. 95

112. Which of the following is equivalent to the expression $3a^2 - 2b^2 + b$?
    A. $2a^2b^2b$
    B. $a^2b^2 + b$
    C. $3a^2 - b(2b + 1)$
    D. $3a^2 - b(2b - 1)$
    E. $3a^2 - 2b(b + 1)$

113. If $x = \frac{1}{2}$, then $(2y - 1)^{-x} =$
    A. $y + \frac{1}{2}$
    B. $2y + \frac{1}{2}$
    C. $\sqrt{y + \frac{1}{2}}$
    D. $\sqrt{-2y + 1}$
    E. $\dfrac{1}{\sqrt{2y - 1}}$

114. Which of the following inequalities has the same solution set as $x - 8 \geq 5x + 1$?
    A. $-x + 8 \leq 5x + 1$
    B. $-x + 8 \leq -5x - 1$
    C. $x - 8 \leq -5x + 1$
    D. $x - 8 \leq -5x - 1$
    E. $-x - 8 \leq -5x - 1$

115. Which operation in place of the Δ in the following equation would make the equation true for all nonzero values of x?
    $$x^2 \Delta 2x = \frac{x}{2}$$
    A. $\times$
    B. $+$
    C. $-$
    D. $\div$
    E. Cannot be determined

116. The product of two numbers is 20, while their sum is 12. What is the difference of the two numbers?
    A. 8
    B. 17
    C. 33
    D. 188
    E. 212

117. For what value(s) of y is $x - y > x + y$ true for any possible value of x?
    A. $y = 0$
    B. $y = 1$
    C. $y < 0$
    D. $y > 0$
    E. $y > 1$

118. If $\log_3 (x - 1) = 2$, what is the value of x?
    A. 3
    B. 4
    C. 7
    D. 9
    E. 10

119. How many roots larger than 5 does $x^2 - 3x + 2$ have?
    A. None
    B. One
    C. Two
    D. Three
    E. Cannot be determined

120. Which of the following represents the solution set to the inequality $-\frac{1}{2}x + 5 \geq 9$?
    A. $x \leq -8$
    B. $x \leq -4$
    C. $x \leq 0$
    D. $x \leq 4$
    E. $x \leq 8$

121. What is the value of x if the following equations are true?
    $$2x - y = -8$$
    $$3x + 2y = 2$$
    A. -4
    B. -2
    C. 4
    D. 10
    E. 12

122. For what value of x is $\log_x 16 = 4$?
    A. 1
    B. 2
    C. 4
    D. 8
    E. 16

123. For positive values of m, $\dfrac{m}{\sqrt{m}}$ is equivalent to which of the following expressions?
    A. 1
    B. m
    C. m^2
    D. $\sqrt{m}$
    E. $m\sqrt{m}$

124. The product of a and $(a - 1)$ is 6. Which of the following is a possible value of a?
    A. 2
    B. $\frac{5}{2}$
    C. 3
    D. $\frac{7}{2}$
    E. 6

125. A number x can be written in the form $k^2 - 2$ for some integer value of k. Which of the following expressions represents x^2 in terms of k?
    A. $k^4 - 4$
    B. $2k^2 - 4$
    C. $k^4 - k^2 + 4$
    D. $k^4 - 4k^2 + 2$
    E. $k^4 - 4k^2 + 4$

126. A factory can produce 100 bracelets every 15 minutes. How many bracelets can the factory produce in three and a half hours?
    A. 300
    B. 350
    C. 550
    D. 1400
    E. 5250

127. $(3x^2 - 5x + 1) - (3x^2 - 2x + 6) =$
   - A. $-3x - 5$
   - B. $-3x + 7$
   - C. $-7x - 7$
   - D. $-7x - 5$
   - E. $-7x + 7$

128. What is the greatest common factor of $2a^4$ and a^3?
   - A. a
   - B. a^3
   - C. $2a$
   - D. $2a^4$
   - E. $2a^7$

129. If $\sqrt{y} + 8 = 3\sqrt{y}$, then $y =$
   - A. 2
   - B. 4
   - C. 16
   - D. 25
   - E. 64

130. Which of the following expressions in place of the square would make the expression $10n^3 - 5n^2 = \square(2n^2 - n)$ true for any value of n?
   - A. 5
   - B. n
   - C. $5n$
   - D. $5n^2$
   - E. n^3

131. Which of the following values of x makes the equation $x - 5 = 9 - x$ true?
   - A. 2
   - B. 4
   - C. 7
   - D. 14
   - E. The equation is not true for any value of x.

132. If $p - 5 > -2$, then which of the following inequalities must be true?
   - A. $p + 5 > -12$
   - B. $p + 5 > -3$
   - C. $p + 5 > 0$
   - D. $p + 5 > 2$
   - E. $p + 5 > 8$

133. If $-k^2 = k$, which of the following is a possible value of k?
   - A. -4
   - B. -3
   - C. -2
   - D. -1
   - E. 1

134. Which of the following is equivalent to the expression $\dfrac{1 - x^2}{x}$ for all nonzero values of x?
   - A. $\dfrac{1}{x}$
   - B. $\dfrac{1}{x} - 1$
   - C. $\dfrac{1}{x} - x$
   - D. $\dfrac{1}{x} - x^2$
   - E. $\dfrac{1}{x} - x^3$

135. A prize of \$$m$ is to be divided evenly among 6 people. In terms of m, which of the following expressions represents the total amount of prize money 2 of the 6 people will receive?
   - A. $\dfrac{m}{6}$
   - B. $\dfrac{m}{5}$
   - C. $\dfrac{m}{4}$
   - D. $\dfrac{m}{3}$
   - E. $\dfrac{m}{2}$

136. If $2x + y^2 = 7$ and $y^2 = 3x$, then $10x =$
   - A. 8
   - B. 10
   - C. 12
   - D. 14
   - E. 19

137. For $x \neq 0, \dfrac{2x}{9} \times \dfrac{3}{x} =$
   - A. $\dfrac{1}{3}$
   - B. $\dfrac{1}{2}$
   - C. $\dfrac{2}{3}$
   - D. $\dfrac{2x^2}{27}$
   - E. $\dfrac{x^2}{4}$

138. If $x > 0$, which of the following expressions will have the smallest value?
   $$-2x, \frac{x}{2}, x^2, \frac{x}{4}, x^3$$
   - A. $-2x$
   - B. $\dfrac{x}{2}$
   - C. x^2
   - D. $\dfrac{x}{4}$
   - E. x^3

139. Given the equation $2(x + 1) = -(y + 2)$, when $y = 0$, which of the following is the value of x?
   - A. -4
   - B. -2
   - C. 0
   - D. 3
   - E. 5

140. What is the least common denominator of $\dfrac{3}{8a}$ and $\dfrac{1}{6a}$?
   - A. $6a$
   - B. $8a$
   - C. $14a$
   - D. $24a$
   - E. $48a$

141. The sum of a number n and 4 is 10. What is the value of the sum of n and -1?

   A. 2
   B. 3
   C. 5
   D. 9
   E. 11

142. Which of the following is a possible value of x if $4x > 3$ and $-x > 3$?

   A. -5
   B. -3
   C. 1
   D. 8
   E. There are no values of x that satisfy both inequalities.

CHAPTER 3
PROBABILITY, STATISTICS, AND SEQUENCES

QUESTIONS 143–213

---

143. If $x > 0$, what is the median of the data set consisting of $-2x$, $-5x$, x, $-8x$, and $4x$?

A. $-2x$
B. $-5x$
C. x
D. $-8x$
E. $4x$

144. A game's card set is made up of 6 blue cards and 9 red cards. If a player randomly selects one of these cards, what is the probability the selected card will be blue?

A. $\frac{1}{15}$

B. $\frac{1}{6}$

C. $\frac{2}{5}$

D. $\frac{3}{5}$

E. $\frac{2}{3}$

145. The average of 5 numbers is 20. What is the sum of these same numbers?

A. 4
B. 5
C. 15
D. 25
E. 100

146. The median of the following data set is 2. Which of the following is a possible value of x?

$x, 2, 1, 6, 7$

A. 2
B. 3
C. 5
D. 6
E. 8

147. A retailer's website allows shoppers to customize the shoes they order. Customers may select one of three different colors, one of two types of laces, and one of eight special logos. With these choices, how many different shoe designs are possible?

A. 14
B. 16
C. 36
D. 48
E. 52

148. The first term of a sequence is 4, and each subsequent term is found by multiplying the previous term by n. What is the 15th term of the sequence?

A. $3n$
B. $4n$
C. $3n + 4$
D. $4n^{14}$
E. n^{15}

149. There are twice as many red pens as there are blue pens in a desk. If a pen is randomly selected, what is the probability it is blue?

A. $\frac{1}{4}$

B. $\frac{1}{3}$

C. $\frac{2}{3}$

D. $\frac{1}{2}$

E. Cannot be determined from the given information

150. The probability of randomly selecting a green marble from a bag is $\frac{4}{5}$. If there are 110 marbles in the bag, how many are NOT green?

A. 20
B. 22
C. 36
D. 80
E. 88

151. Which of the following statements is true of $P(A)$, that is, the probability of A, for any event A?

I. If A is very likely to occur, $P(A) > 1$
II. $P(A) = 1 - P(A \text{ not occurring})$
III. $P(A) \geq 0$

A. I only
B. II only
C. III only
D. I and II only
E. II and III only

152. The average of five numbers is 12.4. The average of four of these numbers is 11. What is the value of the fifth number?

A. 1.4
B. 17.0
C. 18.0
D. 44.0
E. 62.0

153. The tenth term of an arithmetic sequence is 38, and the second term is 6. What is the value of the first term of this sequence?

    A. 0
    B. 2
    C. 4
    D. 14
    E. 26

154. How many different arrangements of the letters A, D, G, and F are possible?

    A. 10
    B. 16
    C. 24
    D. 256
    E. 325

155. The median of a list of seven distinct numbers is 3. If a number $x > 3$ is included in the list, which of the following will be true of the new list?

    A. The median will be zero.
    B. The median will be smaller than three, but not zero.
    C. The median will remain three.
    D. The median will be larger than three.
    E. The median will be larger than x.

156. A fair coin is flipped five times, and each flip results in tails. What is the probability the coin will land on tails on the sixth flip?

    A. $\frac{1}{64}$
    B. $\frac{1}{10}$
    C. $\frac{1}{7}$
    D. $\frac{1}{6}$
    E. $\frac{1}{2}$

157. What is the 35th term of the sequence -1, 5, -2, 1, 5, 2, . . . ?

    A. -2
    B. -1
    C. 1
    D. 2
    E. 5

158. A number is randomly selected from all integers between 1 and 25 inclusive. What is the probability the selected number is prime?

    A. $\frac{1}{10}$
    B. $\frac{1}{9}$
    C. $\frac{9}{25}$
    D. $\frac{2}{5}$
    E. $\frac{12}{25}$

159. The probabilities for five events are listed in the following table. Which event is the LEAST likely to occur?

Event	Probability
Event 1	0.25
Event 2	0.35
Event 3	0.47
Event 4	0.40
Event 5	0.29

    A. Event 1
    B. Event 2
    C. Event 3
    D. Event 4
    E. Event 5

160. The average of four consecutive integers is 14.5. What is the sum of the largest and the smallest of the integers?

    A. 3
    B. 23
    C. 27
    D. 29
    E. 31

161. Two contest winners are chosen by having their names drawn out of a hat one at a time. Once a name is drawn, it is not replaced, and each person is allowed only one entry. In total, seven people entered the contest. If Sara's name was not chosen on the first draw, what is the probability it will be chosen on the second?

    A. $\frac{1}{7}$
    B. $\frac{1}{6}$
    C. $\frac{2}{7}$
    D. $\frac{2}{5}$
    E. $\frac{5}{6}$

162. The sum of the first four terms of an arithmetic sequence is 32. What is the value of the sum of the first and fourth terms of the sequence?

    A. 11
    B. 16
    C. 19
    D. 22
    E. 32

163. In a game, a complete set of cards consists of one situational card, one power card, and one level card. If Blake holds five situational cards, four power cards, and ten level cards, how many different complete sets of cards does he have?

    A. 9
    B. 19
    C. 30
    D. 131
    E. 200

164. If the sum of ten numbers is x, which of the following expressions represents the average of these ten numbers?

    A. $\frac{x}{10}$
    B. x^{10}
    C. $10x$
    D. $x + 10$
    E. $10 - x$

165. What is the first term of the following geometric sequence?

_____, $30, \frac{15}{2}, 1\frac{7}{8}, \ldots$

A. 35

B. $\frac{71}{2}$

C. 60

D. 120

E. $\frac{249}{2}$

166. What is the median of the following set of numbers?

$\{1, 1, 9, 4, 6, 2\}$

A. 1
B. 2
C. 3
D. 4
E. 6

167. A professor kept track of the attendance at his Monday-Wednesday-Friday class for one week. The average daily attendance was 32. How many students attended his class on Friday?

Day	Attendance
Monday	32
Wednesday	34
Friday	?

A. 29
B. 30
C. 31
D. 32
E. 33

168. The 1st term of an arithmetic sequence is m, and each subsequent term is found by adding n to the previous term. Which of the following expressions represents the value of the 99th term?

A. nm^{99}
B. $n^{99} m$
C. $m + 98n$
D. $98m + n$
E. $98mn$

169. Hanna and Jake are hoping to get selected as the host of this year's talent show. The committee chooses a host by random selection, and this year only 29 students entered their name into the drawing. What is the probability either Hanna or Jake is selected as the host this year?

A. $\frac{1}{841}$

B. $\frac{2}{841}$

C. $\frac{1}{58}$

D. $\frac{1}{29}$

E. $\frac{2}{29}$

170. To earn a commission for the workweek (Monday through Friday), a salesperson must have average daily sales of $250 or greater for the week. If a salesperson's sales for Monday through Thursday are $98, $255, $175, and $320, what is the LEAST whole number value of sales the salesperson needs to have on Friday to be eligible to earn a commission?

A. $250
B. $299
C. $402
D. $1250
E. It is not possible for the salesperson to earn a commission this week.

171. A set of numbers contains m numbers, one of which is even. If a number is randomly selected from the set, what is the probability it is NOT even?

A. $\frac{1}{m}$

B. $\frac{1}{m-1}$

C. $\frac{1}{m+1}$

D. $\frac{m-1}{m}$

E. $\frac{m}{m+1}$

172. A governing committee of three is chosen out of 30 people. The committee consists of a president, a treasurer, and a vice president. Only one person may be selected for any given position. Which of the following expressions represents the number of possible combinations of people who could serve in the three positions on the governing committee?

A. 3×30
B. 30^3
C. $30^3 \times 29^2 \times 28$
D. $30 \times 29 \times 28$
E. $30 + 29 + 28$

173. Three telephones in a shipment of eight are known to be defective. A randomly selected telephone is removed from the shipment and tested. It is found not to be defective. If a second telephone is randomly selected from those remaining, what is the probability of it NOT being defective?

A. $\frac{1}{4}$

B. $\frac{4}{7}$

C. $\frac{1}{3}$

D. $\frac{3}{8}$

E. $\frac{3}{7}$

174. An urn contains five white marbles and six green marbles. Which of the following would INCREASE the probability of randomly selecting a white marble from this urn?

I. Increasing the number of white marbles only
II. Increasing the number of green marbles only
III. Decreasing the number of white marbles and green marbles by the same amount

A. I only
B. II only
C. III only
D. I and II only
E. I and III only

175. What is the average of the numbers 228, 219, 202, and 252?

   A. 219.00
   B. 223.50
   C. 225.25
   D. 229.75
   E. 300.25

176. What is the 400th term in the sequence 18, 21, 9, 24, 5, 18, 21, 9, 24, 5, . . .?

   A. 5
   B. 9
   C. 18
   D. 21
   E. 24

177. The fifth term of an arithmetic sequence is $11x^2$, and the seventh term of the same sequence is $17x^2$. What is the third term of this sequence?

   A. $2x^2$
   B. $3x^2$
   C. $5x^2$
   D. $14x^2$
   E. $20x^2$

178. If the median of 1, x, y, 4, and z is x, and $y > z > 4$, which of the following statements MUST be true?

   A. $x < 1$
   B. $x < 4$
   C. $x < z$
   D. $1 < x < 4$
   E. $y < x < z$

179. A coin is selected from a box containing two different types of coins. The probability of selecting the first type of coin is three times the probability of selecting the second type. If there are 240 coins of the first type, how many coins of the second type are in the box?

   A. 80
   B. 110
   C. 243
   D. 720
   E. 832

180. How many distinct arrangements of four letters (without repeats) from the set {A, B, C, D, E} are possible?

   A. 15
   B. 20
   C. 25
   D. 120
   E. 625

181. What is the average of the numbers $\frac{5}{4}, \frac{1}{2}$, and $\frac{x}{2}$?

   A. $\dfrac{2x + 7}{12}$

   B. $\dfrac{4x + 9}{12}$

   C. $\dfrac{x + 6}{6}$

   D. $\dfrac{2x + 7}{4}$

   E. $\dfrac{x + 9}{4}$

182. If $x = 7$, what is the probability a randomly selected number from the set $\{x - 5, 2x + 4, -x, x + 5, x + 3\}$ will be even?

   A. 0

   B. $\dfrac{1}{5}$

   C. $\dfrac{2}{5}$

   D. $\dfrac{3}{5}$

   E. $\dfrac{4}{5}$

183. Aiden's work schedule for the week is represented in the following table. If this schedule remains the same for 4 weeks, and if a day from the 4-week schedule is selected at random, what is the probability that the day selected is a day when Aiden is scheduled to work?

Day	Schedule
Monday	Off duty
Tuesday	8 A.M.–12 noon
Wednesday	8 A.M.–12 noon
Thursday	Off duty
Friday	Off duty
Saturday	4 P.M.–8 P.M.
Sunday	4 P.M.–8 P.M.

   A. $\dfrac{1}{28}$

   B. $\dfrac{1}{7}$

   C. $\dfrac{3}{7}$

   D. $\dfrac{4}{7}$

   E. $\dfrac{5}{7}$

184. On an exam, students must select one short-answer question and one essay question to complete. If the exam has five short-answer and three essay questions, how many distinct combinations of questions can students select?

   A. 2
   B. 7
   C. 8
   D. 15
   E. 45

185. The first term of a sequence is 2, and each subsequent term is found by adding $-\dfrac{5}{4}$ to the previous term. What is the first term that has a value less than zero?

   A. Second term
   B. Third term
   C. Fourth term
   D. Fifth term
   E. Sixth term

186. If the sum of n numbers is m and the average of the same n numbers is p, what is the value of n in terms of m and p?

   A. $\dfrac{p}{m}$

   B. $\dfrac{m}{p}$

   C. mp
   D. $m + p$
   E. $m - p$

187. The average of a set of six numbers is 10. If 5 is added to each number in the set, what is the average of the new set of numbers?

    A. 5
    B. 15
    C. 20
    D. 50
    E. 80

188. If the probability of event A occurring is 0.4 and the probability of event B occurring is 0.2, which of the following probabilities must be greater than 0.5? Assume that events A and B cannot occur at the same time.

    I. The probability of event A not occurring
    II. The probability of event B not occurring
    III. The probability of either event A or event B occurring

    A. I only
    B. II only
    C. III only
    D. I and II only
    E. I, II, and III

189. A box contains red and black cards. The probability of selecting a red card is half the probability of selecting a black card. What is the probability of selecting a black card?

    A. $\frac{1}{4}$
    B. $\frac{1}{3}$
    C. $\frac{1}{2}$
    D. $\frac{2}{3}$
    E. $\frac{3}{4}$

190. Which of the following could NOT represent the probability of an event occurring?

    A. $\frac{1}{1056}$
    B. $\frac{5}{18}$
    C. $\frac{59}{61}$
    D. $\frac{57}{41}$
    E. $\frac{6}{257}$

191. The sum of the first five terms of an arithmetic sequence is 55. What is the value of the sixth term of the sequence if the first term is 3?

    A. 3
    B. 7
    C. 15
    D. 19
    E. 22

192. The first 20 terms of a geometric sequence are less than 60. If the 1st term of the sequence is $\frac{1}{2}$, which of the following is a possible value for the 2nd term?

    A. $\frac{1}{4}$
    B. $\frac{5}{4}$
    C. 2
    D. 3
    E. 6

193. How many three-digit numbers have an odd number as a tens digit?

    A. 25
    B. 200
    C. 450
    D. 500
    E. 620

194. One of three cards must be selected to continue a game. The probability the first card will be selected is $\frac{2}{5}$, while the probability the second card will be selected is $\frac{1}{8}$. What is the probability the third card will be selected?

    A. $\frac{1}{13}$
    B. $\frac{1}{5}$
    C. $\frac{19}{40}$
    D. $\frac{29}{40}$
    E. $\frac{12}{13}$

195. What is the 101st term of the sequence 5, 4, 3, 0, 8, 5, 4, 3, 0, 8, . . .?

    A. 0
    B. 3
    C. 4
    D. 5
    E. 8

196. The list of numbers 1, 1, x, y, 10, 14 is written in order of smallest to largest. If the median of the list is 5, which of the following numbers is a possible value of the product xy?

    A. 8
    B. 17
    C. 20
    D. 24
    E. 29

197. The sum of ten numbers is 250. What is the average of the ten numbers?

    A. 25
    B. 50
    C. 110
    D. 125
    E. 240

198. In a department store, there are x items on sale at a discount. If a total of 171 items are on sale at the store and the probability an item is not on sale at a discount is $\frac{2}{3}$, what is the value of x?

A. 55
B. 57
C. 112
D. 114
E. 118

199. The formula for the nth term of a sequence is $a_n = \frac{1}{5}a_{n-1} + 4$. If the second term of the sequence is 26, what is the first term of the sequence?

A. 22
B. 110
C. 126
D. 130
E. 148

200. Hunter has collected 35 science books over the last two years, and 5 of these science books cover biology. What is the probability a randomly selected science book in his collection covers biology?

A. $\frac{1}{35}$
B. $\frac{1}{30}$
C. $\frac{1}{7}$
D. $\frac{1}{6}$
E. $\frac{1}{5}$

201. Which of the following equations represents a formula for the nth term of the sequence 14, 12, 10, 8, 6, 4, ...?

A. $a_n = 2a_{n-1}$
B. $a_n = \frac{a_{n-1}}{2}$
C. $a_n = a_{n-1} + 2$
D. $a_n = a_{n-1} - 2$
E. $a_n = 2a_{n-1} - 2$

202. The results of a career interest survey of students in a statewide mathematics club are provided in the following table. If a student is randomly selected from this group, what is the probability the student indicated interest in an aviation career?

Career	Number of Students
Medical (doctor, nurse, etc.)	82
Aviation	18
Engineering	22
Computer science and technology	48
Other	30

A. $\frac{1}{200}$
B. $\frac{1}{182}$
C. $\frac{1}{18}$
D. $\frac{9}{100}$
E. $\frac{41}{100}$

203. If the probability of selecting a gray hat from a bin containing gray and black hats is x, which of the following probabilities MUST have a value of $1 - x$?

A. The probability of selecting two gray hats
B. The probability of selecting a black hat
C. The probability of selecting two black hats
D. The probability of selecting a black hat followed by a gray hat
E. The probability of selecting a gray hat followed by a black hat

204. The terms of a sequence are found by multiplying the previous term by 2 and then subtracting 1. Which of the following terms must be the largest in value?

A. The first term
B. The second term
C. The third term
D. The fourth term
E. It depends on the value of the first term.

205. The terms of a geometric series are found by multiplying the previous term by $\frac{1}{3}$. If the first term is a_1, which of the following expressions represents the difference between the third and second terms in terms of a_1?

A. $-\frac{2}{9}a_1$
B. $-\frac{1}{6}a_1$
C. $-\frac{1}{3}a_1$
D. $\frac{1}{3}a_1$
E. $3a_1$

206. What is the median of the data list q, x, y, z, w if the inequality $y < x < w < 8 < z < q$ is true?

A. q
B. x
C. y
D. z
E. w

207. The nth term of a sequence is found using the formula $a_n = 4a_{n-1} + \frac{1}{2}$. If the third term of the sequence is 322.5, what is the value of the first term?

A. 15.5
B. 20
C. 80.5
D. 102
E. 161.5

208. The average daily rainfall for the past six days is 3.22 inches. How many inches of rain must fall on the seventh day for the average daily rainfall over the past week to be 3.40 inches?

A. 2.76
B. 3.25
C. 3.97
D. 4.48
E. 4.72

209. The nth term of a sequence is determined using the formula $a_n = a_{n-1} - r$. If the fifth term of the sequence is 38 and the seventh term of the sequence is 50, what is the value of r?

A. -12
B. -10
C. -6
D. 6
E. 12

210. If the average of twelve numbers is m, which of the following expressions represents the average of these twelve numbers and 5?

A. $m + 5$

B. $m + 13$

C. $13m + 5$

D. $\dfrac{m + 5}{13}$

E. $\dfrac{12m + 5}{13}$

211. What is the median of $\sqrt{2}$, 5, $\sqrt{3}$, 1, and $\sqrt{5}$?

A. $\sqrt{2}$

B. 5

C. $\sqrt{3}$

D. 1

E. $\sqrt{5}$

212. The value of a number x is twice the value of y, and the average of the two numbers is 30. What is the value of x?

A. 30

B. 40

C. 60

D. 120

E. 140

213. If the first term of a series is 4 and the third is 36, what is the value of the second?

A. 3

B. 9

C. 12

D. 13

E. 24

CHAPTER 4

COORDINATE GEOMETRY

214. In the standard (x, y) coordinate plane, what is the distance between $(-1, 1)$ and $(2, 3)$?

A. 5

B. $\sqrt{5}$

C. $2\sqrt{5}$

D. $\sqrt{13}$

E. $\sqrt{29}$

215. What is the slope of a line that is perpendicular to $8x + 4y = 2$?

A. -8

B. -2

C. $-\dfrac{1}{4}$

D. $\dfrac{1}{8}$

E. $\dfrac{1}{2}$

216. In the standard (x, y) coordinate plane, what are the coordinates of the midpoint of the line segment connecting $(2, 7)$ and $(5, 7)$?

A. $(5, 7)$

B. $(3.5, 7)$

C. $(7, 14)$

D. $(3, 0)$

E. $(5, 2)$

217. In the standard (x, y) coordinate plane, the coordinates of the midpoint of a line segment AB are $(2, 5)$. If the coordinates of the point A are $(1, 0)$, what is the length of the line segment AB?

A. $\sqrt{2}$

B. $3\sqrt{3}$

C. $4\sqrt{3}$

D. $\sqrt{26}$

E. $2\sqrt{26}$

218. In the standard (x, y) coordinate plane, at what point does the graph of the line $y - 7x = -10$ cross the y-axis?

A. $y = -10$

B. $y = -7$

C. $y = -3$

D. $y = 7$

E. $y = 10$

219. If the coordinates of the point X have the same sign, then X must be located in which of the four quadrants seen in the following figure?

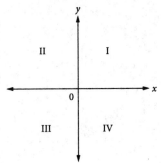

A. I only

B. II only

C. I and II only

D. I and III only

E. III and IV only

220. Line ℓ is parallel to the y-axis in the (x, y) coordinate plane. Which of the following pairs of points could be on line ℓ?

A. $(0, 0), (1, 1)$

B. $(0, 0), (1, 0)$

C. $(1, 4), (1, 7)$

D. $(4, 1), (7, 1)$

E. $(4, 4), (5, 5)$

221. As shown in the following figure, the angle between lines m and ℓ is 90 degrees. What must the product of their slopes equal?

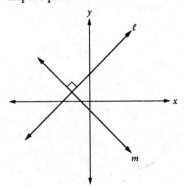

A. -2

B. -1

C. 0

D. 1

E. Cannot be determined

222. For the complex number i such that $i^2 = -1$, which of the following is equal to $i^5 - i^7$?

  A. -2
  B. -1
  C. 0
  D. 1
  E. 2

223. In the following figure, the midpoint of line MN is P, while the midpoint of the line segment QP is R. If the length of QR is 6 and the length of MQ is 4, what is the length of MN?

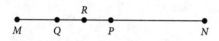

  A. 18
  B. 24
  C. 26
  D. 32
  E. 42

224. Which of the following statements must be true regarding the line graphed in the following figure?

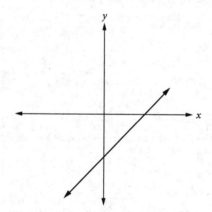

  I. The slope of the line is positive.
  II. The x-intercept of the line is negative.
  III. The y-intercept of the line is positive.

  A. I only
  B. II only
  C. III only
  D. I and II only
  E. I, II, and III

225. Which of the following equations represents a line that is parallel to the x-axis?

  A. $y = \dfrac{1}{2}x$
  B. $y = 18$
  C. $x = -2$
  D. $y = -3x + 1$
  E. $y = 2x - 6$

226. In the following figure, lines m and n are parallel, and the value of x is 36. What is the value of y?

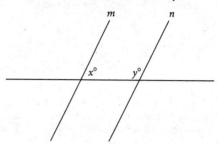

  A. 24
  B. 36
  C. 64
  D. 72
  E. 144

227. The area of a rectangle in the (x, y) coordinate plane is 6. The corners of the rectangle are the points $A(1, 4)$, $B(4, 4)$, $C(4, 6)$, and $D(x, y)$. What are the coordinates of point D?

  A. $(1, 3)$
  B. $(1, 6)$
  C. $(4, 1)$
  D. $(4, 3)$
  E. $(4, 7)$

228. What is the slope of a line that passes through the points $\left(-\dfrac{1}{2}, 2\right)$ and $\left(-\dfrac{1}{4}, \dfrac{1}{4}\right)$ in the (x, y) coordinate plane?

  A. -28
  B. -10
  C. -7
  D. $-\dfrac{5}{2}$
  E. $-\dfrac{7}{4}$

229. In the (x, y) coordinate plane, what is the value of the x-intercept of a line that passes through the points $(0, 5)$ and $(1, 6)$?

  A. -1
  B. -3
  C. -4
  D. -5
  E. -6

230. Which of the following equations represents a line that is perpendicular to the line $5x - 2y = 8$?

  A. $-2x + 2y = 8$
  B. $5x - 2y = -12$
  C. $2x - 5y = 20$
  D. $-2x + 5y = 11$
  E. $-2x - 5y = 10$

231. A line in the (x, y) coordinate plane has a slope of $-\dfrac{5}{4}$ and passes through the point $(-3, 5)$. What is the y-intercept of this line?

  A. -5
  B. $-\dfrac{15}{4}$
  C. $\dfrac{5}{4}$
  D. 14
  E. 20

232. A line in the (x, y) coordinate plane has a positive y-intercept c and a negative slope. Which of the following statements MUST be true about the x-intercept of this line?

A. $x < c$
B. $x < 0$
C. $x = c$
D. $x > c$
E. $x > 0$

233. In the following figure, lines AB and PQ each have a length of 5 units and are parallel to the x-axis. If the coordinates of P are $(3, -2)$, what are the coordinates of Q?

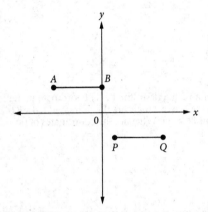

A. $(-8, -7)$
B. $(-2, 3)$
C. $(2, 0)$
D. $(3, 3)$
E. $(8, -2)$

234. Which of the following could be the coordinates of the point M in the (x, y) coordinate plane shown?

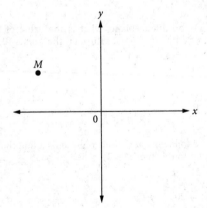

A. $(-2, -3)$
B. $(-2, 2)$
C. $(8, 2)$
D. $(6, -2)$
E. $(10, -3)$

235. For the complex number i such that $i^2 = -1$, which of the following is equal to $\dfrac{i^4 - 5}{i^2}$?

A. -7
B. -6
C. -5
D. 4
E. 24

236. In the following figure, lines m and n are parallel, and line ℓ is a transversal crossing both lines. If the sum of x and y is 160, what is the value of z?

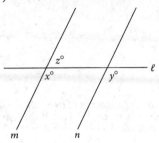

A. 30
B. 80
C. 95
D. 100
E. 200

237. In the (x, y) coordinate plane, a circle with radius 6 is centered at point Q on the x-axis. If the point $(-9, 0)$ is on the circumference of the circle, which of the following could be the x-coordinate of Q?

A. -12
B. -3
C. 3
D. 9
E. 21

238. What is the slope of the line $3x - 8y = 21$?

A. -5
B. $\dfrac{3}{8}$
C. $\dfrac{8}{3}$
D. $\dfrac{21}{8}$
E. 7

239. Which of the following equations represents the same line as the equation $-2x + 6y = 14$?

A. $y = -3x$
B. $y = \dfrac{7}{3}x$
C. $y = -3x + 7$
D. $y = \dfrac{1}{3}x + 14$
E. $y = \dfrac{1}{3}x + \dfrac{7}{3}$

240. A line in the (x, y) coordinate plane is defined such that each y-coordinate is found by multiplying the x-coordinate by three and adding two. What is the y-intercept of this line?

A. 0
B. 2
C. 5
D. 8
E. 10

241. In the (x, y) coordinate plane, what is the x-intercept of the line $2x - 5y = 10$?

A. -5
B. -2
C. 2
D. 5
E. 10

242. In the (x, y) coordinate plane, what is the midpoint of a line segment that starts at $(-4, 0)$ and ends at $(-8, -12)$?
 A. $(2, 6)$
 B. $(6, 2)$
 C. $(6, 12)$
 D. $(-6, -6)$
 E. $(-12, -6)$

243. Which of the following statements must be true of a line in the (x, y) coordinate plane defined by the equation $x = c$ for some constant c?
 I. The line is parallel to the y-axis.
 II. The line is perpendicular to the x-axis.
 III. The line has an x- and y-intercept of c.

 A. I only
 B. II only
 C. III only
 D. I and II only
 E. I, II, and III

244. Which of the following is the slope of a line that is parallel to the line that would pass through the points A and B in the figure shown?

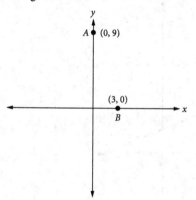

 A. -6
 B. -3
 C. $-\dfrac{1}{3}$
 D. $\dfrac{1}{3}$
 E. 3

245. In the following figure, M is the midpoint of the line segment PQ. What is the value of x?

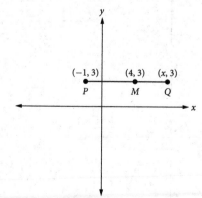

 A. 3
 B. 5
 C. 6
 D. 9
 E. 10

246. What is the slope of the line $y = -6$?
 A. -6
 B. $-\dfrac{1}{6}$
 C. 0
 D. 6
 E. The slope of the line is undefined.

247. The point A lies along the line $7x - 6y = 8$ in the (x, y) coordinate plane. If the x-coordinate of A is 2, what is the y-coordinate?
 A. -6
 B. 1
 C. 3
 D. 8
 E. 14

248. For the complex number i such that $i^2 = -1$, which of the following is equivalent to $\dfrac{(i-1)^2}{(i+1)^2}$?
 A. -2
 B. -1
 C. 0
 D. 1
 E. 2

249. The sides of an equilateral triangle ABC drawn in the (x, y) coordinate plane have sides of length 3. Which of the following pairs of coordinates could represent the endpoints of the line segment AB?
 A. $(-3, 2)$ and $(0, 2)$
 B. $(-1, 4)$ and $(3, 5)$
 C. $(6, 3)$ and $(10, 13)$
 D. $(5, 0)$ and $(10, 0)$
 E. $(8, -3)$ and $(8, 15)$

250. Which of the following equations represents a line with a negative y-intercept in the (x, y) coordinate plane?
 A. $-5x + 2y = -10$
 B. $-2x + y = 1$
 C. $-x - y = -1$
 D. $2x - 5y = -15$
 E. $3x + 4y = 12$

251. If the point $(4, y)$ is on the line $-8x - 4y = 16$, what is the value of y?
 A. -32
 B. -18
 C. -12
 D. 4
 E. 14

252. Lines AB and ℓ intersect at the point C in the following figure. What is the value of x in degrees?

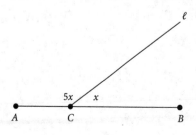

 A. 20
 B. 30
 C. 45
 D. 55
 E. 80

253. A line segment AB in the (x, y) coordinate plane has a midpoint that lies on the y-axis and is perpendicular to that axis. If the coordinates of point A are $(-8, 6)$, which of the following could be the coordinates of point B?

   A. $(-10, 8)$
   B. $(-8, -6)$
   C. $(-4, 3)$
   D. $(4, 6)$
   E. $(8, 6)$

254. In the following figure, lines AB and CD intersect at a point P. If $\angle APD = 80°$, what is the measure of $\angle APC$ in degrees?

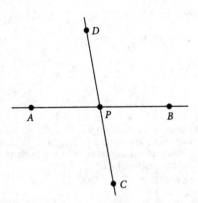

   A. 10
   B. 100
   C. 170
   D. 200
   E. 280

255. Line ℓ is a transversal of the parallel lines m and n. The measures of two angles are given in terms of x and y. What is the value of x, in degrees?

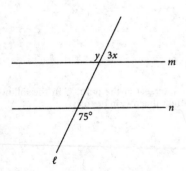

   A. 25
   B. 30
   C. 35
   D. 50
   E. 75

256. If a line in the (x, y) coordinate plane has x-intercept $(x, 0)$ and y-intercept $(0, y)$ such that $x > y$, which of the following could be a graph of the line?

A.

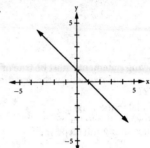

B.

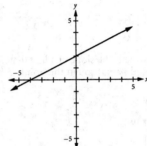

C.

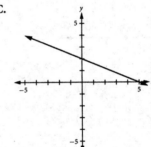

D.

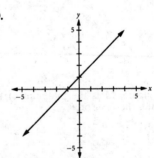

E.

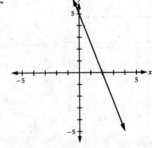

257. What is the slope-intercept form of the line $5x + 8y = 11$?

A. $y = \dfrac{11}{8} - \dfrac{5}{8}x$

B. $y = \dfrac{11}{8} - 5x$

C. $y = 11 - \dfrac{5}{8}x$

D. $y = 11 - 5x$

E. $y = 19 - 40x$

258. If lines AB and CD are perpendicular and intersect at point P, what is the measure of $\angle APB$ in degrees?

A. 30
B. 45
C. 60
D. 90
E. 180

259. In the following figure, the equation of line m is $y = \dfrac{3}{2}x + 1$, and line n, which is parallel to the x-axis, intersects the y-axis at the point A (0, 8). If lines m and n intersect at point B, what is the x-coordinate of point B?

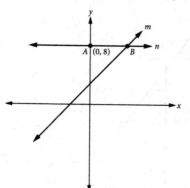

A. $\dfrac{2}{3}$

B. 1

C. $\dfrac{14}{3}$

D. 8
E. 13

260. Which of the following is the equation of a line parallel to the line passing through the points $(-1, 4)$ and $(3, 8)$?

A. $y = x - 10$
B. $y = 2x + 7$
C. $y = -x + 4$

D. $y = -\dfrac{1}{2}x - 6$

E. $y = \dfrac{1}{3}x - 8$

261. Each of the following equations represents a line in the (x, y) coordinate plane EXCEPT

A. $y = \dfrac{x}{4}$

B. $7x - 5x = \dfrac{1}{2}$

C. $y = \dfrac{x - 3}{5}$

D. $y = x(x + 1)$

E. $\dfrac{y}{2} = \dfrac{x}{9}$

262. The points M, N, P, and Q lie on a line in that order such that N is the midpoint of the line segment MP. If the length of MN is 14, the length of NP is $2x$, and the length of PQ is $4x - 9$, what is the length of the line segment MQ?

A. 7
B. 19
C. 21
D. 33
E. 47

263. If the point $(2m, m - 1)$ lies on the line $y = x + 4$ in the (x, y) coordinate plane, then $m =$

A. -5
B. -1
C. 3
D. 5
E. 7

264. In the following figure, the circle centered at point P has a radius of 2, and AB is parallel to the x-axis. If the line segments AB and DC are both diameters such that A has coordinates (1, 4), what are the coordinates of point D?

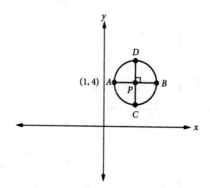

A. $(-1, 4)$
B. $(1, 2)$
C. $(3, 4)$
D. $(3, 6)$
E. $(5, 4)$

265. For the complex number i such that $i^2 = -1$, what is the value of $\dfrac{i^5}{(i - 1)} \times \dfrac{i^8}{(i + 1)}$?

A. $-\dfrac{i}{2}$

B. $\dfrac{i}{2i - 2}$

C. i

D. $2i$

E. $\dfrac{2i}{i - 1}$

266. Every point on a line in the (x, y) coordinate plane has the form $\left(x, \dfrac{x - 1}{4}\right)$. Which of the following is the equation of this line in standard form?

A. $y - 4x = -1$
B. $4y - x = -1$
C. $4y - x = 4$
D. $4y - 4x = 4$
E. $4y - 4x = 1$

267. The distance between points P and Q in the (x, y) coordinate plane is half the distance between $(-4, 2)$ and $(-8, 1)$. What is the distance between points P and Q?

A. $\dfrac{\sqrt{15}}{2}$

B. $\dfrac{\sqrt{17}}{2}$

C. $\dfrac{\sqrt{45}}{2}$

D. $\sqrt{34}$

E. $3\sqrt{10}$

268. The coordinates of a point P are (x, y) such that $xy > 0$. Given the four quadrants of the (x, y) coordinate plane shown, which of the following statements MUST be true?

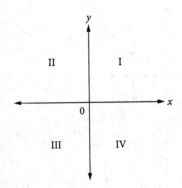

A. Point P must lie in quadrant I.
B. Point P must lie in quadrant II.
C. Point P must lie in quadrant III.
D. Point P must lie in either quadrant I or quadrant II.
E. Point P must lie in either quadrant I or quadrant III.

269. If the x- and y-intercepts of a line in the (x, y) coordinate plane are nonzero and share the same sign, which of the following statements MUST be true?

A. The slope of the line is negative.
B. The slope of the line is positive.
C. The slope of the line is zero.
D. The slope of the line is undefined.
E. The slope of the line is nonzero and defined.

270. Which of the following lines has a slope of zero?

A.

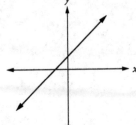

B.

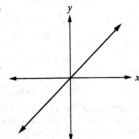

C.

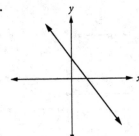

D.

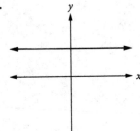

E.

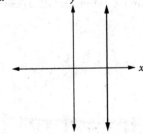

271. What is the slope of the line in the following figure?

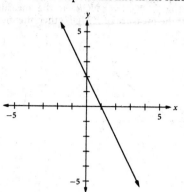

A. −3

B. −2

C. −$\frac{1}{2}$

D. $\frac{1}{2}$

E. 2

272. The points A (1, 0), B (1, 8), and C (5, 0) form a triangle in the (x, y) coordinate plane. In coordinate units, what is the area of triangle ABC?

A. 3

B. 12

C. 16

D. 32

E. 40

273. In the following figure, lines m, n, and ℓ intersect to form angles with the indicated measures. What is the value of $x + y + z$?

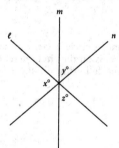

A. 30

B. 60

C. 90

D. 120

E. 180

274. In the (x, y) coordinate plane, which of the following points would lie on the graph of the line $2y - x = 8$?

A. (−2, −3)

B. (−1, 1)

C. (0, 4)

D. (2, 3)

E. (4, 8)

275. A circle is drawn in the (x, y) coordinate plane such that the center of the circle is the point (0, 7). If the radius of the circle is 2, then each of the following points lies on the circle's circumference EXCEPT

A. (−2, 7)

B. (0, 9)

C. (0, 5)

D. (1, 7)

E. (2, 7)

276. Which of the following graphs represents a line with a positive slope and a negative x-intercept?

A.

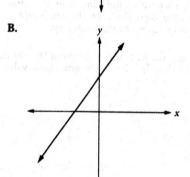

B.

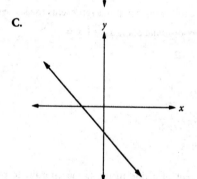

C.

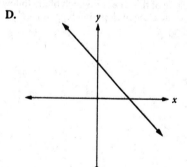

D.

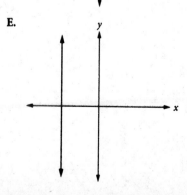

E.

277. In the (x, y) coordinate plane, what is the x-intercept of the line $y = -\frac{1}{4}x + 2$?

A. -8
B. -2
C. $-\frac{1}{4}$
D. 2
E. 8

278. For a line in the (x, y) coordinate plane, which of the following statements is always true of the y-intercept?

A. The coordinates are of the form $(c, 0)$ for some number c.
B. The coordinates are of the form $(0, c)$ for some number c.
C. If the slope is positive, the y-intercept is positive.
D. The larger the slope, the larger the y-intercept.
E. The origin can never be the y-intercept.

279. In the (x, y) coordinate plane, if the point $(x, -5)$ lies on the graph of the line $5y - 2x = -30$, what is the value of x?

A. -10
B. -8
C. $-\frac{23}{5}$
D. $\frac{5}{2}$
E. 15

280. Which of the following equations represents the same line in the (x, y) coordinate plane as $\frac{y}{4} + x = -\frac{1}{2}$?

A. $y = -4x - 2$
B. $y = -x - 2$
C. $y = -\frac{1}{2}x + \frac{1}{4}$
D. $y = -\frac{1}{4}x - \frac{1}{2}$
E. $y = 4x - \frac{1}{2}$

281. The x-intercept of a line in the (x, y) coordinate plane is -6. If the slope of this line is 5, which of the following is the equation of this line in slope-intercept form?

A. $y = 5x + 30$
B. $y = 5x - 6$
C. $y = 5x - 25$
D. $y = -6x + 5$
E. $y = -6x - 6$

282. In the following figure, PR, MQ, and NQ are line segments such that $\angle PQM = \angle NQR$. If the measure of $\angle PQM$ is half the measure of $\angle MQN$, then the measure of $\angle NQR$ is

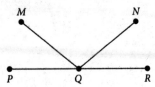

A. $35°$
B. $45°$
C. $90°$
D. $100°$
E. $120°$

283. In the (x, y) coordinate plane, the lines $y = 5x - 1$ and $y = -3x - 17$ intersect at the point with coordinates

A. $(-9, -46)$
B. $(-8, -41)$
C. $(-2, -11)$
D. $(2, 9)$
E. $(8, 39)$

284. If the angle between two perpendicular lines has a measure of $(2x + 2)°$, then $x =$

A. 44
B. 45
C. 89
D. 90
E. 91

285. In the (x, y) coordinate plane, a circle is centered at the point $(2, 5)$. If the point $(4, 9)$ is on the circumference of this circle, then which of the following distances is the radius?

A. 2
B. 4
C. $2\sqrt{5}$
D. $\sqrt{34}$
E. $4\sqrt{5}$

CHAPTER 5
GEOMETRY

QUESTIONS 286–358

---

286. The interior angles of a triangle are x, y, and z. If $x = 45°$ and $y = 90°$, then $z =$

A. 25°
B. 35°
C. 45°
D. 55°
E. 65°

287. In inches, what is the perimeter of a rectangle with a width of 4 inches and a length of 10 inches?

A. 14
B. 18
C. 28
D. 40
E. 160

288. For the triangle shown in the following figure, what is the value of sin x?

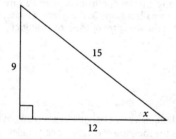

A. $\frac{3}{5}$

B. $\frac{3}{4}$

C. $\frac{4}{5}$

D. $\frac{4}{3}$

E. $\frac{7}{3}$

289. In the following figure, the area of square $ABCD$ is 16 square units. What is the circumference of the circle centered at point B?

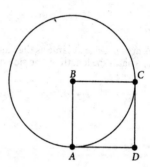

A. 2π
B. 4π
C. 8π
D. 16π
E. 32π

290. If $0° \leq \alpha \leq 90°$ and $\cos\alpha = \frac{9}{7}$, then $\sec\alpha =$

A. $-\frac{9}{7}$

B. $-\frac{7}{9}$

C. $\frac{1}{8}$

D. $\frac{2}{7}$

E. $\frac{7}{9}$

291. The area of a circle is 8π square units. What is the radius of the circle?

A. $2\sqrt{2}$
B. 4
C. $4\sqrt{2}$
D. 8
E. 12

292. The length of the shortest side of an isosceles triangle is 10 meters, and the length of the longest side is 20 meters. If the two smallest angles in the triangle are equal, what is the perimeter of the triangle in meters?

A. 40
B. 45
C. 85
D. 165
E. 185

293. In square units, what is the area of an equilateral triangle with sides of length 6 units?

A. 18
B. 36
C. $9\sqrt{3}$
D. $3\sqrt{5}$
E. $18\sqrt{5}$

294. The value of a square's area is twice as large as the value of its perimeter. In units, what is the length of one side of the square?

A. 4
B. 8
C. 12
D. 16
E. 32

295. A sidewalk is to be placed completely around a rectangular playing field that measures 110 yards by 200 yards. What is the length of the sidewalk, in yards?

A. 220
B. 310
C. 420
D. 510
E. 620

296. In the following figure, triangle ABC is a right triangle such that the sine of angle B is $\dfrac{3}{4}$. What is the value of x?

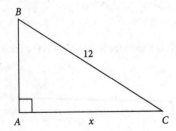

A. 4
B. 6
C. 9
D. 12
E. 16

297. In the (x, y) coordinate plane, which of the following is an equation of the circle with a center at the point $(0, -5)$ and a radius of 2?

A. $x^2 + (y + 5)^2 = 4$
B. $(x + 5)^2 + y^2 = 16$
C. $(x + 5)^2 + (y + 5)^2 = 4$
D. $(x - 5)^2 + (y - 5)^2 = 4$
E. $x^2 + (y - 5)^2 = 16$

298. In the following figure, the length of PR is half the length of QR. What is the length of line segment PQ?

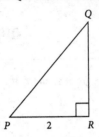

A. $\sqrt{2}$
B. $\sqrt{5}$
C. $2\sqrt{2}$
D. $2\sqrt{5}$
E. $4\sqrt{5}$

299. The length of the diagonal of a rectangle is 20 feet. If the width of the rectangle is 12 feet, what is its area in square feet?

A. 28
B. 144
C. 192
D. 256
E. 400

300. The sides of a triangle have lengths of 3, 3, and 12 meters, respectively. If the smallest angle in the triangle has a measure of 30°, what is the measure of the largest angle?

A. 60°
B. 90°
C. 100°
D. 120°
E. 140°

301. Each of the smallest angles in a parallelogram is 50°. Which of the following is the measure of each of largest angles in the parallelogram?

A. 40°
B. 80°
C. 130°
D. 260°
E. 310°

302. The length of one leg of a right triangle is three times as large as the length of the other leg. If the hypotenuse has a length of 10 inches, which of the following is the perimeter of the triangle in inches?

A. $\sqrt{10}$
B. $4\sqrt{10}$
C. 10
D. $10 + \sqrt{10}$
E. $10 + 4\sqrt{10}$

303. The circles in the following figure are centered at point *O*. In square centimeters, what is the area of the shaded region?

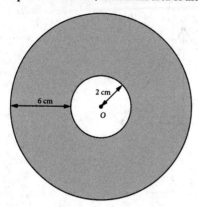

A. 15π
B. 21π
C. 32π
D. 35π
E. 60π

304. Which of the following expressions represents the circumference of a circle with a radius of *x*?

A. $2x$
B. πx
C. $2x\pi$
D. $4x\pi$
E. $4x$

305. Given the trapezoid in the following figure, what is the value of *x*?

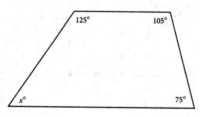

A. 55
B. 65
C. 75
D. 95
E. 105

306. In the following figure, the points *A*, *C*, and *D* lie along the same line, and *ABC* is a triangle with sides of the indicated length. If the measure of angle *CAB* is 85°, what is the measure of angle *BCD*, in degrees?

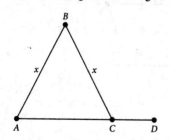

A. 85
B. 95
C. 105
D. 115
E. 120

307. In square units, what is the area of a circle with a circumference of 6π?

A. 3π
B. 6π
C. 9π
D. 12π
E. 36π

308. In the following figure, the square *ABCD* is a single side of a cube with a volume of 8 cubic inches. In inches, what is the length of the line *BD*?

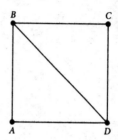

A. 1
B. $\sqrt{2}$
C. 2
D. $2\sqrt{2}$
E. 4

309. Given the right triangle in the following figure, what is the value of *x*?

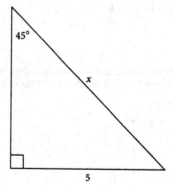

A. $2\sqrt{2}$
B. $5\sqrt{2}$
C. $\sqrt{5}$
D. $2\sqrt{5}$
E. $\sqrt{10}$

310. In inches, what is the radius of a sphere with a volume of 36π?

A. 1
B. 3
C. 6
D. 9
E. 12

311. In the following figure, what is the value of cos *x*?

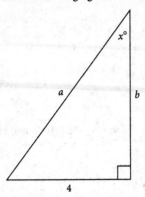

A. $\dfrac{b}{a}$

B. $\dfrac{a}{b}$

C. $\dfrac{4}{a}$

D. $\dfrac{b}{4}$

E. $\dfrac{a}{4}$

312. In the (*x, y*) coordinate plane, the points *A* (6, 0) and *B* (6, 10) are on the circumference of a circle such that the line *AB* is a diameter of the circle. Which of the following is an equation representing the described circle?

A. $(x-6)^2 + (y-5)^2 = 25$
B. $(x-6)^2 + (y-5)^2 = 100$
C. $(x-6)^2 + (y-10)^2 = 25$
D. $(x-6)^2 + (y-10)^2 = 100$
E. $(x-5)^2 + (y-10)^2 = 100$

313. In the following figure, the square *ABCD* is inscribed in the circle centered at point *O*. What is the area of the circle?

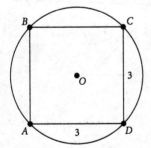

A. $\dfrac{\pi}{4}$

B. $\dfrac{3\pi}{4}$

C. $\dfrac{3\pi}{2}$

D. $\dfrac{9\pi}{4}$

E. $\dfrac{9\pi}{2}$

314. In the following figure, *AB* = *BC* = *AC*, and *BD* bisects the angle *ABC*. What is the value of *x*?

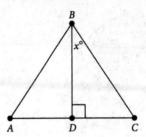

A. 15
B. 20
C. 30
D. 45
E. 60

315. In square meters, what is the area of a rectangle with a diagonal of 25 meters and a width of 15 meters?

A. 200
B. 250
C. 275
D. 300
E. 375

316. In the following figure, *ABCD* is a rectangle such that $\tan x = \dfrac{8}{3}$. In square feet, what is the area of the rectangle?

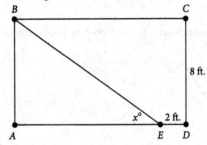

A. 16
B. 24
C. 40
D. 48
E. 52

317. In the following figure, *ABCD* is a parallelogram such that *AB* has a length of 3 centimeters and *BC* has a length of 7 centimeters. What is the perimeter of *ABCD*?

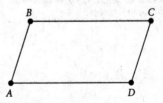

A. 10
B. 20
C. 30
D. 40
E. 50

318. A rectangular container measuring 4 feet wide, 8 feet long, and 3 feet tall is filled with a 1-foot-deep layer of sand. In cubic feet, what volume of the container remains unfilled?

A. 18
B. 32
C. 42
D. 64
E. 72

319. The sides of the rhombus *ABCD* in the following figure all have the same length, and the diagonal *AC* is half the length of the diagonal *BD*. If the length of diagonal *AC* is *m*, which of the following expressions represents the area of *ABCD* in terms of *m*?

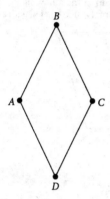

A. $\frac{3}{2}m$

B. m^2

C. $\frac{1}{2}m^2$

D. $\frac{\sqrt{3}}{2}m^2$

E. $\frac{3}{2}m^2$

320. Two squares of the same size overlap such that all three of the resulting rectangles shown in the figure have the same area. If the area of the shaded rectangle is 2, what is the area of one of the original squares?

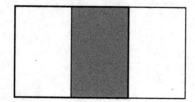

A. 2
B. 4
C. 9
D. 16
E. 25

321. The following figure represents the dimensions of three rooms of a house that are to be completely carpeted. In total, how many square feet of carpet will be needed?

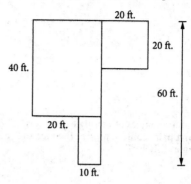

A. 1200
B. 1300
C. 1500
D. 1700
E. 1800

322. Triangle *ABC* in the following figure is an isosceles triangle with height *BD*. What is the value of *a*?

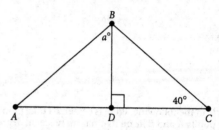

A. 45
B. 50
C. 60
D. 65
E. 90

323. The interior angles of a triangle measure $x°$, $(2x)°$, and $(3x)°$. The value of *x* MUST be

A. 30
B. 35
C. 45
D. 50
E. 65

324. In the following figure, the circles centered at points *B* and *D* are tangent at the point *C*, and each circle has an area of 49π. What is the length of the line segment *AE*?

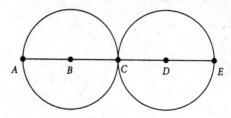

A. 14
B. 28
C. 42
D. 48
E. 56

325. If a right triangle has legs of length $5x$ and x, which of the following expressions represents the length of its hypotenuse in terms of x?

   A. $2x$
   B. $5x$
   C. $x\sqrt{6}$
   D. $2x\sqrt{6}$
   E. $x\sqrt{26}$

326. If one of the interior angles of a triangle measures 72°, each of the following pairs could represent the measures of the remaining angles EXCEPT

   A. 58°, 50°
   B. 42°, 66°
   C. 15°, 93°
   D. 87°, 21°
   E. 36°, 73°

327. The length of a rectangle is 5 times its width. If the width is represented by w, which of the following expressions is the perimeter of the rectangle in terms of w?

   A. $5w$
   B. $6w$
   C. $10w$
   D. $12w$
   E. $14w$

328. The circle in the following figure is centered at the point O, and the points A and B lie on its circumference. In degrees, what is the measure of angle AOB?

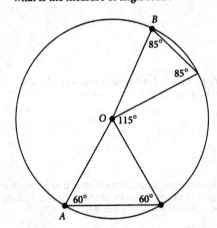

   A. 95
   B. 165
   C. 175
   D. 180
   E. 190

329. In the following figure, $FBCE$ is a rectangle, while ABF and ECD are congruent right triangles. What is the area of the quadrilateral $ABCD$?

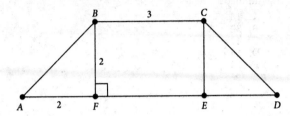

   A. 6
   B. 8
   C. 10
   D. 12
   E. 16

330. The perimeter of the parallelogram in the following figure is 20 feet. In feet, what is the length of the side labeled with an x?

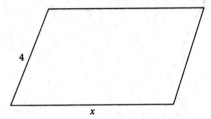

   A. 4
   B. 6
   C. 8
   D. 12
   E. 16

331. A rectangle has an area of 45 square meters and a width of 9 meters. In meters, what is the length of the rectangle?

   A. 5
   B. 7
   C. 14
   D. 27
   E. 36

332. Given the parallelogram in the following figure, what is the value of $x + y$?

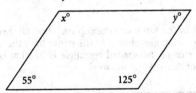

   A. 55
   B. 90
   C. 125
   D. 180
   E. 230

333. Given the right triangle in the following figure, what is the value of *x*?

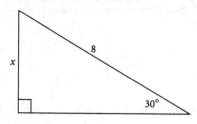

- **A.** 4
- **B.** $2\sqrt{5}$
- **C.** 8
- **D.** $4\sqrt{3}$
- **E.** $8\sqrt{3}$

334. In the following figure, the area of the circle centered at the point *O* is $\frac{29\pi}{4}$ square feet. Given that *AB* has a length of 2 feet, what is the area of triangle *ABC* in square feet?

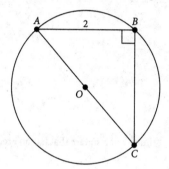

- **A.** 1
- **B.** $\frac{\sqrt{13}}{2}$
- **C.** 5
- **D.** 10
- **E.** $4\sqrt{29}$

335. In square centimeters, what is the area of the parallelogram in the following figure?

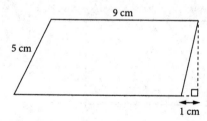

- **A.** $18\sqrt{6}$
- **B.** 45
- **C.** $\frac{95}{2}$
- **D.** $20\sqrt{6}$
- **E.** 50

336. A modern-art piece begins as a special canvas with dimensions shown in the following figure. Initially, the canvas will be painted with a base coat of flat paint. If one tube of the paint can cover four square feet, how many tubes will the artist need in order to apply the base coat?

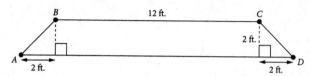

- **A.** 6
- **B.** 7
- **C.** 8
- **D.** 9
- **E.** 10

337. Each of the following pairs of angles could represent the smaller and larger interior angles of a parallelogram EXCEPT

- **A.** 8°, 172°
- **B.** 20°, 160°
- **C.** 35°, 155°
- **D.** 65°, 115°
- **E.** 81°, 99°

338. In the following figure, *ABC* is an equilateral triangle. What is the value of *x*?

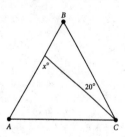

- **A.** 40
- **B.** 60
- **C.** 80
- **D.** 100
- **E.** 120

339. When completely filled, a spherical balloon contains exactly $\frac{32\pi}{3}$ cubic feet of air. In feet, what is the radius of the balloon when it is completely filled?

- **A.** 2
- **B.** $\frac{4\sqrt{6}}{3}$
- **C.** 4
- **D.** $2\sqrt{6}$
- **E.** 8

340. In the following figure, the points A, B, C, and D lie along the same line. What is the difference of x and y?

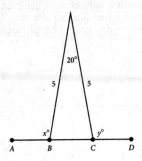

A. 0
B. 20
C. 60
D. 160
E. 200

341. In square meters, what is the area of a single face of a cube that has a volume of 125 cubic meters?

A. $2\sqrt{3}$
B. 5
C. $5\sqrt{5}$
D. 25
E. 63

342. Which of the following expressions represents the area of a right triangle with legs of lengths x and y?

A. $\dfrac{xy}{2}$
B. $\dfrac{x^2 y^2}{2}$
C. $\dfrac{x+y}{2}$
D. $\dfrac{x^2 + y^2}{2}$
E. $\dfrac{\sqrt{x^2 + y^2}}{2}$

343. In the following figure, $ABCD$ is a rectangle, and BD is one of its diagonals. If the area of the triangle ABD is 6 square meters, what is the area of $ABCD$ in square meters?

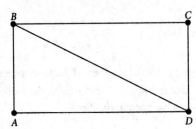

A. 3
B. 6
C. 12
D. 18
E. 24

344. A circle in the (x, y) coordinate plane is determined by the equation $(x - 8)^2 + (y - 10)^2$. Which of the following points lies on the circumference of this circle?

A. $(2, 10)$
B. $(6, 10)$
C. $(8, 6)$
D. $(8, 14)$
E. $(12, 10)$

345. Given the triangle in the following figure, if $x = \dfrac{1}{2}$, then $\sin x =$

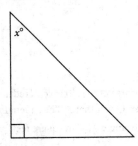

A. $\sqrt{2}$
B. $\sqrt{3}$
C. $\sqrt{5}$
D. $\dfrac{\sqrt{5}}{5}$
E. $\dfrac{\sqrt{3}}{2}$

346. In feet, what is the perimeter of a square that has an area of 49 square feet?

A. 14
B. 28
C. 56
D. 98
E. 196

347. In the following figure, $ABCD$ is a rectangle, and PQR is an equilateral triangle. Given the provided measurements are in inches, what is the area of the rectangle $ABCD$ in square inches?

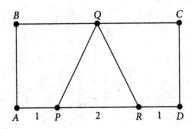

A. $\sqrt{3}$
B. $2\sqrt{3}$
C. 5
D. 8
E. $4\sqrt{3}$

348. If $x \neq y$, which of the following expressions represents the perimeter of the triangle in the following figure in terms of x and y?

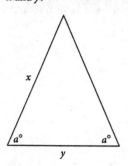

A. $x + y$
B. $x + y + 2$
C. $2x + y$
D. $x + 2y$
E. $2(x + y)$

349. The parallelogram in the following figure has a perimeter of 32 feet. If x is three times as large as y, what is the value of x in feet?

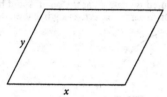

A. 2
B. 4
C. 8
D. 12
E. 24

350. In the following figure, ABC is a triangle such that M is the midpoint of AB and N is the midpoint of AC. If the area of triangle ABC is 12, what is the length of side AB?

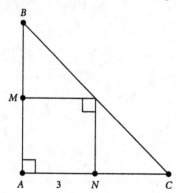

A. 2
B. 4
C. 6
D. 8
E. 10

351. If the circumference of a circle is larger than x, then the circle's radius must be larger than

A. 2π
B. $2\pi x$
C. $x - 2\pi$
D. $\dfrac{x}{2\pi}$
E. $\dfrac{1}{2\pi}$

352. The sides of the rhombus $ABCD$ in the following figure all have the same length, and the dashed line AC is a diagonal of $ABCD$. If the measure of $\angle BCD = 60°$, then $x =$

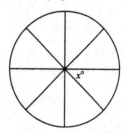

A. 30
B. 40
C. 60
D. 120
E. 180

353. A circle is divided into 8 equal sections, as shown in the following figure. What is the value of x?

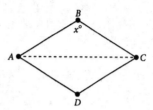

A. 25
B. 36
C. 45
D. 50
E. 55

354. Which of the following values represents the circumference of a circle whose radius is $\dfrac{1}{\pi}$?

A. $\dfrac{1}{2}$
B. 1
C. 2
D. π
E. 2π

355. If the area of the square $ABCD$ in the following figure is 16, what is the value of tan x?

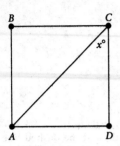

A. $\dfrac{\sqrt{2}}{8}$

B. $\dfrac{1}{4}$

C. 1

D. $\sqrt{2}$

E. $4\sqrt{2}$

356. If the interior angles of a quadrilateral have measures $x°$, $(2x)°$, $(x + 45)°$, and $(x + 55)°$, then $x =$

A. 16

B. 23

C. 52

D. 65

E. 78

357. In the following figure, the height of triangle MNP is 10 units larger than the height of triangle ABC. Both triangles have a base of length x. If the area of triangle ABC is 50 square units and $x = 5$, what is the area of triangle MNP in square units?

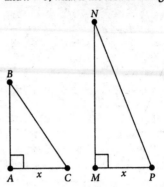

A. 55

B. 60

C. 65

D. 70

E. 75

358. The half circle pictured is centered at the point A and has a radius of 2 meters. In meters, what is the length of the arc PQ?

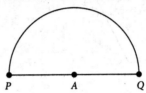

A. π

B. 2π

C. 4π

D. 8π

E. 16π

CHAPTER 6
PROPORTIONS

QUESTIONS 359–428

---

359. The ratio of x to y is 5 to 12. If x is 45, what is the value of y?

A. 38
B. 52
C. 60
D. 84
E. 108

360. If a vehicle is moving at a constant speed of 60 miles per hour, how many miles will it travel in 1 hour and 20 minutes?

A. 60
B. 65
C. 80
D. 90
E. 105

361. If $M\%$ of 135 is 54, then $M =$

A. 2.5
B. 4
C. 25
D. 40
E. 81

362. In a large company, the ratio of full-time to part-time employees is 3:2. If there are 800 total employees, how many are part-time?

A. 260
B. 320
C. 400
D. 480
E. 530

363. If the length of one side of a square is increased by 20%, then the perimeter will increase by

A. 5%
B. 10%
C. 20%
D. 40%
E. 80%

364. A rectangle has a width of 5 meters and a length of 14 meters. If a similar rectangle has a width of 15 meters, what is its perimeter, in meters?

A. 42
B. 58
C. 60
D. 78
E. 114

365. If 5% of x is y and 25% of y is z, then how many times larger than z is x?

A. 4
B. 30
C. 80
D. 95
E. 125

366. A special garden design requires that the garden have three distinct square sections whose areas follow the ratio $2 : 3 : 5$. If such a garden is designed to have a total area of 1550 square feet, then what would be the area of the smallest section in square feet?

A. 155
B. 250
C. 300
D. 500
E. 750

367. In the following figure, triangles ABC and DEF are similar. What is the value of x?

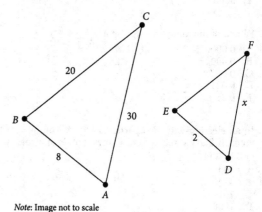

Note: Image not to scale

A. 5.0
B. 7.5
C. 15.0
D. 24.0
E. 36.5

368. If a is inversely proportional to $\frac{b}{2}$ and $a = 1$ when $b = 10$, then what is the value of a when $b = 35$?

A. $\frac{1}{7}$

B. $\frac{1}{5}$

C. $\frac{2}{9}$

D. $\frac{9}{4}$

E. $\frac{7}{2}$

369. If 80% of $x + 1$ is 2, then $x =$

A. 0.975
B. 1.25
C. 1.5
D. 4
E. 5.1

370. If m is directly proportional to n^2 and $m = 2$ when $n = -1$, then which of the following expressions represents the value of m in terms of x when $n = x + 5$?

A. $2x + 5$
B. $2x + 10$
C. $2x^2 + 10$
D. $2x^2 + 10x + 25$
E. $2x^2 + 20x + 50$

371. Greg can read w words a minute. How many minutes will it take Greg to read an n-page document if each page contains 500 words?

A. $\frac{500n}{w}$

B. $\frac{500w}{n}$

C. $500nw$
D. $500(n + w)$
E. $500n + w$

372. Which of the following represents $\frac{1}{2}$% of $\frac{1}{20}$?

A. 0.000025
B. 0.00025
C. 0.0025
D. 0.025
E. 0.25

373. In an election with two parties, Party A won 54% of the votes. If Party B received 874 votes, how many votes were cast in total?

A. 400
B. 472
C. 1619
D. 1900
E. 2102

374. Each side of square A has a length of 3 meters, while each side of square B has a length of 9 meters. What is the ratio of the area of square A to the area of square B?

A. 1:1
B. 1:3
C. 1:6
D. 1:9
E. 1:12

375. The ratio of the lengths of each of the sides of a triangle is 4:12:14. If the shortest side has a length of 2 feet, what is the perimeter of the triangle in feet?

A. 15
B. 24
C. 34
D. 57
E. 68

376. In a college with 14,000 students, 490 are majoring in mathematics. What percentage of the student body does the number of math majors represent?

A. 0.0035%
B. 0.035%
C. 0.35%
D. 3.5%
E. 35%

377. In the following figure, the ratio of the lengths of AB to BC of rectangle $ABCF$ is 2:3, and C is the midpoint of DF. If $AF = FE$, what is the area of triangle DEF?

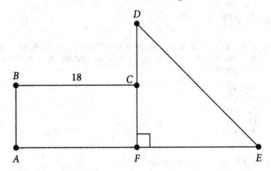

A. 12
B. 28
C. 54
D. 108
E. 216

378. In the following figure, rectangles $ABCD$ and $EFGD$ are similar. What is the perimeter of $EFGD$?

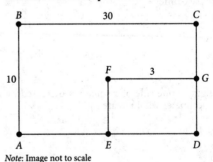

Note: Image not to scale

A. 4
B. 8
C. 26
D. 30
E. 40

379. If x is inversely proportional to y and $x = 12$ when $y = 48$, then what is the value of x when $y = 12$?

A. 2
B. 3
C. 6
D. 12
E. 14

380. If 80% of a number is 122, what is 40% of the number?

A. 48.8
B. 61.0
C. 73.2
D. 83.0
E. 244.0

381. A factory's quality assurance specialist can inspect 28 hard drives in 40 minutes. How many minutes will it take the specialist to inspect 196 hard drives?

A. 47
B. 49
C. 89
D. 137
E. 280

382. If the ratio of A to B is 3:8 and the ratio of B to C is 1:6, what is the ratio of A to C?

A. 1:2
B. 1:14
C. 1:16
D. 1:24
E. 1:48

383. A $154.99 graphing calculator can be purchased with a coupon that gives a 15% discount. What is the price of the calculator if it is purchased with the coupon?

A. $23.25
B. $68.47
C. $131.74
D. $139.99
E. $152.67

384. The length of a rectangle is 40% larger than its width. If the area of the rectangle is 140 square feet, what is the width of the rectangle in feet?

A. 10
B. 22
C. 35
D. 56
E. 64

385. In the following figure, triangles ABC and DEF are similar. Which of the following expressions represents the area of DEF in terms of x and y?

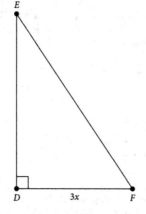

A. $\dfrac{xy}{2}$

B. $\dfrac{3xy}{2}$

C. $3xy$

D. $\dfrac{9xy}{2}$

E. $6xy$

386. For $x > 0$, which of the following represents $x\%$ of $\dfrac{3}{4}$?

A. $\dfrac{3x}{40}$

B. $\dfrac{3x}{400}$

C. $\dfrac{3}{400x}$

D. $\dfrac{30}{4x}$

E. $\dfrac{30x}{4}$

387. What is $\dfrac{1}{4}\%$ of $\dfrac{1}{4}$?

A. 0.000250
B. 0.000625
C. 0.0025
D. 0.0050
E. 1

388. The following table represents the percentages of employees in each of four possible classifications at a certain company. If there are no other possible classifications, what is the value of x?

Classification	Percentage
Part-time	35%
Full-time, hourly	20%
Full-time, salary	24%
Full-time, salary and bonus	$x\%$

A. 1
B. 21
C. 44
D. 79
E. 65

389. If the ratio of x to y is 1:6, what is the difference between y and x when $x = 12$?

A. 5
B. 12
C. 17
D. 60
E. 72

390. In the following figure, the ratio of x to y is 1:4. What is the ratio of the area of the triangle with base x to the area of the triangle with base $x + y$?

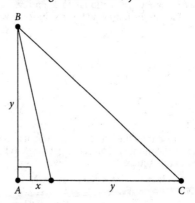

A. 1:2
B. 1:4
C. 1:5
D. 1:7
E. Cannot be determined

391. Rectangles *ABCD* and *PQRS* in the following figure are similar. What is the value of *x*?

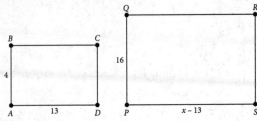

Note: Image not to scale

   A. 13
   B. 25
   C. 38
   D. 52
   E. 65

392. If 95% of $3x$ is 39.9, what is the value of x?

   A. 10
   B. 14
   C. 38
   D. 42
   E. 58

393. The circles in the following figure are centered at points O and P, respectively. If $\frac{AB}{CD} = 3$, what is the ratio of the area of the circle centered at point O to the area of the circle centered at point P?

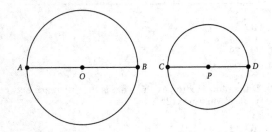

   A. 3:1
   B. 3:2
   C. 6:1
   D. 9:1
   E. 9:2

394. Suppose y^2 is inversely proportional to x and $y^2 = 16$ when $x = 4$. Which of the following is the value of y^2 when $x = 2$?

   A. 4
   B. $\sqrt{21}$
   C. $4\sqrt{2}$
   D. 8
   E. 32

395. The number representing the length of one side of a square is 20% as large as the number representing its area. What is the perimeter of this square?

   A. 5
   B. 15
   C. 20
   D. 34
   E. 60

396. If the ratio of x to y is 2:5, and y is always 30% of z, then for all possible nonzero values of x, y, and z, $\frac{x}{z} =$

   A. $\frac{1}{12}$
   B. $\frac{3}{25}$
   C. $\frac{2}{3}$
   D. $\frac{5}{6}$
   E. $\frac{3}{4}$

397. If $\frac{x}{50} \times 280 = 112$, then x% of 280 is

   A. 23
   B. 56
   C. 102
   D. 188
   E. 224

398. The triangles in the following figure are similar. In terms of x, what is the perimeter of triangle *DEF*?

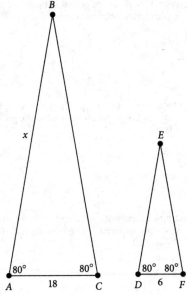

Note: Image not to scale

   A. $\frac{x}{6} + 6$
   B. $\frac{x}{3} + 6$
   C. $\frac{2x}{3} + 6$
   D. $2x + 6$
   E. $6x + 6$

399. A weather station reported that 90% of the days in a 30-day period had measurable snowfall. How many of these days received measurable snowfall?

   A. 3
   B. 12
   C. 18
   D. 27
   E. 29

400. Triangle A and triangle B are equilateral triangles such that the ratio of the length of one side of triangle A to the length of one side of triangle B is 6 to 7. If the perimeter of triangle A is 9, what is the length of a single side of triangle B?

A. $\frac{2}{3}$

B. $\frac{7}{2}$

C. 12

D. 18

E. 21

401. In the following figure, $ABCD$ is a rectangle such that $\frac{x}{y} = \frac{1}{5}$. If the area of $ABPQ$ is 12, what is the area of $ABCD$?

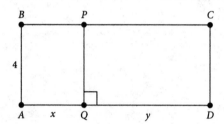

A. 32

B. 56

C. 60

D. 72

E. 112

402. The ratio of x to y is 2 to 3. If the sum of x and y is 125, what is the value of x?

A. 15

B. 25

C. 50

D. 75

E. 100

403. Which of the following represents 0.2% of $\frac{1}{5}$?

A. $\frac{1}{25,000}$

B. $\frac{1}{2500}$

C. $\frac{1}{250}$

D. $\frac{1}{25}$

E. $\frac{1}{10}$

404. For any circle with radius $r > 0$, what is the ratio of the length of its radius to its area?

A. $1 : \pi$

B. $1 : 2\pi$

C. $1 : \pi r$

D. $1 : 2\pi r$

E. $1 : \pi r^2$

405. Every student enrolled in a science course is either a physics major or a biology major. If the ratio of physics majors to biology majors is 3 to 1 and there are 21 physics majors enrolled, how many biology majors are enrolled in the course?

A. 7

B. 15

C. 23

D. 45

E. 63

406. Suppose that m is inversely proportional to n and that $m = \frac{1}{2}$ when $n = 6$. If $n = \frac{2}{3}$, what is the value of m?

A. $\frac{1}{6}$

B. 2

C. 3

D. $\frac{9}{2}$

E. 6

407. The value of a positive number x is 30% of the value of a positive number y. If 20% of y is 8, what is the value of x?

A. 10

B. 12

C. 16

D. 40

E. 70

408. If y is directly proportional to x and if $y = 6$ when $x = \frac{1}{4}$, then which of the following equations describes the relationship between x and y?

A. $y = \frac{1}{4}x$

B. $y = \frac{3}{2}x$

C. $y = \frac{23}{4}x$

D. $y = 6x$

E. $y = 24x$

409. A rectangle has sides of length x and $x + 1$, where x is a positive number. If the area of the rectangle is 12, then which of the following is equivalent to the ratio of x to $x + 1$?

A. 1:6

B. 1:4

C. 1:3

D. 2:3

E. 3:4

410. If the length of one side of a square is 28% of 50, then the area of the square is equal to

A. 70

B. 84

C. 140

D. 196

E. 289

411. If $q\%$ of 30 is 21, then $q =$

A. 50

B. 60

C. 70

D. 80

E. 90

412. This week, the price of a plane ticket is $436.00. Over the next three weeks, suppose the price of the ticket rises 5% in the first week, falls 10% the next week, and then rises 20% in the third week. To the nearest cent, what is the cost of the plane ticket in 3 weeks?

 A. $412.02
 B. $457.80
 C. $494.42
 D. $501.40
 E. $523.20

413. Of 600 items in a storage closet, 40% are pens or pencils, 10% are first-aid items, and 5% are notebooks. How many items in the storage closet have NOT been described?

 A. 45
 B. 60
 C. 240
 D. 270
 E. 300

414. A number a is four times as large as half of a number b. If a and b are nonzero, what percent of a is b?

 A. 20%
 B. 25%
 C. 50%
 D. 100%
 E. 400%

415. A particle can move along the x-axis of the (x, y) coordinate plane at the rate of 3 units every $\frac{1}{2}$ hour. If the particle begins at the origin and moves in the positive x direction, at what point will it be in $2\frac{1}{4}$ hours?

 A. $\left(\frac{9}{8}, 0\right)$

 B. $\left(\frac{27}{8}, 0\right)$

 C. $\left(\frac{9}{2}, 0\right)$

 D. $\left(\frac{27}{4}, 0\right)$

 E. $\left(\frac{27}{2}, 0\right)$

416. In the following figure, the ratio of x to y is 1:4. What is the value of x?

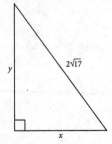

 A. 1
 B. 2
 C. 8
 D. 10
 E. 13

417. Points A, B, and C in the following figure are collinear. If the ratio of m to n is 2:3, what is the value of n in degrees?

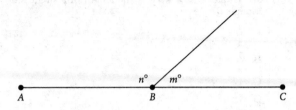

 A. 36
 B. 94
 C. 108
 D. 120
 E. 170

418. If, for nonzero values of m, n, and x, $\frac{m}{n} = \frac{4}{9}$ and $\frac{n}{x} = \frac{4}{3}$, then $\frac{m}{x} =$

 A. $\frac{1}{27}$

 B. $\frac{1}{3}$

 C. $\frac{16}{27}$

 D. $\frac{31}{12}$

 E. $\frac{16}{3}$

419. If $\frac{2}{5}$% of x is 10, then $\frac{1}{5}$% of x must equal

 A. 5
 B. 10
 C. 20
 D. 25
 E. 30

420. Every 6 minutes, a red LED flashes to indicate that a machine is operating correctly. If the machine operates correctly for 800 minutes, how many times will the LED flash?

 A. 133
 B. 134
 C. 135
 D. 136
 E. 137

421. If y is inversely proportional to the square root of x and if y has a value of 18 when x is 4, what is the value of y when x is 12?

 A. $\frac{\sqrt{3}}{9}$

 B. $\frac{\sqrt{6}}{9}$

 C. $\frac{\sqrt{3}}{3}$

 D. $3\sqrt{2}$

 E. $6\sqrt{3}$

422. A circle has a diameter of length d and an area of A. If the diameter of the circle is tripled, the area of the new circle is B. How many times larger than A is B?

A. 3
B. 6
C. 9
D. 12
E. 18

423. In the following figure, $AC = CE = 4$, C is the midpoint of BD, and $ABDE$ is a rectangle. What is the ratio of the area of triangle ACE to the area of triangle ABC?

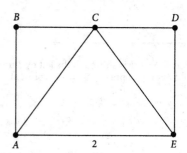

A. 2:1
B. 4:1
C. 8:1
D. 10:1
E. 15:1

424. If $\frac{1}{2}\%$ of $\frac{x}{14}$ is $\frac{1}{4}$, then $x =$

A. 7
B. 70
C. 700
D. 7000
E. 70,000

425. A tenant's monthly rent of \$675 will be increased by 3% every year. To the nearest cent, what will be the tenant's monthly rent in 3 years?

A. \$695.25
B. \$735.75
C. \$737.59
D. \$781.02
E. \$794.66

426. If $\frac{2x}{y} = \frac{4}{7}$, then how many times larger than x is y?

A. $\frac{7}{4}$
B. $\frac{7}{2}$
C. 4
D. 14
E. 28

427. A student's parking pass costs \$45 per semester this year but last year cost only \$38 per semester. To the nearest tenth of a percent, by what percentage has the price of a parking pass increased?

A. 15.6%
B. 18.4%
C. 24.3%
D. 28.6%
E. 31.1%

428. For the first two hours he is at work, Harrison files 14 folders every hour. For the remainder of his seven-hour workday, he files 22 folders every hour. How many folders did Harrison file over the entire day?

A. 28
B. 98
C. 138
D. 182
E. 308

CHAPTER 7
FUNCTIONS

429. Which of the following is a zero of the function $f(x) = x^2 (x - 4) (x + 1)$?

A. -4
B. -2
C. $-\dfrac{1}{2}$
D. 0
E. 1

430. Which of the following is a factor of $x^2 - x - 12$?

A. x
B. $x - 1$
C. $x - 3$
D. $x - 4$
E. $x - 12$

431. If $f(a) = 3a^2 - a^2$, then what is the value of $f(-2)$?

A. -7
B. -4
C. -2
D. 9
E. 20

432. The functions f and g are defined as $g(x) = mx + b$ for nonzero values of m and b, and $f(x) = ax^2 + bx + c$ for nonzero values of a, b, and c. In the standard (x, y) coordinate plane, what is the maximum number of times the graphs of $f(x)$ and $g(x)$ can cross each other?

A. 1
B. 2
C. 3
D. 4
E. 5

433. In the standard (x, y) coordinate plane, a polynomial function $f(x)$ crosses the x-axis at the points $(-3, 0)$, $(-2, 0)$, $(4, 0)$, $(5, 0)$, and $(7, 0)$ only. Each of the following is a factor of $f(x)$ EXCEPT

A. $x - 3$
B. $x - 4$
C. $x - 7$
D. $x - 5$
E. $x + 2$

434. If the graph of $f(x) = x^2 - 1$ is shifted to the left by 3 units, which of the following expressions will represent the resulting graph?

A. $x^2 - 4$
B. $(x - 3)^2 - 1$
C. $x^2 - 2$
D. $(x + 3)^2 - 1$
E. $x^2 - 3$

435. In the standard (x, y) coordinate plane, the graph of the function $f(x) = 3x - 5$ crosses through the point $(q, 4)$. What is the value of q?

A. 2
B. 3
C. 5
D. 7
E. 9

436. The value of an investment grows based on the function $V(t) = 1000(1 + 0.06)^t$, where V is the value in dollars and t is the time in years. To the nearest cent, what is the value of the investment after 8 years?

A. $1068.48
B. $1410.09
C. $1593.85
D. $1604.66
E. $1790.85

437. If $f(x)$ is graphed in the following figure, then which of the following is a possible formula for $f(x)$?

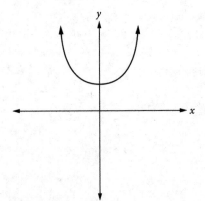

A. x^2
B. $(x - 4)^2$
C. $(x + 3)^2$
D. $x^2 - 2$
E. $x^2 + 4$

438. How many imaginary roots does the function $g(x) = x^2 + 1$ have?

A. 0
B. 1
C. 2
D. 3
E. 4

439. In the standard (x, y) coordinate plane, which of the following statements best describes the graph of $-f(x)$ in terms of the graph of $f(x)$ for any function $f(x)$?

A. It is the graph of $f(x)$ shifted downward by one unit.
B. It is the graph of $f(x)$ shifted upward by one unit.
C. It is the graph of $f(x)$ shifted to the left by one unit.
D. It is the graph of $f(x)$ shifted to the right by one unit.
E. None of these statements are correct.

440. If $f(x) = x^2 + x - 1$, which of the following expressions is equivalent to $f(a - 1)$?

A. $a^2 - a$
B. $a^2 - 3a$
C. $a^2 + a - 2$
D. $a^2 - a - 1$
E. $a^2 - 3a - 2$

441. Which of the following expressions is equivalent to $(2m - 6)^2$ for all values of m?

A. $4m^2 - 12$
B. $4m^2 - 24$
C. $4m^2 - 36$
D. $4m^2 - 24x + 36$
E. $4m^2 - 12x + 36$

442. Given the functions $f(x) = x + 6$ and $g(x) = x^2 - 2$, which of the following is the value of $(f \circ g)\,(3)$?

A. 7
B. 9
C. 10
D. 13
E. 79

443. In the standard (x, y) coordinate plane, the graphs of $f(x) = 8$ and $g(x) = 64x^3$ intersect at the point (a, b) in the first quadrant. What is the value of a?

A. $\frac{1}{8}$
B. $\frac{1}{2}$
C. 2
D. 4
E. 8

444. What is the value of $g(x) = x^4 + x^2$ if $x = \sqrt{3}$?

A. 9
B. $6\sqrt{3}$
C. 12
D. $15\sqrt{3}$
E. 15

445. What is the largest value of x that makes the equation $x^2 + 2x - 35 = 0$ true?

A. 5
B. 7
C. 12
D. 33
E. 35

446. The graph of a polynomial function crosses the x-axis at the points A, B, and C as indicated in the following figure. If the graph does not cross the x-axis at any other point, which of the following could be the formula for the function?

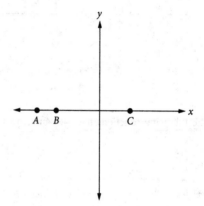

A. $f(x) = (x + 3)(x + 4)(x - 1)$
B. $f(x) = (x + 3)(x - 4)(x - 1)$
C. $f(x) = (x - 3)(x - 4)(x - 1)$
D. $f(x) = (x + 3)(x + 4)(x + 1)$
E. Cannot be determined

447. Given the function $f(x) = x^3 - 3x$, which of the following is true when $x = 1$?

A. $f(x) = -3$
B. $f(x) = -2$
C. $f(x) = 2$
D. $f(x) = 3$
E. $f(x)$ is undefined.

448. What is the value of $9a - a^2$ when $a = 10$?

A. -90
B. -10
C. 70
D. 81
E. 90

449. If $2x^2 - 6x = -4$ and $x < 0$, then $x =$
- **A.** -6
- **B.** -4
- **C.** -2
- **D.** -1
- **E.** There is no such value of x.

450. Which of the following is a factor of $x^4 - 16$?
- **A.** $x - 16$
- **B.** $x - 8$
- **C.** $x - 4$
- **D.** $x - 2$
- **E.** x

451. The following table represents values of a function $f(x)$ for the given values of x. Which of the following must be a solution to the equation $f(x) = 0$?

x	-6	-3	0
$f(x)$	0	1	4

- **A.** -6
- **B.** -4
- **C.** -3
- **D.** 1
- **E.** 4

452. Which of the following functions has the same roots as $f(x) = 3x^2 - 3x - 27$?
- **A.** $f_1(x) = x^2 - 3x - 27$
- **B.** $f_2(x) = 3x^2 - x - 27$
- **C.** $f_3(x) = 3x^2 - 3x - 3$
- **D.** $f_4(x) = x^2 - x - 3$
- **E.** $f_5(x) = x^2 - x - 9$

453. If the following steps evaluate a function g at the value x, then $g(x) =$

Step 1: Add 3 to x.
Step 2: Square the result of step 1.
Step 3: Multiply the result of step 2 by 5.

- **A.** $(5x + 3)^2$
- **B.** $5(x + 3)^2$
- **C.** $5(x^2 + 3)$
- **D.** $(5x)^2 + 3$
- **E.** $5x^2 + 3$

454. If $f(r, s) = rs - r$, then $f(2, -3) =$
- **A.** -8
- **B.** -4
- **C.** 1
- **D.** 6
- **E.** 7

455. If $f(x) = x^3$, which of the following tables would correctly represent the values of $-f(x)$ when x is $-2, -1, 0, 1,$ and 2?

A.

x	-2	-1	0	1	2
$-f(x)$	-8	-1	0	1	8

B.

x	-2	-1	0	1	2
$-f(x)$	-8	-1	0	-1	-8

C.

x	-2	-1	0	1	2
$-f(x)$	-8	-1	0	-1	-8

D.

x	-2	-1	0	1	2
$-f(x)$	8	-1	0	-1	8

E.

x	-2	-1	0	1	2
$-f(x)$	8	1	0	1	8

456. If the point (a, b) lies on the graph of a function $f(x)$ in the standard (x, y) coordinate plane, then which of the following points lies along the graph of $f(x - 2)$?
- **A.** $(-2a, b)$
- **B.** $(a, -2b)$
- **C.** $(a - 2, b)$
- **D.** $(a, b - 2)$
- **E.** $(a + 2, b)$

457. If, for a nonzero value of k, $f(x) = \dfrac{x - 3}{k}$ and $f(x) = 2$, then $k =$
- **A.** -3
- **B.** -2
- **C.** $-\dfrac{1}{2}$
- **D.** $-\dfrac{1}{6}$
- **E.** 6

458. If $f(x) = x^2$ and $g(x) = 72 - x$, what is the smallest value of x for which $f(x) = g(x)$?
- **A.** -9
- **B.** -8
- **C.** 0
- **D.** 8
- **E.** 9

459. If a, b, and c are nonzero real numbers, what is the least number of times a function $f(x) = ax^2 + bx + c$ may cross the x-axis?
- **A.** 0
- **B.** 1
- **C.** 2
- **D.** 3
- **E.** Cannot be determined without the values of a, b, c

460. Given the graph of $g(x)$ shown, which of the following graphs is of the function $-g(x)$?

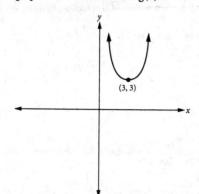

A.

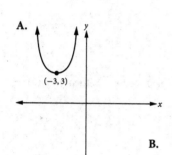

B.

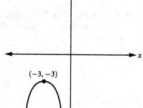

C.

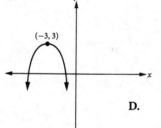

D.

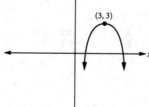

E.

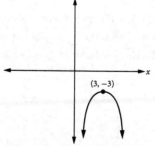

461. If $x > 0$ and $2x^2 - 5x + 3 = x^2 - 5x + 2$, then $x =$
A. 1
B. 2
C. 3
D. 5
E. There are no such real values of x.

462. The following figure represents the graph of a function $f(x)$ whose y-intercept is located at $(0, 2)$ and whose x-intercept is located at $(-4, 0)$. For what values of x must $f(x) > 0$?

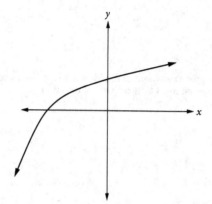

A. $x < -4$
B. $-4 < x < 2$
C. $x < 2$
D. $x > -4$
E. $x > 2$

463. If $f(x) = \dfrac{x-4}{x+1}$ for all nonzero values of x, then $f(5) =$
A. -4
B. $\dfrac{1}{6}$
C. 1
D. $\dfrac{3}{2}$
E. 5

464. The number of patients seen by a doctor over a day is represented by the function $p(t) = 8t - 5$, where P is the total number of patients seen after t hours. Based on this function, how many patients are seen between hours 5 and 6?
A. 3
B. 5
C. 8
D. 10
E. 13

465. For all values of a and b, which of the following expressions is equivalent to $(a - 6)(b + 4)$?
A. $ab - 24$
B. $ab - 2$
C. $a^2b - 2ab - 24$
D. $a^2b - 2ab - 2$
E. $ab + 4a - 6b - 24$

466. Which of the following is a factor of $x^2 - 36$?
A. $x - 36$
B. $x - 9$
C. $x - 6$
D. $x + 3$
E. $x + 12$

467. In the standard (x, y) coordinate plane, the graph of the function $g(x) = \dfrac{3x + 10}{8}$ passes through the point $(4, c)$. What is the value of c?

A. $\dfrac{4}{3}$

B. $\dfrac{3}{2}$

C. $\dfrac{17}{8}$

D. $\dfrac{11}{4}$

E. $\dfrac{22}{3}$

468. If one factor of a polynomial function is $x - k$, then which of the following must be a zero of the function?

A. $-k$

B. $-\dfrac{k}{2}$

C. 0

D. $\dfrac{k}{2}$

E. k

469. For which of the following values of x is the value of $g(x) = -x^2 + 10$ negative?

A. -4

B. -3

C. -2

D. -1

E. 3

470. If $f(x) = \dfrac{1}{2}x^2$ and $g(x) = 2x$, then for what value or values of x is $f(g(x))$?

A. -2 only

B. -2 and 2 only

C. 2 only

D. $2\sqrt{2}$ only

E. $-2\sqrt{2}$ and $2\sqrt{2}$ only

471. The graph of a function $g(x)$ is found by shifting the graph of the function $f(x)$ up by 6 units and to the left by 1 unit. If $f(x) = (x - 5)^3$, then $g(x) =$

A. x^3

B. $(x - 2)^3$

C. $(x + 1)^3 - 1$

D. $(x - 6)^3 + 6$

E. $(x - 4)^3 + 6$

472. If $f(x) = 2x (1 - x)^2$, then $f(1) =$

A. 0

B. 2

C. 4

D. 6

E. 8

473. Let the function $f(x)$ be defined as $f(x) = -x^2 + c$ for a positive value of c. If the function crosses the x-axis at the points -3 and 3, then which of the following must be true about $f(x)$ if $x < -3$?

I. $f(x)$ has the same possible values if $x > 3$.
II. $f(x) < 0$
III. $f(x) > c$

A. I only

B. II only

C. III only

D. I and II only

E. I and III only

474. If $g(a, b) = 4ab - b + a$, then for what values of b is $g(1, b) > 0$?

A. $b < -\dfrac{1}{3}$

B. $b > -\dfrac{1}{5}$

C. $b > -\dfrac{1}{3}$

D. $b > -1$

E. $b < 4$

475. If $f(x) = x + 10$ and $g(x) = -5x - 8$, then $(f \circ g)(7) =$

A. -93

B. -85

C. -43

D. -33

E. -29

476. Given the following graphs of $f(x)$ and $g(x)$ in the standard (x, y) coordinate plane, for what values of x is $g(x) > f(x)$?

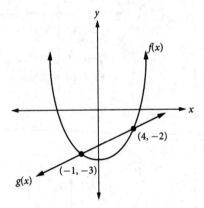

A. $x < -1$ and $x > 4$

B. $-1 < x < 4$

C. $x < -3$

D. $x < 4$

E. $x > -2$

477. For fixed real values of a, b, and c, a solution to the equation $ax^2 + bx + c = 0$ is $-\dfrac{5}{2}$. For the same values of a, b, and c, which of the following is a factor of the expression $ax^2 + bx + c$?

A. $2x - 5$

B. $2x + 5$

C. $-5x - 2$

D. $-5x + 2$

E. $5x - 2$

478. For all values of $x \neq 4$, the function $f(x) = \dfrac{x^2 - 3x - 4}{x - 4}$ has the same value as

A. $-7x$
B. $-3x$
C. $-\dfrac{3}{4}x + 1$
D. $-3x + 1$
E. $x + 1$

479. In the (x, y) coordinate plane, which of the following functions would have a graph that crosses or touches the x-axis at only one point?

A. $x^2 + 5$
B. $x^2 - 6$
C. $x^2 - 8x + 16$
D. $x^2 + 2x + 18$
E. $-x^2 + 4x - 10$

480. Which of the following is equivalent to $g(a^2 - 10)$ when $g(x) = x^2 + x - 5$?

A. $a^4 + 20a^2 + 85$
B. $a^4 + a^2 - 115$
C. $a^4 + a^2 + 85$
D. $a^4 - 19a^2 - 115$
E. $a^4 - 19a^2 + 85$

481. Which of the following points is on the graph of the function $f(x) = (x - 5)(x + 3)(x - 1)(x + 10)$?

A. $(0, 0)$
B. $(5, 0)$
C. $(0, -3)$
D. $(-1, 0)$
E. $(0, 10)$

482. Let a, b, and c represent any three real numbers where $a < 0$. If a quadratic function $f(x) = ax^2 + bx + c$ has x-intercepts of $(3, 0)$ and $(9, 0)$, then which of the following must be true about $f(4)$?

A. The value of $f(4)$ is negative.
B. The value of $f(4)$ is positive.
C. The value of $f(4)$ is zero.
D. The value of $f(4)$ is between -5 and 5.
E. The value of $f(4)$ is undefinable.

483. If $x = 4$ and $y = -1$, then $xy^4 + x^3y =$

A. -8
B. -16
C. -18
D. -60
E. -68

484. If one of the solutions to the equation $(x - 5)(x + 2)$ $(ax - b) = 0$ is -7, then which of the following pairs of values for a and b is possible?

A. $a = -7, b = 1$
B. $a = 1, b = -7$
C. $a = 7, b = 1$
D. $a = 1, b = 7$
E. $a = -1, b = -7$

485. The complete graph of a function $f(x)$ is shown in the following figure. How many real solutions does the equation $f(x) = 0$ have?

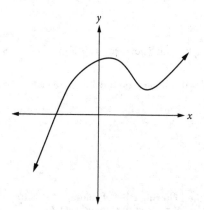

A. 0
B. 1
C. 2
D. 3
E. 4

486. Given the following table of values for a function $f(x)$, which of the following is the solution to the equation $\dfrac{f(2)}{4} = 12x$?

x	1	2	3
$f(x)$	2	8	10

A. $\dfrac{1}{48}$
B. $\dfrac{1}{12}$
C. $\dfrac{1}{6}$
D. $\dfrac{1}{4}$
E. $\dfrac{1}{3}$

487. In the (x, y) coordinate plane, the graphs of $f(x) = 2x^2 + 14$ and $g(x) = x^2 + 30$ intersect at the point (a, b). If $a < 0$, what is the value of b?

A. 22
B. 28
C. 30
D. 39
E. 46

488. For $0 \leq t \leq 19$, the motion of a particle can be modeled by the function $s(t) = -t^2 + 9t$ where s is the height of the particle in feet at time t seconds. What is the height of the particle at a time of 4 seconds?

A. 1 foot
B. 16 feet
C. 18 feet
D. 20 feet
E. 28 feet

489. If the function $f(x) = x^2 - 9x + 8$ is graphed in the (x, y) coordinate plane, then for which of the following values of x will the graph of $f(x)$ be below the x-axis?

A. $x < 1$
B. $x < 8$
C. $x < 1$ and $x > 8$
D. $1 < x < 8$
E. The graph is not below the x-axis for any values of x.

490. How many real number solutions does the equation $2x^3 = 9$ have?

A. 0
B. 1
C. 2
D. 3
E. 9

491. Based on the following table of values, what is the minimum number of zeros of the function $g(x)$?

x	-5	-3	0	1
$g(x)$	0	0	1	8

A. 1
B. 2
C. 3
D. 4
E. Cannot be determined from the given information

492. If $f(m, n) = m^2 - n - 3$ and both m and n are positive numbers, then which of the following statements must be true?

A. $f(m, n) < -3$
B. $f(m, n) < 0$
C. $f(m, n) > -3$
D. $f(m, n) > 0$
E. Cannot be determined from the given information

493. If graphed in the (x, y) coordinate plane, which of the following functions would have a graph that does not intersect the x-axis at any point?

A. $-x^2 + 10$
B. $-x^2 - 15$
C. $x^2 - 8$
D. $x^2 - 4$
E. x^2

494. What is the value of $f(x) = \frac{x^3}{4}$ when $x = \frac{1}{2}$?

A. $\frac{1}{32}$
B. $\frac{1}{16}$
C. $\frac{1}{12}$
D. $\frac{1}{8}$
E. $\frac{1}{2}$

495. The point (q, r) lies on the graph of a function $f(x)$ in the (x, y) coordinate plane. If the graph of $g(x)$ results from shifting the graph of $f(x)$ up 10 units, then which of the following points must lie on the graph of $g(x)$?

A. $(q + 10, r)$
B. $(q - 10, r)$
C. $(q, r + 10)$
D. $(q, r - 10)$
E. $(q + 10, r - 10)$

496. If $f(x) = 20$ when $x = 3$, then which of the following expressions is equivalent to $f(x)$ for this value of x?

A. $17x$
B. $20x$
C. $20x - 10$
D. $10x - 10$
E. $x + 20$

497. If $f(x) = x + 2$ and $g(x) = x^2 - x - 6$, then which of the following is equivalent to $\frac{g(x)}{f(x)}$ for all values of $x \neq -2$?

A. $x - 12$
B. $x - 8$
C. $x - 4$
D. $x - 3$
E. $x + 4$

498. Which of the following expressions represents a polynomial with exactly one real root?

A. $x^2 - 3$
B. $x^2 - 1$
C. $x^2 + 1$
D. $x^2 + 2x + 1$
E. $x^2 + 3x + 2$

499. If $f(x) = 2x + 6$ and $f(b) = 18$, then $b =$

A. 6
B. 12
C. 24
D. 36
E. 42

500. If $x^2 = 8x - 15$, then which of the following is a possible value of x?

A. -15
B. -8
C. -3
D. 0
E. 5

PART I ANSWERS AND EXPLANATIONS

Chapter 1: Numbers

1. **D.** The greatest common factor is the largest number that divides exactly into two or more numbers. With that in mind, this problem is best approached by elimination. Since each number ends in a zero, we know that each is divisible by 10. This means the correct answer must be either D or E. Checking, 130 is not divisible by 30, so the correct answer must be D.

2. **E.** Irrational numbers cannot be written as a fraction of two whole numbers. Each answer choice can be written as a whole number (which is the same as a fraction with a denominator of 1) or a fraction of whole numbers except answer choice E.

3. **B.** The given information indicates that a is negative and both b and c are positive with b being larger than c. The difference $a - c$ (choice A) would be of the form (negative) − (positive), which is always negative. Since answer A states that $a - c > 0$ (is positive), choice A cannot be correct. The difference $c - b$ (choice B) will also always be negative, since b is larger than c. Unlike choice A, choice B states $c - b < 0$ (is negative), so this is the answer. The values of the remaining inequalities depend on the exact values of a, b, and c, which we do not know.

4. **C.** Two facts are important here: First, anything to the zero power is 1. Second, $\frac{1}{n} = a^{-n}$. Using these facts, the given equation becomes $1 = \frac{1}{(1-n)^3}$. The only way this fraction will be equivalent to 1 is if the denominator also is 1. Of the values given, the only value of n for which this is true is 0.

5. **C.** The closest perfect square to 50 is $49 = 7 \times 7$. No integer larger than 7 is smaller than the square root of 50, since $8 \times 8 = 64$.

6. **A.** An even number is defined as any number that can be written as a multiple of 2. Answer choice A is the only choice that can always be written as a multiple of 2 for any m and n, since it already is written in that form.

7. **E.** Careful inspection of the answer choices shows that answer choice E is the same equation with the subtraction written differently. It is always true that $a - b = -b + a$. Since there can be only one correct answer, this must be it. However, the others can be shown to be incorrect by using different examples of x, y, and a.

8. **A.** The correct answer will not be divisible by 7 but will be divisible by 2 and 3. This is the same as saying it is a multiple of 6 but not of 7. Answer choice A is equivalent to -9×6 and is not divisible by 7.

9. **D.** $1 + \sqrt{-(-5)^2} = 1 + \sqrt{-25} = 1 + 5i$. The variable i represents the concept of an imaginary number, and in mathematical terms $i^2 = -1$.

10. **D.** First simplify the expression on the left: $\left(2^{-\frac{1}{2}}\right)^{4y} = 2^{-2y} = \frac{1}{2^{2y}}$. It was given that this expression equals $\frac{1}{8}$, and $8 = 2^3$, so $2y = 3$ and $y = \frac{3}{2}$.

11. **D.** Imaginary numbers are multiples of $i = \sqrt{-1}$. Answer choice D is $\sqrt{-49} = 7\sqrt{-1} = 7i$.

12. **C.** The equation $|x - y| < \frac{1}{2}$ can be interpreted as "the distance between x and y is less than $\frac{1}{2}$." On the provided number line, only points C and D are less than one-half unit apart.

13. **D.** The equation $m^{-3} = 64$ is equivalent to $\frac{1}{m^3} = 64$. To solve for m, cross multiply: $64m^3 = 1$. Collect terms and solve: $m^3 = \frac{1}{64}$, so $m = \frac{1}{4}$. The question asks for the value of $8m$: $8\left(\frac{1}{4}\right) = 2$.

14. **A.** If $3(m + n)$ is even, then $m + n$ must be even, since the product of two odd numbers (that is, 3 and the sum of $m + n$) would be odd. It is possible that both m and n are even, but it is also possible that they are both odd. This eliminates the remaining answer choices.

15. **C.** If a number is a multiple of both 4 and 9, then it is divisible by $4 \times 9 = 36$. All of the answer choices except C are divisible by 36.

16. **C.** The 19 students in both bands are counted in both counts. Therefore, the total in only one band would be the sum of $(45 - 19)$ in performance band and $(30 - 19)$ in jazz band, which is $26 + 11$, or 37.

17. **A.** $-2 \odot 1 = 2(-2) - 3(1) = -4 - 3 = -7$.

18. **E.** The shaded region represents the set, and the open circle at 3 indicates it is not included in the set.

19. **D.** The decimal forms of these numbers are easiest to rank from smallest to largest. Some of these values are

easy to find or should have been memorized (as is true in the case of pi): $\left(\frac{1}{2}\right)^{-2} = 2^2 = 4$, $\frac{1}{3} = 0.\overline{3}$, $\pi \approx 3.14$. To estimate the square root values, consider perfect squares that are close in value: $\sqrt{3} < \sqrt{4} = 2$ and $\sqrt{3} > \sqrt{1} = 1$, and $4 = \sqrt{16} < \sqrt{17}$. The correct order is $\frac{1}{3}$, $\sqrt{3}$, π, $\left(\frac{1}{2}\right)^{-2}$, $\sqrt{17}$.

20. **E.** It is possible that $pq = -2$, since $-2 \times -2 = 4$, so answer choices A and B can be eliminated. For answer choice C, it is possible that if the product of two numbers is 2 or -2, one of the numbers is a fraction. For example it could be that $p = \frac{1}{2}$ and $q = 4$. Similarly, for answer choice D, p and q could have the same sign or different signs, so this may or may not be true. Finally, in choice E, if p is larger than 2, then you would need to multiply it by something smaller to get a final product of 2. As an example, suppose that $p = 3$. Since $pq = 2$, then $q = \frac{2}{3}$. This makes answer choice E the only statement that would always be true.

21. **E.** Exponents distribute over multiplication, and when an exponential term is taken to another exponent, you multiply the exponents to simplify the expression. Therefore, $(2m^3)^4 = 2^4 m^{3 \times 4} = 16m^{12}$.

22. **D.** $|-2(7) - 5| - |-4 + 8| = |-19| - |4| = 19 - 4 = 15$

23. **B.** Start by listing integers whose sum is 21: $1 + 20$, $2 + 19$, $3 + 18$, $4 + 17$, $5 + 16$, etc. The corresponding products keep increasing: 20, 38, 54, etc. Once you see that the products are increasing in this manner, the answer of 20 is the best choice.

24. **C.** A percentage is a "part" out of the "whole." In this case, that is $\frac{120}{500} = 0.24$, or 24%.

25. **E.** Freshmen make up $\frac{125}{500} = \frac{1}{4}$ of the students. Therefore, since a circle has a total of 360 degrees, the portion of the circle graph that would represent this would have a degree measure of $\frac{1}{4}(360) = 90$.

26. **A.** When multiplying terms with exponents and the same base, add the exponents: $(10a^2)(5ab)(2ab^4) = 10 \times 5 \times 2 \times a^{2+1+1} b^{1+4} = 100a^4 b^5$.

27. **A.** $7 \triangle (-2) = \frac{7+1}{-2} = \frac{8}{-2} = -4$

28. **C.** If $\frac{\sqrt{x}}{5}$ is an integer, then any integer multiple of it will also be an integer. Answer choice C is $\frac{1}{5} \times \frac{\sqrt{x}}{5}$, which may or may not be an integer, depending on the value of x.

29. **D.** A total of 20 students received an A or a B in the course out of a total of $5 + 15 + 20 + 3 + 2 = 45$ students. Therefore, the fraction of those who received an A or a B is $\frac{20}{45} = \frac{4}{9}$.

30. **C.** Factor out any perfect squares under both square roots: $\sqrt{48} - \sqrt{27} = \sqrt{3 \times 16} - \sqrt{3 \times 9} = 4\sqrt{3} - 3\sqrt{3} = \sqrt{3}$.

31. **A.** The imaginary number i represents $\sqrt{-1}$. Therefore, $i^2 = (\sqrt{-1})^2 = -1$.

32. **C.** The closest integer value to $\sqrt{26}$ is 5, since $\sqrt{25} = 5$. Similarly, $\sqrt{49} = 7$ is the integer closest to $\sqrt{50}$. Therefore, to satisfy the inequality, a value of x must be larger than 5 but no more than a little larger than 7 (and smaller than 8, since $8 \times 8 = 64$).

33. **A.** $-2|-1 + 5| = -2|4| = -2 \cdot 4 = -8$

34. **C.** Rational numbers can be written as fractions of whole numbers. It is helpful to know some of the common irrational numbers; two of these are $\sqrt{2}$ and $\sqrt{3}$. Since answer choices A, B, D, and E contain these values, check the value of the remaining choice first: $\frac{\sqrt{100}}{5} = \frac{10}{5} = 2$.

35. **E.** Note that y might be negative. If this is the case, it could still be that y^2 is larger than the positive number x, since the square of any negative number is positive. This eliminates answer choices A and B. Answer choices C and D will be true for some values but not for others, while answer choice E is always true, since x is already smaller than y^2.

36. **B.** $\sqrt{-1 + (-(-1))^2} = \sqrt{-1 + 1^2} = \sqrt{-1 + 1} = \sqrt{0} = 0$

37. **B.** The value of $\frac{\sqrt{26}}{5}$ will be a little larger than the value of $\frac{\sqrt{25}}{5} = \frac{5}{5} = 1$. In this case, the next positive integer will be the smallest integer that is larger. In this case, that is 2.

38. **D.** The equation $2^{-m} = \frac{1}{8}$ is equivalent to $2^m = 8$. Since $8 = 2^3$, the value of m must be 3.

39. **A.** Substituting values from the number line into the equation, the point A or $x = -4$ will satisfy the given inequality.

40. **B.** The form of any odd integer is $2k + 1$ where k is any integer. The only answer choice with this form is answer choice B.

41. **E.** Recall that $a^{-n} = \frac{1}{a^n}$. Therefore, $\left(\frac{1}{4m^3}\right)^{-2} = (4m^3)^2 = 4^2 m^{3 \times 2} = 16m^6$.

42. **C.** If there are 1000 students in the school, then there are $0.45 \times 1000 = 450$ freshmen and $0.10 \times 1000 = 100$ juniors. Therefore, the difference is $450 - 100 = 350$.

43. E. Given that a is a positive integer, $\left(\frac{1}{a}\right)^2 < \frac{1}{a}$, since the square is just the product of two fractions, so we can eliminate choice C. Similarly, $\frac{1}{a} < a < a^2$, which eliminates answer choices A and B. Considering answer choices D and E, $\left(\frac{2}{a}\right)^2 = 4\left(\frac{1}{a}\right)^2$, so it is larger, and $\left(\frac{1}{2a}\right)^2 = \frac{1}{4}\left(\frac{1}{a}\right)^2$, so it is smaller.

44. B. Since $16^{\frac{1}{2}} = \sqrt{16} = 4$, we are looking for a power of 2 that is less than 4 but larger than 0. Only the number 2 satisfies this property.

45. D. If a number is in P, it is divisible by 5, and if a number is in Q, it is positive and less than 10. The only number that satisfies both properties is 5.

46. D. $(-2) \,\Xi\, (-3) = (-3)^2 - (-2)^2 + 1 = 9 - 4 + 1 = 6$

47. B. Multiples of 12 include 12, 24, 48, 60, 72, 84, 96, 108, 120, 132, etc.; multiples of 20 include 20, 40, 60, 80, 100, 120, etc.; and multiples of 40 include 40, 80, 120, etc. The smallest multiple shared by all the given numbers is 120.

48. E. The closest values for whole number powers of 2 are $2^5 = 32$ and $2^6 = 64$. Since 41 is between 32 and 64, m must be between 5 and 6.

49. E. It is possible that p is very close to 5 and q is very close to 4. This would make their product very close to 20. The smallest integer that would be greater would have to be 21.

50. E. If a number has prime factors of 2, 3, and 7, it must be divisible by each of these values but by no other prime. In this case, $84 = 2^2 \cdot 3 \cdot 7$.

51. B. For any values of p and q, $\frac{3^p}{3^q} = 3^{p-q}$. Therefore, because $81 = 3^4$, the difference of p and q must be 4.

52. C. If $a^2 < a$, then a must be a fraction, and if $a^2 = a$, then a must be -1, 1, or 0. The values of a that satisfy the inequality $-1 \le a \le 1$ would include some of these values and no others.

53. C. Those signed up for two races are counted in both totals. Therefore, the total who signed up for only one race would be $53 - 12 + 21 - 12 = 50$.

54. A. Another way to state the given information is that $x + 4$ must be a multiple of 4. Of the given possibilities, this is true only when $x = -16$.

55. A. The inequality given is representing the set of numbers between -1 and 5, including the -1 but not including the 5. The set in answer choice A does not include the -1 and contains only negative numbers.

56. B. If $x \triangleright (-1) = \frac{-1}{x}$ is positive, x must be negative, since a negative number divided by a negative number is always positive.

57. B. The number 100 can be factored as $10 \times 10 = 2 \times 5 \times 2 \times 5$. The numbers 2 and 5 are the distinct prime factors of 100, so $m = 2$ and $3m = 6$.

58. D. $(6a^5)^2 = 6^2 a^{5 \times 2} = 36a^{10}$

59. C. The value $|x - y|$ can be thought of as the number of units between x and y on a number line. In this case, x and y are more than 1 unit apart, so $|x - y| > 1$.

60. B. The total is 650, and $147 + 335 + 98 = 580$ are already accounted for, so there must be $650 - 580 = 70$ remaining.

61. B. Since the answer choices are written in terms of square roots, it is helpful to rewrite the given inequality in terms of square roots. Here, $\frac{3}{2} < x < \frac{5}{2}$ is equivalent to $\frac{\sqrt{9}}{2} < x < \frac{\sqrt{25}}{2}$. Of the answer choices, only $\frac{\sqrt{20}}{2}$ is between those values.

62. A. The square of any number is always positive. Therefore, if xy^2 is negative, the value of x must be negative.

63. B. The value of any number taken to the zero power is 1.

64. E. When $x > 1$, $|x| = x$ and $\frac{|x|}{x} = \frac{x}{x} = 1$.

65. A. If the remainder of m divided by 2 is 1, then m must be odd. If m is odd, then $m + 1$ is even and a multiple of 2. Therefore, when $m + 1$ is divided by 2, there will be no remainder.

66. A. $\left(\frac{1}{3}\right)^2 - \left(\frac{1}{2}\right)^{-1} = \frac{1}{9} - 2 = \frac{1}{9} - \frac{18}{9} = -\frac{17}{9}$

67. C. Since the fraction is simplified, a cannot share any factors with 25 other than 1. The factors of 25 are 1, 5, and 25, and only answer choice C appears on this list.

68. D. The expression $\frac{4^m}{4^n}$ is equivalent to the expression 4^{m-n}. For this expression to be smaller than 1, the exponent must be negative, so m must be smaller than n.

69. D. $(-(-2))^2 - (-(-2)) = 2^2 - 2 = 4 - 2 = 2$

70. **C.** Remember that exponents must distribute to everything within the product. Therefore:

$$\left(\frac{1}{2}x^2y\right)^5 = \left(\frac{1}{2}\right)^5 x^{2\times5}y^{1\times5} = \frac{1}{2^5}x^{10}y^5 = \frac{1}{32}x^{10}y^5.$$

71. **A.** The factors of $14a$ will include the factors of a (3 and 2), the factors of 14 (2 and 7), and all of their products. Of the answer choices, only 4 is a product of two of these factors (2 and 2).

Chapter 2: Algebra

72. **B.** Let x represent the number of text messages sent by the customer during the billing period. The bill's total can be expressed as $45 + 0.15x = 61.50$, which has a solution of $x = 110$.

73. **A.** When solving linear equations like these, the goal is to isolate the variable on one side and the constants on the other. By subtracting $3x$ from both sides, we can rewrite the equation as $-5 = x + 9$, which simplifies to $x = -14$ when 9 is subtracted from both sides.

74. **E.** When adding two fractions, we must always have a like denominator. The least common denominator here is ab, and $\frac{1}{a} = \frac{1 \cdot b}{a \cdot b} = \frac{b}{ab}$, while $\frac{1}{b} = \frac{1 \cdot a}{b \cdot a} = \frac{a}{ab}$. Therefore, the sum is $\frac{1}{a} + \frac{1}{b} = \frac{b}{ab} + \frac{a}{ab} = \frac{a+b}{ab}$.

75. **E.** The quadratic function $x^2 - 3x - 10$ factors into $(x-5)(x+2)$. This can equal zero only if $x = 5$ or $x = -2$.

76. **D.** Cross multiplying will provide us with a linear equation to solve: $3m = 4(m-1)$. To solve, distribute the 4 on the right side to get $3m = 4m - 4$, and then subtract $4m$ from both sides: $-m = -4$. If $-m = -4$, then $m = 4$.

77. **A.** This is a system of equations. Adding the two equations gives the equation of one variable, $2x = -4$, which has a solution of $x = -2$. By substituting this value of x into the first equation, we find $-2 - y = -5$ and $y = 3$. Given these two values, we can calculate $xy = -2 \times 3 = -6$.

78. **C.** Use the process of matrix multiplication:
$$\begin{bmatrix} -1 & 2 \\ 4 & 8 \end{bmatrix}\begin{bmatrix} 6 & 3 \\ 7 & -6 \end{bmatrix} = \begin{bmatrix} -1(6)+2(7) & -1(3)+2(-6) \\ 4(6)+8(7) & 4(3)+8(-6) \end{bmatrix}$$
$$= \begin{bmatrix} 8 & -15 \\ 80 & -36 \end{bmatrix}.$$

79. **E.** A root of a function is a solution to the equation formed when setting the function equal to zero. In this case, it would be a solution to $-5x + x^2 = 0$, which is equivalent to $x(-5 + x) = 0$ when x is factored out. Finally, by the zero product rule, the roots are $x = 0$ and $x = 5$.

80. **E.** By factoring the given inequality, we see that it can be rewritten as $(m-5)(m-3) < 0$ and that the function has roots of 3 and 5. This means the function will be negative either before 3 $(m < 3)$, after 5 $(m > 5)$, or in between $(3 < m < 5)$. By testing values, we can determine which is true. For values before 3, testing $m = 0$ yields $0^2 - 8(0) + 15 = 15 > 0$. For values after 5, $m = 6$ yields $6^2 - 8(6) + 15 = 3 > 0$. Finally, for values between 3 and 5, $m = 4$ yields $4^2 - 8(4) + 15 = -1 < 0$, showing us that the function is negative for all of these values.

81. **C.** If we let the first integer be represented by x, then the second integer will be $x + 2$, since they are both odd. Therefore, $x + x + 2 = 256$, which simplifies to $2x + 2 = 256$, and $x = 127$. However, this is the value of the smaller of the pair; the larger is $x + 2 = 129$.

82. **C.** Rewriting the first inequality shows that $2p + q > 5p$. Collecting terms, $q > 3p$. Therefore, when $p > 2$, $q > 6$.

83. **E.** The terms in the numerator all have the same variable and the same degree, so they are like terms and can be added across: $\frac{x^2 - 4x^2 + x^2}{x} = \frac{-2x^2}{x}$. Since the numerator and the denominator share a factor of x, this is equivalent to $-2x$.

84. **D.** For a system of equations to have infinite solutions, one of the equations must be a multiple of the other. Looking at the constant on the right side, the first equation would have to be multiplied by -3 to get from 2 to -6. Therefore, $m = -3(-3) = 9$, and $n = 1(-3) = -3$.

85. **B.** For the inequality to be true, $\frac{x}{4}$ must be more than $\frac{1}{4}$ larger than 1 or simply equal to $1 + \frac{1}{4}$. Since $\frac{4}{4} = 1$, $\frac{4}{4} + \frac{1}{4} = \frac{5}{4}$ will satisfy the greater than or equal to condition, so $x = 5$.

86. **E.** Notice that the expression on the right side of each answer choice is always $3x + 2y$. The only way to clear fractions in this way would be for us to multiply both sides of the equation by 6, which will yield the expression in answer choice E.

87. **A.** Solving inequalities works the same way as solving equations. However, we must remember that multiplying or dividing both sides by a negative value will switch the order of the inequality. Therefore, when we simplify the inequality to $-3x > 2$, the solution becomes $x < -\frac{2}{3}$.

88. **D.** Solving for a in both inequalities gives us $a \geq c + x$ and $a > c + x$. The only difference between these is that $a \geq c + x$ allows for a to equal $c + x$, while $a > c + x$ does not.

89. **B.** If $3^{xy} = \frac{1}{9}$, then xy must be -2. Also, since $2x + y = 0$, $y = -2x$. Substituting this value of y into $xy = -2$ gives us $x(-2x) = -2$ or $-2x^2 = -2$, which has a solution of $x = 1$ or -1, but since the equation states that x is positive, the possibility that $x = -1$ may be discarded. If $x = 1$, then using the first equation, $y = -2$, and $x + y = 1 + (-2) = 1 - 2 = -1$.

90. **C.** When $k = -1$, $\left(\frac{x+y}{k}\right)^2 = (-1)^2(x+y)^2 = (x+y)^2$.

    This expression can be simplified to $x^2 + 2xy + y^2$ by using the FOIL technique.

91. **D.** In general, $\log_b x = a$ is equivalent to $b^a = x$. Here, $\log_2 x = 3$ implies $x = 2^3 = 8$.

92. **B.** Using the FOIL method, $(x-a)(x+a) = x^2 + ax - ax - a^2 = x^2 - a^2$.

93. **A.** We can factor x out of the equation $3x^2 - \frac{1}{2}x = 0$

    to get the equivalent equation $x\left(3x - \frac{1}{2}\right) = 0$. Since this is the product of two terms, we can then apply the zero product rule to find $x = 0$ or $3x - \frac{1}{2} = 0$.

    The second equation has a solution of $x = \frac{1}{6}$.

94. **B.** If, when added, the given equations result in an untrue statement, then the system will have no solutions. The coefficient of x in the second equation is 1, and it is 2 in the first equation. Therefore, if we make b half of 8 and c not equal to half of 2, we will end up with an untrue statement. The choice with this format is $b = 4$ and $c = 3$.

95. **B.** To get $3m - 8$ from the given $3m - 4$, we must subtract 4 from both sides of the equation. On the right side, $6n - 8 - 4 = 6n - 12$.

96. **D.** Substituting the given expression for a, we get $2\left(\frac{x}{y}\right) - \left(\frac{x}{y}\right)^2 = \frac{2x}{y} - \frac{x^2}{y^2}$. To simplify, we must find a common denominator. The common denominator would be y^2, and the resulting expression is $\frac{2x}{y} - \frac{x^2}{y^2} = \frac{2xy}{y^2} - \frac{x^2}{y^2} = \frac{2xy - x^2}{y^2}$.

97. **C.** Subtraction of matrices is performed by subtracting the corresponding entries. Therefore, $z = 4 - 1 = 3$.

98. **A.** Each term in the numerator has a factor of 2. Factoring out this 2 results in the expression $\frac{2(3x-2)}{2} = 3x - 2$.

99. **D.** A good first step here is to divide both sides by 4. This simplifies the equation to $x - 1 = 2(x - 2)$, or $x - 1 = 2x - 4$. To solve, subtract x from both sides and then add 4, resulting in $x = 3$.

100. **E.** The given inequality is equivalent to the inequality $\frac{5}{7} \leq x$, and every positive integer is larger than $\frac{5}{7}$.

101. **B.** The sum of the expressions is $3x + 4x - 1 - 2x = 5x - 1$. Given that this sum is equal to 9, we can write the equation $5x - 1 = 9$ to find the value of x. Adding 1 to both sides, we find $5x = 10$ and $x = 2$.

102. **A.** Begin by simplifying the equation using a like denominator: $\frac{1}{2a} + \frac{1}{a} = \frac{1}{2a} + \frac{2}{2a} = \frac{3}{2a} = 14$. Cross multiplying yields the equation $28a = 3$, so $a = \frac{3}{28}$.

103. **C.** If x represents the size of his original collection, then the statements give us the equation $x + 36 = 2x$. Therefore, $x = 36$, and his current collection has a size of $36 + 36 = 72$.

104. **E.** To solve for x, divide each term in the inequality by 5, and rewrite it as $-\frac{1}{10} \leq x \leq \frac{33}{10}$. Each value given is a solution to this inequality except 4, which is larger than $\frac{33}{10}$.

105. **D.** If the smallest integer is x, then the next is $x + 1$, and the third is $x + 2$. The sum of these expressions is $3x + 3$.

106. **D.** Factoring out a 5 from the given expression leaves us with $5\left(x - \frac{3}{2}\right)$, since $15 = 3 \times 5$.

107. **A.** Adding the two equations, $3a = 6$, so $a = 2$. Substituting this into the first equation gives $2 - b = 7$, so $b = -5$.

108. **A.** If x represents the amount of Type 1 in stock while y represents the amount of Type 2 in stock, $x = 2y$, and $x + y = 21,000$. If you plug the value of x ($x = 2y$) from the first equation into the second equation, you get $3y = 21,000$. Simplifying this yields $y = 7000$.

109. **B.** Being careful to distribute the 2, this equation is equivalent to $6a - 1 = 2a + 2$. Simplifying, $4a = 3$, so $a = \frac{3}{4}$.

110. **C.** After rewriting the equation as $3x^2 - 19x - 14 = 0$, we see that it factors into $(3x + 2)$ and $(x - 7)$. Therefore, the only positive solution will be $x = 7$.

111. **D.** $6(m^2 n^2 - 1) = 6((mn)^2 - 1) = 6(4^2 - 1)$

$= 6(16 - 1) = 6(15) = 90$

112. **D.** Since the terms are not like terms, they cannot be combined at all, and answer choices A and B can be eliminated. In answer choices C and D, the term $-b$ has been factored out of $2b^2 + b$, and only answer choice D does so correctly. Answer choice E tries to factor out $2b$, but 2 is not a factor of b.

113. **E.** $(2y - 1)^{-x} = (2y - 1)^{-\frac{1}{2}} = \dfrac{1}{(2y - 1)^{\frac{1}{2}}} = \dfrac{1}{\sqrt{2y - 1}}$

114. **B.** Each inequality in the answer choices has the reverse direction of the one given. This must mean both sides were multiplied by -1. When both sides are multiplied by -1, the signs on every term will change.

115. **D.** Since the term on the right side of the equation has a lower degree than the first term on the left side of the equation, the operation must have been division.

116. **A.** Let x and y represent the two numbers. Here we can write $xy = 20$, and $x + y = 12$, so $y = 12 - x$. Substituting this expression for y into the first equation, we find that $x(12 - x) = 20$, which can be expressed as $x^2 - 12x + 20 = 0$. This equation factors into $(x - 2)(x - 10) = 0$, which has solutions 2 and 10. Finally, the difference is $10 - 2 = 8$.

117. **C.** Subtracting x from both sides of the inequality yields $-y > y$. This can be true only when $y < 0$.

118. **E.** The equation $\log_3(x - 1) = 2$ is equivalent to $x - 1 = 3^2$, which has a solution of $x = 9 + 1 = 10$.

119. **A.** The roots of an expression are the solutions to that expression set equal to zero. Since this expression factors, the roots can be found by solving $(x - 2)(x - 1) = 0$. Of the roots 2 and 1, neither is larger than 5.

120. **A.** Subtracting 5 from both sides of the inequality yields the inequality $-\dfrac{1}{2}x \geq 4$. To solve, multiply both sides by -2: $x \leq -8$.

121. **B.** Multiplying the first equation by 2 and then adding equations results in the equation $7x = -14$, which has a solution of $x = -2$.

122. **B.** The given log expression is equivalent to $x^4 = 16$. Since $16 = 4 \times 4 = 2 \times 2 \times 2 \times 2$, $x^4 = 2^4$, so $x = 2$.

123. **D.** To rationalize the denominator, we multiply the expression by $\dfrac{\sqrt{m}}{\sqrt{m}}$, so $\dfrac{m}{\sqrt{m}}\left(\dfrac{\sqrt{m}}{\sqrt{m}}\right) = \dfrac{m\sqrt{m}}{m} = \sqrt{m}$.

124. **C.** If the product of a and $(a - 1)$ is 6, then $a^2 - a = 6$, and $a^2 - a - 6 = 0$. This equation factors into $(a - 3)(a + 2)$, which has roots 3 and -2.

125. **E.** To find the square of x, you must use the FOIL technique: $x^2 = (k^2 - 2)^2 = k^4 - 4k^2 + 4$.

126. **D.** There are four 15-minute periods every hour. Therefore, there are fourteen 15-minute periods in $3\dfrac{1}{2}$ hours. Finally, $14 \times 100 = 1400$.

127. **A.** $(3x^2 - 5x + 1) - (3x^2 - 2x + 6) =$

$3x^2 - 5x + 1 - 3x^2 + 2x - 6 = -3x - 5$

128. **B.** The greatest common factor can be thought of as the "largest" term that will divide both terms. In this case, a^3 is the largest term that can divide both terms.

129. **C.** Subtracting $\sqrt{y}$ from both sides simplifies the equation to $8 = 2\sqrt{y}$. Divide both sides by 2 to get $4 = \sqrt{y}$. Squaring both sides of the equation then yields $y = 16$.

130. **C.** On the right side of the equation, both coefficients have been reduced by a factor of 5. Additionally, the power on n was reduced by 1 on each term. Therefore, $5n$ must have been the term factored out.

131. **C.** Adding x and 5 to both sides of the equation yields $2x = 14$, so $x = 7$.

132. **E.** All of the answer choices include the term $p + 5$. The given inequality can be rewritten in terms of $p + 5$ by adding 10 to both sides. The resulting inequality is $p + 5 > 8$.

133. **D.** The equation given is equivalent to $-k^2 - k = 0$, factored to $-k(k + 1) = 0$, which has roots of 0 and -1.

134. **C.** $\dfrac{1 - x^2}{x} = \dfrac{1}{x} - \dfrac{x^2}{x} = \dfrac{1}{x} - x$

135. **D.** Each person will receive $\dfrac{m}{6}$ dollars. Therefore, two people together will receive $\dfrac{m}{6} + \dfrac{m}{6} = \dfrac{2m}{6} = \dfrac{m}{3}$ dollars.

136. **D.** Substituting the value of y^2 from the second equation into the first, $2x + 3x = 7$, which simplifies to $5x = 7$. To find $10x$, we multiply both sides of this equation by 2.

137. **C.** $\dfrac{2x}{9} \times \dfrac{3}{x} = \dfrac{6x}{9x} = \dfrac{2}{3}$

138. **A.** Since x is positive, only $-2x$ will be negative, and a negative number is always smaller than a positive number.

139. **B.** When $y = 0$, $2x + 2 = -2$, which simplifies to $2x = -4$. This equation has a solution of $x = -2$.

140. **D.** Multiples of $8a$ include $16a$, $24a$, $32a$, etc. Multiples of $6a$ include $12a$, $18a$, $24a$, etc. The smallest multiple shared on these two lists is $24a$.

141. **C.** If the sum of n and 4 is 10, then we can write $n + 4 = 10$. Subtracting 5 from both sides, we find $n - 1 = 5$.

142. **E.** The first inequality is equivalent to $x > \frac{3}{4}$, while the second is equivalent to $x < -3$. There are no real numbers that are larger than $\frac{3}{4}$ and at the same time smaller than -3.

Chapter 3: Probability, Statistics, and Sequences

143. **A.** Since we know that x is positive, the terms can be placed in order from smallest to largest: $-8x$, $-5x$, $-2x$, x, $4x$. By definition, the median is the middle term in this list.

144. **C.** There are a total of 15 cards, and 6 are blue. Therefore, the probability will be $\frac{6}{15} = \frac{2}{5}$.

145. **E.** Let x represent the sum of the numbers. Then $\frac{x}{5} = 20$, and by cross multiplying, we see that $x = 100$.

146. **A.** If the median is 2, this means that when the numbers are placed in order from smallest to largest, 2 will be the middle number. Of the given answer choices, this only occurs when $x = 2$.

147. **D.** By the multiplication rule, the number of different combinations will be $3 \times 2 \times 8 = 48$.

148. **D.** The described sequence is geometric, and the nth term of any geometric series is $a_1 \times r^{n-1}$, or the first term times the ratio that each term is being multiplied by. Here the first term is 4, and the ratio is n.

149. **B.** Let B represent the number of blue pens. Then the total number of pens is $B + 2B = 3B$, and the probability of selecting a blue pen is $\frac{B}{3B} = \frac{1}{3}$.

150. **B.** The bag must contain $\frac{4}{5}(110) = 88$ green marbles and $110 - 88 = 22$ marbles that are not green.

151. **E.** The probability of any event is always between zero and one inclusive. Additionally, the probability of event A occurring is always equal to one minus the probability of the event not occurring (also called the complementary event).

152. **C.** Let the five numbers be represented by a, b, c, d, and e. Since the average of all five is 12.4, we know that $\frac{a+b+c+d+e}{5} = 12.4$, or $a+b+c+d+e = 12.4 \times 5 = 62$. We can say the four numbers that have an average of 11 are a, b, c, and d. This means that $\frac{a+b+c+d}{4} = 11$, or $a+b+c+d = 44$. Combining these equations, $(a+b+c+d) + e = 62 = 44 + e$, so $e = 62 - 44 = 18$.

153. **B.** Arithmetic sequences are formed when each number in the sequence is the sum of some fixed number and the number before it. Suppose the fixed number being added to every term is x. Then for us to get from the second term to the tenth term, x must have been added to eight terms. Expressed as an equation, $6 + 8x = 38$, so $8x = 32$. This equation has a solution of $x = 4$. Finally, because the second term was found by adding 4 to the first term, the first term must have been $6 - 4 = 2$.

154. **C.** By the multiplication rule, there are $4 \times 3 \times 2 \times 1$ ways to arrange the letters.

155. **D.** The median is the middle number when the numbers in the list are placed in order. Since there are seven numbers in the original list, 3 must be the fourth number when the list is placed in order. When the new number is added, the new median will be the average of the fourth and fifth numbers. The numbers are distinct, so the fifth number must be larger than 3, and the median will therefore also be larger than 3.

156. **E.** Coin flips are independent of each other. Although the flips so far have resulted in tails, the probability that a fair coin will land on tails in an individual flip is always $\frac{1}{2}$.

157. **E.** Since the sequence repeats every 6 numbers, the 6th, 12th, 18th, 24th, and 30th numbers in the sequence will be 2. Therefore the next 5 terms will be $-1, 5, -2, 1, 5$.

158. **C.** Out of the total of 25 numbers between 1 and 25, there are 9 prime numbers (2, 3, 5, 7, 11, 13, 17, 19, and 23).

159. **A.** The lower the probability, the less likely an event is to occur.

160. **D.** Let x be the smallest of the integers. The remaining integers are therefore $x + 1$, $x + 2$, and $x + 3$. Given the average, we can say that $\frac{x+(x+1)+(x+2)+(x+3)}{4} = 14.5$, which is equivalent to $\frac{4x+6}{4} = 14.5$. Therefore, $x + \frac{3}{2} = 14.5$, or

$x = 13$. This means the largest integer is $13 + 3 = 16$, and the sum of x and $x + 3$ is $13 + 16 = 29$.

161. **B.** After the first entry is drawn, only 6 are left. One of these entries is Sara's, giving a probability of $\frac{1}{6}$ it will be selected.

162. **B.** The sum of the first n terms of any arithmetic sequence can be found using the formula $\frac{n}{2}(a_1 + a_n)$. In this case, $32 = \frac{4}{2}(a_1 + a_4)$, and $a_1 + a_4 = 16$.

163. **E.** By the multiplication rule, he has $5 \times 4 \times 10$ complete sets.

164. **A.** The average of any set of numbers is the sum of those numbers divided by how many numbers are in the set.

165. **D.** The terms of a geometric series are found by multiplying the previous term by some fixed ratio. For us to get from 30 to $\frac{15}{2}$, we would have to multiply 30 by $\frac{1}{4}$. Therefore, 30 is $\frac{1}{4}$ times the first term, and one-fourth of 120 is 30.

166. **C.** The median is the middle value when the numbers are placed in order. Since the number of values in the set is even, the middle will be the average of 2 and 4 (the two middle numbers), which is 3.

167. **B.** If x is the number in attendance on Friday, we can use the formula $\frac{32 + 34 + x}{3} = 32$ to find x. This formula is equivalent to $66 + x = 96$, which has a solution of $x = 30$.

168. **C.** The nth term of any arithmetic sequence is found with the formula $a_n = a_1 + d(n - 1)$, where d is the common difference. In this equation a_1 would be m, the variable n would be the difference, and it would be multiplied by $99 - 1$, yielding $m + 98n$.

169. **E.** Since it is not possible to choose both Hanna and Jake, the probability of one or the other being chosen is the sum of the probabilities of each of them being chosen individually: $\frac{1}{29} + \frac{1}{29} = \frac{2}{29}$.

170. **C.** The smallest average that would allow for the salesperson to get a commission is $250. Therefore, if x represents the person's sales on Friday, it must be that $\frac{98 + 255 + 175 + 320 + x}{5} = 250$, and $848 + x = 1250$. This equation has a solution of $x = 402$.

171. **D.** The probability of an event not occurring is one minus the probability it will occur. Here, $P(\text{not even}) = 1 - P(\text{even}) = 1 - \frac{1}{m} = \frac{m}{m} - \frac{1}{m} = \frac{m - 1}{m}$.

172. **D.** By the multiplication rule and the fact that a person cannot hold two positions, the total is $30 \times 29 \times 28$.

173. **B.** In the initial shipment of eight phones, five are not defective. After one good phone is removed, there are seven total phones, four of which are not defective.

174. **A.** Increasing the number of green marbles would decrease the probability of selecting a white marble, and decreasing both by the same number would leave the probability unchanged.

175. **C.** $\frac{228 + 219 + 202 + 252}{4} = 225.25$

176. **A.** The sequence repeats every five terms, so for example, the 5th, 10th, 15th, 20th, and 25th terms will all be 5. Further, since 400 is a multiple of 5, the sequence will "restart" at 18 on the 401st term, and the 400th term will be 5.

177. **C.** To get from the fifth to the seventh term requires that the common difference of the arithmetic sequence be added twice. If this difference is d, then $11x^2 + 2d = 17x^2$, and $d = 3x^2$. Therefore, the third term is $11x^2 - 3x^2 - 3x^2 = 5x^2$.

178. **C.** If x is the median, it must be in the middle of the list when the items are placed in order. This means two numbers must be smaller than x, and since z and y are larger than 4, the smaller numbers must be 1 and 4. Given this information, the correct order of the list would be 1, 4, x, z, y, and only the inequality in answer choice C holds.

179. **A.** If the probability is three times as large, the number of the first type must be three times the number of the second type. Therefore, the box must contain $\frac{240}{3}$ coins of the second type.

180. **D.** By the multiplication rule, there are $5 \times 4 \times 3 \times 2$ ways to arrange four of these letters.

181. **A.**
$$\frac{\left(\frac{5}{4} + \frac{1}{2} + \frac{x}{2}\right)}{3} = \frac{5}{12} + \frac{1}{6} + \frac{x}{6} = \frac{5}{12} + \frac{2}{12} + \frac{2x}{12}$$
$$= \frac{2x + 7}{12}$$

182. **E.** Given that $x = 7$, the set can be written as {2, 18, −7, 12, 10}, which contains four even numbers. Since there are a total of five numbers in the set, the probability of selecting an even number is $\frac{4}{5}$.

183. **D.** Given this schedule, Aiden will work 16 (or 4×4) of the 28 (or 7×4) days.

184. **D.** By the multiplication rule, there are $5 \times 3 = 15$ choices.

185. **B.** The second term of the sequence is $2 - \frac{5}{4} = \frac{3}{4}$, and the third term of the sequence is $\frac{3}{4} - \frac{5}{4} = -\frac{2}{4} = -\frac{1}{2}$.

186. **B.** The average is found by taking the total of the values and dividing by how many values there are. In this case, we would have an average of $\frac{m}{n} = p$, which simplifies to $np = m$. Next, to write n in terms of m and p, divide both sides by p to get $n = \frac{m}{p}$.

187. **B.** Let x represent the sum of the six numbers. Then, since the average is 10, $\frac{x}{6} = 10$, and $x = 60$. When 5 is added to each number in the set, the new average is $\frac{60 + (6 \times 5)}{6} = \frac{90}{6} = 15$.

188. **E.** The probability of an event not occurring is 1 minus the probability of the event occurring. Therefore, probability I is 0.6, and probability II is 0.8. Finally, if both events cannot occur at the same time, the probability that one or the other will occur is the sum of their individual probabilities. Thus, probability III is $0.4 + 0.2 = 0.6$. All of these probabilities are greater than 0.5.

189. **D.** Since only red and black cards are in the box, the probability of selecting a red card or a black card must have a sum of 1. If x is the probability of selecting a black card, then $\frac{1}{2}x$ is the probability of selecting a red card, and $x + \frac{1}{2}x = \frac{3}{2}x = 1$. Therefore, $x = \frac{2}{3}$.

190. **D.** The probability of any event occurring must be smaller than or equal to 1.

191. **E.** The sum of the first n terms of an arithmetic sequence is found with the formula $S_n = \frac{n}{2}(a_1 + a_n)$.

Using the information given, $55 = \frac{5}{2}(3 + a_5)$, and this simplifies to $a_5 = \frac{110}{5} - 3 = 19$. Therefore, the sixth term must be $19 + 3 = 22$.

192. **A.** If the first 20 terms are all less than 60, the common ratio used to find terms must be quite small. If we check 2 (choice C) first, we see that to get from the 1st term to 2, we would have to multiply by 4. Thus the 20th term will be $\frac{1}{2}4^{19}$, which is much larger than 60. Therefore, we can eliminate answer choices C, D, and E as being too large. A similar check eliminates answer choice B as well.

193. **C.** Because the three-digit number has an odd number in the tens digit, there are 5 possible values for that digit. Further, the first digit can be any value 1–9, and the last digit can be any value 0–9.

Using the multiplication rule, there are $9 \times 5 \times 10 = 450$ possibilities.

194. **C.** The total of all the probabilities must be 1, since the events represent all possible choices: $1 - \frac{2}{5} - \frac{1}{8} = \frac{40}{40} - \frac{16}{40} - \frac{5}{40} = \frac{19}{40}$.

195. **D.** Every 5th term is 8. Therefore, the 100th term will be 8, since 100 is a multiple of 5, and the next term will be 5.

196. **D.** Since the list has an even number of values, the median is the average of x and y: $\frac{x+y}{2} = 5$, and the sum of x and y must be 10. Therefore the product of x and y must be the product of two numbers that add up to 10. Only answer choice D satisfies this property.

197. **A.** $\frac{250}{10} = 25$

198. **B.** Given that the probability an item is not on sale at a discount is $\frac{2}{3}$, then there must be $\frac{2}{3} \times 171 = 114$ items not on sale at a discount and $171 - 114 = 57$ items on sale at a discount.

199. **B.** Using the formula, $a_2 = 26 = \frac{1}{5}a_1 + 4$, and simplifying, $\frac{1}{5}a_1 = 22$. Therefore, $a_1 = 110$.

200. **C.** There are 5 biology books of 35 total books, so the probability is $\frac{5}{35} = \frac{1}{7}$.

201. **D.** By inspection, each term is found by subtracting 2 from the previous term.

202. **D.** The total number of students in the group is $82 + 18 + 22 + 48 + 30 = 200$. Of these, 18 indicated interest in an aviation career, so the probability is $\frac{18}{200} = \frac{9}{100}$.

203. **B.** Hats in the bin are either black or gray. Therefore, the probability of selecting a gray hat and the probability of selecting a black hat must total 1. In other words, $P(\text{gray}) + P(\text{black}) = 1$, so $P(\text{black}) = 1 - P(\text{gray}) = 1 - x$.

204. **E.** If the first term is negative, then each of the following terms will be more negative, and the first term will be the largest. If the first term is positive, then of those selections, the fourth term will be the largest.

205. **A.** The third term of this sequence can be represented by the formula $a_3 = a_1\left(\frac{1}{3}\right)^2$, and the second term can be represented by $a_2 = a_1\left(\frac{1}{3}\right)$. Therefore,

$$a_3 - a_2 = a_1\left(\frac{1}{3}\right)^2 - a_1\left(\frac{1}{3}\right) = a_1\left(\frac{1}{9} - \frac{1}{3}\right) = a_1\left(\frac{1}{9} - \frac{3}{9}\right)$$
$$= a_1\left(-\frac{2}{9}\right).$$

206. E. The median is the middle value if the list items are put in order from smallest to largest. Using the inequality, w would be the middle number of the data list.

207. B. The third term is $322.5 = 4a_2 + \frac{1}{2}$. Solving this, we find the second term is $80.5 = a_2$. Using the formula, the second term can be written as $80.5 = 4a_1 + \frac{1}{2}$, which has a solution of 20 for a_1, the first term.

208. D. If x is the total rain over the past six days and the average is 3.22, then $\frac{x}{6} = 3.22$, so $x = 19.32$. For the average over seven days to be 3.40, it must be true that $\frac{19.32 + y}{7} = 3.4$, where y is the rainfall on the seventh day. This equation has a solution of 4.48.

209. C. Based on the formula, to get from the fifth to the seventh term requires that r be subtracted twice. This yields the equation $38 - 2r = 50$, which has a solution of -6.

210. E. Given that the average of 12 numbers is m and if x represents the total of those numbers, then $\frac{x}{12} = m$ and $x = 12m$. Therefore, the average of these 12 numbers and 5 would be $\frac{12m + 5}{13}$.

211. C. The list written in order from smallest to largest is $1, \sqrt{2}, \sqrt{3}, \sqrt{5}, 5$. The median is the middle value of this list.

212. B. If $x = 2y$, then $\frac{1}{2}x = y$ and $\frac{x + y}{2} = \frac{x + \frac{1}{2}x}{2} = \frac{\frac{3}{2}x}{2} = \frac{3}{4}x = 30$. Solving this equation yields the solution $x = 40$.

213. C. It is possible that the series is increasing by addition, but if so, the second term would be 20, the number equidistant from both 4 and 36. Since this is not an answer choice, you can assume the series is increasing by multiplication. Getting from the first to the third term requires that a number x be multiplied by the first term and then the second term. Therefore, $4x^2 = 36$ and $x = 3$. To get the second term, 4 is multiplied by 3, and the result is 12.

Chapter 4: Coordinate Geometry

214. D. Using the distance formula, $\sqrt{(2 - (-1))^2 + (3 - 1)^2} = \sqrt{9 + 4} = \sqrt{13}$.

215. E. The slope of the given line can be found by solving for y. The result is $y = \frac{1}{2} - 2x$, which has a slope of -2. The slope of any perpendicular line will be the negative reciprocal of -2, which is $\frac{1}{2}$.

216. B. Using the midpoint formula, $M = \left(\frac{2 + 5}{2}, \frac{7 + 7}{2}\right) = \left(\frac{7}{2}, 7\right)$.

217. E. If M is the midpoint, the length of AM will be $\sqrt{(2 - 1)^2 + (5 - 0)^2} = \sqrt{1 + 25} = \sqrt{26}$. Since M is the midpoint, this is half the length of the line AB.

218. A. The point where the line crosses the y-axis is the y-intercept and can be found by putting the line in slope-intercept form (solving for y). This is written as $y = mx + b$, with m as the slope and b as the y-intercept. The resulting equation is $y = -10 + 7x$, and $b = -10$.

219. D. In quadrant I, the signs on x and y are positive, while in quadrant III, the signs on x and y are negative. In quadrant II, the sign on y is positive, while the sign on x is negative, and in quadrant IV, the sign on x is positive, while the sign on y is negative.

220. C. If a line is parallel to the y-axis, it is of the form $x = c$ for some constant c. In that case, any points on the line will have the same x value.

221. B. Since the angle between the lines is 90 degrees, the lines are perpendicular, and the slopes are negative reciprocals of each other.

222. C. $i^5 - i^7 = i \times i^4 - i \times i^6 = i(-1) - i(-1) = -i + i = 0$

223. D. Since R is the midpoint of QP, the length of QP is $2(6) = 12$. Further, since MQ has a length of 4, MP has a length of $12 + 4 = 16$. Finally, P is the midpoint of MN, so the length of MN is $16 \times 2 = 32$.

224. A. Since the line rises from left to right, the slope is positive. However, the line crosses the x-axis to the right of the origin, so its x-intercept is positive. It crosses the y-axis below the origin, so its y-intercept is negative.

225. B. If a line is parallel to the x-axis, it will be of the form $y = c$ for some constant c.

226. E. Since m and n are parallel, the sum of angles x and y must be 180, and since x is 36, $y = 180 - 36 = 144$.

227. **B.** Quite often on a geometry question with no figures given, it helps if you make a quick sketch. Plotting out points A, B, and C should give you a clear idea of where point D must be. Since the figure is a rectangle, point D will have the same x-coordinate as point A and the same y-coordinate as point C. This leads to the answer of $(1, 6)$.

228. **C.** Using the slope formula, $m = \dfrac{\dfrac{1}{4} - 2}{-\dfrac{1}{4} - \left(-\dfrac{1}{2}\right)}$
$= \dfrac{\dfrac{1}{4} - \dfrac{8}{4}}{-\dfrac{1}{4} + \dfrac{2}{4}} = \dfrac{-\dfrac{7}{4}}{\dfrac{1}{4}} = -7.$

229. **D.** The slope of the line would be $m = \dfrac{6-5}{1-0} = 1$, and because the line passes through $(0, 5)$, the y-intercept is 5. Therefore, the equation of the line is $y = x + 5$. To find the x-intercept, let $y = 0$ and solve for x.

230. **E.** The slope of a line in the form $ax + by = c$ is $-\left(\dfrac{a}{b}\right)$. In this case, the slope is $\dfrac{5}{2}$, and any line perpendicular to this line will have a slope of $-\dfrac{2}{5}$. Only the equation in choice E satisfies this condition.

231. **C.** Using the point-slope formula, $y - 5 = -\dfrac{5}{4}(x - (-3))$. This equation simplifies to $y = -\dfrac{5}{4}x + \dfrac{5}{4}$.

232. **E.** With a negative slope, the line will fall from left to right. Starting with the positive y-intercept, this leaves the only possibility for an x-intercept as being along the positive x-axis.

233. **E.** The line PQ is parallel to the x-axis. Therefore, the y-coordinates of P and Q must be the same. Since the length of the line is 5, the x-coordinate is $3 + 5 = 8$.

234. **B.** The point M is in the second quadrant, where x values are negative and y values are positive. Only choice B satisfies those conditions.

235. **D.** $\dfrac{i^4 - 5}{i^2} = \dfrac{(i^2)^2 - 5}{-1} = \dfrac{(-1)^2 - 5}{-1} = \dfrac{1 - 5}{-1} = \dfrac{-4}{-1} = 4$

236. **D.** Because lines m and n are parallel, angles x and y must have the same value; that is, $x = y$. So $x + y = x + x = 2x = 160$, and $x = 80$. The angles x and z must have a sum of 180, so $z = 100$.

237. **B.** The distance from Q to the given point must be 6. Since both points lie on the x-axis, the x-coordinate must be within 6 of -9.

238. **B.** Solving for y, the line can be written as $y = -\dfrac{21}{8} + \dfrac{3}{8}x$. This is the slope-intercept form for the line, and the slope is the coefficient of x, or $\dfrac{3}{8}$.

239. **E.** Each of the lines in the answer choices is in slope-intercept form. Solving for y in the given equation will give us the equivalent equation in slope-intercept form. In this case, that would yield $y = \dfrac{1}{3}x + \dfrac{7}{3}$.

240. **B.** The process described can be written as $y = 3x + 2$ for an x-coordinate of x. This equation is in slope-intercept form, so it indicates that the resulting line would have a y-intercept of 2.

241. **D.** The x-intercept is the point where $y = 0$. In this case, $2x - 5(0) = 10$, and $x = \dfrac{10}{2} = 5$.

242. **D.** Using the midpoint formula, the coordinates would be $\left(\dfrac{-4 + (-8)}{2}, \dfrac{0 + (-12)}{2}\right)$. Each fraction simplifies to -6.

243. **D.** Any line of the form $x = c$ is parallel to the y-axis, which is equivalent to being perpendicular to the x-axis. The x-intercept is c, but there is no y-intercept because the line is parallel to the y-axis, so III is not true.

244. **B.** A line through AB would have a slope of $\dfrac{9-0}{0-3} = -3$, and any line parallel to this line will have the same slope by definition.

245. **D.** The length of line PM is $4 - (-1) = 5$. Since M is the midpoint of PQ, the length of MQ must also be 5. Therefore, $x - 4 = 5$, and $x = 9$.

246. **C.** Any line of the form $y = c$ will have a slope of zero, since the y-coordinates will not change.

247. **B.** Solving the given equation for $x = 2$, $14 - 6y = 8$, and $y = 1$.

248. **B.** $\dfrac{(i-1)^2}{(i+1)^2} = \dfrac{i^2 - 2i + 1}{i^2 + 2i + 1} = \dfrac{-1 - 2i + 1}{-1 + 2i + 1} = \dfrac{-2i}{2i} = -1$

249. **A.** Since ABC is an equilateral triangle, each side must have a length of 3. The distance between the points in answer choice A is 3, as the difference along the x-axis between $(-3, 2)$ and $(0, 2)$ would be 3.

250. **A.** Dividing the constant on the right side of each equation by the coefficient of y will give the value of the y-intercept. This is because it will transform the equation into standard line-slope form. In answer

choice A, the y-intercept is $\frac{-10}{2} = -5$. This is the only choice with a negative y-intercept.

251. **C.** Given that the point $(4, y)$ is on the line, solving the given equation for $x = 4$ will give us the value of y. This yields the equation $-32 - 4y = 16$, which has a solution $y = -12$.

252. **B.** Since AB is a line, the sum of $5x$ and x must be 180 degrees. Thus, $5x + x = 6x = 180$, and $x = 180/6 = 30$.

253. **E.** If the midpoint of line AB is on the y-axis, then the distance from A to the y-axis must be the same as the distance from B to the y-axis. Additionally, since the line must be perpendicular to the y-axis, the y-coordinate of the two points will be the same. The point A is 8 units from the y-axis, so the point B must be as well.

254. **B.** The sum of the measures of angles APD and APC must be 180 degrees, since DPC lies on the same line. Since the measure of APD is 80 degrees, angle APC must have a measure of $180 - 80 = 100$ degrees.

255. **C.** Since the lines m and n are parallel, $y = 75$ (corresponding angles). And since the angles lie on the same line, $y + 3x = 180$. Therefore, $75 + 3x = 180$, and $x = 35$.

256. **C.** The x-intercept for the line in answer choice C is 5, while the y-intercept is 2.

257. **A.** Solving for y, $8y = 11 - 5x$, and $y = \frac{11}{8} - \frac{5}{8}x$.

258. **D.** By definition, the angle between two perpendicular lines is 90 degrees.

259. **C.** The lines will intersect where $y = 8$. Substitute this value of y into the given equation: $8 = \frac{3}{2}x + 1$, which can be simplified to $7 = \frac{3}{2}x$. To solve for x, multiply both sides by $\frac{2}{3}$: $x = \frac{2}{3}(7) = \frac{14}{3}$.

260. **A.** The slope of the line passing through the given points is $\frac{8-4}{3-(-1)} = \frac{4}{4} = 1$. Any line parallel to this line will also have a slope of 1. The answer choices are of the form $y = mx + b$, so the coefficient of x will be the slope. The only equation in which the coefficient of x is 1 is choice A.

261. **D.** In all of the equations except answer choice D, y and x are by themselves with an exponent of 1. In answer choice D, the exponent of x is 2 when the expression $x(x + 1)$ is multiplied.

262. **E.** Since N is the midpoint of MP, we know that MN and NP have the same length. Therefore, $2x = 14$, and $x = 7$. This means the length of the line is the sum of the lengths of MN, NP, and PQ, or $14 + 14 + 4(7) - 9 = 47$.

263. **A.** Using $x = 2m$ and $y = m - 1$, substitute for x and y in the equation of the line: $m - 1 = 2m + 4$, so $m = -5$.

264. **D.** If the radius is 2, then the lengths of line segments AP and PD are 2. Since AB is parallel to the x-axis, P has coordinates $(3, 4)$. Further, since DC is perpendicular to AB, the coordinates of D are $(3, 4 + 2)$, or $(3, 6)$.

265. **A.** $\dfrac{i^5}{(i-1)} \times \dfrac{i^8}{(i+1)} = \dfrac{i(i^4)(i^2)^4}{i^2 - 1} = \dfrac{i(1)(1)}{-1-1} = -\dfrac{i}{2}$

266. **B.** We are given the point $y = \dfrac{x-1}{4} = \dfrac{x}{4} - \dfrac{1}{4} = \dfrac{1}{4}x - \dfrac{1}{4}$. To put the equation in standard form, multiply both sides by 4, and bring the x and y terms to the same side: $4y - x = -1$.

267. **B.** To find the answer, you can use the distance formula for two points and then divide by two, since the question states that the distance being looked for is half the distance between P and Q. Placing the values of P and Q into this formula yields $\dfrac{\sqrt{(-8-(-4))^2 + (1-2)^2}}{2} = \dfrac{\sqrt{(-4)^2 + (-1)^2}}{2} = \dfrac{\sqrt{17}}{2}$.

268. **E.** If $xy > 0$, then the individual values of x and y must have the same sign. Only points in the first and the third quadrants have the same sign.

269. **A.** If both are positive, then the line will have to fall from left to right. If both are negative, the same is true.

270. **D.** Any line with a slope of zero will be parallel to the x-axis.

271. **B.** The line passes through the points $(1, 0)$ and $(0, 2)$, so the slope is $\dfrac{2-0}{0-1} = -2$.

272. **C.** Sketching this triangle, you will see that it is a right triangle. The base is the line segment AC, and the height is the line segment AB. These line segments have lengths of 4 and 8, respectively. Using the formula for the area of a triangle, the area is thus $\frac{1}{2}(4)(8) = 16$ square units.

273. **E.** For each of the given angles, the angle directly across from it will have the same measure. Moving up along line m, this gives the angles as z, x, and y. Since these angles are all along the same line, $x + y + z = 180$.

274. **C.** Solving for y, this equation is $y = \frac{1}{2}x + 4$, and any point along this line must have the form $\left(x, \frac{1}{2}x + 4\right)$. Only the point (0, 4) is of this form.

275. **D.** To be along the circumference of the circle, the point must be exactly 2 units away from the point (0, 7). Only the point (1, 7) is not exactly 2 units from (0, 7), as it is 1 unit away.

276. **B.** A line with positive slope will rise from left to right, and a line with a negative x-intercept will cross the x-axis to the left of the origin.

277. **E.** To find the x-intercept, let $y = 0$, and solve for x. The equation $0 = -\frac{1}{4}x + 2$ is equivalent to the equation $-2 = -\frac{1}{4}x$, which has a solution of $x = 8$.

278. **B.** The y-intercept always occurs at the point where $x = 0$.

279. **D.** In the equation, let $y = -5$. This yields $-25 - 2x = -30$, or $-2x = -5$, which has a solution of $x = 5/2$.

280. **A.** All of the equations in the answer choices are in point-slope form, so rewrite the equation in the question in that form. Start by subtracting x from both sides to get $\frac{y}{4} = -\frac{1}{2} - x$, and then finish by multiplying both sides of the equation by 4. The resulting equation is $y = -2 - 4x$.

281. **A.** If the x-intercept is -6, then the line passes through the point $(-6, 0)$. Using the point-slope equation, the line is $y - 0 = 5(x + 6)$, which simplifies to $y = 5x + 30$.

282. **B.** The angles discussed all lie along the same line. Therefore, if x is the measure of angle MQN, then $\frac{1}{2}x + x + \frac{1}{2}x = 180$, which simplifies to $2x = 180$, so $x = 90$. Therefore, the measure of PQM is 45 degrees, which is the same as the measure of angle NQR.

283. **C.** To find the point that is on both lines, set the two equations equal: $5x - 1 = -3x - 17$. Collecting terms, $8x = -16$, and $x = -2$. Therefore, the equations intersect at the point with x-coordinate -2. Only choice C has this value for the x-coordinate.

284. **A.** The angle between any two perpendicular lines is 90 degrees. Therefore, we can write the equation

$2x + 2 = 90$. Simplifying, $2x = 88$, which yields a solution of $x = 44$.

285. **C.** The radius is the distance from the center of the circle to any point on the circumference. Here, that distance is $\sqrt{(4-2)^2 + (9-5)^2} = \sqrt{4+16} = \sqrt{20} = 2\sqrt{5}$.

Chapter 5: Geometry

286. **C.** The interior angles of any triangle must sum to 180. Therefore, the missing angle has a measure of $180 - 45 - 90 = 45$ degrees.

287. **C.** The perimeter is the total distance around the rectangle. Here that distance is $4 + 10 + 4 + 10 = 28$.

288. **A.** By definition, $\sin x = \dfrac{\text{opposite}}{\text{hypotenuse}}$, where "opposite" means the length of the side opposite the angle and "hypotenuse" is the length of the hypotenuse. Here, $\sin x = \frac{9}{15} = \frac{3}{5}$.

289. **C.** The sides of a square all have the same length, so if the area is 16, the length of any side, including the side AB, is 4. The line segment AB is also the radius of the circle, which is required to find the circumference. Using the formula, the circumference is $2\pi r = 8\pi$.

290. **E.** For all angles, $\sec\alpha = \dfrac{1}{\cos\alpha}$.

291. **A.** The area of any circle is πr^2, where r is the radius. The radius of this circle is therefore $\sqrt{8} = 2\sqrt{2}$.

292. **A.** The shortest side must be opposite the smallest angle, and the longest side must be opposite the largest angle. Since an isosceles triangle has two sides of the same length, the sides must have lengths 10, 10, and 20, giving a perimeter of 40.

293. **C.** To find the area, we must first find the height of the triangle. If we draw the triangle and draw a line from its apex to the base, we will form a right triangle with sides of 6, 3, and h, where h is the height. Using the Pythagorean theorem, $3^2 + h^2 = 6^2$, so $h = \sqrt{36 - 9} = \sqrt{27} = 3\sqrt{3}$. Now use the formula for the area of the triangle: $A = \frac{1}{2}bh = \frac{1}{2}(6)(3\sqrt{3}) = 9\sqrt{3}$.

294. **B.** If the length of any one side of the square is x, then the area is x^2, and the perimeter is $4x$. If the area is twice the perimeter, $x^2 = 2(4x)$, and $x^2 - 8x = 0$. By factoring, we see this equation is equivalent to $x(x - 8) = 0$, which has solutions 0 and 8. The length cannot be 0, so it must be 8 units.

295. **E.** The sidewalk will cover the perimeter, which is $110 + 200 + 110 + 200 = 620$ yards.

296. **C.** Using the definition of sine as the opposite side divided by the hypotenuse, $\sin B = \frac{3}{4} = \frac{x}{12}$. Cross multiplying yields the equation $36 = 4x$, so $x = 9$.

297. **A.** The standard form of the equation of a circle is $(x-h)^2 + (y-k)^2 = r^2$, where (h, k) is the center and r is the radius. Using the given values, the equation of this circle is $(x-0)^2 + (y-(-5))^2 = 2^2$. The first term can be simplified to x^2, and the second term to $(y + 5)^2$.

298. **D.** If the legs have lengths 2 and 4, then the hypotenuse has a length of $\sqrt{2^2 + 4^2} = \sqrt{20} = 2\sqrt{5}$.

299. **C.** To find the area of the rectangle, we need to know the length of the rectangle. The diagonal, the width, and the length form a right triangle. Further, since the hypotenuse of this triangle has a measure of 4(5) and one of the legs has a measure of 4(3), the triangle must be a 3-4-5 triangle, and the remaining leg has a measure of $4(4) = 16$. Finally, the area of the rectangle will be $16 \times 12 = 192$.

300. **D.** The smallest angle will correspond to one of the smallest sides, or to a side with length 3. Since the two smallest sides are equal, the triangle is isosceles, and there will be two angles with the given measure. Therefore, the remaining angle will have a measure of $180 - 30 - 30 = 120$, confirming that it is the largest angle.

301. **C.** Opposite angles in a parallelogram are congruent, so there are two angles of 50 degrees. Because a parallelogram is a quadrilateral, its interior angles sum to 360 degrees. Accounting for the two angles we already know, the remaining two angles must sum to $360 - 2(50) = 260$ degrees. Each of the larger angles therefore measures $\frac{260}{2} = 130$ degrees.

302. **E.** If the length of the smaller leg is x, then the larger leg is $3x$, and by the Pythagorean theorem, the hypotenuse is $\sqrt{x^2 + 9x^2} = x\sqrt{10} = 10$, the given length. Solving for x, $x = \frac{10}{\sqrt{10}} = \frac{10\sqrt{10}}{10} = \sqrt{10}$, and the perimeter is $\sqrt{10} + 3\sqrt{10} + 10$.

303. **E.** The largest circle has a radius of 8 and therefore an area of 64π, while the inner circle has a radius of 2 and therefore an area of 4π. The area of the shaded region is the difference between these two areas: $64\pi - 4\pi = 60\pi$.

304. **C.** The circumference of any circle is $2\pi r$, where r is the radius.

305. **A.** The interior angles of any quadrilateral sum to 360 degrees. Therefore, $x = 360 - 125 - 75 - 105 = 55$.

306. **B.** Given that the measure of CAB is 85 degrees, then the measure of ACB is as well, since $AB = BC$. Further, A, C, and D lie on the same line, so the angle BCD is $180 - 85 = 95$ degrees.

307. **C.** The circumference is 6π, so for a radius r, $2\pi r = 6\pi$, and $r = 3$. The area is then $\pi(3^2) = 9\pi$.

308. **D.** The volume of any cube is s^3, where s is the length of any one side. Here, $s^3 = 8$, so $s = 2$ (the cube root of 8). This means that $AB = AD = 2$, and by the Pythagorean theorem, $BD = \sqrt{2^2 + 2^2} = \sqrt{8} = 2\sqrt{2}$.

309. **B.** The right triangle is a 45-45-90 triangle, and with such a triangle the two equal sides (which are across from the 45-degree angles) will always have the same value—we can call it s—while the hypotenuse will always be $\sqrt{2}$ times larger than the value of either of these sides, or $s\sqrt{2}$. Looking at the figure, since the value of the identical sides is 5, you know that x will be $\sqrt{2}$ times larger than that, or $5\sqrt{2}$.

310. **B.** The volume of any sphere is $\frac{4}{3}\pi r^3$, where r is the radius. In this case, $\frac{4}{3}\pi r^3 = 36\pi$, and $r^3 = \frac{3}{4}(36) = 27$. Finally, r, the cube root of 27, is 3.

311. **A.** The cosine of x is the ratio of the lengths of the side adjacent to the angle and the hypotenuse. Here, those sides have lengths b and a, respectively.

312. **A.** The formula of a circle in the (x, y) coordinate plane is $(x-h)^2 + (y-k)^2 = r^2$, where (h, k) is the center and r is the radius. The line AB is a diameter with a length of 10 (which can be found by looking at the y-coordinates of A and B), so the radius must be 5. Further, the center will occur at the halfway point along the line, which is $(6, 5)$.

313. **E.** The diagonal AC is also the diameter of the circle, which we can use to find the radius and thus the area. In a square, the diagonal and two sides form a 45-45-90 triangle with sides x, x, and $x\sqrt{2}$. Therefore, the diameter of the circle is $3\sqrt{2}$, and the radius is $\frac{3\sqrt{2}}{2}$. Using the area formula for a circle, $A = \pi\left(\frac{3\sqrt{2}}{2}\right)^2 = \pi\left(\frac{9(2)}{4}\right) = \pi\left(\frac{9}{2}\right) = \frac{9\pi}{2}$.

314. **C.** ABC is an equilateral triangle, so each angle has a measure of 60 degrees. The angle with a measure of x degrees is the result of bisecting, or halving, this 60-degree angle, so $x = 30$.

315. **D.** The diagonal forms a right triangle with the width and the length acting as legs. Using the Pythagorean theorem, the length of the triangle will be $\sqrt{25^2 - 15^2} = \sqrt{400} = 20$, and the area will be $20 \times 15 = 300$.

316. **C.** Let w be the width of the rectangle and l be the length. We are given that $\tan x = \frac{8}{3} = \frac{l}{AE}$. From the figure, $w = AE + 2$; substituting AE from the solution to $\tan x$, $3 + 2 = 5$. The area is thus $w \times l = 5 \times 8 = 40$.

317. **B.** Opposite sides of a parallelogram are congruent. Therefore, $AB = CD = 3$, and $BC = AD = 7$. The perimeter of $ABCD$ is then $3 + 3 + 7 + 7 = 20$.

318. **D.** The total volume of the container is $8 \times 4 \times 3 = 96$ cubic feet, and the volume of the sand is $8 \times 4 \times 1 = 32$ cubic feet. This leaves $96 - 32 = 64$ cubic feet of the container unfilled.

319. **B.** The area of a rhombus is $\frac{a \times b}{2}$, where a and b are the diagonals. In this case, the diagonals are m and $2m$, so substitute to solve for the area: $\frac{m \times 2m}{2} = \frac{2m^2}{2} = m^2$.

320. **B.** The overlap is shared by both of the squares and has an area of 2. Using the left square, the unshaded portion is said to be the same size. These two pieces make up the square, so it must have an area of 4.

321. **E.** The total area of all the individual rectangles representing rooms will represent the total square footage of carpet needed. The largest rectangle has dimensions of 40 ft. × 30 ft. and an area of 1200 sq. ft. The smallest has dimensions 10 ft. × 20 ft. = 200 sq. ft. Finally, there is a square with dimensions of 20 ft. × 20 ft. and an area of 400 sq. ft. The resulting total is $1200 + 200 + 400 = 1800$ sq. ft.

322. **B.** As an isosceles triangle, ABC will have two sides of the same length and two angles of the same measure. Here it must be that angle BAC is also 40 degrees, so angle ABC is $180 - 40 - 40 = 100$ degrees. The height BD will bisect this angle, meaning $a = 50$.

323. **A.** Since the angles are the interior angles of a triangle, their sum is 180 degrees: $x + 2x + 3x = 6x = 180$, and $x = 180/6 = 30$.

324. **B.** Using the circle centered at B, the radius is $\sqrt{49} = 7$. This is also the length of AB and BC.

Since the circle centered at D has the same area, $CD = DE = 7$, and the length of AE is $4(7) = 28$.

325. **E.** By the Pythagorean theorem, the hypotenuse will have a length of $\sqrt{(5x)^2 + x^2} = \sqrt{26x^2} = x\sqrt{26}$.

326. **E.** The sum of each pair must be $180 - 72 = 108$ degrees. This is true of every pair except the pair in answer choice E.

327. **D.** If the width is w, then $l = 5w$, and the perimeter is $w + 5w + w + 5w = 12w$.

328. **C.** In the triangle with two 60-degree angles, the missing angle is $180 - 120 = 60$ degrees. In the triangle with two angles of 85 degrees, the missing angle is $180 - 170 = 10$ degrees. Since the central angle of any circle has a measure of 360 degrees, the angle AOB is $360 - 60 - 10 - 115 = 175$ degrees.

329. **C.** The area is the total of the area of the two triangles and the rectangle $FBCE$: $\frac{1}{2}(2)(2) + 3(2) + \frac{1}{2}(2)(2) = 2 + 6 + 2 = 10$.

330. **B.** Since opposite sides of a parallelogram are congruent, the perimeter is $8 + 2x = 20$. To solve for x, subtract 8 from both sides and then divide by 2: $x = \frac{12}{2} = 6$.

331. **A.** The area is found with the formula lw, where l is the length and w is the width. Therefore, $45 = 9l$, and $l = \frac{45}{9} = 5$.

332. **D.** In a parallelogram, opposite angles are congruent. Here, $x = 125$, and $y = 55$.

333. **A.** The triangle is a 30-60-90 triangle, which always has legs x (opposite the 30-degree angle) and $x\sqrt{3}$ (opposite the 60-degree angle), along with a hypotenuse of $2x$. Since the hypotenuse here is 8, $x = 4$, and this is equal to the length of the side opposite the 30-degree angle.

334. **C.** Using the formula for the area of a circle, $\frac{29\pi}{4} = \pi r^2$, so $r = \sqrt{\frac{29}{4}} = \frac{\sqrt{29}}{2}$. The hypotenuse of the triangle ABC is also the diameter of the circle, which is $2r = \sqrt{29}$. Therefore, by the Pythagorean theorem, $(\sqrt{29})^2 = 2^2 + (BC)^2$, and $BC = 5$. Finally, the area of the triangle is $\frac{1}{2}(2)(5) = 5$.

335. **A.** The area is the base (9) times the height, which is unknown. The height is a leg of the right triangle with a hypotenuse of 5 and a second leg of 1. Therefore, by the Pythagorean theorem, $1^2 + h^2 = 5^2$, where h is the unknown height.

Solving for h, $h = \sqrt{24} = 2\sqrt{6}$, and the area of the parallelogram is $9(2\sqrt{6}) = 18\sqrt{6}$.

336. **B.** The total area of the surface to be painted is $\frac{1}{2}(2)(2) + 12(2) + \frac{1}{2}(2)(2) = 28$. If each tube can cover four square feet, the artist will need $\frac{28}{4} = 7$ tubes of paint.

337. **C.** Since the figure is a parallelogram, the pair of angles must sum to 180 degrees. The only pair of angles whose sum is not 180 degrees is the pair in choice C.

338. **C.** Because ABC is an equilateral triangle, each of its interior angles has a measure of 60 degrees. The angle at point C has been split into two angles; one has a measure of 20 degrees, so the other has a measure of $60 - 20 = 40$ degrees. Finally, the triangle containing the angle labeled x has interior angles of 40 degrees and 60 degrees, so $x = 180 - 40 - 60 = 80$.

339. **A.** Using the formula for the volume of a sphere and the given volume, $\frac{4}{3}\pi r^3 = \frac{32}{3}\pi$, and $\frac{32}{3} = \frac{4}{3}(8)$, so $r = 2$.

340. **A.** The triangle has two sides of equal length, so it is isosceles, and the angles opposite these sides have the same measure. Since B and C lie along the same line as these angles, $x = y$, and $x - y = 0$.

341. **D.** If s is a single side of the cube, $s^3 = 125$, and $s = 5$. Therefore, a single face would have an area of $5 \times 5 = 25$.

342. **A.** Area $= \frac{1}{2}$(base)(height) $= \frac{1}{2}xy = \frac{xy}{2}$

343. **C.** Since BD is a diagonal, ABD is exactly half of the rectangle, and the area of $ABCD = 2(6) = 12$ square meters.

344. **B.** Using the standard form of the equation of a circle, $(x-h)^2 + (y-k)^2 = r^2$, you can determine that the radius of the circle is 2, and the center is at the point (8, 10). Any point exactly two units from (8, 10) will lie on the circumference of the circle. You can then use the distance formula between two points to determine the answer is B.

345. **D.** Given that $\tan x = \frac{1}{2} = \frac{\text{opposite}}{\text{adjacent}}$ and h = the length of the hypotenuse, then $h^2 = 1^2 + 2^2$, and $h = \sqrt{5}$. Therefore, $\sin x = \frac{\text{opposite}}{\text{hypotenuse}} = \frac{1}{\sqrt{5}} = \frac{\sqrt{5}}{5}$.

346. **B.** If s is one side of the square, then $s^2 = 49$, and $s = 7$. Therefore, the perimeter is $4(7) = 28$.

347. **E.** The height of triangle PQR will equal the length of BA and allow us to find the area. Because the sides of an equilateral triangle are equal, we can determine that the height h is a leg of a right triangle with hypotenuse of 2 and a leg of 1. Using the Pythagorean theorem, $1^2 + h^2 = 2^2$, so $h = \sqrt{3}$. The area is then $4\sqrt{3}$.

348. **C.** The given triangle has two angles with the same measure, but one of its sides has a different value (x is not equal to y). The triangle is therefore an isosceles triangle and has two sides of length x. The perimeter is then $x + x + y = 2x + y$.

349. **D.** The perimeter can be written as $2x + 2y = 32$. To simplify and solve for y, divide both sides by 2: $x + y = 16$. Given $x = 3y$, substitute and solve: $3y + y = 4y = 16$, and $y = 4$. Therefore, $x = 16 - 4 = 12$.

350. **B.** Since N is the midpoint of AC, AC has a length of $2(3) = 6$. Using the area formula and the given area, $\frac{1}{2}(6)(AB) = 12$, and $AB = 4$.

351. **D.** Let r represent the radius of a circle. Using the formula for circumference, the given inequality is $2\pi r > x$. Solving for r, $r > \frac{x}{2\pi}$.

352. **D.** The diagonal AC bisects the angle at point C. You can attempt to determine the interior angles of the triangle ABC, but if you recall that the adjacent angles of a rhombus always sum to 180 degrees, then you can simply use the equation $x = 180 - 60 = 120$.

353. **C.** As a circle has 360 degrees total, to find x you must divide this amount by 8: $x = \frac{360}{8} = 45$.

354. **C.** Circumference $= 2\pi r = 2\pi\left(\frac{1}{\pi}\right) = 2$

355. **C.** Since the area is 16 and $ABCD$ is a square, $AD = CD = 4$, and $\tan x = \frac{4}{4} = 1$.

356. **C.** The sum of the interior angles of any quadrilateral is 360 degrees. Therefore, $x + 2x + x + 45 + x + 55 = 360$, and $5x + 100 = 360$. This equation has a solution of $x = 52$.

357. **E.** Let h be the height of triangle ABC. Given the area, $\frac{1}{2}(5)h = 50$, and $h = 20$. For triangle MNP, the area is $\frac{1}{2}(5)(20 + 10) = 75$.

358. **B.** Using the formula for circumference and dividing by 2 because this is a half circle, arc $PQ = \frac{1}{2}(2\pi(2)) = 2\pi$.

Chapter 6: Proportions

359. **E.** As an equation, the ratio is written as $\frac{x}{y} = \frac{5}{12}$. If $x = 45$, then this is nine times larger than 5, so $y = 12 \times 9 = 108$.

360. **C.** One hour and 20 minutes is equivalent to 80 minutes. At 60 miles per hour, the vehicle is moving at 1 mile per minute and will therefore cover 80 miles.

361. **D.** $M\%$ can be written as $\frac{M}{100}$, giving us the equation $\frac{M}{100}(135) = 54$ or $1.35M = 54$, which has a solution of $M = \frac{54}{1.35} = 40$.

362. **B.** Let F represent the number of full-time employees and P represent the number of part-time employees. Since there are 800 employees, $F + P = 800$. Also, given the ratio $\frac{F}{P} = \frac{3}{2}$, we can cross multiply and solve for F: $3P = 2F$, and $F = \frac{3}{2}P$. Finally, substitute this value of F into the first equation, and solve for P: $F + P = \frac{3}{2}P + P = \frac{5}{2}P = 800$, and $P = 800\left(\frac{2}{5}\right) = 320$.

363. **C.** If one side of the square is x, then the perimeter is $4x$. If we increase x by 20%, the new length of a side will be $1.2x$, and the perimeter will be $4.8x$. The percent increase is then $100\left(\frac{4.8x - 4x}{4x}\right) = 100\left(\frac{0.8x}{4x}\right) = 20\%$.

364. **E.** Since the rectangles are similar and $3(5) = 15$, the length of the larger rectangle is $3(14) = 42$, and the perimeter is $15 + 42 + 15 + 42 = 114$.

365. **C.** Stated as equations, the information provided says $0.05x = y$ and $0.25y = z$. Substituting the value of y from the first equation into the second, $0.25(0.05x) = z$, which simplifies to $0.0125x = z$. Solving for x, divide both sides by 0.0125, so $x = 80z$.

366. **C.** Let x represent the area of the largest section, y the area of the middle section, and z the area of the smallest section. We will find the largest area first, since it is easiest to work with. Given the total area, $x + y + z = 1550$. Also, given the ratios $2x = 3y$ and $2x = 5z$, we can solve these equations for y and z respectively: $y = \frac{2}{3}x$ and $z = \frac{2}{5}x$. Our original equation can now be written as $x + \frac{2}{3}x + \frac{2}{5}x = 1550$. Collecting terms,

$\frac{31}{15}x = 1550$, and $x = 750$. The smallest section, z, will have an area of $\frac{2}{5}(750) = 300$.

367. **B.** The ratio of BA to ED is 4:1, so $x = \frac{30}{4} = 7.5$.

368. **E.** If a is inversely proportional to $\frac{b}{2}$, then for some k, $a = \frac{1}{k}\left(\frac{b}{2}\right) = \frac{b}{2k}$. Using the given values to find k, $1 = \frac{10}{2k}$ and $k = 5$. Therefore, we can write $a = \frac{b}{10}$, and when $b = 35$, $a = \frac{35}{10} = \frac{7}{2}$.

369. **C.** $0.8(x + 1) = 2$ is equivalent to $0.8x = 2 - 0.8 = 1.2$, and $x = \frac{1.2}{0.8} = 1.5$.

370. **E.** For some value of k, $m = kn^2$. Using the given values to find k, $2 = k(-1)^2$ and $k = 2$. Therefore, $m = 2n^2$, and when $n = x + 5$, $m = 2(x + 5)^2 = 2(x^2 + 10x + 25) = 2x^2 + 20x + 50$.

371. **A.** The document will contain a total of $500n$ words, since this is the number of pages multiplied by the number of words per page. Since Greg can read w words per minute, he will need $\frac{500n}{w}$ minutes to read it.

372. **B.** First restate each term as a decimal: $\frac{1}{2}\% = 0.5\% = 0.005$, and $\frac{1}{20} = 0.05$. Therefore, $\frac{1}{2}\%$ of $\frac{1}{20}$ is $0.005(0.05) = 0.00025$.

373. **D.** Party B received 46% of the votes, so $0.46x = 874$, where x is the total number of votes. Solve for x to find the total: $x = \frac{874}{0.46} = 1900$.

374. **D.** The area of square A is $3 \times 3 = 9$, and the area of square B is $9 \times 9 = 81$. The ratio 9:81 is equivalent to 1:9.

375. **A.** If x is the next largest side, then $\frac{2}{x} = \frac{4}{12}$ and $x = 6$. If y is the largest side, then $\frac{2}{y} = \frac{4}{14}$ and $y = 7$. Therefore the perimeter is $2 + 6 + 7 = 15$.

376. **D.** To determine this answer, you must divide the number of math majors (490) by the total number of students (14,000), and then multiply the amount by 100 to get the percentage: $100\left(\frac{490}{14,000}\right) = 3.5$.

377. E. Given the ratio, $\dfrac{AB}{18}=\dfrac{2}{3}$, and $AB=12$. Since C is the midpoint of DF, $DF=2(12)=24$. Finally, the area is $\dfrac{1}{2}(24)(18)=216$.

378. B. Since $10FG=BC$, $(1/10)AB=FE$, and $FE=1$. Therefore, the perimeter is $1+3+1+3=8$.

379. B. For some k, $x=\dfrac{1}{k}y$. Using the values given, $12=\dfrac{1}{k}(48)$, which means $k=4$. Therefore, when $y=12$, $x=\dfrac{1}{4}(12)=3$.

380. B. 40% is half of 80%, so 40% of the number is $\dfrac{122}{2}=61$.

381. E. $\left(\dfrac{40\ \text{min.}}{28\ \text{hard drives}}\right)(196\ \text{hard drives})=7(40)\ \text{min.}$
$=280\ \text{min.}$

382. C. Expressing the given ratios as equations, $\dfrac{A}{B}=\dfrac{3}{8}$ and $\dfrac{B}{C}=\dfrac{1}{6}$. Solving for B in the second equation, $6B=C$ and $B=\dfrac{C}{6}$. When we substitute this value of B in the first equation, we find $\dfrac{A}{\left(\dfrac{C}{6}\right)}=\dfrac{6A}{C}=\dfrac{3}{8}$.

Dividing both sides by 6, $\dfrac{A}{C}=\dfrac{3}{48}=\dfrac{1}{16}$.

383. C. $(1-0.15)(154.99)=0.85(154.99)=131.74$

384. A. If the width is w, then the length is $1.4w$. Since area of a rectangle is length times width, the area is: $w(1.4w)=1.4w^2=140$. Solving this equation, $w^2=\dfrac{140}{1.4}=100$, and $w=10$.

385. D. Since the triangles are similar, $ED=3y$, and the area is $\dfrac{1}{2}(3x)(3y)=\dfrac{9xy}{2}$.

386. B. $\dfrac{x}{100}\left(\dfrac{3}{4}\right)=\dfrac{3x}{400}$

387. B. Convert the fractions to decimals and solve: $0.0025(0.25)=0.000625$.

388. B. The total percentage must be 100, so $x=100-(35+20+24)=21$.

389. D. When $x=12$, $\dfrac{12}{y}=\dfrac{1}{6}$ and $y=72$. The difference is $72-12=60$.

390. C. Given the ratio of x to y, $4x=y$, and the area of the larger triangle is $\dfrac{1}{2}(AB)(x+y)=\dfrac{1}{2}(AB)(x+4x)=\dfrac{1}{2}(AB)(5x)$. The area of the smaller triangle is $\dfrac{1}{2}(AB)(x)$, or $\dfrac{1}{5}$ as large. Therefore, the ratio of the areas is 1:5.

391. E. The length of QP is four times the length of BA. Since the rectangles are similar, this implies $4(13)=x-13$, or $52=x-13$. Therefore, $x=65$.

392. B. Given that $0.95(3x)=39.9$, dividing both sides yields $x=\dfrac{39.9}{0.95(3)}=14$.

393. D. The radius is half the diameter, so the area of the circle centered at point O is $\pi\left(\dfrac{AB}{2}\right)^2=\dfrac{\pi}{4}(AB)^2$.

Using the given ratio, $AB=3CD$, so $CD=\dfrac{AB}{3}$, and the area of the circle centered at P is $\pi\left(\dfrac{CD}{2}\right)^2=\dfrac{\pi}{4}(CD)^2=\dfrac{\pi}{4}\left(\dfrac{AB}{3}\right)^2=\dfrac{\pi}{36}(AB)^2$. The ratio of the two areas is then $\dfrac{\dfrac{\pi}{4}(AB)^2}{\dfrac{\pi}{36}(AB)^2}=\dfrac{\pi}{4}\left(\dfrac{36}{\pi}\right)=\dfrac{36}{4}$, which we see is equivalent to 9:1.

394. E. For some constant k, $y^2=\dfrac{k}{x}$. Using the given values, $16=\dfrac{k}{4}$ and $k=64$. Therefore, when $x=2$, $y^2=\dfrac{64}{2}=32$.

395. C. Let A be the area of the square and s be the length of one side. We are told that $s=0.2A$; since this is a square, $A=s^2$ and $s=0.2s^2$. Bringing all the terms to one side and factoring, we have $s(0.2s-1)=0$. The solutions are $s=0$ and $s=\dfrac{1}{0.2}=5$. The sides can't have a length of zero, so each side has a length of 5, and the perimeter is $4\times5=20$.

396. B. Assuming x and y are nonzero, we can write $\dfrac{x}{y}=\dfrac{2}{5}$ and $y=0.3z$. Using substitution, $\dfrac{x}{y}=\dfrac{2}{5}=\dfrac{x}{0.3z}$ and $\dfrac{x}{z}=\dfrac{2(0.3)}{5}=\dfrac{0.6}{5}=\dfrac{6}{50}=\dfrac{3}{25}$.

397. B. Taking $x\%$ of something is the same as multiplying by $\dfrac{x}{100}$. Therefore, if $\dfrac{x}{50}(280)=112$, then to find $x\%$ of 280, we multiply both sides by $\dfrac{1}{2}$

to get $\frac{1}{2}\left(\frac{x}{50}\right)(280)=\frac{1}{2}(112)$. This is equivalent to $\frac{x}{100}(280)=56$.

398. **C.** The length of AC is 3 times larger than the length of DF. Since the triangles are similar, this pattern will be true for each pair of sides. Further, since the triangles are isosceles, $BC = AB = x$, and $ED = EF = \frac{x}{3}$. The perimeter of DEF is then

$$6+\frac{x}{3}+\frac{x}{3}=6+\frac{2x}{3}.$$

399. **D.** $0.9(30) = 27$

400. **B.** Since A is equilateral, one side of A has a length of $\frac{9}{3} = 3$. Using the ratio, with b representing the length of one side of triangle B, $\frac{3}{b}=\frac{6}{7}$, or $21 = 6b$. Therefore, $b=\frac{21}{6}=\frac{7}{2}$.

401. **D.** The given equation can be rewritten as $5x = y$. Further, since the area of $ABPQ$ is $4x = 12$, we can find $x = 3$, which means $y = 5(3) = 15$. Therefore, the area of $ABCD$ is $4(3 + 15) = 4(18) = 72$.

402. **C.** Because $\frac{x}{y}=\frac{2}{3}$, we can find $3x = 2y$ and $y=\frac{3}{2}x$. Given that $x + y = 125$, we can write $x+\frac{3}{2}x=\frac{5}{2}x=125$, so $x=\frac{2}{5}(125)=50$.

403. **B.** Since the answer choices are given as fractions, express the percentage in fraction form:

$$\frac{0.2}{100}\left(\frac{1}{5}\right)=\frac{2}{1000}\left(\frac{1}{5}\right)=\frac{1}{500}\left(\frac{1}{5}\right)=\frac{1}{2500}.$$

404. **C.** The ratio $r:\pi r^2$ is equivalent to $1:\pi r$.

405. **A.** If P is the number of physics students and B is the number of biology students, then $3B = P$. Given $P = 21$, we can substitute and solve: $21 = 3B$, so $B = 7$.

406. **D.** For some constant k, $m=\frac{k}{n}$. Given the initial values, $\frac{1}{2}=\frac{k}{6}$, so $k = 3$. When $n=\frac{2}{3}$, $m=\frac{3}{\left(\frac{2}{3}\right)}=3\left(\frac{3}{2}\right)=\frac{9}{2}$.

407. **B.** With the given information, we can write the equations $x = 0.3y$ and $0.2y = 8$. Solving the second equation, $y = 40$. Using this value of y in the first equation, $x = 0.3(40) = 12$.

408. **E.** If y is directly proportional to x, then for some constant k, $y = kx$. Given the initial values, $6=k\left(\frac{1}{4}\right)$ and $k = 24$. Therefore, $y = 24x$.

409. **E.** Using the area of the rectangle, we can write $x(x + 1) = 12$, or $x^2+x-12=0$. Factoring, we see that $(x + 4)(x - 3) = 0$, and the equation has the solutions $x = -4$ and $x = 3$. Since the length must be positive, $x = 3$, and the ratio of x to $x + 1$ is 3 to 4.

410. **D.** The length of one side of the square is $0.28(50) = 14$, so the area is $14 \times 14 = 196$.

411. **C.** If $\frac{q}{100}(30)=21$, then $q=21\left(\frac{100}{30}\right)=70$.

412. **C.** After the first week, the price is $1.05(436) = 457.8$. After the second, the price is $0.9(457.8) = 412.02$, and after the third, $1.2(412.02) = 494.42$.

413. **D.** The question describes $40\% + 10\% + 5\% = 55\%$ of the items, so the remaining items will be 45% of the total: $0.45(600) = 270$.

414. **C.** The equation $a=4\left(\frac{b}{2}\right)$ describes the relationship between a and b, and it can be simplified to $a = 2b$; solving for b, we have $b=\frac{1}{2}a$. Therefore, the percentage is $100\left(\frac{b}{a}\right)\%=100\left(\frac{\frac{1}{2}a}{a}\right)\%=50\%$.

415. **E.** To find the distance the particle will have moved in $2\frac{1}{4}$ hours, multiply the rate by the time:

$$\frac{3\text{ units}}{\frac{1}{2}\text{ hr.}}\left(2\frac{1}{4}\text{ hr.}\right)=\frac{6\text{ units}}{1\text{ hr.}}\left(\frac{9}{4}\text{ hr.}\right)=6\left(\frac{9}{4}\right)\text{ units}$$

$=\frac{27}{2}$ units. It is moving along the x-axis from the origin, so the y-coordinate remains at zero, and in $2\frac{1}{4}$ hours it will arrive at the point with coordinates $x=\frac{27}{2}$, $y = 0$.

416. **B.** Given the ratio, we can write $\frac{x}{y}=\frac{1}{4}$, or $4x = y$.

Using the Pythagorean theorem, $x^2+y^2=\left(2\sqrt{17}\right)$. Substituting the value for y from the first equation, $x^2+(4x)^2=4(17)$, and $17x^2=68$. Finally, dividing both sides by 17 gives us $x^2=4$, and since x must be positive, $x = 2$.

417. **C.** Because they lie on the same line, $m + n = 180$. Using the given ratio, $\frac{m}{n}=\frac{2}{3}$, so $3m = 2n$ and

$m = \frac{2}{3}n$. Combining equations, $m + n = \frac{2}{3}n + n = \frac{5}{3}n = 180$, and $n = 180\left(\frac{3}{5}\right) = 108$.

418. **C.** The second equation can be written as $3n = 4x$ or $n = \frac{4}{3}x$. Therefore, $\frac{m}{n} = \frac{4}{9} = \frac{m}{\left(\frac{4}{3}x\right)}$. Multiplying both sides by $\frac{4}{3}$ gives us $\frac{m}{x} = \left(\frac{4}{3}\right)\frac{4}{9} = \frac{16}{27}$.

419. **A.** $\frac{1}{5}$ is half as large as $\frac{2}{5}$, and half of 10 is 5.

420. **A.** $\frac{1 \text{ flash}}{6 \text{ min.}}(800 \text{ min.}) = 133.33$ flashes, or 133 complete flashes

421. **E.** For some constant k, $y = \frac{k}{\sqrt{x}}$. Using the given values, $18 = \frac{k}{\sqrt{4}}$ and $k = 36$. Therefore, when $x = 12$, $y = \frac{36}{\sqrt{12}} = \frac{36}{2\sqrt{3}} = \frac{18}{\sqrt{3}} = \frac{18\sqrt{3}}{3} = 6\sqrt{3}$.

422. **C.** The area for the smaller circle is $A = \pi\left(\frac{d}{2}\right)^2 = \frac{\pi}{4}d^2$, while the area of the larger circle is $B = \pi\left(\frac{3d}{2}\right)^2 = \frac{9}{4}\pi d^2$. The value of B is 9 times the value of A.

423. **A.** The length of AB is the height of ABC and ACE, so it is best to find it first. Since $AC = 4$ and $BC = 1$, by the Pythagorean theorem, $(AB)^2 + 1^2 = 4^2$ and $AB = \sqrt{15}$. Substitute this value of the height to find the areas of ACE and ABC: area of $ACE = \frac{1}{2}bh = \frac{1}{2}(2)(\sqrt{15}) = \sqrt{15}$; area of $ABC = \frac{1}{2}(1)(\sqrt{15}) = \frac{\sqrt{15}}{2}$. The ratio is therefore $1:\frac{1}{2}$, or 2:1.

424. **C.** Simplify the expression for the information given: $\frac{\left(\frac{1}{2}\right)}{100}\left(\frac{x}{14}\right) = \frac{1}{200}\left(\frac{x}{14}\right) = \frac{x}{2800}$. Next solve the given equation: $\frac{x}{2800} = \frac{1}{4}$, so $4x = 2800$ and $x = 700$.

425. **C.** $1.03 \times 1.03 \times 1.03 \times \$675 = \$737.59$

426. **B.** Cross multiply and solve for y: $14x = 4y$, and $y = \frac{14}{4}x = \frac{7}{2}x$.

427. **B.** $100\left(\frac{45 - 38}{38}\right)\% = 18.4\%$

428. **C.** In the first two hours, he filed $14(2) = 28$ folders. In the next five hours, he filed $22(5) = 110$ folders. Therefore, he filed a total of $28 + 110 = 138$ folders.

Chapter 7: Functions

429. **D.** Using the zero product rule, the zeros of the function are the solutions to $x^2 = 0$, $x - 4 = 0$, and $x + 1 = 0$. These solutions are 0, 4, and -1.

430. **D.** In order to determine the binomials that make up this trinomial, you must experiment with some values. Since the middle value x has a -1 in front of it, it helps to work with two factors of -12 that might add up to -1 when combined. The numbers -4 and 3 fit this description. $x^2 - x - 12 = (x - 4)(x + 3)$.

431. **E.** $f(-2) = 3(-2)^2 - (-2)^3 = 3(4) + 8 = 20$

432. **B.** The graph of $g(x)$ is a line, while the graph of $f(x)$ is a parabola (both ends either rising or falling). Therefore, the graphs of the functions may intersect 0, 1, or 2 times, meaning 2 is the maximum number of times.

433. **A.** If $f(x)$ is a polynomial with the given zeros, then $(x + 3)$, $(x + 2)$, $(x - 4)$, $(x - 5)$, and $(x - 7)$ are factors of $f(x)$.

434. **D.** A shift of $f(x)$ to the left c units is always represented by $f(x + c)$.

435. **B.** We are given the y value and must find the x value. Substituting the given value into the function, $4 = 3q - 5$, and $9 = 3q$. Therefore, $q = 3$.

436. **C.** $V(8) = 1000(1 + 0.06)^8 = 1593.85$

437. **E.** The graph of x^2 crosses the x-axis at the origin, so choice A is not correct. Since this graph is centered along the y-axis, it must be a vertical translation of x^2. Further, since it has a positive y-intercept, it must be of the form $x^2 + c$, where c is positive, as in choice E.

438. **C.** If $x^2 + 1 = 0$, then $x^2 = -1$ and $x = \pm\sqrt{-1} = \pm i$.

439. **E.** The graph of $-f(x)$ will be a reflection of the graph of $f(x)$.

440. **D.** $f(a - 1) = (a - 1)^2 + (a - 1) - 1 = a^2 - 2a + 1 + a - 1 - 1 = a^2 - a - 1$

441. **D.** Using the FOIL method, $(2m-6)^2 = 4m^2 - 12m - 12m + 36 = 4m^2 - 24m + 36$.

442. **D.** $(f \circ g)(3) = f(g(3)) = f(3^2 - 2) = f(7) = 7 + 6 = 13$.

443. **B.** To find the x value of the point where the graphs intersect, we set the expressions equal to each other and solve for x. Given that $64x^3 = 8$, we see that $x^3 = \dfrac{8}{64} = \dfrac{1}{8}$ and $x = \dfrac{1}{2}$.

444. **C.** $g(\sqrt{3}) = (\sqrt{3})^4 + (\sqrt{3})^2 = 9 + 3 = 12$

445. **A.** Factoring gives $x^2 + 2x - 35 = (x+7)(x-5) = 0$. By the zero product rule, $x + 7 = 0$ and $x - 5 = 0$. Therefore, the roots are -7 and 5. The question asks for the largest value, which is 5.

446. **A.** Since the function is a polynomial that does not cross the x-axis at any other point, it will be of the form $(x + a)(x + b)(x - c)$ for positive a, b, and c, since the x-coordinates of A and B are negative while the x-coordinate of C is positive. Only choice A meets this condition.

447. **B.** When $x = 1$, then $f(1) = 1^3 - 3(1) = -2$.

448. **B.** $9(10) - 10^2 = 90 - 100 = -10$.

449. **E.** Dividing both sides of the equation by 2 gives an equivalent equation, $x^2 - 3x = -2$, which can be restated as $x^2 - 3x + 2 = 0$. Factor the equation to get $(x - 2)(x - 1) = 0$. By the zero product rule, $x = 2$ and $x = 1$. Therefore, there is no value $x < 0$ that makes the equation true.

450. **D.** The expression $x^4 - 16$ is a difference of squares, so it factors into $(x^2 + 4)(x^2 - 4)$, which factors further into $(x^2 + 4)(x + 2)(x - 2)$.

451. **A.** Given the table, $f(x) = 0$ when $x = -6$.

452. **E.** The function $f(x) = 3x^2 - 3x - 27 = 0$ is equivalent to $\dfrac{1}{3}(3x^2 - 3x - 27) = \dfrac{1}{3}(0)$, or $x^2 - x - 9 = 0$.

453. **B.** The 3 is added to the x before the term is squared, so the first two steps are $(x + 3)^2$. In the next step, this term is multiplied by 5.

454. **A.** $f(2, -3) = 2(-3) - 2 = -6 - 2 = -8$

455. **C.** Given that $-f(x) = -x^3$, then for $x = -2$, we find $-f(-2) = -(-2)^3 = -(-8) = 8$. For $x = -1$, we find $-f(-1) = -(-1)^3 = -(-1) = 1$. For $x = 0$, the solution is $-f(0) = -(0)^3 = 0$. For $x = 1$, it is $-f(1) = -(1)^3 = -(1) = -1$, and for $x = 2$, it is $-f(2) = -(2)^3 = -8$.

456. **E.** The graph of $f(x - 2)$ would be the graph of $f(x)$ shifted to the right by 2 units. Therefore, every x-coordinate would be increased by 2.

457. **C.** If $f(2) = 2$, then $\dfrac{-1}{k} = 2$ and $2k = -1$. Therefore, $k = \dfrac{1}{2}$.

458. **A.** If $x^2 = 72 - x$, then $x^2 + x - 72 = 0$. Factoring, $(x + 9)(x - 8) = 0$, and by the zero product rule, $x = -9$ and $x = 8$. The question asks for the smaller of these values.

459. **A.** The resulting graph would be a parabola, which could be completely within the first quadrant.

460. **E.** The graph of $g(x)$ will be reflected over the x-axis. Further, if $g(3) = 3$, then $-g(3) = -3$.

461. **E.** The equation $2x^2 - 5x + 3 = x^2 - 5x + 2$ is equivalent to the equation $x^2 + 1 = 0$. This equation is equivalent to $x^2 = -1$, which has no real solutions.

462. **D.** After $f(x)$ crosses the x-axis, it stays above it. Therefore, the function is positive for every x value after -4.

463. **B.** $f(5) = \dfrac{5 - 4}{5 + 1} = \dfrac{1}{6}$

464. **C.** $P(6) - P(5) = [8(6) - 5] - [8(5) - 5] = 43 - 35 = 8$

465. **E.** Using the FOIL method, $(a - 6)(b + 4) = ab + 4a - 6b - 24$.

466. **C.** The given expression is a difference of squares, so $x^2 - 36 = (x + 6)(x - 6)$.

467. **D.** We are given the x value and must find the corresponding y value. Given the expression for the function, $c = g(4) = \dfrac{3(4) + 10}{8} = \dfrac{22}{8} = \dfrac{11}{4}$.

468. **E.** By the zero product rule, if the function is $(x - k)(f(x))$, then $x - k = 0$ and $f(x) = 0$ can be used to find the zeros of the function. Using the first equation, $x = k$ must be a zero of the function.

469. **A.** Substituting each of the values, $g(-4) = -6$.

470. **B.** The equation $f(g(x)) = 8$ is equivalent to $\dfrac{1}{2}(2x)^2 = 8$, or $\dfrac{1}{2}(4x^2) = 8$. Dividing both sides by 2, $x^2 = 4$, so $x = \pm\sqrt{4} = \pm 2$.

471. **E.** In general, if a function $f(x)$ is shifted up by 6 units, the graph will be described by $f(x) + 6$. If that same graph is shifted to the left one unit, then the graph will be represented by $f(x + 1) + 6$. Applying this to the given expression, $(x - 5 + 1)^3 + 6 = (x - 4)^3 + 6$.

472. **A.** $f(1) = 2(1)(1 - 1)^2 = 0$

473. **D.** The graph will be a downward-facing parabola with a line of symmetry through the x-axis. Since c is positive, $f(x) > 0$ when x is between -3 and 3 and

$f(x) < 0$ otherwise. Finally, because of the symmetry, $f(-c) = f(c)$.

474. C. For $a = 1$, substitute and simplify: $g(1, b) = 4b - b + 1 = 3b + 1 > 0$. For the inequality where $g(1, b) > 0$, solve for b: $3b + 1 > 0$, so $b > -\dfrac{1}{3}$.

475. D. $(f \circ g)(7) = f(g(7)) = f(-5(7) - 8) = f(-43) = -43 + 10 = -33$

476. B. The function $g(x)$ is greater than $f(x)$ whenever the graph of $g(x)$ is above the graph of $f(x)$. This occurs between the x values of -1 and 4.

477. B. At some point in solving the given equation, the equation $x = -\dfrac{5}{2}$ must have been found. Work backward by adding $\dfrac{5}{2}$ to both sides and multiplying both sides by 2: $x + \dfrac{5}{2} = 0$, and $2x + 5 = 0$.

478. E. $\dfrac{x^2 - 3x - 4}{x - 4} = \dfrac{(x - 4)(x + 1)}{x - 4} = x + 1, x \ne 4$

479. C. To touch the x-axis at only one point and be a quadratic function as shown in the answer choices, the function would have to be of the form $(x + c)^2 = x^2 + 2xc + c^2$ or $(x - c)^2 = x^2 - 2xc + c^2$ for some value of c. The function in answer choice (C) is of this form, since $8 = 2(4)$ and $4^2 = 16$.

480. E. $g(a^2 - 10) = (a^2 - 10)^2 + (a^2 - 10) - 5 = a^4 - 20a^2 + 100 + a^2 - 10 - 5 = a^4 - 19a^2 + 85$

481. B. Since $x - 5$ is a factor, 5 must be a zero of the function, and $(5, 0)$ is on its graph.

482. B. If $a < 0$, the graph is facing downward, and for any x value between 3 and 9, $f(x) > 0$.

483. D. $xy^4 + x^3 y = (4)(-1)^4 + 4^3(-1) = 4 - 64 = -60$

484. B. If $ax - b = 0$, then $ax = b$ and $x = \dfrac{b}{a}$. Therefore, a and b can have any values where $\dfrac{b}{a} = -7$. Of the pairs of values given, you need a pair where b is 7 or -7 and a has the opposite sign; only choice B meets these conditions.

485. B. The equation crosses the x-axis at one point, so there will be one real solution to $f(x) = 0$.

486. C. Using the table, $f(2) = 8$. Therefore, $\dfrac{f(2)}{4} = \dfrac{8}{4} = 2 = 12x$, so $x = \dfrac{2}{12}$, or $\dfrac{1}{6}$.

487. E. Setting the equations equal to each other, $2x^2 + 14 = x^2 + 30$. Collecting terms gives us $x^2 = 16$. This equation has solutions $x = 4, x = -4$. But since $a < 0$, we will use $x = -4$. At $x = -4$, $b = f(-4) = 2(16) + 14 = 46$.

488. D. $s(4) = -4^2 + 9(4) = -16 + 36 = 20$

489. D. Since the coefficient on the first term is positive, the graph of the function is a parabola opening up. Additionally, since $x^2 - 9x + 8 = (x - 8)(x - 1)$, the function crosses the x-axis at $x = 8$ and $x = 1$. Therefore, for values of x between 1 and 8, $f(x)$ will be negative.

490. B. The given equation is equivalent to $x^3 = \dfrac{9}{2}$, which has one solution, $x = \sqrt[3]{\dfrac{9}{2}}$.

491. B. While there may be more zeros, there must be at least two, since the table shows two instances where $g(x) = 0$.

492. E. If n is larger than m^2, the expression will be negative. Otherwise, as long as m^2 is larger than $n + 3$, the expression will be positive.

493. B. The equation $-x^2 - 15 = 0$ is equivalent to the equation $x^2 = -15$, which has no real solutions.

494. A. $f\left(\dfrac{1}{2}\right) = \dfrac{\left(\dfrac{1}{2}\right)^3}{4} = \dfrac{\left(\dfrac{1}{8}\right)}{4} = \dfrac{1}{32}$

495. C. The graph of the function $f(x)$ moved up 10 units will be represented by the function $f(x) + 10$. This means every y-coordinate will be increased by 10 units.

496. D. Substituting 3 in each of the expressions in the answer choices, we find that $10(3) - 10 = 30 - 10 = 20$.

497. D. $\dfrac{g(x)}{f(x)} = \dfrac{x^2 - x - 6}{x + 2} = \dfrac{(x - 3)(x + 2)}{x + 2} = x - 3$, $x \ne -2$

498. D. $x^2 + 2x + 1 = (x + 1)^2$, which has a single root of $x = -1$

499. A. If $f(b) = 18$, then $2b + 6 = 18$, and $2b = 12$. Therefore, $b = \dfrac{12}{2} = 6$.

500. E. The equation $x^2 = 8x - 15$ is equivalent to $x^2 - 8x + 15 + 0$, or $(x - 3)(x - 5) = 0$. The possible values of x are then solutions to the equations $x - 3 = 0$ and $x - 5 = 0$; those solutions are $x = 3$ and $x = 5$.

PART II

READING

QUESTIONS 1–69

PROSE FICTION
"LOVE OF LIFE" *BY JACK LONDON*

This selection is the end of a story about a man who had starved in the wilderness for several days. Hungry and sick, he crawled to a beach, where he was taken aboard a ship filled with scientists.

He was lost and alone, sick and injured too badly to walk upright. He crawled on. There came frightful days of snow and rain. He did not know when he made camp, when he broke camp. He traveled in the night as much
5 as in the day. He rested wherever he fell and crawled on whenever the dying life in him flickered up and burned less dimly. He did not try. It was the life in him, unwilling to die, that drove him on. He didn't suffer. His nerves had become blunted and numb, while his mind was filled with
10 weird visions and delicious dreams.

There were some members of a scientific expedition on the whaleship *Bedford*. From the deck they saw a strange object on the shore. It was on the beach, moving towards the water. They couldn't tell what it was. Being scientists,
15 they took a boat to see. They saw something alive, but it hardly looked like a man. It was blind, unconscious, and crawled on the beach like a giant worm. Most of its effort to crawl was useless, but it kept trying. It turned and twisted, moving about 20 feet an hour.
20 Three weeks afterwards the man lay in a bunk on the whaleship, and with tears streaming down his wasted cheeks told who he was and what he had undergone. He also babbled words that made no sense: about his mother, of sunny Southern California, and a home among the
25 orange groves and flowers.

The days were not many after that when he sat at table with the scientific men and ship's officers. He was happy over the sight of so much food, watching it anxiously as it went into the mouths of others. With the disappearance of
30 each mouthful, an expression of deep regret came into his eyes. He was quite sane, yet he hated those men at mealtimes because they ate so much food. He was haunted by a fear that it would not last. He inquired of the cook, the cabin-boy, the captain concerning the food stores. They
35 reassured him countless times; but he could not believe them and pried cunningly about the food storage chest to see with his own eyes.

It was noticed that the man was getting fat. He grew stouter with each day. The scientific men shook their heads
40 and theorized. They limited the man at his meals, but still his girth increased and his body grew fatter under his shirt.

The sailors grinned. They knew. And when the scientific men followed the man, they knew, too. They saw him bent over after breakfast, and like a mendicant, with

45 outstretched palm, stop a sailor. The sailor grinned and passed him a fragment of sea biscuit. He clutched it avariciously, looking at it as a miser looks at gold, and thrust it inside his shirt. Similar were the donations from other grinning sailors.
50 The scientific men respected the man's privacy. They left him alone. But they secretly examined his bunk. It was lined with seamen's crackers; the mattress was stuffed with crackers; every nook and cranny was filled with crackers. Yet he was sane. He was taking precautions against another
55 possible famine—that was all. He would recover from it, the scientific men said; and he did, 'ere the *Bedford*'s anchor rumbled down in San Francisco.

1. The point of view from which the passage is told can best be described as that of a
   A. scientist who traveled on the *Bedford* and met the man in the story.
   B. narrator who is able to see and understand every aspect of the main character.
   C. friend of the man who learned of the man's plight and helped him recover.
   D. narrator who is describing his own experiences and how he was affected by them.

2. When the author describes the man by saying that "the dying life in him flickered up and burned less dimly," he is comparing the man's life to
   A. death.
   B. dimness.
   C. insanity.
   D. a candle.

3. It can reasonably be inferred from the second paragraph (lines 11–19) that the man
   A. was trying to get their attention.
   B. was unhappy to see the scientists.
   C. looked more like an animal than a human.
   D. was a dangerous person.

4. Which of the following best describes the man's predicament?
   A. There wasn't enough food on the ship.
   B. The scientists aboard the ship were too harsh with him.
   C. The man needed to recover from a terrible ordeal.
   D. The man needed transportation to San Francisco.

5. When the author says that the man looked at a piece of sea biscuit "as a miser looks at gold," he means that the man
   A. thought the sea biscuit was inedible.
   B. wanted to hoard it.
   C. wanted nothing to do with it.
   D. got sick just looking at it.

6. It can reasonably be inferred from the passage that the man stored biscuits in his mattress because

   A. he wanted to make sure he always had food.
   B. he knew that biscuits were in short supply and would soon run out.
   C. he was a thief.
   D. he was very fond of sea biscuits.

7. In the sixth paragraph (lines 42–49), the author compares the man to a mendicant, which means that he was

   A. begging.
   B. crying.
   C. arguing.
   D. experimenting.

8. It can reasonably be inferred from the fourth paragraph (lines 26–37) that the man hated the people eating with him because

   A. he disliked scientists.
   B. they were unfriendly to him.
   C. he thought they were taking food that he would need.
   D. they had few manners.

9. Which of the following statements about the sailors is supported by the passage?

   A. They thought he might hurt them if they didn't help him.
   B. They thought he was a curiosity and went along with his requests.
   C. They wanted the man to gain weight, since he had been starving.
   D. They hoped that the man would help them when they were in need.

10. The passage discusses everything about the man EXCEPT his

    A. appearance.
    B. name.
    C. past.
    D. attitude toward food.

11. It can reasonably be inferred that the man could be seen as a symbol of

    A. greed and unpleasantness.
    B. humanity's desire to survive.
    C. the failures of humankind.
    D. the power of science.

12. According to the passage, what would most likely happen to the man?

    A. He would lose his obsession with food.
    B. He would never recover his sanity.
    C. He would stay convinced that he will starve.
    D. He would steal more and more.

13. It can reasonably be inferred that the main theme of the passage is that

    A. scientists are kind people.
    B. starvation can affect a person's mind.
    C. sailors are helpful to sick people.
    D. some people are unable to control their desire for food.

SOCIAL SCIENCES
THE GREAT STILT RACE

This account of a bizarre event in the late 1800s is true, proving that truth can be stranger than fiction.

One of the most unusual and grueling races ever to be run was the great stilt race that took place in southwestern France in the late 1800s. Walking on stilts requires a good sense of balance and a great deal of practice, but the men
5   who competed in the great stilt race were experts. They had to be, because the race called for them to walk almost 300 miles. It may seem that it would be difficult for the organizers of a stilt race to gather enough contestants to compete in such an unusual contest. But this was not the case in the
10 particular area of France where the race took place.

In southwestern France, there is a large, flat section of land known as "Les Landes." The people who live there are shepherds, and in order to keep a close watch over their herds, they have to overcome one formidable obstacle—
15 the undrained lagoons and marshes covering Les Landes, which make normal walking impossible. So that they could navigate these ditches and wet areas, the shepherds of Les Landes took to wearing stilts. They strapped the stilts to their thighs so that their hands were left free. And
20 since most of their waking hours were spent four feet off the ground on stilts, they became adept at this mode of transportation.

The stilt race was organized because a local newspaper was looking for a way to increase its circulation. When a
25 journalist happened to see two shepherds from Les Landes on stilts heading at top speed down a country road, an idea began to form in his mind. Shortly afterward, the newspaper was offering a prize of $170 and a gold medal to the winner of a race run on stilts. The response from
30 the local people was overwhelming—before long, 75 men had entered the competition. For days before the race, they practiced and held small competitions among themselves so that they would be ready for the big day. Among other preparations, they made necessary improvements to their
35 stilts. They added rubber tips to the bottoms of the stilts to deaden the shock of walking on hard cobblestone pavements. They also fashioned special chafeproof bindings that would lessen the wear and tear on their thighs.

The rules of the race were simple. The contestants were
40 to walk on stilts along a 305-mile-long course across the French countryside. Estimates put the time necessary to complete the trip at eight and a half days. At 9:22 on the morning of May 26, the 75 contestants took off, covering about two yards with each step. Hundreds of spectators
45 lined the road, eyeing the contestants and eagerly placing bets on their favorites.

The course took the men first along paved roads, then over dirt roads farther out in the country, and finally into the hills. All along the route, proprietors of local cafés
50 rushed out with glasses of wine to refresh the parched throats of the competitors. Stopping for just a moment, but without dismounting, a racer would reach down, take the glass, quickly down its contents, and continue on his way. The same was true of food offered to the competitors, who
55 quickly devoured it.

The biggest problems the racers encountered were fatigue, blisters, and chafed legs. These problems took their toll: about halfway through the race, the field had narrowed to only 32 contestants, a fact that did not surprise
60 the organizers.

Finally, on May 30, the first weary and dust-covered competitor dragged himself over the finish line in Bordeaux. He had completed the course in just over 100 miles, averaging about three miles per hour over the
65 entire trip. This was several days under the time the organizers had estimated it would take to complete the race.

Hundreds of fans and a brass band were there to greet the winner. As for the rest of the competitors—well, by the time they got to the finish line, the festivities honoring the
70 winner were well underway. They were certainly welcome to join in, but most of them were too tired.

14. The main point of this passage is to
   A. illustrate the difficulties of walking long distances on stilts.
   B. recount the story of a strange race with stilts that took place in the late 1800s.
   C. deliberate why the winner was so much faster than the other competitors.
   D. illustrate how many newspapers try to increase their readership by sponsoring events.

15. When the race is described as *grueling* (line 1), the author means it was
   A. lengthy.
   B. extremely demanding.
   C. comical.
   D. very unusual.

16. Which of the following best states why the people of Les Landes used stilts?
   A. Les Landes is an extremely flat area.
   B. A newspaper was offering a prize for a stilt race.
   C. The shepherds could see their sheep more easily.
   D. The land was filled with ditches and marshes.

17. The shepherds had become *adept* at walking on stilts (lines 21–22), which means that they
   A. enjoyed it.
   B. found it difficult.
   C. were unaccustomed to it.
   D. were skilled at it.

18. The most likely reason that the author says that the "response from the local people was overwhelming" (lines 29–30) was that
   A. 75 men entered the race.
   B. bets were made on who would win.
   C. the contestants got tired.
   D. the café owners greeted the competitors.

19. Which of the following most completely gives the reasons that the race was difficult?
   A. The route was long and covered various types of terrain.
   B. The route was chosen by the organizers for its many cafés.
   C. The route was unknown to the participants.
   D. The route included large areas that were well populated.

20. Which of the following was a problem that the racers faced?
   A. Blistering sun
   B. Lack of food
   C. Rain and sleet
   D. Lack of sleep

21. One concession that the competitors made prior to the race was to
   A. change aspects of the stilts so that they were more comfortable.
   B. study the type of land they would be walking over.
   C. wear heavy clothing to protect their skin from chafing.
   D. sleep for several hours before they started the race.

22. Which of the following statements is true of the competitors?

    A. They were determined to win the race.
    B. They were unprepared for the terrain of the race.
    C. They did not have the best equipment.
    D. They were unaccustomed to racing.

23. Which of the following statements would the author of the passage be MOST likely to make?

    A. Cultural differences matter little.
    B. More newspapers should organize races.
    C. People who like a challenge will go all out.
    D. Time is a relative thing.

24. One expectation of the race organizers that did not materialize was

    A. the number of spectators.
    B. the competitors' averaging two miles per hour.
    C. 43 of the competitors dropping out.
    D. the cafés serving food to the competitors.

25. Which of the following statements best explains "halfway through the race, the field had narrowed to only 32 contestants" (lines 58–59)?

    A. The course was not as wide as it was at the beginning.
    B. The marshy land was flooded.
    C. There were fewer racers.
    D. Some racers had been cheating.

26. It can reasonably be inferred from the passage that

    A. the joy of competing is what motivated the competitors.
    B. the prize was a large amount of money at the time.
    C. there were bad feelings between the winner and the losers.
    D. the competitors had bonded because of the race.

27. Which of the following statements explains why the competitors put rubber tips on the bottom of their stilts?

    A. The rubber tips made the stilts faster.
    B. The rubber tips made it easier to climb hills.
    C. The rubber tips made it easier to walk on pavement.
    D. The rubber tips made the shepherds' strides longer.

HUMANITIES
UP FROM SLAVERY BY BOOKER T. WASHINGTON

Booker T. Washington (1856–1915), the first principal of Tuskegee Institute in Alabama, was born into slavery. The following passage is from his autobiography.

The cabin was not only our living-place, but was also used as the kitchen for the plantation. My mother was the plantation cook. The cabin was without glass windows; it had only openings in the side which let in the light, and also the cold, chilly air of winter. There was a door to the cabin—that is, something that was called a door—but the uncertain hinges by which it was hung, and the large cracks in it, to say nothing of the fact that it was too small, made the room a very uncomfortable one.

In addition to these openings there was, in the lower right-hand corner of the room, the "cat-hole,"—a contrivance which almost every mansion or cabin in Virginia possessed during the antebellum period. The "cat-hole" was a square opening, about seven by eight inches, provided for the purpose of letting the cat pass in and out of the house at will during the night. In the case of our particular cabin, I could never understand the necessity for this convenience, since there were at least a half-dozen other places in the cabin that would have accommodated the cats.

There was no wooden floor in our cabin, the naked earth being used as a floor. In the center of the earthen floor there was a large, deep opening covered with boards, which was used as a place in which to store sweet potatoes during the winter. An impression of this potato-hole is very distinctly engraved upon my memory, because I recall that during the process of putting the potatoes in or taking them out, I would often come into possession of one or two, which I roasted and thoroughly enjoyed. There was no cooking-stove on our plantation, and all the cooking for the whites and slaves my mother had to do over an open fireplace, mostly in pots and skillets. While the poorly built cabin caused us to suffer with cold in the winter, the heat from the open fireplace in summer was equally trying.

The early years of my life, which were spent in the little cabin, were not very different from those of thousands of other slaves. My mother, of course, had little time in which to give attention to the training of her children during the day. She snatched a few moments for our care in the early morning before her work began, and at night after the day's work was done. One of my earliest recollections is that of my mother cooking a chicken late at night, and awakening her children for the purpose of feeding them. How or where she got it I do not know. I presume, however, it was procured from our owner's farm. Some people may call this theft. If such a thing were to happen now, I should condemn it as theft myself. But taking place at the time it did, and for the reason that it did, no one could ever make me believe that my mother was guilty of thieving. She was simply a victim of the system of slavery.

I cannot remember having slept in a bed until after our family was declared free by the Emancipation Proclamation. Three children—John, my older brother, Amanda, my sister, and myself—had a pallet on the dirt floor, or, to be more correct, we slept in and on a bundle of filthy rags laid upon the dirt floor.

I had no schooling whatever while I was a slave, though I remember on several occasions I went as far as the schoolhouse door with one of my young mistresses to carry her books. The picture of several dozen boys and girls in a schoolroom engaged in study made a deep impression upon me, and I had the feeling that to get into a schoolhouse and study in this way would be about the same as getting into paradise.

So far as I can now recall, the first knowledge that I got of the fact that we were slaves, and that freedom of the slaves was being discussed, was early one morning before day, when I was awakened by my mother kneeling over her children and fervently praying that Lincoln and his armies might be successful, and that one day she and her children might be free.

In this connection I have never been able to understand how the slaves throughout the South, completely ignorant as were the masses so far as books or newspapers were concerned, were able to keep themselves so accurately and completely informed about the great national questions that were agitating the country. From the time that Garrison, Lovejoy, and others began to agitate for freedom, the slaves throughout the South kept in close touch with the progress of the movement.

Though I was a mere child during the preparation for the Civil War and during the war itself, I now recall the many late-at-night whispered discussions that I heard my mother and the other slaves on the plantation indulge in. These discussions showed that they understood the situation, and that they kept themselves informed of events by what was termed the "grape-vine" telegraph.

28. Which of the following statements explains why Washington did not understand why the cabin had a cat-hole?
A. They had no cat.
B. The hole was too small for people to pass through.
C. There were a number of holes in the walls.
D. The sweet potatoes covered it up.

29. It can reasonably be inferred that Washington's early years were
A. something he tried to forget.
B. free of any major problems.
C. a large influence on him.
D. difficult to remember.

30. It can reasonably be inferred that Washington told the story of his mother's cooking a chicken so that the reader would
A. reflect on whether she stole the chicken or not.
B. understand the desperate situation the family was in.
C. be sympathetic toward their masters.
D. realize the difficult work his mother did.

31. In the third paragraph (lines 20–33), the author most nearly characterizes his experience eating sweet potatoes as
A. a thoughtful moment in his young life.
B. a funny occurrence that he never forgot.
C. a fond memory among many depressing ones.
D. a confusing event that led to his desire to achieve.

32. In the context of the passage, the fifth paragraph (lines 51–56) is best described as
A. giving the reader a realistic understanding of Washington's living conditions.
B. comparing the lives of slaves and masters.
C. complaining to the reader about his life as a child.
D. being careful how he talks about the conditions that he encountered in the cabin.

33. Based on Washington's experience of seeing the classroom in the sixth paragraph (lines 57–64), it can reasonably be inferred that he thought that school was
A. beyond his reach.
B. useful in becoming a lawyer.
C. something he would be fearful of trying.
D. a goal he had to attain.

34. Washington discusses many of his earliest memories EXCEPT

   A. what kind of food he ate.
   B. what kind of place he lived in.
   C. what he thought about school.
   D. what his owner's name was.

35. Which aspect of life as a slave seemed most surprising to Washington?

   A. The fact that slaves knew what was going on in the country
   B. The idea that slaves could spend time with their families
   C. The idea that slaves enjoyed talking to each other when they weren't working
   D. The fact that slaves may have stolen from their owners

36. In the last paragraph, Washington refers to the "grape-vine" telegraph (line 87) in order to show

   A. how unaware the slaves were.
   B. how hopeful the slaves were.
   C. how the slaves spent their time.
   D. how the slaves found things out.

37. The main point of this passage is to

   A. indicate the results of the Civil War.
   B. show the harsh realities of the slaves' lives.
   C. criticize the way Washington's mother treated her children.
   D. prove that education is valuable.

38. It could reasonably be inferred that the author's attitude toward his past was

   A. one of anger and resentment.
   B. one of sensitivity and acceptance.
   C. one of fear and deception.
   D. one of indifference and boredom.

39. Why was it possible for Washington to see the schoolhouse?

   A. He was performing a job for the owner's daughter.
   B. He was being taught by the teacher who ran the school.
   C. He was allowed to go to the school and do errands for the teacher.
   D. He was able to sneak out of the cabin in the early morning.

40. Based on the seventh paragraph (lines 65–71), what effect did Washington's mother's praying have on him?

   A. It made him want to stand up to his owner.
   B. It made him realize that he was not free.
   C. It made him fear his mother.
   D. It made him want to go to war.

41. When the author speaks of the "cat-hole" as a *contrivance* (lines 11–12), he means that it was a(n)

   A. adaptor.
   B. concession.
   C. device.
   D. generator.

NATURAL SCIENCES
THE PROGRESSION OF WRITTEN LANGUAGE

Once we learn to write at an early age, we take writing for granted. But as this passage shows, writing has a long and complicated history.

The fact that we can speak to one another and exchange complicated information may seem like a miracle. But if spoken language is a miracle, the ability to write using an alphabet seems almost incredible. Everyone who speaks
5   English knows tens of thousands of words—out of a total of 1,500,000 words in the English language—and all those words can be represented by just 26 letters.

How did people ever learn to write? We know that spoken languages existed long before writing was invented.
10   How did people get the idea of representing all the words of a whole language, big words and little words, with just a small number of letters? How did they decide to ignore the tone of voice and pay attention only to the words? Indeed, who got the idea of writing? How did it all begin?

15   No one knows for sure. One theory is that the first writing was employed by rich people to keep track of all their possessions, for example, their sheep and jars of grain. Another theory is that writing was developed as a means of recording payment of taxes. The theory goes
20   like this: a man must pay four jars of wine as his tax. He brings the tax to a tax collector, who has to find a way of recording this information. The tax collector asks a man who keeps the records—a scribe—to record the information that the taxes were paid. The scribe draws four jars of
25   wine. This was the beginning of written language.

After a while, a clever scribe doesn't draw four jars of wine. He draws just one jar and makes four lines under it. Still later, a smart scribe doesn't draw the whole jar; he just draws a mark to stand for the whole jar. At this point, the
30   scribe's record might look like this: ^//// (where ^ stands for "jar" and the four lines stand for "four"). He draws a different mark to stand for "olives," and yet another mark to stand for "wheat." His record for three jars of olives might look like this: *////. The scribe has to remember, of
35   course, what all the marks stand for.

In the beginning, scribes agreed on hundreds of pictures or marks that stood for words like *king* or *built* or *jar*. They might learn thousands of word pictures, such as the ones in Egyptian hieroglyphics, which originated about
40   53 centuries ago. Scribes, who spent years learning this way of writing, were important people, sometimes priestly rulers or well-paid representatives of the king. Some countries had only a few dozen scribes, because the job was so demanding. Of course, anyone who has finished seventh
45   grade today and knows our alphabet, would be a lot more skilled at writing than the best scribes of ancient times.

There were some advantages to this kind of written language. Sometimes, people in different parts of the country—or in different countries altogether—spoke different lan-
50   guages. But they could use the same sign for *king* or *jar* or *fight*, so scribes from all parts of the country could communicate, at least a little, in the written language.

This works even today. The language we call Chinese is actually several different languages. But people in
55   China can always communicate through writing, because Chinese writing uses word signs instead of letters that represent sounds. Our own writing system contains a few word signs—numerals, for example. So people in Sweden or Russia can read signs like *4* or *5* as easily as you can.
60   There are also signs for places to sleep or eat and to give warnings on highways that make use of symbols or pictures that people all over the world can recognize.

We don't know who made the first alphabet. In the fall of 1999, two scientists published a study of carvings found
65   in an Egyptian desert. They theorized that merchants in the Middle East, in what is now Lebanon, Israel, and Syria, made a very simple alphabet about 3,900 years ago. Instead of taking two years to learn thousands of picture marks, these merchants could learn the new alphabet in less than
70   a week. This was a great discovery. The written language could now be learned by far greater numbers of people.

Alphabets slowly spread to other countries, including Greece. Our modern term *alphabet* is derived from the first two Greek letters, alpha and beta. English words are con-
75   fusing to spell, because there are only 26 letters to represent 40 sounds and because the spelling of many words is based on several other languages that the words come from. Even so, large numbers of people around the world are able to communicate by reading and writing English.

80   We don't know the identity of the Middle Eastern merchants who developed the simple alphabet, and no one has translated their message yet. We cannot even be sure that other scientific findings in the future won't disprove this whole account of a simple alphabet. We don't even
85   know the dates of any of the great inventions in writing, nor the names of any of the early geniuses who developed writing thousands of years ago. But all that is immaterial. What we do know is that writing is an amazing achievement.

42. The main point of the passage is that

A. writing a language is the same as speaking it.
B. all written languages use letters to stand for sounds.
C. written languages were invented before spoken languages.
D. written language evolved slowly over many years.

43. According to the passage, writing may have developed

A. to keep track of possessions.
B. to write down religious ceremonies.
C. to record the best times to plant and to harvest.
D. to record victories of the king and his army.

44. According to the passage, one advantage of using picture symbols for writing rather than an alphabet was that it

A. was cheaper.
B. used only 26 symbols.
C. could be read by people who speak different languages.
D. meant that scribes were important people.

45. According to the fifth paragraph (lines 26–33), scribes were well-paid, important people because they

A. were the rulers.
B. kept track of collected taxes.
C. taught the alphabet to other people.
D. could speak many languages.

46. It can reasonably be inferred that scribes began to use symbols instead of pictures because it

A. cost less money.
B. made more sense.
C. looked better.
D. was much faster.

47. People in the United States and Sweden can read the numeral 4, because

A. the symbol is used in the same way in both countries.
B. the Swedish language uses an alphabet.
C. Swedish and Russian use the same alphabet.
D. people around the world use the English alphabet to communicate.

48. According to the passage, the idea of writing with an alphabet may have first developed in
    A. China and Japan.
    B. Lebanon, Israel, and Syria.
    C. Peru and Mexico.
    D. Egypt and Greece.

49. According to the passage, the first alphabet was probably invented before
    A. picture writing.
    B. the Greek alphabet.
    C. any spoken language.
    D. hieroglyphics.

50. It can reasonably be inferred that the language for which a writing system was developed last was
    A. English.
    B. Egyptian.
    C. Greek.
    D. Chinese.

51. According to the passage, why are English words confusing to spell (lines 74–77)?
    A. There are 40 sounds that make up words.
    B. There are 26 letters in the alphabet.
    C. English words are very long.
    D. English words are difficult to pronounce.

52. According to the passage, which language uses a writing system based on pictures rather than letters?
    A. Russian
    B. Swedish
    C. English
    D. Chinese

53. It can reasonably be inferred that the author of the passage probably holds the opinion that
    A. knowing how to write creates problems for people.
    B. countries that use picture writing are better than countries that use alphabets.
    C. it is good for people to be able to communicate with one another.
    D. all countries should use the same alphabet.

54. According to the passage, in what way is a writing system of letters superior to a system of pictures?
    A. People can learn an alphabet more quickly than symbols.
    B. An alphabet allows people who speak different languages to understand each other.
    C. People can learn to record information more quickly with an alphabet.
    D. An alphabet has more letters than a system of pictures.

55. When the author states that knowing the names of those who developed writing thousands of years ago is *immaterial* (line 87), the author means that it is
    A. vital to know them.
    B. not easy to know them.
    C. unimportant to know them.
    D. acceptable to know them.

PROSE FICTION
"HEARTS AND HANDS" BY O. HENRY

O. Henry (1862–1910) lived in the American West as a young man. Accused of embezzling money while working in a bank, he began writing while in federal prison. He became famous for short stories with surprise endings. See if the ending of this story surprises you.

At Denver there was an influx of passengers into the coaches on the eastbound express. In one coach there sat a very pretty young woman dressed in elegant taste and surrounded by all the luxurious comforts of an experienced
5 traveler. Among the newcomers were two young men, one of handsome presence with a bold, frank look and manner, the other a ruffled, glum-faced person, heavily built and roughly dressed. The two were handcuffed together.

As they passed down the aisle of the coach, the only
10 vacant seat offered was a reversed one facing the attractive young woman. Here the linked couple seated themselves. The young woman's glance fell upon them with a distant, swift disinterest. Then with a lovely smile brightening her face and a tender pink coloring her rounded cheeks, she
15 held out a little gray-gloved hand. When she spoke her voice, full, sweet, and deliberate, proclaimed that its owner was accustomed to speak and be heard.

"Well, Mr. Easton, if you *will* make me speak first, I suppose I must. Don't you ever recognize old friends when
20 you meet them in the West?"

The younger man roused himself sharply at the sound of her voice, seemed to struggle with a slight embarrassment which he threw off instantly, and then clasped her fingers with his left hand.

25 "It's Miss Fairchild," he said, with a smile. "I'll ask you to excuse the other hand; it's otherwise engaged just at present."

He slightly raised his right hand, bound at the wrist by the shining "bracelet" to the left one of his companion.
30 The glad look in the girl's eyes slowly changed to a bewildered horror. The glow faded from her cheeks. Her lips parted in a vague distress. Easton, with a little laugh, as if amused, was about to speak again, when the other man interrupted him. The glum-faced man had been watching
35 the girl's countenance with veiled glances from his keen, shrewd eyes.

"You'll excuse me for speaking, miss, but I see you're acquainted with the marshal here. If you'll ask him to speak a word for me when we get to the pen he'll do it,
40 and it'll make things easier for me there. He's taking me to Leavenworth prison. It's seven years for counterfeiting."

"Oh!" said the girl, with a deep breath and returning color. "So that is what you are doing out here? A marshal!"

"My dear Miss Fairchild," said Easton, calmly, "I had
45 to do something. Money has a way of taking wings unto itself, and you know it takes money to keep in step with our crowd in Washington. I saw this opening in the West, and—well, a marshalship isn't quite as high a position as that of ambassador, but—"

50 "The ambassador," said the girl, warmly, "doesn't call any more. He needn't ever have done so. You ought to know that. And so now you are one of these dashing Western heroes, and you ride and shoot and go into all kinds of dangers. That's different from the Washington life.
55 You have been missed from the old crowd."

The girl's eyes, fascinated, went back, widening a little, to rest upon the glittering handcuffs.

"Don't you worry about them, miss," said the other man. "All marshals handcuff themselves to their prison-
60 ers to keep them from getting away. Mr. Easton knows his business."

"Will we see you again soon in Washington?" asked the girl.

"Not soon, I think," said Easton. "My butterfly days are
65 over, I fear."

"I love the West," said the girl. Her eyes were shining softly. She looked out the car window. She began to speak truly and simply, without the gloss of style and manner: "Mamma and I spent the summer in Denver. She went home
70 a week ago, because Father was slightly ill. I could live and be happy in the West. I think the air here agrees with me. Money isn't everything. But people always misunderstand things and remain stupid—"

"Say, Mr. Marshal," growled the glum-faced man. "This
75 isn't quite fair. I haven't had a smoke all day. Haven't you talked long enough? Take me in the smoker now, won't you? I'm half dead for a pipe."

The bound travelers rose to their feet, Easton with the same slow smile on his face.

80 "I can't deny a petition for tobacco," he said lightly. "It's the one friend of the unfortunate. Good-bye, Miss Fairchild. Duty calls, you know." He held out his hand for a farewell.

"It's too bad you are not going East," she said, recloth-
85 ing herself with manner and style. "But you must go on to Leavenworth, I suppose?"

"Yes," said Easton, "I must go on to Leavenworth."

The two men sidled down the aisle into the smoker.

The two passengers in a seat nearby had heard most of
90 the conversation. Said one of them: "That marshal's a good sort of chap. Some of these Western fellows are all right."

"Pretty young to hold an office like that, isn't he?" asked the other.

"Young!" exclaimed the first speaker, "why—Oh, didn't
95 you catch on? Say—did you ever know an officer to handcuff a prisoner to his *right* hand?"

56. Based on the information in the introduction, which of the following is most likely true?

A. O. Henry was familiar with the foreign service.
B. O. Henry knew something about going to prison.
C. O. Henry wrote poetry about traveling through the West.
D. O. Henry served as marshal in the western United States.

57. In the sixth paragraph (lines 28–36), the *bracelet* worn by Easton was

A. a handcuff.
B. a present from Miss Fairchild.
C. worth a lot of money.
D. something only women usually wear.

58. Which of the following is the most likely description of Easton's relationship to the ambassador?

A. He was a good friend of the ambassador and misses him.
B. He left Washington because he fought with him.
C. He wanted to become ambassador instead.
D. He was jealous about his seeing Miss Fairchild in Washington.

59. It can reasonably be inferred that Miss Fairchild

A. was never interested in Easton.
B. would like to see more of Easton.
C. thinks Easton has changed a good deal.
D. worries that Easton will try to see her more.

60. When the author says that Easton "seemed to struggle with a slight embarrassment" (lines 22–23), he is referring to the fact that Easton was

   A. a marshal.
   B. handcuffed.
   C. unhappy to be on the train.
   D. displeased with Miss Fairchild.

61. When Easton says, "My butterfly days are over, I fear" (lines 64–65), he means that he

   A. is no longer popular.
   B. can no longer be frivolous.
   C. is busy with traveling.
   D. has a lot of prisoners he needs to see.

62. Based on the information in the passage, the real reason the older man asks to be taken to the smoking car is that he

   A. is tired of the conversation.
   B. wants to save Easton from embarrassment.
   C. doesn't like Miss Fairchild.
   D. is trying to escape.

63. In the last paragraph, the significance of the passenger saying "Oh, didn't you catch on?" (lines 94–95) is that it tells the reader that he

   A. knew that Easton was not the real marshal.
   B. realized that Easton was really the marshal.
   C. knew Easton.
   D. had met Miss Fairchild.

64. When Easton says, "Money has a way of taking wings unto itself" (lines 45–46), he means that he

   A. is not interested in money.
   B. saved money in the West.
   C. has a lot of money.
   D. spent most of his money.

65. Which of the following statements best describes Miss Fairchild's initial reaction on seeing Easton with handcuffs?

   A. She was uninterested.
   B. She thought it was funny.
   C. She was horrified.
   D. She was angry.

66. When the author says that the "glum-faced man had been watching the girl's countenance with veiled glances from his keen, shrewd eyes" (lines 34–36), he is suggesting that the man

   A. was interested in what was going on between Miss Fairchild and Easton.
   B. was looking for a way to impress Miss Fairchild.
   C. wanted to tell Miss Fairchild why Easton came to the West.
   D. thought Miss Fairchild should be careful of Easton.

67. By the end of the story, the reader is able to realize that

   A. Easton had been in prison for several years.
   B. Easton was the prisoner.
   C. Easton never was in Washington.
   D. Easton does not like Miss Fairchild.

68. Based on his actions in the passage, the glum-faced man can be best described as

   A. compassionate.
   B. detached.
   C. malicious.
   D. squeamish.

69. The first three paragraphs (lines 1–20) establish all of the following about Miss Fairchild EXCEPT

   A. what she looks like.
   B. why she is on the train.
   C. that she knows Easton.
   D. that she is well-mannered.

QUESTIONS 70–125

PROSE FICTION
"MR. TRAVERS'S FIRST HUNT" *BY RICHARD HARDING DAVIS*

Richard Harding Davis (1864–1916) wrote humorous short stories about people who were rich enough to own dogs and horses for the sport of fox hunting. This is an adaptation of one story.

Young Travers, who had been engaged to a girl down on Long Island, only met her father and brother a few weeks before the day set for the wedding. The father and son talked

5 about horses all day and until one in the morning, for they owned fast thoroughbreds, and entered them at race-tracks. Old Mr. Paddock, the father of the girl to whom Travers was engaged, had often said that when a young man asked him for his daughter's hand he would ask him in return, not if he had lived straight, but if he could ride straight.

10 Travers had met Miss Paddock and her mother in Europe, while the men of the family were at home. He was invited to their place in the fall when the fox-hunting season opened, and spent the evening most pleasantly and satisfactorily with his fiancée in a corner of the

15 drawing-room.

But as soon as the women had gone, young Paddock joined him and said, "You ride, of course?" Travers had never ridden; but he had been prompted how to answer by Miss Paddock, and so said there was nothing he liked better.

20 "That's good," said Paddock. "I'll give you Monster tomorrow morning at the meet. He is a bit nasty at the start of the season; and ever since he killed Wallis, the second groom, last year, none of us care much to ride him. But you can manage him, no doubt."

25 Mr. Travers dreamed that night of taking large, desperate leaps into space on a wild horse that snorted forth flames, and that rose at solid stone walls as though they were haystacks.

He was tempted to say he was ill in the morning—

30 which was, considering his state of mind, more or less true—but concluded that, as he would have to ride sooner or later during his visit, and that if he did break his neck, it would be in a good cause, he determined to do his best.

He came downstairs looking very miserable indeed.

35 Monster had been taken to the place where they were to meet, and Travers viewed him on his arrival there with a sickening sense of fear as he saw him pulling three grooms off their feet.

Travers decided that he would stay with his feet on solid

40 earth just as long as he could, and when the hounds were sent off and the rest had started at a gallop, he waited until they were all well away. Then he scrambled up onto the saddle. His feet fell quite by accident into the stirrups, and the next instant he was off after the others, with a feeling that he

45 was on a locomotive that was jumping the ties. Monster had passed the other horses in less than five minutes.

Travers had taken hold of the saddle with his left hand to keep himself down, and sawed and swayed on the reins with his right. He shut his eyes whenever Monster jumped,

50 and never knew how he happened to stick on; but he did stick on, and was so far ahead that no one could see in the misty morning just how badly he rode. As it was, for daring and speed he led the field, and not even young Paddock was near him from the start.

55 There was a broad stream in front of him, and a hill just on its other side. No one had ever tried to take this at a jump. It was considered more of a swim than anything else, and the hunters always crossed it by the bridge, towards the left. Travers saw the bridge and tried to jerk Monster's head

60 in that direction; but Monster kept right on as straight as an express train over the prairie.

Travers could only gasp and shut his eyes. He remembered the fate of the second groom and shivered. Then the horse rose like a rocket, lifting Travers so high in the air

65 that he thought Monster would never come down again; but he did come down, on the opposite side of the stream. The next instant he was up and over the hill, and had stopped panting in the very center of the pack of hounds that were snarling and snapping around the fox.

70 And then Travers showed that he was a thoroughbred, even though he could not ride, for he hastily fumbled for his cigar case, and when the others came pounding up over the bridge and around the hill, they saw him seated nonchalantly on his saddle, puffing critically at a cigar, and

75 giving Monster patronizing pats on the head.

"My dear girl," said old Mr. Paddock to his daughter as they rode back, "if you love that young man of yours and want to keep him, make him promise to give up riding. A more reckless and more brilliant horseman I have never seen.

80 He took that jump at that stream like a centaur. But he will break his neck sooner or later, and he ought to be stopped."

Young Paddock was so delighted with his prospective brother-in-law's great riding that that night in the smoking-room he made him a present of Monster before

85 all the men.

"No," said Travers, gloomily, "I can't take him. Your sister has asked me to give up what is dearer to me than anything next to herself, and that is my riding. She has asked me to promise never to ride again, and I have given

90 my word."

A chorus of sympathy rose from the men.

"Yes, I know," said Travers to her brother, "it is rough, but it just shows what sacrifices a man will make for the woman he loves."

70. The point of view from which the passage is told can best be described as that of
    A. a narrator who rode with Travers on the fox hunt.
    B. a narrator who is aware of Travers's problem.
    C. a narrator who is a member of the Paddock family.
    D. a narrator who has no riding ability.

71. Which of the following statements best indicates why Travers tells his future brother-in-law that he likes to ride horses?
    A. He is an excellent horseman.
    B. His fiancée told him to say that.
    C. He wants to ride in the fox hunt.
    D. He likes a challenge.

72. All of the following are reasons to fear riding Monster EXCEPT
    A. that Travers had never ridden a horse.
    B. that Monster had killed a groom.
    C. that young Paddock gave Monster to Travers.
    D. that young Paddock said that Monster was nasty.

73. It can reasonably be inferred that Travers had the dream described in the fifth paragraph (lines 25–28) because he
    A. was anxious about getting married.
    B. was afraid of riding Monster.
    C. had a fever.
    D. had indigestion from the food he ate at dinner.

74. Which of the following statements best describes Travers's predicament?
    A. He was worried that his fiancée didn't really care for him.
    B. He was fearful of asking young Paddock how to ride.
    C. He wanted to impress young Paddock, but he didn't know how.
    D. He wanted to impress his fiancée's family, but he was afraid.

75. Travers gives the impression that he is a great rider by
    A. managing to stay on Monster as the horse goes wildly onward.
    B. showing that he is skilled in handling the horse.
    C. getting Monster to do several jumps.
    D. bragging a lot about his riding ability after the hunt.

76. Which of the following statements best explains why Travers did not take the bridge over the stream?
    A. He preferred to jump over it.
    B. He couldn't get Monster to go over to it.
    C. He wanted to show off his courage and skill.
    D. His fiancée warned him not to.

77. When the author says that Travers felt as though "he was on a locomotive that was jumping the ties" (lines 44–45), he means that Travers
    A. realized that the horse was galloping.
    B. could not control the horse.
    C. was getting hurt.
    D. was enjoying the ride.

78. In the fourth paragraph (lines 20–24), what is one probable reason that young Paddock chooses Monster for Travers to ride?
    A. He thinks Travers deserves the best horse.
    B. He wants to upset his sister.
    C. He wants to please Travers.
    D. He wants to test Travers.

79. When the author says that Monster "rose like a rocket" (line 64), he means that the horse
    A. went up in the air with a great force.
    B. made a loud sound.
    C. went up in the air slowly at first.
    D. was startled.

80. The sacrifice that Travers refers to in the last paragraph is most likely
    A. that he had to ride Monster.
    B. that he had decided to marry.
    C. that he was starting a new life.
    D. that he was giving up Monster.

81. When the author says that after Monster came to a stop, the others found Travers seated *nonchalantly* on his saddle (lines 73–74), he means that Travers
    A. looked like a great horseman.
    B. acted unconcerned.
    C. acted nervously.
    D. worked hard to keep control.

82. It can reasonably be inferred that this story is
    A. highly improbable.
    B. filled with significant meaning.
    C. very moral.
    D. extremely serious.

83. Which of the following descriptions best characterizes Travers?
    A. Delusional and irrational
    B. Full of regret for what he pretended to be
    C. Intelligent and predictable
    D. Willing to try anything in order to please others

SOCIAL SCIENCES
"I HAVE A DREAM" *BY MARTIN LUTHER KING, JR.*

This is an excerpt from the famous speech that Martin Luther King, Jr. (1929–1968) gave on August 28, 1963, in Washington, DC, before a quarter of a million supporters of his civil rights stance.

Five score years ago, a great American, in whose symbolic shadow we stand, signed the Emancipation Proclamation. This momentous decree came as a great beacon light of hope to millions of Negro slaves who had 5 been seared in the flames of withering injustice. It came as a joyous daybreak to end the long night of captivity.

But one hundred years later, we must face the tragic fact that the Negro is still not free. One hundred years later, the life of the Negro is still sadly crippled by the mana- 10 cles of segregation and the chains of discrimination. One hundred years later, the Negro lives on a lonely island of poverty in the midst of a vast ocean of material prosperity. One hundred years later, the Negro is still languishing in the corners of American society and finds himself an exile 15 in his own land. So we have come here today to dramatize an appalling condition.

In a sense we have come to our nation's capital to cash a check. When the architects of our republic wrote the magnificent words of the Constitution and the Declaration 20 of Independence, they were signing a promissory note to which every American was to fall heir. This note was a promise that all men would be guaranteed the inalienable rights of life, liberty, and the pursuit of happiness.

It is obvious today that America has defaulted on 25 this promissory note insofar as her citizens of color are concerned. Instead of honoring this sacred obligation, America has given the Negro people a bad check which has come back marked "insufficient funds." But we refuse to believe that the bank of justice is bankrupt. We refuse to 30 believe that there are insufficient funds in the great vaults of opportunity of this nation. So we have come to cash this check—a check that will give us upon demand the riches of freedom and the security of justice. We have also come to this hallowed spot to remind America of the fierce urgency 35 of now. This is no time to engage in the luxury of cooling off or to take the tranquilizing drug of gradualism. Now is the time to rise from the dark and desolate valley of segregation to the sunlit path of racial justice. Now is the time to open the doors of opportunity to all of God's children. 40 Now is the time to lift our nation from the quicksands of racial injustice to the solid rock of brotherhood. . . .

I am not unmindful that some of you have come here out of great trials and tribulations. Some of you have come fresh from narrow cells. Some of you have come from 45 areas where your quest for freedom left you battered by the storms of persecution and staggered by the winds of police brutality. You have been the veterans of creative suffering. Continue to work with the faith that unearned suffering is redemptive.

50 Go back to Mississippi, go back to Alabama, go back to Georgia, go back to Louisiana, go back to the slums and ghettos of our northern cities, knowing that somehow this situation can and will be changed. Let us not wallow in the valley of despair.

55 I say to you today, my friends, that in spite of the difficulties and frustrations of the moment, I still have a dream. It is a dream deeply rooted in the American dream.

I have a dream that one day this nation will rise up and live out the true meaning of its creed: "We hold these 60 truths to be self-evident: that all men are created equal."

I have a dream that one day on the red hills of Georgia the sons of former slaves and the sons of former slave owners will be able to sit down together at a table of brotherhood.

65 I have a dream that one day even the state of Mississippi, a desert state, sweltering with the heat of injustice and oppression, will be transformed into an oasis of freedom and justice.

I have a dream that my four children will one day live 70 in a nation where they will not be judged by the color of their skin but by the content of their character.

I have a dream today.

I have a dream that one day the state of Alabama, whose governor's lips are presently dripping with the words 75 of interposition and nullification, will be transformed into a situation where little black boys and black girls will be able to join hands with little white boys and white girls and walk together as sisters and brothers.

I have a dream today.

80 I have a dream that one day every valley shall be exalted, every hill and mountain shall be made low, the rough places will be made plain, and the crooked places will be made straight, and the glory of the Lord shall be revealed, and all flesh shall see it together.

85 This is our hope. This is the faith with which I return to the South. With this faith we will be able to hew out of the mountain of despair a stone of hope. With this faith we will be able to transform the jangling discords of our nation into a beautiful symphony of brotherhood. With this faith 90 we will be able to work together, to pray together, to struggle together, to go to jail together, to stand up for freedom together, knowing that we will be free one day.

This will be the day when all of God's children will be able to sing with a new meaning, "My country, 'tis of thee, 95 sweet land of liberty, of thee I sing. Land where my fathers died, land of the pilgrim's pride, from every mountainside, let freedom ring."

84. The main point of the second paragraph (lines 7–16) is to

A. determine the meaning of freedom.
B. recount the way in which slavery was eradicated.
C. illustrate the ways in which prejudice is manifested.
D. show that race issues were not resolved by the end of slavery.

85. When King says that Negro slaves were "seared in the flames of withering injustice" (line 5), he means that slaves were

A. unpaid.
B. treated cruelly.
C. went to jail very often.
D. expected to be loyal.

86. According to the second paragraph (lines 7–16), what was the purpose of the demonstration?

A. King wants to make the public aware of the injustices that exist.
B. King wants to incite the public into taking action.
C. King wants to meet with the governors of the southern states to talk.
D. King hopes to raise funds to create grants for those in need.

87. Which of the following sentences from the speech best supports the idea that King has hope for a better world?

A. It came as a joyous daybreak to end the long night of captivity.
B. It is obvious today that America has defaulted on this promissory note insofar as her citizens of color are concerned.
C. Continue to work with the faith that unearned suffering is redemptive.
D. With this faith we will be able to transform the jangling discords of our nation into a beautiful symphony of brotherhood.

88. When King says, "One hundred years later, the life of the Negro is still sadly crippled by the manacles of segregation and the chains of discrimination" (lines 7–8), he is comparing segregation and discrimination to being

    A. in a hospital.
    B. tied to work.
    C. in jail.
    D. kept safe.

89. In the third paragraph, what does King suggest by his use of the word *architects* (line 18)?

    A. The founders of the United States enjoyed designing buildings.
    B. Most of the buildings in the country were built by slaves.
    C. The writers of the Constitution and Declaration designed and built the country.
    D. The people in charge of bureaucracy built the country.

90. Based on the information in the fourth paragraph (lines 24–41), it can reasonably be inferred that King wanted to

    A. quickly make changes in civil rights.
    B. slowly change the way blacks are treated.
    C. keep segregation as the law of the country.
    D. hold a countrywide vote on civil rights.

91. Which of the following statements best describes the meaning of the last two lines of the fifth paragraph (lines 42–49)?

    A. Continue, knowing that suffering is productive.
    B. Continue, knowing that suffering is evil.
    C. Continue, knowing that you have faith.
    D. Continue, knowing that suffering is godly.

92. When King says, "Let us not wallow in the valley of despair" (lines 53–54), he means that he

    A. does not want his supporters to stumble.
    B. is encouraging his supporters to go back to their homes.
    C. does not want his supporters to be self-indulgent.
    D. wants the situation to change.

93. King mentions the many hardships that African-Americans endure EXCEPT

    A. returning to slums in the northern cities.
    B. experiencing police brutality.
    C. enduring years of racial injustice.
    D. still not being free.

94. When King says, "It is a dream deeply rooted in the American dream" (line 57), he means that

    A. his dream is difficult to understand.
    B. the American dream is the same as the African-American's dream.
    C. like the American dream, his dream is of freedom.
    D. his dream is of returning to the South.

95. It can reasonably be inferred from the thirteenth paragraph (lines 73–78) that

    A. there is little hope for progress in Alabama.
    B. the governor of Alabama wants white and black children to play together.
    C. there is blood on the governor's lips.
    D. the governor in Alabama intends to block any progress toward King's dream.

96. The phrase "hew out of the mountain of despair a stone of hope" (lines 86–87) is best described as creating a metaphor for

    A. a step toward freedom.
    B. a symbolic sculpture.
    C. the work that needs to be done.
    D. the impossibility of what King wants to have happen.

97. The last paragraph suggests that

    A. King feels that music is liberating.
    B. the words of the patriotic song will finally apply to all Americans.
    C. children need to learn the meaning of the song.
    D. the song will take on a new and different meaning.

HUMANITIES
THE STORY OF MY LIFE BY HELEN KELLER

Helen Keller (1880–1968) became deaf and blind as the result of an illness at the age of 19 months. In the following passage from her autobiography, she describes how she learned to communicate despite her disabilities, with the help of her teacher, Anne Sullivan. Keller went on to attend college, write several books, and work in many programs to help people.

The morning after my teacher came, she led me into her room and gave me a doll. The little blind children at the Perkins Institution had sent it; but I did not know
5 this until afterward. When I had played with it a little while, Miss Sullivan slowly spelled into my hand the word "d-o-l-l." I was at once interested in this finger play and tried to imitate it. When I finally succeeded in making the letters correctly, I was flushed with childish pleasure and pride.

Running downstairs to my mother, I held up my hand
10 and made the letters for *doll*. I did not know that I was spelling a word or even that words existed; I was simply making my fingers go in monkey-like imitation. In the days that followed I learned to spell in this uncomprehending way a great many words, among them *pin, hat,*
15 *cup* and a few verbs like *sit, stand,* and *walk*. But my teacher had been with me several weeks before I understood that everything has a name.

One day, while I was playing with my new doll, Miss Sullivan put my big rag doll into my lap also, spelled
20 "d-o-l-l" and tried to make me understand that "d-o-l-l" applied to both. Earlier in the day we had had a tussle over the words "m-u-g" and "w-a-t-e-r." Miss Sullivan had tried to impress it upon me that "m-u-g" is mug and that "w-a-t-e-r" is water, but I persisted in confounding the two. In
25 despair she had dropped the subject for the time, only to renew it at the first opportunity. I became impatient at her repeated attempts and, seizing the new doll, I dashed it upon the floor.

I was keenly delighted when I felt the fragments of the
30 broken doll at my feet. Neither sorrow nor regret followed my passionate outburst. I had not loved the doll. In the still, dark world in which I lived, there was no strong sentiment or tenderness. I felt my teacher sweep the fragments to one side of the hearth, and I had a sense of satisfaction that
35 the cause of my discomfort was removed. She brought me my hat, and I knew I was going out into the warm sunshine. This thought, if a wordless sensation may be called a thought, made me hop and skip, with pleasure.

We walked down the path to the well-house, attracted
40 by the fragrance of the honeysuckle with which it was covered. Someone was drawing water and my teacher placed my hand under the spout. As the cool stream gushed over one hand she spelled into the other the word *water* first slowly, then rapidly. I stood still, my whole attention fixed
45 upon the motions of her fingers. Suddenly I felt a misty consciousness as of something forgotten—a thrill of returning thought; and somehow the mystery of language was revealed to me. I knew then that "w-a-t-e-r" meant the wonderful cool something that was flowing over my hand.
50 That living word awakened my soul, gave it light, hope, joy, set it free! There were barriers still, it is true, but barriers that could in time be swept away.

I left the well-house eager to learn. Everything had a name, and each name gave birth to a new thought. As
55 we returned to the house, every object which I touched seemed to quiver with life. That was because I saw everything with the strange, new sight that had come to me. On entering the door I remembered the doll I had broken. I felt my way to the hearth and picked up the pieces. I tried
60 vainly to put them together. Then my eyes filled with tears; for I realized what I had done, and for the first time I felt repentance and sorrow.

I learned a great many new words that day. It would have been difficult to find a happier child than I was as I lay
65 in my crib at the close of that eventful day and lived over the joys it had brought me, and for the first time longed for a new day to come.

98. The main point of the passage is to
   A. show that the author liked playing with dolls.
   B. argue against funding to educate people with disabilities.
   C. persuade people to support laws regarding disabilities.
   D. describe an important event in the author's life.

99. When Keller writes that she "persisted in confounding" (line 24) the words *mug* and *water*, she means that she
   A. understood them.
   B. confused them.
   C. worried about them.
   D. could write them.

100. Which of the following statements is the most likely reason that the author says she "was flushed with childish pleasure and pride" (line 8)?
   A. She wanted to show that she was capable of feeling good about herself.
   B. She wanted to show that she knew she was intelligent.
   C. She wanted to show that she liked her teacher.
   D. She wanted to show that she had learned what a doll was.

101. The second paragraph contains evidence that Helen had a good sense of
   A. hearing.
   B. loyalty.
   C. touch.
   D. justice.

102. According to the passage, when Helen first learned to make the signs for the word *doll*, she
   A. realized that she could communicate with others at last.
   B. knew that it meant a plaything that resembles a person.
   C. didn't realize it was the name of the object she was holding.
   D. couldn't imitate her teacher's motions very well.

103. It can reasonably be inferred that Helen broke the new doll into pieces because she
   A. was frustrated by her teacher's efforts to make her learn.
   B. often had temper tantrums and broke things.
   C. thought the doll was ugly.
   D. wanted her mother's attention.

104. In the sixth paragraph (lines 53–62), which of the following statements best describes the significance of Helen's trying to put the doll back together again?
   A. It shows that she now understands language.
   B. It shows that she has feelings about things.
   C. It shows that she cares a good deal for her teacher.
   D. It shows that she is ready to go to a formal school.

105. It can reasonably be inferred that as a teacher, Anne Sullivan was
   A. strict and demanding.
   B. caring and persistent.
   C. lenient and careless.
   D. misinformed and erratic.

106. When Helen says, "There were barriers still, it is true, but barriers that could in time be swept away" (lines 51–52), she is most likely referring to

   A. her future teachers.
   B. the way in which she thought about her teacher.
   C. her feeling of closeness to her family.
   D. her future success in life.

107. Helen discusses many memories of herself EXCEPT

   A. how she learned what words meant.
   B. what she thought about her new doll.
   C. whether she enjoyed being outside.
   D. what games she liked to play.

108. It could reasonably be inferred that Helen's attitude as a grown-up toward her teacher was one of

   A. regret.
   B. appreciation.
   C. confusion.
   D. indifference.

109. It can reasonably be inferred that Helen's childhood was

   A. something she did not concentrate on.
   B. full of significance for the rest of her life.
   C. similar to the childhood of other girls of her time.
   D. filled with great sadness.

110. According to the passage, Helen began to comprehend language when she

   A. threw her new doll on the floor.
   B. realized the substance that poured from the spout was water.
   C. spelled the word *doll* into her mother's hand.
   D. began to care about her teacher.

111. In the last part of the passage, the author most nearly characterizes her experience of learning the names of things as

   A. an impossible feat.
   B. an upsetting moment.
   C. an inevitability.
   D. an extraordinary event.

NATURAL SCIENCES
LEFT-HANDED IN A RIGHT-HANDED WORLD

It's an everyday question: why are some people left-handed and others right-handed? Scientists haven't been able to determine the answer. Meanwhile, there are problems and opportunities for the minority of people who are left-handed. This passage presents what we know today about handedness.

About 90 percent of the world's people are right-handed. The criterion employed by scientists who study handedness is which hand a person uses to throw a ball,
5 saw, sew, shoot marbles, cut with a knife, bowl, or strike with a hammer. Fewer than 10 percent of people studied perform all of these activities with their left hand—the genuine lefties of the world. A few people have no handedness preference, freely using either hand as convenience dictates.

10 Scientists who study this phenomenon are unable to agree on the etiology of hand preference. Renowned geneticist Dr. A. Klar, interviewed in spring 2000, argued that right-handedness is almost entirely determined by traits inherited from one's parents. Dr. Stanley Coren, a promi-
15 nent psychologist who has studied many left-handed people, disagrees with the inheritance point of view. He thinks that mild brain injury causes people to grow up with a preference for the left hand. And still other scientists, like Daniel Geschwind, feel that the traits you are born with,
20 plus your parents' preferences, plus injury, plus early events in your life must all be taken into account to determine handedness.

While we know little about what causes people to prefer the left hand, we know several interesting facts about
25 left-handed people. Although no careful statistical studies of the success rate of lefties vs. righties have ever been published, informal observation suggests that lefties are often leaders in their fields. Most recent American presidents have been left-handed. Many of the most successful
30 sports figures have been left-handed, including Babe Ruth, the home-run hitter who was also a great pitcher and was named the greatest athlete of the last hundred years.

Left-handed people are dominant in many fields. World conquerors like Alexander the Great, Julius Caesar,
35 and Napoleon, and the two most glamorous actresses of the twentieth century, Marilyn Monroe and Greta Garbo, were lefties. Leonardo da Vinci, Raphael, and Michelangelo are often called our greatest artists, Beethoven our greatest musician, Mark Twain our most popular writer, and Albert
40 Einstein our greatest scientist. All were lefties. And then there's Paul McCartney of the Beatles, baseball star Ted Williams, tennis stars Monica Seles and John McEnroe, and Benjamin Franklin and Helen Keller. Left-handed television and film performers include Jay Leno, Julia Roberts,
45 Bruce Willis, Tom Cruise, Robert DeNiro, Angelina Jolie, and Whoopi Goldberg. Even renowned criminals like Billy the Kid and John Dillinger were lefties.

Left-handedness runs in families. In the British royal family, Queen Elizabeth, Prince Charles, and Prince
50 William are lefties. The Kerr clan in Scotland supposedly had so many lefties that their castles were built with counterclockwise spiral stairways, which someone who held a sword in his left hand could defend more easily. Several scientists are busily analyzing blood samples of parents
55 and children to identify genetic markers of handedness. More men (12.6 percent) are left-handed than women (9.9 percent), and left-handedness is found less often among Asians and Hispanics than among whites, blacks, and Native Americans.

60 Some people don't want their children to grow up left-handed, because so many tools and apparatus are made for right-handed people. They tie the child's left hand behind its back, where it can't be used, thereby forcing the child to use the right hand, which consequently grows stronger.
65 This procedure is usually effective in shifting competence and power to the right hand, but scientists are almost unanimous in arguing against this technique. Either hand is satisfactory, and no child should be forced to change against its will. In some cases, being left-handed may be an
70 advantage. Baseball players think that left-handed batters have an advantage, since pitchers aren't used to pitching to lefties.

An organization of lefties exists to help children deal with the many minor problems connected with growing up
75 slightly different from other people. It's called Lefthanders International, and membership is free for lefties. The club provides a magazine, books on topics such as how to play the guitar left-handed, and left-handed playing cards, scissors, and toothbrushes. You can join the pen club and cor-
80 respond with lefties all over the world. There are also many organizations for left-handed adults, and many stores stock products specifically devoted to people who favor the left hand. The phone book lists 60 American companies that specialize in the manufacture of leftie products; the most
85 popular products are cooking pots and scissors.

A right-handed person may gain some understanding of the problems lefties have in daily life by trying to write with the left hand in a spiral-bound notebook or at a desk with a writing arm on the right side. A computer can
90 solve most writing problems for a lefty—but you must first change the mouse from right-hand to left-hand operation. Many power tools are built for right-handed operation. It can be dangerous for a left-handed person to use such a tool with the right hand, since he or she is less skillful using
95 the right hand.

Many scientific efforts are underway to determine the causative factors in handedness. Within the next 50 years, we will probably learn more about what makes people lefties than we learned in the last 2,000 years.

---

112. When the author says in the first paragraph that "a few people have no handedness preference, freely using either hand as convenience dictates" (lines 7–9), the author means that

  A. a few people want to impress their friends with their abilities.
  B. some people are happier using the left hand.
  C. these people can use either hand to write and work with.
  D. some people are not good with either hand.

113. As used in the second paragraph (lines 10–22), etiology can best be defined as

  A. custom.
  B. essence.
  C. effect.
  D. cause.

114. The third paragraph (lines 23–32) suggests that

  A. left-handed people live happier lives.
  B. the causes of hand preference are still undetermined.
  C. too much effort is devoted to the topic of handedness.
  D. musicians are usually left-handed.

115. The main point of the fourth paragraph (lines 33–47) is that

  A. people who are left-handed often excel at what they do.
  B. left-handedness runs in families.
  C. most recent American presidents have been left-handed.
  D. a majority of actors are left-handed.

116. In the fifth paragraph (lines 48–59), what is the most likely reason the author included information about Queen Elizabeth?

   A. To show that there are left-handed people who are royal
   B. To try to convince people that being left-handed is not a liability
   C. To indicate that royals are closely related
   D. To give an example of how left-handedness is hereditary

117. The author would probably agree with all of the following statements EXCEPT that

   A. left-handedness is hereditary.
   B. left-handed people can reach high office.
   C. most lefties have trouble using computers.
   D. many great artists, athletes, and criminals have been left-handed.

118. According to the passage, the theory that a preference for the right hand is largely inherited is associated with

   A. Daniel Geschwind.
   B. Dr. Stanley Coren.
   C. Dr. A. Klar.
   D. Albert Einstein.

119. Based on the information in the passage, which of the following statements is true?

   A. More people are left-handed than right-handed.
   B. Most people are right-handed.
   C. Many people can use both hands equally well.
   D. Many people are changed from being left-handed.

120. According to the passage, how do most scientists view trying to change a left-handed child to a right-handed one?

   A. They worry that the child will become confused if the handedness is changed from left to right.
   B. They almost completely oppose the practice.
   C. Most think it is best to leave the child alone, although they realize that lefties have a harder time of it.
   D. They feel it may be justified in some cases, such as when a parent wants the child to become a doctor or scientist.

121. According to the passage, left-handed people are as skilled as right-handed people at all of the following EXCEPT

   A. cooking.
   B. playing the guitar.
   C. working on a computer.
   D. using a power tool.

122. According to the passage, which of the following factors is important to scientists in deciding whether a person is right-handed or left-handed?

   A. Which leg the person kicks with
   B. Which hand the person sews with
   C. Which hand is most bitten, if the person bites his or her nails
   D. Which hand is larger

123. Based on the information in the passage, it could reasonably be inferred that left-handed people

   A. have large families.
   B. have trouble using ordinary scissors.
   C. dislike sports.
   D. are more intelligent than right-handed people.

124. Based on the information in the seventh paragraph (lines 74–86), it can reasonably be inferred that

   A. making products for left-handed people is profitable.
   B. many products cannot be changed to accommodate left-handed people.
   C. life for left-handed people is less enjoyable than for right-handed people.
   D. many people feel that left-handedness is a liability.

125. According to the passage, which of the following could schools do to make life easier for left-handed students?

   A. Seat left-handed students together in the classroom.
   B. Provide desks with writing arms on the left side.
   C. Allow left-handed students more leeway when it comes to homework.
   D. Invest in a counselor to meet with left-handed students.

CHAPTER 10
SET 3 READING QUESTIONS

QUESTIONS 126–194

PROSE FICTION
"THE LOTTERY TICKET" *BY ANTON CHEKHOV*

The following passage is adapted from a short story written by the Russian author and playwright Anton Chekhov (1860–1904).

Ivan Dmitritch, a middle-class man who lived with his family and was very well satisfied with his lot, sat down on the sofa after supper and began reading the newspaper.

"I forgot to look at the newspaper today," his wife said
5   to him as she cleared the table. "Look and see whether the list of drawings is there."

"Yes, it is," said Ivan Dmitritch.

"What is the number?"

"Series 9,499, number 26."

10   "All right . . . we will look . . . 9,499 and 26."

Ivan Dmitritch had no faith in lottery luck, and would not, as a rule, have consented to look at the lists of winning numbers, but now, as he had nothing else to do and as the newspaper was before his eyes, he passed his finger down-
15   wards along the column of numbers. And immediately, as though in mockery of his skepticism, his eye was caught by the figure 9,499! Unable to believe his eyes, he hurriedly dropped the paper on his knees without looking to see the number of the ticket.

20   "Masha, 9,499 is there!" he said in a hollow voice.

His wife looked at his astonished and panic-stricken face, and realized that he was not joking.

"9,499?" she asked, turning pale and dropping the folded tablecloth on the table.

25   "Yes, yes . . . it really is there!"

"And the number of the ticket?"

"Oh yes! There's the number of the ticket too. But stay . . . wait! No, I say! Anyway, the number of our series is there!"

30   Looking at his wife, Ivan Dmitritch gave a broad, senseless smile, like a baby when a bright object is shown it. His wife smiled too; it was as pleasant to her as to him that he only mentioned the series, and did not try to find out the number of the winning ticket. To torment and tan-
35   talize oneself with hopes of possible fortune is so sweet, so thrilling!

"It is our series," said Ivan Dmitritch, after a long silence. "So there is a probability that we have won. It's only a probability, but there it is!"

40   "Well, now look!"

"Wait a little. We have plenty of time to be disappointed. The prize is seventy-five thousand. And in a minute I shall look at the list. I say, what if we really have won?"

The husband and wife began laughing and staring at
45   one another in silence. The possibility of winning bewildered them; they could not have said, could not have dreamed, what they both needed that seventy-five thousand for, what they would buy, where they would go.

"And if we have won," he said— "why, it will be a new
50   life, it will be a transformation! The ticket is yours, but if it were mine I should, first of all, of course, spend twenty-five thousand on real property in the shape of an estate; ten thousand on immediate expenses, new furnishings . . . traveling . . . paying debts, and so on. . . . The other forty
55   thousand I would put in the bank and get interest on it."

And pictures came crowding on his imagination, each more gracious and poetical than the last. And in all these pictures he saw himself well-fed, serene, healthy, felt warm, even hot!

60   "Yes, it would be nice to buy an estate," said his wife, also dreaming, and from her face it was evident that she was enchanted by her thoughts.

Ivan Dmitritch pictured to himself autumn with its rains and its cold evenings. At that season he would have
65   to take longer walks about the garden and beside the river, so as to get thoroughly chilled. It rains day and night, the bare trees weep, the wind is damp and cold. It is dreary!

Ivan Dmitritch stopped and looked at his wife.

"I should go abroad, you know, Masha," he said.

70   And he began thinking how nice it would be in late autumn to go abroad somewhere to the South of France . . . to Italy . . . to India!

"I should certainly go abroad too," his wife said. "But look at the number of the ticket!"

75   "Wait, wait! . . ."

He walked about the room and went on thinking. It occurred to him: what if his wife really did go abroad? Ivan Dmitritch imagined his wife on the train with a multitude of parcels, baskets, and bags; she would be sighing over
80   some-thing, complaining that the train made her head ache, that she had spent so much money. . . .

"She would begrudge me every farthing," he thought, with a glance at his wife. "The lottery ticket is hers, not mine! She would shut herself up in the hotel, and not let
85   me out of her sight . . . I know!"

And for the first time in his life his mind dwelt on the fact that his wife had grown elderly and plain, while he was still young, fresh, and healthy.

90   And he looked at his wife, not with a smile now, but with hatred. She glanced at him too, and also with hatred and anger. She had her own daydreams, her own plans, her own reflections; she understood perfectly well what her husband's dreams were. She knew who would be the first to try to grab her winnings.

95   "It's very nice making daydreams at other people's expense!" is what her eyes expressed. "No, don't you dare!"

Her husband understood her look; and in order to annoy his wife he glanced quickly, to spite her, at the fourth page on the newspaper and read out triumphantly:

100   "Series 9,499, number 46! Not 26!"

Hatred and hope both disappeared at once, and it immediately began to seem to Ivan Dmitritch and his wife that their rooms were dark and small and low-pitched, that the supper they had been eating was not doing them good, 105 but lying heavy on their stomachs, that the evenings were long and wearisome.

126. The main conflict in this passage can best be described as Ivan's

  A. believing his wife will not give him any money if she has won the lottery.
  B. waiting to see whether his wife won the lottery.
  C. wanting to go abroad in the autumn because the weather isn't very good then.
  D. wanting to buy an estate when his wife doesn't want to.

127. When the author says that Ivan "gave a broad, senseless smile, like a baby when a bright object is shown it" (lines 30–32), he means that Ivan was

  A. reacting to something instinctually.
  B. happy about the prospect of winning the lottery.
  C. unaware of how the lottery works.
  D. very much in love with his wife.

128. The point of view from which the passage is told can best be described as that of

  A. a narrator who has been in the position of almost winning the lottery.
  B. a narrator who has a good grasp of human nature.
  C. a friend of Ivan and his wife who hoped that the couple would win the lottery.
  D. a person who had just met Ivan and his wife.

129. The image of "autumn with its rains and its cold evenings" (lines 63–64) suggests that Ivan

  A. is fascinated by that season.
  B. finds that season troublesome.
  C. likes to walk in the rain.
  D. wishes it were autumn.

130. Based on the information in the passage, if the lottery ticket is a winner,

  A. Masha wants to give the money to her husband.
  B. Ivan wants to buy a house and put money away.
  C. Ivan wants to buy his wife fine clothing.
  D. Masha would leave her husband.

131. It can reasonably be inferred that the author contrasts how Ivan thinks his wife looks as opposed to how he thinks he looks to show that

  A. his wife is no longer in love with him.
  B. his wife has worked harder than he has.
  C. he has an unrealistic picture of himself.
  D. he is much younger than his wife.

132. It can reasonably be inferred that Ivan imagines that his wife

  A. prefers not to win the money.
  B. will take all the money and leave him nothing.
  C. will share the money with him happily.
  D. wants to go abroad to buy him new clothes.

133. Masha mirrors her husband's feelings by showing that she

  A. has daydreams of her own.
  B. has difficulty with the weather too.
  C. wants them to stay at home.
  D. is also sensitive to criticism.

134. What does the author mean when he has Ivan say, "She would begrudge me every farthing" (line 82)?

  A. Masha no longer thought Ivan was competent when it came to money.
  B. Masha would be cautious when it came to buying things.
  C. Masha was good with budgets and liked to keep track of their money.
  D. Masha would be stingy with her money once she won the lottery.

135. Based on the information in the passage, what is the most likely reason Ivan wanted to wait before looking to see if they had the winning number?

  A. He hoped he was not the winner.
  B. He did not want his wife to be disappointed.
  C. He wanted to tease his wife.
  D. He wanted to savor the feeling of not knowing.

136. It may reasonably be inferred that Ivan and his wife both

  A. have strong fantasy worlds.
  B. want to give the money away.
  C. are extremely generous.
  D. want to tear up the lottery ticket.

137. At the end of the passage, what is the relevance of the author's saying that the rooms of their home seemed "dark and small and low-pitched" (line 103)?

  A. It shows that they finally appreciate their lives.
  B. It suggests that they are no longer interested in winning the lottery.
  C. It shows that they are living in a terrible place.
  D. It suggests how their perception about their lives has changed.

138. The theme of the passage is best described as

  A. money can help cement a relationship.
  B. husbands are less aware of things than wives are.
  C. life without imagination is not worth living.
  D. greed can bring out the worst in people.

SOCIAL SCIENCES
DIRECT ELECTION OF THE PRESIDENT

This passage is based on testimony before the U.S. Senate in 1997 by Becky Cain, then-president of the League of Women Voters. Her organization wanted to abolish the electoral college vote and have the presidential election determined by popular vote.

I am pleased to be here today to express the League's support for a constitutional amendment to abolish the Electoral College and establish the direct election of the President and Vice President of the United States by popu-
5 lar vote of the American people.

Since 1970, the League has supported an amendment to the Constitution that would abolish the Electoral College and establish a direct, popular vote for the President and Vice President of the United States. . . . Our method of
10 electing a President must be changed to ensure a more representative government.

Political developments since the 1970s have only underscored the need for the elimination of the Electoral College system. The downward trend in voter participa-
15 tion, coupled with increased cynicism and skepticism amongst the public about the ability of elected leaders to provide meaningful representation, are the warning signs of a potential electoral fiasco.

Picture if you will a future national election in which
20 a presidential candidate receives a majority of the popular vote, but is denied the 270 votes necessary for election by the Electoral College. This has already happened once in our nation's history, when, in 1888, Grover Cleveland out-polled Benjamin Harrison in the popular vote but lost
25 the Electoral College vote by 233 to 168. It caused a public furor then, when political office was often gained through backroom deals and closed-door maneuvering. Imagine the public outcry today, after a long primary campaign and a grueling race for the Presidency. Imagine the public's rage
30 at being denied their candidate of choice.

Now go one step further. Consider a close three-way race for President in which no candidate earns the necessary Electoral College votes to win. This has happened twice before in our nation's history, in 1801 and 1825, when the
35 House of Representatives chose Thomas Jefferson and John Quincy Adams, respectively. While the League believes both of these men were great presidents, we are troubled about the potential for a future presidential candidate with the highest number of popular votes to lose the election in a House of
40 Representatives dominated by one or another political party.

In the twentieth century, we have only narrowly avoided a series of constitutional crises in which the Electoral College could have overruled the popular vote.

In the 1916 presidential election, a shift of only
45 2,000 votes in California would have given Charles Evans Hughes the necessary electoral votes to defeat Woodrow Wilson, despite Wilson's half-million-vote nationwide plurality.

In 1948, a shift of only 30,000 votes in three states
50 would have delivered the White House to Governor Dewey, in spite of the fact that he trailed President Truman by some 2.1 million popular votes.

In 1960, a shift of only 13,000 votes in five states would have made Richard Nixon president.

55 In 1968, a shift of 42,000 votes in three states would have denied Nixon an Electoral College victory and thrown the election into the House of Representatives.

In 1976, a shift of only 9,300 votes would have elected Gerald Ford, even though he trailed Jimmy Carter in the
60 popular vote by 1.6 million ballots. . . .

In a nation where voting rights are grounded in the one-person, one-vote principle, the Electoral College is a hopeless anachronism.

The current system is unfair for two reasons.

65 First, a citizen's individual vote has more weight if he or she lives in a state with a small population than if that citizen lives in a state with a large population. . . .

The system is also unfair because a citizen's individual vote has more weight if the percentage of voter participa-
70 tion in the state is low. . . .

Moreover, the electoral vote does not reflect the volume of voter participation within a state. If only a few voters go to the polls, all the electoral votes of the state are still cast.

75 Finally, the Electoral College system is flawed because the Constitution does not bind presidential electors to vote for the candidates to whom they have been pledged. For example, in 1948, 1960, and 1976, individual electors pledged to the top two vote-getters cast their votes for
80 third-place finishers and also-rans.

Defecting electors in a close race could cause a crisis of confidence in our electoral system.

For all these reasons, the League believes that the presidential election method should incorporate the one-
85 person, one-vote principle. The President should be directly elected by the people he or she will represent, just as the other federally elected officials are in this country. Direct election is the most representative system. It is the only system that guarantees the President will have
90 received the most popular votes. It also encourages voter participation by giving voters a direct and equal role in the election of the President.

When the Constitution was first written, our nation was a vastly different kind of democracy than it is today.
95 Only white, male property owners could vote. The 15th Amendment gave black men the right to vote. The 19th Amendment gave women the vote. The 26th Amendment established the right of citizens 18 years of age and older to vote.

100 The time has come to take the next step to ensure a broad-based, representative democracy. Fairness argues for it. Retaining the fragile faith of American voters in our representative system demands it. We urge the House and the Senate to pass a constitutional amend-
105 ment abolishing the Electoral College system and establishing the direct popular election of our President and Vice President.

139. When Cain says that political developments have "underscored the need for the elimination of the Electoral College system" (lines 12–14), she means that these developments have

A. denied the need for elimination of the Electoral College system.
B. ignored the need for elimination of the Electoral College system.
C. emphasized the need for elimination of the Electoral College system.
D. forgotten the need for elimination of the Electoral College system.

140. Which of the following statements best describes what happens when no candidate in a three-way race for president gets enough Electoral College votes to win?

A. The Senate decides between the candidates with the largest number of electoral votes.
B. The election is decided by the popular vote.
C. The candidate with the least amount of electoral votes must give up his or her votes to the candidates with the most electoral votes.
D. The House of Representatives decides who will be president.

141. Which of the following statements best expresses the main point of the passage?

   A. The Electoral College system is flawed and should be changed.
   B. Electors do not have to vote for candidates to whom they have been pledged.
   C. The 26th Amendment established the right of citizens 18 years of age and older to vote.
   D. Fewer people are voting today, because they feel out of touch with government.

142. When the author says that "the Constitution does not bind presidential electors to vote for the candidates to whom they have been pledged" (lines 76–77), she means that

   A. no one can predict who will win a particular state's electors.
   B. people have control over whom electors will vote for.
   C. electors do not have to vote for the candidate that voters picked.
   D. elections are often determined by the electors and not the people.

143. Based on the information in the passage, in a presidential election, what happens to a person's vote for Candidate A if Candidate B carries the state?

   A. It is not counted.
   B. It becomes a vote for Candidate B.
   C. The vote is recorded under protest.
   D. The person has a chance to vote in another state.

144. When the author calls the Electoral College "a hopeless anachronism" (lines 62–63), she means that the Electoral College is

   A. not large enough.
   B. outdated.
   C. voted into office.
   D. not strong enough.

145. Which of the following positions is supported by the statement that "the 19th Amendment gave women the vote" (lines 96–97)?

   A. A citizen's individual vote has more weight if he or she lives in a state with a small population.
   B. Political office has been gained through backroom deals.
   C. The Constitution has been updated.
   D. The president should be directly elected by the people.

146. According to the author, all of the following are reasons for abandoning the Electoral College system EXCEPT

   A. the problem that could arise if there is a three-way race.
   B. the possibility that the Electoral College could overrule the popular vote.
   C. the problem of some votes having more weight than others.
   D. the idea that popular votes should be made more significant.

147. When Cain refers to "defecting electors" who did not cast their votes for the winners in their states' elections, she means that the electors

   A. feared following the voters' choice.
   B. abandoned their responsibility.
   C. were less than perfect.
   D. gave up too easily.

148. When the author says that "retaining the fragile faith of American voters in our representative system" (lines 102–103) demands changing the electoral system, she seems to suggest that the voters are

   A. committed to our present form of democracy.
   B. losing trust in the way that they are represented.
   C. not interested in the democratic process.
   D. more inclined to vote for new candidates.

149. It can reasonably be inferred that the author would most likely support

   A. reviewing all procedures to see if they need updating.
   B. having senators decide who the president will be.
   C. having presidents appointed by the House of Representatives.
   D. giving more power to the Electoral College.

150. In the last paragraph, the author makes it clear that the amendment should be passed because

   A. people would be more likely to vote for newcomers as presidents.
   B. people would ultimately choose more capable presidents.
   C. presidential elections would most likely be run in an orderly fashion.
   D. voters would take more interest in the process of electing a president.

151. It can reasonably be inferred that the author mentions the presidential race between Gerald Ford and Jimmy Carter in order to

   A. emphasize the lack of consistency in the electoral process for choosing a president.
   B. explain why Carter won the presidential race.
   C. discuss the values of each candidate.
   D. show how little it would have taken to change who won the presidency.

152. Based on the information in the passage, the purpose of the author is to

   A. explain why the Electoral College system should be abandoned.
   B. explain how the president is voted into office.
   C. instruct on the proper method of casting electoral votes.
   D. tell how many electoral votes are needed to become president.

HUMANITIES
INDIAN BOYHOOD *BY CHARLES A. EASTMAN*

This excerpt is from the memoir of Charles A. Eastman (1858–1939), born Hakadah and later named Ohiyesa. Part Native American and part Anglo-American, Eastman was a doctor, writer, and activist who accomplished a great deal for Native Americans. He is considered the first person to write from a Native American perspective.

With the first March thaw the thoughts of the Indian women of my childhood days turned promptly to the annual sugarmaking. This industry was chiefly followed by the old men and women and the children. The rest of
5　the tribe went out upon the spring fur-hunt at this season, leaving us at home to make the sugar.

The first and most important of the necessary utensils were the huge iron and brass kettles for boiling. Everything else could be made, but these must be bought, begged or
10　borrowed. A maple tree was felled and a log canoe hollowed out, into which the sap was to be gathered. Little troughs of basswood and birchen basins were also made to receive the sweet drops as they trickled from the tree.

As soon as these labors were accomplished, we all pro-
15　ceeded to the bark sugar house, which stood in the midst of a fine grove of maples on the bank of the Minnesota river. We found this hut partially filled with the snows of winter and the withered leaves of the preceding autumn, and it must be cleared for our use. In the meantime a tent was
20　pitched outside for a few days' occupancy. The snow was still deep in the woods, with a solid crust upon which we could easily walk; for we usually moved to the sugar house before the sap had actually started, the better to complete our preparations.

25　My grandmother worked like a beaver in these days (or rather like a muskrat, as the Indians say; for this industrious little animal sometimes collects as many as six or eight bushels of edible roots for the winter, only to be robbed of his store by some of our people). If there
30　was prospect of a good sugaring season, she now made a second and even a third canoe to contain the sap. These canoes were afterward utilized by the hunters for their proper purpose.

My grandmother did not confine herself to
35　canoe-making. She also collected a good supply of fuel for the fires, for she would not have much time to gather wood when the sap began to flow. Presently the weather moderated and the snow began to melt. The month of April brought showers which carried most of it off into
40　the Minnesota river. Now the women began to test the trees—moving leisurely among them, axe in hand, and striking a single quick blow, to see if the sap would appear. The trees, like people, have their individual characters; some were ready to yield up their life-blood, while oth-
45　ers were more reluctant. Now one of the birchen basins was set under each tree, and a hardwood chip driven deep into the cut which the axe had made. From the corners of this chip—at first drop by drop, then more freely—the sap trickled into the little dishes.

50　It is usual to make sugar from maples, but several other trees were also tapped by the Indians. From the birch and ash was made a dark-colored sugar, with a somewhat bitter taste, which was used for medicinal purposes. The box-elder yielded a beautiful white sugar, whose only fault was
55　that there was never enough of it!

A long fire was now made in the sugar house, and a row of brass kettles suspended over the blaze. The sap was collected by the women in tin or birchen buckets and poured into the canoes, from which the kettles were
60　kept filled. The hearts of the boys beat high with pleasant

anticipations when they heard the welcome hissing sound of the boiling sap! Each boy claimed one kettle for his especial charge. It was his duty to see that the fire was kept up under it, to watch lest it boil over, and finally, when the
65　sap became syrup, to test it upon the snow, dipping it out with a wooden paddle. So frequent were these tests that for the first day or two we consumed nearly all that could be made; and it was not until the sweetness began to pall that my grandmother set herself in earnest to store up sugar
70　for future use. She made it into cakes of various forms, in birchen molds, and sometimes in hollow canes or reeds, and the bills of ducks and geese. Some of it was pulverized and packed in rawhide cases. Being a prudent woman, she did not give it to us after the first month or so, except
75　upon special occasions, and it was thus made to last almost the year around. The smaller candies were reserved as an occasional treat for the little fellows, and the sugar was eaten at feasts with wild rice or parched corn, and also with pounded dried meat. Coffee and tea, with their substitutes,
80　were all unknown to us in those days.

153. The point of view from which the passage is told can best be described as that of

　A. an outsider who lived briefly with Native Americans.
　B. a young person who lives with the tribe.
　C. a person who recalls his childhood.
　D. a person who wants to watch maple sugar being made.

154. It can reasonably be inferred that the grandmother needed to make the sugar last the entire year because

　A. there was no way to get more until the next March thaw.
　B. sugar was a special treat for the little children.
　C. it was too much work to make more sugar.
　D. the tribe moved away from the sugar maple trees.

155. When the author says, "Now the women began to test the trees . . . axe in hand, and striking a single quick blow, to see if the sap would appear" (lines 40–42), the author means that the women were

　A. making canoes from the trees.
　B. gathering wood for the fires.
　C. checking to see if the trees should be tapped.
　D. getting ready to make the fires.

156. It is most likely that the author says that there is snow in the sugar house to show that the sugar house

　A. did not have a roof.
　B. was made of concrete.
　C. was very cold.
　D. had a source for water.

157. It can reasonably be inferred that the boys tested the syrup so frequently because

　A. the sap had to be stirred constantly.
　B. each boy had to test many kettles at once.
　C. the sap kept boiling over and putting out the fire.
　D. the syrup tasted good because it was so sweet.

158. The grandmother can best be described as

　A. austere and cold.
　B. diligent and productive.
　C. lenient and forgiving.
　D. moral and demanding.

159. When Eastman was no longer a child, during maple syrup season he probably
    A. took over making the canoes for his grandmother.
    B. kept the young people working hard.
    C. went on the fur-hunt instead of making sugar.
    D. took over the job of collecting sap from the trees.

160. In the last paragraph, it can be reasonably be inferred that the boys were happy because they
    A. enjoyed being outside.
    B. liked to keep the fires going.
    C. were learning new skills.
    D. were anticipating tasting the syrup.

161. Based on the passage, what feelings did Eastman have toward his grandmother?
    A. He thought she worked too hard.
    B. He wanted to help her more.
    C. He admired her strength.
    D. He worried she might hurt herself.

162. In the last paragraph, the author says that some sugar "was pulverized and packed in rawhide cases," which means that the sugar was
    A. cut into shapes and stored.
    B. put into molds.
    C. made into candy.
    D. crushed into tiny pieces and stored.

163. According to the sixth paragraph (lines 50–55), which tree yielded the finest sugar?
    A. The ash
    B. The birch
    C. The box-elder
    D. The maple

164. It can reasonably be inferred that the grandmother
    A. would have preferred not participating in the sugar gathering.
    B. did not want her grandson working so hard.
    C. felt she needed more important work to do.
    D. was in charge of the maple sugar project.

165. In the last paragraph, the author says that the Indians ate sugar with everything EXCEPT
    A. corn.
    B. meat.
    C. rice.
    D. tea.

166. Which of the following statements best describes the author's attitude toward his childhood?
    A. He has warm feelings about his childhood.
    B. He feels that it was a difficult time for him.
    C. He wonders if his past was a bad influence on him.
    D. He thinks that his past presented many challenges that were beyond him.

NATURAL SCIENCES
EFFECTS OF BLUE LIGHT

With the advent of so many electronic devices, this passage on blue light is extremely timely. Perhaps in the future, more effort will be made to control this form of light.

Blue light is the light emitted from TV screens and computer monitors. It is also emitted from the backlit, luminous screens of tablet computers and iPads, e-readers, and smartphones, as well as from energy-saving fluo-
5   rescent lights. As the number of electronic devices has increased exponentially in recent years, there has been a considerable amount of research conducted on what effect, if any, increased exposure to blue light has on humans. There is also an increased concern, because these devices
10 are held much closer to the eye than a TV screen, or even a computer monitor.

Light consists of electromagnetic particles that move in waves. Radio waves have the longest wavelength, and gamma rays have the shortest. Visible light, which can be
15 discerned by the human eye, makes up only a very small part of the entire electromagnetic spectrum, ranging from red with the longest wavelength to violet with the shortest. Blue light has a wavelength of about 450 to 500 nanometers. A nanometer is equivalent to one billionth of a meter.

20 Researchers at the University of Basel in Switzerland recently studied the effects of evening use of computer monitors with light-emitting diode (LED)–backlit screens that emitted blue light. Thirteen male volunteers were studied in a controlled setting, where they were exposed
25 to five hours of computer light in the evening and night-time hours. Some used blue light LED monitors; others used white, non-LED–backlit screens. Compared to the volunteers using white screens, those exposed to blue light showed a significant, measurable decrease in cognitive per-
30 formance, attention span, and alertness. Most importantly, the results showed a significant inhibition of the normal nighttime rise of endogenous (built-in) melatonin in the blue-light user group.

Melatonin is a hormone secreted by the pineal gland,
35 located in the forebrain. It is how the body regulates what is defined as circadian timing, an approximately 24-hour cycle that both animals and plants are governed by. The word *circadian* comes from the Latin words *circa* ("around") and *dies* ("day"). Melatonin is released when it grows dark;
40 during daylight hours, the hormone is not released. The hormone therefore is utilized to regulate daily sleep/wake cycles; light is the factor that synchronizes the circadian system. According to the National Sleep Foundation, stud-ies have linked a host of illnesses, ranging from depression,
45 obesity, diabetes, and cardiovascular disease to poor sleep-ing habits. In addition, not getting enough sleep can cause irritability, and even anger or rage.

Engineers at Rensselaer Polytechnic Institute (RPI) in Troy, New York, conducted a thorough study of the effects
50 of blue light from self-luminous, backlit electronic devices at the Lighting Research Center. Adolescents and young adults were given tablet computers, which they used for reading, playing games, and watching movies during the evening hours.

55 The participants were divided into three groups. The first group wore no glasses, the second (the control group) wore clear goggles fitted with blue-light LEDs, and the third group wore orange-tinted goggles. The orange tint filters out shorter-wavelength light. Each of the partici-
60 pants wore a dimesimeter, a data-logging device developed at RPI that records light levels for up to a month; it is very portable—about the size of a dime.

The three groups were monitored and had their mel-atonin levels measured. The findings built on what the
65 Basel researchers discovered: extensive use of these devices interferes with the body's normal nighttime increase in the release of endogenous melatonin. The group with the orange glasses had the least suppression of melatonin, those with no glasses fell in the middle range, and those
70 with the LED goggles had the greatest suppression of mela-tonin. In fact, using these devices two hours before retiring lowered melatonin levels by 22% in the control group. It is precisely this age bracket, adolescents and young adults, who are most prone to sleep disruption and the consequent
75 pattern of behavior changes. The task being performed on the device, as well as its distance from the retina, affected the level of melatonin suppression by as much as a factor of 10.

The engineers at RPI hope that the results of the
80 study will encourage manufacturers to develop circadian-friendly electronic devices, which would reduce circadian stimulation in nighttime use for a better night's sleep and increase circadian stimulation during daytime use for more alertness. A software engineer has developed a pro-
85 gram, called f.lux, that decreases the blue light emanating from a screen; screen color is adjusted automatically. To use the software, which can be downloaded for free, the user simply enters his longitude and latitude. This program is a step in the right direction for night owls who stare at a
90 screen late at night.

167. The word *spectrum*, as used in the second paragraph (line 16), most nearly means

A. distribution of energy.
B. collection of molecules.
C. social association.
D. saline solution.

168. According to the passage, visible light

A. has a wavelength of 450 to 500 nanometers.
B. is not detected by the human eye.
C. travels in waves.
D. has the shortest wavelength.

169. The main point of the third paragraph (lines 20–33) is that

A. blue light is emitted from LED screens.
B. the research in Basel was conducted in a controlled setting.
C. exposure to blue light can have physical and mental side effects.
D. endogenous melatonin is increased after five hours of computer use.

170. The phrase *cognitive performance*, as used in the third paragraph (lines 29–30), most nearly means

A. state of ignorance.
B. mental process.
C. personality trait.
D. successful conclusion.

171. When the author states that the number of handheld elec-tronic devices has "increased exponentially" (line 6), the author is most likely concerned that

A. the deleterious effects of blue-light exposure are greater because the devices are held closer.
B. it is another sign that young people spend too much time texting on their smartphones.
C. manufacturers will not develop circadian-friendly electronic devices.
D. adolescents don't read books before they go to bed like they used to.

172. The main point of the fourth paragraph (lines 34–47) is that
    A. circadian timing is an approximately 24-hour cycle.
    B. melatonin governs daily cycles of sleeping and waking.
    C. melatonin is released when night falls.
    D. the pineal gland is located in the forebrain.

173. According to the passage, researchers in both Basel, Switzerland, and Troy, New York, noticed that
    A. a host of illnesses can be linked to poor sleeping habits.
    B. the pineal gland is responsible for the secretion of melatonin.
    C. there is a computer program called f.lux that decreases blue light.
    D. using computers at night measurably lowers melatonin levels.

174. The author of the passage would most likely recommend all of the following actions to reduce the melatonin-lowering effects of blue light EXCEPT
    A. watching movies on TV rather than on a tablet.
    B. cutting down on nighttime computer use.
    C. wearing a dimesimeter while using the computer.
    D. using the software known as f.lux.

175. When the author states that "studies have linked a host of illnesses, ranging from depression, obesity, diabetes, and cardiovascular disease to poor sleeping habits" (lines 43–46), the author is most likely suggesting that readers
    A. add a melatonin supplement to their diet.
    B. try to get as much sleep as they can.
    C. replace their energy-efficient fluorescent lighting.
    D. be cognizant of this link when using a computer a lot at night.

176. The main point of the seventh paragraph (lines 63–78) is that
    A. adolescents and young adults are prone to sleep problems.
    B. it is a good idea to wear orange-tinted goggles.
    C. the Basel and RPI research yielded similar results.
    D. an electronic device should be held as far as possible from the eyes.

177. When the author says that f.lux software is "a step in the right direction" (line 89), it can reasonably be inferred that the author
    A. feels that not enough research is being done by scientists on blue light.
    B. thinks electronic devices should have f.lux software already installed.
    C. wants parents to make sure their children download the f.lux software.
    D. is hopeful about new ways of controlling blue light.

178. According to the passage, all of the following statements are true about blue light EXCEPT that
    A. it has the shortest wavelength of all light.
    B. it cannot be seen by the human eye.
    C. its rays interfere with the production of melatonin.
    D. it is used in most electronic devices.

179. The last paragraph of the passage suggests that the RPI engineers
    A. believe manufacturers are working on devices that reduce circadian stimulation.
    B. feel that their study offers useful information to computer users.
    C. hope that computer users discontinue excessive nighttime use.
    D. will continue their research into the effects of blue-light emission.

180. Which of the following statements is the main point of the passage?
    A. There is a growing body of evidence that users of handheld electronic devices should use them with caution, especially at night.
    B. Melatonin plays an important role in regulating the body's response to getting the proper amount of sleep.
    C. Adolescents and young adults should not hold handheld electronic devices too close to their eyes.
    D. If you are going to use a handheld electronic device for a long period of time, download and install f.lux software.

PROSE FICTION
"THE MOUSE" BY SAKI

H. H. Munro (1870–1916), whose pen name was Saki, wrote many short stories about unusual subjects and with comic twists. This passage, adapted from Saki's short story "The Mouse," is no exception.

Theodoric Voler had been brought up by a fond mother, whose chief concern had been to keep him away from what she called the coarser realities of life. To a man of his temperament and upbringing, even a simple railway
5 journey was crammed with petty annoyances and minor discords. As he settled himself down in a second-class compartment one September morning, he was aware of ruffled feelings and general mental discomfort.

He had been staying at a country vicarage with friends.
10 The pony carriage that was to take him to the station had never been properly ordered. When the moment for his departure drew near, Theodoric found himself obliged to ask the vicar's daughter for help with harnessing the pony. That meant groping about in an ill-lighted outbuilding
15 called a stable that smelled very like one—except where it smelled of mice.

As the train glided out of the station, Theodoric's nervous imagination brought up the image of a strange stable yard odor escaping from him. Fortunately, the only other
20 occupant of the compartment, a lady of about the same age as himself, was sleeping. The train was not due to stop till the terminal was reached, in about an hour's time. And yet the train had scarcely attained its normal speed before he became aware that he was not alone with the slumbering
25 lady. He was not even alone in his own clothes.

A warm, creeping movement over his flesh betrayed the unwelcome presence of a stray mouse, which had evidently dashed into his clothes while he was in the stable. Stamps and shakes and pinches failed to get rid of the
30 mouse, and the lawful occupant of the clothes lay back against the cushions and endeavored rapidly to evolve some means for putting an end to the dual ownership. Nothing less drastic than partial undressing would ease him of his tormentor. But to undress in the presence of a
35 lady was an idea that made his eartips tingle in a blush of shame. The mouse kept climbing up his leg, and then it would lose its footing and slip for half an inch or so. And then, in fright, or more probably temper, it bit. Theodoric was forced to undertake the most bold undertaking of his
40 life. Keeping an agonized watch on his slumbering fellow traveler, he swiftly and noiselessly put the ends of his railway rug on the racks on either side of the carriage.

In the narrow dressing room that he had thus improvised he proceeded to get himself partially and the mouse
45 entirely from the pant leg. As the mouse gave a wild leap to the floor, the rug slipped down and the noise woke the sleeper. With a movement almost quicker than the mouse's, Theodoric jumped on the rug and hauled it chin-high over himself. The blood raced and beat in the veins
50 of his neck and forehead, while he waited dumbly for the communication cord to be pulled. The lady, however, contented herself with a silent stare at her strangely muffled companion. How much had she seen, Theodoric queried to himself; and in any case, what on earth must she think
55 of his present posture? The lady, however, just sat back and stared at him.

"I think I have caught a chill," he said to her desperately.

"Really, I'm sorry," she replied. "I was just going to ask you if you would open this window."

60 "I think it's malaria," he added, his teeth chattering slightly, as much from fright as from a desire to support his theory.

"I suppose you caught it in the tropics?"

Theodoric, whose acquaintance with the tropics was
65 limited to an annual present of a chest of tea from an uncle in Ceylon, felt that even the malaria was slipping from him. Would it be possible, he wondered, to explain the real state of affairs to her?

"Are you afraid of mice?" he ventured, growing, if pos-
70 sible, more scarlet in the face.

"Not unless they came in quantities. Why do you ask?"

"I had one crawling inside my clothes just now," said Theodoric in a voice that hardly seemed his own. "It was a most awkward situation."

75 "It must have been, if you wear your clothes at all tight," she observed. "But mice have strange ideas of comfort."

"I had to get rid of it while you were asleep," he continued. Then, with a gulp, he added, "It was getting rid of it that brought me to—to this."

80 "Surely getting rid of one small mouse wouldn't bring on a chill," she exclaimed, with a lightheartedness that Theodoric thought abominable.

Evidently she had realized a bit of his predicament and was enjoying his confusion. With every minute that passed,
85 the train was rushing nearer to the terminal. There, dozens of eyes would be watching him instead of just the eyes in the corner of the carriage. There was only one chance. That was the hope that his fellow traveler might fall back asleep. But as the minutes passed by, that chance ebbed away.
90 The glance which Theodoric gave her from time to time showed that she was still awake.

"I think we must be getting near now," she commented.

Theodoric had already noticed with growing terror the small, ugly dwellings passing by. They were almost there.
95 Like a hunted beast breaking cover, he threw aside his rug, and struggled into his disheveled clothes. Then, as he sank back in his seat, clothed and almost delirious, the train slowed down to a final crawl, and the woman spoke.

"Would you be so kind," she asked, "as to get me a por-
100 ter to put me into a cab? It's a shame to trouble you when you're feeling unwell, but being blind makes one so helpless at a railway station."

181. It can reasonably be inferred that Theodoric
A. travels a good deal.
B. was an only child.
C. was protected as a child.
D. enjoys meeting new people.

182. Which of the following statements best describes the theme of the passage?
A. People learn from their mistakes.
B. Traveling allows for new adventures.
C. Things are not always as they appear.
D. People are apt to do odd things when traveling.

183. The event that most significantly affects the outcome of the story is
A. the disclosure that the companion is blind.
B. the rug falling to the floor.
C. Theodoric's removing his clothes.
D. Theodoric's being bitten by the mouse.

184. It can reasonably be inferred that the reason Theodoric tells his traveling companion he has malaria (line 60) is to
A. amuse himself during the long trip.
B. show that he knows a lot about the tropics.
C. make it appear that he had lived in the tropics.
D. make up an excuse for being wrapped up in a rug.

185. What is the most likely reason that Theodoric decided to put his clothes back on?

   A. He realized the rug looked silly on him.
   B. He thought the conductor would be coming shortly.
   C. He realized he would have to get off the train in a little while.
   D. He thought he should straighten up for the sake of his companion.

186. The situation with the mouse caused Theodoric to become

   A. more observant than he was before.
   B. more forgiving than he was before.
   C. more reasonable than he was before.
   D. more daring than he was before.

187. When the author says that "the lawful occupant of the clothes lay back against the cushions and endeavored rapidly to evolve some means for putting an end to the dual ownership" (lines 22–24), he means that

   A. the mouse was nesting in Theodoric's clothes.
   B. Theodoric's clothes were borrowed.
   C. Theodoric's clothes were old.
   D. the mouse was inside Theodoric's clothes.

188. Based on the information in the sixth paragraph (line 57), Theodoric tells his traveling companion that he has a chill in order to

   A. suggest that it is cold on the train.
   B. explain why he is covered by a rug.
   C. suggest that he needs her help.
   D. explain why he is fully clothed.

189. Which of the following statements best describes the author's perspective on Theodoric in the story?

   A. He finds Theodoric humorous.
   B. He thinks Theodoric is overly cynical.
   C. He believes that Theodoric has a great deal of potential.
   D. He worries that Theodoric may suffer physically because of his nerves.

190. In the fifth paragraph (lines 43–56), why does Theodoric think that his traveling companion will pull the communication cord?

   A. He thinks that she wants to order some food.
   B. He is worried that she has seen him without his clothes.
   C. He knows that she is blind and is seeking help.
   D. He wants her to call for help.

191. Based on the information in the seventeenth paragraph (lines 83–91), what does Theodoric think of his traveling companion?

   A. He believes that she is not well.
   B. He thinks she is making fun of him.
   C. He thinks that she may be odd.
   D. He believes that she wants him to be friendlier.

192. It can reasonably be inferred that the author waits until the end of the story to reveal that the traveling companion is blind because the author

   A. does not think it is an important detail.
   B. does not want to upset the reader earlier.
   C. wants to surprise the reader with the information.
   D. wants to make the reader feel compassion for the companion.

193. The tone of the passage is best described as

   A. bitter and acrid.
   B. sarcastic.
   C. tongue-in-cheek.
   D. whimsical.

194. The probable effect that the words of his traveling companion had on Theodoric was that he felt

   A. betrayed.
   B. relieved.
   C. angered.
   D. troubled.

CHAPTER 11

SET 4 READING QUESTIONS

QUESTIONS 195–250

PROSE FICTION
"THE LAST CLASS—THE STORY OF A LITTLE ALSATIAN"
BY ALPHONSE DAUDET

This passage is adapted from a short story by Alphonse Daudet (1840–1897). It takes place in 1870, when Prussian forces under King Otto Bismarck attacked France. As a result, the French districts of Alsace and Lorraine, which bordered Prussia (modern Germany), came under Prussian rule.

I was very late for school that morning, and I was terribly afraid of being scolded, especially as Monsieur Hamel had told us that he should examine us on participles, and I did not know the first thing about them. For a moment
5 I thought of staying away from school and wandering about the fields. I could hear the blackbirds whistling on the edge of the wood, and in the field, behind the sawmill, the Prussians going through their drill. All that was much more tempting to me than the rules concerning participles;
10 but I had the strength to resist, and I ran as fast as I could to school.

Usually, at the beginning of school, there was a great uproar which could be heard in the street, desks opening and closing, lessons repeated aloud in unison, with our
15 ears stuffed in order to learn quicker, and the teacher's stout ruler beating on the desk.

I counted on all this noise to reach my bench unnoticed; but as it happened, that day everything was quiet, like a Sunday morning. I had to open the door and enter,
20 in the midst of that perfect silence.

Monsieur Hamel looked at me with no sign of anger and said very gently:

"Go at once to your seat, my little Frantz; we were going to begin without you."

25 I stepped over the bench and sat down at once at my desk. Not until then, when I had partly recovered from my fright, did I notice that our teacher had on his handsome blue coat, which he wore only on days of inspection or of distribution of prizes. Moreover, there was something
30 extraordinary, something solemn about the whole class. But what surprised me most was to see at the back of the room, on the benches which were usually empty, some people from the village sitting, as silent as we were. They all seemed depressed.

35 While I was wondering at all this, Monsieur Hamel had mounted his platform, and in the same gentle and serious voice with which he had welcomed me, he said to us:

"My children, this is the last time that I shall teach you. Orders have come from Berlin to teach nothing but
40 German in the schools of Alsace and Lorraine. The new teacher arrives tomorrow. This is the last class in French, so I beg you to be very attentive."

Those few words overwhelmed me. My last class in French!

45 And I barely knew how to write! So I should never learn! How angry I was with myself because of the time I had wasted, the lessons I had missed! And it was the same about Monsieur Hamel. The thought that he was going away, that I should never see him again, made me forget
50 the punishments, the blows with the ruler.

I was at that point in my reflections, when I heard my name called. What would I not have given to be able to say from beginning to end that famous rule about participles without a slip! But I got mixed up at the first words, and I
55 stood there swaying against my bench, with a full heart, afraid to raise my head. I heard Monsieur Hamel speaking to me:

"I will not scold you, my little Frantz; you must be punished enough; that is the way it goes; every day we say to
60 ourselves: 'Pshaw! I have time enough. I will learn tomorrow.' And then you see what happens."

Then, passing from one thing to another, Monsieur Hamel began to talk to us about the French language, saying that it was the most beautiful language in the world; that
65 we must always retain it among ourselves, and never forget it, because when a people falls into servitude, "so long as it clings to its language, it is as if it held the key to its prison."

Then he took the grammar and read us our lesson. I was amazed to see how readily I understood. Everything
70 that he said seemed so easy to me, so easy. I believed, too, that I had never listened so closely, and that he had never been so patient with his explanations.

When the lesson was at an end, we passed to writing.

From time to time, when I raised my eyes from my
75 paper, I saw Monsieur Hamel sitting motionless in his chair and staring at the objects about him as if he wished to carry away in his glance the whole of his little schoolhouse. Think of it! For forty years he had been there in the same place, with his yard in front of him and his class just as
80 it was! What a heart-rending thing it must have been for that poor man to leave all those things, and to hear his sister walking back and forth in the room overhead, packing their trunks! For they were to go away the next day—to leave the province forever.

85 However, he had the courage to keep the class to the end. After the writing, we had the lesson in history; then the little ones sang all together.

Suddenly the church clock struck twelve. At the same moment, the bugles of the Prussians returning from drill

90   blared under our windows. Monsieur Hamel rose, pale as
      death, from his chair. Never had he seemed to me so tall.

      "My friends," he said, "my friends, I—I—"

      But he could not finish the sentence.

      Thereupon he turned to the blackboard, took a piece of
95   chalk, and wrote in the largest letters he could:

      "VIVE LA FRANCE!"*

      Then he stood there, with his head resting against the
      wall, and without speaking, he motioned to us with his
      hand:
100   "That is all; go."

195. The point of view from which the passage is told can best
be described as that of

A. a narrator who is good at his studies, but not sensitive
   to the moment.
B. a narrator who realizes that his world will never be
   the same.
C. a friend of Monsieur Hamel who is transcribing what
   his last French class was like.
D. a person who was in the classroom observing, but who
   is new to the town.

196. When Frantz says, "but I had the strength to resist, and I ran
as fast as I could to school" (lines 10–11), he means that he

A. wanted to get to school to help Monsieur Hamel.
B. was strong enough to be able to run to school.
C. resisted saying something to the Prussians.
D. overcame his desire to skip school.

197. It can reasonably be inferred that the villagers attended the
class to

A. pay their respects to Monsieur Hamel.
B. decide whether Monsieur Hamel should be fired.
C. learn to speak French better.
D. find out how well the students were doing with their
   French.

198. When Frantz says, "there was something extraordinary,
something solemn about the whole class" (lines 29–30), it
can reasonably be inferred that Frantz

A. was upset about being late.
B. was worried about French grammar.
C. thought something bad was happening.
D. believed Monsieur Hamel's sister was sick.

199. Based on the information in the passage, what effect did
the villagers' presence in the class have on Frantz?

A. It made Frantz think he was in trouble.
B. It told Frantz that something odd was going on.
C. It made Frantz even more nervous.
D. It caused Frantz to forget his lesson.

200. From comments made by Frantz, it can be assumed that
Monsieur Hamel's treatment of Frantz during the last
class was

A. more critical of Frantz than usual.
B. more sympathetic than before.
C. less interested in Frantz than before.
D. less kindly than usual.

201. It can reasonably be inferred that when Frantz heard that
this was the last French class, he was

A. worried about learning German.
B. sure that he would do better learning German than
   French.
C. brokenhearted because Monsieur Hamel would be gone.
D. relieved that he would no longer be punished by
   Monsieur Hamel.

202. The theme of the passage is that

A. school teachers are emotional.
B. young men should be more studious.
C. some changes can be painful.
D. life holds many joys.

203. Monsieur Hamel says that Frantz "must be punished
enough" (lines 58–59), because

A. Frantz had been punished by Monsieur Hamel a great
   deal before.
B. Monsieur Hamel feels that he was wrong to have punished Frantz.
C. Frantz would not have the chance to study French
   again.
D. Monsieur Hamel thinks Frantz will cry.

204. In the fourteenth paragraph (lines 68–72), why was the
lesson different from other lessons for Frantz?

A. It was an easier lesson than the others.
B. He concentrated on it more than the others.
C. He was less concerned about doing well.
D. It was a lesson that they had done before.

205. What was the author's intention for including the sentence
"At the same moment, the bugles of the Prussians returning from drill blared under our windows" (lines 88–90)?

A. To show that the Prussians were orderly
B. To suggest that the Prussians marched only in the
   morning
C. To show how much people were interested in the
   Prussians
D. To suggest how intrusive the Prussians were

206. You can tell that Monsieur Hamel's attitude toward the
Prussians was one of

A. respect.
B. dislike.
C. fear.
D. indifference.

207. When Frantz says that Monsieur Hamel "rose, pale as
death" (lines 90–91), he is suggesting that

A. Monsieur Hamel was dying of a disease.
B. Monsieur Hamel was embarrassed to be losing his job.
C. Monsieur Hamel was anemic.
D. it was like a death for Monsieur Hamel to lose his job.

208. In the twentieth paragraph (line 93), it can be reasonably
be inferred that Monsieur Hamlin could not finish his sentence because he

A. forgot what he needed to say.
B. didn't know what to say.
C. was losing his voice.
D. was overcome by emotion.

*French for "Long live France!"

SOCIAL SCIENCES
THE JOURNEYS OF MARCO POLO

Marco Polo (1254–1324) was born in the Republic of Venice (known today as Venice, Italy). He is considered one of the greatest explorers in history, traveling to China and learning much about its customs. He is also known to have brought the first spaghetti noodles from China to Venice.

Marco Polo's father, Niccolo, and his uncle, Maffeo, were merchants who traveled and were away from home much of the time; they returned from a trip to China in 1269. There they had met the ruler Kublai Khan, grandson
5 of the Mongol warlord Genghis Khan. Kublai had conquered China in 1215, burning the capital city Zhongdu (now called Beijing and the capital of the People's Republic of China) to the ground.

Kublai had expressed interest in learning more about
10 Christianity. He asked Niccolo and Maffeo to return to China with 100 missionaries, so that his people could learn about the religion. Marco wanted to go with them, so in 1271, seventeen-year-old Marco set off with his father and uncle on the long overland route that had become known
15 as the Silk Road: 4,000 miles of very inhospitable terrain with some of the harshest conditions on Earth, vast deserts, and steep mountains. Only two missionaries had agreed to come, but after only a few days, they turned back to Italy. Marco and his party finally arrived after four long
20 years at Xanadu, the summer palace of Kublai Khan, in Inner Mongolia.

The Europeans were awed by what they saw: walls were covered with silver and gold, and there was a great hall where 6,000 people could dine. The emperor had
25 10,000 pure white horses.

Kublai had established the Yuan Dynasty with the Mongolian conquest of China. The sophisticated culture that Marco saw around him dwarfed the Holy Roman Empire. He quickly learned four languages, and Kublai
30 became captivated by the young Venetian. He appointed Marco a special envoy. Marco traveled all over China, Burma, India, and Tibet. Many of the places he traveled were not seen by a European again until the nineteenth century. He wrote a history of the Mongols and about the
35 wonders of Chinese civilization. He marveled at the wealth he saw, the magnificent porcelain and silk, and the complex structure of Chinese society. The Chinese manufactured iron, mined coal, and produced salt on a scale unheard of in Europe. Kublai had introduced paper money, also
40 unknown in Europe, and he developed a fast and efficient postal system to link together the millions of square miles of his vast empire. Couriers could travel up to 300 miles a day, using fresh horses supplied for them at intervals.

After 17 years, Marco wanted to return to Venice.
45 Kublai was getting old; it was feared that if he died, the fortune that the Polo family had amassed over the years would be confiscated. After much badgering, the emperor relented; he would let them depart if they would escort a Mongol princess to Persia to marry a young prince there.
50 In 1292, they left Hangchow to return by sea. The trip lasted three years, and many of the travelers perished in storms or from scurvy. The princess and the Polos did survive, however, and they landed at the port of Hormuz in Persia in 1295.

55 After returning to Venice, Marco was captured in 1298 while he was commanding a galley in a war against the rival Republic of Genoa, and he was thrown into a Genoese prison. While in prison, he met the writer Rusticello of Pisa. Marco dictated his adventures to him. When they
60 were released in 1299, Rusticello went on to publish *Description of the World*. Nobody believed the book; they couldn't conceive that such a world as China existed. In

Venice, it was called *Il Milione* ("The Million"); the public thought it was made up of a million lies. Marco got the
65 nickname Marco Milione.

A hundred years after his death, handwritten manuscript editions of the book continued to be produced. It was realized that *Description of the World*, or *The Travels of Marco Polo*, as it came to be called, was the most com-
70 plete rendering of life in Asia that was available in medieval Europe. Christopher Columbus is known to have had a manuscript; it was an inspiration to him as he planned his trip to reach Asia by sailing west.

A few historians have questioned whether Marco
75 Polo really did go to China, suggesting that he may have only talked with other travelers. There is no mention in the book of the Great Wall of China, for instance, or the custom of binding the feet of women that was prevalent at the time. Nevertheless, *The Travels of Marco Polo* has
80 had a profound influence on how Europeans understand a culture so different from their own. In addition, Chinese historians value the book for its detailed insights into thirteenth-century life in China. Marco summed it up for himself, speaking on his deathbed to a priest in 1324, "I
85 have not told half of what I saw."

209. In the second paragraph (lines 7–15), it can reasonably be inferred that the two missionaries turned back because they

  A. decided the trip would be too long and hazardous.
  B. were called back by their superiors.
  C. became ill from the strange food.
  D. decided to take a trip elsewhere.

210. The main point of the fifth paragraph (lines 44–54) is that

  A. the Polos finally got Kublai Khan to let them go home.
  B. the Polos took a Mongol princess to Persia.
  C. Kublai Khan was getting old.
  D. the trip home took three years.

211. According to the passage, the Yuan Dynasty offered all of the following EXCEPT

  A. iron and coal.
  B. a fleet of ships.
  C. a postal system.
  D. paper money.

212. Based on the information in the fourth paragraph (lines 26–43), how did Europe compare with the Yuan Dynasty?

  A. Europe had more artists than the Yuan Dynasty had.
  B. Europe was more skilled in metal production.
  C. Europe lacked many of the facilities that the Yuan Dynasty had.
  D. Europe was not as old as the Yuan Dynasty.

213. According to the passage, it could reasonably be inferred that Christopher Columbus considered *The Travels of Marco Polo* inspiring because

  A. he had been to China.
  B. they were both explorers.
  C. they were both writers.
  D. he wanted to write a book.

214. The Venetians thought that Marco Polo's book was

  A. beautifully written.
  B. a sham.
  C. too long.
  D. hard to read.

215. Based on the information in the passage, what was most likely true of Khan?

    A. He was a cruel dictator.
    B. He wanted to become a Christian.
    C. He was a man ahead of his time.
    D. He was kind to his subjects.

216. A major reason that the Polos stayed in Kublai Khan's empire was that they

    A. wanted to help Kublai Khan.
    B. were getting rich.
    C. were not well enough to travel.
    D. hoped to become part of the royalty themselves.

217. According to the sixth paragraph (lines 55–65), it can reasonably be inferred that Marco Polo

    A. had few skills as a commander.
    B. did not enjoy fighting.
    C. had never been in a fight before.
    D. was a good sailor.

218. What is the most likely reason that the Mongol princess needed to be escorted to Persia?

    A. She did not like traveling by herself.
    B. The trip was too dangerous for a young woman to take on her own.
    C. She was hesitant to leave her homeland.
    D. Kublai Khan wanted to make sure she did not run away while traveling.

219. Based on the information in the sixth paragraph (lines 55–65), Marco Polo was jailed because he

    A. had written about his travels.
    B. was a pirate.
    C. angered Kublai Khan.
    D. lost a naval battle.

220. Based on the information in the last paragraph, why do some historians wonder if Marco Polo actually traveled to China?

    A. He did not bring many things back with him from his travels.
    B. He was known to make up stories.
    C. He did not write about the Great Wall of China.
    D. He was extremely rich.

221. Probably the best proof that Marco Polo did travel to China was

    A. what he said to the priest.
    B. the fact that he knew so much about Kublai Khan.
    C. the fact that he knew how to speak many languages.
    D. what he told his fellow prisoner.

222. Which of the following statements best describes the author's attitude toward Marco Polo?

    A. The author feels that Marco Polo was an exceptional person who had far-reaching influence on the world.
    B. The author thinks that Marco Polo was an excellent merchant who was able to amass a great deal of wealth.
    C. The author worries that Marco Polo's name will be blemished by some historians.
    D. The author believes that Marco Polo made up most of the stories in his book.

HUMANITIES
"THE SNOW-WALKERS" BY JOHN BURROUGHS

This excerpt is adapted from an essay in *In the Catskills* by John Burroughs (1837–1921), an American naturalist and essayist. Burroughs built a cabin in the woods in the Catskill Mountains area of New York State. He did most of his writing at the cabin, called Slabsides, which is now a National Historic Landmark.

He who marvels at the beauty of the world in summer will find equal cause for wonder and admiration in winter. It is true the pomp and the pageantry are swept away, but the essential elements remain,—the day and the night, the
5   mountain and the valley, the elemental play and succession and the perpetual presence of the infinite sky. In winter the stars seem to have rekindled their fires, the moon achieves a fuller triumph, and the heavens wear a look of a more exalted simplicity. Summer is more wooing and seductive,
10 more versatile and human, appeals to the affections and the sentiments, and fosters inquiry and the art impulse. Winter is of a more heroic cast, and addresses the intellect. The severe studies and disciplines come easier in winter. One imposes larger tasks upon himself, and is less tolerant of
15 his own weaknesses.

The tendinous part of the mind, so to speak, is more developed in winter; the fleshy, in summer. I should say winter had given the bone and sinew to Literature, summer the tissues and blood.

20 The simplicity of winter has a deep moral. The return of nature, after such a career of splendor and prodigality, to habits so simple and austere, is not lost either upon the head or the heart. It is the philosopher coming back from the banquet and the wine to a cup of water and a crust of
25 bread.

And then this beautiful masquerade of the elements,— the novel disguises our nearest friends put on! Here is another rain and another dew, water that will not flow, nor spill, nor receive the taint of an unclean vessel. And if we
30 see truly, the same old beneficence and willingness to serve lurk beneath all.

Look up at the miracle of the falling snow,—the air a dizzy maze of whirling, eddying flakes, noiselessly trans- forming the world, the exquisite crystals dropping in ditch
35 and gutter, and disguising in the same suit of spotless livery all objects upon which they fall. How novel and fine the first drifts! The old, dilapidated fence is suddenly set off with the most fantastic ruffles, scalloped and fluted after an unheard-of fashion! Looking down a long line of decrepit
40 stone wall, in the trimming of which the wind had fairly run riot, I saw, as for the first time, what a severe yet mas- ter artist old Winter is. Ah, a severe artist! How stern the woods look, dark and cold and as rigid against the horizon as iron!

45 All life and action upon the snow have an added emphasis and significance. Every expression is under- scored. Summer has few finer pictures than this winter one of the farmer foddering his cattle from a stack upon the clean snow,—the movement, the sharply defined fig-
50 ures, the great green flakes of hay, the long file of patient cows, the advance just arriving and pressing eagerly for the choicest morsels, and the bounty and providence it sug- gests. Or the chopper in the woods,—the prostrate tree, the white new chips scattered about, his easy triumph over
55 the cold, his coat hanging to a limb, and the clear, sharp ring of his axe. The woods are rigid and tense, keyed up by the frost, and resound like a stringed instrument. Or the road-breakers, sallying forth with oxen and sleds in the still, white world, the day after the storm, to restore the lost
60 track and demolish the beleaguering drifts.

All sounds are sharper in winter; the air transmits better. At night I hear more distinctly the steady roar of the North Mountain. In summer it is a sort of complacent purr, as the breezes stroke down its sides; but in winter always
65 the same low, sullen growl.

A severe artist! No longer the canvas and the pig- ments, but the marble and the chisel. When the nights are calm and the moon full, I go out to gaze upon the wonderful purity of the moonlight and the snow. The air
70 is full of latent fire, and the cold warms me—after a differ- ent fashion from that of the kitchen stove. The world lies about me in a "trance of snow." The clouds are pearly and iridescent, and seem the farthest possible remove from the condition of a storm,—the ghosts of clouds, the indwell-
75 ing beauty freed from all dross. I see the hills, bulging with great drifts, lift themselves up cold and white against the sky, the black lines of fences here and there obliterated by the depth of the snow. Presently a fox barks away up next the mountain, and I imagine I can almost see
80 him sitting there, in his furs, upon the illuminated sur- face, and looking down in my direction. As I listen, one answers him from behind the woods in the valley. What a wild winter sound, wild and weird, up among the ghostly hills! Since the wolf has ceased to howl upon these moun-
85 tains, and the panther to scream, there is nothing to be compared with it. So wild! I get up in the middle of the night to listen to the ear, and one delights to know that such wild creatures are among us. At this season Nature makes the most of every throb of life that
90 can withstand her severity. How heartily she indorses this fox! In what bold relief stand out the lives of all walkers of the snow! The snow is a great tell-tale, and blabs as effec- tually as it obliterates. I go into the woods, and know all that has happened. I cross the fields, and if only a mouse
95 has visited his neighbor, the fact is chronicled.

223. According to the author, what effect does winter have on the moon?

   A. It seems more silver.
   B. Its terrain looks smoother.
   C. It seems bigger.
   D. Its light is dimmed.

224. It can reasonably be inferred that "the tendinous part of the mind" (line 16) refers to the

   A. imagination that creates beauty.
   B. ligaments that hold things together.
   C. passion that creates drama.
   D. sadness that causes intensity.

225. Summer is described by the author in all of the following ways EXCEPT

   A. intelligent.
   B. seductive.
   C. versatile.
   D. human.

226. According to the author, which of the following activities is most likely done during the winter?

   A. Reading philosophy
   B. Writing a play
   C. Falling in love
   D. Holding a seminar

227. The main point of the third paragraph (lines 20–25) is that winter

    A. is a victim of summer.
    B. gives less joy than summer.
    C. cleanses the individual.
    D. is harder to live through.

228. Which words best describe the author?

    A. Overwrought and tense
    B. Pragmatic and intellectual
    C. Romantic and deep-seeing
    D. Cynical and despairing

229. The main point of the fifth paragraph (lines 32–44) is that the snow

    A. makes the stone fence look like iron.
    B. transforms ordinary objects into something wonderful.
    C. is difficult to describe.
    D. makes everything look cold.

230. When the author speaks of the chopper's "easy triumph over the cold" (lines 54–55), he means that

    A. the chopper wears a heavy sweater.
    B. the work of cutting trees keeps the chopper warm.
    C. the trees protect the chopper from the wind.
    D. it is not very cold.

231. From the information in the seventh paragraph (lines 61–65), it can reasonably be inferred that cold air

    A. helps sound travel.
    B. keeps noises quieter.
    C. makes higher sounds.
    D. helps create strong feelings.

232. When the author says that "the air is full of latent fire" (lines 69–70), he means that the air

    A. makes it easier to build a fire.
    B. is extremely dry.
    C. burns the lungs when a person breathes.
    D. contains a hidden warmth.

233. The author views the sound of the fox as

    A. annoying at night.
    B. frightening to hear in the winter.
    C. chilling.
    D. inspiring.

234. The author likens winter to a(n)

    A. fox.
    B. artist.
    C. poet.
    D. farmer.

235. The author describes winter in all of the following ways EXCEPT

    A. austere.
    B. severe.
    C. sentimental.
    D. essential.

236. When the author says, "if only a mouse has visited his neighbor, the fact is chronicled" (lines 94–95), he means that

    A. no one would ever know.
    B. there is food in the snow.
    C. it would make noises.
    D. its footprints would be recorded in the snow.

NATURAL SCIENCES
EATERS OF LIGHT

Black holes are a part of the universe that have intrigued scientists for many years. This passage addresses what scientists have slowly uncovered about these phenomena.

What is a black hole? A black hole is an area in space where the force of gravity is so strong that light cannot get out. It is basically a dead star. The star itself has disappeared; what is left is the gravity. An enormous amount of
5 matter is intensely compressed and squeezed into a small space.

The phrase "black hole" was first used by physicist John Archibald Wheeler in 1967. Until that time, black holes were just a theory; their existence had not been proven,
10 nor had a black hole been observed, since there is nothing to "see." The existence of black holes was foreshadowed by Albert Einstein. In his *General Theory of Relativity*, published in 1915, he proposed that gravity is not a force, as had previously been accepted since the time of Sir Isaac
15 Newton in the seventeenth century, but a consequence of distortion in space and time—what he called "space-time."

Einstein's theory led scientists to ponder what the effect of matter enormously compressed would have on gravity and energy. At the time, it was presumed that this was
20 impossible. In the 1960s, theoretical scientists confirmed that black holes were a prediction of general relativity.

Since that time, by studying how stars and interstellar gases orbit black holes and by using radio telescopes, scientists have been able to measure black holes. By measur-
25 ing the speed of the material orbiting the black hole and the size of the orbit, scientists can determine the mass of the black hole using the laws of gravity. What they have found is that the size of black holes ranges from tiny to supermassive.

30 As a dead star collapses on itself, the mass becomes so tremendous that it bends space and time around itself. Nothing can get out. This infinitely dense region is called a singularity. It cannot be measured, since it is equal to infinity. An event horizon is a spherical boundary outside the
35 black hole where the gravitational attraction nearly equals the speed of light.

It is now believed that every large galaxy has at least one supermassive black hole at its center. Our own galaxy, the Milky Way, has one. Called Sagittarius A* (read
40 as "Sagittarius A Star" and abbreviated *Sgr A**), it is 27,000 light years from Earth and has a mass equal to four million suns, with a diameter (event horizon) of 24 million miles. In comparison, Earth is 93 million miles from the sun.

Scientists have been able to analyze event horizons in
45 space using the Chandra X-ray Observatory. Launched by NASA in 1999 by the Space Shuttle *Columbia* (under the command of the first woman to command a mission, Eileen Collins), Chandra has a resolution so acute that it is equivalent to being able to read a stop sign from a distance
50 of 12 miles. X-rays have a shorter wavelength than visible light, so X-rays transmitted from space cannot be measured on Earth—they are absorbed by the atmosphere. The Chandra X-ray Observatory orbits the Earth at a distance of 86,500 miles; it can observe X-rays from particles heated
55 to 180 million degrees Fahrenheit right up to the last second before they are sucked into a black hole.

NASA's Nuclear Spectroscopic Telescope Array (NuSTAR), launched in 2012, measures high-energy X-ray light. It has recorded flares on the surface of Sgr A* as the
60 black hole gobbles up matter. NuSTAR will conduct a census of black holes and probe the origin of cosmic rays.

Some people believe that black holes are "wormholes" that lead to another dimension and another universe.

65 There is no way to prove such a theory, because nothing would be able to enter a black hole and survive. One physicist, Nikodem Popławski, has put forth a theory that the matter contained in such infinite density at the center of a black hole is actually spewn out the other side, which he calls a white hole, where it forms the basic building blocks
70 for another universe in a reality different from ours. It is possible that there may be an infinite number of universes in addition to the one we call home.

Dr. Wheeler summed up existing knowledge about black holes in his 1999 autobiography, *Geons, Black Holes,*
75 *and Quantum Foam: A Life in Physics:* A black hole "teaches us that space can be crumpled up like paper into an infinitesimal dot, that time can be extinguished like a blown-out flame, and that the laws of physics that we regard as 'sacred,' as immutable, are anything but."

237. According to the passage, a black hole has all of the following characteristics EXCEPT

A. a distortion in space and time.
B. a tremendous force of gravity.
C. intensely compressed matter.
D. the inability of light to get out.

238. Which of the following scientists is credited with first theorizing the existence of black holes?

A. John Wheeler
B. Isaac Newton
C. Nikodem Popławski
D. Albert Einstein

239. Which of the following statements best describes the function of NuSTAR?

A. It predicts the existence of compressed matter.
B. It calculates the event horizon.
C. It measures high-energy X-rays.
D. It maps the event horizon of Sgr A*.

240. According to the passage, scientists measure black holes by

A. bending space and time around them.
B. studying the movement of stars around them.
C. observing X-ray emissions from flares.
D. defining the singularity of a black hole.

241. As described in the passage, Chandra allows scientists to

A. read a stop sign from a distance of 12 miles.
B. confirm Einstein's theory of relativity.
C. analyze data that cannot be obtained on Earth.
D. prove that wormholes exist.

242. It can reasonably be inferred that the author of the passage believes that

A. black holes cannot be seen, but they can be measured.
B. Einstein was a genius, truly a man ahead of his time.
C. the nature of the universe may never be fully understood.
D. the size of supermassive black holes boggles the mind.

243. According to the passage, when a dead star collapses, it

A. becomes unbelievably dense in mass.
B. emits measurable high-energy X-rays.
C. becomes a supermassive black hole.
D. reaches a temperature of 180 million degrees Fahrenheit.

244. It can reasonably be inferred from the sixth paragraph (lines 37–43) that

   A. Sgr A* has a diameter of about one fourth the distance between Earth and the sun.
   B. the Milky Way has a supermassive black hole at its center.
   C. Sgr A* has a mass equivalent to 27,000 suns.
   D. the event horizon of a black hole is the same as its diameter.

245. According to the passage, Isaac Newton

   A. first coined the phrase "black hole."
   B. defined gravity as a force.
   C. discovered the Milky Way.
   D. had a satellite named after him.

246. According to the passage, the difference between a wormhole and a black hole is that

   A. black holes cannot be seen.
   B. black holes eject matter out the other side.
   C. wormholes could lead to a parallel universe.
   D. wormholes are just a fantasy.

247. In the passage, the author refers to physicist John Archibald Wheeler as being best known for

   A. *Geons, Black Holes, and Quantum Foam: A Life in Physics*.
   B. confirming that Einstein predicted black holes.
   C. the invention of the radio telescope.
   D. first using the term "black hole" in scientific circles.

248. The main point of the ninth paragraph (lines 62–72) is that

   A. there is at least one other universe in existence besides ours.
   B. so-called wormholes have yet to be discovered.
   C. black holes contain the building blocks for new universes.
   D. any theory about where a black hole might lead cannot be proved.

249. Based on the information in the passage, it can reasonably be inferred that if you were to approach a black hole in a spaceship and you traveled inside the event horizon,

   A. you would be able to see if wormholes actually exist.
   B. you could measure the X-rays emitted from the singularity.
   C. the gravitational pull would overwhelm you.
   D. space-time would no longer exist.

250. When Dr. Wheeler says that "the laws of physics that we regard as 'sacred,' as immutable, are anything but" (lines 78–79), he means that the laws of physics are

   A. ignorant.
   B. permanent.
   C. variable.
   D. itinerant.

PART II ANSWERS AND EXPLANATIONS

Chapter 8: Set 1 Reading Questions

1. **B.** The narrator isn't a scientist, so answer choice (A) is incorrect. There is no mention of a friend of the man, so answer choice (C) is incorrect. The narrator is clearly not the man himself, so answer choice (D) is incorrect.

2. **D.** This is a metaphor and uses words that would typically describe a candle.

3. **C.** The language that is used to describe the man sounds more like a description of some beast. The other answer choices aren't suggested by the passage.

4. **C.** There is enough food onboard, so answer choice (A) is incorrect. The scientists treated the man with respect, so answer choice (B) is incorrect. The ship is going to San Francisco, but that isn't the man's concern, so answer choice (D) is incorrect.

5. **B.** This is what the simile suggests, that to the man the food was like gold.

6. **A.** The man feared that he would run out of food.

7. **A.** A *mendicant* is a beggar—someone who has nothing and asks for money or food.

8. **C.** They were eating food that he thought he would need when there was another famine.

9. **B.** The sailors smiled and gave him their biscuits; they thought he was a curiosity. There is no indication that the sailors were afraid of the man, so answer choice (A) is incorrect. Neither answer choice (C) nor answer choice (D) is supported by the passage.

10. **B.** Although it is suggested that he told the scientists his name, it isn't revealed in the passage.

11. **B.** This is what the experiences of the man suggest. The other answer choices aren't consistent with the passage.

12. **A.** This is what the scientists thought would happen and what did happen.

13. **B.** The fact that the man nearly starved to death has impacted the way he thinks and acts. The other answer choices refer to aspects of the story, but they aren't the main theme.

14. **B.** This is the main reason the passage was written and what the author wanted to achieve.

15. **B.** Although the other words could be used to describe the race, they don't mean the same as *grueling*.

16. **D.** A close reading of the passage makes this the clear answer choice. While (C) is probably true, the passage notes that the stilts were helpful in navigating undrained marshes.

17. **D.** This is the meaning of *adept*. They may have enjoyed it or found it difficult, but these don't mean that they were adept at it.

18. **A.** This shows how well the race was greeted by the people of the area. The other answer choices don't reflect their enthusiasm.

19. **A.** While the route was chosen by the organizers of the race, they did not choose it because of the number of cafés. Familiarity with the route is not discussed in the passage, making answer choice (C) unlikely, and the passage also does not state whether the route went through well-populated areas, making answer choice (D) incorrect.

20. **D.** The competitors did not stop to sleep and were exhausted.

21. **A.** While the men did practice before the race, the passage says nothing about them studying the type of land they would be walking over, so answer choice (B) is incorrect. The passage does talk about chafe-proof clothing, but whether this is heavy or light is not mentioned. Answer choice (D) is incorrect, because the passage does not discuss the sleep habits of the contestants before the race.

22. **A.** The competitors were determined. It appears the competitors knew the land where the race took place, so answer choice (B) is incorrect. Whether there was better equipment available is unknown, so answer choice (C) is incorrect. The passage suggests that the shepherds liked to race each other, so answer choice (D) is incorrect.

23. **C.** There was little talk or comparison of different cultures, making answer choice (A) unlikely. The passage states that one newspaper organized this race, but the passage does not go on to make any statements along the lines of answer choice (B). Since the author discusses how the contestants practiced and modified their equipment in order to compete, answer choice (C) is correct. Answer choice (D) is a rather abstract statement that the author never fully discusses.

24. **B.** The winner actually averaged three miles per hour.

25. **C.** The word *narrowed* means "became fewer" in this case.

26. **B.** This is the most likely of the four answer choices, since the race occurred so long ago. Answer choice (A) is doubtful; the money was probably the motivating force.

27. **C.** The tips cushioned the stilts from the shock of walking over hard cobblestone pavements.

28. **C.** Specifically, Washington notes that "there were at least a half-dozen other places in the cabin that would have accommodated the cats" (lines 18–19). Based on this information, as well as on an earlier description of the room as having "openings in the side" (line 4), answer choice (C) is most supported by information in the passage.

29. **C.** This is the best answer choice. Since Washington is telling about his childhood in detail, answer choices (A) and (D) are unlikely. Washington addresses his family's desperate situation, so answer choice (B) is incorrect.

30. **B.** The family did not have enough food, and the mother was trying to feed them.

31. **C.** Eating the roasted sweet potatoes was a joy to Washington.

32. **A.** This is the intent of the paragraph. There is no comparison, so answer choice (B) is incorrect. Washington isn't complaining, so answer choice (C) is incorrect. He isn't being careful about how he talks about the conditions—he is blunt—so answer choice (D) is incorrect.

33. **A.** He thought it was similar to being in paradise, not an easy option for a young slave. Answer choice (B) doesn't relate to the passage. Washington doesn't seem fearful of trying school, so answer choice (C) is incorrect. The passage doesn't mention answer choice (D).

34. **D.** This is the one memory that Washington doesn't reveal.

35. **A.** This was surprising to Washington; the other answer choices were not.

36. **D.** This was the means by which the slaves acquired information.

37. **B.** This is the author's intent. While the Civil War is mentioned, it isn't the main point of the passage, so answer choice (A) is incorrect.

38. **B.** This seems to be the attitude the author has as he talks about his youth; there is no sense of anger or fear, so answer choices (A) and (C) are incorrect. Certainly, the author doesn't have an attitude of indifference or boredom about the hardships he endured in the past, so answer choice (D) is incorrect.

39. **A.** Washington states that he "went as far as the schoolhouse door with one of my young mistresses" (lines 58–59). The daughter of the plantation owner would be referred to by a slave as "my young mistress," making answer choice (A) the most plausible.

40. **B.** The passage says that this was the first time that Washington realized he was a slave and, therefore, not free.

41. **C.** A *contrivance* is a device or gadget.

42. **D.** Answer choices (A), (B), and (C) are all contradicted in the passage.

43. **A.** A close reading of the passage makes this the clear answer choice. The subjects in the other answer choices may have been written down, but the passage says that keeping track of personal possessions was a likely impetus for the development of writing.

44. **C.** This was the advantage of picture symbols.

45. **B.** Scribes helped rulers keep track of the collection of taxes, but the scribes were not rulers themselves, so answer choice (B) is more accurate than answer choice (A). Answer choice (C) covers a later topic, alphabets. Answer choice (D) may be true, but it is not supported by the passage.

46. **D.** Although this isn't directly stated in the passage, this conclusion is probable. Writing a symbol instead of drawing a jar would be a much faster way to keep track of what has been paid.

47. **A.** Both the United States and Sweden use the same signs for numbers; this can be inferred from the information in the passage.

48. **B.** It is theorized that merchants in the Middle East (in modern Lebanon, Israel, and Syria) made the first alphabet. Answer choice (D) is tempting, since both of these ancient countries had alphabets, but they were not the first.

49. **B.** Picture writing and hieroglyphics both preceded an alphabet. No alphabet was created before any language was spoken, so answer choice (C) is incorrect.

50. **A.** Logically, it would have to be English; all of the other languages predate English.

51. **A.** This is the reason that English is difficult to spell.

52. **D.** The passage clearly states that written Chinese is composed of picture symbols.

53. **C.** Certainly, the author doesn't believe that knowing how to write creates problems, so answer choice (A) is incorrect, nor would the author agree with answer choice (B) or answer choice (D).

54. **A.** This is the main reason that an alphabet is superior to a system of symbols. More people can learn it more easily, which means more people can learn to read and write.

55. **C.** This is the meaning of the word *immaterial*.

56. **B.** The reader is told about O. Henry's background being in federal prison, so this is an easy inference to make.

57. **A.** This is a figurative use of *bracelet*. There is no mention of a present, so answer choice (B) is incorrect. There is no mention that the bracelet was worth a lot of money, so answer choice (C) is incorrect.

58. **D.** Soon after Easton bemoans his lack of money and high social standing, he implies that the ambassador does not have these problems. Miss Fairchild interrupts him to state that the ambassador "doesn't call any more." The exchange makes it plausible that both men were vying for Miss Fairchild's attention and that Easton was jealous of the ambassador's money and social prominence.

59. **B.** The reader can determine this from the clues that the author gives about how Miss Fairchild feels about Easton, such as in the tenth paragraph, when the author says that she answers Easton "warmly."

60. **B.** The fact that he was handcuffed and a prisoner of the marshal was embarrassing to him.

61. **B.** Easton tells Miss Fairchild that the days of having fun are over for him; he is serious now. This is the figurative meaning of "butterfly days."

62. **B.** The marshal feels that if the conversation continues, Miss Fairfield will realize that Easton is the prisoner, not the marshal.

63. **A.** He notices the handcuff is on Easton's right hand.

64. **D.** This is the figurative meaning of money "taking wings," that is, flying away.

65. **C.** The passage says that the "look in the girl's eyes slowly changed to a bewildered horror" (lines 30–31).

66. **A.** The man is following the conversation and then reacts to it. It is unlikely he was trying to impress Miss Fairchild, so answer choice (B) is incorrect. He probably doesn't know why Easton came to the West, so answer choice (C) is incorrect.

67. **B.** This surprise ending is typical of O. Henry.

68. **A.** We can see through his actions that he is trying to help Easton in a difficult situation.

69. **B.** The paragraphs don't mention why she is on the train.

Chapter 9: Set 2 Reading Questions

70. **B.** This is the point of view from which the story is told. There is no evidence that the narrator rode on the fox hunt, is a member of the Paddock family, or has no riding ability.

71. **B.** The sentence "Travers had never ridden; but he had been prompted how to answer by Miss Paddock" (lines 18–19) makes answer choice (B) the best response.

72. **C.** This doesn't pose a reason to fear riding Monster; the other answer choices do.

73. **B.** Travers was worried about what he was told about the horse. There is no evidence that he was anxious about getting married, had a fever, or had indigestion.

74. **D.** Before the ride, Travers is worried about his riding skills, since he knows he will be judged by his fiancée's family in that regard. Once Travers learns that he will be riding a horse that has killed a man, his fear grows even worse.

75. **A.** For much of the ride, as Monster races ahead of the other horses, Travers has his eyes closed and is more or less clinging to the horse for dear life. Answer choice (A) best conveys this state of affairs.

76. **B.** The passage indicates that Travers tried to get Monster to the bridge, but the horse would not comply.

77. **B.** A locomotive "jumping the ties" is out of control and cannot be controlled.

78. **D.** Although the passage doesn't explicitly state young Paddock's motivation, this reason must be closest to the truth. Clearly, Monster was not the best horse, so answer choice (A) is incorrect. The passage doesn't mention a desire to upset his sister, so answer choice (B) is incorrect. It is doubtful that, considering what young Paddock said about Monster, he was trying to please Travers, so answer choice (C) is incorrect.

79. **A.** This is what the simile means.

80. **A.** The sacrifice was what he endured to gain the respect of his fiancée's family. The other answer choices would not have been sacrifices.

81. **B.** This is what *nonchalant* means.

82. **A.** The story is extremely amusing, but highly improbable.

83. **D.** This is the correct description of Travers. He was willing to do anything to please his bride-to-be and gain the admiration of her family.

84. **D.** The other answer choices are mentioned in the speech, but they aren't the main point of the second paragraph.

85. **B.** This is the meaning of the metaphor.

86. **A.** King wants to dramatize the situation.

87. **D.** This sentence speaks of transforming our nation into a symphony of brotherhood; it is hopeful. The other sentences don't support the idea that King has hope for a better world.

88. **C.** Manacles and chains evoke the image of a jail. A person would not be chained in a hospital or at work, and chains would not keep him safe.

89. **C.** This is what King is suggesting. The other answer choices aren't supported by the passage.

90. **A.** He repeats three times, "Now is the time . . .". He doesn't use the word *slowly*, so answer choice (B) is incorrect. He doesn't advocate preserving segregation, so answer choice (C) is incorrect. There is no mention in the speech of holding a vote on civil rights, so answer choice (D) is incorrect.

91. **D.** King is saying that the suffering endured by African-Americans at the hands of the police can be called godly. There is no mention of suffering being productive, so answer choice (A) is incorrect. King doesn't use the word *evil*, so answer choice (B) is incorrect. While it could be inferred that those who have suffered have faith (answer choice (C)), answer choice (D) is more accurate.

92. **C.** Here, the verb *wallow* means "to roll about lazily." *Self-indulgent* is a close synonym.

93. **A.** There is no indication that going back to the slums and ghettos in the North would be a hardship. The hardships are police brutality, racial injustice, and the fact that, 100 years after the Emancipation Proclamation, African-Americans are still not free.

94. **C.** Just as Americans in colonial days dreamed of freedom from British rule, King dreams of freedom from oppression for his people. He doesn't mention that his dream is difficult to understand, so answer choice (A) is incorrect. He doesn't talk of an African-American dream, so answer choice (B) is incorrect. He exhorts the audience to return to wherever they are from, South or North, and work to make the dream of freedom a reality.

95. **D.** King paints a grim portrait of the governor of Alabama. *Interposition* and *nullification* are strong words. Indeed, two months earlier, the governor had blocked the enrollment of African-American students at the University of Alabama. There is no sign of giving up hope in the paragraph, so answer choice (A) is incorrect. Certainly, the last thing the governor wants to see are white and black children playing together, so answer choice (B) is incorrect. Although the word *dripping* is suggestive, King is merely using a strong metaphor, so answer choice (C) is incorrect.

96. **A.** The metaphorical "sculpture" is a huge task, but it does represent the beginning of hope for freedom for all African-Americans. Creation of an actual sculpture isn't discussed, so answer choice (B) is incorrect.

97. **B.** King means that freedom will ring for all Americans; "God's children" refers to all human beings. King doesn't say that music is liberating, so answer choice (A) is incorrect. The song wouldn't have a new meaning, so answer choice (D) is incorrect.

98. **D.** The author does like the doll, but that isn't the main point of the passage, so answer choice (A) is incorrect. The passage doesn't argue against funding for people with disabilities, so answer choice (B) is incorrect. The passage doesn't support laws that protect people with disabilities, so answer choice (C) is incorrect.

99. **B.** When something is confounded, it is confused or mixed up. The other answer choices don't signify *confounding*.

100. **A.** This is why Helen felt pleasure and pride: she could copy her teacher and spell *doll* in her hand.

101. **C.** Helen quickly learned to mimic the way her teacher wrote words in her hand. She was deaf, so answer choice (A) is incorrect.

102. **C.** Although Helen could copy her teacher, she had no idea that the word referred to the doll she played with. She realized only later that she could communicate with others, so answer choice (A) is incorrect. The passage indicates that Helen could copy her teacher, so answer choice (D) is incorrect.

103. **A.** Although this isn't directly stated in the passage, there are clues that Helen was frustrated. There is no indication that she had many tantrums, so answer choice (B) is incorrect. The passage doesn't suggest that she thought the doll was ugly, so answer choice (C) is incorrect. The passage doesn't suggest that she wanted her mother's attention, so answer choice (D) is incorrect.

104. **B.** Prior to this incident, Helen showed little attachment to things.

105. **B.** This is the best description of Anne Sullivan. She was somewhat demanding but not particularly strict, so answer choice (A) is incorrect. Answer choices (C) and (D) are clearly incorrect.

106. **D.** Those barriers were swept away, and Helen went on to have a remarkable career.

107. **D.** The passage doesn't indicate the games that Helen liked to play.

108. **B.** Helen shows how much she appreciated Anne Sullivan for teaching her about language and how to communicate.

109. **B.** The entire passage concentrates on Helen's childhood, so answer choice (A) is incorrect. Her childhood was most likely quite different from that of girls who could see and hear, so answer choice (C) is incorrect. While there was sadness in her childhood, it was not overwhelming, so answer choice (D) is incorrect.

110. **B.** A key piece of information is the sentence "I knew then that "w-a-t-e-r" meant the wonderful cool something that was flowing over my hand." This statement, and the text surrounding it, makes answer choice (B) correct.

111. **D.** The experience created a sense of joy in Helen; it set her free. Communication was not impossible, as she found out, so answer choice (A) is incorrect; it certainly wasn't upsetting (answer choice (B)) or inevitable (answer choice (C)).

112. **C.** These people are ambidextrous and can use either hand for any purpose.

113. **D.** *Etiology* is the cause of a condition or a disease. *Custom* (answer choice (A)) and *essence* (answer choice (B)) don't make sense in the context of the paragraph. While *effect* (answer choice (C)) could possibly be correct, a close reading makes *cause* the best answer.

114. **B.** This is clearly stated in the third paragraph. Nowhere does the article state that left-handed people are happier (answer choice (A)) or that too much effort is given to the topic (answer choice (C)). The passage does say that a large preponderance of successful sports figures are left-handed, but doesn't make the same claim for musicians, so answer choice (D) is incorrect.

115. **A.** The fourth paragraph states that "lefties are often leaders in their fields." Answer choices (B) and (C) are touched on, but they aren't the main point of the passage; they are only examples that support the main point.

116. **D.** The author uses Queen Elizabeth and her family as an example of how left-handedness runs in families. Answer choices (A), (B), and (C) may be true, but none of them is the reason for including the Queen in the passage.

117. **C.** Handedness isn't a significant factor in computer use.

118. **C.** Dr. A. Klar argued in 2000 that right-handedness is determined by traits inherited from parents. Dr. Coren (answer choice (B)) thinks that preference for the left hand is due to mild brain injury, while Daniel Geschwind (answer choice (A)) believes that both of these, in addition to events early in life, are the cause. The passage states that Albert Einstein was left-handed, but he didn't focus on the study of left-handedness, so answer choice (D) is incorrect.

119. **B.** The first paragraph states that 90 percent of people are right-handed.

120. **B.** The passage states that scientists are "almost unanimous in arguing against" (lines 67–68) tying "the child's left hand behind its back" (lines 62–63).

121. **D.** The passage states that most power tools are made for right-handed people. The passage states that there are cooking utensils for left-handed people, so answer choice (A) is incorrect. The passage states that there are books on how to play the guitar with the left hand, so answer choice (B) is incorrect. The passage states that lefties can use a computer if the mouse is switched to the left side, so answer choice (C) is incorrect.

122. **B.** The passage doesn't mention legs, biting fingernails, or the size of one's hand.

123. **B.** While answer choice (D) may be tempting, nothing in the passage indicates that left-handed people are more intelligent, although it strongly suggests that many lefties excel at what they do. The passage does say that left-handed scissors are available, so one can infer that lefties have trouble with ordinary scissors.

124. **A.** Judging from the number of left-handed people and their need for products that are easier to use, this answer choice makes the most sense. Answer choice (B) may be true, but it is impossible to infer this from the seventh paragraph.

125. **B.** The desk problem is pointed out in the passage. Seating left-handed students together in the classroom would be of no benefit, although it might benefit them in the cafeteria, so answer choice (A) is incorrect.

Chapter 10: Set 3 Reading Questions

126. **A.** This is what Ivan fears if his wife wins the lottery. Answer choice (B) obviously doesn't pose a problem. Answer choices (C) and (D) are mentioned in the passage, but they aren't the main conflict.

127. **A.** Ivan responded to the number as a baby would—a baby who did not really know what was going on, but reacted instinctually.

128. **B.** The narrator certainly understands human nature and how it affects the situation.

129. **B.** Ivan is contemplating how rainy and miserable autumn is.

130. **B.** Masha doesn't want to give the money to her husband, so answer choice (A) is incorrect. Ivan doesn't want to buy his wife clothing, so answer choice (C) is incorrect. Nothing in the passage suggests that Masha would leave her husband, so answer choice (D) is incorrect.

131. **C.** There is no indication that his wife no longer is in love with him, so answer choice (A) is incorrect. It is unlikely that his wife has worked harder than Ivan has, so answer choice (B) is incorrect. There is no evidence that Ivan is younger than his wife, so answer choice (D) is incorrect.

132. **B.** This is what Ivan imagines will happen (lines 82–85).

133. **A.** Both Ivan and Masha have daydreams of what it would be like to win the lottery.

134. **D.** The word *begrudge* means "to resent," so it is clear that the author means that Ivan thought that Masha would be stingy.

135. **D.** This is the reason Ivan did not immediately look to find out the winning number. Nothing in the passage suggests that the other answer choices are correct.

136. **A.** Both Ivan and Masha fantasize about winning the lottery, and both go from being positive about each other to being angry with each other.

137. **D.** After Ivan and Masha learn that they have not won the lottery, their notion about their lives has changed for the worse.

138. **D.** Greed in this case pitted husband against wife.

139. **C.** Cain uses the word *underscored* to emphasize the need.

140. **D.** A close reading of the passage indicates that in the event that no candidate has received enough Electoral College votes, the House of Representatives decides who the next president will be.

141. **A.** This is Cain's main point. The other answer choices are merely details.

142. **C.** Electors aren't bound to vote for the choice of the people, which means they are free to vote for whomever they want. Answer choice (A) isn't relevant, and answer choice (B) isn't true. Answer choice (D) could happen but doesn't happen often.

143. **B.** The candidate who wins the popular vote in a state gets all of the state's electoral votes, so in effect the vote is a vote for Candidate B.

144. **B.** The word *anachronism* means something that is out-of-date or old-fashioned.

145. **C.** The Constitution is updated by adopting amendments. The other answer choices are mentioned in the passage, but they don't support this statement.

146. **D.** This isn't one of the reasons that the Electoral College system should be abandoned.

147. **B.** The word *defecting* means "abandoning."

148. **B.** She worries that American voters are losing faith in a system that they cannot directly affect.

149. **A.** Cain would be most likely to support a thorough review, because she is suggesting that the Constitution be updated.

150. **D.** The League of Women Voters wants to reinvigorate the voters in the country so they will be more interested in having their voices heard.

151. **D.** Cain uses this example to demonstrate how little it would take to change the outcome of elections and bypass the choice of the people.

152. **A.** This is the author's main point; she wants Congress to adopt an amendment that would abandon the Electoral College system.

153. **C.** Eastman is recalling the details of his youth. The narrator isn't an outsider, so answer choice (A) is incorrect. The narrator isn't a young person, so answer choice (B) is incorrect.

154. **A.** It is only in the spring that the sap runs in the trees.

155. **C.** The women wanted to see if the sap was flowing so they could tap the trees. The sentence doesn't refer to making canoes, gathering wood, or making fires, so the other answer choices are incorrect.

156. **C.** Answer choices (A) and (B) are irrelevant to the passage. The passage doesn't suggest that water was needed, so answer choice (D) is incorrect.

157. **D.** Prior knowledge makes this the clear answer choice. While the sap had to be stirred (answer choice (A)), this isn't the reason the boys tasted the syrup so often. Answer choices (B) and (C) are untrue.

158. **B.** While the grandmother does seem lenient about the boys' tasting the syrup (answer choice (C)), this isn't her chief quality.

159. **C.** The passage states that the sugar gathering was left to women, children, and old men, so it is probable that Eastman would join the other men on the fur-hunt.

160. **D.** The boys were looking forward to tasting the syrup.

161. **C.** The author was proud of his grandmother's industry. None of the other answer choices is suggested by the passage.

162. **D.** *Pulverize* means "to crush into tiny pieces."

163. **C.** The sentence "The box-elder yielded a beautiful white sugar, whose only fault was that there was never enough of it!" (lines 53–55) points to answer choice (C) as correct.

164. **D.** The grandmother seemed to be the one who was running the maple sugar project. There is no evidence that she did not want to participate in the sugar gathering, so answer choice (A) is incorrect. There is no evidence that she thought her grandson was working too hard, so answer choice (B) is incorrect.

165. **D.** The passage clearly states that the tribe didn't have tea and coffee. The items in the other answer choices were all eaten with sugar.

166. **A.** The author thinks back on his childhood with warmth.

167. **A.** Answer choice (A) is the only answer choice that fits the context of the second paragraph.

168. **C.** Like all electromagnetic particles, light travels in waves. Only blue light has a wavelength of 450 to 500 nanometers, so answer choice (A) is incorrect.

169. **C.** The main point isn't that LED screens emit blue light (answer choice (A)) or that the research was conducted in a controlled setting (answer choice (B)).

170. **B.** *Cognitive* most nearly means "mental" and includes the areas of perception, memory, and reasoning, and *performance* means "process."

171. **A.** The huge increase in the use of tablets, e-readers, and smartphones causes concern, because they are held closer to the eyes, with increased exposure to blue-light emissions.

172. **B.** The entire paragraph is about melatonin, and the key point is that the hormone regulates our daily sleep/wake cycle. The other answer choices are merely supporting details.

173. **D.** The National Sleep Foundation is cited as the source for answer choice (A), so this answer choice is incorrect. While answer choices (B) and (C) are mentioned in the passage, neither is associated with the two research projects.

174. **C.** Wearing a dimesimeter, a recording device, would not accomplish anything. Watching movies on TV (answer choice (A)), cutting down on nighttime use of the computer (answer choice (B)), and using f.lux (answer choice (D)) are all ways to reduce the melatonin-lowering effects of blue light.

175. **D.** The author cites data from the National Sleep Foundation to make readers aware of the possible consequences of excessive nighttime computer use. Melatonin supplements (answer choice (A)) aren't discussed in the passage, and nowhere does the passage suggest that replacing fluorescent lighting (answer choice (C)) would help readers get more sleep.

176. **C.** The first lines of the paragraph state that the RPI findings "built on what the Basel researchers discovered."

177. **D.** The author hopes that f.lux software is only the first step in finding ways to control blue light.

178. **A.** While blue light's rays are shorter than those of visible light, they aren't the shortest. The other answer choices accurately describe blue light.

179. **B.** It is logical to assume that the RPI engineers feel that their study offers useful information to computer users, especially those who often use the computer at night.

180. **A.** The other answer choices are found in the passage, but they are details—not the main idea.

181. **C.** This deduction is based on information in the early part of the passage. Answer choice (B) might be correct, but there isn't any evidence to support it. Based on what the author tells the reader about Theodoric, answer choice (D) is incorrect.

182. **C.** Theodoric didn't realize that his traveling companion was blind until the end of the passage. Although answer choice (D) is appealing, most people don't do odd things when they travel.

183. **A.** While all of the events were important, the disclosure affects the outcome of the story the most.

184. **D.** The other answer choices aren't indicated by the information in the passage.

185. **C.** This is the reason that Theodoric decided to put his clothes back on; the train was approaching the station and he would be seen by many people.

186. **D.** The mouse's crawling in his pants and biting him forced Theodoric to do something he would never have done otherwise.

187. **D.** The author uses a somewhat figurative way to express that the mouse was inside Theodoric's clothes. There is no suggestion that the mouse was nesting in Theodoric's clothes, so answer choice (A) is incorrect.

188. **B.** Theodoric is embarrassed and wants to give a logical reason why he has the rug over himself. Theodoric doesn't suggest that it is cold on the train, so answer choice (A) is incorrect.

189. **A.** It is clear from the way in which the author writes about Theodoric that he finds him humorous.

190. **B.** Theodoric is worried that his traveling companion will be horrified that he doesn't have all his clothes on and will call for help.

191. **B.** Theodoric thinks that the traveling companion is having a good time at his expense.

192. **C.** The author knows that the traveling companion's blindness is a very important detail, so answer choice (A) is incorrect.

193. **C.** The author obviously has fun writing the story and uses a tongue-in-cheek tone.

194. **B.** Theodoric was surprised and perhaps somewhat angry, but he most certainly was relieved.

Chapter 11: Set 4 Reading Questions

195. **B.** The narrator sees that he will never study French again and that Monsieur Hamel will be leaving; his life will never be the same.

196. **D.** Frantz wanted to skip school, but he did not. Nothing in the passage suggests that he wanted to help his teacher (answer choice (A)) or that he wanted to speak to the Prussians (answer choice (C)).

197. **A.** The villagers came to show respect to the teacher and say goodbye to him. The Prussians, not the villagers, decided that the teacher should be let go, so answer choice (B) is incorrect.

198. **C.** This is an example of foreshadowing. Frantz understood that something was not right because of how solemn the class was.

199. **B.** There is no indication of a tradition of the villagers' presence when Frantz was in trouble, so answer choice (A) is incorrect. There is no evidence that the villagers' presence caused Frantz to become even more nervous (answer choice (C)) or to forget his lesson (answer choice (D)).

200. **B.** Monsieur Hamel showed greater patience with Frantz than before, when he punished him with his ruler.

201. **C.** Frantz was extremely upset that Monsieur Hamel would be gone.

202. **C.** This is the main point of the passage and the lesson that it teaches.

203. **C.** Monsieur Hamel realizes that Frantz has lost his chance to study French and that Frantz feels badly.

204. **B.** The lesson was not easier, so answer choice (A) is incorrect. Frantz was not less concerned about doing well, so answer choice (C) is incorrect. There is no indication that it was a repeated lesson, so answer choice (D) is incorrect.

205. **D.** The use of *blared* tells the reader that the author didn't look favorably on the Prussians.

206. **B.** Monsieur Hamel's attitude might have been even stronger: he may have hated the Prussians.

207. **D.** The fact that he must leave after teaching and living in the building for 40 years was like a death to him.

208. **D.** Since Monsieur Hamel wrote his message on the board, it is unlikely that he forgot what he needed to say (answer choice (A)) or didn't know what to say (answer choice (B)). There is no indication that he was losing his voice (answer choice (C)).

209. **A.** This is the most likely reason that they turned back.

210. **A.** This is the main point of the paragraph. The other answer choices are details—not the main idea.

211. **B.** The passage doesn't mention a fleet of ships, but does state that the Yuan Dynasty offered the items in the other three answer choices.

212. **C.** A close reading of the paragraph makes this the clear answer choice. There is no mention of the number of artists, so answer choice (A) is incorrect. Europe was older than the Yuan Dynasty, so answer choice (D) is incorrect.

213. **B.** It is logical that Columbus admired Polo and wanted to be a great explorer too.

214. **B.** A close reading of the passage makes it clear that the Venetians thought his book was all lies.

215. **C.** Nothing in the passage suggests that Khan was cruel (answer choice (A)) or kind (answer choice (D)). While he expressed an interest in Christianity, this doesn't mean that he wanted to become a Christian, so answer choice (B) is incorrect.

216. **B.** The passage refers to the wealth that the Polos amassed—an indication that they had a good reason to stay there. They may have wanted to help Khan (answer choice (A)), but this was not the main reason they stayed.

217. **D.** In the sixth paragraph, the reader learns that Marco Polo was the commander of a galley.

218. **B.** Nothing in the passage suggests that the princess did not enjoy traveling by herself (answer choice (A)), that she was hesitant to leave her homeland (answer choice (C)), or that she might run away (answer choice (D)).

219. **D.** According to the sixth paragraph, Marco Polo commanded a ship and lost a naval battle.

220. **C.** The paragraph identifies the failure to mention the Great Wall of China as one of the historians' reasons.

221. **A.** This is probably the best proof; there is a saying that dying men tell no lies.

222. **A.** While the author mentions that Marco Polo did have great wealth (answer choice (B)), this isn't his overall feeling toward Polo.

223. **C.** The author says that in winter "the moon achieves a fuller triumph," that is, it seems bigger.

224. **B.** Winter brings out the sinewy part of the mind, not imagination (answer choice (A)), passion (answer choice (C)), or sadness (answer choice (D)).

225. **A.** Answer choice (A) describes winter, not summer.

226. **A.** According to the author, winter is a time for "studies and disciplines."

227. **C.** There is no mention in the paragraph that winter is a victim of summer (answer choice (A)), that it gives less joy than summer (answer choice (B)), or that it is harder to live through (answer choice (D)).

228. **C.** The author is romantic, but sees deeply into things. There is no suggestion that the author is overwrought and tense, so answer choice (A) is incorrect. The author might be considered intellectual, but he is hardly pragmatic, so answer choice (B) is incorrect. There is no suggestion that the author is cynical and despairing (answer choice (D))—quite the opposite.

229. **B.** The paragraph does state that snow makes the fence look like iron (answer choice (A)), but that is a detail—not the main idea.

230. **B.** The work that the chopper does warms his body. He may be wearing a heavy sweater (answer choice (A)), but that isn't the point that the author is making.

231. **A.** The first sentence of the paragraph states, "All sounds are sharper in winter; the air transmits better" (lines 61–62). This is reinforced in the next sentence, which states that another sound is heard "more distinctly."

232. **D.** The author makes it clear that he isn't talking about conventional heat. There is no mention of making a fire more easily (answer choice (A)) or the air being dry (answer choice (B)).

233. **D.** The author enjoys the sound of the fox and imagines things about the animal. It doesn't annoy (answer choice (A)) or frighten (answer choice (B)) him. Nor does he find it chilling (answer choice (C)).

234. **B.** The author likens winter to an artist several times in the passage.

235. **C.** Winter isn't sentimental; summer is.

236. **D.** The snow keeps a record of the footprints of animals and people.

237. **A.** Gravity is a consequence of distortion in space and time, according to Einstein. The other answer choices are all characteristics of black holes.

238. **D.** The passage states that Einstein foreshadowed the possibility of the existence of black holes in 1915.

239. **C.** NuSTAR measures high-energy X-ray light (lines 58–59).

240. **B.** By measuring the speed and orbit of stars and interstellar gases as they orbit a black hole, scientists can measure the mass of the black hole.

241. **C.** The Chandra X-ray Observatory can measure X-rays that are absorbed by the atmosphere and cannot be detected on Earth. The phrase "read a stop sign from a distance of 12 miles" (answer choice (A)) is used by the author merely to indicate the acuity of the telescope.

242. **C.** By quoting from the autobiography of Dr. Wheeler at the end of the passage, the author makes clear that the nature of the universe may never be fully understood.

243. **A.** When the star collapses on itself, its mass becomes infinitely dense and is known as a singularity.

244. **A.** The paragraph states this statistic as 24 million miles vs. 93 million miles, or slightly more than 25%. Sgr A* has a mass equivalent to 4 million suns, so answer choice (C) is incorrect. Answer choices (B) and (D) are facts, not inferences.

245. **B.** Newton defined gravity as a force, a theory that was superseded by Einstein's *General Theory of Relativity*.

246. **C.** The first sentence of the ninth paragraph states that "some people believe that black holes are 'wormholes' that lead to another dimension and another universe." Answer choices (A) and (B) are false statements. Wormholes might be a fantasy (answer choice (D)), but there is no way to prove the theory.

247. **D.** Although his autobiography is quoted in the last paragraph, Dr. Wheeler is best known for first using the term "black hole."

248. **D.** Because nothing can enter a black hole without being destroyed, there is no way to prove any theory about whether black holes lead anywhere.

249. **C.** According to the passage, "the gravitational attraction nearly equals the speed of light" at the event horizon (lines 35–36), so you would be overwhelmed.

250. **C.** Dr. Wheeler is saying that these laws aren't permanent.

PART III

ENGLISH

CHAPTER 12
SET 1 ENGLISH QUESTIONS

QUESTIONS 251-375

In the passages that follow, certain words and phrases are underlined and numbered. Each number refers to a question that offers alternatives for the underlined word or phrase. In most cases, you are to choose the answer that best expresses the idea, makes the statement appropriate for standard written English, or is worded most consistently with the style and tone of the passage as a whole. If you think that the original version is best, choose "NO CHANGE."

There are also questions about a section of the passage or about the passage as a whole. These questions do not refer to an underlined portion of the passage, but are identified by numbers in boxes.

Alice Paul: Suffragette

Suffragette Alice Paul was born in New Jersey in 1885. She went on to found the National Women's Party and dedicate
251
her entire life to the cause that men and women should be

equal in society. Although raised as a Quaker, she believed, like
252
all Quakers, in gender equality. Even as a child, she attended meetings of the American Suffrage Association. Paul had an exceptionally keen mind. She earned a B.A. from Swarthmore College in 1905, an M.A. and a Ph.D. from the University of Pennsylvania in 1907 and 1912 and three law degrees from
253
American University—a bachelor, masters, and doctor of law in the 1920s.

Paul having traveled to England in 1907. It was there that
254
she met the militant suffragette Emmeline Pankhurst, who

believed that prayers and petitions were not enough and that
255

action was needed. As they were arrested and imprisoned
256
several times, but their actions resulted in newspaper stories

251. **A.** NO CHANGE
   B. Party, and
   C. Party; and
   D. Party and,

252. **A.** NO CHANGE
   B. While
   C. When
   D. OMIT the underlined portion.

253. **A.** NO CHANGE
   B. 1912; and
   C. 1912: and
   D. 1912, and

254. **A.** NO CHANGE
   B. had traveled
   C. was traveling
   D. OMIT the underlined portion.

255. **A.** NO CHANGE
   B. believing
   C. having believed
   D. was believing

256. **A.** NO CHANGE
   B. After
   C. When
   D. OMIT the underlined portion.

that brought their struggle out into the open. In prison, Paul
                                                        257
would take comfort from Thomas Jefferson's words, "Resistance

to tyranny is obedience to God."

[1] Paul returned to the U.S. in 1910. [2] It was in 1916 that

she founded the National Women's Party. [3] She and others

became famous for what the press called "Silent Sentinels." 258

[4] They were arrested many times, while the tactic brought
                                                        259
them publicity, and ceding to the public outcry, President

Woodrow Wilson reversing his position against equal rights.
                          260
[5] The women would stand outside the White House day after

day bearing banners demanded equal rights. [6] Congress
                           261
passed the Nineteenth Amendment: "The right of citizens of

the United States to vote shall not be, denied or abridged, by
                                       262
the United States or by any State on account of sex." [7]

The amendment was ratified and
                 263

became law on August 26, 1920. 264

In the 1920s, Paul continues to champion women's rights,
                        265
proposing an Equal Rights Amendment that guaranteed

absolute equality. She founded the Women's World Party in

1938, based in Geneva, Switzerland, and traveled all over the

world. She worked to ensure that gender equality was included

in the United Nations Charter.

The Equal Rights Amendment (ERA) was finally passed by

Congress in 1972. Paul died on July 9, 1977.

The ERA yet has not been ratified, needing approval by
        266
three more states before it can become the Twenty-eighth

Amendment.

257. **A.** NO CHANGE
     B. When in prison
     C. After being in prison
     D. While in prison

258. The writer is considering revising the last part of the
     preceding sentence ("for what the press called 'Silent
     Sentinels'") to read as "for their demonstrations." If the
     writer did this, the essay would primarily lose
     A. Paul's purpose for the demonstrations.
     B. the idea that Paul was not demonstrating alone.
     C. Paul's description of the demonstrations.
     D. the name given to the demonstrations by the media.

259. **A.** NO CHANGE
     B. but
     C. since
     D. OMIT the underlined portion.

260. **A.** NO CHANGE
     B. reversed
     C. was reversing
     D. has reversed

261. **A.** NO CHANGE
     B. demanding
     C. are demanding
     D. was demanding

262. **A.** NO CHANGE
     B. not be denied or abridged, by
     C. not be, denied or abridged by state on
     D. not be denied or abridged by

263. **A.** NO CHANGE
     B. amendment ratified
     C. amendment is being ratified
     D. amendment is ratified

264. For the sake of the logic and coherence of the paragraph,
     Sentence 5 should be
     A. placed where it is now.
     B. placed after Sentence 3.
     C. placed after Sentence 6.
     D. OMITTED from the paragraph.

265. **A.** NO CHANGE
     B. is continuing
     C. continued
     D. will continue

266. **A.** NO CHANGE
     B. ERA but has
     C. ERA still has
     D. ERA that has

Life at the South Pole

The Amundsen-Scott South Pole Station is situated at the Geographic South Pole on the Antarctic Continent. It is absolutely the most southern place on the Earth. The
267
facility is named after the first two men to reach the South

Pole just months apart: they were the Norwegian explorer
268
Roald Amundsen, who arrived on December 14, 1911, and Robert F. Scott of Great Britain, who reached the South Pole on January 17, 1912. Tragically, Scott and his party died from exposure on their return journey. It wasn't until 1956 that
269
the United States opened a research facility at the South Pole. The current station, the third on the site, was completed in 2008 and is elevated on stilts so it cannot be buried by drifting snow.

Located at an elevation of just exactly 9,306 feet, the station
270
sits above a sheet of ice 9,000 feet thick. Conditions are

difficult; during the six months from April to September, which
271
is winter in the South Pole, the sun never shines and the

temperature falls to 100 degrees below zero. Consequently,
272
during this period 50 or so scientists remain at the station,

but during the summer, the population gets to over 150.
273
In spite of being located in such a remote place, the Amundsen-Scott South Pole Station is alive with numerous scientific studies. 274 This is because the station is a prime location for research for a number of scientific disciplines,

all of which are represented with experiments.
275
The Martin A. Pomerantz Observatory, known as MAPO, was named after the astronomer who first realized the value of Antarctica for telescopes because of its cleaner, thinner

267. **A.** NO CHANGE
    B. so very far south
    C. just the most southern point
    D. the southernmost point

268. **A.** NO CHANGE
    B. they had been
    C. they were being
    D. OMIT the underlined portion.

269. **A.** NO CHANGE
    B. from the very cold weather they were having
    C. from not having enough warm clothes
    D. from the way they had to travel over ice

270. **A.** NO CHANGE
    B. exactly around 9,306 feet
    C. about 9,306 feet
    D. 9,306 feet

271. Given that all of the choices are true, which one best emphasizes the extent of the difficulty of the weather in the South Pole?
    A. NO CHANGE
    B. extremely severe and life-threatening
    C. hard to deal with
    D. freezing cold most of the time

272. Which of the following alternatives to the underlined portion would NOT be acceptable?
    A. As a result
    B. Accordingly
    C. Because of this
    D. In spite of this

273. **A.** NO CHANGE
    B. swells
    C. grows
    D. increases

274. If the writer were to delete the words *remote* and *numerous* from the preceding sentence, the sentence would primarily lose
    A. a feeling that the station is open to everyone.
    B. a suggestion of the nature of the scientific research that goes on in the station.
    C. a contrast between the location and the number of scientists working there.
    D. a sense of where the station is in Antarctica.

275. Given that all of the choices are true, which one best supports the sentence's claim about the Amundsen-Scott South Pole Station's being a prime location for a number of scientific disciplines?
    A. NO CHANGE
    B. all of which come from many countries.
    C. such as geology, biology, astrophysics, and oceanography.
    D. but no one owns the continent of Antarctica.

and has no light <u>light pollution atmosphere,</u> spends the long winter
276
night searching the skies. The observatory is a two-story

elevated structure and is home to equipment that operates

and supports four projects: the Antarctic Muon and Neutrino

Detector Array (AMANDA), the South Pole Infrared Explorer

(SPIREX), the Cosmic Background Radiation Anisotropy

(COBRA) experiment, and the Advanced Telescope Project

(ATP). 277

    Nearby, the radio telescope probes the universe for dark

matter. Not far from the observatory is the world's largest

neutrino detector. Called <u>IceCube it</u> is buried one and a half
278
miles below the surface identifying neutrinos, charged, sub-

atomic particles that arise from exploding stars, black holes,

<u>and, also,</u> neutron stars and travel at the speed of light. The
279
electromagnetic radiation they emit when they hit the ice is

analyzed by computers on the surface. <u>However,</u> scientists are
280
hoping to discover the origin of high-energy cosmic rays.

    Scientists from all over the world <u>takes</u> advantage of the
281
unique conditions the continent provides to conduct their

research. Altogether, 30 countries maintain permanent or

seasonal facilities on the Antarctic Ice Shelf. 282

276. A. NO CHANGE
    B. and a no light pollution atmosphere,
    C. atmosphere with no pollution,
    D. atmosphere that has no light pollution at all,

277. At this point, the writer is considering adding the following true statement:

> Pomerantz was one of the pioneers in balloon-borne cosmic ray research in the 1940s and 1950s.

Should the writer make this addition here?
    A. Yes, because it tells more about who Pomerantz was.
    B. Yes, because it fits in with the overall point of the essay.
    C. No, because it doesn't tell enough about why the observatory was named for Pomerantz.
    D. No, because the information would be off the main topic of what the observatory does.

278. A. NO CHANGE
    B. IceCube, it
    C. IceCube. It
    D. IceCube; it

279. A. NO CHANGE
    B. and
    C. and as well,
    D. and too

280. A. NO CHANGE
    B. Because
    C. As a result,
    D. OMIT the underlined portion.

281. A. NO CHANGE
    B. take
    C. has taken
    D. OMIT the underlined portion.

282. If the writer were to delete the phrase "permanent or seasonal" from the preceding sentence, the sentence would primarily lose
    A. the feeling that many scientists prefer not to use the facilities.
    B. the notion that most facilities are permanent.
    C. the suggestion that most scientists work during the winter months.
    D. the idea that not all of the scientific facilities operate full-time.

El Yunque

El Yunque National Forest is the only tropical rain forest in the United States. This marvelous attraction, located near the eastern end of Puerto Rico, has been a part of the U.S. National Forest Service <u>from as long ago as</u> 1903. Part of the Sierra de
283

Luquillo Mountain <u>Range, El Yunque</u> covers over 28,000 acres.
284
The mountain itself has an elevation of 3,543 feet and offers

<u>some of the better</u> views of the surrounding areas.
285
The name "El Yunque" comes from a Taino word, *Yuque*, meaning "white lands." The Taino, who were native to the island, named the rain forest "Yuque" because there were always <u>big flowing</u> white clouds surrounding the mountain at
286
the center of the forest. These people believed that a god

<u>in the mountain</u> lived and that he would protect them.
287

Climbing up the <u>mountains slope</u>, visitors can see Yokahu
288
Tower. At an elevation of 1,900 feet and 70 feet high, the tower offers a magnificent panoramic view of the Atlantic Ocean and San Juan, the capital of Puerto Rico. El Yunque's peak,

<u>which was earlier noted,</u> is almost always
289

<u>within</u> clouds and mist, averages over 240 inches of rain a year.
290

<u>Incredibly,</u> there are 175 tree species in El Yunque, 23 of which
291
are only found there, and 150 species of ferns. Exotic vegetation like the Palo Colorado Palm and the Giant Tree Fern thrive, and dozens of brightly colored bromeliad varieties abound. 292

283. A. NO CHANGE
B. as far back as
C. since
D. OMIT the underlined portion.

284. A. NO CHANGE
B. Range El Yunque
C. Range. El Yunque
D. Range; El Yunque

285. A. NO CHANGE
B. long vistas
C. astonishing
D. OMIT the underlined portion.

286. A. NO CHANGE
B. many
C. large
D. billowy

287. The best placement for the underlined portion would be
A. where it is now.
B. before the word *god*.
C. before the word *and*.
D. before the word *that*.

288. A. NO CHANGE
B. mountains slope
C. mountains' slope,
D. mountain's slope,

289. A. NO CHANGE
B. which the writer had earlier stated about the mountain
C. which the reader learned in the preceding paragraph
D. which was mentioned earlier on in the essay

290. A. NO CHANGE
B. shrouded in
C. covered up with
D. OMIT the underlined portion.

291. A. NO CHANGE
B. However
C. Realistically
D. OMIT the underlined portion.

292. If the writer were to delete the word *exotic* from the preceding sentence, the sentence would primarily lose
A. a firm understanding of the extent of vegetation in El Yunque.
B. the contrast between the forms of vegetation and tree variety.
C. the thought that El Yunque has many forms of vegetations.
D. the suggestion that these are not everyday forms of vegetation.

Visitors can explore the many hiking trails in the park,

of which there are many. El Yunque Rock, a massive outcrop-
_____
293

ping rising above the forest, is a popular destination. Other

attractions include the many waterfalls and rocky pools.

La Coca Falls has a spectacular drop of 185 feet. The water

temperature remains at about 60 degrees all year round, and

visitors often enjoy a dip in the crystal waters at its base before

continuing their hike.

[1] So many creatures abound in El Yunque. [2] Its home to
                                                      ‾‾‾
                                                      294
the Puerto Rican Parrot, *Amazona vittata,* which is bright

green, with white-ringed eyes and around the beak a brilliant red.
                                        _____
                                              295
[3] Puerto Rico once was filled with the bird. [4] Conservation

efforts began in 1968, and today there are more than 40

in El Yunque and over 100 in captivity. [5] But civilization

encroached and, by the 1960s, there were only two dozen left.

[6] El Yunque also has 13 species of coquí, the tiny tree frog

found all over the island, and loved for its unique call, which

sounds like its name. [7] The call rings out from dusk until
                                 ‾‾‾‾‾‾‾‾‾
                                   296

dawn each night. It is a sound that all Puerto Ricans love. 297

A visit to El Yunque will give one a sense of the way that the

early Taino people must have viewed this special place, which

they thought of as magical; it is certainly a must-see for every

visitor. 298

293. Given that all of the choices are true, which one provides the most significant new information?
  A. NO CHANGE
  B. which are rated at levels from easy to strenuous.
  C. which are found all over the forest.
  D. which are enjoyed by many people.

294. A. NO CHANGE
  B. It's
  C. Its'
  D. OMIT the underlined portion.

295. The best placement for the underlined portion would be
  A. where it is now.
  B. after the word *eyes.*
  C. after the word *brilliant.*
  D. after the word *red.*

296. A. NO CHANGE
  B. continues
  C. says
  D. declares

297. For the sake of the logic and coherence of the paragraph, Sentence 5 should be placed
  A. where it is now.
  B. after Sentence 1.
  C. after Sentence 3.
  D. after Sentence 6.

298. If the writer were to change the pronoun *one* to *you* in the preceding sentence, this closing sentence would
  A. suggest that the writer is trying to tell the reader what to do.
  B. make the essay's audience feel uncomfortable.
  C. create a more appealing and personal tone.
  D. indicate that the writer is confused.

The Life of Abdul Rahman

The story of the life of Abdul Rahman is a strange and tragic one. He was born in Timbuktu, a famous city in western Africa
<u>299</u>
in 1769. His father was the king of Futa Jallon, a small

kingdom near Timbuktu. Abdul was heir to the throne and

was educated to be a <u>king, he</u> studied geography, mathematics,
<u>300</u>
astronomy, and the history and laws of his country.

<u>He was also a student of Islam, his religion.</u>
<u>301</u>

The first white man Abdul <u>ever seen</u> was John C. Cox, an
<u>302</u>
English surgeon who traveled through their kingdom. Cox

became ill with malaria and recuperated at the court of Abdul's

father. Cox stayed for <u>six months time.</u> During that time, Cox
<u>303</u>

<u>learned about the culture.</u> When he felt better and wanted to
<u>304</u>

return to England, the king <u>paying his fare</u> and sent men to
<u>305</u>
escort him safely to the ship.

[1] Seven years later, Abdul <u>was taking</u> prisoner
<u>306</u>
and sold as a slave in Natchez, Mississippi. [2] Abdul,

<u>that was called Prince,</u> worked in the fields with other slaves.
<u>307</u>
[3] John Cox happened to visit Mississippi and found Abdul.

[4] Seventeen years passed. [5] He tried to buy his friend's

freedom, but was unsuccessful. <u>308</u>

Abdul's master would not sell this slave, his <u>more productive</u>
<u>309</u>
one. Finally, in 1829, Abdul and his wife were freed and sent

---

299. A. NO CHANGE
B. Timbuktu, a famous city in western Africa,
C. Timbuktu; a famous city in western Africa
D. Timbuktu a famous city in Western Africa

300. A. NO CHANGE
B. king; he
C. king—he
D. king. He

301. Which choice would most effectively conclude this paragraph?
A. NO CHANGE
B. The history of his country was complicated.
C. He was a good student and became knowledgeable about many things.
D. Islam was the predominant religion of his country.

302. A. NO CHANGE
B. ever saw
C. ever had seen
D. ever had been seen

303. A. NO CHANGE
B. six months' time
C. six month's time
D. six month times

304. Given that all of the choices are true, which choice provides more information that is relevant and that makes the rest of the essay understandable?
A. NO CHANGE
B. Cox became good friends with young Abdul.
C. Cox met with many different people.
D. Cox learned about Islam.

305. A. NO CHANGE
B. paid his fare
C. was paying his fare
D. has paid his fare

306. A. NO CHANGE
B. was taken
C. had been taken
D. taken

307. A. NO CHANGE
B. who was called Prince
C. whom was called Prince
D. which was called Prince

308. Which of the following sequences of sentences makes the paragraph most logical?
A. NO CHANGE
B. 1, 4, 2, 5, 3
C. 2, 1, 3, 4, 5
D. 1, 2, 4, 3, 5

309. A. NO CHANGE
B. most
C. mostest
D. OMIT the underlined portion.

with 160 other African-Americans to live in Liberia, a country
<u>310</u>
on the west coast of Africa. Liberia was a new country set up in

1822 by the American Colonization Society to provide a home

for freed slaves from America. [311] Abdul's job in his new

country was developing trade and good relations with nearby

African nations <u>through diplomacy.</u>
312

<u>He wrote to his relatives to get money to free his children</u>
313
<u>and grandchildren from enslavement in America.</u> Some men
313

were given $7,000 in gold to bring to Abdul. <u>However before</u>
314
they reached Liberia, they were told that Abdul was dead.

Unfortunately for Abdul's children, they decided to return

home with the gold.

The African historian Professor Kazembe has said, "The sad

story of Abdul Rahman symbolizes the tragedy of slavery." This

tragedy was recently featured in a made-for-TV movie that

depicted the importance of Abdul's life.

310. A. NO CHANGE
B. to be living
C. who live
D. to lived

311. If the writer were to delete the phrase "by the American Colonization Society," the passage would lose a detail that
A. shows that Liberians were magnanimous about accepting freed slaves.
B. lends historical accuracy to the paragraph.
C. is critical of the efforts of Americans to colonize Liberia.
D. provides an origin for the meaning of the word *Liberia*.

312. The best placement for the underlined portion would be
A. where it is now.
B. after the word *developing*.
C. after the word *country*.
D. after the word *relations*.

313. A. NO CHANGE
B. Wanting to get his children and grandchildren free from slavery in America, he wrote to his relatives to get money.
C. To get his children and grandchildren freed from slavery in America, he wanted to write to his relatives to get money.
D. To get money, he wrote to his relatives to free his children and grandchildren from enslavement in America.

314. A. NO CHANGE
B. However, before
C. However—before
D. However; before

Tsunamis

Note: The following paragraphs may not be in the most logical order. Each paragraph is numbered; question 330 asks you to choose where Paragraph 2 would most logically be placed.

[1] Tsunamis can occur in any <u>ocean, most</u> are in the Pacific
                                    315

Ocean, where there <u>were</u> many quakes in the sea and on land.
                          316

The Pacific Ocean <u>strongly affected</u> by volcanoes. A volcano
                          317
or earthquake may create a tsunami in the ocean thousands

of miles away. The majority of tsunamis occur near Hawaii,

Alaska, Japan, and the West Coast of the United States. The

explosion of the volcano <u>Krakatoa, near Java, in 1883,</u> resulted
                                318
in a tsunami that killed 36,000 people many miles from there.

[2] Imagine a wall of ocean water reaching 100 feet high.

This wave crashes onto the shore, crushing buildings and

washing thousands of people out to sea. Scientists

<u>call this amazing phenomenon of the ocean a tsunami;</u>
                          319

<u>Japanese for "storm wave."</u> It destroys towns and kills thousands
        320

of people. Tsunamis are also known as tidal waves, although <u>it has</u>
                                                                        321

nothing to do with actual tides. ⬚322⬚

[3] What causes this horrifying disaster? The cause

can be either an undersea earthquake, called a seaquake

<u>more often,</u> or a volcanic eruption or earthquake on land.
    323
Oceanographer Patrick Martin says, "A tsunami is created

315. A. NO CHANGE
B. ocean most
C. ocean. Most
D. ocean—most

316. A. NO CHANGE
B. have been
C. will be
D. are

317. A. NO CHANGE
B. will be strongly affected
C. strongly affect
D. can be strongly affected

318. A. NO CHANGE
B. Krakatoa; near Java in 1883,
C. Krakatoa near Java, in 1883,
D. Krakatoa, near Java; in 1883.

319. Which of the choices best emphasizes the damage a tsunami can cause?
A. NO CHANGE
B. call this terror of the ocean
C. label this force of nature
D. have given it a name—

320. A. NO CHANGE
B. . Japanese for "storm wave."
C. : Japanese for "storm wave."
D. Japanese for "storm wave."

321. A. NO CHANGE
B. it had
C. they had
D. they have

322. At this point, the writer is considering adding the following true statement:

Tides are caused by the gravitational forces of the sun and moon.

Should the writer make this addition here?
A. Yes, because it informs the reader as to the cause of tides.
B. Yes, because it reinforces in the reader's mind that the writer is knowledgeable.
C. No, because it contradicts what the writer states in the rest of the paragraph.
D. No, because it distracts the reader from the main focus of the passage.

323. The best placement for the underlined portion would be
A. where it is now.
B. before the word *called*.
C. after the word *land* (before the period).
D. before the word *The*.

when a quake causes land shifted underwater." When a tsunami
                                   324
begins, it creates low waves that speed along at up to 500 miles

per hour. However, this doesn't immediately cause huge waves
           325
to form out on the ocean. Instead, these small swells of water

rush along and then turn into a huge wave near land. As the

ocean becomes shallowest, the tsunami near the shore builds
                 326

up, pulling water up with it and exposes the sea bottom. Then
                                  327
the tsunami strikes the shore with devastating force.

[4] The Pacific Tsunami Warning Center in Hawaii monitors

seaquakes and sent out warnings of tsunamis. Scientists use
                 328
seismographs (machines that detect and measure quakes)

to predict where and when a tsunami will strike. This early

warning system cannot prevent tsunamis, although

it's been successful in saving lives. One of the newest ways
329
to track tsunamis is with satellites. Scientists use satellites to

track the beginnings and movements of tsunamis all over the

world. 330

---

324. A. NO CHANGE
    B. shifting
    C. to shift
    D. having shifted

325. A. NO CHANGE
    B. hour—however,
    C. hour, however,
    D. hour, however.

326. A. NO CHANGE
    B. shallower
    C. most shallowest
    D. shallow

327. A. NO CHANGE
    B. exposed
    C. expose
    D. exposing

328. A. NO CHANGE
    B. send out
    C. did send out
    D. sends out

329. A. NO CHANGE
    B. its been
    C. it been
    D. it be

330. For the sake of the logic and coherence of the essay, Paragraph 2 should be placed

    A. where it is now.
    B. after Paragraph 4.
    C. after Paragraph 3.
    D. before Paragraph 1.

Determining Personality Types

A <u>noted thinker, named</u> Joseph Campbell gave some
      331
excellent and thought-provoking advice about choosing a

career. 332 Campbell said, "Follow your bliss." By this he

meant that you should let your <u>most deepest</u> interests and
                                    333
needs lead you to a career that you will enjoy. It may be difficult

to decide which career <u>for a young person about to graduate</u>
                                    334
<u>from high school</u> will make one's life happy and productive.
      334

Career choice can be <u>hard.</u> But most experts in the field of
                          335
career counseling agree that the most important step you

can take is to find a career that <u>suits to your</u> personality.
                                        336
According to psychologist John Holland, there are six basic

personality types that match most <u>people, the</u> six types are the
                                          337

realistic, the investigative, the <u>artistic: the</u> social, the enter-
                                        338
prising, and the conventional. The realistic personality is often

interested in machines and how they work. This kind of person

is suited to such skilled trades as machine <u>and as</u> computer
                                                    339
repairman, auto mechanic, and electrician. Investigative people

enjoy research in science and other fields. Artistic people can be

creative in a variety of jobs, such as interior design, illustration,

and clothes design. Social people have a strong need to help

others and make good social workers, teachers, and counsel-

ors. Enterprising people love adventure and challenges; they

often start their own businesses and prefer to be managers and

331. A. NO CHANGE
       B. noted thinker named
       C. noted, thinker, named
       D. noted thinker; named

332. If the writer were to delete the words *excellent* and *thought-provoking* from the preceding sentence, the passage would primarily lose
       A. what the writer's opinion is of Joseph Campbell's advice.
       B. why Joseph Campbell talked about career choice.
       C. the reason why Joseph Campbell became a noted thinker.
       D. the idea that young people are troubled.

333. A. NO CHANGE
       B. deeper
       C. most deeper
       D. deepest

334. The best placement for the underlined portion would be
       A. where it is now.
       B. after the word *difficult*.
       C. after the word *decide*.
       D. after the word *happy*.

335. Which choice best emphasizes the problems of career choice for young people?
       A. NO CHANGE
       B. most stressful
       C. confusing
       D. uncomfortable

336. A. NO CHANGE
       B. suited your
       C. suited to your
       D. suits your

337. A. NO CHANGE
       B. people: the
       C. people. The
       D. people, the

338. A. NO CHANGE
       B. the artistic. The
       C. the artistic; the
       D. the artistic, the

339. A. NO CHANGE
       B. as,
       C. yet
       D. OMIT the underlined portion.

bosses. Conventional people feel most comfortable in a job in which they know exactly what is expected of them. 340 Jobs

that suit them include clerical work accounting, and
 341
banking. People in the military are often both realistic and conventional.

[1] Many careers also call for a combination of personality traits. [2] You can find out which type describes your personality by taking the Vocational Preferences Inventory, a test invented by Holland. [3] However, many people find that they
                                            342
have elements of two or more of these personality types. [4] For example, a psychologist who treats patient's problems needs to be investigative (research-oriented). [5] As well as social
                                            343
(wanting to help others). [6] A writer who works in advertising might be both artistic and enterprising, or business-oriented. 344

340. The writer is considering adding the following sentence here: They have a strong need for order and rules. Should the writer include the sentence?

A. Yes, because it tells more about conventional people.
B. Yes, because it helps the reader understand what conventional people do.
C. No, because it contradicts what the rest of the essay says about personality types.
D. No, because it distracts from the overall message of the essay.

341. A. NO CHANGE
B. clerical, work accounting
C. clerical, work, accounting
D. clerical work, accounting

342. A. NO CHANGE
B. Although
C. In spite of
D. OMIT the underlined portion.

343. A. NO CHANGE
B. (research-oriented): as well as
C. (research-oriented), as well as
D. (research-oriented) as well as

344. For the sake of the logic and coherence of the paragraph, Sentence 1 should be placed

A. where it is now.
B. after Sentence 3.
C. after Sentence 5.
D. after Sentence 6.

345. Suppose that the writer had set out to write a brief essay on the age at which people should decide which aspect of a career is most important to them. Has the writer been successful at his goal?

A. Yes, because the essay addresses the problems that young people have in choosing a career.
B. Yes, because the essay talks about the different personality types.
C. No, because the essay doesn't talk about the various aspects of a career, only personality types.
D. No, because the essay doesn't go into detail about which people are good at which jobs.

Remembering Sherbro Island

Note: The following paragraphs may not be in the most logical order. Each paragraph is numbered; question 359 asks you to choose where Paragraph 2 would most logically be placed.

[1] Bonthe was a day's travel by lorry from Joru, the town
                        346
that I lived in. I was excited to see the island, because my friend
had told me that there were no cars and everyone walked to
their destinations. It turned out to be very picaresque, with
houses that were unusual because they were built on stilts.
                                              347
I guess it flooded a lot. I remember too the wonderful
beaches there.

[2] Sherbro Island is located in the Atlantic Ocean,
off the coast of West Africa. The primary town is the port
of Bonthe. It is accessible from the mainland at Mattru Jong
by ferry along the Jong River. Sherbro Island is part of
the country that is called Sierra Leone and was its first capital,
          348
when it was settled by the British toward the end of the
eighteenth century. I learned about Sherbro Island from
another volunteer who was stationed there when I was in the
Peace Corps, teaching English as a Second Language. I decided
to visit him and see the island.

[3] Twenty years later, I decided I would return to Sierra
Leone to see what had changed. A problem in the country had
                                        349
prevented me from going earlier. I knew it would be a nostalgic

trip for me. 350 Bonthe would be my first stop of a
ten-day trip.

[4] I had decided to forgo public transportation on my trip,

and bravely rented a car in Freetown they drive on the wrong
                                351
side of the road there, so it would be a challenge. After two
hours, I turned off the main road onto a secondary road that
was unpaved, rough, and uncared for. Sections were still eroded
from rainy season. From Koribundu to Mattru Jong, the road
was even worse, but I got through. I was glad I had chose the
                                              352
four-wheel-drive upgrade.

346. **A.** NO CHANGE
     B. days travel
     C. days' travel
     D. day travel

347. **A.** NO CHANGE
     B. because they used stilts to put their houses on
     C. because the houses stood on stilts in the ground
     D. OMIT the underlined portion

348. **A.** NO CHANGE
     B. the country that people know as
     C. the country known today as
     D. OMIT the underlined portion.

349. Given that all of the choices are true, which one provides
     the most significant new information?
     A. NO CHANGE
     B. difficulty in the country
     C. situation that could not be resolved
     D. long and dangerous civil war

350. If the word *nostalgic* were deleted from the preceding
     sentence, the essay would primarily lose
     A. the fact that he wants to reenlist in the Peace Corps.
     B. why the writer waited so long to take the trip.
     C. the reason for going to Bonthe.
     D. an idea of what the writer feels about his trip.

351. **A.** NO CHANGE
     B. Freetown. They
     C. Freetown, they
     D. Freetown—they

352. **A.** NO CHANGE
     B. was chosen
     C. has chosen
     D. had chosen

[5] The ferry was <u>crowded with everything</u>, but the
                              353
40-minute ride was peaceful; the mangrove swamps were

just as I remembered. The sound of the birds in the jungle

was cacophonous and mysterious. We all piled off the boat

in Bonthe. I asked directions for Bonthe Holiday Village,

a resort that wasn't there the last time I had come, but

<u>that I had been reading about.</u> The rooms were small, but clean.
                        354
After a delicious feast of groundnut stew, I slept deeply.

[6] The next day, I walked through the sleepy town. [355]

It hadn't changed after all these years. Barefoot children

ran and played in the sandy streets. Women leaned

<u>stirring fragrant fish stews</u> over big iron pots. The fisher-
                  356
men had all gone out to sea. The Anglican church was still

there, looking as dilapidated as it had before. I walked out to

Peninsular Beach. It was all just as I remembered, mile after

mile of pure white sand, palm trees, crystal clear water. There

wasn't another soul on the beach.

[7] Far out at sea I could see the fishermen casting their

nets. <u>However,</u> I was glad I had come. Lying on the sand,
        357
looking up at the cloudless dry-season sky, I tapped into

all the memories of my life as it was so long ago when I first

visited the island. Tomorrow I would drive to <u>Joru but now</u>
                                                          358

I was going for a swim. [359]

353. Given that all of the choices are true, which one provides
the most significant additional information?
 A. NO CHANGE
 B. filled with people, chickens, and children
 C. had a lot of people
 D. filled to capacity

354. A. NO CHANGE
 B. that I read about
 C. that I had read about earlier
 D. OMIT the underlined portion.

355. If the word *sleepy* were deleted from the preceding sen-
tence, the essay would primarily lose
 A. an idea of what the town was like.
 B. the sense that the writer was tired.
 C. the suggestion that residents often napped during the
day.
 D. the idea that people did not walk around much.

356. The best placement for the underlined portion would be
 A. where it is now.
 B. after the word *Women*.
 C. after the word *over*.
 D. after the word *pots*.

357. A. NO CHANGE
 B. Yet,
 C. Moreover,
 D. OMIT the underlined portion.

358. A. NO CHANGE
 B. Joru, but
 C. Joru—but
 D. Joru: but

359. For the sake of the logic and coherence of the essay,
Paragraph 2 should be placed
 A. where it is now.
 B. before Paragraph 1.
 C. after Paragraph 3.
 D. after Paragraph 4.

360. Suppose that the writer had wanted to write an essay that
captured his feelings about a place that he had visited
many years before. Was he successful in doing that?
 A. Yes, because he had the chance to revisit his past and
relive his memories.
 B. Yes, because he was able to describe in detail what his
life was like while in the Peace Corps.
 C. No, because he failed to tell about his feelings about
the past.
 D. No, because the essay was not descriptive enough.

Born to Be a Vet

Its strange, but
___
361

true, ever since I was little, I knew
___
362

I been a veterinarian when I grew up. I just loved animals.
___
363

I grew up on a small farm in Minnesota, and I like to watch as
                                                              _____
                                                                 364
the vet treated a sick cow that wouldn't get up. The vet gave the

cow an IV saline solution, before the bag was empty and the
                            _____
                                        365
cow would rise right up. My parents had 34 dairy cows, but

there were also lots of chickens and geese. We had three dogs

and four cats and two horses too. When I was five, my father let

me help milk the cows.

I helped him every day until I started going to school.

My parents' farm was way out in the country and

the school bus picked me up at 6:30 in the morning,

since our house was first on the route. When I was in high
_____
            366
school, I volunteered at the local humane society. I cleaned

the dirtier cages and washed blankets. I learned how to groom.
    ___
    367
I took the dogs for walks and played with the cats. I stuffed

envelopes with brochures about being a foster parent for young

puppies and kittens. On weekends, I went to the local mall with

dogs and cats who needed homes that would provide affection
            ___
            368
and love, and talked to people, encouraging them to adopt a

pet because they needed love. 369

After graduating from high school, I was fortunate to

receive a scholarship at State. I found that I possess a natural
                                            _____
                                              370
flair for science, and I enrolled in Biology and Chemistry

---

361. A. NO CHANGE
   B. Its'
   C. It's
   D. They're

362. A. NO CHANGE
   B. true. Ever
   C. true ever
   D. true . . . ever

363. A. NO CHANGE
   B. I have been
   C. I will be
   D. I would be

364. A. NO CHANGE
   B. liked to watch
   C. liked to have watched
   D. liked to be watching

365. The best placement for the underlined portion would be
   A. where it is now.
   B. before the word *would*.
   C. after the word *vet*.
   D. after the word *up*.

366. Given that all of the choices are true, which one provides the most significant new information?
   A. NO CHANGE
   B. which was very early.
   C. so I couldn't help.
   D. and the driver always smiled.

367. A. NO CHANGE
   B. more dirty
   C. dirty
   D. dirtiest

368. A. NO CHANGE
   B. whom
   C. that
   D. OMIT the underlined portion.

369. If the writer were to delete the phrase "because they needed love" from the preceding sentence, the sentence would primarily lose
   A. the idea that the pets need affection.
   B. a description of what pets need.
   C. an indication that the writer loves pets.
   D. nothing, because the phrase is redundant.

370. A. NO CHANGE
   B. possessed
   C. possessing
   D. to possess

classes. After my first year, I decided to major in Biology. That summer, I found a local animal hospital where I could intern. I learned how to perform lab tests, and the technicians taught me how to use the equipment and interpret the test results. Whenever I could find the time, I returned home to the farm, I was an only child, and my parents were always
<u>371</u>
overjoyed to see me.

[1] I was worried that it would be difficult for me to get in, because I was female and from a small midwestern farming community. [2] During my senior year, I decided to apply to a Veterinary Medicine graduate school. [3] <u>However,</u> I was
<u>372</u>
surprised when I talked to one of the deans to hear that that

years graduating class was 82% female. [4] So
<u>373</u>

I crossed my fingers and sent in my application. [5] A month
<u>374</u>
later, I received my acceptance letter. [6] In four years

I would become a Doctor of Veterinary Medicine. 375

It was difficult, but it happened. I opened a practice in my hometown, where I have so many friends and wonderful memories, and I couldn't be happier in my work.

371. **A.** NO CHANGE
    B. farm. I
    C. farm I
    D. farm: I

372. Which of the following alternatives to the underlined portion would NOT be acceptable?
    A. Yet
    B. Consequently
    C. Still
    D. Nevertheless

373. **A.** NO CHANGE
    B. year
    C. years'
    D. year's

374. **A.** NO CHANGE
    B. I cross
    C. I was crossing
    D. I had crossed

375. For the sake of the logic and coherence of the paragraph, Sentence 2 should be
    A. placed where it is now.
    B. placed before Sentence 1.
    C. placed before Sentence 4.
    D. OMITTED from the paragraph.

CHAPTER 13

SET 2 ENGLISH QUESTIONS

QUESTIONS 376–500

The Aviatrix

Amelia Earhart, born in 1897 in Atchison, Kansas was a
pioneer in the early days of aviation. Called "the Lady of the
Air," she was a role model to women all around the world.
However, Amelia was the first woman, and the second person
after Charles Lindbergh, to fly solo across the Atlantic Ocean
in 1932, and the first woman to fly alone from Hawaii to
California in 1935. At a time when men dominated aviation,
she was truly a celebrated aviatrix. 378

In 1937, Amelia decides she wanted to be the first
person to fly around the world at the equator, a distance

totaling 29,000 miles. Funding from Purdue University,
she outfitted a twin-engine Lockheed Electra

with oversized fuel tanks and special radio equipment. This was
before radar had been invented, so she would have to rely on
radio communication for direction. Realizing she would need

help, she recruited Fred Noonan, an experienced navigator who

376. **A.** NO CHANGE
B. Kansas, was
C. Kansas: was
D. Kansas; was

377. **A.** NO CHANGE
B. While
C. Although
D. OMIT the underlined portion.

378. The writer is considering revising the first part of this sentence ("At a time when men dominated aviation,") to read as follows:

At a time when flying was new,

If the writer did this, the essay would primarily lose

A. an indication that planes were not very safe at the time.
B. a detail that helps the reader understand how special Amelia Earhart was.
C. a detail that gives the reader more information about how popular aviation was at the time.
D. a possibly confusing issue over what aviation was like at the time.

379. **A.** NO CHANGE
B. deciding
C. has decided
D. decided

380. **A.** NO CHANGE
B. With funding from Purdue University
C. After funds were given by Purdue University
D. With funds that came from a university called Purdue

381. **A.** NO CHANGE
B. oversized fuel tanks and special radio equipment
C. having oversized fuel tanks and special radio equipment
D. OMIT the underlined portion.

382. **A.** NO CHANGE
B. help; she
C. help she
D. help. She

was charting air routes across the Pacific for the fledgling
383
commercial airline industry.

[1] Earhart and Noonan set out on their trip on June 1, 1937,
departing from Miami, Florida. [2] They made its way eastward
384
and, by early July, they had reached New Guinea, having flown
22,000 miles. [3] On July 2, they took off from Lae Airport.
[4] They had a distance of over 2,500 miles to get to Howland
Island, a tiny uninhabited island which the U.S. government had
385
built an airfield and fuel tanks for her. [5] The U.S. Coast Guard
had stationed the cutter *Itasca* by the island to maintain radio
contact with the plane. [6] Despite a massive search-and-rescue
operation that covered 250,000 square miles, no trace was ever
found of the plane or its crew. [7] Their plane, though, was
386
having difficulty maintaining radio contact with the *Itasca*;
transmissions were faint and broken by static. [8] At 8:45 that
morning, Amelia radioed, "We are running north and south."
[9] Those were her last words. [387]

Many people have put forth theories of Amelia's
disappearance and conducted searches, all to no avail
over the years. In August 2012, a search team using a remote
388
operating vehicle (ROV) took pictures of what is purported
to be part of a wheel assembly: a strut, wheel, gear, and fender,
found far below the surface of the sea near Nikumaroro Island,
a tiny atoll of less than two square miles, located 400 miles
southwest of Howland Island. The next step would be to send an
unmanned submarine to retrieve the parts then see if they do
389
indeed belong to a Lockheed Electra, but that has not happened.

Possibly one day, we will all find out what was happening
390

to Amelia Earhart and Fred Noonan. [391]

383. A. NO CHANGE
B. charting
C. charted
D. charts

384. A. NO CHANGE
B. his
C. her
D. their

385. A. NO CHANGE
B. that
C. where
D. OMIT the underlined portion.

386. Which of the following alternatives to the underlined portion would NOT be acceptable?
A. however
B. since
C. nonetheless
D. nevertheless

387. For the sake of the logic and coherence of the paragraph, Sentence 6 should be placed
A. where it is now.
B. after Sentence 1.
C. after Sentence 9.
D. OMITTED from the paragraph.

388. The best placement for the underlined portion would be
A. where it is now.
B. after the word *people.*
C. after the word *disappearance.*
D. after the word *searches.*

389. A. NO CHANGE
B. parts and then
C. parts, then
D. parts and, then

390. A. NO CHANGE
B. have happened
C. were happening
D. happened

391. At this point, the writer is considering adding the following true statement:

Noonan joined the Merchant Marine in 1906.

Should the writer make this addition here?
A. Yes, because it provides further details about Noonan before he was lost.
B. Yes, because it strengthens the idea that Noonan was a resourceful person.
C. No, because it has no bearing on what the passage is mostly about.
D. No, because it creates confusion about what Noonan was like.

History of Advertising

Note: The following paragraphs may not be in the most logical order. Each paragraph is numbered; question 406 asks you to choose where Paragraph 4 would most logically be placed.

[1] It is thought commonly that merchants did not advertise
                           392
before the twentieth century, but the truth is that people were

advertising for hundreds of years before that. In the Middle

Ages, European merchants returned from the Orient with

silk and spices that had never been ever seen before.
                           393

Instead of peddling their goods from door to door, they hired a
394
man to run through the streets of the city shouting that exotic

silks and spices from the East could be bought. 395 The man

who ran through the streets was called a "crier."

[2] Very few people could read then, so advertising was

done exclusively by criers for many years. Later, merchants'
                                              396
painted signs for the front of their shops. But instead of

words, they used pictures of their merchandise. The invention
397
of the printing press in the fifteenth century meant that more

people learned to read. Nevertheless, printed posters became
                          398
more commonplace advertising tools. The first newspaper ad

was published in 1704, the *Boston News-Letter* ran an ad for a
                   399
house for sale in Oyster Bay, Long Island. In 1742, Benjamin

Franklin published *The General Magazine and Historical Chronicle*

for all the British Plantations in America with the first magazine

ads. The first advertising agency opened in Philadelphia in 1843.

[3] Today, television dominates the advertising world, with

total revenues in 2011 of $190 billion. 400 Internet ad sales

are growing by leaps and bounds. Magazine and newspaper

392. The best placement for the underlined portion would be
- **A.** where it is now.
- **B.** after the word *is*.
- **C.** after the word *merchants*.
- **D.** after the word *advertise*.

393. A. NO CHANGE
- **B.** never ever seen before
- **C.** never been seen before
- **D.** never seen before

394. A. NO CHANGE
- **B.** While
- **C.** In spite of
- **D.** OMIT the underlined portion.

395. If the writer were to delete the word *exotic* and the phrase "from the East" from the preceding sentence, the sentence would primarily lose
- **A.** the reasoning behind the use of a crier.
- **B.** the suggestion that the items were not easily obtained.
- **C.** the idea that Eastern silks and spices were commonplace.
- **D.** a comparison between the silk and the spices.

396. A. NO CHANGE
- **B.** Later merchants'
- **C.** Later, merchant's
- **D.** Later, merchants

397. A. NO CHANGE
- **B.** words they
- **C.** words. They
- **D.** words; they

398. A. NO CHANGE
- **B.** Consequently,
- **C.** However,
- **D.** OMIT the underlined portion.

399. A. NO CHANGE
- **B.** 1704. The
- **C.** 1704 the
- **D.** 1704—the

400. The writer is considering revising the preceding sentence to read as follows:

Nowadays, television gets a great deal of revenue from advertising.

If the writer does this, the essay would primarily lose
- **A.** a feeling for which kind of advertising is the most lucrative.
- **B.** an actual idea of the amount of money that is spent on television advertising.
- **C.** the idea that television advertising might be replaced by Internet advertising.
- **D.** the concept that political advertising is increasing.

advertising has declining, especially with the advent of tablet
$\underline{\hspace{2cm}}$
                      401
computers and e-readers, as more and more people prefer

reading on electronic devices. [402] Although the methods

may have changed and more likely will continue to change,
                      $\underline{\hspace{2cm}}$
                               403
advertising one's products is certainly here to stay.

[4] In 1922, a New York City radio station, WEAF

(which later became WNBC) broadcast the first

advertisement on radio, promoting a new apartment

complex in Jackson Heights. [404] And in 1941,

as well in New York City, the first television broadcast aired on
$\overline{405}$
July 1. At this time, advertising cost $120 an hour for an evening

show. Compare that to the average network cost in 2011 for a

"prime-time" 30-second slot of $110,000. With the advent of the

Internet in the 1990s, another advertising avenue opened. [406]

---

401. A. NO CHANGE
 B. have declining
 C. been declining
 D. has declined

402. If the writer were to delete the phrase "especially with the advent of tablet computers and e-readers" from the preceding sentence, the sentence would primarily lose

 A. the reason why magazine and newspaper advertising revenues have declined.
 B. an awareness of why people prefer tablet computers and e-readers.
 C. a knowledge of how much revenue has been lost by magazines and newspapers.
 D. the idea that people are whimsical when it comes to watching advertisements.

403. A. NO CHANGE
 B. much likely
 C. likelier
 D. most likely

404. At this point, the writer is considering adding the following true statement:

 Jackson Heights is a community in Queens, one of New York City's six boroughs, and is known for its garden apartment buildings.

 Should the writer make this addition here?

 A. Yes, because it informs the reader about what Jackson Heights is known for.
 B. Yes, because it informs the reader that the writer knows how many boroughs there are in New York City.
 C. No, because the information does not fit in with the main focus of the paragraph, which is about how advertising evolved.
 D. No, because the reader could be confused by the information about how many boroughs there are in New York City.

405. A. NO CHANGE
 B. too
 C. also
 D. OMIT the underlined portion.

406. For the sake of the logic and coherence of the essay, Paragraph 4 should be placed

 A. where it is now.
 B. before Paragraph 1.
 C. before Paragraph 2.
 D. before Paragraph 3.

407. Suppose the writer had intended to write a brief essay showing how important advertising has been throughout history. Would this essay successfully fulfill the writer's goal?

 A. Yes, because the essay shows how integral advertising has been since early times when someone wanted to sell something.
 B. Yes, because the essay shows how much income was made from advertising in the past and in modern times.
 C. No, because the focus of the essay is on income rather than the history of advertising.
 D. No, because the essay fails to cover fully why advertising came into existence.

The Sioux Nation

South Dakota was the home of the great Sioux Nation. In all, there were about 20,000 Sioux in three groups, the Lakota, Dakota, and Nakota comprising 14 different tribes throughout the Great Plains. They were nomads riding the plains on horses that were brought to this country by the Spanish conquistador Hernán Cortés in 1519. The horses were a great help to the Sioux as they traveled about hunting the buffalo. By using these horses, they could easily transport their teepees and equipment from place to place.

The Sioux people were their own masters, not having rules. Their lives were based on hunting, gathering

foodstuffs; and caring for their young. Children were considered special and were called *wakanisha*, or sacred ones. The Sioux passed down to their children the stories that were the foundation of their civilization. Their central belief was the principle of living in harmony with nature and the environment. The area known as the Black Hills was considered holy ground. Through their relationship with nature, and particularly the animals they hunted, the Sioux developed a unique and sophisticated culture.

[1] Their connection with nature is most evident in stories that have handed down generation after generation, and that are still told on the reservations today. [2] These stories are meant to explain the origins of the world and the Sioux's relationship to these origins. [3] A typical story tells how the rainbow came to be. [4] It was said to be made from colorful summer flowers that die in the fall. [5] The young artist ran out of paint, so the loons are gray, as the story goes. [6] Another explains why ducks have so many different-colored feathers. [7] An Indian brave painted them and each one is, consequent, different.

408. **A.** NO CHANGE
     B. Nakota, comprising
     C. Nakota, comprised
     D. Nakota,

409. **A.** NO CHANGE
     B. These horses,
     C. In using these horses,
     D. With these horses,

410. Given that all of the choices are true, which one provides the most significant new information?
     A. NO CHANGE
     B. without any restraints on them.
     C. roaming freely as they pleased.
     D. with no place to call home.

411. **A.** NO CHANGE
     B. foodstuffs. And caring
     C. foodstuffs, and caring
     D. foodstuffs and caring

412. **A.** NO CHANGE
     B. and particularly the animals they hunt,
     C. in particularly the animals they hunted,
     D. and particularly with the animals they hunted,

413. **A.** NO CHANGE
     B. have been handed
     C. were being handed
     D. are being handed

414. **A.** NO CHANGE
     B. comes to be
     C. came to have been
     D. came to being

415. **A.** NO CHANGE
     B. consequently,
     C. consequencely,
     D. with consequence,

[8] Many of their stories are about the buffalo, which was an important <u>part</u> of their lives and culture. [9] The buffalo
416
provided them with everything from food to clothing to housing. [10] It was also the basis of many of the Sioux's myths and legends. ⊡417⊡

During the mid-1800s, the culture of the Sioux, which was nomadic and centered on the buffalo and the horse, increasingly conflicted with the culture of the white man, which was <u>industrial and agricultural based</u>. Tensions flared when gold
418
was discovered in the Black Hills in 1874 by an expedition led by George Custer. The U.S. government offered the Sioux $6 million for the Black Hills, which was refused. A series of battles ensued, <u>concomitant</u> in the Battle of the Little
419
Bighorn in Greasy Grass, Montana. On June 25, 1876, General Custer and over 200 soldiers of the 7th U.S. Army Cavalry Regiment perished fighting the Sioux, <u>led by their famous chief, Sitting Bull,</u> and their allies, the
420
Cheyenne. The victory was short-lived, however, as other soldiers invaded the hunting grounds of the Sioux. Within five years, all the Sioux and Cheyenne would be restricted to living on reservations.

Today the Sioux <u>has</u> a renewed sense of pride. Children are
421

taught <u>their native</u> customs and language. Native American
422
artists produce buffalo hide paintings, beadwork, and pottery. In 2012, over $9 million was raised by Hollywood stars and musicians, and the revered and sacred site of Pe' Sla in the Black Hills was reacquired. ⊡423⊡ The great Sioux Nation can once again host annual ceremonies at the site that is central to the Lakota Creation Myth.

416. **A.** NO CHANGE
　　 B. an integral part
　　 C. a big part
　　 D. an occurring part

417. For the sake of logic and coherence of the paragraph, Sentence 5 should be placed
　　 A. where it is now.
　　 B. before Sentence 2.
　　 C. after Sentence 3.
　　 D. after Sentence 7.

418. **A.** NO CHANGE
　　 B. industry and agricultural base
　　 C. industrially and agriculturally based
　　 D. based on industry and agriculture

419. **A.** NO CHANGE
　　 B. culminating
　　 C. cascading
　　 D. collaterally

420. The best placement for the underlined phrase would be
　　 A. where it is now.
　　 B. after the word *Regiment*.
　　 C. at the beginning of the sentence.
　　 D. after the word *soldiers*.

421. **A.** NO CHANGE
　　 B. had
　　 C. have
　　 D. are having

422. **A.** NO CHANGE
　　 B. the native
　　 C. the natives'
　　 D. native

423. At this point, the writer is considering adding the following true statement:

　　 Pe' Sla was considered to be "The Heart of Everything That Is" by the Sioux.

　　 Should the writer make this addition here?

　　 A. Yes, because it informs the reader how the Sioux feel about Pe' Sla.
　　 B. Yes, because it shows the reader that the writer did a lot of research.
　　 C. No, because it distracts the reader from the main focus of the paragraph.
　　 D. No, because it contradicts the writer's statement in the following sentence.

A Memory of Marco and Polo

Note: The following paragraphs may not be in the most logical order. Each paragraph is numbered; question 438 asks you to choose where Paragraph 3 would most logically be placed.

[1] One sunny and hot afternoon in July when I was 12, I played in the backyard of our house, when I spotted two small
424

turtles slowly walking through the grass, they were about an
425
inch or so across. They had a hard shell that was green with little yellow stripes. Excitedly, I ran into the house to tell my mother. [426] We came out a few minutes later and found the turtles lounging on some rocks by our garden. They were clearly sunning themselves.

[2] My mom looked the turtles up on her computer. From their markings, it appeared they belonged to a species of
427

turtle called the river cooter. The species accesses rivers and
428
wetlands, and since our house was less than a half mile from

the Satilla River, that must being where they had come
429
from. We read that cooters often could be domesticated as pets

as long as you had an aquatic environment to support them.
430
Since we had an aquarium in our house, I begged my

mom to let us keep them. She agreed, on the condition that I

am responsible for taking care of them. I carefully picked the
431
turtles up and carried them to the aquarium.

[3] We had a 100-gallon fish tank in the house. My mother was really into fish. She had neon tetras and knife fish, but her favorite were two red bettas. Lifting up the lid, I gently slipped the turtles into the warm water. They seemed happy and quickly start swimming around. They didn't chase the fish
432
and the fish didn't seem to mind the turtles. I read some more about my river cooters. I learned that they were herbivorous,

424. **A.** NO CHANGE
  B. did play
  C. was playing
  D. could play

425. **A.** NO CHANGE
  B. grass—they
  C. grass they
  D. grass. They

426. If the word *excitedly* were deleted from the previous sentence, the essay would primarily lose
  A. a suggestion that the writer was afraid.
  B. a detail that changes the meaning of the sentence.
  C. evidence that the writer did not like the turtles.
  D. support for the previous sentence.

427. **A.** NO CHANGE
  B. From their markings, it appears
  C. It appears, from their markings
  D. From their markings it appeared

428. **A.** NO CHANGE
  B. claims
  C. inhabits
  D. dominates

429. **A.** NO CHANGE
  B. must have was
  C. must have been
  D. must been

430. The best placement for the underlined phrase is
  A. where it is now.
  B. after the word *them*.
  C. after the word *domesticated*.
  D. before the word *We*.

431. **A.** NO CHANGE
  B. would be responsible
  C. are responsible
  D. was responsible

432. **A.** NO CHANGE
  B. start to swim
  C. started swimming
  D. starts swimming

which means they ate plants. [433] I took some lettuce from the refrigerator and cut it into little pieces. They were clearly hungry and gobbled it all up.

[4] I named my turtles Marco and Polo. Since I didn't know if they were male or female, I decided on the names from my favorite swimming pool game. I went to the pet store and got turtle food. I made a basking area out of some bark and floated it on the surface of the water. They loved laying under the heat
                                                                 434
lamp. As the summer wore on, Marco and Polo grew, and little pieces of their carapace, or shell, would come off and new shell would replace it.

[5] School began again. I came home every day and fed the turtles. They were growing very fast, almost three
                                                        435
inches in diameter. I read that the river cooter could measure
435
as much as 13 inches across as an adult.

They were becoming much too big, even for our enormous fish
        436
tank. I went to my mom and we discussed the future for Marco and Polo. There was only one thing to do. Together we put my turtles into a shoebox and walked down to the edge of the river. I put them on a rock. They seemed to look back at me and then quietly slipped into the water. I was a little sad after that, but I
                                                          437
knew it was best for them. One night a few months later, I had a dream. I dreamt that Marco was pregnant. She would have a baby turtle in the spring and she thanked me for taking care of her and Polo. I felt proud that I had helped them. [438]

433. At this point, the writer is considering adding the following true statement:

> I also read that young turtles love to eat fresh lettuce.

Should the writer make this addition here?

A. Yes, because it tells what kind of plant turtles will eat.
B. Yes, because it informs the reader that the writer needed to cut the lettuce up.
C. No, because the writer previously stated that the turtles ate plants.
D. No, because it distracts the reader and doesn't fit logically in the passage.

434. A. NO CHANGE
B. lain
C. lying
D. to lay

435. A. NO CHANGE
B. very fast, nearly three inches in diameter.
C. very fast. They were nearly three inches in diameter.
D. very fast, but they were nearly three inches in diameter.

436. A. NO CHANGE
B. would become
C. would have become
D. would be becoming

437. Which of the following choices best emphasizes how the writer responded to letting the turtles go free?
A. NO CHANGE
B. I felt a little funny.
C. It was odd at first.
D. It wasn't so bad after that.

438. For the sake of the logic and coherence of the essay, Paragraph 3 should be placed
A. where it is now.
B. before Paragraph 1.
C. before Paragraph 2.
D. after Paragraph 4.

439. Suppose that the writer had intended to write a brief essay about a child's learning to accept the fact that life is often full of change. Would this essay successfully fulfill that goal?
A. Yes, because the essay shows that the writer felt that the mother was a good parent.
B. Yes, because the essay shows that the writer accepted the loss of the turtles by having a positive dream.
C. No, because the focus of the essay was primarily on river cooters.
D. No, because the essay was not about change, but a summer in the life of a young boy.

Superman

During all of time, people have enjoyed myths about heroes
                440
with amazing powers. The ancient Greeks had Hercules with

his mighty strength. The Middle Ages produced Beowulf,

a fearless warrior who defeated the monster Grendel. Paul

Bunyan was a giant lumberjack in early American folklore

who becomes a symbol of might. But the superhero to end all
        441
superheroes was Superman. The comic book hero Superman

was created by two imaginative 17-year-olds named Jerry Siegel

and Joe Shuster in 1933. ☐442 He was the first superhero.

With his special powers, he was able to fight any evildoers.
                                           443
Originally, Superman couldn't fly, but he could leap an

eighth of a mile at a time. That was fast enough to catch a

criminal. He had X-ray vision and supersharp hearing,

which were excellent tools for tracking down criminals.
     444
As time went on, he was given more powers, including the abil-

ity to fly. He could travel through time at the speed of light. By

the end of World War II, Superman would even survive a
                                   445

nuclear blast unharmed. In fact, Superman took the identity
                       446

of mild-mannered newspaper reporter Clark Kent. Ordinary
      447
people saw themselves in Clark Kent. They saw injustice and

suffering all around them and felt helpless about it.

But when Clark Kent took off his tie and business shirt

so as to reveal the blue-and-red-caped uniform of Superman,
     448
every reader felt a thrill. This was the perfect way for ordinary

people to feel powerful. They could feel since they were
                                    449

440. A. NO CHANGE
    B. In time
    C. Throughout time
    D. All along time

441. A. NO CHANGE
    B. became a symbol
    C. becoming a symbol
    D. is becoming a symbol

442. If the word *imaginative* were deleted from the previous sentence, the essay would primarily lose
    A. a suggestion that Jerry Siegel and Joe Shuster were talented.
    B. evidence that Jerry Siegel and Joe Shuster worked together.
    C. a hint about Superman's nature.
    D. evidence that Superman was created as a joke.

443. Given that all the choices are true, which one best supports the sentence's claims about Superman's powers?
    A. NO CHANGE
    B. he could overcome any problems.
    C. he was better than everyone else.
    D. he had the chance to defend himself.

444. A. NO CHANGE
    B. which were handy
    C. which could be excellent
    D. OMIT the underlined portion.

445. A. NO CHANGE
    B. could even survive
    C. could even survives
    D. would have even survived

446. A. NO CHANGE
    B. For instance
    C. Therefore
    D. OMIT the underlined portion.

447. If the writer were to delete the word *mild-mannered*, the sentence would primarily lose
    A. a comparison between Superman and other superheroes.
    B. a detail that stresses how ordinary people feel about Superman.
    C. the suggestion that Superman and Clark Kent were similar in nature.
    D. a contrast to the powers of Superman.

448. A. NO CHANGE
    B. to reveal
    C. and revealing
    D. OMIT the underlined portion.

449. A. NO CHANGE
    B. as if they were
    C. as though they'd be
    D. although they were

Superman, fighting for the innocent and prostrate against
450
the villains of the world. As Superman said, "There is a

right and a wrong in the universe and that distinction is not

hard to make."*

    Americans weren't the only ones to follow the adventures

of the Man of Steel. Superman became popular all around the

world. From his origin as a comic book hero, Superman moved

on to radio and then television and movies. 451 He can be

found in cartoons and computer games. His adventures have

been recorded on audiotapes and DVDs. Why has Superman

stayed popular for nearly 80 years? Other action heroes have

come and gone, but Superman has remained a
452

favorite. Some people think the reason is that Superman
453

seemingly cares about people. He wants to protect ordinary
454
people against evil. To many Americans, Superman stands for

the values and beliefs that Americans care about. Superman

represents "truth, justice, and the American way."
455

450. A. NO CHANGE
    B. servile
    C. rejected
    D. helpless

451. At this point, the writer is considering adding the following true statement:

> The film *Superman Returns* was released to critical acclaim in 2006.

Should the writer make this addition here?

    A. Yes, because it provides an important detail for the paragraph.
    B. Yes, because it reinforces the paragraph's statement that Superman is in movies.
    C. No, because it distracts attention from the paragraph's focus on the different media Superman appears in.
    D. No, because it isn't timely information.

452. Which of the following alternatives to the underlined portion would NOT be acceptable?

    A. besides
    B. nevertheless, preceded by a semicolon instead of a comma and followed by a comma
    C. yet
    D. however, preceded by a semicolon instead of a comma and followed by a comma

453. A. NO CHANGE
    B. think why the reason is
    C. think that is
    D. think which the reason is

454. A. NO CHANGE
    B. apparently
    C. truly
    D. OMIT the underlined portion.

455. If the writer were to delete the quotation marks around the phrase "truth, justice, and the American way," the sentence would primarily lose a feature that suggests

    A. the writer is putting words in Superman's mouth.
    B. those words are what Superman lives for.
    C. the words are a direct quote from Superman.
    D. Superman doesn't believe in those words.

*Superman: Last Son of Krypton by Elliot S. Maggin (New York: Warner Books, 1978).

Sojourner Truth

Sojourner Truth was one of the more remarkable women
456
leaders America has produced. Although there are no records
of her birth, historians believe that Sojourner was probably
born in 1797 in Ulster County, New York. We do know
that this African-American was born a slave named
Isabella Baumfree. She was sold away from her parents
when she was just a child. She took the name Sojourner Truth
457

after she was free by the New York State Emancipation Act of
458

1827. Her new name represented the ideals, for which she lived
459
and fought. Sojourner moved to New York City, where she

began to work with a plethora of organizations that helped
460

women. Later, she became a leading abolitionist who fought
461
against slavery. Fighting for freedom and for equality for
women, Sojourner Truth became a leader in these struggles.
In 1850, she published *The Narrative of Sojourner Truth: A
Northern Slave.* Her book provided a small income, and
she was often invite to speak about anti-slavery and
462

womens rights topics.
463
Sojourner was a powerful speaker with a quick wit and
strong presence. She drew huge crowds with her speeches.
Never intimidated by opposition, Sojourner Truth was always
looking for people of whom she could convince of the truth.
464
As she once said, "I feel safe in the midst of my enemies, for the
truth is all powerful and will prevail." Her most famous speech,
"Ain't I a woman?", was given in 1851 at a women's rights con-
465
vention in Ohio. It urged those at the convention not to ignore
the plight of African-American women.

456. A. NO CHANGE
B. more remarkable woman
C. most remarkable women
D. OMIT the underlined portion.

457. Given that all the choices are true, which one provides the most significant new information?
A. NO CHANGE
B. when she was young
C. while she was still growing
D. when she was only nine years old

458. A. NO CHANGE
B. when she was freed
C. after she was freed
D. after she was freer

459. A. NO CHANGE
B. ideals for which
C. ideals: for which
D. ideals under which

460. A. NO CHANGE
B. a profusion of
C. a scarcity of
D. OMIT the underlined portion.

461. A. NO CHANGE
B. would become
C. was becoming
D. would have become

462. A. NO CHANGE
B. often invited
C. was often invited
D. was oft invited

463. A. NO CHANGE
B. women's rights
C. womens' rights
D. women's right

464. A. NO CHANGE
B. of who
C. that
D. OMIT the underlined portion.

465. A. NO CHANGE
B. woman"?, was
C. woman?," was
D. woman?" was

[1] This brave woman challenged injustice wherever she
saw them. [2] One example was her fight for the desegregation
of public transportation in Washington, D.C. [3] When all the
slaves were liberated after the Civil War, Sojourner worked in
the Freedmen's Bureau. [4] One day, Sojourner and a white
woman were walking down the street and became tired.
[5] Even though the Washington streetcars were supposed to
integrated, they remained segregated. [6] Sojourner had her
friend hail the trolley, and they both got on. [7] A conductor
grabbed Sojourner and tried to keep her from getting on.
[8] He grabbed her so hard that he injured her shoulder.
[9] Sojourner took the trolley company to court and received
$125 in damages, a large amount in those days. [10] This
government agency was set up to help former slaves learn skills.
[11] The conductor was fired. [12] The next day, the trolley
system was declared open to all passengers. 469 Sojourner
lived a long and productive life and won much respect and
admiration. She even spoke before President Lincoln. Age and

ill health caused her retiring from the lecture circuit. She spent
her last days in Battle Creek, Michigan, where she died in 1883.

In 2009, Sojourner Truth became the first African-
American woman to have a bust in the U.S. Capitol. The statue
is in Emancipation Hall, named in honor of all the slaves who
worked on the construction of the Capitol.

466. A. NO CHANGE
     B. when she saw them
     C. whenever she saw that
     D. whenever she saw it

467. A. NO CHANGE
     B. were supposed to been integrated
     C. were supposed to have been integrated
     D. were supposed to have been integrate

468. A. NO CHANGE
     B. so hardly that
     C. so harder that
     D. so much hard that

469. For the sake of the logic and coherence of this paragraph,
     Sentence 10 should be placed
     A. where it is now.
     B. after Sentence 1.
     C. after Sentence 3.
     D. before Sentence 6.

470. A. NO CHANGE
     B. having retired from
     C. retired from
     D. to retire from

On Motherhood

Note: The following paragraphs may not be in the most logical order. Each paragraph is numbered; question 484 asks you to choose where Paragraph 2 would most logically be placed.

[1] Let us consider motherhood. [471] There is no greater

joy on Planet Earth. <u>Since there are endless duties to the job,</u>
₄₇₂
the rewards are numerous. Still, with the fast-paced lifestyle

so common today, mothers can feel challenged by external

societal factors, like peer pressure and entertainment media.

<u>For instance,</u> it is sometimes difficult to be patient. A survey by
₄₇₃

the Pew Research Center in 2007 <u>finds</u> that 70 percent of adults
₄₇₄
surveyed said it was harder to be a mother today than it was in

the 1970s or 1980s.

[2] When my son called to ask if I could drop off his track

uniform for an unscheduled track meet that afternoon, I raced

to the school to give it to <u>him and to find</u> out what time he
₄₇₅
would need to be picked up afterwards. I arrived and asked the

secretary if she could call him to the office. Classes were just

finishing and the hall <u>were filled</u> with high school students.
₄₇₆
When my son saw me, his face at once lit up with a huge smile.

<u>As he took</u> his uniform and gave me the information about
₄₇₇
pickup times, he just kept smiling as if we hadn't met in

ages [478] and he was really glad to see me. He didn't seem

to be embarrassed at all about being there in the high school

<u>with all of his friends around</u> talking to his mother. In fact,
₄₇₉
he seemed quite proud. The harried pace I'd been keeping fell

away as I enjoyed this small moment. That smile brightened the

rest of my day every time I thought of it.

471. If the writer were to change the pronoun *us* to *me* in the preceding sentence, this opening sentence would
   A. take on a less formal tone.
   B. indicate that the writer feels isolated.
   C. show that the topic is not personal.
   D. suggest that the writer has strong feelings.

472. A. NO CHANGE
   B. Because
   C. Moreover,
   D. While

473. A. NO CHANGE
   B. As an example,
   C. Considering
   D. OMIT the underlined portion.

474. A. NO CHANGE
   B. found
   C. was finding
   D. was found

475. A. NO CHANGE
   B. him. And to find
   C. him and find
   D. him, and find

476. A. NO CHANGE
   B. filled
   C. were filled
   D. was filling

477. A. NO CHANGE
   B. While taking
   C. After he took
   D. As he was taking

478. The writer is considering revising the preceding part of the sentence ("as if we hadn't met in ages") to read as follows:

   as if we hadn't seen each other in a long time

   If the writer did this, the passage would primarily lose
   A. nothing of significance, since they mean the same thing.
   B. a detail that adds depth, as the expression "ages" connotes an extremely long time.
   C. a point that helps set the time and place of the passage.
   D. an indication that the mother feels old around her son.

479. The best placement for the underlined portion would be
   A. where it is now.
   B. at the beginning of the sentence, with a capital *W*.
   C. after the word *embarrassed*.
   D. after the word *mother*.

[3] Sometimes we don't always feel the fruition of being a
                                              _____
                                               480
mother. But I remember one incident that brought to mind

how special motherhood is. I been having a very busy day.
                            _____
                               481
It was filled with a doctor's appointment, a meeting with my

daughter's teacher, mounds of work at the office, deadlines,

and pressure. Plus there was still grocery shopping to be done.
    _____
       482
Career and motherhood were on a collision course.

[4] I think motherhood is summed up best by a line from

Karen Maezen Miller's book *Momma Zen: Walking the Crooked*

Path of Motherhood: "The life of the mother is the life of the

child: you are two blossoms on a single branch." My son's smile

brought back those words to me, and my joy was immeasurable.
                                                 _____
                                                     483
[484]

480. A. NO CHANGE
    B. laxity
    C. confluence
    D. loquaciousness

481. A. NO CHANGE
    B. had been having
    C. had been
    D. having

482. A. NO CHANGE
    B. pressure: plus
    C. pressure plus
    D. pressure, plus

483. Which of the alternatives to the underlined portion would NOT be acceptable?
    A. infinitesimal
    B. impressive
    C. boundless
    D. never-ending

484. For the sake of the logic and coherence of the essay, Paragraph 2 should be placed
    A. where it is now.
    B. at the beginning of the passage.
    C. after Paragraph 3.
    D. after Paragraph 4.

485. Suppose that the writer had intended to write a brief essay showing why the simplest and littlest things in life can surprise anybody and change the course of things. Would this essay satisfy that goal?
    A. Yes, because the essay shows that the writer finally learned how to be a good parent.
    B. Yes, because the essay shows that her son's smiling at her in school was so unexpected but, at the same time, so joyful, that her stress dissolved.
    C. No, because the focus of the essay is on how hard it is to be a mother these days.
    D. No, because the essay is not about her, but about how motherhood is different now than it was in simpler times.

The American Cowboy

Cowboys are an integral part of our history. While the
<u>486</u>
first cowboys in North America were the Mexican vaqueros.

Vaquero means "cattle driver" in Spanish. The vaqueros were

very skilled on horseback and had been herding cattle since

the sixteenth century, when the conquistadors (soldiers of the

Spanish Empire) arrived from Spain [487] with horses and

cattle. Many Anglos, or <u>English-speaking pioneers',</u> moved
<u>488</u>
into Texas beginning in 1821. They came to round up the

cattle that <u>roam free</u> on the plains. At that time, Texas was
<u>489</u>

part of Mexico. <u>Texas won its independence from Mexico in</u>
<u>490</u>
<u>1836; after the Battle of San Jacinto,</u> when the Mexican general
<u>490</u>

Santa Anna was defeated. <u>For instance,</u> the Anglos took over
<u>491</u>

the ranches that the Mexican owners <u>left behind them</u> when
<u>492</u>
they fled to Mexico. The Anglos hired the vaqueros to teach

them the cattle business. <u>These vaqueros trained Anglo</u>
<u>493</u>
<u>cowboys.</u> They also gave the English language new names for
<u>493</u>
cowboys' equipment and activities. *Hacienda* was the estate.

Rancho was the ranch, and the *ranchero* worked on the

ranch. The leather pants called "chaps," which cowboys

<u>wore protecting</u> their legs while riding, got their name from the
<u>494</u>
Spanish word *chaparajos*. So many Anglos mispronounced the

word *vaquero* <u>until it became</u> *buckaroo*, another name for
<u>495</u>

486. A. NO CHANGE
    B. Besides
    C. Indeed
    D. OMIT the underlined portion.

487. The writer is considering revising the preceding part of the sentence ("conquistadors [soldiers of the Spanish Empire] arrived from Spain") to read as follows:

    Spanish soldiers arrived from Spain

    If the writer did this, the essay would primarily lose
    A. an historical detail that adds texture to the essay.
    B. a possible point of confusion over the word *conquistadors*.
    C. an indication that the Spanish Empire was far-reaching.
    D. nothing.

488. A. NO CHANGE
    B. English-speaking pioneer's
    C. English-speaking pioneers
    D. English pioneers

489. A. NO CHANGE
    B. roaming free
    C. roamed free
    D. roamed freely

490. A. NO CHANGE
    B. Texas won its independence from Mexico in 1836. After the Battle of San Jacinto,
    C. Texas won its independence from Mexico in 1836, after the Battle of San Jacinto.
    D. Texas won its independence from Mexico in 1836, after the Battle of San Jacinto,

491. A. NO CHANGE
    B. Consequently,
    C. As an example,
    D. OMIT the underlined portion.

492. A. NO CHANGE
    B. leave behind them
    C. left behind
    D. leaving behind

493. A. NO CHANGE
    B. This vaquero trained Anglo cowboys.
    C. Those vaqueros trained Anglo cowboys.
    D. Whose vaqueros trained Anglo cowboys.

494. A. NO CHANGE
    B. wore protected
    C. protected
    D. wore to protect

495. A. NO CHANGE
    B. when it became
    C. that it became
    D. it became

cowboy. The lariat that cowboy used to rope cattle got its name
                              _____
                                 496
from the Spanish *la reata*, which means "the long rope." *Rodeo*
came from the Spanish word *rodear*, which means "to round up
cattle." The funny slang word for "jail": hoosegow, was a
                                   _____
                                            497
garbled version of the Spanish word for "courtroom," *juzgado*
(pronounced /hooz-GAH-doh/).

    When the end of the Civil War came, many flocked to
    _____
                 498
the West for a new life. The cowboy became a symbol of
freedom, living on the open range, sleeping under the stars.
Independently and self-reliantly, the cowboy represented a
_____
             499
rugged individualism, a symbol of hard work and honor,
freedom and strength. There were cowgirls too, just as skilled
as their male counterparts, handling cattle on horseback.

    In recognition of the cowboy's place in history, in 2005 the
U.S. Senate declared the fourth Saturday in July to be National
Day of the American Cowboy.

    [1] In the twentieth century, this fascination with the life of
the cowboy was reflected in hundreds of movies, with classic
films like *3:10 to Yuma*, *Rio Grande*, and *High Noon*. [2] Even
to this day, boys and girls dream of growing up to become a
cowboy or a cowgirl. [3] Cowboys had their impact on TV also;
shows like *Bonanza*, *The Lone Ranger*, and *Annie Oakley* were
favorites. 500

496. **A.** NO CHANGE
     B. the cowboy use
     C. the cowboy used
     D. cowboys used

497. **A.** NO CHANGE
     B. "jail"—hoosegow—
     C. "jail," hoosegow—
     D. OMIT the underlined portion.

498. **A.** NO CHANGE
     B. When came the end of the Civil War,
     C. With the end of the Civil War,
     D. With the ending of the Civil War,

499. **A.** NO CHANGE
     B. Independent and self-reliant,
     C. More independent and self-reliant,
     D. Most independent and self-reliant,

500. Which of the following sequences of sentences makes the
     paragraph most logical?
     A. NO CHANGE
     B. 2, 1, 3
     C. 1, 3, 2
     D. 3, 2, 1

PART III ANSWERS AND EXPLANATIONS

Chapter 12: Set 1 English Questions

251. **A.** No comma or semicolon is required between *Party* and *and*, because *and* joins two parallel phrases and doesn't require any punctuation; nor is there a need for a comma after *and*.

252. **D.** No transition word is required here, because the sentence introduces information about Alice Paul that isn't directly linked to the preceding sentence.

253. **D.** A serial comma is required before *and*, because this is a series of degrees that Paul received.

254. **B.** Since the action took place in the past, the verb should reflect that. The verb form *having traveled* creates a phrase rather than a sentence; a sentence is required.

255. **A.** This simple past verb form is correct. Answer choices (B) and (C) change the sentence to a phrase.

256. **D.** No transition word is required here.

257. **D.** The transition word *while* makes the most sense, since it links the time of Paul's being in prison to what she was doing.

258. **D.** Including the name that the press gave the demonstrations shows that the press was characterizing them.

259. **B.** The word *but* shows the correct relationship between the two parts of the sentence.

260. **B.** Since the action took place in the past, the verb should reflect that. Answer choice (A) is incorrect, because this verb form creates a phrase rather than a sentence. Answer choice (C) is an incorrect past tense, since it shows an ongoing action. Answer choice (D) is also an incorrect past tense.

261. **B.** This verb form introduces a phrase that modifies *banners*.

262. **D.** The verb forms *denied* and *abridged* are part of the sentence and should not be set off by commas.

263. **A.** This is the correct past-tense verb form. Answer choice (B) is incorrect, because an amendment cannot *ratify*; it can only *be ratified*. Answer choices (C) and (D) are incorrect verb forms; they are in the present tense.

264. **B.** This is where the sentence logically belongs. It is too important a detail to omit, so answer choice (D) is incorrect.

265. **C.** The action takes place in the past, so a past-tense verb form is required.

266. **C.** The conjunction *still* creates the correct relationship between the two parts of the sentence.

267. **D.** This is the most concise way to express the idea. The other answer choices are awkward and wordy.

268. **D.** There is no need for the words *they were*; all that needs to follow the colon is the names of the explorers.

269. **A.** The word *exposure* succinctly incorporates the concepts of very cold weather and lack of warm clothing.

270. **D.** This is the most concise and exact way to communicate how high the station is above sea level.

271. **B.** This is the strongest description of the weather at the South Pole; it gives the reader a sense of danger by using the words *severe* and *life-threatening*.

272. **D.** Answer choice (D) isn't acceptable as an alternative to *Consequently*. All of the other answer choices could be substituted for *Consequently*.

273. **B.** *Swells* is much more precise and descriptive than the other answer choices of what happens to the population of scientists.

274. **C.** By eliminating these two words, the reader would lose the sense of a contrast between where the station is located and how many scientists work there.

275. **C.** This gives more specific information about the scientific disciplines that make use of the research station.

276. **C.** This is the most succinct and direct way to include information about light pollution. The other answer choices are wordy or convoluted.

277. **D.** This information is of minor importance to the main topic of the paragraph.

278. **B.** A comma is necessary after this opening phrase. Answer choices (C) and (D) would make the opening phrase an incomplete sentence.

279. **B.** This is the most succinct and direct way to link the series. The other answer choices include unnecessary and repetitive adverbs.

280. **D.** The word *However* should be omitted, since there is no relationship between this sentence and the preceding one. Answer choice (B) is incorrect, since the word *Because* would make the sentence incomplete.

281. **B.** This word agrees in number with the subject of the sentence, *scientists*. Answer choice (D) is incorrect, because it would leave the sentence without a verb.

282. **D.** There is no basis for the other three answer choices.

283. **C.** This is the most succinct way to express this idea. Answer choices (A) and (B) are overly wordy and awkward. The sentence wouldn't make sense if the preposition were removed, so answer choice (D) is incorrect.

284. **A.** A comma is required after the opening phrase, which describes El Yunque. Answer choices (C) and (D) would make the opening phrase an incomplete sentence.

285. **C.** This provides the strongest and most precise description of the views. Answer choice (A) is rather vague. Answer choice (B) would be ungrammatical. Answer choice (D) would leave the views without a description.

286. **D.** This provides a vivid image of the clouds. The other answer choices are imprecise and weak descriptors.

287. **C.** The sentence only makes sense using this word sequence.

288. **D.** This is a possessive form. Answer choice (B) is incorrect for two reasons: lack of a possessive form and omission of the necessary comma. There is only one mountain, so answer choice (C) is incorrect.

289. **A.** This is the most succinct and direct way of communicating this information. The other answer choices are unwieldy and awkward.

290. **B.** This language is strong and provides a vivid image, making the writing much more interesting and colorful. Answer choices (A) and (C) are vague and uninteresting. Answer choice (D) would result in an incomplete phrase.

291. **A.** This word alerts the reader to information that is amazing. Answer choice (B) is incorrect, since it implies a negative relationship with the preceding sentence. Answer choice (C) is contrary to the meaning of the sentence. Answer choice (D) would leave out an important clue about the large number of tree varieties found in El Yunque.

292. **D.** Without the word *exotic*, the reader would not realize that these varieties of vegetation are unusual.

293. **B.** This provides important information about the trails. The other answer choices add little or no new information.

294. **B.** This sentence needs a subject and a verb, and the contraction *it's*, for *it is*, provides these. Answer choice (A) is a possessive form, not a contraction. Answer choice (C) is grammatically incorrect. Answer choice (D) would result in an incomplete sentence.

295. **D.** This placement is the most logical and helps the reader understand what the bird looks like. The other answer choices render the sentence extremely confusing or ungrammatical.

296. **A.** This fits the notion of the coquí calling out during the evening hours. Answer choice (B) is mundane. Answer choices (C) and (D) would apply to a person, not an animal.

297. **C.** The idea expressed in Sentence 5 naturally follows the idea expressed in Sentence 3.

298. **C.** The use of *you* would personalize the sense that the writer wants to convey. The other answer choices are not accurate.

299. **B.** The phrase describing Timbuktu, "a famous city in western Africa," should be set off by commas.

300. **D.** Since these clauses contain two distinct thoughts, each one should be its own sentence.

301. **C.** This is the most effective closing sentence; it sums up the information in the preceding sentences. The other answer choices provide details, but not a summary.

302. **B.** The simple past verb form fits the context here.

303. **B.** A possessive form is required to show that this represents a time (period) of six months. Since "six months" is plural, the singular possessive in answer choice (C) is incorrect.

304. **B.** This tells of Cox and Abdul becoming friends—important information for understanding the rest of the essay.

305. **B.** The simple past verb form fits the context here.

306. **B.** The past participle *taken* matches *sold*. The simple past form *was* fits the context.

307. **B.** The pronoun *who* refers to a person (in this case, Abdul); *that* and *which* are used with objects, so answer choices (A) and (D) are incorrect. *Whom* isn't used when the pronoun is the subject of its clause, so answer choice (C) is incorrect.

308. **D.** This sequence shows that 17 years passed between Abdul's enslavement and Cox's discovery of him in Mississippi.

309. **B.** The superlative form of the adjective makes the most sense. *Mostest* isn't grammatical, so answer choice (C) is incorrect.

310. **A.** The simple infinitive form is correct in this construction with *sent*.

311. **B.** The phrase is evidence that the writer researched the subject.

312. **D.** The phrase "through diplomacy" modifies "developing trade and good relations" and should be placed with it.

313. **A.** Although answer choice (B) expresses the same thought as answer choice (A), it isn't as well written. The other answer choices are convoluted.

314. **B.** A comma is required after the conjunctive adverb *however*.

315. **C.** Since these clauses contain two distinct ideas, each one should be its own sentence and they should be separated by a period.

316. **D.** The tense of the verb in the subordinate clause should agree with the tense of the main verb (the present tense).

317. **D.** The past participle *affected* needs a verb to make this a complete sentence; *can be* makes the most sense.

318. **A.** The underlined portion is correctly punctuated.

319. **B.** The word *terror* most effectively indicates the intense fear that a tsunami evokes.

320. **C.** The colon introduces an explanation of what a tsunami is.

321. **D.** The antecedent is "tidal waves," so the pronoun should be *they*. Since the verb in the main clause is in the present tense, the verb in this clause should also be in the present tense.

322. **D.** Although this information doesn't contradict earlier statements, it doesn't advance the main idea of the essay; it distracts the reader.

323. **B.** This phrase modifies *called* and should be placed immediately before it.

324. **C.** The infinitive is required in the construction with *causes*.

325. **A.** The conjunctive adverb *however* introduces a new and complete idea and therefore needs to be part of a separate sentence.

326. **B.** Use of the comparative form of *shallow* is correct, since only two items are being compared: the depth of the ocean farther and closer to shore.

327. **D.** The present participle matches the earlier verb form *pulling*.

328. **D.** Since the subject ("The Pacific Tsunami Warning Center") is singular, the verb must be singular. The tense of the verb should be the same as that of the earlier verb, *monitors*, that is, present tense.

329. **A.** *It's* is the contracted form of *it has*, which is grammatically correct. The other answer choices are ungrammatical.

330. **D.** Paragraph 2 logically introduces the essay and therefore should be placed first.

331. **B.** Since "noted thinker" and "Joseph Campbell" are in apposition, there should be no comma after *thinker*.

332. **A.** The writer is letting the reader know what he thinks of the advice that follows.

333. **D.** A superlative comparison is being made, so answer choice (B) is incorrect. Answer choices (A) and (C) are ungrammatical.

334. **B.** This is where the phrase logically belongs. The other answer choices make the sentence confusing and illogical.

335. **B.** *Stressful* is a strong descriptor. The other answer choices are weak and vague.

336. **D.** The word *to* is incorrect in this construction. Since the tense of the verb should match that of the main clause, answer choices (B) and (C) are incorrect.

337. **C.** The original construction is a run-on sentence and needs to be made into two sentences by inserting a period and capitalizing the first word of the second sentence.

338. **D.** Since the items in this serial list are separated by commas, there should be a comma after *artistic*.

339. **D.** The word *as* is incorrect, because *machine* and *computer* both modify *repairman*.

340. **A.** This is valuable information about conventional people and why they choose the jobs they do, so it should be included.

341. **D.** This is a serial list of the kinds of jobs that conventional personality types do, so there needs to be

a comma between the job possibilities *clerical work* and *accounting*.

342. **A.** The transition word *However* contrasts the information in the preceding sentence with the information in its sentence.

343. **D.** *As well as* introduces an incomplete sentence and needs to be joined to the preceding sentence.

344. **A.** This is where Sentence 1 logically belongs.

345. **C.** The article doesn't discuss various career aspects; it discusses personality types and which careers are most suitable for certain personalities.

346. **A.** A possessive form is required to show that this represents a trip of one day. Since "a day" is singular, the plural possessive in answer choice (C) is incorrect.

347. **A.** This is the clearest and most succinct way to express this fact. Answer choice (D) is incorrect, because it would delete important information.

348. **D.** The phrases in answer choices (A), (B), and (C) are unnecessary and cumbersome.

349. **D.** This adds significant information to the essay. The other answer choices are vague.

350. **D.** The word *nostalgic* tells the reader that the writer was feeling wistful about the past.

351. **B.** The original construction is a run-on sentence and needs to be made into two sentences by inserting a period and capitalizing the first word of the second sentence.

352. **D.** The past perfect tense (with the correct past participle, *chosen*) is correct.

353. **D.** This provides concise and important information. Answer choice (B) is incorrect, since children are people.

354. **B.** This clause is direct and concise. Answer choice (A) is slightly awkward, and answer choice (C) is wordy. Answer choice (D) is ungrammatical.

355. **A.** This descriptive word gives the reader an idea of what the town was like.

356. **D.** This is where the phrase logically belongs, since it tells what the women were doing with the pots.

357. **D.** The word *However* suggests a contrasting relationship between this sentence and the preceding one, but none exists, so it should be deleted.

358. **B.** A comma is required between two clauses that are connected by a transition word.

359. **B.** Paragraph 2 logically introduces the essay and therefore should be placed first.

360. **A.** The writer contrasts his memories of Sherbro Island with his feelings as he revisits it.

361. **C.** *It's* is the contracted form of *it is*, which is grammatically correct. *Its'* is ungrammatical, so answer choice (B) is incorrect. *They're* (answer choice (D)) is plural and makes no sense in this context.

362. **B.** The original construction is a run-on sentence and needs to be made into two sentences by inserting a period and capitalizing the first word of the second sentence.

363. **D.** The conditional verb *would* is correct after *knew*.

364. **B.** The simple past verb form *liked* matches the simple past form *grew* earlier in the sentence. Answer choice (C) is ungrammatical, and answer choice (D) is awkward.

365. **D.** The clause is logically placed at the end of the sentence.

366. **A.** The other answer choices add little detail.

367. **C.** There is no reason to suppose that the writer cleaned only the *dirtier* or *dirtiest* cages, so answer choices (A) and (D) are incorrect. Answer choice (B) isn't grammatical.

368. **C.** The relative pronoun *who* refers to people, while *that* refers to animals and objects; therefore, answer choices (A) and (B) are incorrect. Since the pronoun is necessary, answer choice (D) is incorrect.

369. **D.** This information is included earlier in the sentence.

370. **B.** The tense of the verb in the subordinate clause must match that of the main verb (the simple past tense).

371. **B.** The original construction is a run-on sentence and needs to be made into two sentences by inserting a period. Answer choice (C) also creates a run-on sentence.

372. **B.** *Consequently* doesn't make sense in this context. The other answer choices have the approximate meaning of *however*.

373. **D.** The singular possessive of *year* is required here.

374. **A.** The simple past tense matches the tense of *sent* later in the sentence.

375. **B.** This is where Sentence 2, as an introductory sentence, logically belongs.

Chapter 13: Set 2 English Questions

376. **B.** A comma is required after the name of the state.

377. **D.** The word *However* suggests a contrasting relationship between this sentence and the preceding one, but none exists, so it should be deleted.

378. **B.** The inclusion of the fact that women were rare in early aviation shows how special Amelia Earhart was.

379. **D.** Since the decision took place in the past, the verb should be in the simple past tense.

380. **B.** This is the most concise way to provide the information. Answer choice (A) doesn't modify any element in the rest of the sentence. Answer choices (C) and (D) are wordy.

381. **A.** The word *with* completes the meaning of the verb *outfitted*. Answer choices (B) and (C) would create an ungrammatical sentence. Answer choice (D) is incorrect, because it would eliminate important information.

382. **A.** A comma is required between the opening phrase, which modifies *she*, and the main clause. Answer choice (D) would create an incomplete sentence before the period.

383. **C.** The simple past tense is the correct form of the verb. Answer choice (A) is incorrect, since Noonan was not in the act of charting.

384. **D.** Since the antecedent of this word is *they*, the plural possessive form is required.

385. **C.** *Where* is required, because the clause that follows concerns the location of the airfield and fuel tanks. The other answer choices are ungrammatical.

386. **B.** This is the only answer choice of transition words that cannot be substituted for *though*.

387. **C.** This is where Sentence 6 logically belongs. Answer choice (D) is incorrect, because it would delete important information.

388. **D.** This is where the phrase logically belongs. The other answer choices are awkward or confusing.

389. **B.** A conjunction is required to connect *to send* and *(to) see*.

390. **D.** The simple past tense form of the verb is required.

391. **C.** This statement about Noonan's career is an unimportant detail in an essay about the ill-fated flight of Earhart and Noonan.

392. **B.** This placement makes the most sense. The other answer choices are awkward or change the meaning of the sentence.

393. **C.** This is the simplest and most straightforward way of stating the information. The other answer choices are ungrammatical or contain redundant words.

394. **A.** The other answer choices change the meaning of the sentence.

395. **B.** Elimination of *exotic* and "from the East" would remove the idea that the items were not easily obtained because they came from far away.

396. **D.** A comma is required after the opening adverb. Since *merchants* is the subject of the sentence, the possessive form is not used.

397. **A.** A comma is required after the opening phrase. Answer choices (C) and (D) would create an incomplete sentence.

398. **B.** This transition word correctly shows a cause-and-effect relationship between the preceding sentence and this sentence. Answer choices (A) and (C) incorrectly suggest a contrasting relationship. Answer choice (D) incorrectly suggests that there is no relationship between the two sentences.

399. **B.** The sentence contains two distinct ideas and should be separated into two sentences.

400. **B.** The actual figures spent on television advertising provide a sense of the huge amount of money involved.

401. **D.** Since the subject (*advertising*) is singular, the verb must be singular. Answer choice (B) is plural, so it is incorrect. Answer choices (A) and (C) are ungrammatical.

402. **A.** This important information would be lost.

403. **D.** A superlative form of the adverb is required, since there is a range of probabilities, not just two. Answer choice (B) is ungrammatical. Answer choice (C) is a comparative adjective.

404. **C.** This information is unnecessary and distracts from the main focus of the paragraph.

405. **C.** This reads smoothly. Answer choice (A) is awkward, and answer choice (B) is ungrammatical. Answer choice (D) would eliminate the word that links the location of this sentence with that of the preceding one.

406. **D.** This is where the paragraph belongs in terms of sequence and logic. The other answer choices wouldn't make sense.

407. **A.** The writer has successfully fulfilled his goal by demonstrating the significance of advertising through the years.

408. **B.** A comma is required after *Nakota* to separate the serial list from the phrase beginning with *comprising*.

409. **D.** This is the clearest and most direct of the answer choices. Answer choice (B) is ungrammatical.

410. **D.** This phrase provides the most significant information.

411. **C.** This is a serial list of gerunds, so there needs to be a comma between the second and third gerund phrases, "gathering foodstuffs" and "caring for their young." Answer choice (B) would create an incomplete sentence.

412. **D.** The preposition *with* is required to show the relationship between "nature" and "the animals they hunted."

413. **B.** The action has occurred for generations up to the present, and the verb form must be in the passive voice.

414. **A.** The story of the rainbow happened in the past, and *to be* correctly follows *came* in this idiom.

415. **B.** The adverb *consequently*, formed by adding *-ly* to the adjective *consequent*, is correct. *Consequence* is a noun and cannot be converted to an adverb, so answer choice (C) is incorrect. The phrase *with consequence* makes no sense, so answer choice (D) is incorrect.

416. **B.** The adjective *integral*, meaning "essential to completeness," is more precise than answer choices (A) and (C). Answer choice (D) makes no sense.

417. **D.** Sentence 5 should be placed after Sentence 7.

418. **D.** This phrase is clear and straightforward. The other answer choices are awkward or ungrammatical.

419. **B.** *Culminating* means "coming to a climax or ending" and describes *series*. *Concomitant* and *cascading* don't make sense in this context. The adverb *collaterally* would make the sentence ungrammatical.

420. **A.** Sitting Bull was chief of the Sioux. The other answer choices obscure or contradict this fact.

421. **C.** *The Sioux* is a collective plural, and the verb must be in the present tense because the reference is to *today*. Answer choice (D) is awkward.

422. **A.** The phrase "their native" is specific and clear.

423. **A.** The statement explains why the site is revered and sacred.

424. **C.** The progressive tense is used to express an ongoing action when another action took place.

425. **D.** Since these clauses contain two distinct thoughts, each one should be its own sentence.

426. **B.** The word *excitedly* adds the nuance that the writer was thrilled by the discovery of the turtles.

427. **A.** The simple past tense is required to match the tense of *looked up* and *belonged*, so answer choices (B) and (C) are incorrect. Answer choice (D) is incorrect, because a comma is required to separate the initial adverbial phrase from the rest of the sentence.

428. **C.** *Inhabits*, which means "lives in," makes the most sense here.

429. **C.** *Must have been* is the only answer choice that is grammatical.

430. **A.** The phrase should be placed where it is now, because the phrase "to support them" must immediately follow "an aquatic environment," which it modifies.

431. **B.** *Would* is required in a clause that begins "on the condition that."

432. **C.** The simple past tense *started* matches the tense of *seemed*.

433. **A.** This additional information is important, because it helps the reader understand why the writer fed the turtles lettuce.

434. **C.** *Lying* is the gerund of the verb *to lie*, which means "to be in a reclining position." *Laying* means "putting down," so answer choice (A) is incorrect. *Lain* is the past participle of *lie*, so answer choice (B) is incorrect. *To lay* means "to put down," so answer choice (D) is incorrect.

435. **C.** It is best to divide the awkward sentence into two separate sentences; this makes the meaning clearer.

436. **B.** *Would become* is the correct verb form; it shows the writer's speculation based on the preceding sentence.

437. **A.** This answer choice reveals the writer's feelings most effectively. Answer choices (B) and (C) are vague, and answer choice (D) is inaccurate.

438. **A.** Paragraph 1 sets the stage for the essay, and paragraph 2 provides more details about the turtles. Paragraph 4 relates events that occurred after the events of paragraph 3.

439. **B.** The essay tells of the writer's acceptance of change and fulfills the goal of illustrating that life is full of unexpected turns.

440. **C.** The preposition *throughout* is most appropriate and makes the meaning clearest. The other answer choices are awkward or misleading.

441. **B.** The tense of the verb in the subordinate clause must match the simple past tense of the verb in the main clause, *was*.

442. **A.** *Imaginative* suggests that the two teenagers were talented.

443. **A.** This answer choice best substantiates the claims about Superman's powers. The other answer choices are vague.

444. **A.** This answer choice adds an important description of Superman's powers. The other answer choices are awkward or less specific.

445. **B.** *Could*, which indicates possibility, matches *could* in the preceding sentence.

446. **D.** No transition word is required, since the sentence is unrelated to the preceding sentence.

447. **D.** As his alter ego, Superman purposefully chose to be *mild-mannered*.

448. **B.** This is the most direct expression; it reads more clearly than answer choice (A). Answer choices (C) and (D) would make the sentence ungrammatical.

449. **B.** The phrase "as if" makes the most sense after *feel*.

450. **D.** *Helpless* is the most appropriate word in this context. *Prostrate* means "lying face down," *servile* means "submissive," and *rejected* means "spurned" or "abandoned."

451. **C.** The statement would distract the reader without adding any important information.

452. **A.** The transition word *besides* makes no sense. Answer choices (B), (C), and (D) mean about the same as *but*.

453. **A.** *Think the reason is* makes sense and is grammatically correct; the other answer choices are ungrammatical.

454. **C.** *Truly*, which means "really" or "doubtlessly," best completes the sentence. *Seemingly* and *apparently* imply doubt, so answer choices (A) and (B) are incorrect. Omission of *seemingly* would weaken the notion that Superman cares about people.

455. **B.** The quotation marks add authenticity to Superman's mission in life.

456. **C.** The superlative form of the adjective is required for clarity, and *one of* requires the plural *women*. Answer choice (D) would result in a nonsensical sentence.

457. **D.** This answer choice provides specific, relevant information.

458. **C.** It is logical that she took the name afterward. Answer choices (A) and (D) are ungrammatical.

459. **B.** No comma is used before a restrictive clause. The use of *under* changes the meaning of the sentence, so answer choice (D) is incorrect.

460. **D.** The underlined phrase should be eliminated. *Plethora* means "excess," which is clearly not the writer's intention. Answer choice (B) means about the same thing, while answer choice (C) means the opposite.

461. **A.** Since the preceding verbs are in the simple past tense, it would be awkward to use another tense here.

462. **C.** The passive voice requires the past participle *invited*. Answer choice (B) is ungrammatical. *Oft*, while sometimes acceptable in poetry, is archaic and inappropriate in this essay, so answer choice (D) is incorrect.

463. **B.** The possessive plural, *women's*, must be used before *rights*.

464. **D.** Answer choices (A) and (B) are ungrammatical. Since the relative pronoun *that* is used with animals and things, but not with people, answer choice (C) is incorrect. In this construction, *whom* may be understood.

465. **A.** When a question mark is part of a title that is followed by a comma, the comma is placed after the closing quotation mark, so answer choice (C) is incorrect. Answer choice (B) is incorrect, because the question mark is part of the title of the speech and must be placed inside the closing quotation mark. Since the title must be set off by commas before and after, answer choice (D) is incorrect.

466. **D.** The antecedent is *injustice*, so the singular pronoun *it* is used.

467. **C.** The other answer choices are ungrammatical.

468. **A.** The other answer choices are awkward and ungrammatical.

469. **C.** Sentence 10 explains the purpose of the Freedmen's Bureau, which is mentioned in Sentence 3.

470. **D.** The infinitive of *retire* is required in the construction with *caused*. The other answer choices are ungrammatical.

471. **A.** *Let us* has a very formal tone in this context; changing *us* to *me* would make the tone less formal and more personal.

472. **D.** The preposition *while* establishes the proper relationship between *duties* and *rewards*.

473. **D.** No transition phrase is required, since the ideas in the preceding sentence and this one aren't connected. Answer choice (C) makes no sense.

474. **B.** The survey took place in the past, so the simple past tense is required. The passive voice in answer choice (D) would create an ungrammatical sentence.

475. **A.** No punctuation is necessary. Answer choice (B) creates an incomplete sentence.

476. **D.** The past progressive tense is used to match *were finishing* earlier in the sentence.

477. **C.** The conjunction *after* makes the most sense in this context, because he continued smiling after he took his uniform. *Taking* in answer choices (B) and (D) don't match the tense of the verb *gave*.

478. **B.** The phrase "in ages" is much stronger than "in a long time."

479. **D.** This placement makes the most sense. Answer choice (A) makes it appear that the friends are talking to the mother. Answer choices (B) and (C) are awkward.

480. **A.** *Fruition*, which means "achievement" or "fulfillment," is appropriate here. The other words don't make sense.

481. **B.** The other answer choices are ungrammatical or nonsensical.

482. **A.** Beginning a new sentence with *Plus* highlights the fact that there is even more work to do. Answer choices (C) and (D) would create run-on sentences.

483. **A.** *Infinitesimal* means "exceedingly small"—the opposite of *immeasurable*. The other answer choices are close in meaning to *immeasurable*.

484. **C.** Paragraph 3 sets the stage for the events of paragraph 2.

485. **B.** The essay clearly demonstrates that life can change quickly due to an emotional experience; in this case, the mother's harried day turned into a day of joy.

486. **D.** The sentence is complete and coherent without a conjunction at the beginning; in fact, the conjunction creates an incomplete sentence.

487. **A.** "Conquistadors (soldiers of the Spanish Empire)" adds texture and detail to the essay.

488. **C.** *Pioneers* is an appositive of the subject *Anglos* and therefore is not possessive, so answer choices (A) and (B) are incorrect. Answer choice (D) incorrectly suggests that all Anglos were English.

489. **D.** The tense of *roam* must match the simple past tense of the main verb *came*. The adverbial form *freely* modifies the verb *roamed*.

490. **D.** "After the Battle of San Jacinto" is a subordinate clause set off by commas. The other answer choices would create incomplete sentences.

491. **B.** *Consequently* correctly links this sentence to the preceding one. Answer choices (A) and (C) establish an incorrect relationship between these sentences. Omitting the linking word reduces the clarity of the paragraph.

492. **C.** The simple past tense is used to match *took* earlier in the sentence, so answer choices (B) and (D) are incorrect. *Them* is redundant, so answer choice (A) is incorrect.

493. **A.** "These vaqueros" refers to "the vaqueros" in the preceding sentence. *Vaqueros* is plural, so answer choice (B) is incorrect. *Those* in answer choice (C) makes it appear that they are different vaqueros. Answer choice (D) is an incomplete sentence.

494. **D.** They wore chaps in order to protect their legs. The other answer choices are ungrammatical.

495. **C.** *That* is used to complete the thought introduced by *so many*. The other answer choices are awkward or ungrammatical.

496. **D.** The simple past tense is used to match the other verbs in the paragraph, so answer choice (B) is incorrect. The plural *cowboys* must be used to match other uses of the word in the paragraph, so answer choices (A) and (C) are incorrect.

497. **B.** Setting *hoosegow* off with dashes is grammatically correct. (It could also be set off with commas.)

498. **C.** This answer choice is simple and direct. The other answer choices are awkward or wordy.

499. **B.** *Independent* and *self-reliant* are adjectives modifying *cowboy*. No comparison is being made, so using the comparative or superlative forms of these adjectives is incorrect.

500. **C.** Sentence 1 is the best opening sentence. The word *also* in Sentence 3 links it to Sentence 1. Sentence 2 is the best closing sentence.

PART IV
SCIENCE

QUESTIONS 1–45

PASSAGE 1

A corn seed, or kernel, is made up of pericarp, aleurone, and endosperm layers. Figure 14.1 shows the basic anatomy of a corn seed. The endosperm layer may be yellow or white. The aleurone layer may be purple, red, or colorless. Unless the aleurone is colorless, the color of the aleurone layer masks the color of the endosperm layer.

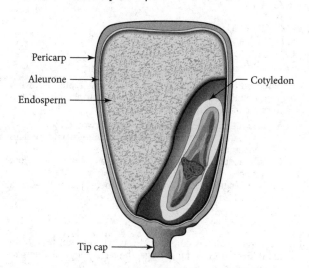

Figure 14.1

Endosperm color is determined by a single gene with two versions, or *alleles*. A corn seed's specific combination of alleles, or *genotype*, determines the physical color of the endosperm (*phenotype*). Aleurone color is determined by the interactions of three independently assorting genes. A genotype that contains at least one aleurone color allele *R* and one aleurone color inhibitor allele *C* will produce a purple aleurone. A genotype that contains at least one *R*, one *C*, and two aleurone color modifier alleles *pp* will produce a red aleurone. All other allele combinations will produce a colorless aleurone.

Table 14.1 shows the phenotypes that result from all possible allele combinations for each of the four corn seed color genes.

In a single ear of corn, each individual kernel is a separate seed representing an independent outcome from the cross of the parental corn. This means that individual kernels on the same ear of corn can have different genotypes and phenotypes.

Students in a biology class examined several ears of corn that resulted from three different parental crosses. Students were told the parental phenotypes for each cross and were instructed to count the number of kernels of each color present on each ear of corn. Table 14.2 shows the students' kernel color data for each of the three crosses.

Table 14.1 Corn Seed Color			
Gene	**Allele Relationships**	**Genotype**	**Phenotypic Outcome**
Aleurone color	$R > r$	*RR* or *Rr*	Purple aleurone in presence of *C* allele
		rr	Colorless aleurone
Aleurone color inhibitor	$C' > C > c$	*C'C', C'C*	Colorless aleurone or *C'c*
		CC or *Cc*	Purple aleurone in presence of *R* allele
		Cc	Colorless aleurone
Aleurone color modifier	$P > p$	*PP* or *Pp*	No effect on aleurone color
		pp	Changes purple aleurone to red
Endosperm color	$Y > y$	*YY* or *Yy*	Yellow endosperm
		yy	White endosperm

Table 14.2 Corn Seed Genetic Cross		
	Parental Phenotypes	**Phenotypic Outcomes**
Cross 1	Yellow × white	Ear 1 503 yellow Ear 2 510 yellow Ear 3 506 yellow
Cross 2	Red × red	Ear 1 381 red; 126 yellow Ear 2 384 red; 124 yellow Ear 3 380 red; 123 yellow
Cross 3	Purple × yellow	Ear 1 256 purple; 249 yellow Ear 2 255 yellow; 253 purple Ear 3 257 yellow; 251 purple

1. Which structure's color is only visible when the aleurone layer is colorless?

A. Pericarp
B. Tip cap
C. Cotyledon
D. Endosperm

2. It can most logically be inferred that the pericarp layer of a corn seed:

A. is colorless.
B. is beneath the aleurone and endosperm layers.
C. has the same phenotype as the endosperm layer.
D. is absent in most corn seeds.

3. According to Table 14.1, which trait has more than two alleles?

A. Aleurone color modifier
B. Aleurone color
C. Aleurone color inhibitor
D. Endosperm color

4. According to Table 14.1, how many unique kernel color phenotypes are possible?

A. Two
B. Four
C. Five
D. Nine

5. Based on the information in Table 14.1, a corn seed with the genotype *rrCʹcPPyy* would appear:

A. white.
B. purple.
C. yellow.
D. colorless.

6. Based on the information in Table 14.1, which of the following genotypes would produce a red kernel?

A. *rrCCppyy*
B. *rrCCPpyy*
C. *RRCCppyy*
D. *RRCCPpyy*

7. The term *allele relationships* describes how multiple alleles for the same gene interact. Based on the information in Table 14.1, which statement accurately describes the relationship between the alleles of the aleurone color modifier gene?

A. When both *P* and *p* are present, an intermediate phenotype is produced.
B. When *P* is present, the phenotype of *p* is masked.
C. When *p* is present, the phenotype of *P* is masked.
D. The relationship between *P* and *p* cannot be determined from the information in the table.

8. Table 14.2 shows two different kernel colors on the same ear of corn. This is possible because:

A. different kernels have different parent plants.
B. some kernels do not have an aleurone layer.
C. each kernel only gets two of the four seed color genes.
D. each kernel represents a separate offspring.

9. If the genotype of the yellow parent in Cross 1 is *rrCCppYY*, which of the following could be the genotype of the white parent?

A. *rrCCppyy*
B. *rrccppYY*
C. *RrCCppYY*
D. *rrCCPPYY*

10. In Cross 2, two red parents are shown to produce yellow kernels. What is the most likely explanation for this outcome?

A. A mutation occurring when the two parent plants were crossed resulted in a new color phenotype.
B. The crossing of parent alleles resulted in some kernels with a colorless aleurone phenotype.
C. The two parent plants for Cross 2 were incorrectly identified, resulting in mismatched phenotypes.
D. One of the parent plants passed on a yellow allele instead of a red aleurone color modifier allele.

11. The ratio of red to yellow kernels in Cross 2 is approximately:

A. 2:1.
B. 3:2.
C. 3:1.
D. 4:1.

12. To have the greatest probability of producing a yellow kernel, it would be most appropriate to repeat Cross(es):

A. 1.
B. 3.
C. 1 and 3.
D. 1, 2, and 3.

13. Based on the relationships information in Table 14.1, what would be the outcome if the yellow parent plant in Cross 3 were replaced with a white parent?

A. The ratio of purple to yellow kernels would increase.
B. The ratio of purple to yellow kernels would remain constant.
C. The resulting ears would contain purple and white kernels.
D. The resulting ears would contain purple, yellow, and white kernels.

14. Corn seed color is considered a polygenic trait. Based on the information in the passage, the term *polygenic* refers to a trait that:

A. results from a single gene with multiple alleles.
B. can exhibit a variety of phenotypes over time.
C. has a phenotype that is influenced by multiple genes.
D. affects many different functions of an organism.

15. Most of the corn sold in grocery stores is yellow. This means that an ear of corn seen at the grocery store possesses:

A. a different combination of genes than is shown in Table 14.1.
B. fewer color genes than the corn in the crosses shown here.
C. the same genotype as the yellow kernels produced in Cross 2.
D. a genotype that produces a colorless aleurone.

PASSAGE 2

Four basic aerodynamic forces act on an airplane, whether it is a passenger jet or a model made of paper. *Thrust* is the forward force and *drag* is the backward force, both of which act parallel to the airplane's motion. *Lift* is the upward force that acts perpendicular to the airplane's motion. *Gravity* is the downward force.

Students performed three experiments to determine the effects of different physical modifications on the flying ability of paper airplanes. In each experiment, students used printer paper to create a set of identical paper dart planes. They then modified the airplanes' design to investigate the effect on flight distance.

In each experiment, a single student gently threw each airplane. A second student then measured the horizontal distance covered by each plane. The students performed each experiment three times for each airplane.

Experiment 1

Students created three identical paper airplanes. The first plane's flat wings were left unaltered. The second plane's wings were modified to curve upward in a U shape. The third plane's wings were modified to curve downward in an inverted U shape. The results are shown in Table 14.3.

Table 14.3 Airplane Wing Curvature Data	
Wing Curvature	Horizontal Distance (m)
Trial 1	
Flat wings	9.5
Wings curved up	10.2
Wings curved down	9.1
Trial 2	
Flat wings	10.4
Wings curved up	10.3
Wings curved down	9.9
Trial 3	
Flat wings	10.8
Wings curved up	10.6
Wings curved down	10.8

Experiment 2

Students created three identical paper airplanes. They left the first plane's flat wings unaltered. The second plane's wingtips were bent slightly upward. The third plane's wingtips were bent slightly downward. The results are shown in Table 14.4.

Table 14.4 Airplane Wingtip Position Data	
Wingtip Position	Horizontal Distance (m)
Trial 1	
Flat wingtips	10.6
Wingtips bent up	12.4
Wingtips bent down	3.2
Trial 2	
Flat wingtips	11.1
Wingtips bent up	12.9
Wingtips bent down	3.5
Trial 3	
Flat wingtips	10.9
Wingtips bent up	12.8
Wingtips bent down	3.3

Experiment 3

Students created four identical paper airplanes. The first plane remained unaltered. Two paperclips were placed on either side of the second plane's nose. Two paperclips were placed on either side of the third plane at midwing. Two paperclips were placed on either side of the fourth plane's tail. The results are shown in Table 14.5.

Table 14.5 Airplane Paperclip Position Data	
Paperclip Position	Horizontal Distance (m)
Trial 1	
No paperclips	10.8
Nose	9.1
Midwing	10.6
Tail	6.3
Trial 2	
No paperclips	10.7
Nose	9.4
Midwing	10.5
Tail	6.2
Trial 3	
No paperclips	10.8
Nose	9.3
Midwing	10.7
Tail	6.0

16. Which aerodynamic force is the result of friction as an airplane moves through the air?

   A. Thrust
   B. Lift
   C. Drag
   D. Gravity

17. Which pair of aerodynamic forces directly oppose each other?

   A. Lift and drag
   B. Thrust and lift
   C. Gravity and thrust
   D. Drag and thrust

18. To keep a paper airplane in the air, the forces of thrust and lift:

   A. cannot be less than the forces of drag and gravity.
   B. must be equal to each other.
   C. cannot be equal to each other.
   D. must be less than the forces of drag and gravity.

19. Experiments 1 and 3 differed in the:

   A. type of paper used.
   B. number of airplanes tested.
   C. number of students involved.
   D. number of trials performed.

20. Which of the following statements about Experiment 1 is most accurate?

   A. Curving the wings slightly upward appears to improve airplane performance.
   B. Altering the curvature of the wings appears to have little impact on airplane performance.
   C. Curving the wings slightly downward appears to impede airplane performance.
   D. Flat wings appear to result in poor airplane performance.

21. In Experiment 2, bending the wingtips slightly downward most likely increased the effect of which force?

   A. Drag
   B. Lift
   C. Thrust
   D. Gravity

22. Which condition represents the control group in Experiment 2?

   A. Wingtips bent down
   B. Wingtips bent up
   C. Flat wingtips
   D. No wingtips

23. Based on the data from Experiment 3, which paperclip placement had the least effect on flight distance?

   A. At the tail
   B. On the wingtips
   C. At the nose
   D. Midwing

24. Based on the data from the three experiments, which of the following is the approximate average horizontal distance traveled by an unaltered airplane?

   A. 9.5 m
   B. 10.0 m
   C. 10.5 m
   D. 11.5 m

25. Which modification had the most positive effect on airplane performance?

   A. Bending wingtips slightly upward
   B. Adding paperclips to the midwing
   C. Curving wings upward
   D. Bending wingtips slightly downward

26. A student produces the graph shown in Figure 14.2. This graph best represents the data contained in:

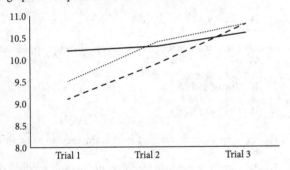

Figure 14.2

   A. Table 14.3.
   B. Table 14.4.
   C. Table 14.5.
   D. all three tables.

27. An object's *center of gravity* identifies the average location of the object's weight. In which experiment did students alter the center of gravity of the paper airplanes?

   A. All three experiments
   B. Experiment 2
   C. Experiment 1
   D. Experiment 3

28. Which modification changed an airplane's average horizontal distance the most?

   A. Adding paperclips to the tail
   B. Adding paperclips to the nose
   C. Curving wings downward
   D. Bending wingtips slightly downward

29. In Table 14.3, the horizontal distance of each individual airplane is shown to increase with each subsequent trial. The most reasonable explanation for this trend is that the:

   A. student measuring the distance used different meter sticks with each trial.
   B. three airplanes became more aerodynamic with each trial.
   C. student throwing increased the amount of initial thrust with each trial.
   D. effects of gravity on all three airplanes were decreased with each trial.

30. Based on the data from the three experiments, which combination of features would be expected to produce the longest flight?

   A. Wings curved down, flat wingtips, and paperclips at the nose
   B. Flat wings, wingtips bent up, and no paperclips
   C. Wings curved up, wingtips bent down, and paperclips at the tail
   D. Flat wings, flat wingtips, and no paperclips

PASSAGE 3

Bacteria species are differentiated into two large groups, gram-positive and gram-negative, based on the properties of their cell walls. *Peptidoglycan*, a sugar–amino acid polymer, is a structural component of the cells walls of both types of bacteria, though the peptidoglycan layer is significantly thicker in gram-positive bacteria. Gram-negative bacteria have an extra lipid bilayer, called the *outer membrane*, that surrounds the entire cell. Figure 14.3 shows a structural comparison of the cell walls of gram-positive and gram-negative bacteria.

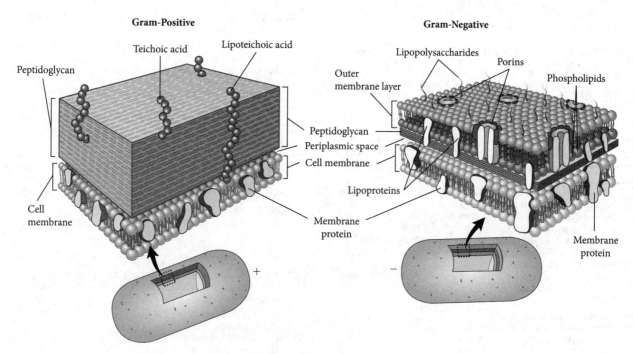

Figure 14.3

Gram staining is a technique used to identify to which group a particular bacteria species belongs based on its ability to retain a dye when rinsed with a solvent. First, the primary stain, crystal violet, is applied to the bacteria culture. An iodine solution is then added to form a complex with the crystal violet inside the cells. A decolorizer (ethyl alcohol or acetone) is added next. In gram-positive bacteria, the decolorizer dehydrates and shrinks the thick peptidoglycan layer. This traps the large crystal violet–iodine complex inside the cell, staining the cell purple. In gram-negative bacteria, the decolorizer degrades the outer membrane. This prevents the thin peptidoglycan layer from retaining the crystal violet–iodine complex, and the dye is washed out of the cell. A counterstain (safranine or fuchsin) is then added to the culture, giving decolorized gram-negative cells a red color. The counterstain is lighter colored than the primary stain, so it does not affect the outcome for gram-positive cells. After the staining procedure is completed, the treated cells are examined under a microscope to determine their color, thus identifying the group to which they belong.

Gram staining is typically the first test in a series of laboratory tests used to identify an unknown bacteria sample. Table 14.6 is a dichotomous key of characteristics that can be used to identify members of five common bacteria genera.

Table 14.6 Bacteria Dichotomous Key		
1a.	Gram-positive cells	Go to Step 2
1b.	Gram-negative cells	Go to Step 3
2a.	Rod-shaped cells	Gram-positive bacilli
2b.	Sphere-shaped cells	Go to Step 4
3a.	Rod-shaped cells	Go to Step 5
3b.	Sphere-shaped cells	Gram-negative cocci
4a.	Produces catalase	*Staphylococcus* spp.
4b.	Does not produce catalase	*Streptococcus* spp.
5a.	Ferments lactose	Go to Step 6
5b.	Does not ferment lactose	*Pseudomonas* spp.
6a.	Can use citric acid as sole carbon source	*Enterobacter* spp.
6b.	Cannot use citric acid as sole carbon source	*Escherichia* spp.

31. Which statement accurately describes a structural difference between gram-positive and gram-negative bacteria?

    A. Gram-positive bacteria have a thicker layer of peptidoglycan but lack an outer membrane.
    B. Both types of bacteria have a cell wall, but gram-negative bacteria lack a cell membrane.
    C. Gram-negative bacteria have an outer membrane instead of a peptidoglycan layer.
    D. The outer membrane is located beneath the peptidoglycan layer in gram-positive bacteria.

32. Which structural feature is present in both gram-positive and gram-negative cells?

    A. Porins
    B. Lipoteichoic acid
    C. Periplasmic space
    D. Lipopolysaccharides

33. Which of the following statements is most logically supported by the presence of porins in gram-negative bacteria?

    A. Cells walls are not permeable, so all substances entering a bacteria cell must travel through porins.
    B. The lipopolysaccharide and phospholipid bilayer is less permeable than peptidoglycan.
    C. In bacteria cells, a thicker peptidoglycan layer is more permeable than a thin peptidoglycan layer.
    D. Gram-negative bacteria transport larger molecules into their cells than do gram-positive bacteria.

34. Which substance does not act as a tissue stain in the Gram staining technique?

    A. Safranine
    B. Crystal violet
    C. Fuchsin
    D. Ethyl alcohol

35. According to the Gram staining technique, a bacteria species is identified as gram-negative if its cells:

    A. appear purple after the staining procedure.
    B. have not been exposed to any stain.
    C. appear colorless after the staining procedure.
    D. appear red after the staining procedure.

36. In the Gram staining technique, which step must be performed before the addition of the iodine solution?

    A. Staining with safranine
    B. Washing with acetone
    C. Staining with crystal violet
    D. Washing with ethyl alcohol

37. Based on the information about the Gram staining technique, the most logical reason for applying a counterstain is to:

    A. intensify the appearance of gram-positive cells under a microscope.
    B. prevent the primary stain from affecting gram-negative cells.
    C. counteract the effects of the primary stain on gram-positive cells.
    D. allow gram-negative cells to be seen more easily under a microscope.

38. Based on the information about the Gram staining technique, it is most reasonable to expect a chain of which type of molecule to degrade in the presence of ethyl alcohol?

    A. Lipids
    B. Nucleotides
    C. Sugars
    D. Amino acids

39. Based on the information in Table 14.6, bacteria belonging to which genus would appear purple after a Gram staining test?

    A. Streptococcus
    B. Escherichia
    C. Pseudomonas
    D. Enterobacter

40. In Table 14.6, Steps 2 and 3 list the same cell shape characteristics because:

    A. gram-positive and gram-negative bacteria can both be rod- or sphere-shaped.
    B. gram-positive bacteria can switch between rod and sphere shapes.
    C. cell shape depends on the results of the bacteria's Gram staining test.
    D. the cell shape of many gram-positive and gram-negative bacteria is unknown.

41. Of the five bacteria genera listed in Table 14.6, how many have a cell wall composed of a thick peptidoglycan layer?

    A. One
    B. Two
    C. Three
    D. Five

42. Based on the information in Table 14.6, which genera contains gram-negative, rod-shaped bacteria that do not ferment lactose?

    A. Pseudomonas
    B. Enterobacter
    C. Staphylococcus
    D. Escherichia

43. Based on the information in Table 14.6, which characteristic is shared by Pseudomonas and Enterobacter bacteria?

    A. Gram-positive cells
    B. Lactose fermentation
    C. Use of citric acid as sole carbon source
    D. Rod-shaped cells

44. A laboratory technician is examining a bacteria sample belonging to the genus Escherichia under a microscope and notes that the sample remains colorless after performing the Gram staining procedure. It is most reasonable to assume that an error occurred during the:

    A. application of the primary stain.
    B. application of the counterstain.
    C. decolorization of the cells.
    D. bonding of iodine to the primary stain.

45. Since gram-negative bacteria are generally more resistant to antibiotics such as penicillin, Gram staining can be used to inform appropriate antibiotic treatment for patients with bacterial infections. Based on the information in Table 14.6, infections caused by bacteria belonging to which genera would be most effectively treated with penicillin?

    A. Staphylococcus and Streptococcus
    B. Enterobacter and Escherichia
    C. Staphylococcus and Enterobacter
    D. Streptococcus and Escherichia

CHAPTER 15
TEST 2

QUESTIONS 46–88

PASSAGE 4

An organism's genetic information is stored within the nuclei of its cells as a set of chromosomes. The number of chromosomes in a cell varies from species to species. In some species, the number of chromosomes can vary between individuals. Table 15.1 lists the chromosome count for a variety of species.

Table 15.1   Species Chromosome Count

Organism	Scientific Name	Diploid Number of Chromosomes
Adder's-tongue fern	*Ophioglossum reticulatum*	1,260
Coyote	*Canis latrans*	78
Dog	*Canis lupus familiaris*	78
Horse	*Equus ferus caballus*	64
Donkey	*Equus africanus asinus*	62
Bengal fox	*Vulpes bengalensis*	60
Silkworm	*Bombyx mori*	54
Pineapple	*Ananas comosus*	50
Zebra fish	*Danio rerio*	50
Potato	*Solanum tuberosum*	48[1]
Human	*Homo sapiens*	46
Oats	*Avena sativa*	42[2]
Mouse	*Mus musculus*	40
Earthworm	*Lumbricus terrestris*	36
Red fox	*Vulpes vulpes*	34
Alfalfa	*Medicago sativa*	32[1]
European honeybee	*Apis mellifera*	32[3]
Yeast	*Saccharomyces cerivisiae*	32

Table 15.1   Species Chromosome Count (*Continued*)

Organism	Scientific Name	Diploid Number of Chromosomes
Slime mold	*Dictyostelium discoideum*	12
Swamp wallaby	*Wallabia bicolor*	10/11[4]
Fruit fly	*Drosophila melanogaster*	8
Jack jumper ant	*Myrmecia pilosula*	2[3]

[1]Organism is a tetraploid.
[2]Organism is a hexaploid.
[3]Males are haploid.
[4]Males have one less chromosome than females.
Source: http://en.wikipedia.org/wiki/List_of_organisms_by_chromosome_count.

Ploidy is the number of sets of chromosomes present in the cell of an organism. The *monoploid* number (x) is the number of chromosomes an organism has in one set.

In most species, a *gamete* (sex cell) contains one complete set of an organism's chromosomes. The number of chromosomes in a gamete is referred to as the *haploid* number (n). The fusing of two gametes into a zygote during sexual reproduction produces *somatic cells* (body cells) containing two complete sets of chromosomes. The total number of chromosomes in a somatic cell is referred to as the *diploid* number ($2n$). In most species, the monoploid number (x) and the haploid number (n) are the same.

Some species have more than two sets of chromosomes present in their cells, a condition referred to as *polyploidy*. The somatic cells of *triploid* organisms have three sets of chromosomes, for example, and *tetraploids* have four. In polyploidy organisms, the term *haploid* is still used to describe the number of chromosomes in a gamete, and *diploid* is used to describe the number of chromosomes in a somatic cell. However, the monoploid number and the haploid number are not the same in a polyploidy organism.

46. Based on the information in Table 15.1, which species does not exhibit variation in chromosome numbers between individuals?

   A. European honeybee
   B. Swamp wallaby
   C. Slime mold
   D. Jack jumper ant

47. The first part of an organism's scientific name identifies the *genus* to which it belongs. Which statement about the members of a genus is best supported by the information in Table 15.1?

A. An organism's genus determines the number of chromosomes it has.
B. Organisms in the same genus tend to have similar chromosome counts.
C. No two organisms in the same genus can have the same number of chromosomes.
D. Chromosome count can vary greatly between organisms in the same genus.

48. Based on the information in Table 15.1, the relationship between diploid chromosome count and organism complexity can best be described as exhibiting:

A. a direct correlation.
B. no correlation.
C. an inverse correlation.
D. a linear correlation.

49. To which kingdom does the organism exhibiting the greatest diploid number of chromosomes in Table 15.1 belong?

A. Animalia
B. Plantae
C. Eubacteria
D. Protista

50. Which species has more chromosomes than a human but fewer chromosomes than a dog?

A. *Bombyx mori*
B. *Canis latrans*
C. *Ophioglossum reticulatum*
D. *Mus musculus*

51. Cells from which pair of organisms have the same number of chromosomes in their nuclei?

A. Horse and donkey
B. Zebra fish and pineapple
C. Earthworm and European honeybee
D. Oats and potato

52. A team of scientists have discovered three previously unknown insect species in the Amazon rain forest. Which statement about the genetic information of these species is best supported by the data in Table 15.1?

A. The largest species is most likely to have the highest number of diploid chromosomes.
B. There is no way to determine the diploid chromosome count of each species.
C. The three species are highly likely to have the same number of diploid chromosomes.
D. It is not easy to predict the diploid chromosome count of each species.

53. Based on the information in the passage, which species produces gametes that each contain 32 chromosomes?

A. *Apis mellifera*
B. *Saccharomyces cerivisiae*
C. *Equus ferus caballus*
D. *Drosophila melanogaster*

54. According to the information in Table 15.1, how many more total chromosomes does a female European honeybee have than a male?

A. 1
B. 2
C. 16
D. 32

55. Based on the information in the passage, the total number of chromosomes in a somatic cell is represented by which of the following terms?

A. n
B. x
C. $2x$
D. $2n$

56. Which statement about polyploidy is supported by the information in the passage?

A. The number of chromosomes varies among the somatic cells of a polyploid organism.
B. The gametes and somatic cells of a polyploid organism contain the same number of chromosomes.
C. The gametes of a polyploid organism contain more than one complete set of chromosomes.
D. The somatic cells of a polyploid organism contain too many chromosomes to be considered diploid.

57. Which of the following organisms has four complete sets of chromosomes in its somatic cells?

A. Alfalfa
B. Slime mold
C. Oats
D. Earthworm

58. Table 15.1 identifies the oat species *Avena sativa* as a hexaploid, containing six sets of chromosomes. The numerical representation $2n = 6x = 42$ describes the total number of chromosomes in a somatic cell of this hexaploid species. How many chromosomes does *Avena sativa* have in one set?

A. 6
B. 7
C. 21
D. 42

59. Which of the following correctly identifies the relationship between the diploid number ($2n$), haploid number (n), and monoploid number (x) of *Solanum tuberosum*?

A. $2n$ is twice n, but 4 times x.
B. $2n$ is twice the sum of n and x.
C. $2n$ is the sum of n and x.
D. $2n$ is twice x, but 4 times n.

PASSAGE 5

The majority of scientists agree that global temperatures are rising, leading to a host of climate changes that will produce significant worldwide effects over time. Still subject to debate are the type and severity of effects that these climate changes will have on various industries. Two scientists present their viewpoints regarding the effects of climate change on agriculture in the United States.

Scientist 1

Climate change is likely to have mixed effects on U.S. agriculture over time. Every crop has a set of optimal conditions under which it grows and reproduces best. For many crops, the growth rate increases as temperature increases, suggesting that the progressive increase in average temperatures will have a beneficial effect on many types of crops. On the other hand, a faster growth rate means less time for the seeds of certain crops to mature, hindering their reproductive ability. Average temperatures will eventually surpass the optimal growth temperature for some crops, causing their yields to decline.

Crop yields also increase with carbon dioxide levels. The positive growth effect of carbon dioxide can be suppressed, however, if the optimal growth temperature is surpassed. The potential effects of climate change on other environmental conditions, including soil moisture, nutrient levels, and water availability must be taken into account as well.

Scientist 2

Agriculture in the United States will be adversely affected by climate change over the next several decades. Many weeds, pests, and fungi thrive in warm, wet climates and with increased levels of carbon dioxide. As average temperatures continue to increase and these conditions become more widespread, the habitat ranges for these organisms will spread northward. This will pose challenges to northern crops that have not previously been exposed to certain competitors and pests.

The predicted increase in extreme weather events will also negatively impact crop yields. An increase in the frequency of floods will destroy crops and potentially deter farming along major waterways altogether. In areas in which drought conditions are projected to become more common, a water supply capable of sustaining even modest crop yields is a very real concern.

60. According to Scientist 1, how will a change in average temperature affect the growth rates of crops?

A. As average temperature increases, all crops will begin to grow faster.

B. A change in average temperature will benefit some crops and harm others.

C. If average temperature changes too quickly, many crops will stop growing.

D. An increase in average temperature will hinder growth until crops adapt.

61. If Scientist 1 is correct, which of the following trends will most likely occur over the next several decades?

A. The agriculture industry will experience no significant change in crop yields.

B. The depletion of soil nutrients will cause yields of all crops to decline.

C. Crops with chemical defenses against pests will exhibit increased yields.

D. Crops with higher optimal growth temperatures will produce greater yields.

62. Which environmental change was discussed by Scientist 2, but not Scientist 1?

A. Elevated carbon dioxide levels

B. Increasing average temperatures

C. Limited water availability

D. Increased frequency of flooding

63. Scientist 2 did not predict that climate change would cause an increase in which of the following factors affecting crop yields?

A. Fungi

B. Pests

C. Seeds

D. Weeds

64. Based on the passage, the major difference between the opinions of Scientists 1 and 2 is that:

A. Scientist 2 does not predict any positive effects of climate change on agriculture.

B. Scientist 1 discusses the effects of increased temperature but not carbon dioxide.

C. Scientist 2 expects agriculture in southern areas to be unaffected by climate change.

D. Scientist 1 focuses only on the effects of climate change on crop reproductive rates.

65. Scientist 2 states that high:

A. carbon dioxide levels will benefit crop yields.

B. carbon dioxide levels will lead to decreased crop yields.

C. average temperatures will improve crop yields.

D. average temperatures will hinder the growth of fungi.

66. An industry-wide increase in agricultural pesticide use over the next several decades would support the opinion of:

A. Scientist 1.

B. Scientist 2.

C. both scientists.

D. neither scientist.

67. According to Scientist 1, what happens when a crop's optimal growth temperature is surpassed?

A. The crop maintains growth at its maximum rate.

B. The crop continues to grow but at a reduced rate.

C. The crop experiences growth at an exponential rate.

D. The crop can no longer grow in that environment.

68. Based on the information in the passage, both scientists would agree with which of the following statements?

   A. The greatest threat posed by climate change to the U.S. agriculture industry is the projected increase in extreme weather events.
   B. Southern crops are better adapted than northern crops to withstand the effects of elevated carbon dioxide levels associated with climate change.
   C. The effects of climate change will have a greater negative impact on the reproductive ability of crops than on their growth rate.
   D. Increasing average temperatures associated with climate change will provide an advantage to some organisms.

69. It can be inferred that Scientist 1 believes elevated levels of carbon dioxide will directly lead to crops with a(n):

   A. shortened growing season.
   B. higher optimal growth temperature.
   C. decreased need for soil nutrients.
   D. increased rate of photosynthesis.

70. Which of the following does Scientist 2 identify as potential competitors to northern crops?

   A. Invasive species of weeds
   B. Newly introduced crop species
   C. Other industries that use land
   D. Migrating pest species

71. The hypothesis of Scientist 1 could best be tested by recording data over the next decade on:

   A. crop yields, average temperatures, and soil nutrient availability worldwide.
   B. seed production, soil nutrient availability, and water availability worldwide.
   C. seed production, carbon dioxide levels, and water availability in the United States.
   D. crop yields, average temperatures, and carbon dioxide levels in the United States.

72. If Scientist 2 is correct, over time, the range of:

   A. northern crops will become narrower.
   B. southern crops will move farther south.
   C. northern crops will overtake southern crops.
   D. southern crops will remain constant.

73. Assuming that increasing carbon dioxide levels cause average temperature to increase, which graph best represents the relationship between carbon dioxide level and crop yields, according to Scientist 1?

A.

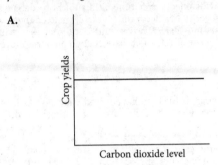

Figure 15.1

B.

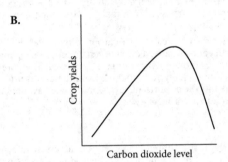

Figure 15.2

C.

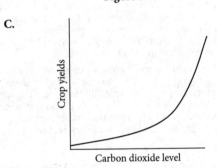

Figure 15.3

D.

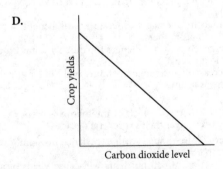

Figure 15.4

PASSAGE 6

The leaves of green plants use the energy in sunlight to convert atmospheric carbon into organic carbon through the reactions of photosynthesis. These reactions can be summarized by the following equation:

$$6CO_2 + 6H_2O + light \rightarrow C_6H_{12}O_6 + 6O_2$$

Gas exchange between the leaf and the environment is an integral part of the photosynthesis reactions. As carbon dioxide enters the leaf, the oxygen produced as a by-product of photosynthesis is released into the environment in a 1:1 ratio. Enclosing a leaf within a lighted chamber allows for the rate of this exchange, and therefore the rate of photosynthesis, to be measured.

Students in a biology class used lighted chambers to measure the photosynthetic rate of leaves from four common plant species: sunflower, water hyacinth, rhoeo, and pothos. A leaf was placed inside the chamber, and a flow of air was introduced. Sensors within the chamber recorded data on light intensity (LED irradiance), carbon dioxide concentration, air temperature, and relative humidity.

The leaf was initially exposed to a constant light intensity of 300 μE/m²/s to stimulate photosynthesis. After this initial period, students incrementally increased the light intensity to investigate the relationship between light intensity and photosynthetic rate.

Figure 15.5 shows the light intensity (LED irradiance) over time for a chamber containing a water hyacinth.

Figure 15.6 shows the change in carbon dioxide concentration over time for a chamber containing a water hyacinth.

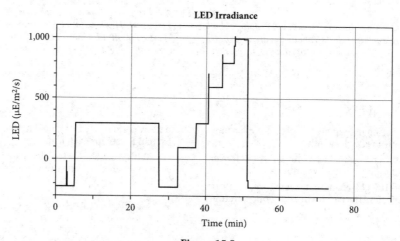

Figure 15.5
Source: "BISC 111/113: Introductory Organismal Biology," by Jocelyne Dolce, Jeff Hughes, Janet McDonough, Simone Helluy, Andrea Sequeira, and Emily A. Bucholtz. http://openwetware.org/wiki/Lab_5:_Measurement_of_Chlorophyll_Concentrations _and_Rates_of_Photosynthesis_in_Response_to_Increasing_Light_Intensity.

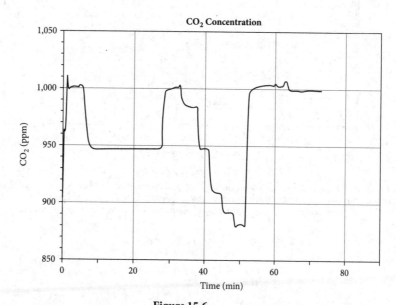

Figure 15.6
Source: "BISC 111/113: Introductory Organismal Biology," by Jocelyne Dolce, Jeff Hughes, Janet McDonough, Simone Helluy, Andrea Sequeira, and Emily A. Bucholtz. http://openwetware.org/wiki/Lab_5:_Measurement_of_Chlorophyll_Concentrations _and_Rates_of_Photosynthesis_in_Response_to_Increasing_Light_Intensity.

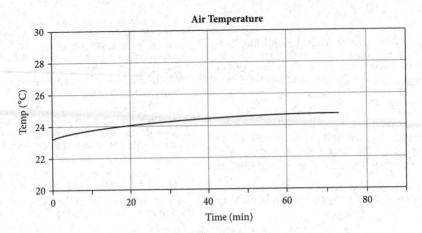

Figure 15.7

Source: "BISC 111/113: Introductory Organismal Biology," by Jocelyne Dolce, Jeff Hughes, Janet McDonough, Simone Helluy, Andrea Sequeira, and Emily A. Bucholtz. http://openwetware.org/wiki/Lab_5:_Measurement_of_Chlorophyll_Concentrations_and_Rates_of_ Photosynthesis_in_Response_to_Increasing_Light_Intensity.

Figure 15.7 shows the change in air temperature over time for a chamber containing a water hyacinth.

Figure 15.8 shows the change in relative humidity (RH) over time for a chamber containing a water hyacinth.

Students performed 10 light-chamber trials with leaves from each of the four plant species. The carbon dioxide concentration

data was then used to calculate the maximum carbon dioxide exchange rate for each leaf.

Table 15.2 shows the calculated and mean carbon dioxide exchange rates for each of the four plant species.

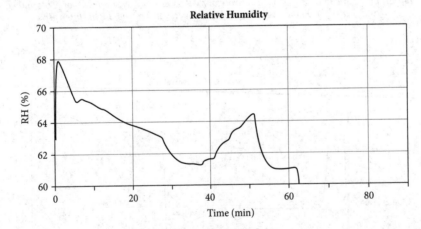

Figure 15.8

Source: "BISC 111/113: Introductory Organismal Biology," by Jocelyne Dolce, Jeff Hughes, Janet McDonough, Simone Helluy, Andrea Sequeira, and Emily A. Bucholtz. http://openwetware.org/wiki/Lab_5:_Measurement_of_Chlorophyll_Concentrations _and_Rates_of_Photosynthesis_in_Response_to_Increasing_Light_Intensity.

Table 15.2 Carbon Dioxide Exchange Rates

Trial	Plant	CO$_2$ Exchange Rate (μmol/m^2/s)	Plant	CO$_2$ Exchange Rate (μmol/m^2/s)	Plant	CO$_2$ Exchange Rate (μmol/m^2/s)	Plant	CO$_2$ Exchange Rate (μmol/m^2/s)
1	Sunflower	14	Water hyacinth	16	Rhoeo	2	Pothos	8
2		19		19		3		3
3		27		12		5		12
4		20		13		4		8
5		24		12		5		4
6		11		15		3		4
7		17		12		4		10
8		17		16		2		4
9		10		13		2		5
10		15		15		5		2
	Mean	17.4	Mean	14.3	Mean	3.5	Mean	6.0
	Standard Deviation	5.4	Standard Deviation	2.3	Standard Deviation	1.3	Standard Deviation	3.3

Source: http://openwetware.org/wiki/Lab_5:_Measurement_of_Chlorophyll_Concentrations_and_Rates_of_Photosynthesis_in_Response_to_Increasing_Light_Intensity.

74. The atmospheric carbon absorbed by green plants is in the form of:

A. carbon monoxide.
B. carbon dioxide.
C. carbohydrates.
D. water.

75. Which molecule is formed as a by-product of the photosynthesis reactions?

A. Carbon dioxide
B. Glucose
C. Water
D. Oxygen

76. According to Figure 15.5, the initial photosynthesis-stimulating period lasted approximately:

A. 5 minutes.
B. 20 minutes.
C. 50 minutes.
D. 80 minutes.

77. The slight increase in air temperature indicated in Figure 15.7 is most likely related to the:

A. increasing light intensity as the study progressed.
B. peak in relative humidity at the 50-minute mark.
C. increase in CO$_2$ concentration at the end of the study.
D. heat generated by the sensors in the light chamber.

78. Sensors within the lighted chamber monitor the presence of which chemical reactant of the photosynthesis reactions?

A. Carbon dioxide
B. Oxygen
C. Sunlight
D. Glucose

79. Which graph represents the independent variable in the students' study?

A. Figure 15.6
B. Figure 15.7
C. Figure 15.5
D. Figure 15.8

80. Based on the data in Figures 15.5 and 15.6, which light intensity causes a water hyacinth leaf to absorb carbon dioxide at the fastest rate?

A. 0 μE/m^2/s
B. 300 μE/m^2/s
C. 100 μE/m^2/s
D. 1,000 μE/m^2/s

81. The data in the table would best support the assertion that sunflower plants:

A. require less intense light than the other three species.
B. release more oxygen than the other three species.
C. are the fastest growing of the four species studied.
D. have the shortest life cycle of the four species studied.

82. According to Table 15.2, which plant showed the least variability across trials?

A. Water hyacinth
B. Pothos
C. Rhoeo
D. Sunflower

83. Based on the information in the passage, if the oxygen concentration within the chamber had been recorded, its graph would most closely resemble which figure?

    A. Figure 15.6
    B. Figure 15.7
    C. Figure 15.5
    D. Figure 15.8

84. According to the data in Table 15.2, which plant species perform(s) photosynthesis at a faster rate than pothos?

    A. Sunflower only
    B. Sunflower and water hyacinth
    C. Rhoeo only
    D. Rhoeo and water hyacinth

85. Which of the following generalizations is supported by the data in Figures 15.5 through 15.8?

    A. Photosynthesis occurs at a faster rate in a highly humid environment.
    B. The rate of photosynthesis varies directly with air temperature.
    C. The greater the light intensity, the faster the rate of photosynthesis.
    D. The rate of photosynthesis depends on the level of carbon dioxide available.

86. Which of the following statements is supported by the data in Table 15.2?

    A. The single leaf with the fastest gas exchange rate was from a sunflower plant.
    B. The single leaf with the slowest gas exchange rate was from a water hyacinth plant.
    C. No two leaves from different species exhibited the same gas exchange rate.
    D. No two leaves from the same species exhibited the same gas exchange rate.

87. Based on the data in Table 15.2, which plant could be expected to be most tolerant of a low-light environment?

    A. Rhoeo
    B. Pothos
    C. Sunflower
    D. Water hyacinth

88. The passage states that the rates recorded in Table 15.2 represent the maximum carbon dioxide exchange rates observed for each trial. Assuming that light intensity was increased at the same intervals for each trial, at approximately which point during each trial were the exchange rates recorded in the table most likely observed?

    A. 30 minutes
    B. 70 minutes
    C. 10 minutes
    D. 50 minutes

PASSAGE 7

Antigens occur on the surface of many cell types and provide a unique chemical signature that allows the body to determine the cell's identity. *Antibodies* are proteins that attack foreign substances that may pose an immune threat to the body. Antibodies identify a substance as foreign by recognizing and binding to its surface antigens. Each type of antibody is antigen-specific, attacking only one type of antigen.

Human blood is classified into different blood groups based on the presence of certain antigens on the red blood cells. The most commonly used blood group system is ABO. This system classifies blood into four groups (types) according to the presence or absence of A and/or B antigens on the blood cells. Cells may contain A antigens only, B antigens only, both A and B antigens, or neither antigen. Blood also contains antibodies against the antigens that are absent from the red blood cells. For example, type A blood contains A antigens and anti-B antibodies. Table 16.1 identifies the antigens and antibodies present in each blood type.

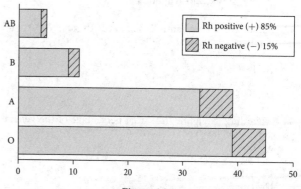

Figure 16.1
Source: https://www.armydogtags.com.

Table 16.1 ABO Blood Types		
Blood Type	**Antigens Present**	**Antibodies Present**
A	A	Anti-B
B	B	Anti-A
AB	A and B	None
O	None	Anti-A and Anti-B

Blood can also be classified as Rh-positive (Rh+) or Rh-negative (Rh−), based on the presence or absence of a different antigen on the red blood cells. Table 16.2 identifies whether the Rh antigen or antibody is present in each blood type.

Table 16.2 Rh Blood Types		
Blood Type	**Antigens Present**	**Antibodies Present**
Rh+	Yes	No
Rh−	No	Yes

The ABO and Rh blood group systems are combined to determine an individual's medical blood type. Figure 16.1 illustrates the distribution of medical blood types in the general population of the United States.

Table 16.3 indicates the distribution of medical blood types by ethnicity in the United States. The values listed represent the percentage of individuals within the given ethnic group that exhibit each blood type.

Table 16.3 Blood Type Demographics				
Blood Type	**Percentage of Individuals with Blood Type (%)**			
	Caucasian	**African American**	**Hispanic**	**Asian**
O+	37	47	53	39
O−	8	4	4	1
A+	33	24	29	27
A−	7	2	2	0.5
B+	9	18	9	25
B−	2	1	1	0.4
AB+	3	4	2	7
AB−	1	0.3	0.2	0.1

89. What is the total number of medical blood types possible for a human being?

A. Two
B. Four
C. Six
D. Eight

90. The name of each ABO blood type is derived from the:

    A. antibodies that are present in the blood.
    B. antigens that are present on the red blood cells.
    C. prevalence of each blood type in the general population.
    D. antigens that are absent from the red blood cells.

91. According to the passage, antigens:

    A. distinguish one cell type from another.
    B. recognize and attack antibodies.
    C. are only found on harmful cells.
    D. block antibodies from attacking cells.

92. Rh+ blood always contains:

    A. Rh antigen.
    B. anti-Rh antibodies.
    C. A and B antigens.
    D. anti-A and anti-B antibodies.

93. Blood containing anti-A and anti-Rh antibodies and B antigens would be identified as which blood type?

    A. A+
    B. B−
    C. AB−
    D. B+

94. According to Figure 16.1, what percentage of the general population has type B blood?

    A. 9%
    B. 2%
    C. 11%
    D. 16%

95. The least common blood type in the United States is type:

    A. O+.
    B. AB+.
    C. B−.
    D. AB−.

96. Based on the data in Table 16.3, which continent's population can be inferred to have the greatest incidence of blood type B+?

    A. Asia
    B. Europe
    C. Africa
    D. South America

97. In what percentage of the general population are A antigens present on red blood cells?

    A. 39%
    B. 33%
    C. 44%
    D. 37%

98. The data in Table 16.3 support the statement that more than half of the:

    A. Caucasian population has type O blood.
    B. Hispanic population has type O+ blood.
    C. general population with type O blood is Caucasian.
    D. general population with type O+ blood is Hispanic.

99. An individual of African-American ethnicity has a greater chance of having a B+ blood type than:

    A. the general population.
    B. an A+ blood type.
    C. an individual of Asian ethnicity.
    D. an O+ blood type.

100. Based on the information in Table 16.1, if an individual with an AB blood type receives donated type A blood, the donated blood will cause:

    A. the conversion of existing B antigens to A antigens, altering the individual's blood type.
    B. an immune reaction because the existing B antigens will attack the new A antigens.
    C. no immune reaction because the individual has no antibodies against the new blood.
    D. the individual's body to begin producing anti-A antibodies in response to the new blood.

101. Blood type O− is often referred to as the "universal donor" because it can be donated to any of the other blood types. This is because it has:

    A. no antibodies to attack antigens.
    B. no antigens to trigger an attack by antibodies.
    C. both A and B antibodies to attack antigens.
    D. both A and B antigens to prevent attack by antibodies.

102. An individual with blood type A− can safely receive a transfusion of which of the following blood types?

    A. A+ or A−
    B. A− or AB−
    C. A− or O−
    D. O− or O+

103. The percentage of the Caucasian population that has blood type AB− is:

    A. the same as the percentage for the Hispanic population.
    B. less than the percentage for the African-American population.
    C. equal to the percentage for the general population.
    D. greater than the percentage for the general population.

PASSAGE 8

Agarose gel electrophoresis is a technique in which an electric field is used to separate fragments of DNA by size. Figure 16.2 illustrates a common setup of an electrophoresis apparatus. A square of agarose gel is prepared and placed in a tray of buffer solution. DNA in solution is loaded into small slits (*wells*) in the top of the gel. A solution of DNA fragments of known length, called a *DNA ladder*, is loaded in the first well. DNA samples to be studied are loaded in the remaining wells, and an electric current is applied to the apparatus. Since DNA is negatively charged, the DNA molecules in the wells travel toward the opposite, positive end of the gel. Smaller DNA fragments are able to move through the gel more easily and thus move faster than longer fragments. This causes the fragments to separate according to size as the procedure runs. Comparison to the DNA ladder provides an estimate of the separated fragments' sizes.

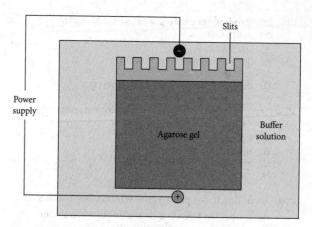

Figure 16.2

Table 16.4	Factors Affecting Fragment Migration	
Factor	**Variations**	**Effect on Fragment Migration**
Agarose gel concentration		
(0.5–2%)	Low	Sharper resolution of larger DNA fragments
		Longer run time (may be days)
		Possibly weak/fragile gel
	High	Sharper resolution of smaller DNA fragments
		Shorter run time
		Possibly brittle gel
Voltage of electric current		
(0.25–7 V/cm)	Low	Sharper resolution of larger DNA fragments
		Longer run time (may be days)
		Possibility of DNA fragments <1 kb diffusing horizontally through gel
	High	Shorter run time
		Possible smearing of DNA fragments >10 kb
		Possibility of overheating gel, causing low-concentration gels to melt

In addition to fragment size, several factors can affect the rate of migration of DNA fragments through the agarose gel. Table 16.4 provides a summary of the effects of agarose gel concentration and voltage of the electric current.

Table 16.5 identifies the agarose gel concentration needed for optimum resolution of DNA fragments within various size ranges.

Table 16.5	Agarose Concentrations
Agarose Concentration (%)	**DNA Size Range for Optimum Resolution (kilobases)**
0.5	1–30 kb
0.7	0.8–12.0 kb
1.0	0.5–10.0 kb
1.2	0.4–0.7 kb
1.5	0.2–0.5 kb

Source: http://www.idtdna.com/pages/decoded/decoded-articles/pipet-tips /decoded/2011/06/17/running-agarose-and-polyacrylamide-gels.

One application of the gel electrophoresis technique is to identify the *alleles* an individual carries for a particular gene. Although there may be multiple possible alleles (versions) for a specific gene, each individual carries exactly two copies. When subjected to electrophoresis, each allele separates out into a distinct band, allowing that individual's pair of alleles to be identified. A single darker band indicates two copies of the same allele.

Figure 16.3 shows electrophoresis results for a gene with three possible alleles. Allele 2 is known to contain extra bases as compared to Allele 1. Allele 3 is known to be missing bases as compared to Allele 1. DNA samples from 16 different individuals are loaded in Lanes A through P. The sizes of the known fragments in the DNA ladder are listed along the left.

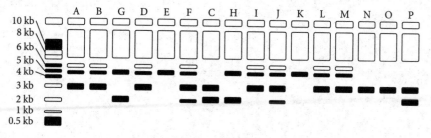

Figure 16.3

104. In a standard gel electrophoresis procedure, the first well is generally reserved for:

A. a DNA ladder.
B. the buffer solution.
C. smaller DNA fragments.
D. the DNA sample of greatest interest.

105. Applying an electric current to the electrophoresis apparatus causes the DNA fragments to travel:

A. toward the wells.
B. toward the cathode.
C. away from the anode.
D. away from the cathode.

106. According to the passage, the role of a DNA ladder is to:

A. propel the DNA fragments through the agarose gel.
B. provide an approximation of a DNA fragment's size.
C. identify the base sequence in a DNA fragment.
D. determine the total number of bases in a DNA fragment.

107. Which of the following would be a disadvantage of running a gel electrophoresis at a voltage of 6 V/cm?

A. Poor resolution of large DNA fragments
B. A short total run time for the procedure
C. A total run time of more than one day
D. Brittleness of the agarose gel

108. According to Table 16.5, as the concentration of agarose increases, the range of DNA fragment sizes that can be resolved:

A. expands.
B. is constant.
C. shrinks.
D. expands, then shrinks.

109. Which combination of factors would provide the best results for DNA fragments of 0.5–0.7 kb?

A. 0.7% agarose and 0.5 V/cm
B. 1.0% agarose and 0.5 V/cm
C. 1.2% agarose and 5 V/cm
D. 1.5% agarose and 5 V/cm

110. When observing electrophoresis results, the largest DNA fragments will appear:

A. closest to the cathode.
B. closest to the anode.
C. as the largest bands.
D. as the smallest bands.

111. Based on the information in the passage, Allele 2 traveled through the agarose gel faster than:

A. Allele 1 but slower than Allele 3.
B. neither Allele 1 nor Allele 3.
C. Allele 3 but at the same rate as Allele 1.
D. both Alleles 1 and 3.

112. According to the passage, a single darker band, as seen in Lane E, most likely indicates an:

A. error during the electrophoresis process.
B. error when collecting the DNA sample.
C. individual missing an allele due to mutation.
D. individual with two copies of the same allele.

113. What is the approximate size of Allele 1?

A. 3.0 kb
B. 1.0 kb
C. 8.0 kb
D. 0.5 kb

114. What is the most common allele combination represented in the DNA samples shown in Figure 16.3?

A. Two copies of Allele 2
B. Allele 1 and Allele 2
C. Two copies of Allele 1
D. Allele 1 and Allele 3

115. Which of the following provides the best explanation for the result shown in Lane J?

A. Individual J carries Alleles 1 and 3.
B. Individual J carries Alleles 2 and 3.
C. Lane J contains the DNA ladder.
D. Sample J contains DNA from two individuals.

116. Which allele combination is not represented in the DNA samples shown in Figure 16.3?

A. Allele 1 and Allele 3
B. Allele 1 and Allele 2
C. Two copies of Allele 3
D. Allele 2 and Allele 3

117. Which agarose concentration was most likely used in the electrophoresis in Figure 16.3?

A. 1.5%
B. 2.0%
C. 1.0%
D. 1.2%

118. Which combination of factors would cause the slowest migration of DNA fragments?

A. 0.5% agarose and 7 V/cm
B. 2.0% agarose and 7 V/cm
C. 2.0% agarose and 0.25 V/cm
D. 0.5% agarose and 0.25 V/cm

PASSAGE 9

A student wanted to test human reaction time to different stimuli to determine the conditions that cause the fastest reaction. The student conducted three experiments to test reaction time.

Experiment 1

The student used a computer program to record the time between the sounding of a tone and the student pressing the spacebar on the keyboard. This process was repeated 10 times per trial. The program then averaged the 10 response times to produce an average for the trial. The student conducted three trials using a tone length of 200 milliseconds (ms) and three trials with a tone length of 400 ms. Results are shown in Table 16.6.

Table 16.6 Experiment 1		
Trial	**Response Time (ms)**	**Tone Length (ms)**
1	158 ms	200 ms
2	154 ms	200 ms
3	152 ms	200 ms
4	144 ms	400 ms
5	142 ms	400 ms
6	143 ms	400 ms

Experiment 2

The student then used the same computer program to record the time between the sounding of a tone *or* the appearance of an image on the screen and the student pressing the spacebar. This process was repeated 10 times per trial, with the computer again averaging the 10 response times for each trial. The student conducted three trials using the tone as the stimulus and three trials using the image. Each stimulus lasted for a duration of 400 ms. Results are shown in Table 16.7.

Table 16.7 Experiment 2		
Trial	**Response Time (ms)**	**Stimulus**
1	145 ms	Auditory
2	142 ms	Auditory
3	142 ms	Auditory
4	193 ms	Visual
5	189 ms	Visual
6	188 ms	Visual

Experiment 3

The student repeated the previous experiment but alternated the stimulus (tone versus image) with each trial. Results are shown in Table 16.8.

Table 16.8 Experiment 3		
Trial	**Response Time (ms)**	**Stimulus**
1	143 ms	Auditory
2	195 ms	Visual
3	152 ms	Auditory
4	199 ms	Visual
5	151 ms	Auditory
6	199 ms	Visual

119. In the three experiments, response time is measured as the time between:

   A. exposures to two consecutive stimuli.
   B. exposure to a stimulus and the subsequent response.
   C. the registering of two consecutive responses.
   D. the beginning and end of one trial.

120. The stimulus in Experiment 1 was the:

   A. sounding of a tone.
   B. appearance of a screen image.
   C. pressing of the spacebar.
   D. use of a computer program.

121. How do Experiments 2 and 3 differ?

   A. Experiments 2 and 3 used different stimuli to test response times.
   B. The length of exposure to the stimulus was greater in Experiment 2.
   C. Experiment 3 included more trials than Experiment 2.
   D. In Experiment 3, the type of stimulus was alternated with each trial.

122. Based on the data in Table 16.7, the sense of hearing is:

   A. twice as fast as sight.
   B. more complex than sight.
   C. not as readily testable as sight.
   D. more acute than sight.

123. A stimulus duration of 400 ms was used during which experiment(s)?

   A. Experiments 2 and 3 only
   B. Experiment 1 only
   C. Experiments 1 and 2 only
   D. Experiments 1, 2, and 3

124. The fastest reaction time occurred in response to:

   A. an auditory stimulus lasting 200 ms.
   B. an auditory stimulus lasting 400 ms.
   C. a visual stimulus lasting 400 ms.
   D. a visual stimulus lasting 200 ms.

125. Based on the data in Table 16.6, what is the relationship between reaction time and length of stimulus exposure?

   A. Lengthening the stimulus improves reaction time.
   B. A shorter stimulus produces the fastest reaction time.
   C. Stimulus length has no measurable effect on reaction time.
   D. A longer stimulus produces the slowest reaction time.

126. Scientists have found that it takes 20–40 ms for a visual signal to reach the brain. Based on the data in Experiments 2 and 3, how long can an auditory signal be expected to take to reach the brain?

   A. 25–45 ms
   B. 50–55 ms
   C. 8–10 ms
   D. 20–40 ms

127. The data in Tables 16.7 and 16.8 best support the conclusion that alternating between two stimuli:

   A. increases the average response time for both stimuli.
   B. improves auditory response time but not visual response time.
   C. decreases the average response time for both stimuli.
   D. improves visual response time but not auditory response time.

128. Scientists have found that a specific response time range exists for each particular sense. Which of the following would be the range for auditory stimuli?

   A. 140–160 ms
   B. 180–200 ms
   C. 150–170 ms
   D. 125–145 ms

129. How many total responses were recorded during Experiment 2?

   A. 10

   B. 6

   C. 60

   D. 30

130. Which graph best represents the data collected during Experiment 3?

   A.

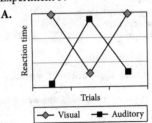

Figure 16.4

   B.

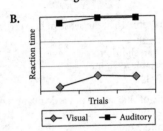

Figure 16.5

   C.

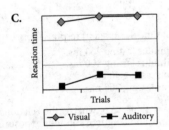

Figure 16.6

   D.

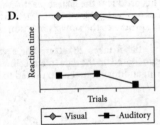

Figure 16.7

131. The student wants to test how varying the length of exposure to a visual stimulus affects response time. The best way to do this is to repeat:

   A. all three experiments using visual stimuli only.

   B. Experiment 1, replacing the tone with an image.

   C. Experiment 3, using a visual stimulus only.

   D. Experiment 2, using a stimulus duration of 200 ms.

132. What was the slowest auditory response time recorded during the three experiments?

   A. 199 ms

   B. 152 ms

   C. 142 ms

   D. 158 ms

133. Based on the data from the three experiments, what can be done to improve response time?

   A. Alternate exposure to two different stimuli.

   B. Decrease the duration of each exposure to a stimulus.

   C. Repeat exposure to the same stimulus.

   D. Increase the number of stimuli used at one time.

CHAPTER 17

TEST 4

PASSAGE 10

Organic molecules (carbohydrates, lipids, proteins, and nucleic acids) compose and are produced by living organisms. Scientists believe that simple organic molecules originally formed from inorganic molecules on primitive Earth. This step is considered a key precursor to the development of life on our planet. Two leading theories on the origin of the first organic molecules are described here.

Primordial Soup

The theory that organic molecules formed in the atmosphere of primitive Earth using energy from lightning is often called the "primordial soup theory." Evidence for this theory includes the Miller-Urey experiment, in which the conditions

believed to exist in the primitive atmosphere were reproduced to create organic molecules.

The major components of the primitive atmosphere were believed to be methane (CH_4), ammonia (NH_3), hydrogen (H_2), and water (H_2O). These gases were put into a closed system and exposed to a continuous electrical charge to simulate lightning storms. After one week, samples taken from the apparatus contained a variety of organic compounds, including some amino acids (components of proteins). Figure 17.1 is a diagram of the apparatus used in the Miller-Urey experiment.

Hydrothermal Vents

The theory that organic molecules originally formed in the deep oceans using energy from inside the earth focuses on the existence of hydrothermal vents. Evidence for this theory

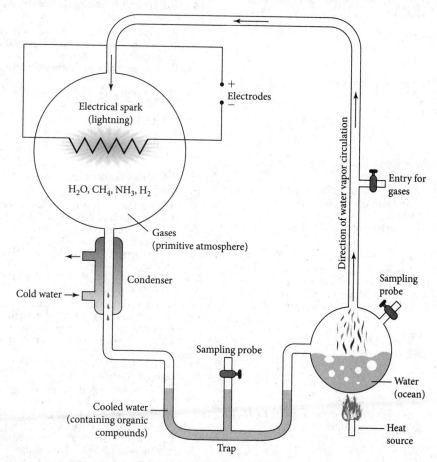

Figure 17.1

includes the fact that ecosystems of diverse organisms have been found to exist around hydrothermal vents in the deep ocean. These ecosystems thrive without any energy input from the sun.

Organic molecules are only stable within a very narrow temperature range. Hydrothermal vents release hot (300°C) gases originating from inside the earth into the otherwise cold (4°C) water of the deep ocean. This release of gases causes a temperature gradient to exist around deep-sea vents. Scientists believe that within this temperature gradient exist the optimal conditions to support the formation of stable organic compounds. Figure 17.2 shows a diagram of the gradient produced by deep-sea vents.

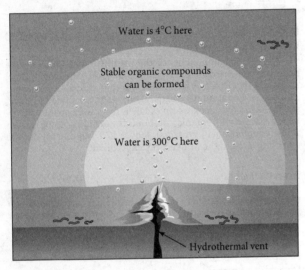

Figure 17.2

134. Which of the following is NOT an organic molecule?

A. Carbohydrates
B. Water
C. Lipids
D. Nucleic acids

135. Both theories on the origin of organic molecules are based on the assumption that those molecules:

A. contain different atoms than inorganic molecules.
B. only exist in the atmosphere and deep ocean.
C. have not yet been produced in the laboratory.
D. can be produced from inorganic molecules.

136. In Figure 17.1, the purpose of the heat source is to:

A. produce water vapor for the simulated atmosphere.
B. simulate hydrothermal vents in the deep ocean.
C. reduce inorganic compounds to organic compounds.
D. generate an electrical charge to stimulate the reaction.

137. Ammonia (NH_3) is an:

A. inorganic compound.
B. element.
C. amino acid.
D. organic compound.

138. In Figure 17.1, the reaction that produces organic molecules occurs in which part of the Miller-Urey apparatus?

A. Condenser
B. Large sphere
C. Trap
D. Small sphere

139. Based on the hydrothermal vents theory, which of the following would most likely be the optimal temperature range for organic molecule formation?

A. Between 0°C and 4°C
B. Higher than 300°C
C. Lower than 300°C
D. Between 4°C and 25°C

140. Which of the following statements would scientists supporting either theory most likely agree on?

A. At least some organic compounds on Earth likely originated in meteorites from space.
B. The production of amino acids requires the existence of a temperature gradient.
C. The existence of water on Earth was essential to the original formation of organic compounds.
D. A single method most likely produced the original versions of all organic molecules.

141. The specific source of energy used to form simple organic molecules is:

A. addressed in the primordial soup theory only.
B. not discussed in either of the two theories.
C. a major difference between the two theories.
D. the only similarity between the two theories.

142. According to the primordial soup theory, which of the following gases is not believed to have been a major component of the primitive atmosphere?

A. Methane
B. Hydrogen
C. Water vapor
D. Helium

143. The greatest limitation in the design of the Miller-Urey experiment is the:

A. use of a condenser to cool water vapor.
B. production of a variety of organic compounds.
C. presence of a constant electrical charge.
D. recycling of water throughout the apparatus.

144. The hydrothermal vents theory states that organic molecules originally formed:

A. inside the earth.
B. in the earth's atmosphere.
C. in the deep ocean.
D. within volcanoes.

145. Scientists consider the outcome of the Miller-Urey experiment to be evidence:

A. that refutes the primordial soup theory.
B. in support of the primordial soup theory.
C. that refutes both the primordial soup and the hydrothermal vents theories.
D. in support of the hydrothermal vents theory.

146. According to the passage, temperature gradients exist in the deep ocean due to the:

A. constant release of hot gases into cold water.
B. decreased availability of sunlight at greater depths.
C. existence of ecosystems made up of diverse organisms.
D. reactions that produce organic molecules.

147. Which of the following is a key assumption of the primordial soup theory?

A. Sunlight provided the energy needed to convert inorganic compounds to organic compounds.
B. The composition of the primitive atmosphere was different than that of the current atmosphere.
C. Amino acids can be produced from inorganic compounds in the laboratory.
D. Organic compounds can only be produced by the reaction of other organic compounds.

PASSAGE 11

As a liquid evaporates, the vapors on the surface of the liquid exert a *vapor pressure*. Vapor pressure varies with the liquid's temperature.

When vapor pressure equals the surrounding atmospheric pressure, boiling occurs. The *normal boiling point* of a liquid is defined as the temperature at which vapor pressure is equal to the standard atmospheric pressure of 760 mmHg (1 atm). If atmospheric pressure changes, a liquid's boiling point will also change.

Figure 17.3 illustrates the relationship between vapor pressure and temperature for four organic compounds belonging to the alkane group. The normal boiling point is indicated by a horizontal dashed line.

Organic compounds are composed of various functional groups attached to a hydrocarbon backbone. A *functional group* is a specific grouping of atoms that exhibits a characteristic set of properties. These properties remain consistent, regardless of the overall size of the compound.

Figure 17.4 compares the normal boiling points of organic compounds of increasing size for eight different functional groups, including the alkane group.

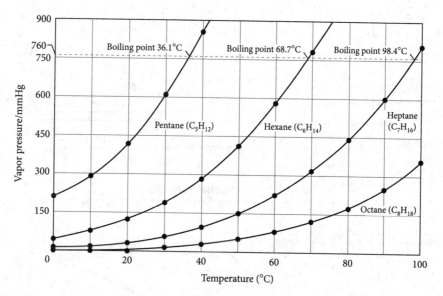

Figure 17.3
Source: http://wiki.chemprime.chemeddl.org.

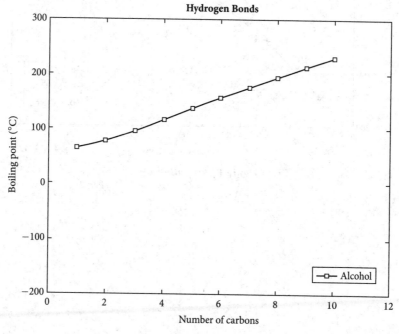

Figure 17.4

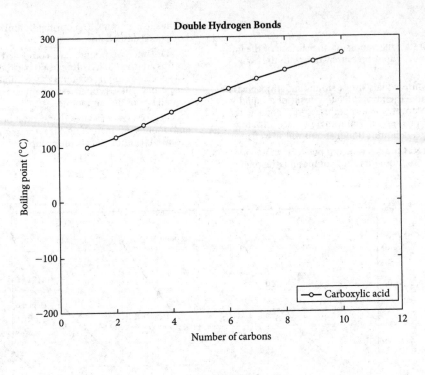

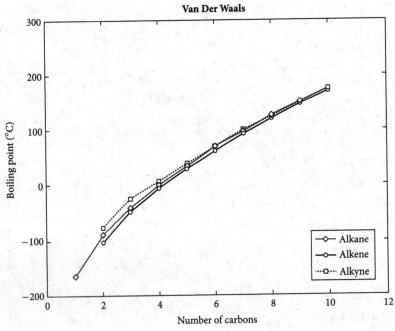

Figure 17.4 (*Continued*)

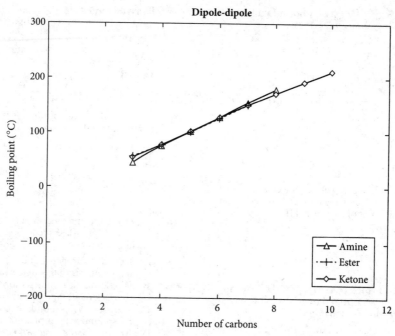

Figure 17.4 (Continued)

Table 17.1 lists the types of chemical bonds each of the eight functional groups are capable of forming. Stronger bonds are more difficult to break, thus requiring a higher temperature for phase changes.

Table 17.1	Functional Group Bonds
Functional Group	**Type of Bonds**
Alcohol	Hydrogen bonds
Alkane	Van der Waals
Alkene	Van der Waals
Alkyne	Van der Waals
Amine	Dipole-dipole
Carboxylic acid	Double hydrogen bonds
Ester	Dipole-dipole
Ketone	Dipole-dipole

Table 17.2 lists characteristics of four common organic compounds with similar molecular weights. The temperatures listed represent the normal boiling point for each molecule.

Table 17.2	Molecular Weight		
Molecule	**Molecular Formula**	**Molecular Weight (g/mol)**	**Boiling Point (°C)**
Propanoic acid	$C_3H_6O_2$	74	140
n-Butanol	$C_4H_{10}O$	74	117
Butanone	C_4H_8O	72	80
Pentane	C_5H_{12}	72	36

148. A compound's normal boiling point is the:

   A. minimum temperature at which the compound boils.
   B. average temperature at which the compound boils across all possible atmospheric pressures.
   C. maximum temperature at which the compound boils.
   D. temperature at which the compound boils under standard atmospheric pressure.

149. According to Figure 17.3, an organic compound will boil at a lower temperature if:

   A. vapor pressure increases.
   B. atmospheric pressure decreases.
   C. atmospheric and vapor pressures become unequal.
   D. vapor pressure is greater than atmospheric pressure.

150. At a vapor pressure of 50 mmHg, which alkane in Figure 17.3 would boil closest to 0°C?

   A. Heptane
   B. Hexane
   C. Pentane
   D. Octane

151. According to Figure 17.3, what vapor pressure will cause pentane's boiling point to be closest to 40°C?

   A. 760 mmHg
   B. 600 mmHg
   C. 400 mmHg
   D. 850 mmHg

152. What is the best approximation for the normal boiling point of octane in Figure 17.3?

   A. 126°C
   B. 100°C
   C. 145°C
   D. 98°C

153. According to Figure 17.4, the alkanes exhibit normal boiling points most similar to which other group?

   A. Alkynes
   B. Alcohols
   C. Carboxylic acids
   D. Amines

154. Based on the data in Figure 17.4, a 2-carbon alcohol would exhibit a normal boiling point closest to that of a:

   A. 3-carbon alkane.
   B. 9-carbon alkene.
   C. 4-carbon ketone.
   D. 2-carbon carboxylic acid.

155. Based on the data in Figure 17.4, which type of bond listed in Table 17.1 is the weakest?

   A. Dipole-dipole
   B. Double hydrogen
   C. Van der Waals
   D. Single hydrogen

156. Caproic acid is a carboxylic acid with a molecular formula of $C_6H_{12}O_2$. Which of the following temperatures is closest to the normal boiling point of caproic acid?

   A. 200°C
   B. 250°C
   C. 100°C
   D. 125°C

157. Based on the data in Figure 17.4, which of the following lists the bonds in Table 17.1 from the highest to the lowest boiling point required to break them?

   A. Van der Waals, dipole-dipole, single hydrogen, double hydrogen
   B. Double hydrogen, single hydrogen, dipole-dipole, Van der Waals
   C. Single hydrogen, double hydrogen, dipole-dipole, Van der Waals
   D. Dipole-dipole, Van der Waals, single hydrogen, double hydrogen

158. Which of the following generalizations about the relationship between an organic compound's molecular weight and its boiling point is best supported by the data in Table 17.2?

   A. The boiling point varies directly with molecular weight.
   B. As molecular weight increases, the boiling point decreases.
   C. As molecular weight decreases, the boiling point increases.
   D. The boiling point is not determined by molecular weight.

159. Based on the data in Figure 17.4, n-Butanol (see Table 17.2) most likely contains which functional group?

   A. Alcohol
   B. Ester
   C. Amine
   D. Alkyne

160. Which of the four compounds in Table 17.2 is most likely to contain double hydrogen bonds?

   A. Pentane
   B. Butanone
   C. Propanoic acid
   D. n-Butanol

161. Based on the information in the passage, which of the following can be inferred about the type of bonds in an organic compound?

   A. Double hydrogen bonds are easier to break at high temperatures than single hydrogen bonds.
   B. Dipole-dipole bonds require the highest boiling point to break of all four types of bonds.
   C. Van der Waals bonds become easier to break as a compound's vapor pressure is increased.
   D. At the same vapor pressure, single hydrogen bonds require a higher boiling point to break than dipole-dipole bonds.

162. Which of the following generalizations is best supported by the data in Figures 17.3 and 17.4?

   A. Organic compounds containing the same number of carbon atoms have similar boiling points.
   B. The boiling point increases with the number of carbon atoms among organic compounds within the same group.
   C. The number of carbon atoms in an organic compound cannot be used to predict the compound's relative boiling point.
   D. The greater the number of carbon atoms in an organic compound, the lower that compound's boiling point is.

PASSAGE 12

Shebay Park has been the site of ongoing population dynamics studies since the 1960s. Consisting of a group of isolated islands, the park provides ecologists with a unique, closed ecosystem in which to analyze the relationship between predator and prey populations. Figure 17.5 illustrates the food web for the Shebay Park ecosystem.

Ecological research in the park has focused mainly on the predator-prey relationship between the jaguar and peccary

(a type of pig) populations. In addition to the typical selective pressures each species exerts on the other, scientists have observed specific events over the years that have affected population sizes. The inadvertent introduction of feline leukemia by humans in the late 1980s severely reduced the jaguar population. In 2004, the severest winter on record and an outbreak of ticks did the same to the peccary population. Figure 17.6 compares the annual population sizes for both species observed between 1968 and 2012.

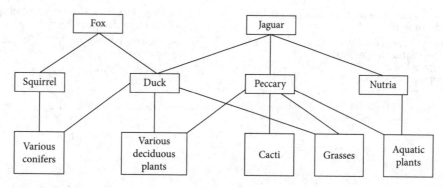

Figure 17.5

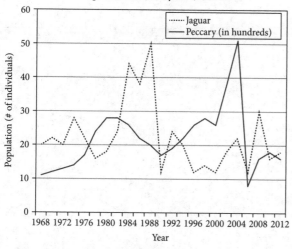

Figure 17.6

163. Shebay Park is considered a closed ecosystem because:
    A. organisms cannot easily migrate in from other ecosystems.
    B. population sizes within the ecosystem do not fluctuate.
    C. scientists have never had the opportunity to study the ecosystem.
    D. predator-prey is the only type of relationship that exists in the ecosystem.

164. According to the food web in Figure 17.5, peccary can be categorized as which type of consumer?
    A. Scavengers
    B. Herbivores
    C. Carnivores
    D. Omnivores

165. According to Figure 17.6, what has been the maximum size of the jaguar population since 1968?
    A. 20
    B. 60
    C. 50
    D. 10

166. The peccary population reached its smallest size in which year?
    A. 2006
    B. 2003
    C. 1995
    D. 1988

167. It can be inferred that the 13-year trend in the peccary population that began after 1990 was largely influenced by a sharp decline in:
    A. the jaguar population caused by disease.
    B. cactus growth caused by disease.
    C. the jaguar population during a severe winter.
    D. cactus growth during a severe winter.

168. According to Figure 17.5, how many secondary consumer species are present in the Shebay Park ecosystem?
    A. 0
    B. 1
    C. 6
    D. 2

169. Organisms that compete for many of the same resources within an ecosystem are said to occupy similar niches. Based on the information in Figure 17.5, which populations occupy a niche most similar to that of the peccary population?
    A. Nutria and squirrel
    B. Fox and jaguar
    C. Duck and fox
    D. Nutria and duck

170. Based on the data in Figure 17.6, a sharp decline in a population's size most commonly occurs in response to:

A. a sharp increase in another population's size.
B. an event that reduces individuals' immediate survival.
C. a parallel decline in the size of other populations.
D. an event that limits individuals' reproductive ability.

171. Ecologists believe that an increase in parasites is partially responsible for the shift in:

A. the peccary population after 2004.
B. the peccary population before 2004.
C. the jaguar population after 1990.
D. the jaguar population before 1990.

172. Which of the following statements is best supported by the information in the passage?

A. Predation is the single greatest factor affecting peccary population size.
B. Food availability is the single greatest factor affecting peccary population size.
C. Peccary population size varies independently of the predator population size.
D. Predation is one of several factors that impact the size of the peccary population.

173. Based on Figure 17.5, which population is least likely to be affected by a change in the peccary population?

A. Aquatic plants
B. Squirrel
C. Cacti
D. Duck

CHAPTER 18

TEST 5

PASSAGE 13

An *invasive species* is a species that is not native to an ecosystem and whose introduction has harmful environmental, economic, and/or human health effects.

Eichhornia crassipes (water hyacinth) is an invasive species of floating aquatic weed found in freshwater waterways in tropical and temperate regions worldwide. It is highly tolerant of fluctuations in water level, nutrient availability, pH, and temperature. This allows it to grow rapidly and outcompete native aquatic plant species for resources. Dense floating mats of *E. crassipes* further alter aquatic communities by reducing dissolved oxygen levels and access to light. Decomposing matter from *E. crassipes* mats increases sediment deposition in waterways.

Ecological studies have shown that the growth of a plant can be influenced by competition with different species of neighboring plants. A group of scientists carried out the following studies to determine the effects on the growth of *E. crassipes* when paired with three other, more benign, aquatic weed species.

Study 1

Scientists collected growth data on *E. crassipes* mats in the Kagera River in Tanzania. Scientists marked off 1 square meter (m^2) sample areas containing *E. crassipes* alone and in combination with three other aquatic weeds common to the Kagera River.

To determine the effects of the other three weed species on *E. crassipes* growth, scientists analyzed five growth parameters. *Fresh weight* was determined by removing and immediately weighing 10 *E. crassipes* plants from each area. *Plant height* was measured from the base of the plant to the tip of the tallest leaf. The total number of *E. crassipes* plants within a sample area was recorded as *plant density*, which was then multiplied by fresh weight to determine *total biomass*. The number of leaves per plant was also recorded. Table 18.1 lists the averages for each

Table 18.1 Kagera River Data					
Weed Combination	**Fresh Weight (g)**	**Plant Height (cm)**	**Leaves per Plant**	**Plant Density (per m²)**	**Total Biomass (per m²)**
E. crassipes	652.7	38.4	9.3	51.7	30.98
E. crassipes + *Commelina* sp.	452.2	33.7	9	38.9	16.09
E. crassipes + *Justicia* sp.	320.2	26.5	8.6	37.9	12.3
E. crassipes + *V. cupsidata*	332.7	21.8	8.6	26	7.77
E. crassipes + *Commelina* sp.					
+ *Justicia* sp. + *V. cupsidata*	342	29.2	9	28.3	9.50

Source: http://www.academicjournals.org/ijbc/fulltext/2011/August/Katagira%20et%20al.htm.

growth parameter for *E. crassipes* growing alone and in combination with the three other aquatic weed species.

Study 2

Scientists transplanted young *E. crassipes*, *Commelina* sp., *Justicia* sp., and *V. cupsidata* plants from the Kagera River to a greenhouse. In the greenhouse, *E. crassipes* potted alone and in combination with the other three weed species were allowed to grow in water from the Kagera River for four months. At the end of the four-month growth period, the parameters of fresh weight, plant height, and leaves per plant were all determined by the same methods used in Study 1.

Table 18.2 lists the averages for each growth parameter for *E. crassipes* growing in the greenhouse alone and in combination with the other aquatic weed species.

Table 18.2	Greenhouse Experiment Data		
Weed Combination	Fresh Weight (g)	Plant Height (cm)	Leaves per Plant
E. crassipes	180.80	8.69	10.54
E. crassipes + Commelina sp.	129.08	8.80	10.70
E. crassipes + Justicia sp.	151.66	8.88	9.90
E. crassipes + V. cupsidata		8.24	9.75

Source: http://www.academicjournals.org/ijbc/fulltext/2011/ August/Katagira%20et%20al.htm.

174. According to the passage, species identified as invasive are always:

A. aggressively growing plants.
B. disruptive to an ecosystem.
C. introduced by humans.
D. economically profitable.

175. According to the passage, water hyacinths upset freshwater ecosystems by doing all of the following EXCEPT:

A. increasing sediment deposition in waterways.
B. outcompeting native plants for resources.
C. altering the pH of aquatic environments.
D. limiting aquatic organisms' access to sunlight.

176. Which weed combination was tested in Study 1 but not Study 2?

A. Water hyacinth alone
B. All four aquatic weeds together
C. Water hyacinth with V. cupsidata
D. Water hyacinth with Justicia sp.

177. In Study 1, plant density was measured as:

A. the total number of E. crassipes plants in 1 m^2.
B. the total number of weed plants in 1 m^2.
C. fresh weight divided by water volume in 1 m^2.
D. fresh weight divided by plant volume in 1 m^2.

178. Which weed combination serves as the control group in Study 1?

A. E. crassipes with Justicia sp.
B. E. crassipes with all three other weeds
C. E. crassipes with V. cupsidata
D. E. crassipes alone

179. In Study 1, V. cupsidata caused the greatest reduction in:

A. all E. crassipes growth parameters.
B. E. crassipes fresh weight only.
C. all growth parameters except fresh weight.
D. E. crassipes height and density only.

180. Based on the data in Table 18.1, which weed exerts the least competitive pressure on E. crassipes?

A. Justicia sp.
B. V. cupsidata
C. Commelina sp.
D. The combination of all three weeds.

181. In Table 18.2, Commelina sp. and Justicia sp. are both shown to have:

A. a stronger effect on fresh weight than V. cupsidata.
B. no effect on E. crassipes plant height.
C. the same effect on fresh weight as V. cupsidata.
D. a positive effect on E. crassipes plant height.

182. In Study 2, the water hyacinths grown alone exhibited a greater average:

A. number of leaves than in Study 1.
B. plant height than in Study 1.
C. fresh weight than in Study 1.
D. total biomass than in Study 1.

183. Total biomass was not included as a growth parameter in Table 18.2 because:

A. plant density was not measured in Study 2.
B. the fresh weight values recorded in Table 18.2 were too low.
C. the plants used in Study 2 had no biomass.
D. total biomass is not a good indicator of plant growth.

184. Which of the following statements is supported by the data collected in both studies?

A. V. cupsidata has the most negative effect on water hyacinth growth.
B. Commelina sp. has a positive effect on water hyacinth growth.
C. Water hyacinth growth is not affected by the presence of other weed species.
D. Justicia sp. has no effect on water hyacinth growth.

185. Based on the data in Table 18.2, the most significant impact of growing E. crassipes in combination with other weeds in a greenhouse environment appears to be the production of:

A. shorter plants.
B. lighter plants.
C. fewer leaves per plant.
D. fewer plants.

186. The greatest advantage of the experimental design in Study 2 is that scientists were able to:

A. choose on which weed species to focus their observations.
B. record data more frequently than could be done at the Kagera River.
C. control for other environmental factors that may affect plant growth.
D. obtain more precise measurements for each of the growth parameters.

187. According to Table 18.1, the presence of all three competitor weeds within the same square meter appears to have:

A. a greater effect on E. crassipes fresh weight than the presence of any single competitor weed.
B. an effect approximately equal to the sum of the effects of each single competitor weed on fresh weight.
C. a lesser effect on E. crassipes fresh weight than the presence of any single competitor weed.
D. an effect approximately equal to the mean of the effects of each single competitor weed on fresh weight.

188. Ecologists have found that introducing a competitor to an ecosystem is sometimes more effective in reducing an unwanted population than introducing a predator. Based on the results of this pair of studies, increasing the presence of which of the following species can be predicted to best reduce the water hyacinth population?

A. Justicia sp.
B. V. cupsidata and Commelina sp.
C. Commelina sp. and Justicia sp.
D. V. cupsidata

PASSAGE 14

A rollercoaster car is often used as a model of energy transformations. Resting at its starting point, the car has gravitational potential energy. As it moves along the track, the potential energy is converted to kinetic energy and then back to potential energy as the car approaches the rollercoaster's ending point.

An object's gravitational potential energy can be calculated as the product of the object's mass, acceleration due to gravity, and the object's height above the ground ($PE_g = m \times g \times h$). In a frictionless system, the amount of potential energy at the beginning and end of the rollercoaster would be equal. However, friction between the car and the track causes *frictional dissipation* to transform some of the energy to heat and sound. The amount of energy dissipated due to friction can be calculated as the product of the frictional force on an object and the distance traveled by the object ($F_f d$).

A group of students built a marble rollercoaster out of foam pipe insulation tubing and tried to determine the conditions that would maximize the height of the rollercoaster's hill. The students conducted two experiments to study the effects of gravitational potential energy and frictional dissipation on the marble.

Experiment 1

Figure 18.1 shows the initial setup for the marble rollercoaster. A indicates the starting height (drop height) and C indicates the ending height (hill height) of the marble. B is the lowest point located halfway between A and C.

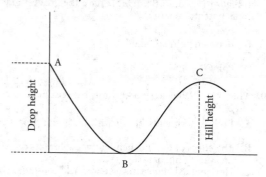

Figure 18.1

Students started with a drop height of 0.6 m and stretched the rollercoaster tubing out to a horizontal length of 1 m. They then varied the hill height until the marble was able to successfully reach the top of the hill without going over. To study the effects of the marble's initial gravitational potential energy, students conducted three more trials using different drop heights. Table 18.3 shows the results for each trial.

Table 18.3 Experiment 1		
Trial	**Drop Height (m)**	**Hill Height (m)**
1	0.6	0.52
2	0.3	0.25
3	0.9	0.78
4	1.2	1.06

Experiment 2

Students started with a drop height of 1.2 m and stretched the rollercoaster tubing out to a horizontal length of 1.0 m. Students then varied the hill height until the marble was able to reach the top of the hill successfully without going over. To study the effects of frictional dissipation, students conducted two more trials using different horizontal track lengths. Table 18.4 shows the results for each trial.

Table 18.4 Experiment 2			
Trial	**Drop Height (m)**	**Horizontal Distance (m)**	**Hill Height (m)**
1	1.2	1.0	1.06
2	1.2	0.5	1.15
3	1.2	1.5	0.97

189. When determining the gravitational potential energy of various objects on Earth, which variable would be considered a constant?

   A. h
   B. m
   C. PE_g
   D. g

190. According to the formula provided in the passage, doubling the height of an object should:

   A. double that object's potential energy.
   B. half that object's mass.
   C. double that object's mass.
   D. halve that object's potential energy.

191. In a frictionless environment, with a drop height of A, the marble should be able to reach a hill height (C in Figure 18.1) of:

   A. 1.0 m.
   B. 0.6 m.
   C. 1.2 m.
   D. 0.5 m.

192. In Experiment 1, students altered the drop height of the marble to test the effect of which of the following variables on hill height?

   A. Frictional dissipation
   B. Horizontal distance traveled
   C. Initial gravitational potential energy
   D. Mass of the marble

193. What was the maximum drop height used in either experiment?

   A. 0.6 m
   B. 1.2 m
   C. 1.15 m
   D. 1.5 m

194. Which of the following graphs best represents the relationship between drop height and hill height in Experiment 1?

A.

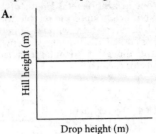

Figure 18.2

B.

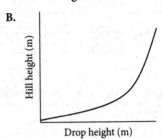

Figure 18.3

C.

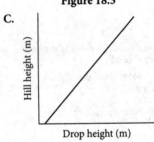

Figure 18.4

D.

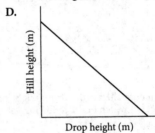

Figure 18.5

195. The data in Table 18.4 indicate that lengthening the rollercoaster's track:

  A. causes the effects of frictional dissipation to increase.
  B. causes the effects of frictional dissipation to decrease, then increase.
  C. has no effect on the amount of frictional dissipation.
  D. causes the effects of frictional dissipation to decrease.

196. What was the smallest hill height recorded by the students in Experiment 2?

  A. 0.5 m
  B. 1.2 m
  C. 1.06 m
  D. 0.97 m

197. The students used drop height as the dependent variable in:

  A. Experiment 1 only.
  B. Experiment 2 only.
  C. both Experiments 1 and 2.
  D. neither Experiment 1 nor 2.

198. If the students were to carry out a third experiment to study the relationship between marble mass and hill height, how would the data table for this new experiment compare to Table 18.3?

  A. They would need to add an extra column between drop height and hill height for marble mass.
  B. They would need to replace the hill height column with a column for marble mass.
  C. They would need to add extra rows to the bottom of the table for additional trials.
  D. They would need to replace the horizontal distance column with a column for marble mass.

199. Based on the data for the two experiments, at which point in Figure 18.1 does the marble have the greatest gravitational potential energy?

  A. Point A
  B. Between points A and B
  C. Point C
  D. Point B

200. Which of the following is a similarity between Experiments 1 and 2?

  A. Both experiments began with an initial drop height of 0.6 m.
  B. The effect of the independent variable was studied by measuring hill height.
  C. Horizontal distance traveled was held constant in both experiments.
  D. The initial gravitational potential energy increased with each trial.

201. Which of the following energy transformations is not demonstrated by the marble rollercoaster in either Experiment 1 or Experiment 2?

  A. Mechanical energy to thermal energy
  B. Mechanical energy to sound
  C. Mechanical energy to chemical energy
  D. Potential energy to kinetic energy

202. In Experiment 2, a fourth trial using a horizontal distance of 1.75 m would most likely result in a hill height:

  A. greater than the hill height recorded in Trial 2.
  B. less than the hill height recorded in Trial 3.
  C. close to the hill height recorded in Trial 1.
  D. between the hill heights recorded in Trials 2 and 3.

PASSAGE 15

The scientific classification of organisms provides information about the relative level of relatedness between species. Biologists use a hierarchical grouping system to classify organisms into various *taxa* (groups) based on shared physiological, developmental, and genetic characteristics. Table 18.5 identifies the scientific classification of five common species.

Biologists use a *phylogenetic tree* to illustrate the evolutionary history of related species. In a typical tree, currently living species called *extant taxa* are listed along the right. Moving to the left, the point at which two or more extant taxa meet is called a *node*. A node indicates an *ancestral taxon*, or a common ancestor shared by the extant taxa.

Horizontal line length in a phylogenetic tree indicates relative *divergence time*, an estimation of how long ago the extant taxa are thought to have diverged into separate species. Figure 18.6 shows a phylogenetic tree of the species listed in Table 18.5.

Table 18.5   Taxonomic Classification

	American		European		
	Badger	**Coyote**	**Otter**	**Gray Wolf**	**Leopard**
Kingdom	Animalia	Animalia	Animalia	Animalia	Animalia
Phylum	Chordata	Chordata	Chordata	Chordata	Chordata
Class	Mammalia	Mammalia	Mammalia	Mammalia	Mammalia
Order	Carnivora	Carnivora	Carnivora	Carnivora	Carnivora
Family	Mustelidae	Canidae	Mustelidae	Canidae	Felidae
Genus	*Taxidea*	*Canis*	*Lutra*	*Canis*	*Panthera*
Species	*taxus*	*latrans*	*lutra*	*lupis*	*pardus*

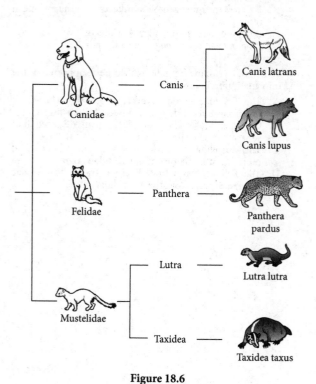

Figure 18.6

203. The phylogenetic tree in Figure 18.6 identifies evolutionary relationships between which type of organisms?

   A. Mammals
   B. Arthropods
   C. Invertebrates
   D. Amphibians

204. To which family does *Panthera pardus* belong?

   A. Mustelidae
   B. Canidae
   C. Felidae
   D. Carnivora

205. All organisms in Table 18.5 are members of the same:

   A. genus.
   B. order.
   C. species.
   D. family.

206. *Canis latrans* is the scientific name of which organism?

   A. American badger
   B. Gray wolf
   C. Leopard
   D. Coyote

207. According to Figure 18.6, the European otter is most closely related to which species?

   A. *Panthera pardus*
   B. *Canis lupus*
   C. *Taxidea taxus*
   D. *Canis latrans*

208. According to Figure 18.6, how many common ancestors does *Panthera pardus* share with *Taxidea taxus*?

   A. Three
   B. One
   C. Two
   D. Four

209. According to Figure 18.6, which pair of species have the most recent divergence time?

   A. *Lutra lutra* and *Panthera pardus*
   B. *Canis latrans* and *Lutra lutra*
   C. *Taxidea taxus* and *Lutra lutra*
   D. *Canis lupus* and *Canis latrans*

210. Based on the information in the passage and Figure 18.6, *Taxidea taxus* would be considered:

   A. an extant taxon.
   B. a node.
   C. an ancestral taxon.
   D. an order.

211. Which of the following inferences can be made about the seven-level classification system used in Table 18.5?

   A. Organisms classified in the same kingdom are classified in the same phylum.
   B. Organisms within the same class share a common kingdom and phylum.
   C. Organisms that share a common order cannot be classified in the same family.
   D. Organisms within the same family must share a common genus and species.

212. The scientific classification of the lynx is shown in Table 18.6. With which species would the lynx share the most recent ancestor?

Table 18.6	Lynx Classification
Kingdom	Animalia
Phylum	Chordata
Class	Mammalia
Order	Carnivora
Family	Felidae
Genus	*Lynx*
Species	*lynx*

   A. *Lutra lutra*
   B. *Canis latrans*
   C. *Panthera pardus*
   D. *Taxidea taxus*

213. How many taxonomic levels does the lynx have in common with the gray wolf?

   A. One
   B. None
   C. Two
   D. Four

214. Based on the information in Table 18.5, it can be predicted that the common ancestor shared by all five species belonged to which taxon?

   A. Mustelidae
   B. Carnivora
   C. Canidae
   D. Felidae

215. A *clade* is the taxonomic term for a grouping composed of all the descendants of a single ancestral taxon. According to Figure 18.6, which of the following groupings would not constitute a clade?

   A. *Canis latrans* and *Canis lupus*
   B. *Taxidea taxus* and *Lutra lutra*
   C. *Canis latrans*, *Canis lupus*, and *Lutra lutra*
   D. *Canis latrans*, *Canis lupus*, *Taxidea taxus*, and *Lutra lutra*

216. The wolverine (*Gulo gulo*) belongs to the family Mustelidae. Which of the following assumptions can be made about the wolverine?

   A. It is most closely related to the American badger.
   B. It shares the most genetic similarity with the European otter.
   C. It belongs to the same family as the gray wolf.
   D. It belongs to the same order as the coyote.

217. Which of the following statements is best supported by the information in Figure 18.6?

   A. The Canidae taxon diverged from the Mustelidae taxon more recently than from the Felidae taxon.
   B. Canidae, Mustelidae, and Felidae all diverged into separate taxa at the same time.
   C. The Mustelidae taxon diverged from the Felidae taxon more recently than from the Canidae taxon.
   D. The Felidae taxon first diverged from the Canidae taxon and then from the Mustelidae taxon.

QUESTIONS 218–261

PASSAGE 16

A gene is composed of a series of exon and intron segments. *Exons* are the coding regions of a gene, the segments that contain the instructions for building a protein. A gene's exons are connected by noncoding regions, or *introns*.

To build a protein, the cell must first transcribe the gene into messenger RNA (mRNA). Then a process called *RNA splicing* removes the noncoding introns and connects all of the exons to produce an mRNA transcript that can be used to build the protein.

Tropomyosins are a family of proteins that help maintain the cytoskeleton structure in all cells and support the contraction of muscle cells. In the late 1980s, a group of scientists discovered that the alpha-tropomyosin (α-TM) gene can code for several different tropomyosin proteins within different tissues of the same organism.

Figure 19.1 shows the structure of the seven mRNA transcripts identified as the result of the scientific study. In each transcript, each box represents an exon. Each transcript was found to be a product of the same α-TM gene.

α–TM mRNA Transcripts

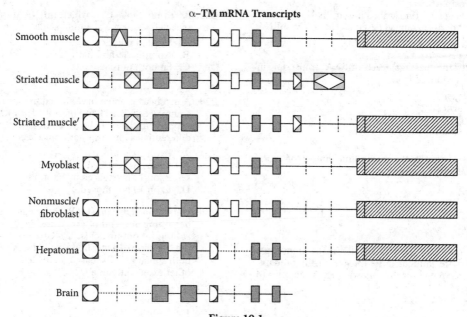

Figure 19.1
Source: *http://www.bio.utexas.edu/research/tuckerlab/bright/phylo_3_10_04/index.html.*

Scientists continue to study the α-TM gene as a model of *alternative splicing*, in which mRNA transcripts containing different combinations of exons can lead to the production of different proteins. Figure 19.2 shows the structure of the α-TM gene, which is composed of 12 exons connected by 11 introns.

Each exon in a gene codes for a specific series of amino acids in the corresponding protein. The complete α-TM gene codes for a protein composed of 284 total amino acids. Table 19.1 shows the series of amino acids coded by each of the 12 exons in the α-TM gene.

α–TM Gene

Figure 19.2
Source: *http://www.bio.utexas.edu/research/tuckerlab/bright/phylo_3_10_04/index.html.*

Table 19.1 Alpha-Tropomyosin Exon	
Exon	**Amino Acids**
1	1–38
2	39–80
3	39–80
4	81–125
5	126–164
6	165–188
7	189–213
8	214–234
9	235–257
10	258–284
11	None
12	258–284

218. To produce a tropomyosin protein, which of the following steps must occur first?

A. The introns are removed from the α-TM mRNA.
B. Exons are alternatively spliced to code a specific tropomyosin.
C. The α-TM gene is transcribed into mRNA.
D. Amino acids are arranged based on the α-TM mRNA sequence.

219. According to the passage, each mRNA transcript in Figure 19.1 is produced from:

A. the same gene.
B. multiple genes.
C. an independent gene.
D. the same tissue.

220. In Figure 19.1, what is the maximum number of exons present in an mRNA transcript?

A. 10
B. 7
C. 9
D. 11

221. *Constitutive exons* are present in all mRNA transcripts of a gene and are thought to be integral in the proteins' basic structure. Which of the following exons appears to be constitutive?

A. Exon 3
B. Exon 7
C. Exon 12
D. Exon 4

222. *Alternatively spliced exons* (ASEs) are those that only appear in certain mRNA transcripts. Which of the following cell types appears to have the least number of ASEs?

A. Myoblast
B. Brain
C. Nonmuscle/fibroblast
D. Smooth muscle

223. Which exons do NOT appear in any of the same mRNA transcripts?

A. Exons 10 and 12
B. Exons 7 and 11
C. Exons 2 and 3
D. Exons 3 and 11

224. Two types of muscle tissues—skeletal and cardiac—are both striated. Based on Figure 19.1, how do the α-TM mRNA transcripts of skeletal and cardiac muscle tissues differ?

A. One transcript contains a greater total number of exons.
B. The exons present in one transcript are absent in the other.
C. One contains Exon 2, while the other contains Exon 3.
D. Each transcript contains a different final exon.

225. The total number of exons in the α-TM gene is:

A. unknown.
B. 12.
C. variable.
D. 11.

226. Based on the data in Table 19.1, which α-TM exon codes for the longest sequence of amino acids?

A. Exon 8
B. Exon 4
C. Exon 11
D. Exon 6

227. Which α-TM mRNA transcript is missing amino acids 258–284?

A. Hepatoma
B. Myoblast
C. Smooth muscle
D. Brain

228. Based on Table 19.1, which mRNA transcript contains a repeated sequence of amino acids?

A. Striated muscle
B. Nonmuscle/fibroblast
C. Smooth muscle
D. Brain

229. A myoblast is an embryonic cell that can differentiate into a muscle cell. Based on Figure 19.1, which of the following happens to the α-TM mRNA transcript when a myoblast differentiates into a smooth muscle cell?

A. Exon 10 is added.
B. Exon 3 is replaced by Exon 2.
C. Exon 12 is replaced by Exon 11.
D. Exon 10 is removed.

230. *Untranslated regions* (UTRs) are sequences that exist at the beginning and end of every mRNA transcript. Instead of coding for amino acids, UTRs regulate the expression of the transcribed gene. In the α-TM mRNA, Exons 1 and 12 both contain UTRs. Based on the data in Table 19.1, which other exon contains a UTR?

A. Exon 5
B. Exon 8
C. Exon 11
D. Exon 3

231. The passage states that in addition to their function in all cells, tropomyosins also support contraction in muscle cells. It can be inferred that this extra function is related to which of the following sequences of amino acids?

A. Amino acids 39–80
B. Amino acids 81–125
C. Amino acids 258–284
D. Amino acids 1–38

232. A hepatoma is a tumor that forms within the liver. Based on Figure 19.1, it can be inferred that tumor formation may correlate to a loss of which exon?

A. Exon 2
B. Exon 10
C. Exon 11
D. Exon 7

PASSAGE 17

Over the past several decades, scientists have seen a rapid decline in honeybee populations worldwide. In an effort to boost population sizes, the European Union recently instituted a temporary two-year ban on *neonicotinoids*, a class of pesticides thought to be harmful to honeybees.

Two scientists present their viewpoints regarding the value of instituting a similar ban in the United States.

Scientist 1

A short-term ban on the class of pesticides called *neonicotinoids* is a viable option that should seriously be considered by the United States. Studies have found neonicotinoid concentrations in pollen and nectar that can be lethal to pollinators. Although research has not identified a direct link between neonicotinoids and a reduction in honeybee populations, recent studies suggest that these pesticides may increase honeybees' susceptibility to parasites and diseases. The health of honeybee populations directly affects the agriculture industry and the overall ecosystem. Twenty-three percent of crops grown in the United States are pollinated by honeybees. Some crops, such as almonds, apples, onions, and carrots, are pollinated almost exclusively by honeybees. The reproductive rates of these crops vary directly with the availability of honeybees. Many of the plants that make up the base of the food web in the natural ecosystem also rely on these pollinators. Because the honeybee's role as pollinator is so pervasive, any measures that have the potential to support the health of honeybee populations should be taken.

Scientist 2

Honeybees are important pollinators for both natural ecosystems and the agriculture industry, and the health of their populations should be monitored closely. Instituting a ban on neonicotinoids, however, is unnecessary. Based on current research, the benefits of neonicotinoid use to the agriculture industry outweigh the threat to honeybee health. Though the exact causes are difficult to identify, researchers attribute the decrease in honeybee populations in recent years to weather, environmental stress, disease, and varroa mites. Environmental stressors include nectar and water that is scarce or of poor quality and exposure to pesticides, although researchers have found the latter to have the weakest correlation to honeybee loss of all stressors. Therefore, a ban on neonicotinoids will not be an effective approach for improving the health of honeybee populations. A more effective method should address varroa mites and disease, the greatest known threats to honeybee health.

233. According to the passage, neonicotinoids are a type of:

    A. parasite.
    B. pollinator.
    C. pesticide.
    D. pathogen.

234. According to Scientist 1, neonicotinoids:

    A. have been directly linked to declines in honeybee populations.
    B. affect honeybees by increasing their vulnerability to parasites.
    C. provide agricultural benefits that outweigh the risk to honeybees.
    D. are the greatest threat to honeybee health in the United States.

235. Scientist 1 identifies all of the following crops as being highly dependent on pollination by honeybees except:

    A. cherries.
    B. almonds.
    C. carrots.
    D. apples.

236. The major difference between the two scientists' viewpoints is that:

    A. Scientist 1 believes honeybee populations should be saved, while Scientist 2 believes humans should not interfere with honeybee populations.
    B. Scientist 1 believes all threats to honeybee health should be addressed, while Scientist 2 believes that efforts should focus on the greatest threats to these populations.
    C. Scientist 1 believes honeybee populations are declining in the United States, while Scientist 2 believes that honeybee populations are stable.
    D. Scientist 1 believes neonicotinoids are harmful to honeybees, while Scientist 2 believes neonicotinoids do not pose any threat.

237. According to Scientist 1, which of the following graphs best represents the relationship between honeybees and producers in an ecosystem?

A.

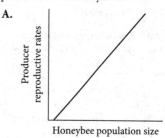

Figure 19.3

B.

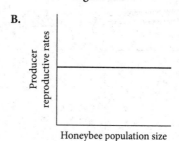

Figure 19.4

C.

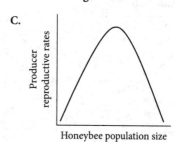

Figure 19.5

D.

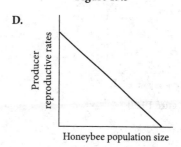

Figure 19.6

238. Which of the following does Scientist 2 identify as the greatest threats to honeybee populations in the United States?

   A. Varroa mites and disease
   B. Neonicotinoids and weather
   C. Disease and nectar quality
   D. Water and nectar scarcity

239. Which factor affecting honeybee health was discussed by Scientist 2 but not by Scientist 1?

   A. Pesticides
   B. Disease
   C. Parasites
   D. Water quality

240. It can be inferred that Scientist 1 believes honeybees' most important role in natural ecosystems is to:

   A. act as a host for varroa mites.
   B. provide a food source for birds.
   C. transfer pollen between plants.
   D. compete with other bee species.

241. According to Scientist 2, which graph best represents the relationship between neonicotinoid exposure and honeybee health?

   A.
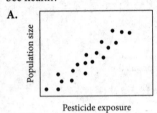
   Figure 19.7

   B.
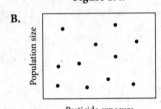
   Figure 19.8

   C.
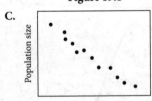
   Figure 19.9

   D.
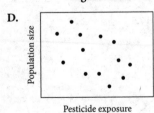
   Figure 19.10

242. A doubling of the average honeybee population size in Europe over the next five years would support the opinion of:

   A. both scientists.
   B. neither scientist.
   C. Scientist 1.
   D. Scientist 2.

243. Based on the information in the passage, both scientists would support efforts to:

   A. institute a one-year ban on neonicotinoids in the United States.
   B. improve disease and parasite prevention in honeybee populations.
   C. reduce private consumer use of pesticides near honeybee habitats.
   D. monitor changes in the size of honeybee populations without interfering.

244. According to Scientist 1, approximately what proportion of the agriculture industry in the United States is dependent on honeybees?

   A. $\frac{1}{4}$
   B. $\frac{1}{20}$
   C. $\frac{1}{3}$
   D. $\frac{1}{23}$

245. If Scientist 2 is correct, which of the following trends is most likely to be seen if a ban on neonicotinoids is enacted in the United States?

   A. Honeybee populations will continue to decline at the preban rate.
   B. Honeybee populations will begin to increase at a rapid rate.
   C. Honeybee populations will continue to decline but at a slower rate.
   D. Honeybee populations will begin to increase at a moderate rate.

246. If Scientist 2 is correct, it can be inferred that honeybee health is most strongly affected by:

   A. seasonal conditions.
   B. resource availability.
   C. human interference.
   D. biotic factors.

PASSAGE 18

Corals build the habitat that is the home for the fish and other marine species that live on the reef. The corals grow by creating aragonite forms of calcium carbonate cups in which the polyp sits. Figure 19.11 identifies the anatomy of a coral polyp.

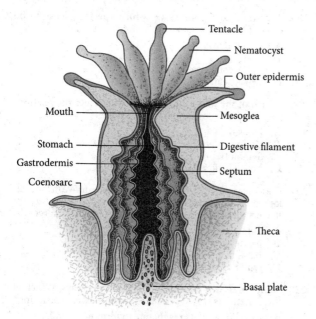

Figure 19.11
Source: http://oceanservice.noaa.gov/education/kits/corals/
media/supp_coral01a.html.

Millions of photosynthetic algae, called zooxanthellae, reside inside polyp tissues. They serve as an energy source for corals as well as providing the coloration for which corals are known.

Current research indicates that increasingly acidic waters may be to blame for the decline in coral populations. Oceans absorb atmospheric carbon dioxide. Table 19.2 depicts changes to ocean chemistry and pH estimated using scientific models calculated from surface ocean measurement data.

Table 19.2 Ocean Chemistry and pH			
	Preindustrial (1750)	**Today (2013)**	**Projected (2100)**
Atmospheric concentration of CO_2	280 ppm	380 ppm	560 ppm
Carbonic acid, H_2CO_3 (mol/kg)	9	13	19
Bicarbonate ion, HCO^{3-} (mol/kg)	1,768	1,867	1,976
Carbonate ion, CO_3^{2-} (mol/kg)	225	185	141
Total dissolved inorganic carbon (mol/kg)	2,003	2,065	2,136
Average pH of surface oceans	8.18	8.07	7.92
Calcite saturation	5.3	4.4	3.3
Aragonite saturation	3.4	2.8	2.1

Some coral become less successful at reproducing sexually in acidic waters. Studies also show links between ocean acidification and coral bleaching. Figure 19.12 summarizes the physiological responses of marine organisms to biological ocean acidification experiments done by various scientists.

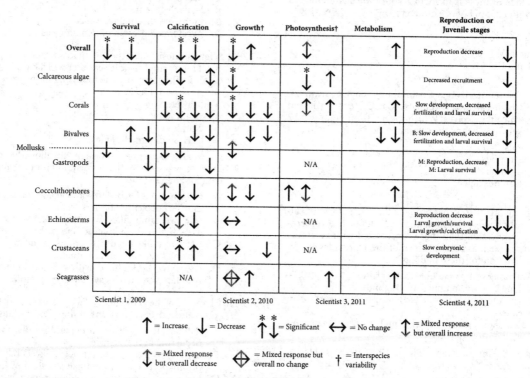

Figure 19.12
Source: Data adapted from "Recognising Ocean Acidification in Deep Time: An Evaluation of the Evidence for Acidification across the Triassic-Jurassic Boundary," Sarah E. Greene, Rowan C. Martindale, Kathleen A. Ritterbush, David J. Bottjer, Frank A. Corsetti, and William M. Berelson, Earth-Science Reviews, volume 113 (1–2), copyright © 2012 by Elsevier.

247. Zooxanthenellae would logically inhabit which part of a coral?

A. Stomach
B. Basal plate
C. Outer epidermis
D. Stinging nematocyst

248. The data in Table 19.2 indicates that as the concentration of carbon dioxide in the water rises:

A. the pH decreases and the balance shifts toward bicarbonate instead of carbonate.
B. the pH increases and the carbonate ion concentration increases.
C. both the pH and the bicarbonate concentration decrease.
D. the pH increases and the balance shifts toward carbonate instead of bicarbonate.

249. Based on the information in Table 19.2, what conclusions can be drawn about ocean chemistry?

A. Future emissions of carbon dioxide are less likely to significantly impact ocean chemistry over time.
B. Increased atmospheric carbon dioxide will have little impact on the concentration of carbonate ions.
C. Chemical changes in oceans are a result of the water absorbing atmospheric carbon dioxide produced by human activities.
D. Ocean acidification is an unpredictable response that is unlikely to be linked to human activities that increase the atmospheric concentration of carbon dioxide.

250. Factors that might impact the data found in Table 19.2 include:

I. seasonal changes in temperature.
II. variations in photosynthesis.
III. runoff from rivers.
IV. fluctuations in respiration.

Which of these is likely to account for fluctuations in the geographic pH of ocean waters?

A. II
B. III
C. I and IV
D. II and III

251. The saturation horizon is a natural boundary in seawater, above which calcium carbonate ($CaCO_3$) can form and below which it dissolves. Which species from Figure 19.12 most likely lives below the saturation horizon?

A. Corals
B. Gastropods
C. Crustaceans
D. Calcareous algae

252. Calcifying organisms that produce the calcite form of calcium carbonate, such as foraminifera, can be less vulnerable to acidification than those constructed with aragonite structures, such as corals. Which of these provides a logical explanation for these findings?

A. Aragonite is more soluble than calcite.
B. Calcite is more soluble than aragonite.
C. Aragonite saturation is farther from the surface of oceans.
D. Calcite saturation is farther from the surface of oceans.

253. Based on the information in Figure 19.12, decreased fertilization affects corals as well as:

A. echinoderms.
B. bivalves.
C. crustaceans.
D. calcareous algae.

254. In Figure 19.12, the most significant data with regard to the health of marine ecosystems is:

A. the decline in coral calcification.
B. the rise in crustacean calcification.
C. the declining metabolism of bivalves.
D. the decreased larval survival in gastropods.

255. According to Figure 19.12, which species appear to be most affected by ocean acidification?

A. Echinoderms
B. Gastropods
C. Calcareous algae
D. Crustaceans

256. Which of the following terms best describes the relationship between zooxanthellae and corals?

A. Parasitic
B. Codependent
C. Symbiotic
D. Mutualistic

257. Corals have several features that help them survive in the shallow ocean. Which part of a coral's anatomy may protect against fluctuating environmental changes such as temperature?

A. Stomach
B. Nematocysts
C. Basal plate
D. Outer epidermis

258. Some corals can reproduce in a variety of ways. Which of these methods would produce the most diverse offspring?

A. Coral fragments regenerate to form new coral.
B. Adult coral sprouts tiny buds to form new coral.
C. Adult coral divides and both pieces grow new coral.
D. Coral eggs join with coral sperm to form new coral.

259. Which of the following is most likely to result from declines in a coral polyp's zooxanthellae population?

A. Bleaching
B. Hyperpigmentation
C. Increased thermal tolerance
D. Accelerated growth of nematocysts

260. Scientists design an experiment in an attempt to predict the effect increasingly acidic seawater will have on coral reproduction. They may use the following in the experiment:

- Aquarium tanks
- Seawater
- Tap water
- Corals
- Carbon dioxide bubbles

Which experimental design will allow the scientists to investigate their hypothesis fairly and produce high-quality data for analysis?

A. Use two tanks filled with seawater and corals. Add carbon dioxide bubbles to one tank.
B. Use two tanks filled with tap water and corals. Add carbon dioxide bubbles to one tank.
C. Use two tanks filled with corals. Add tap water to one tank and seawater to the other.
D. Use three tanks filled with carbon dioxide bubbles. Add tap water and seawater to each tank.

261. Changes in the biological processes in the surface ocean water affect deeper portions of the ocean because:

A. habitats at deeper levels depend on dissolved oxygen occurring at the surface.
B. organisms living at lower ocean levels rely mainly on products created by organisms at shallow levels.
C. the pH of organisms in shallow waters is altered and becomes non-nutritious to deep-water organisms.
D. the calcification of shallow-water organisms provides an additional layer of protection that prevents predation.

CHAPTER 20

TEST 7

PASSAGE 19

Lenses are made of transparent materials such as glass and plastic and are used in eyeglasses, cameras, and telescopes, as well as other applications. When light rays enter a curved lens from a distant object, the rays are bent into new angles. A *convex lens*, which is thicker in the middle, takes parallel light rays and converges them toward a common point called the focal point. The *focal length* is defined as the distance from the center of the lens to the point where the bent rays converge. A *concave lens*, on the other hand, is thinner in the middle and diverges parallel light rays as if they came from a point ahead of the lens (this point is one focal length from the lens). Both lenses are shown in Figure 20.1.

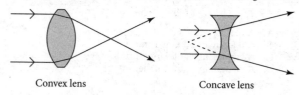

Convex lens   Concave lens

Figure 20.1

In conventional ray diagrams, the source of light (the object) is to the left of the lens and the rays move to the right through the lens. Light rays leave objects at various angles and are bent by the lens to form an image of the distant object. *Real images* are formed when actual light rays converge to a common point to the right of the lens. *Virtual images* are formed when the observer looks backward through the lens and sees an image on the same side of the lens as the object. Table 20.1 summarizes the images observed by these lenses.

		Table 20.1	
Lens Type	**Distance of Object to the Left of Lens**	**Image Description**	**Image Location**
Convex	More than two focal lengths	Inverted, smaller	Between one and two focal lengths to the right of lens
Convex	Two focal lengths	Inverted, same size	Two focal lengths to the right of lens
Convex	Between one and two focal lengths	Inverted, larger	More than two focal lengths to the right of lens
Convex	One focal length	No image	No image
Convex	Within one focal length	Upright, larger	To the left of lens
Concave	Any position	Upright, smaller	To the left of lens

262. When the human eye views distant objects, the light rays go through a lens that is thicker in the middle. An image forms on the retina, which is the inner back surface of the eye. Which of the following best identifies the eye's lens and the characteristics of the image?

   A. Convex; real, inverted, and smaller
   B. Concave; virtual, upright, and smaller
   C. Convex; virtual, upright, and larger
   D. Concave; real, inverted, and smaller

263. According to the information provided in the passage and Table 20.1, which of the following statements is true?

   A. A lens that is thinner in the middle is capable of forming inverted images.
   B. Convex lenses form a real image when the object is one focal length to the left of the lens.
   C. Concave lenses can form images with many characteristics.
   D. All real images are inverted.

264. A particular convex lens in a camera has a focal length of 10 cm. If the object for the picture is 30 cm from the lens, what type of image will form on the film?

   A. A real, inverted, smaller image
   B. A real, inverted, larger image
   C. A real, inverted, same-size image
   D. A virtual, upright, smaller image

265. Rays of light from the distant sun reach the earth nearly parallel with each other. A child wishes to take these rays of light and use them to burn a piece of paper. What type of lens should the child use, and how far from the center of the lens should the paper be?

   A. A convex lens two focal lengths away from the paper
   B. A concave lens two focal lengths away from the paper
   C. A convex lens one focal length away from the paper
   D. A concave lens one focal length away from the paper

266. A slide projector uses a convex lens with a focal length of 120 mm. A small picture on a transparent slide is placed upside down in the projector, 125 mm in front of the lens. What will the image on the screen look like?

   A. Larger than the slide and right side up
   B. Larger than the slide and upside-down
   C. Same size as the slide and right side up
   D. Same size as the slide and upside-down

267. Eyeglass lenses may be used to correct both nearsighted and farsighted vision. Someone who is farsighted has difficulty seeing tiny objects that are close to the lens. As farsighted patients look through corrective lenses toward the object, they are able to see a larger image clearly on the same side of the lens as the object. What type of lens corrects farsighted vision, and what is the orientation of the image to that of the object?

   A. Convex; inverted
   B. Convex; upright
   C. Concave; inverted
   D. Concave; upright

268. A copy machine has a lens with a focal length of 30 cm. How far from the lens must a document (the object) be placed if the copy (the image) is to be exactly the same size?

   A. More than 60 cm from the lens
   B. 60 cm from the lens
   C. Between 30 and 60 cm from the lens
   D. 30 cm from the lens

269. A child looks through a lens at the distant trees, and the trees still look distant but appear smaller. What type of lens is the child looking through, and is the image upright or inverted?

   A. Convex; upright
   B. Convex; inverted
   C. Concave; upright
   D. Concave; inverted

270. A 15-cm focal-length lens is used to focus a sharp image on a piece of paper that is 20 cm to the right of the lens. What information is known about the lens and the object?

   A. The lens is convex, and the object is 30 cm to the left of the lens.
   B. The lens is concave, and the object may be any distance from the lens.
   C. The lens is convex, and the object is between 15 and 30 cm to the left of the lens.
   D. The lens is convex, and the object is more than 30 cm to the left of the lens.

271. In Figure 20.2, Point "F" represents the focal point of the lens. If the candle is placed as shown in the figure, what type of image will be seen?

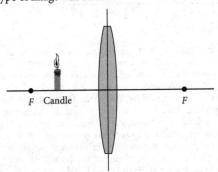

Figure 20.2

   A. A real, inverted, smaller image
   B. A real, inverted larger image
   C. A virtual, upright, larger image
   D. A virtual, upright, smaller image

PASSAGE 20: THE KAIBAB PLATEAU[*1]

In 1906, the Kaibab Plateau in northern Arizona was declared a federal game refuge by President Theodore Roosevelt. Before this time, the Kaibab was home to mule deer, cattle, sheep, and a variety of predators. The approximately 4,000 Rocky Mountain deer were an important source of food for the wolves, coyotes, bears, mountain lions, and bobcats that lived on the Kaibab and competed with sheep, horses, and cattle for the limited grass resources of the plateau.

When the game refuge was created, all deer hunting was banned in an attempt to protect the "finest deer herd in America." In 1907, the U.S. Forest Service began to exterminate the natural predators of the deer. With the deer freed from the checks and balances of predators, the population began to multiply. By the early 1920s, scientists estimated that there were as many as 100,000 deer on the plateau.

Sheep and cattle were also banned from the Kaibab. Signs of overgrazing were everywhere, and disease began to attack the crowded deer population. Hunting was reopened, but it was not enough to reduce the number of deer. Some estimate that as many as 60,000 deer starved to death in the winters of 1925 and 1926.

Two scientists exchange views about "The Kaibab Deer Incident: A Long-Persisting Myth."

Scientist A

The Kaibab Plateau should be a lesson to everyone about the disruption of the predator-prey relationship. This is a classic example of predator control hurting the very species that the wildlife biologists are attempting to help. If the predators had not been removed from the Kaibab Plateau, the deer population would have grown under normal conditions and would not have been subjected to the cruel fate of starvation and disease. This is a moral case that should be heeded by all biologists when considering predator control and presented to biology students in their studies of predator checks in population dynamics.

Scientist B

Predator removal is only a small part of the disaster on the Kaibab and has been grossly overdramatized. The deer population on the plateau grew rapidly because of the increase in food supply after the removal of competitive species. With no sheep and cattle to compete with for grazing, the environment could readily support more deer. The increased food supply allowed the population to grow quickly and to fall just as quickly due to the density-dependent factors of starvation and disease. In fact, data about the peak total number of deer on the plateau are unreliable, and there may have only been 30,000. The factors are more complex than early ecologists believed, but the lesson is still valuable.

272. Which of the following pieces of information would Scientist A use to support his claim?

A. Before 1906, the Kaibab Plateau had already been overgrazed by the herbivores in the area.

B. It is estimated that between 1907 and 1939, 816 mountain lions, 20 wolves, 7,388 coyotes, and more than 500 bobcats were killed.

C. The U.S. Forest Service reduced the number of livestock grazing permits.

D. In 1924, a committee formed to oversee the situation recommended that all livestock not owned by local residents be removed immediately.

273. Which of the following reflects evidence presented by both Scientist A and Scientist B about the deer situation on the Kaibab Plateau?

A. Competition among herbivores was reduced due to restrictions on grazing.

B. The food chain was disrupted when secondary consumers were reduced.

C. Starvation and disease reduced the herd during the winters of 1925 and 1926.

D. Human intervention in the predator population was the cause of the upsurge in the deer population.

274. Which statement would LEAST likely be attributed to Scientist B?

A. "Data about the deer herd are unreliable and inconsistent, and the factors that may have led to an upsurge are hopelessly confounded."

B. "Conclusions that have been made about the Kaibab are based on the maximum estimate and evolved by unjustified tampering with original data."

C. "This is a classic example of how the effects of disruption of the predator-prey relationship can be seen plainly."

D. "The reduction in sheep alone from 1889 to 1908 might have totaled 195,000."

275. The following statements have been made by biologists to describe the Kaibab Plateau situation. On which statement would Scientists A and B be likely to agree?

A. "The plateau represents the unforeseen and disastrous possibilities of ignorant interference in natural communities."

B. "The Kaibab is a classic example of what happens when people set out to protect prey from their 'enemies' (sometimes only to preserve them for their human ones) by killing the predators."

C. "Man is the most destructive predator alive."

D. "This situation is a well-documented example of what can happen when predators are removed from an ecosystem."

276. The views of Scientist A:

A. minimize the role of the bounty placed on predators.

B. emphasize the lack of competition for resources.

C. show a more balanced view of the problem by taking into account all factors that led to the increase in population.

D. are likely to be used by someone trying to illustrate the dangers of removing a species from the food chain.

277. Scientist A would be most likely to support:

A. the introduction of non-native species into an area where there are no natural predators.

B. controlled hunting of predators to protect endangered species.

C. future efforts to reorganize natural ecosystems through human intervention.

D. the view that predators help preserve ecosystems.

1* Based on data from C. John Burk, "The Kaibab Deer Incident: A Long-Persisting Myth," *BioScience* 23, no. 2 (1973): 113–14.

278. Scientists A and B tend to agree on:

   A. the role of an increase in grass abundance in the increase of the deer population.

   B. the role that disease and starvation played in reducing the population.

   C. the role of predation in the increase of the deer population.

   D. the data to be used to represent the situation on the Kaibab.

279. Which of the following facts would support the view of Scientist B regarding the cause for rapid increase in the deer population?

   A. Coyotes were hunted in the thousands.

   B. Starvation and disease were rampant from 1924 to 1926.

   C. Hunters killed 674 deer in 1924.

   D. Sheep and cattle were banned during this time period.

280. Lethal reduction of midsized mammal predators that target duck nests is a method used to increase the duck population available for sport hunters. Which of the following statements would Scientist A most likely make regarding this practice?

   A. Hunting will keep the duck population from increasing unchecked and limit growth.

   B. The removal of mammals such as foxes and skunks will disrupt other areas of the food chain, such as the population of mice.

   C. The duck population will have greater nesting success as a result of reduced predatory concerns.

   D. Other waterfowl will enjoy the benefits of less predation.

281. On which of the following conclusions would Scientists A and B agree?

   A. Human intervention in natural ecosystems is a necessary step to protect populations.

   B. Caution should be taken when creating an ecological situation that favors a single species.

   C. Humans can make a change involving a single species with little or no effect on other species in the area.

   D. The Kaibab Plateau does not offer any lessons applicable to modern-day issues in ecology.

PASSAGE 21

A group of students gathered data to determine the factors that affect the speed of a wave pulse as it travels down a spring. They studied springs with their coils stretched out (high tension) against springs with looser coils (low tension) to determine how changing the characteristics of the medium affect wave speed.

They also studied the effect of wave amplitude on the speed of the wave. *Amplitude* is the size of the disturbance.

The students conducted slow-motion video analysis of a wave pulse traveling down the spring and graphed the total distance the pulse traveled versus the total travel time, as shown in Figure 20.3.

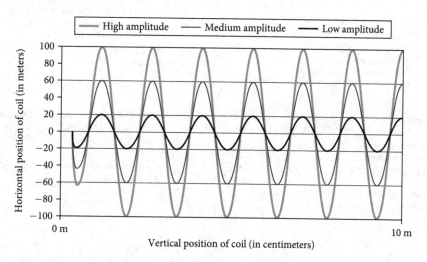

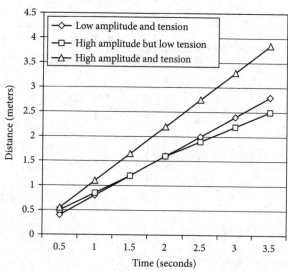

Figure 20.3
Source: *U.S. Geological Survey and www.thinkquest.org. http://earthquake.usgs.gov/ learn /glossary/?term=amplitude.*

282. To properly determine the effect of wave amplitude on wave speed, the students must:

   A. make the spring tighter as they change the amplitude.
   B. keep the tension the same but change the amplitude.
   C. keep the amplitude and tension the same.
   D. change both the tension and the amplitude.

283. According to Figure 20.3, the average speed of the high-tension/high-amplitude wave is closest in value to:

   A. 0.50 m/s.
   B. 0.72 m/s.
   C. 0.91 m/s.
   D. 1.10 m/s.

284. According to Figure 20.3, the low-tension/low-amplitude wave:

   A. gained speed with time.
   B. lost speed with time.
   C. maintained a constant speed.
   D. accelerated at first and then slowed down.

285. According to Figure 20.3, what is the effect of the tension of the spring on wave speed?

   A. An increase in tension results in a greater wave speed.
   B. An increase in tension results in a smaller wave speed.
   C. Tension has no significant effect on wave speed.
   D. Tension increases the amplitude of the wave.

286. What is the effect of amplitude on wave speed?

   A. An increase in amplitude results in a greater wave speed.

   B. An increase in amplitude results in a smaller wave speed.

   C. Amplitude has no significant effect on wave speed.

   D. Amplitude increases the tension of the wave.

287. Because sound behaves like a wave, one can infer from the results in Figure 20.3 that loud sounds:

   A. travel at the same speed as soft sounds.

   B. travel faster than soft sounds.

   C. gain speed as they move through the air.

   D. lose speed as they move through the air.

288. It is believed that light has the same characteristics as waves. From the results in Figure 20.3, one can infer that:

   A. the speed of light depends on the characteristics of the material it goes through.

   B. the speed of light depends on the brightness of the light.

   C. light loses speed as it moves away from its source.

   D. increased light frequency increases wave speed.

289. Water waves behave like spring waves in many ways. From the results in Figure 20.3, one can conclude that a water wave:

   A. gains speed as it travels.

   B. loses speed as it travels.

   C. gains speed at first before slowing down to rest.

   D. maintains a constant speed as it travels.

290. Assuming the low-tension/low-amplitude wave was able to keep moving, what is the approximate distance it would travel in 6.0 seconds?

   A. 0.77 m

   B. 1.6 m

   C. 4.8 m

   D. 6.4 m

291. In another experiment with springs, a large wave travels 10.2 m along a spring in 5.3 seconds. Approximately how much time would it take a small ripple to travel the same distance?

   A. 1.9 seconds

   B. 4.9 seconds

   C. 5.3 seconds

   D. 10.2 seconds

PASSAGE 22

The *boiling point* of a liquid is commonly defined as the temperature at which the vapor pressure of the liquid is equal to the atmospheric pressure that surrounds the liquid. When a liquid is brought to a temperature at or above its boiling point, it quickly changes from the liquid phase to the gaseous phase. This can easily be observed in vapor bubbles that form in the liquid and rise to the top.

The boiling point of a substance depends on many different factors, such as the composition of the substance, its molar mass, and the atmospheric pressure surrounding it. The names, molar masses, and skeletal models of a variety of *alkanes* and three *alcohols* were identified and recorded in Table 20.2.

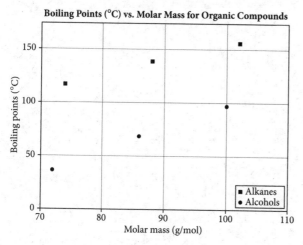

Table 20.2			
	Name	**Molar Mass (g/mol)**	**Skeletal Model**
Alkanes	Pentane	72	
	Hexane	86	
	Heptane	100	
Alcohols	Butanol	74	
	Pentanol	88	
	Hexanol	102	

Figure 20.4 shows the boiling points of these six substances versus their molar mass. All temperatures are in degrees Celsius and have been recorded at a standard atmospheric pressure of 1 atm.

Figure 20.4

292. What is the boiling point of heptane?
   A. 37°C
   B. 97°C
   C. 117°C
   D. 156°C

293. Based on Figure 20.4, what is the best summary of the relationship between the molar mass and boiling point of an alkane?
   A. The molar mass of a substance seems to have little effect on its boiling point.
   B. As the molar mass of a substance increases, its boiling point tends to increase.
   C. As the molar mass of a substance increases, its boiling point tends to decrease.
   D. The relationship between the molar mass and boiling point of a substance is not clear from the data in the figure.

294. The organic substance propanol has a molar mass of about 60 g/mol. Which temperature is most likely the boiling point of propanol?
   A. 11°C
   B. 52°C
   C. 97°C
   D. 117°C

295. In which physical state would pentanol be if the atmospheric pressure were 1.0 atm and the temperature were 150°C?
   A. Solid
   B. Liquid
   C. Gaseous
   D. Cannot be determined

296. Based on the skeletal models shown in Table 20.2, which statement best describes the effect of a hydroxyl group (OH^-) on the boiling point of a substance?
   A. When the molar mass of a substance is controlled, the addition of a hydroxyl group tends to increase the substance's boiling point.
   B. When the molar mass of a substance is controlled, the addition of a hydroxyl group tends to decrease the substance's boiling point.
   C. When the molar mass of a substance is controlled, the addition of a hydroxyl group tends to have no effect on the substance's boiling point.
   D. The figure does not show a relationship between the presence of a hydroxyl group and the boiling point of a substance.

297. Based on the skeletal models shown in Table 20.2, which of the following images shows the skeletal model for hexanol?
   A.
   B.
   C. OH
   D. OH

298. Organic chemists draw skeletal models to simplify the actual atoms and connections that exist within a molecule. Each short line segment represents the connection between two carbon atoms. In alkane molecules, hydrogen atoms surround each carbon atom in such a way that there are three hydrogen atoms on each end carbon and two hydrogen atoms on each middle carbon. These molecules can also be represented by ball-and-stick models or chemical formulas. An example for the molecule hexane is shown in Figure 20.5.

 C_6H_{14}

Figure 20.5

The alkane molecule, decane, has the following skeletal structure.

What is the chemical formula for decane?

A. $C_{10}H_{20}$
B. $C_{10}H_{22}$
C. $C_{10}H_{24}$
D. $C_{10}H_{30}$

299. Decane has a molar mass of 142 g/mol. What could a person expect its boiling point to be?

A. 212°C
B. 185°C
C. 156°C
D. 142°C

CHAPTER 21
TEST 8

PASSAGE 23: UVB BLOCKING

The sun is a source of many wavelengths of radiation that reach the earth. The earth's atmosphere absorbs some of these wavelengths, while others are able to penetrate and reach the planet's surface. Ultraviolet radiation from the sun comes in three different categories based on wavelength and penetration: UVA, UVB, and UVC.

UVB radiation has wavelengths of 280 to 320 nm and is partially absorbed by the earth's ozone layer. The UVB rays that do reach the surface can be absorbed by human skin and have been known to cause sunburn and many forms of skin cancer. Many products, from glasses to sunscreen, have been created to help protect humans from UVB radiation. Two groups of students set out to test the ability of materials to block UVB light, using a computer and a sensor specifically designed to detect UVB radiation.

Group 1
The members of Group 1 placed a sensor in full sunlight and shielded the sensor with a variety of sunglasses claiming to offer UVB protection. A reading was taken on the UVB sensor for each product, and the data were recorded in Table 21.1.

Group 2
The members of Group 2 placed a sensor in the sun and shielded that sensor with a piece of glass. They tested sunscreens of increasing SPF (sun protection factor) on the glass, and the data were recorded in Table 21.2.

Table 21.1				
	Approx. Retail Cost of Glasses ($)	UVB Reading Before Shielding (mW/m²)	UVB Reading After Shielding (mW/m²)	Shielding (%)
Pair A	10	742.3	2.7	99.6
Pair B	350	742.3	3.2	99.6
Pair C	1	742.3	4.2	99.4
Pair D	25	742.3	3.5	99.5
Pair E	90	742.3	2.1	99.7
Clear plastic	n/a	742.3	423.1	43.0

Table 21.2				
Description	SPF	UVB Reading with Sunscreen (mW/m²)	UVB Reading without Sunscreen (mW/m²)	Cost per Bottle of Sunscreen ($)
Dark tanning	4	72.1	742.3	8.99
Waterproof	8	35.6	742.3	4.99
Sport	15	20.2	742.3	7.99
Oil-free	30	19.8	742.3	15.99
Baby	50	18.5	742.3	10.99

300. In Group 2's experiment, SPF is the independent variable being manipulated and UVB is the dependent variable being measured. Which of the following graphs best represents the relationship between the SPF and UVB data from this experiment?

A.

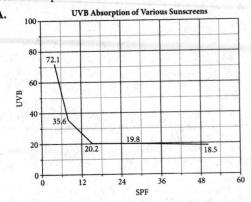

Figure 21.1

B.

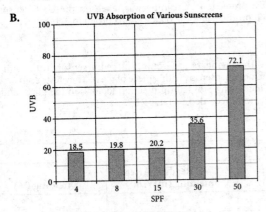

Figure 21.2

C.

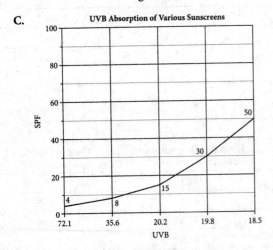

Figure 21.3

D.

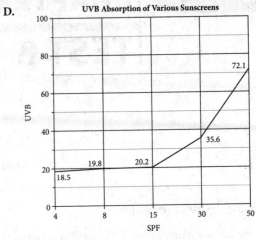

Figure 21.4

301. Which of the following questions could the students in Group 2 be attempting to answer using the data from their experiment?
  A. Does the cost of sunscreen affect the amount of UVB that is blocked?
  B. Which brand of sunscreen is the best?
  C. Is there a relationship between SPF and the amount of UVA radiation blocked?
  D. Can sunscreen protect humans from skin cancer?

302. According to the findings of Group 1:
  A. there is a negative correlation between price and the ability to protect from UVB radiation.
  B. there is a positive correlation between price and the ability to protect from UVB radiation.
  C. there is no correlation between the price of a pair of sunglasses and their ability to protect the eyes from UVB radiation.
  D. sunglasses do not protect the eyes from UVB radiation.

303. Assuming that the sunscreen being tested was purchased in 10-oz bottles, which sunscreen had the best cost for the amount of UVB protection (use the formula $/mW/m^2$ of UVB blocked)?
  A. SPF 50
  B. SPF 30
  C. SPF 8
  D. SPF 4

304. Which of the following is MOST likely to represent a control that would have been used to ensure reliability of data in the experiment done by Group 2?
  A. The distance from the sunglasses to the sensor
  B. The ingredients in the sunscreen being used
  C. A longer time for the sensor readings as SPF increased
  D. The amount and thickness of sunscreen being spread on the glass

305. According to the results of Group 1's experiment, what percentage of UVB rays would a $200 pair of sunglasses block?
    A. 99.5%
    B. 99.7%
    C. 99.6%
    D. There is not enough information to determine this answer.

306. Based on the results of Group 2's experiment, what would the UVB reading most likely be if SPF 60 sunscreen were to be tested?
    A. 18 mW/m^2
    B. 19.25 mW/m^2
    C. 9.25 mW/m^2
    D. 4.5 mW/m^2

307. Which of the following is the experimental variable that Group 1 manipulated?
    A. The time of day
    B. The type of sunglasses
    C. The amount of UVB rays
    D. The distance of the materials from the sensor

308. Which of the following implies the correct relationship between SPF and UVB blockage?
    A. Sunscreens with SPFs higher than 30 provide only a marginal increase in sun protection over their counterparts with lower SPFs.
    B. As SPF increases, the ability to block UVB light decreases.
    C. There is no correlation between SPF and UVB blockage.
    D. Sunscreens with higher SPFs provide less sun protection than those with low SPFs.

309. What other experiment could the students in Group 2 conduct using the same equipment?
    A. The effect of sunscreen on shielding UVA rays
    B. The ability of sunscreen to prevent cancer
    C. How the amount of sunscreen applied can impact the SPF
    D. The margin of benefit of SPF sunscreens higher than 60

PASSAGE 24

A study was conducted to identify the factors that affect the evaporation rates of various liquids in air. Throughout the experiment, the amount of liquid was varied, and the surface area exposed to the air was also manipulated. Table 21.3 displays the results.

The experiment was continued over a period of seven weeks for water and alcohol. Figure 21.5 shows the results graphically.

Table 21.3						
Type of Liquid	**Surface Area Exposed (cm²)**	**Initial Amount (mL)**	**Amount Evaporated after 1 Week of Exposure (mL)**			
			Trial 1	**Trial 2**	**Trial 3**	**Average**
Water	16	20.0	12.3	11.5	12.4	12.1
Water	12	40.0	9.3	9.2	8.8	9.1
Water	8	60.0	6.3	5.9	6.2	6.1
Water	4	80.0	2.8	3.1	2.9	2.9
Orange juice	4	80.0	2.7	3.2	3.2	3.0
Liquid bleach[1]	4	80.0	3.1	3.3	3.0	3.1
Vegetable oil	4	80.0	0.1	0.0	0.0	0.0
Rubbing alcohol	4	80.0	9.1	8.8	8.9	8.9
Rubbing alcohol	8	80.0	18.6	18.1	17.8	18.2
Rubbing alcohol	12	80.0	27.1	28.0	26.9	27.3
Rubbing alcohol	16	80.0	38.0	37.1	34.0	36.4

[1]The liquid bleach was approximately 5% sodium hypochlorite and 95% water.

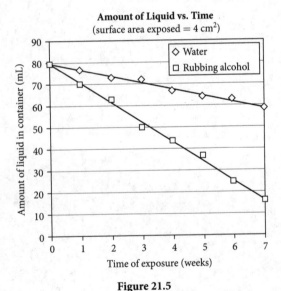

Amount of Liquid vs. Time
(surface area exposed = 4 cm²)

Figure 21.5

310. Based on the data for water in Table 21.3, which of the following statements do the data NOT support?

 A. The trials with larger surface areas of exposed water had greater evaporation rates.
 B. The evaporation rate for water is less than that for rubbing alcohol.
 C. Water had approximately the same evaporation rate as orange juice.
 D. Larger amounts of water correlate to higher evaporation rates.

311. In the experiment, 80 mL of orange juice with 4 cm² exposed was left in the open for one week. Using the data in Table 21.3, how much of the original liquid was left at the end of the week?

 A. 3.0 mL
 B. 77.0 mL
 C. 80.0 mL
 D. 83.0 mL

312. Before the experiment, students made the following hypotheses:

Student 1: "Since I can smell rubbing alcohol as soon as I open the bottle, I expect it to have a greater rate of evaporation in air."
Student 2: "Since orange juice and liquid bleach are composed primarily of water, their evaporation rates will be close to that of water."
Student 3: "Surface area should not affect the rate of evaporation of a liquid because only the total amount of liquid affects evaporation rates."

Which of the hypotheses are supported by the data collected?

 A. Student 1 only
 B. Students 1 and 2
 C. Students 1, 2, and 3
 D. None of the students' hypotheses are supported by the data.

313. If 80.0 mL of rubbing alcohol are placed in a container with 20 cm² exposed, what would be the approximate amount of liquid left in the container after one week?

 A. 9 mL
 B. 15 mL
 C. 36 mL
 D. 45 mL

314. Using Figure 21.5, what is the approximate number of weeks required for 80 mL of rubbing alcohol to evaporate completely from a container with a 4 cm² exposure?

    A. 9 weeks
    B. 12 weeks
    C. 28 weeks
    D. The data does not provide enough evidence to make a reasonable prediction.

315. According to Figure 21.5, what is the rate of evaporation of water with a 4 cm² exposed surface area?

    A. 3 mL of water each week
    B. 10 mL of water each week
    C. 20 mL of water each week
    D. 80 mL of water each week

316. Which of the following conclusions may be supported by Figure 21.5?

    A. The rate of evaporation for alcohol increases with time.
    B. The rate of evaporation for alcohol decreases with time.
    C. The rate of evaporation for alcohol is fairly steady with time.
    D. The rate of evaporation for water is greater than that for alcohol.

317. If data for vegetable oil were added to Figure 21.5, one would most likely see:

    A. data with a steeper negative slope than that of rubbing alcohol.
    B. data very similar to the line for water.
    C. data with a flat line.
    D. data very similar to the line for rubbing alcohol.

318. Which of the following statements about rubbing alcohol is supported by the data?

    A. The variability between the trials increases with the surface area exposed.
    B. A decrease in surface area of exposure increases the evaporation rate.
    C. An increased amount of liquid in the container increases the evaporation rate.
    D. The rate of evaporation for rubbing alcohol is greater than that for ethyl alcohol.

319. Although the graph for rubbing alcohol displays a general downward trend, the variations in the data could possibly be attributed to all of the following EXCEPT:

    A. fluctuations in temperature in the room in which the containers were located.
    B. variations in the air flow in the room in which the containers were located.
    C. inaccuracies in the measurement of liquid volume.
    D. varying amounts of initial liquid in the containers.

PASSAGE 25

A simple pendulum consists of a mass (the *pendulum bob*) suspended by a string, as shown in Figure 21.6. In an experiment, the mass of the bob, the radius of the arc, and the release height (measured vertically from the bottom of the swing) were varied. Rather than measuring the speed at the bottom of the swing, energy analysis was used to predict the speed of the pendulum bob at the bottom of the swing. The results are shown in Table 21.4.

Mass of Pendulum Bob (kg)	Radius of Arc (m)	Release Height (m)	Gravitational Energy at Top of Swing (J)	Kinetic Energy at Bottom of Swing (J)	Speed at Bottom of Swing (m/s)
0.010	0.05	0.05	0.005	0.005	0.99
0.010	0.10	0.05	0.005	0.005	0.99
0.010	0.20	0.05	0.005	0.005	0.99
0.010	0.30	0.05	0.005	0.005	0.99
0.010	0.40	0.05	0.005	0.005	0.99
0.010	0.40	0.10	0.010	0.010	1.40
0.010	0.40	0.15	0.015	0.015	1.71
0.010	0.40	0.20	0.020	0.020	1.98
0.010	0.40	0.25	0.025	0.025	2.21
0.020	0.40	0.25	0.049	0.049	2.21
0.030	0.40	0.25	0.074	0.074	2.21
0.040	0.40	0.25	0.098	0.098	2.21
0.050	0.40	0.25	0.123	0.123	2.21

Table 21.4

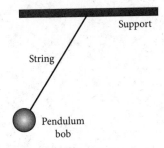

Figure 21.6

A second experiment used the same scenario, but it included the measurement of the centripetal force and calculation of centripetal acceleration. *Centripetal force* is a real, unbalanced force pointed toward the center of an object's circular motion. Likewise, *centripetal acceleration* is defined as the component of acceleration directed toward the center. As a pendulum bob swings through the bottom of its arc, the string force dominates the gravitational force, thus providing the centripetal force that gives the pendulum bob its upward centripetal acceleration. The results are shown in Table 21.5.

Mass of Pendulum Bob (kg)	Radius of Arc (m)	Release Height (m)	Speed at Bottom of Swing (m/s)	Centripetal Force (N)	Centripetal Acceleration (m/s/s)
0.010	0.05	0.05	0.99	0.196	19.6
0.010	0.10	0.05	0.99	0.098	9.8
0.010	0.20	0.05	0.99	0.049	4.9
0.010	0.30	0.05	0.99	0.033	3.3
0.010	0.40	0.05	0.99	0.025	2.5
0.010	0.40	0.10	1.40	0.049	4.9
0.010	0.40	0.15	1.71	0.074	7.4
0.010	0.40	0.20	1.98	0.098	9.8
0.010	0.40	0.25	2.21	0.123	12.3
0.020	0.40	0.25	2.21	0.245	12.3
0.030	0.40	0.25	2.21	0.368	12.3
0.040	0.40	0.25	2.21	0.490	12.3
0.050	0.40	0.25	2.21	0.613	12.3

Table 21.5

320. According to the data in Table 21.4, increasing the mass of the pendulum bob:

   A. has no effect on the gravitational energy at the top of the swing.
   B. decreases the gravitational energy at the top of the swing.
   C. increases the radius of the arc.
   D. has no effect on the speed at the bottom of the swing.

321. A 0.010-kg pendulum has an arc radius of 0.40 m. Using the data trends shown in Table 21.4, predict the kinetic energy at the bottom of the swing if it is released from a height of 0.35 m.

   A. 0.025 J
   B. 0.030 J
   C. 0.035 J
   D. 0.040 J

322. According to Table 21.4, when the release height doubles, the gravitational energy at the top of the swing:

   A. doubles.
   B. quadruples.
   C. decreases to one-half its value.
   D. decreases to one-fourth its value.

323. Which of the following conclusions about energy is supported by Table 21.4?

   A. Kinetic energy at the bottom of the swing is directly proportional to speed.
   B. Gravitational energy at the top of the swing is inversely proportional to release height.
   C. Kinetic energy at the bottom of the swing is directly proportional to the radius of the arc.
   D. Gravitational energy at the top of the swing equals kinetic energy at the bottom of the swing.

324. When the mass of the pendulum bob doubles, the kinetic energy at the bottom of the swing:

   A. doubles.
   B. quadruples.
   C. decreases to one-half its value.
   D. decreases to one-fourth its value.

325. When the pendulum bob's kinetic energy doubles, its speed:

   A. doubles.
   B. decreases to one-half its value.
   C. increases by a factor of 1.4.
   D. increases by a factor of 2.2.

326. According to Table 21.5, centripetal acceleration is

   A. independent of mass.
   B. directly proportional to mass.
   C. inversely proportional to mass.
   D. directly proportional to the radius of the arc.

327. When the radius of the arc doubles, the centripetal force:

   A. doubles.
   B. quadruples.
   C. decreases to one-half its value.
   D. decreases to one-fourth its value.

328. A car approaches a school zone with a speed limit of 20 miles per hour. Using the data trends shown in Table 21.4, how does the kinetic energy of a car speeding at 40 miles per hour compare to that of a car moving at the speed limit?

   A. The speeding car's kinetic energy is one-half that of the other car.
   B. The speeding car's kinetic energy is one-fourth that of the other car.
   C. The speeding car's kinetic energy is twice that of the other car.
   D. The speeding car's kinetic energy is four times that of the other car.

329. Using Table 21.5, predict the centripetal force on a 0.060-kg bob with a 0.40-m arc radius that is released from a height of 0.25 m.

   A. 0.613 N
   B. 0.736 N
   C. 1.226 N
   D. 9.800 N

PASSAGE 26: DATA INTERPRETATION

Phosphorus is an essential nutrient that can negatively affect water quality, primarily by promoting excessive plant and algae growth. When this occurs, plants and animals that live in the water are affected by the reduced sunlight and lower oxygen levels that develop as organic matter decomposes. For humans, algal blooms lead to a reduction in the quality of drinking water, a decrease in the use of the water source for recreational activities, and a decline in property value along waterfront areas.

Lakes are often classified according to their *trophic state*, which indicates their biological productivity. The least productive lakes are called *oligotrophic*. Bodies of water classified as oligotrophic are typically cool and clear, have relatively low nutrient concentrations, and provide excellent drinking water. The most productive lakes are called *eutrophic* and are characterized by high nutrient concentrations that result in algal growth, cloudy water, and low dissolved oxygen levels. Table 21.6 shows the phosphorus levels that are found in lakes with different trophic classifications.

Table 21.6	
Trophic Classification	**Phosphorus (mg/L)**
Oligotrophic	0–12
Mesotrophic	12–24
Eutrophic	24–96
Hypereutrophic	96+

Lake managers collected data over approximately two decades in four different ecological areas of a large lake. Each area had a different target phosphorus level based on the natural ecological factors of the area, as indicated in Figures 21.7 through 21.10. For proper lake health, the level must be at or below the target amount. Levels in excess of the target amount lead to an imbalance in nutrient flow.

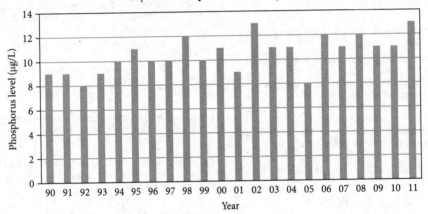

Figure 21.7

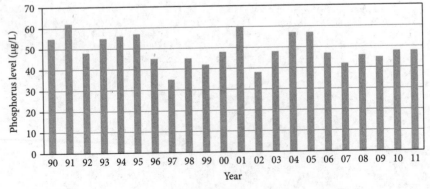

Figure 21.8

Bay Area 2 Phosphorus Levels Target: 14 µg/L

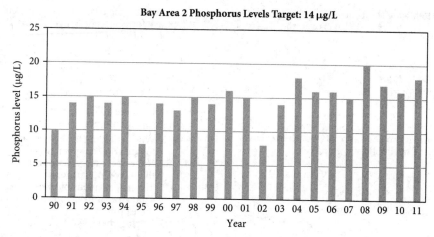

Figure 21.9

North Lake Phosphorus Levels Target: 25 µg/L

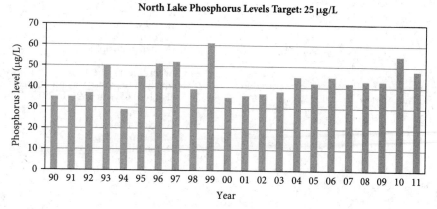

Figure 21.10

330. In which area of the lake did the scientists fail to attain the target phosphorus level in *any* of the years of the study?

  A. Bay Area 1
  B. North Lake
  C. Bay Area 2
  D. South Lake

331. The target for Bay Area 2 falls in the trophic category of:

  A. oligotrophic.
  B. mesotrophic.
  C. eutrophic.
  D. hypereutrophic.

332. In 2011, flooding occurred in the region surrounding the lake. This caused:

  A. all areas of the lake to exceed their target phosphorus levels.
  B. all areas of the lake to meet the standard for target phosphorus level.
  C. all but one of the lake areas to exceed the recommended phosphorus levels.
  D. two of the four lake areas to exceed the target phosphorus level.

333. In 2005, ecologists managing the lake began a concentrated effort to reduce agricultural runoff. This appears to have had the greatest effect on phosphorus levels in:

  A. Bay Area 1.
  B. North Lake.
  C. Bay Area 2.
  D. South Lake.

334. In 2002, the South Lake area had a trophic classification of:

  A. oligotrophic.
  B. mesotrophic.
  C. eutrophic.
  D. hypereutrophic.

335. For how many years of the study was Bay Area 2 found to be mesotrophic?

  A. 0
  B. 3
  C. 9
  D. 19

336. During which of the following years did Bay Area 1 have a trophic classification of mesotrophic?

  A. 1992
  B. 1995
  C. 2009
  D. 2011

337. Which of the following best describes the range in phosphorus levels in the North Lake over the 21-year period?

    A. 32 μg/L
    B. 62 μg/L
    C. 25 μg/L
    D. 45 μg/L

338. Which lake had the narrowest range of phosphorus levels over the time period of the study?

    A. Bay Area 1
    B. North Lake
    C. Bay Area 2
    D. South Lake

339. During how many years did Bay Area 1 meet or surpass the standard for proper lake health?

    A. 4
    B. 10
    C. 10
    D. 15

340. What was the difference in phosphorus concentration between Bay Area 1 and North Lake in 1993?

    A. 9 μg/L
    B. 41 μg/L
    C. 50 μg/L
    D. 59 μg/L

341. A neighboring lake was tested in 2005 and found to have a phosphorus level of 10 μg/L. It was most likely taken from a body of water similar to:

    A. Bay Area 1.
    B. North Lake.
    C. Bay Area 2.
    D. South Lake.

342. Which of the following statements is best supported by the information in the passage and figures?

    A. When studying the North Lake area, one would expect to find cool, clear water and high oxygen levels.
    B. None of the target levels for any of the lake areas fell in the eutrophic category.
    C. The management of phosphorus levels does not have a positive impact on humans who use the lake for recreation.
    D. During the 21-year period of the study, none of the lakes could be classified as hypereutrophic.

343. The category of lake classification appearing most frequently in the North and South Lake areas was:

    A. oligotrophic.
    B. mesotrophic.
    C. eutrophic.
    D. hypereutrophic.

344. According to the information provided in the passage, which of the areas was the most likely to have the lowest dissolved oxygen levels in 2010?

    A. Bay Area 1
    B. North Lake
    C. Bay Area 2
    D. South Lake

PASSAGE 27

There is some evidence that ancient civilizations knew placing various metals together could create an electrical current. In the year 1800, Alexander Volta published experiments outlining his discovery of the *voltaic pile*, a device commonly referred to as the first electric battery. Volta stacked two different metals on either side of a wet felt disk and found that certain combinations produced an electrical voltage. By the early 1800s, many scientists were expanding on the idea of the voltaic pile by making apparatuses now known as *voltaic cells*. These cells generally contain two separate jars connected by a *salt bridge*, or porous membrane. Each jar contains a certain metal and a solution of the positive ions of the same metal. When different jars containing different metals are connected, an electrical voltage can be produced. A theoretical example of a copper/zinc voltaic cell is shown in Figure 22.1.

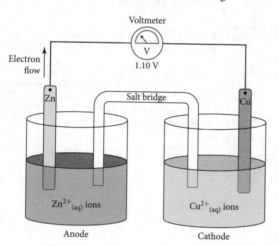

Voltmeter

V

1.10 V

Electron flow

Zn

Salt bridge

Cu

$Zn^{2+}_{(aq)}$ ions

$Cu^{2+}_{(aq)}$ ions

Anode

Cathode

Figure 22.1

The last two centuries have seen a marked spike in demand for smaller batteries that can produce higher voltages for longer periods of time. This led a chemistry student to become interested in how using different metals in the voltaic cell could increase the voltage output of that cell. To conduct the experiment she chose four different types of metals that were available in strips from her local hardware store. These metals were zinc (Zn), lead (Pb), copper (Cu), and silver (Ag). She used 1-molar concentrated solutions of each of the various metal ions. She then made a salt bridge out of filter paper soaked in a potassium chloride brine solution. Many different combinations of metals were attempted, and the voltage output was measured with a standard voltmeter. The results of the experiment are recorded in Table 22.1.

Table 22.1			
Experiment Number	**Jar 1 Contents**	**Jar 2 Contents**	**Measured Output Voltage (V)**
1	Zn metal/Zn^{2+}	Pb metal/Pb^{2+}	0.63
2	Zn metal/Zn^{2+}	Cu metal/Cu^{2+}	1.10
3	Zn metal/Zn^{2+}	Ag metal/Ag^+	1.56
4	Cu metal/Cu^{2+}	Ag metal/Ag^+	0.47
5	Cu metal/Cu^{2+}	Pb metal/Pb^{2+}	0.65
6	Pb metal/Pb^{2+}	Ag metal/Ag^+	0.73
7	Pb metal/Pb^{2+}	Pb metal/Pb^{2+}	0.00

After the experiment was completed, the chemistry student looked at the literature to make sense of her results. She found two definitions particularly helpful. The *anode* was defined as the metal strip where oxidation occurs. The metal atoms were losing electrons and dissolving into the solution as metal ions. Electrons from the anode were free to move through the wire toward the cathode. The *cathode* was defined as the metal strip where reduction occurs. The cathode had an abundance of electrons from the anode. Metal ions in the solution around the cathode accepted those electrons and joined the strip as additional solid metal atoms.

The student also found tables of standard reduction potentials (Table 22.2). These tables compared how much voltage

Table 22.2			
Cathode (Reduction)	**Standard Potential (Volts)**	**Anode (Oxidation)**	**Standard Potential (Volts)**
$Al^{3+}_{(aq)} + 3e^- \rightarrow Al_{(s)}$	−1.66	$Ag_{(s)} \rightarrow Ag^+_{(aq)} + e^-$	−0.80
$Zn^{2+}_{(aq)} + 2e^- \rightarrow Zn_{(s)}$	−0.76	$Cu_{(s)} \rightarrow Cu^{2+}_{(aq)} + 2e^-$	−0.34
$Pb^{2+}_{(aq)} + 2e^- \rightarrow Pb_{(s)}$	−0.13	$Pb_{(s)} \rightarrow Pb^{2+}_{(aq)} + 2e^-$	0.13
$Cu^{2+}_{(aq)} + 2e^- \rightarrow Cu_{(s)}$	0.34	$Zn_{(s)} \rightarrow Zn^{2+}_{(aq)} + 2e^-$	0.76
$Ag^+_{(aq)} + e^- \rightarrow Ag_{(s)}$	0.80	$Al_{(s)} \rightarrow Al^{3+}_{(aq)} + 3e^-$	1.66

should be produced when the metal is placed in an electrochemical cell with a standard electrode. One table showed each metal as a cathode, and the other showed each as an anode. The student learned that these tables were used to calculate the theoretical voltage output of any electrochemical cell. (Any electrochemical cell has to have both a cathode and an anode.)

The theoretical output voltage of an electrochemical cell is the sum of the standard potentials of the anode and the cathode.

345. Which of the following best describes the independent variables of this investigation?

A. The types of metal used for the cathode and anode
B. The type of metal ion solution used in the anode jar
C. The amount of output voltage produced by various electrochemical cell configurations
D. The concentration of metal ion solution used in each electrochemical cell

346. Which variable should NOT be controlled for this experiment?

A. The surface area of the metal strip used for the anode
B. The type of metal strip used for the anode
C. The amount of time the electrochemical cell is allowed to operate
D. The concentration of potassium chloride used to make the salt bridge

347. A lead/silver electrochemical cell is expected to have an output voltage of 0.93 V. However, Experiment 6 from Table 22.1 shows a measured output voltage of 0.73 V. Which of the following might account for the difference?

A. Silver should have been the cathode, and lead should have been the anode, but the experimenter switched them.
B. Experiment 6 was the third time the silver ion solution had been used, and the concentration of silver ions had been diminished.
C. The experimenter mistakenly switched a lead strip with a zinc strip for the anode.
D. The experimenter used a 1.5-inch-wide strip of lead as the anode instead of the standard 1-inch strip.

348. Experiment 1 from Table 22.1 shows a zinc/lead cell with a measured output voltage of 0.63 V. Which of the following best describes the cell?

A. Zinc is the cathode and lead is the anode.
B. Zinc is the cathode and zinc ions are the anode.
C. Zinc is the anode and lead is the cathode.
D. Zinc is the anode and zinc ions are the cathode.

349. Figure 22.1 shows the electrochemical cell the student used for Experiment 2 where zinc was the anode and copper was the cathode. What can be inferred about the mass of the zinc and copper strips as the experiment progressed?

A. The mass of both strips increased.
B. The mass of both strips decreased.
C. The mass of the zinc strip increased, but the mass of the copper strip decreased.
D. The mass of the zinc strip decreased, but the mass of the copper strip increased.

350. Experiment 8 was conducted with an aluminum strip in Jar 1 and a copper strip in Jar 2. Which metal would be the anode?

A. Aluminum would be the anode.
B. Copper would be the anode.
C. Aluminum would be the anode until the metal dissolved to a certain point, and then copper would become the anode.
D. There is not enough information to determine which would be the anode.

351. Experiment 8 was conducted with an aluminum strip in Jar 1 and a copper strip in Jar 2. What would be the expected output voltage of the electrochemical cell?

A. 1.10 V
B. 1.66 V
C. 1.32 V
D. 2.00 V

352. Further experimentation finds that when electrochemical cells are hooked together in a series configuration, their output voltage is added together for total output voltage. How many copper/zinc electrochemical cells are required to light a diode that needs a minimum of 12.0 V to operate?

A. 2 cells
B. 10 cells
C. 11 cells
D. 12 cells

PASSAGE 28

Every time a lightbulb is switched on, an electrical circuit is formed. When plugged into outlets that provide a certain voltage, current begins to flow through the bulbs. Current depends on the resistance of the bulb and the voltage of the power supply. The power output of a bulb is a measure of the amount of energy the bulb requires each second. Power is calculated by multiplying current and voltage. Table 22.3 contains data that relate these variables for a basic circuit consisting of one lightbulb and a power supply.

Table 22.3				
Resistance of Single Bulb (ohm)	Voltage across Bulb (V)	Current through Bulb (A)	Power Output (W)	Energy Usage/ Hour (kJ)
120	120	1.00	120	432
240	120	0.50	60	216
360	120	0.33	40	144
480	120	0.25	30	108
480	180	0.38	68	243
480	240	0.50	120	432
480	300	0.63	188	675

Figure 22.2 shows three configurations of bulbs. When the bulbs are connected in series, they form one path to the power supply. If any bulb in the pathway breaks, all the lights go out because the circuit is no longer complete. In contrast, bulbs connected in parallel are all independently connected to the power supply—in essence, forming their own circuits. Bulbs wired in parallel across a power supply continue to work even when one bulb goes out because each branch forms an independent circuit.

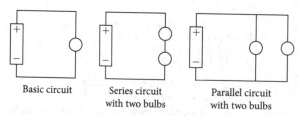

Basic circuit   Series circuit with two bulbs   Parallel circuit with two bulbs

Figure 22.2

Table 22.4 shows how the number of bulbs in series and parallel affect the current and power values. It gives data for 240-ohm bulbs connected to a 120-V power supply.

Table 22.4					
Arrangement of Bulbs	Number of Bulbs	Current in Each Bulb (A)	Current through Battery (A)	Power Output of Each Bulb (W)	Power Output of Circuit (W)
Series	2	0.25	0.25	15.0	30
Series	3	0.17	0.17	6.7	20
Series	4	0.13	0.13	3.8	15
Parallel	2	0.5	1.0	60	120
Parallel	3	0.5	1.5	60	180
Parallel	4	0.5	2.0	60	240

353. Based on the data in Table 22.3, describe the relationship between current, voltage, and resistance.

   A. Current is the ratio of voltage to resistance.
   B. Current is the product of voltage and resistance.
   C. Current is the ratio of resistance to voltage.
   D. Current is proportional to the square of voltage and independent of resistance.

354. Using information provided in the passage, determine the power output of a 50.0-ohm bulb connected to a 150-V socket that has 3.0 A flowing through it.

   A. 3 W
   B. 50 W
   C. 150 W
   D. 450 W

355. For a fixed voltage, what happens to the power output of a bulb when its resistance triples?

   A. The power triples.
   B. The power increases by a factor of 9.
   C. The power decreases to one-third of its value.
   D. The power decreases to one-ninth of its value.

356. For a bulb with a given resistance, what happens to the flow of current through the bulb when the voltage of the power supply doubles?

   A. The current doubles.
   B. The current quadruples.
   C. The current decreases to one-half its value.
   D. The current decreases to one-fourth its value.

357. A 480-ohm bulb is screwed into a 120-V socket. How much energy does it need to stay lit for four hours?

   A. 108 kJ
   B. 120 kJ
   C. 216 kJ
   D. 432 kJ

358. Predict the power required to operate a 600-ohm light bulb when it is plugged into a 120-V outlet.

   A. 20 W
   B. 24 W
   C. 30 W
   D. 120 W

359. According to Tables 22.3 and 22.4, when a fifth bulb is added to a parallel circuit, each bulb will:
    A. output the same amount of energy per second as a bulb in a basic circuit.
    B. output more energy per second than a bulb in a basic circuit.
    C. output less energy per second than a bulb in a basic circuit.
    D. make the other bulbs get brighter.

360. When a fifth bulb is added to a series circuit, how will the bulb's power output compare to that of a bulb in a four-bulb series circuit?
    A. It will produce the same amount of power.
    B. It will produce twice the power.
    C. It will produce less power.
    D. It will produce no power.

361. According to the information in Tables 22.3 and 22.4, adding an additional bulb to a parallel circuit:
    A. increases the circuit's power output by decreasing the total resistance of the entire circuit.
    B. decreases the circuit's power output by decreasing the total resistance of the entire circuit.
    C. increases the circuit's power output by increasing the total resistance of the entire circuit.
    D. decreases the circuit's power output by increasing the total resistance of the entire circuit.

362. The circuit in Figure 22.3 shows Bulbs 2 and 3 wired in parallel. That combination is wired in series with Bulb 1 and the battery. Which of the following statements is FALSE?

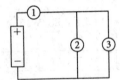

Figure 22.3

    A. If Bulb 1 breaks, the other two bulbs will go out.
    B. If Bulb 2 breaks, the other two bulbs will go out.
    C. If both Bulbs 2 and 3 break, Bulb 1 will go out.
    D. If Bulb 3 breaks, the other bulbs will stay lit.

363. As bulbs are added to a parallel circuit:
    A. more current flows through each bulb.
    B. less current flows through each bulb.
    C. less power is output from the circuit.
    D. more current flows through the battery.

364. A child noticed that five bulbs in her electric toy went out simultaneously, but four other bulbs remained lit. What is the most likely circuit arrangement in the toy?
    A. The five bulbs that went out are wired in parallel.
    B. Each of the five bulbs that went out are broken.
    C. The five bulbs that went out are wired in series.
    D. All nine bulbs are wired in parallel.

365. Adding additional bulbs to a series circuit:
    A. increases the resistance of the entire circuit.
    B. decreases the resistance of the entire circuit.
    C. decreases the power output of the entire circuit.
    D. increases the flow of current in each bulb.

366. A watt (W) of power is the total joules (J) of electrical energy transferred by a circuit element each second. Given a circuit with three 240-ohm bulbs wired in series to a 120-V power supply, how much energy is transferred by the circuit if it operates for 10 seconds?
    A. 6.7 J
    B. 67 J
    C. 150 J
    D. 200 J

367. How much power does a parallel circuit require if it has six 240-ohm resistors connected to a 120-V power supply?
    A. 60 W
    B. 120 W
    C. 360 W
    D. 1,440 W

PASSAGE 29

Since ancient times, scientists, philosophers, and other thinkers considered the smallest pieces of matter to be tiny spherical structures called atoms that were stacked in various arrangements. The ancient Greek philosopher Democritus also suggested that these atoms were indivisible and indestructible. The turn of the twentieth century brought with it a renewed interest in exploring atoms. Two ground-breaking experiments challenged the idea that atoms are the smallest constituent of matter. These experiments were very different, but both pointed to the fact that atoms contained even smaller parts.

Experiment 1: The 1897 Cathode Ray Tube Experiments

Scientists in the late 1890s investigated a curious new device known as a cathode ray tube (CRT). The CRT consisted of a glass tube with a metal wire coming out of each end. When all of the air was removed from the tube and a voltage was applied across the wires, mysterious green rays appeared at one end of the tube. These rays were called cathode rays. It was not immediately known if these rays were a type of wave or a type of particle, but several experiments were conducted on them. First it was discovered that the rays would always be attracted to an area of excess positive charge and away from an area of excess negative charge. Precise measurements could not determine the exact mass of the cathode rays, but it was determined that they did have mass. After that discovery, the rays were considered a particle instead of a wave.

The mass-to-charge ratio of the cathode rays was determined to be more than 1,000 times smaller than the same ratio for any known atom or ion. After subsequent experiments, researchers determined that cathode rays were small particles that broke off of an atom when a voltage was applied.

Experiment 2: The 1911 Gold Foil Experiment

At the time, the accepted model of the atom was a relatively solid sphere, similar to a ball of chocolate chip cookie dough. An experiment in 1911 brought that model into question. A beam of alpha particles (small, high-energy, positively charged particles) was shot into a piece of gold foil approximately 8.6×10^{-8} m in thickness. The alpha particles were thought to have enough energy to pass straight through the foil and hit a detector on the other side, and most of the particles did just that. However, a small fraction of alpha particles were deflected a few degrees as they passed through the foil. Upon closer examination of the data, a more startling fact was found—some alpha particles never hit the detector.

More detectors were added around the gold foil, and it was discovered that a tiny portion of the alpha particles, 1 out of every 20,000 particles, was deflected 90 degrees or more from the beam. Some particles even bounced straight back toward the alpha particle source. The scientist was so surprised by the results that he stated, "It was as if you fired a 15-inch shell at a sheet of tissue paper and it came back to you." It was concluded that there must be some particle inside an atom causing these major deflections of alpha particles.

368. Which of the following best describes what each experiment concluded about the newly discovered small particles that make up atoms?

	Experiment 1	Experiment 2
A.	Dense and sturdy	Positively charged
B.	Negatively charged	Dense
C.	Positively charged	Negatively charged
D.	Small	Low energy

369. Which of the following is the best conclusion concerning why the cathode rays in Experiment 1 had a mass-to-charge ratio 1,000 times smaller than that of any known atom?

A. Cathode ray particles are 1,000 times less massive than any known atom.

B. Cathode ray particles have 1,000 times less charge than any known atom.

C. Cathode ray particles have 1,000 times more charge than any known atom.

D. Cathode ray particles could either be less massive or have a greater charge than any known atom.

370. Modern chemistry books discuss several subatomic particles. Figure 22.4 offers a common diagram of such particles. The symbol (−) means negative, (+) means positive, and (Ø) means neutral. Which particle would have an undefined mass-to-charge ratio?

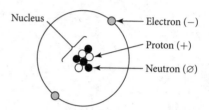

Figure 22.4

A. Electron
B. Proton
C. Neutron
D. Nucleus

371. Which of the following statements do the data from both experiments support?

A. Atoms are highly charged particles.
B. Atoms are composed of a dense core known as a nucleus.
C. Atoms are not indestructible and indivisible.
D. The mass-to-charge ratio of atoms is much smaller than was originally thought.

372. Atoms, once thought to be solid spheres, have instead been proven to be mostly empty space with just a few tiny particles giving each atom its properties. Which data from either Experiment 1 or Experiment 2 best explains this fact?

A. Experiment 1: Cathode rays are attracted to areas of positive electric charge.
B. Experiment 1: Cathode rays have a small mass-to-charge ratio.
C. Experiment 2: Some alpha particles were deflected from the beam at wide angles.
D. Experiment 2: One out of every 20,000 particles got deflected to a large extent.

373. A micrometer (μm) is a common unit to measure small objects. One micrometer is equivalent to 0.000001 m. How thick was the gold foil in Experiment 2?

A. 8,600 μm
B. 86 μm
C. 0.86 μm
D. 0.086 μm

374. Which scientists would be most likely to write the following in their lab notebook: "I can see no escape from the conclusion that they are charges of negative electricity carried by particles of matter"?

  A. Scientists working on Experiment 1
  B. Scientists working on Experiment 2
  C. Scientists working on either experiment
  D. Scientists working on both experiments

375. Which headline best matches the conclusions of the experiment?

  A. Gold Foil: Alpha Particles Are Found Inside Atoms
  B. Cathode Rays Destroy Atoms
  C. Gold Foil: Solid Particle in Atom Incredibly Small
  D. Cathode Rays: Most Go through but a Few Bounce Off

PASSAGE 30

The moon is the earth's only natural satellite and is the fifth-largest moon in the solar system. Believed to be around 4.5 billion years old, the moon was a deity worshipped by ancient civilizations and the first object in the solar system besides Earth that human beings set foot on. It has played a special role in human history, yet despite its ubiquity, the origin of this celestial body remains surrounded by mystery. Theories about the origin of the moon have long been debated among scientists. The following are summaries of the most recent major theories of moon formation. The first three theories are known as the Big Three and represent the predominant ideas before the mid-1970s. The fourth theory represents the most recent school of thought, developed in light of evidence gained from the Apollo space program.

Theory 1: Fission

The moon was spun off from the earth when the planet was young and rotating rapidly on its axis. The empty space the moon left behind became the Pacific Ocean basin.

Theory 2: Capture

The moon formed elsewhere in the universe. At some point, it came near enough to be affected by the earth's gravitational field. The moon was pulled into permanent orbit by the earth's gravity.

Theory 3: Coaccretion

The earth and moon and all other bodies of the solar system condensed independently out of the huge cloud of cold gases and solid particles that constituted the primordial solar nebula. The moon then fell into orbit around the earth.

Theory 4: Giant Impact

The earth was struck by a body about the size of Mars very early in its history. A ring of debris from the impact containing primarily Earth materials and some materials from the impacting object eventually coalesced to form the moon.

376. In which of the theories would the rocks on the moon NOT necessarily bear any similarity to the rocks on the earth?

A. Fission
B. Capture
C. Both fission and coaccretion
D. Both capture and fission

377. In which *two* of the theories would the rocks on the moon be nearly identical to those on the earth?

A. Capture and fission
B. Capture and coaccretion
C. Coaccretion and fission
D. Giant impact and capture

378. Which of the following statements would best support the argument of a proponent of the capture theory?

A. Planets are incredibly small compared to the vastness of space.
B. Jupiter and Saturn (the giant gas planets) have captured moons.
C. The moon and the earth have the same oxygen isotope composition.
D. The moon does not have a regular-size core.

379. The Big Three theories have cleverly been dubbed the Daughter theory, the Sister theory, and the Spouse theory by scientists who compared the relationship of the moon and the earth to familial relationships. Based on the information in the passage, which of the following would most accurately associate the theories to their nickname: Daughter, Sister, and Spouse?

A. Fission, coaccretion, and capture
B. Capture, fission, and coaccretion
C. Capture, coaccretion, and fission
D. Fission, capture, and coaccretion

380. The following description of the formation of the moon is from a children's radio program in the 1930s. Which of the four moon theories does this seem to illustrate?

Once upon a time—a billion or so years ago—when the earth was still young—a remarkable romance developed between the earth and the sun—according to some of our ablest scientists. . . . In those days, the earth was a spirited maiden who danced about the princely sun, was charmed by him, yielded to his attraction, and became his bride. . . . The sun's attraction raised great tides upon the earth's surface . . . the huge crest of a bulge broke away with such momentum that it could not return to the body of Mother Earth. And this is the way the moon was born!

A. Fission
B. Capture
C. Condensation
D. Giant impact

381. The fission theory is refuted by which of the following pieces of evidence?

A. The moon lacks a large core.
B. There is a striking similarity between the oxygen isotopes present on the earth and those on the moon.
C. Studies of isotopes found in rocks put the age of the earth and moon at 4.5 billion years.
D. The Pacific Ocean basin was formed 70 million years ago.

382. The moon's crust is thinner on the side nearest the earth. Scientists believe that this is because the moon was close to the earth when it formed. As the moon's mantle cooled, the earth's gravitational field pulled slightly more mantle closer to the planet before it "set." A thicker mantle made for a thinner crust on the side nearest the earth. This piece of evidence contradicts the capture theory because:

A. in the capture theory, the moon broke off from the earth.
B. in the capture theory, the moon formed close to the earth.
C. in the capture theory, the moon formed in another part of the solar system.
D. this piece of evidence supports the coaccretion theory.

383. The evidence that rock samples from the moon match rocks from the earth's crust and mantle but bear no resemblance to the earth's interior rock refutes all of the following theories EXCEPT:

A. fission.
B. capture.
C. coaccretion.
D. giant impact.

384. The giant impact theory:

    A. is not likely to change with the discovery of new evidence.

    B. completely explains the origin of the moon.

    C. is unable to account for why the moon is made mostly of rock.

    D. is the theory best supported by the most current scientific evidence.

385. Which of the theories is best supported by the evidence that the earth and moon are both 4.5 billion years old and provide isotopic evidence that indicates they were formed in the same "neighborhood" of the solar system?

    A. Fission

    B. Capture

    C. Coaccretion

    D. Giant impact

386. A fifth theory of moon formation, called the colliding planetesimals theory, exists. In this theory, an asteroid-like chunk of rock orbiting the sun collided with an asteroid-like chunk of rock orbiting the earth. The moon then condensed from the debris of this collision. This theory would be weakened by which of the following pieces of evidence?

    A. Moon rock matches the rock from the earth's crust and mantle.

    B. The moon's crust is thinner on the side nearest the earth.

    C. The moon is made of mostly rock.

    D. Isotopes indicate that the earth and moon formed in the same area of the solar system.

PASSAGE 31

When the effect of air on a falling object is negligible and gravity is the only significant force on that object, the object is considered to be in freefall. A scientist can create a free-fall scenario by removing all air from a chamber (thus creating a vacuum) and allowing an object to drop freely. When objects are not falling freely, air affects them in different ways, depending on variables such as speed, mass, and size. If objects are able to fall for enough time through the air, they will eventually reach *terminal velocity*, a point at which their velocity stops increasing. Table 23.1 and Figures 23.1 and 23.2 show the effect of air on falling balls of different mass and radius.

Table 23.1						
	10-g Ball Freefalling (R = 1 cm)			10-g Ball Falling with Air (R = 1 cm)		
Time (s)	Distance Fallen (m)	Velocity (m/s)	Air Drag Force (N)	Distance Fallen (m)	Velocity (m/s)	Air Drag Force (N)
0	0.0	0.0	0	0.0	0.0	0.000
1	4.9	9.8	0	4.8	9.5	0.009
2	19.6	19.6	0	19.1	18.7	0.033
3	44.1	29.4	0	41.0	25.1	0.061
4	78.4	39.2	0	68.1	28.9	0.080
5	123.0	49.0	0	97.8	30.7	0.090
6	176.0	58.8	0	129.0	31.5	0.095
7	240.0	68.6	0	161.0	31.8	0.097
8	314.0	78.4	0	192.0	31.9	0.098
9	397.0	88.2	0	224.0	32.0	0.098
10	490.0	98.0	0	256.0	32.0	0.098
11	593.0	108.0	0	288.0	32.0	0.098
12	706.0	118.0	0	320.0	32.0	0.098

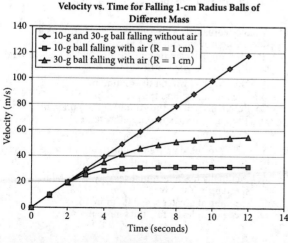

Figure 23.1

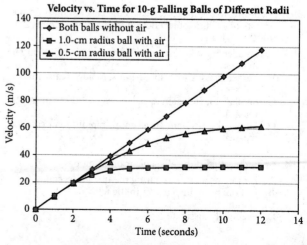

Figure 23.2

387. According to Table 23.1, which of the following is a correct statement about the velocity of a 10-g freefalling ball?

   A. The velocity is constant.
   B. The velocity increases 9.8 m/s each second.
   C. The velocity increases 4.9 m/s each second.
   D. The velocity steadily decreases.

388. According to Table 23.1, which of the following is a correct statement about the distance a 10-g ball freefalls?

   A. The distance increases constantly.
   B. The distance increases 9.8 m each second.
   C. The distance increases more each second compared to the previous second.
   D. The distance increases 4.9 m each second.

389. According to Table 23.1, how much does the air drag force on the ball (10 g, 1 cm) increase during the fourth second of falling through air?

   A. 0.000 N
   B. 0.019 N
   C. 0.061 N
   D. 0.080 N

390. Using the trends in Table 23.1, predict the velocity of the 10-g ball at the instant it has fallen freely from rest for 14 seconds.

   A. 9.8 m/s
   B. 19.6 m/s
   C. 118.0 m/s
   D. 138.0 m/s

391. After comparing the data for the falling ball with and without air, which of the following is a correct statement about the effect of air on velocity?

   A. The presence of air reduces the rate at which velocity increases.
   B. The presence of air increases the rate at which velocity increases.
   C. When air is not present, the velocity eventually stops increasing.
   D. When air is present, the velocity eventually stops decreasing.

392. For the 10-g ball falling with air, Table 23.1 indicates that the force of air drag:

   A. increases steadily with time.
   B. plateaus initially and then decreases.
   C. increases more each second compared to the previous second.
   D. increases more rapidly early in the fall and eventually plateaus.

393. According to Figure 23.1, what is the effect of mass on the velocity of a falling object during the first five seconds as it falls through air?

   A. Smaller masses lose speed more rapidly than larger masses.
   B. Larger masses lose speed more rapidly than smaller masses.
   C. Smaller masses gain speed more rapidly than larger masses.
   D. Larger masses gain speed more rapidly than smaller masses.

394. As an object falls, the effect of air on its motion:

   A. is more pronounced during the first few seconds.
   B. is more pronounced later in the fall.
   C. is minimal.
   D. eventually dissipates.

395. When air is present, what is the effect of the radius of the ball on the velocity of a falling object during the first five seconds?

   A. Smaller radii lose speed more rapidly than larger radii.
   B. Larger radii lose speed more rapidly than smaller radii.
   C. Smaller radii gain speed more rapidly than larger radii.
   D. Larger radii gain speed more rapidly than smaller radii.

396. According to Figures 23.1 and 23.2, the terminal velocity of the 10-g ball with the 0.05-cm radius is most nearly:

   A. 9.8 m/s.
   B. 32 m/s.
   C. 55 m/s.
   D. 62 m/s.

397. In the absence of air drag, a ball with a larger radius:

   A. has the same motion as one with a smaller radius.
   B. reaches terminal velocity sooner than one with a smaller radius.
   C. obtains a larger terminal velocity.
   D. obtains a smaller terminal velocity.

398. According to Figures 23.1 and 23.2, the ball with less mass (but the same radius) falling through the air:

   A. reaches terminal velocity later than a ball with more mass.
   B. reaches terminal velocity within the first second it is dropped.
   C. reaches terminal velocity sooner than a ball with more mass.
   D. has the same terminal velocity as the ball with more mass.

399. Suppose one skydiver jumps out of an airplane feet first toward the ground. Her identical twin sister jumps out at the same time with her arms and legs extended and her stomach parallel to the ground. According to the passage, what can you infer about their subsequent motion?

   A. The feet-first twin will reach terminal velocity first.
   B. The belly-first twin will reach terminal velocity first.
   C. Both twins will reach terminal velocity at the same time.
   D. The belly-first twin will obtain a greater terminal velocity.

400. A table-tennis ball with a mass of 3 g is dropped side by side with an identical-sized wooden ball with a mass of 30 g. Based on the information provided, what can you conclude if the balls fall in a vacuum (no air)?

   A. The 30-g ball will hit the ground first.
   B. The 3-g ball will hit the ground first.
   C. Both balls will hit the ground at the same time.
   D. The 3-g ball will speed up more at first.

401. A table-tennis ball with a mass of 3 g is dropped side by side with an identical-sized wooden ball with a mass of 30 g. If both balls are dropped from rest and fall through the air, what can you conclude?

   A. The 30-g ball will hit the ground first.
   B. The 3-g ball will hit the ground first.
   C. Both balls will hit the ground at the same time.
   D. The 3-g ball will speed up more at first.

402. According to the data trends illustrated in the passage, a ball dropped in a vacuum without air will:

   A. eventually reach terminal velocity as it's falling.
   B. speed up at a steady rate as long as it has room to drop.
   C. speed up at greater rate if it's more massive.
   D. speed up at lesser rate if it's more massive.

PASSAGE 32

A chemistry student was given the task of determining what percentage of hydrated magnesium sulfate sample was water. Many chemical compounds exist in nature as hydrates instead of in a dry (or anhydrous) state. A sample of hydrated magnesium sulfate ($MgSO_4 \cdot nH_2O$) is a solid white powder that contains a certain number (n) of water molecules bonded to each magnesium sulfate crystal. One accepted method of isolating magnesium sulfate from the water molecules is by heating the sample in an open porcelain crucible. Magnesium sulfate has a very high boiling temperature, but water molecules can easily be turned into gas. When sufficiently heated, the water molecules are driven away from the container, leaving only anhydrous magnesium sulfate ($MgSO_4$).

The student cautiously heated the sample over a Bunsen burner. He then removed the crucible, allowed it to cool, and measured the mass. He returned the crucible to the burner and heated it again, allowed it to cool, and measured the mass again. The student repeated this procedure until he was certain all of the water had been removed. His data are found in Table 23.2.

Table 23.2	
Mass of empty crucible	26.449 g
Mass of crucible + $MgSO_4 \cdot nH_2O$ sample	32.569 g
Mass of crucible and sample after first heating	32.558 g
Mass of crucible and sample after second heating	31.943 g
Mass of crucible and sample after third heating	29.439 g
Mass of crucible and sample after fourth heating	29.440 g

403. What mass of hydrated magnesium sulfate sample did the student place in the crucible at the start of the experiment?
    A. 32.569 g of $MgSO_4 \cdot nH_2O$
    B. 6.120 g of $MgSO_4 \cdot nH_2O$
    C. 29.440 g of $MgSO_4 \cdot nH_2O$
    D. 3.129 g of $MgSO_4 \cdot nH_2O$

404. How was the student certain that all of the water had been removed from the sample after the fourth heating?
    A. He had heated the sample for a sufficient amount of time.
    B. The mass of the sample and empty crucible remained at less than 30.00 g for two consecutive heatings.
    C. The mass did not change appreciably between the third and fourth heatings.
    D. The sample would have started to gain mass if more heating had occurred.

405. Which equation is the appropriate way to determine the percent mass of water in a sample of hydrated magnesium sulfate?

    A. $\dfrac{\text{Mass of water driven off}}{\text{Mass of sample before heating}} = 100$

    B. $\dfrac{\text{Mass of water driven off}}{\text{Mass of anhydrous } MgSO_4} = 100$

    C. $\dfrac{\text{Mass of water driven off}}{\substack{\text{Mass of crucible and sample after} \\ \text{fourth heating}}} = 100$

    D. $\dfrac{\text{Mass of sample before heating}}{\text{Mass of water driven off}} = 100$

406. From the data in Table 23.2, which is closest to the percent mass of the sample that is made up of water?
    A. 10% water molecules
    B. 25% water molecules
    C. 50% water molecules
    D. 90% water molecules

407. How would the calculated percent mass of water in the sample be affected if some of the sample splattered out of the crucible while it was being heated?
    A. The calculated percent mass of water would be too high.
    B. The calculated percent mass of water would be too low.
    C. The calculated percent mass of water would be too high or too low, depending on outside conditions.
    D. The calculated percent mass of water would remain unchanged.

408. The student left the crucible and the sample on the balance after the fourth heating. Forty minutes later, he came back and noticed the mass of the sample had changed again, as shown in Table 23.3. What is the best conclusion the student can reach about the additional change in mass?

Table 23.3	
Mass of empty crucible	26.449 g
Mass of crucible + $MgSO_4 \cdot nH_2O$ sample	32.569 g
Mass of crucible and sample after first heating	32.558 g
Mass of crucible and sample after second heating	31.943 g
Mass of crucible and sample after third heating	29.439 g
Mass of crucible and sample after fourth heating	29.440 g
Mass of crucible and sample 40 minutes later	32.139 g

    A. More water molecules were able to evaporate during the additional 40 minutes.
    B. During the additional 40 minutes, the contents cooled to room temperature, which caused the mass to increase.
    C. Water molecules were able to reattach to the $MgSO_4$ crystals during the additional 40 minutes.
    D. The magnesium sulfate crystals had time to expand during the additional 40 minutes.

409. The student repeated the procedure but placed a lid on the crucible during the entire experiment. Which statement best describes the expected results?
    A. More water would be driven off because the crucible would get to a higher temperature.
    B. Drops of water would be found on the lid, but the mass of the sample would not change.
    C. Less water would be driven off because the heat could not get to the sample.
    D. The mass change of this experiment would be identical to the change in mass recorded in the initial experiment.

410. The student did a follow-up experiment by completely dissolving 50 g of anhydrous $MgSO_4$ in 100 mL of distilled water in Beaker 1 and 50 g of $MgSO_4 \cdot 7H_2O$ hydrate in 100 mL of distilled water in Beaker 2. How would the concentration of magnesium (Mg) in each beaker compare?
    A. Both beakers would have identical concentrations of magnesium.
    B. Beaker 1 would have a higher concentration of magnesium.
    C. Beaker 2 would have a slightly higher concentration of magnesium.
    D. Beaker 2 would have a concentration approximately 7 times higher than that of magnesium.

PASSAGE 33

Astronomers have identified more than 170 moons in the solar system. For centuries, many of these scientists have used telescopic observations to measure the time it takes each moon to complete each orbit (the *period*). Using proportions and geometry, the radius of each orbit has also been determined. With these data in place, the speed of each moon in its orbit may be found by taking the circumference of each orbit ($2 \times \pi \times$ radius, assuming a circular orbit, with π, or *pi*, approximately equal to 3.14159) divided by the period. The acceleration of each moon in its respective orbit is equivalent to its centripetal acceleration, which is found by dividing the square of its speed by the radius of its orbit. Table 23.4 provides data for various moons in our solar system.

Table 23.4						
Central Planet Name	**Central Planet Mass (earth masses)**	**Moon Name**	**Radius of Moon's Orbit (millions of m)**	**Period of Moon (days)**	**Orbital Speed of Moon (km/s)**	**Gravitational Acceleration of Moon in Orbit (m/s/s)**
Earth	1	Moon	385	27.30	1.0	0.00273
Jupiter	318	Andrastea	129	0.30	31.5	7.67
Jupiter	318	Amalthea	181	0.50	26.5	3.87
Saturn	95	Atlas	138	0.60	16.6	2.01
Saturn	95	Epimetheus	151	0.69	15.8	1.66
Saturn	95	Mimas	186	0.94	14.3	1.11
Saturn	95	Enceladus	238	1.37	12.6	0.671
Saturn	95	Telesto	295	1.88	11.4	0.441
Saturn	95	Helene	378	2.74	10.0	0.267
Saturn	95	Rhea	527	4.52	8.4	0.137
Saturn	95	Hyperion	1,480	21.30	5.1	0.0173
Saturn	95	Iapetus	3,560	79.30	3.2	0.00299
Saturn	95	Phoebe	13,000	550.00	1.7	0.000226
Uranus	15	Miranda	129	1.40	6.7	0.343
Uranus	15	Ariel	191	2.52	5.5	0.159

In an attempt to find the relationships in the data, the gravitational acceleration versus the inverse of the orbital radius squared was graphed in Figure 23.3.

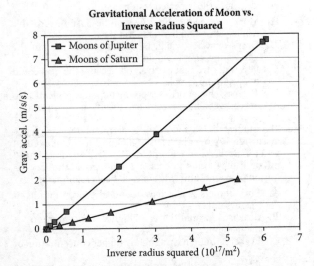

Figure 23.3

411. Which moon has a period closest in value to the period of Earth's moon?

   A. Andrastea
   B. Miranda
   C. Rhea
   D. Hyperion

412. Given just the data in the table, which two moons are most appropriate for studying the effect of central planet mass on gravitational acceleration?

   A. The moon and Atlas
   B. Andrastea and Miranda
   C. Atlas and Phoebe
   D. Iapetus and Arial

413. What is the best description of the relationship between radius of orbit and the period of the moon?

   A. The period is independent of the radius of orbit.
   B. The period has no consistent relationship with the radius of orbit.
   C. The larger the radius of orbit, the less the period.
   D. The larger the radius of orbit, the greater the period.

414. Figure 23.3 indicates that the gravitational acceleration of moons is:

   A. inversely proportional to the square of the radius.
   B. directly proportional to the radius.
   C. directly proportional to the square of the radius.
   D. independent of planet mass.

415. A particular moon orbits a planet that is 318 times more massive than Earth. If that moon has a radius of orbit of 422 million meters, what is a possible value for the moon's speed?

- **A.** 52 km/s
- **B.** 31 km/s
- **C.** 26 km/s
- **D.** 17 km/s

416. Using Figure 23.3, along with information in Table 23.4, what conclusion can be made about the effect of a planet's mass on the acceleration of its moons?

- **A.** Greater planet masses result in greater gravitational acceleration.
- **B.** Greater planet masses result in lesser gravitational acceleration.
- **C.** Gravitational acceleration is independent of planet mass.
- **D.** Gravitational acceleration is directly proportional to the inverse-square of planet mass.

417. According to the passage, which columns were calculated from data gathered by scientists?

- **A.** Period of moon orbit and central planet mass
- **B.** Central planet mass and radius of orbit
- **C.** Speed and gravitational acceleration
- **D.** Gravitational acceleration and period

418. About how many times does the moon orbit the earth while Phoebe completes one orbit of Saturn?

- **A.** 1.7
- **B.** 34
- **C.** 20
- **D.** 27

419. How far does Helene travel in 15 seconds?

- **A.** 10 km
- **B.** 41 km
- **C.** 150 km
- **D.** 2,400 km

420. If the moons of Mars (a planet with a mass 0.107 times that of Earth) were placed on the graph in Figure 23.3, where would they most likely appear?

- **A.** Above the line for the moons of Jupiter
- **B.** Below the line for the moons of Jupiter but above the line for the moons of Saturn
- **C.** Above the line for the moons of Jupiter initially, but then below that same line
- **D.** Below the line for the moons of Saturn

PASSAGE 34

A sample of solid lauric acid was placed in a test tube and heated in a Bunsen burner in a chemistry classroom. The lauric acid melted. A thermometer was carefully placed in the test tube to measure the temperature of the sample. The burner was then turned off, and the sample was allowed to cool; the temperature was recorded in Figure 23.4. The warm liquid sample crystallized into a solid while the temperature was being recorded.

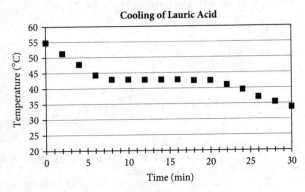

Figure 23.4

The *melting point* of a substance is the temperature at which that substance changes from the solid to the liquid phase. The *boiling point* of a substance is the temperature at which that substance changes from the liquid to the gaseous phase. Table 23.5 shows the boiling and melting points of other common substances.

Table 23.5		
Substance	**Melting Point (°C)**	**Boiling Point (°C)**
Water	0	100
Isopropyl alcohol	–90	82
Paraffin wax	59	343

421. Based on Figure 23.4, the temperature of the lauric acid sample decreased most rapidly during which time interval?

    A. 0 to 6 minutes
    B. 15 to 20 minutes
    C. 20 to 25 minutes
    D. 25 to 30 minutes

422. The thermometer was carefully placed in the test tube to measure the temperature of the lauric acid. If the thermometer was allowed to rest on the bottom of the test tube, what temperature may have been recorded at the start of the experiment (0 minutes)?

    A. 80°C
    B. 50°C
    C. 20°C
    D. 0°C

423. During the experiment, particles of lauric acid could either decrease in temperature or change from a liquid to a solid—they could not do both at the same time. In which time interval(s) did the particles' temperature decrease?

    A. 0 to 6 minutes
    B. 6 to 20 minutes
    C. 20 to 30 minutes
    D. Both 0 to 6 minutes and 20 to 30 minutes

424. What is the melting point of lauric acid?

    A. 55°C
    B. 43°C
    C. 34°C
    D. 0°C

425. What phase(s) of matter is present in the sample of lauric acid at 25°C?

    A. Only solid
    B. Only liquid
    C. Only gaseous
    D. Both solid and liquid

426. The sample of lauric acid was allowed to remain in the room, and the clock continued to run. If the trend found in Figure 23.4 continued, what would the stopwatch read when the sample reached room temperature of 25°C?

    A. About 32 minutes
    B. About 40 minutes
    C. About 50 minutes
    D. About 60 minutes

427. If twice the amount of lauric acid were heated in the test tube, at what temperature would one expect the lauric acid to crystallize into a solid?

    A. 43°C
    B. 86°C
    C. Somewhere between 43°C and 86°C
    D. A little lower than 43°C

428. What would most likely have occurred if this experiment had been conducted in an oven set at 50°C?

    A. The sample would have taken much longer to turn to a solid.
    B. The sample would have turned to a solid much more quickly.
    C. The sample would never have turned into a solid.
    D. The sample would not have decreased in temperature.

429. According to the data in Table 23.5, what phase(s) of matter is present in the sample of isopropyl alcohol at 25°C?

    A. Only solid
    B. Only liquid
    C. Only gaseous
    D. Both solid and liquid

430. The same experiment was conducted with a sample of water in a test tube. It was heated to 55°C and then removed from the heat and allowed to cool in the classroom. Which of the following graphs would most likely represent the results?

A.

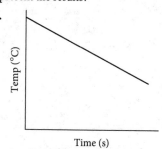

Figure 23.5

B.

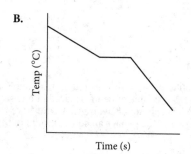

Figure 23.6

C.

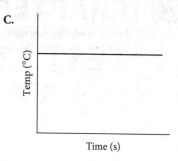

Figure 23.7

D.

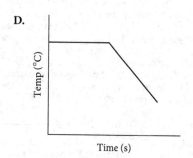

Figure 23.8

PASSAGE 35

In the early 1800s, chemists started experimenting with different chemicals. They had the ability to measure the temperature, pressure, and mass of a sample of gas. In 1911, a chemist named Amadeo Avogadro published an observation that came to be known as Avogadro's law. This law states that any two gasses that are held under the same pressure, temperature, and volume will contain the same number of molecules (measured in moles) regardless of the identity of the gasses. Table 24.1 shows data collected from various gas samples at 1 atm and 0°C.

Table 24.1			
Sample	Gas	Volume (L)	Mass of Gas (g)
1	Hydrogen (H_2)	11.2	1.0
2	Hydrogen (H_2)	5.6	0.5
3	Neon (Ne)	11.2	10.1
4	Neon (Ne)	22.4	20.2
5	Helium (He)	22.4	4.0
6	Helium (He)	44.8	8.0
7	Oxygen (O_2)	11.2	16.0
8	Oxygen (O_2)	5.6	8.0

431. According to Table 24.1, which sample of gas took up the most space?

A. Sample 1
B. Sample 4
C. Sample 6
D. Sample 7

432. Comparing Samples 1 and 3, one can state that:

A. Samples 1 and 3 are the same size and the same mass.
B. Sample 1 is larger, but Sample 3 is more massive.
C. Sample 3 is larger, but Sample 1 is more massive.
D. Samples 1 and 3 are the same size, but Sample 3 is more massive.

433. Referring to Table 24.1, how does the number of gas molecules in Sample 4 compare to the number of gas molecules in Sample 5?

A. Sample 4 has more molecules.
B. Sample 5 has more molecules.
C. Samples 4 and 5 have the same number of molecules.
D. It is impossible to determine from the data given.

434. How much mass would a 22.4-L sample of oxygen gas have when measured at 1 atm and 0°C?

A. 4.0 g
B. 20.2 g
C. 32.0 g
D. 44.8 g

435. In the early 1800s, mass was measured with a double-pan balance. If a 11.2-L sample of neon is placed in one side of the balance, what volume of hydrogen would have to be placed on the other side to have an equal amount of mass?

A. 224.0 L
B. 112.0 L
C. 22.4 L
D. 11.2 L

436. Referring to Avogadro's law and Table 24.1, which of the following places the samples of gas in order from the least number of molecules to the most?

A. Sample 1, Sample 3, Sample 7
B. Sample 7, Sample 3, Sample 1
C. Samples 3 and 1 have an equal number of molecules, but Sample 7 has more.
D. All the samples have an equal number of molecules.

437. What can be said about the mass of one molecule of helium and one molecule of oxygen gas?

A. One molecule of helium has the same mass as one molecule of hydrogen gas.
B. One molecule of oxygen is 8 times more massive than one molecule of helium.
C. One molecule of helium is 8 times more massive than one molecule of oxygen gas.
D. One molecule of oxygen gas is 4 times more massive than one molecule of helium.

438. Chemists counted molecules in the unit of *moles*. Avogadro stated that 1 mole (mol) of gas particles at 1 atm and 0°C takes up a volume of 22.4 L. What is the mass of 1 mol of oxygen gas molecules?

A. 32.0 g
B. 16.0 g
C. 8.0 g
D. 4.0 g

PASSAGE 36: THE ABSORPTION SPECTRA OF CHLOROPHYLL

Photosynthesis is the process by which organisms such as green plants, algae, and cyanobacteria convert light energy from the sun to chemical energy stored in the bonds of carbohydrates. Chlorophyll is a pigment employed by many autotrophic organisms to absorb the various wavelengths of visible light from the sun for use in photosynthesis. A variety of photosynthetic pigments exist; they are specifically adapted for absorbing different ranges of the visible light spectrum and reflecting others. The absorption spectrum of chlorophyll and accessory pigments can be obtained through spectrophotometry and later used to gain insight into plant growth, determine the abundance of photosynthetic organisms in fresh- or saltwater, and evaluate water quality.

The data in Figure 24.1 and Table 24.2 were collected by students measuring the absorption spectra of three commonly encountered photosynthetic pigments.

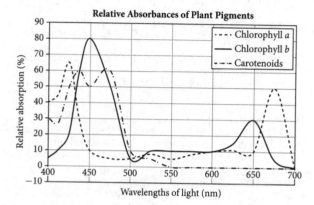

Figure 24.1

Table 24.2	
Color	**Wavelength**
Red	620–750 nm
Orange	590–620 nm
Yellow	570–590 nm
Green	495–570 nm
Blue	450–495 nm
Violet	380–450 nm

439. Which of the following statements represents a valid assessment of the data?

- **A.** Chlorophyll *a* and *b* absorb the most green light.
- **B.** Neither chlorophyll *a*, *b*, nor the carotenoids absorb light in the wavelengths of 425 to 475 nm.
- **C.** Chlorophyll *a* and *b* have the most reflection in the wavelengths of 525 to 625 nm.
- **D.** Carotenoids absorb the most light in the red portion of the spectrum.

440. Using the information in Table 24.2, which of the following wavelengths of light would phycocyanin, a pale blue-colored accessory pigment, reflect most?

- **A.** 400 nm
- **B.** 460 nm
- **C.** 550 nm
- **D.** 750 nm

441. Based on Figure 24.1, which of the following wavelengths of visible light would be absorbed to promote the most photosynthetic activity in green plants?

- **A.** 400 nm
- **B.** 440 nm
- **C.** 550 nm
- **D.** 625 nm

442. Based on the information in Figure 24.1 and Table 24.2, which pigment has the highest relative absorbance in the red portion of the spectrum?

- **A.** Chlorophyll *a*
- **B.** Chlorophyll *b*
- **C.** Carotenoids
- **D.** All pigments absorb the same amount of light in this portion of the spectrum.

443. Which of the following statements about the relative absorbance levels of the pigments is most accurate?

- **A.** Chlorophyll *a* absorbs 8 times as much light as chlorophyll *b* at 450 nm.
- **B.** Carotenoids behave similarly to chlorophyll *a* and *b* at wavelengths greater than 550 nm.
- **C.** Chlorophyll *b* has the lowest relative absorbance of violet light.
- **D.** Carotenoids absorb approximately 60% as much light as chlorophyll *b* at 450 nm.

444. Which pigment would absorb the most violet light at a wavelength of 425 nm?

- **A.** Chlorophyll *a*
- **B.** Chlorophyll *b*
- **C.** Carotenoids
- **D.** All pigments absorb violet light equally.

445. Which wavelength represents the maximum absorbance of chlorophyll *b*?

- **A.** 425 nm
- **B.** 450 nm
- **C.** 515 nm
- **D.** 650 nm

446. From the information in the passage, one can conclude that chlorophyll appears green to the human eye because:

- **A.** wavelengths of light between 550 and 600 nm are highly absorbed.
- **B.** wavelengths in the green portion of the visible spectrum are absorbed.
- **C.** wavelengths in the green portion of the visible spectrum are reflected.
- **D.** wavelengths in the red portion of the visible spectrum are reflected.

447. Phycoerythrin is a photosynthetic pigment that is found in marine algae. It has absorption peaks at 495 nm and 566 nm and reaches its lowest values over 600 nm. Based on this information, one would expect phycoerythrin to:

- **A.** appear very similar to chlorophyll *a* and *b* to the naked eye.
- **B.** reflect green light and absorb red light.
- **C.** reflect red light and absorb green light.
- **D.** absorb red and green light equally.

PASSAGE 37: LIGHT WAVES VERSUS LIGHT PARTICLES

In the late 1600s, scientists developed theories about the nature of light. Sir Isaac Newton theorized that light consisted of tiny particles. Christiaan Huygens, on the other hand, believed that light consisted of waves. What do we know about particles? Particles are small, localized objects that typically have certain physical properties like mass, color, or volume. They move in straight lines unless some outside force is acting on them.

Waves, on the other hand, consist of energy that moves through a medium (material). When waves hit a boundary from one material into another, some of that energy bounces back into the original material (reflection); some of the energy moves into the new material (refraction or transmission); and some of the energy transfers to thermal energy through heating (absorption). When waves encounter one another, they will increase in size and strength if similar parts of them overlap (constructive interference) and will decrease in size and strength if opposite parts of them overlap (destructive interference); after the interference, the waves continue moving in their original direction. Waves also spread out (diffract) when they hit a sharp edge or a tiny opening.

448. The front view in Figure 24.2 shows the image projected on a screen by the light from a tiny lightbulb placed in front of a square card. What can you conclude about the nature of light from the image shown?

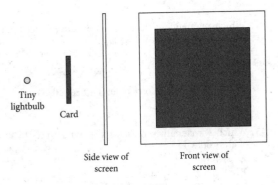

Figure 24.2

A. Light behaves like a wave because it moves in all directions from the lightbulb.
B. Light behaves like a wave because it does not move through the card.
C. Light behaves like a particle because it moves in straight lines from the bulb to form the larger shadow on the screen.
D. Light behaves like a particle because it reflects, refracts, and absorbs in this scenario.

449. Which of the following does NOT support Huygens's wave theory of light?
A. A laser light reflects off a mirror and strikes the wall in the back of the lab.
B. Light hits a black shirt and heats it up.
C. Sunlight transmits through a thick pane of glass, illuminating a room.
D. The smallest unit of light is a bundle of energy called a photon.

450. In the 1600s, it was believed that waves required a medium to travel. Which of the following observations did Huygens have difficulty explaining with his wave theory?
A. Light travels from the sun to the earth through the vacuum of space.
B. Light spreads out when it encounters a thin slit in a sheet of paper.
C. When light hits an opaque surface, the surface heats up.
D. White light separates into a rainbow of colors when it strikes a prism.

451. In the early 1800s, Thomas Young shone light through two tiny slits and observed an image on the screen that consisted of many regions of alternating bright and dark patterns. This provided evidence that light is:
A. a wave because the light from one slit overlapped with the light from the other slit in areas that were strong and weak.
B. a particle because it was able to make it through the two slits.
C. a wave because it refracted through the slits, bent in multiple directions, and reflected and absorbed at the screen.
D. multiple particles bouncing off the slits and moving to certain locations on the screen to make the bright areas and avoiding the dark areas.

452. When a laser beam of light strikes a penny, one might expect a sharp shadow to form. Instead, a circular, fuzzy-edged shadow forms with a bright spot in the middle. Which of the following best explains this phenomenon?
A. Laser light particles move in straight lines, and some of those particles are blocked by the penny.
B. The beam of laser light is a result of stimulated emission of electrons, and the electron particles are able to travel through the material of the penny.
C. The light bounces off the edge of the penny and hits the middle of the shadow, causing the bright spot.
D. The light diffracts around the sharp edge of the penny and interferes constructively at the center of the penny.

453. Figure 24.3 was most likely created by Huygens because:

Figure 24.3
Source: Christiaan Huygens, Treatise on Light. *Translated by Silvanus P. Thompson. The Project Gutenberg eBook, http://www.gutenberg.org/files/14725/14725-h/14725-h.htm#Page_4.*

A. the circles show the pathways that particles take when they leave the candle flame.
B. light is moving in all directions from the candle flame.
C. the circles coming from Points A, B, and C are like ripples in a pond.
D. light is coming from different points on the candle flame.

454. Is the following more likely to be attributed to Newton or Huygens and why?

If you consider the extreme speed with which light spreads on every side, as well as the fact that when it comes from different regions—even those directly opposite—the rays traverse one another without being hindered, you may well understand that when a person sees a luminous object, it cannot be by any transport of matter coming to that person from the object, in the same way that a shot or an arrow flies through the air. Therefore, light must spread in some other way, and that which can lead us to comprehend it is the knowledge we have of the spreading of sound in the air.

A. Newton, because of the reference to the way light spreads
B. Huygens, because it claims that light cannot travel like matter does
C. Newton, because the emphasis is on the extreme speed of light
D. Huygens, because it explains how we can see images of luminous objects

455. In the 1900s, Albert Einstein and others determined that the basic unit of light consists of a photon. Among other properties, this unit has a fixed amount of energy, depending on its location on the visible color spectrum. The fact that light can be broken down to fixed units is most consistent with:

A. Newton's particle theory of light.
B. Huygens's wave theory of light.
C. Newton's wave theory of light.
D. Huygens's particle theory of light.

456. A beam of direct sunlight moves along an axis through the middle of two polarizing filters, where the axis remains perpendicular to the filters. When the light passes through the first polarizing filter, its brightness reduces to 50%, regardless of its orientation. The light will remain at the same brightness after the second polarizing filter if that filter is aligned the same way as the first. If the second filter twists, however, the light passing through it will gradually be eliminated. Which of the following statements CANNOT be supported by this information?

A. Because wave energy may be absorbed at a boundary, it is feasible that only 50% of the light energy passes through the first filter.
B. Light particles may be blocked by objects; therefore, it is feasible that only 50% of the light passes through the first filter.
C. Polarizing filters may be used to control the intensity of light.
D. The change in the light intensity as the second filter is rotated may be explained by the particle theory of light.

PASSAGE 38

Two investigations were conducted on a sample of green nickel sulfate ($NiSO_4$) that was dissolved in water. The first investigation placed a sample of the nickel sulfate into a spectrometer. Most solutions absorb some wavelengths of light and allow other wavelengths to pass right through. The spectrometer changed the wavelength of light shining into the solution and recorded how much of the light was absorbed by the solution. An *absorbance* of 0.00 would indicate that all of the light shone into the solution passed through with no light being absorbed. Figure 24.4 shows the result of absorbance versus wavelength for a sample of $NiSO_{4(aq)}$.

The next experiment used five different solutions of $NiSO_{4(aq)}$ at different known concentrations (measured in molarity). Each solution was placed in a spectrometer set at 740 nm, and light was shone into each sample to determine the absorbance of each of the five solutions. Table 24.3 shows the results.

Table 24.3		
Sample	Concentration of $NiSO_{4(aq)}$ (mol/L)	Absorbance
1	0.08	0.091
2	0.16	0.182
3	0.24	0.273
4	0.32	0.363
5	0.40	0.451

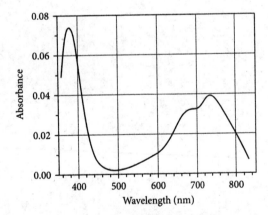

Figure 24.4

457. Which wavelength of light was absorbed to the greatest degree in the first investigation?

- **A.** 380 nm
- **B.** 500 nm
- **C.** 740 nm
- **D.** 830 nm

458. The wavelength of 490 nm is green light. Why is the absorbance of $NiSO_4$ low at 490 nm?

- **A.** The spectrometer is not accurate at the wavelength of 490 nm.
- **B.** The $NiSO_{4(aq)}$ is green in color, so green light from the spectrometer passes through the solution.
- **C.** The $NiSO_{4(aq)}$ is green in color, so the green light from the spectrometer is absorbed to a large extent.
- **D.** The green light gets reflected back to the spectrometer when it contacts the green $NiSO_{4(aq)}$ solution.

459. What conclusions can be drawn from the data collected in Table 24.3?

- **A.** As the wavelength of light aimed at the sample increases, the absorbance increases.
- **B.** Light with a wavelength of 740 nm is not absorbed to a great extent by $NiSO_{4(aq)}$.
- **C.** Concentration of solution is inversely proportional to absorbance of light.
- **D.** As the concentration of $NiSO_{4(aq)}$ increases, the absorbance of light increases.

460. Which of the following statements accurately describes the trend found in Table 24.3?

- **A.** Light with a wavelength of 740 nm increases absorbance by about 0.09.
- **B.** Doubling the concentration of $NiSO_{4(aq)}$ causes an increase in absorbance of about 0.90.
- **C.** An increase of 0.08 mol/L causes an increase in the absorbance of about 0.90.
- **D.** The absorbance of $NiSO_{4(aq)}$ stops increasing at a concentration of 0.40 mol/L.

461. Which set of data would best represent the results if Investigation 2 were repeated with a wavelength of 490 nm instead of 740 nm?

	Sample	Concentration $NiSO_{4(aq)}$ (mol/L)	Absorbance
A.	1	0.08	0.091
	2	0.16	0.182
	3	0.24	0.273
	4	0.32	0.363
B.	1	0.08	0.049
	2	0.16	0.098
	3	0.24	0.147
	4	0.32	0.196
C.	1	0.08	0.003
	2	0.16	0.006
	3	0.24	0.009
	4	0.32	0.012
D.	1	0.08	0.25
	2	0.16	0.51
	3	0.24	0.76
	4	0.32	0.99

462. The process of spectrometry works well on colored solutions such as green nickel sulfate ($NiSO_4$) and cupric sulfate ($CuSO_4$). Why might spectrometry not work well on solutions such as table salt dissolved in water ($NaCl_{(aq)}$)?

- **A.** Table salt is clear, so it will absorb all wavelengths of light.
- **B.** Table salt is clear, so all colors of light will pass through the solution.
- **C.** The researcher cannot vary the concentration of table salt.
- **D.** Spectrometry is not appropriate for food-grade substances.

463. Experiment 2 was repeated with a sixth sample of $NiSO_4$ solution with a concentration of 0.48 mol/L. However, the test tube had fingerprints on the glass where the light passed through. The fingerprints absorbed some light from the spectrometer. What would be an expected value for the absorbance?

- **A.** 0.451
- **B.** 0.522
- **C.** 0.542
- **D.** 0.622

464. What would be the results of Investigation 1 if a more concentrated solution of $NiSO_{4(aq)}$ were used to make the graph in the table?

A.

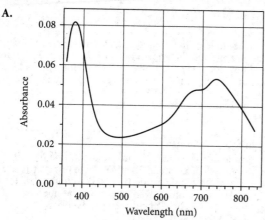

Figure 24.5

B.

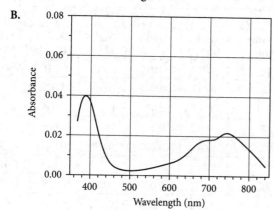

Figure 24.6

C.

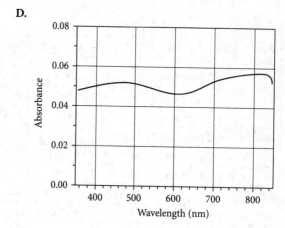

Figure 24.7

D.

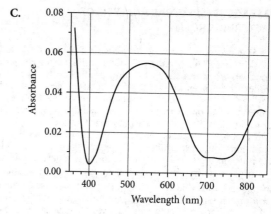

Figure 24.8

PASSAGE 39: SPECTRAL ANALYSIS OF BACTERIAL GROWTH

Staphylococcus aureus (*S. aureus*) is a bacterium found on the skin of 25% of healthy individuals with no adverse effects. However, when transferred to food products, the toxins it can produce have been known to cause food-borne illness, particularly in cooked and cured meats. It is important to determine conditions that promote the growth of pathogenic species of bacteria and apply that knowledge in food preparation and handling. Two groups of students set out to determine the ideal growth conditions for *S. aureus*. In each group, bacteria were inoculated in a nutrient broth and allowed to grow over a period of time.

When analyzing the growth of bacteria in a liquid medium, an increase in turbidity corresponds to an increase in the bacteria growing in suspension. Because the bacterial cells scatter light, spectrophotometry can be used to determine bacterial growth. Changes in the logarithmic absorbance scale on the spectrophotometer correspond to changes in the number of cells, and a growth curve can be plotted by graphing the absorbance readings from the spectrophotometer versus time. The rate of growth can be determined by the slope of the lines, and the type of growth occurring at a given time can be determined by the shape of the curve.

Group 1

The students in Group 1 set out to determine whether temperature affected the growth rate of *S. aureus* in a nutrient-rich medium. They tested *S. aureus* by inoculating a flask of nutrient-rich broth with a pH of 6 at the following temperatures: 3°C, 20°C, 37°C, 45°C, and 60°C. The spectrophotometer absorbance readings are shown in Table 24.4.

Group 2

Students in Group 2 planned to determine the effect of pH on the growth of *S. aureus*. They wanted to test growth at a range of values from highly acidic (low pH) to highly basic/alkaline (high pH). The cultures were grown at a temperature of 37°C, and the pH levels of each culture were as follows: 3, 5, 6, 7, and 9. Table 24.5 shows their data.

	Table 24.4				
Time (min)	Trial 1 (3°C)	Trial 2 (20°C)	Trial 3 (37°C)	Trial 4 (45°C)	Trial 5 (60°C)
0	0.011	0.011	0.011	0.012	0.013
48	0.011	0.030	0.022	0.045	0.013
62	0.011	0.067	0.035	0.081	0.013
68	0.011	0.072	0.047	0.056	0.013
82	0.011	0.085	0.070	0.075	0.013
88	0.011	0.090	0.081	0.078	0.013
97	0.011	0.098	0.099	0.078	0.013
108	0.011	0.108	0.109	0.079	0.013
118	0.011	0.117	0.137	0.088	0.013
128	0.011	0.126	0.149	0.089	0.013
138	0.011	0.135	0.167	0.098	0.013
148	0.011	0.144	0.174	0.106	0.013
157	0.011	0.152	0.190	0.109	0.013
168	0.011	0.162	0.207	0.114	0.013
180	0.011	0.173	0.222	0.117	0.013
188	0.011	0.180	0.297	0.118	0.013
198	0.011	0.189	0.288	0.126	0.013
600	0.011	0.551	0.800	0.125	0.013
1,470	0.011	0.553	0.800	0.130	0.013

	Table 24.5				
Time (min)	Trial 1 (pH 3)	Trial 2 (pH 5)	Trial 3 (pH 6)	Trial 4 (pH 7)	Trial 5 (pH 9)
0	0.012	0.012	0.011	0.011	0.013
48	0.012	0.026	0.022	0.045	0.013
62	0.012	0.031	0.035	0.054	0.013
68	0.012	0.032	0.047	0.059	0.013
82	0.012	0.037	0.070	0.068	0.013
88	0.012	0.038	0.081	0.073	0.013
97	0.012	0.041	0.099	0.079	0.013
108	0.012	0.044	0.109	0.087	0.013
118	0.012	0.047	0.137	0.094	0.013
128	0.012	0.050	0.149	0.101	0.013
138	0.012	0.053	0.167	0.108	0.013
148	0.012	0.056	0.174	0.115	0.013
157	0.012	0.059	0.190	0.121	0.013
168	0.012	0.062	0.207	0.129	0.013
180	0.012	0.066	0.222	0.137	0.013
188	0.012	0.068	0.297	0.143	0.013
198	0.012	0.071	0.288	0.150	0.013
600	0.012	0.192	0.800	0.431	0.013
1,470	0.012	0.195	0.851	0.440	0.013

465. Which of the following is a valid assessment of the data from Group 1?

   A. As temperature increases, the growth rate of *S. aureus* increases proportionally.
   B. *S. aureus* grows optimally at a temperature of 37°C.
   C. As temperature decreases, so does the growth rate of *S. aureus*.
   D. *S. aureus* exhibits exponential growth at a temperature of 37°C.

466. The stationary phase of growth is entered as the nutrients in the medium begin to run out and the growth of bacteria changes the conditions in the flask. Cell division slows, and the turbidity ceases to increase because the overall population remains unchanged. When did the bacteria in Group 1/Trial 3 likely begin the stationary phase of growth?

   A. 97 minutes
   B. 148 minutes
   C. 600 minutes
   D. 1,470 minutes

467. Which of the following statements is most accurate?

    A. *S. aureus* responds well to increases in pH above 7.
    B. pH factor does not have an effect on the growth of *S. aureus*.
    C. *S. aureus* is viable at pH levels below 2.
    D. pH is a control for Group 1 and an experimental variable for Group 2.

468. *Generation time* is the amount of time it takes for the bacterial population to double. Some bacteria, such as *E. coli*, have a doubling time of 20 minutes under ideal conditions, while other bacteria may take days to double their population size. Which of these is most likely the approximate generation time for the bacteria in Group 1/Trial 3 during the first 100 minutes of the experiment?

    A. 6 minutes
    B. 29 minutes
    C. 75 minutes
    D. 100 minutes

469. Which of the following does NOT represent a controlled variable for both groups?

    A. The nature of the nutrient media
    B. The temperature of incubation
    C. The strain of *S. aureus* used
    D. The wavelength of light set on the spectrophotometer

470. Which of the following is a valid assessment of the data in Table 24.5?

    A. *S. aureus* has a faster growth rate at pH 7 than at pH 5.
    B. *S. aureus* achieves a higher overall turbidity at pH 5 than at pH 7.
    C. *S. aureus* achieves maximum growth at pH levels below 4.
    D. *S. aureus* has a faster growth rate at pH 5 than at pH 7.

471. The data for Group 2/Trial 5 indicate that:

    A. at this high level of acidity, *S. aureus* bacteria cannot grow.
    B. at this high level of alkalinity, *S. aureus* bacteria cannot grow.
    C. at this low level of alkalinity, *S. aureus* bacteria cannot grow.
    D. at this high level of alkalinity, *S. aureus* bacteria thrive.

472. Which of the following trials were run under the same conditions for Groups 1 and 2?

    A. Group 1/Trial 1 and Group 2/Trial 1
    B. Group 1/Trial 2 and Group 2/Trial 4
    C. Group 1/Trial 3 and Group 2/Trial 3
    D. Group 1/Trial 5 and Group 2/Trial 5

473. If scientists wanted to do further testing on the growth of *S. aureus* to inform food processing and handling decisions, such as the effect of salinity, what conditions would be best as the controls for their test?

    A. 37°C and pH 6
    B. 37°C and pH 5
    C. 20°C and pH 6
    D. 45°C and pH 7

474. Which of the following graphs most closely resembles the shape of a graph that could be drawn for Group 1/Trial 3?

    A.
    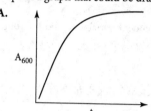

    Figure 24.9

    B.
    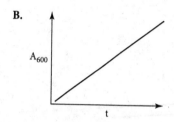

    Figure 24.10

    C.
    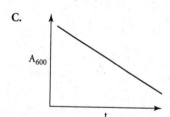

    Figure 24.11

    D.
    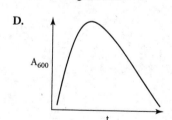

    Figure 24.12

475. Chemical inhibitors such as sodium benzoate are often used as food preservatives because of their ability to retard, although not completely inhibit, bacterial growth. If a study were done on the effects of sodium benzoate on the growth of *S. aureus* at 37°C, one would expect to see results similar to those of:

A. Group 2/Trial 1.
B. Group 1/Trial 5.
C. Group 2/Trial 2.
D. Group 1/Trial 3.

476. What is the independent variable for both Group 1 and Group 2?

A. Time
B. pH
C. Temperature
D. The type of bacteria being tested

477. Meat in a delicatessen tested positive for the presence of bacteria, and this bacteria was to be identified using spectrophotometry. Which of the following test results would most clearly indicate that the bacteria found was *S. aureus*?

A. The bacteria died at temperatures above 55°C.
B. The bacteria experienced rapid growth at temperatures below 20°C.
C. The bacterial generation time was determined to be approximately 30 minutes at 37°C.
D. The bacteria showed no increase in turbidity when incubated in an ice bath.

478. Which of the following statements is the best explanation for what occurred in Group 2/Trial 2 between 10 and 24 hours?

A. The bacterial population grew exponentially.
B. The birth and death rate of bacterial cells were relatively equal during this time.
C. The bacteria were dying more rapidly than new bacteria could be generated.
D. No new bacteria were generated or died during this time.

CHAPTER 25
TEST 12

PASSAGE 40

In 1922, Niels Bohr revised the atomic model to include a positively charged nucleus surrounded by negatively charged electrons that traveled in well-defined shells around the nucleus. The shells can be thought of as concentric circles around the nucleus. A neutral atom contains the same number of protons in the nucleus as electrons surrounding the nucleus. The inside shell can hold two electrons, and the second shell can hold eight electrons. An electrostatic attraction occurs between the positively charged protons in the nucleus and the negatively charged electrons. A representation of Bohr's shell model is shown in Figure 25.1.

Partial evidence for this atomic shell model comes from the study of ionization energies of different elements. *Ionization energy* is the amount of energy required to remove an electron from an atom or ion in the gaseous state. The first ionization energy removes the electron farthest from the nucleus and can be represented by the following formula:

$$X + \text{Ionization energy} \rightarrow X^{+1} + \text{Electron}^{-1}$$

where X represents a neutral atom.

The nth ionization energy removes additional electrons from an already charged ion. For example, the third ionization energy can be represented by the following formula:

$$X^{+2} + \text{Ionization energy} \rightarrow X^{+3} + \text{Electron}^{-1}$$

The ionization energies in kJ/mol of the first 10 elements can be found in Table 25.1.

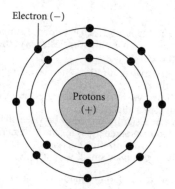

Electron (−)

Protons (+)

Figure 25.1

Table 25.1										
Atom	Protons	First	Second	Third	Fourth	Fifth	Sixth	Seventh	Eighth	Ninth	Tenth
H	1	1,312									
He	2	2,372	5,250								
Li	3	520	7,298	11,815							
Be	4	900	1,757	14,849	21,007						
B	5	801	2,427	3,659	25,025	32,827					
C	6	1,087	2,353	4,621	6,223	37,831	47,277				
N	7	1,402	2,856	4,578	7,475	9,445	53,267	64,360			
O	8	1,314	3,388	5,300	7,469	10,990	13,327	71,330	84,078		
F	9	1,681	3,374	6,050	8,408	11,023	15,164	17,868	92,038	10,6434	
Ne	10	2,081	3,952	6,122	9,371	12,177	15,238	19,999	23,070	115,380	131,432

479. How much energy does it take to remove the outermost electron from beryllium (Be)?

A. 900 kJ/mol
B. 1,757 kJ/mol
C. 14,849 kJ/mol
D. 21,007 kJ/mol

480. Which of the following statements regarding the ionization energy of the third proton of the elements listed is true?

A. There is a general and consistent increase as the elements get larger.
B. There is a general and consistent decrease as the elements get larger.
C. Increases are then followed by a decrease.
D. After an early dip, there is a general increase.

481. How much energy is required to remove an electron from nitrogen as shown in the following equation?

$$N^{+3} + \text{Ionization energy} \rightarrow N^{+4} + \text{Electron}^{-1}$$

A. 1,402 kJ/mol
B. 2,856 kJ/mol
C. 4,578 kJ/mol
D. 7,475 kJ/mol

482. The first ionization energy of Element 2, hydrogen, is much larger than the first ionization energy for Element 3, lithium. Which statement best explains this trend?

A. Helium has only two electrons while lithium has three.
B. Helium is a very light element; therefore, it is very hard to remove its electrons.
C. Both of helium's electrons are the first shell, while one of lithium's electrons is found in the second shell.
D. Helium has two protons providing the positive electrostatic attraction, while lithium has three protons providing a larger attraction.

483. Which best explains why there is no seventh ionization energy listed for the element carbon?

A. It is hard to measure the energy required to remove carbon's seventh electron.
B. Carbon does not have seven electrons surrounding its nucleus.
C. The seventh ionization energy of carbon is equal to the first ionization energy of nitrogen, so it does not need to be listed.
D. The seventh, eighth, ninth, and tenth ionization energies of carbon are all equal to the sixth, so they do not need to be listed.

484. Figure 25.2 shows an electron being removed from the element oxygen. How much energy is associated with the image shown?

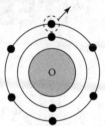

Figure 25.2

A. 1,314 kJ/mol
B. 3,388 kJ/mol
C. 71,330 kJ/mol
D. 84,078 kJ/mol

485. According to Table 25.1, how many electrons must the element nitrogen have in its outermost shell?

A. Two
B. Five
C. Seven
D. Eight

486. Referring to Table 25.1, what evidence supports the fact that each element has only two electrons in the first, innermost shell?

A. The first two ionization energies are always smaller than the rest.
B. The last two ionization energies are always significantly larger than the rest.
C. There is a significant jump between the second and third ionization energies for most elements.
D. The first two ionization energies of helium and lithium are both relatively small.

487. Which set of ionization energy (IE) data represents an atom that has one electron in its outermost electron shell?

	First IE	Second IE	Third IE	Fourth IE
A.	300	600	1,801	2,230
B.	700	2,892	3,019	3,299
C.	1,121	1,398	4,456	4,876
D.	854	1,981	2,765	3,344

488. Helium and lithium are isoelectronic. This means their electron structure is identical. They both have two electrons in the first shell outside of the nucleus. Why does it take less energy to remove an electron from helium than it does to remove an electron from lithium?

A. Helium has two protons, but lithium has three.
B. Lithium has already had the outermost electron removed.
C. The first ionization energy of lithium is smaller than that of helium.
D. Lithium has a positive charge so removing electrons is more difficult.

489. How many kJ of energy would be required to remove *all* of the electrons from 1 mol of helium atoms?

A. 2,372 kJ
B. 5,250 kJ
C. 7,622 kJ
D. 10,500 kJ

PASSAGE 41

Many companies advertise that their brand of battery outlasts the competitors' batteries. A series of experiments were conducted to compare batteries from different manufacturers. Figure 25.3 shows the results of tests of four different brands of batteries. Two AA batteries were tested in an incandescent bulb flashlight, and the combined voltage was tested for continuous use over time. The flashlight operated effectively for voltage values greater than 2.2 V.

Table 25.2 compares how Brands D and E alkaline batteries performed in different devices. The table displays the time the combined voltage of two batteries remained above 2.2 V. The voltages were checked every quarter-hour.

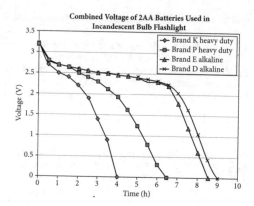

Figure 25.3

Table 25.2						
	Time Two AA Alkaline Batteries Exceeded 2.2 V (hours)					
Device	Brand D Trial 1	Brand D Trial 2	Brand D Trial 3	Brand E Trial 1	Brand E Trial 2	Brand E Trial 3
Incandescent bulb flashlight	7.00	6.75	6.75	6.75	6.50	6.50
LED bulb flashlight	24.25	25.50	24.00	23.75	25.75	24.75
Remote-control toy car	2.00	8.50	6.50	14.25	4.50	8.50
Plug-and-play video game	11.50	12.50	13.50	13.50	12.25	13.25

490. According to Figure 25.3, how did the performance of Brands D and E alkaline batteries compare?

   A. Brand E performed significantly better than Brand D.
   B. Brand D performed significantly better than Brand E.
   C. There was no significant difference between the performance of the brands.
   D. Neither Brand D nor Brand E was capable of lighting the flashlight for more than an hour.

491. According to Figure 25.3, the Brand P battery was capable of operating the incandescent flashlight for approximately:

   A. 0.5 hours.
   B. 2.0 hours.
   C. 3.5 hours.
   D. 6.5 hours.

492. Which of the following conclusions is plausible from the information provided in Figure 25.3?

   A. Heavy-duty batteries perform better than alkaline batteries when used in medium-drain devices such as incandescent bulb flashlights.
   B. In the experiment, there was more consistency in the performance of alkaline batteries than in that of heavy-duty batteries.
   C. Alkaline batteries perform better than heavy-duty batteries in high-drain devices such as camera flashes.
   D. The Brand P heavy-duty battery is the best value for the money spent.

493. What can one conclude about the performance of Brands D and E batteries when they were used in the remote-control car?

   A. Brand E performed significantly better than Brand D.
   B. Brand D performed significantly better than Brand E.
   C. The two brand's performances were approximately the same.
   D. The variability of the data prevents any valid comparison.

494. When used in the incandescent bulb flashlight, how much time did Brand K's heavy-duty battery sustain a voltage between 2 and 3 V?

   A. 0.5 hours
   B. 2.0 hours
   C. 3.0 hours
   D. 6.5 hours

495. Using the data in Table 25.2, how do the averages of the three trials compare when Brands D and E are used in the plug-and-play video game?

   A. Brand D's average was 0.75 hours more than Brand E's.
   B. Brand E's average was 0.5 hours more than Brand D's.
   C. Brand E's average was 1.5 hours more than Brand D's.
   D. Brands E and D had the same average.

496. Which of the following statements is true according to Figure 25.3?

    A. In the first few hours of testing, the voltage drop for Brand D was greater than that for Brand K.

    B. Brand P's performance over the first four hours was nearly identical to that of Brand E.

    C. At voltages under 2.2 V, the voltage of Brand E drops more rapidly than that of Brand P.

    D. Brand K lasts longer than Brand P.

497. Which of the following steps in the experimental procedure is MOST IMPORTANT in the comparison of battery performance between brands?

    A. The batteries tested were manufactured in the same year.

    B. The batteries tested were not previously used in any other device.

    C. The temperature was controlled in the testing room.

    D. The time intervals for measuring voltages were the same for each brand.

498. Which of the following devices is most likely classified as a low-drain device?

    A. Incandescent bulb flashlight

    B. LED bulb flashlight

    C. Remote-control toy car

    D. Plug-and-play video game

499. Approximately how much longer than the incandescent bulb flashlight does the LED bulb flashlight last?

    A. Twice as long

    B. Four times as long

    C. Six times as long

    D. Twenty-four times as long

500. In terms of just the Brand E tests, which of the following devices is most likely classified as a high-drain device?

    A. Incandescent bulb flashlight

    B. LED bulb flashlight

    C. Remote-control toy car

    D. Plug-and-play video game

■ PART IV ANSWERS AND EXPLANATIONS

Chapter 14: Test 1

1. **D.** The endosperm may be yellow or white. Since the endosperm is located underneath the aleurone layer, its color is only visible when the aleurone is colorless. A purple or red aleurone masks the endosperm.

2. **A.** The pericap is the outermost layer of the corn seed, as shown in Figure 14.1. Since no color phenotypes related to the pericap are mentioned, it can be inferred that the pericap is colorless, allowing the color phenotype of the aleurone and endosperm to be visible.

3. **C.** Table 14.1 lists three alleles (*C'*, *C*, and *c*) for the aleurone color inhibitor trait. The other traits listed each have two alleles (*Y* or *y*, *R* or *r*, and *P* or *p*).

4. **B.** The aleurone may have a purple, red, or colorless phenotype. Colorless is not itself a kernel color phenotype because a colorless aleurone allows the endosperm color, either yellow or white, to be visible. Thus, there are 4 possible unique kernel color phenotypes (purple, red, yellow, and white).

5. **A.** The endosperm color genotype *yy* produces a white kernel when the aleurone phenotype is colorless. According to Table 14.1, the aleurone color genotype *rr* and the aleurone color inhibitor genotype *C'c* both produce a colorless aleurone, and the aleurone color modifier genotype *PP* has no effect on aleurone color.

6. **C.** The aleurone color modifier genotype *pp* changes a purple kernel to red. A purple kernel results from a genotype that includes at least one *R* and one *C*. *RRCCppyy* is the only answer choice that satisfies these conditions. The endosperm color genotype (*yy*) does not matter in this case because the aleurone color masks it.

7. **B.** The notation *P > p* in the Allele Relationships column of Table 14.1 indicates that the allele *P* is dominant to the allele *p*, and thus the phenotype of *p* will be masked when *P* is present. This is supported by the fact that the genotypes *PP* and *Pp* both produce the same phenotypic outcome, while *pp* produces a different phenotypic outcome.

8. **D.** Each kernel is a separate seed, or offspring, produced from the same pair of parents. Each seed gets the same genes, but the two specific alleles of each gene that each seed receives can be different.

9. **A.** According to Table 14.1, a white phenotype can only result from a genotype containing the endosperm color combination *yy*. *rrCCppyy* is the only genotype listed that corresponds to a white phenotype.

10. **B.** To have a yellow color, a kernel must have a colorless aleurone. Since both parents are red (and based on the relationships information in Table 14.1), the only genotype information known for certain about the kernels in Cross 2 is that each must have received the aleurone color modifier alleles *pp* from the parents. It is possible that the offspring kernels could receive from the parents some combination of *R* and *C* alleles that would produce a colorless aleurone, allowing the yellow endosperm to be visible.

11. **C.** The ratio can be found by dividing the number of red kernels by the number of yellow kernels. Using the data from Ear 1, 381 red kernels ÷ 126 yellow kernels = approximately 3. This means that the ratio of red to yellow is 3 to 1, or 3:1. This same ratio can be found using the data from Ear 2 or 3, or by combining all of the data from Cross 2.

12. **A.** Cross 1 produced 100% yellow kernels. Repeating this cross will provide the greatest chance of producing more yellow kernels. Since Crosses 2 and 3 both produced lower percentages of yellow kernels, repeating either or both crosses would lower the overall probability of producing yellow kernels.

13. **C.** Because yellow and white are two different alleles of the same gene (endosperm color), substituting a white parent for the yellow parent in Cross 3 would produce an ear with white kernels instead of yellow. Since endosperm color is masked by aleurone color, the kernels exhibiting purple aleurone color would not be affected by a change in endosperm color.

14. **C.** The passage presents corn seed color as a trait that is influenced by four different genes whose influences are listed in Table 14.1. The passage does not mention an ability to change phenotype over time or any other functions of genes besides the influence on seed color.

15. **D.** The only statement that can be completely supported by the information in the passage is that corn with a yellow phenotype must have a genotype that produces a colorless aleurone. Excluding mutations, all corn should have the same number and types of genes, though an exact genotype match to the yellow kernels in Cross 2 cannot be supported with the information available.

16. **C.** The amount of friction between the airplane's surface and the air molecules determines the amount of drag, or backward force, on the plane. Like any other type of friction, drag opposes the motion of the airplane.

17. **D.** Forces that oppose each other work on the same object but in opposite directions. Drag and thrust both act parallel to the motion of the airplane but in opposite directions. Lift and gravity also oppose each other.

18. **A.** Thrust and lift are both positive forces acting on the airplane, while drag and gravity are both negative forces. To keep a paper airplane in the air, the magnitude of the positive forces cannot be less than that of the negative forces.

19. **B.** According to the passage, students tested three airplanes in Experiment 1 and four airplanes in Experiment 3. The type of paper used, number of students involved, and number of trials performed were constants in all three experiments.

20. **B.** Based on the data in Table 14.3, no significant difference in horizontal distance can be identified among the three airplanes tested. In each trial, flat wings were the control group. Curving the wings upward appeared to cause a slight increase in distance in Trial 1, but a decrease in Trials 2 and 3. Curving the wings downward appeared to cause a slight decrease in distance in Trials 2 and 3, but no change in Trial 3.

21. **A.** Bending the wingtips downward would increase the effects of air resistance, or friction, on the airplane. This would increase the force of drag, which results from friction and opposes the airplane's motion.

22. **C.** Flat wingtips represents the control group in Experiment 2 because this was the design that was unaltered from the original. Bending the wingtips up and down created two experimental groups to be compared to the flat-winged control group.

23. **D.** Based on the data in Table 14.5, the paperclips placed midwing produced results closest to the results of the control group (no paperclips). This means that placing paperclips midwing had the least effect on the airplane's horizontal distance.

24. **C.** Flat wings (Experiment 1), flat wingtips (Experiment 2), and no paperclips (Experiment 3) represent the unaltered airplanes. The horizontal distance traveled by these three planes ranged from 9.5 m (Table 14.3) to 11.1 m (Table 14.4). The approximate average horizontal distance of 10.5 m falls within the data range for the unaltered airplanes. The calculated average horizontal distance is 10.62 m.

25. **A.** As shown in Table 14.4, curving the wingtips slightly upward increased the horizontal distance by approximately 2 m when compared to flat wingtips. This is the greatest positive effect of any variable in all three experiments.

26. **C.** The student graph displays data for three airplanes. The line representing each airplane maintains a positive slope, indicating that the horizontal distance for all three airplanes increased with each subsequent trial. This corresponds to the data displayed in Table 14.5.

27. **D.** In Experiment 3, adding paperclips to each paper airplane increased the plane's total weight. Adding weight to different locations along the airplanes altered their center of gravity by causing the location of the average weight to shift toward the paperclips.

28. **D.** As shown in Table 14.4, bending the wingtips slightly downward decreased the horizontal distance by approximately 7 m when compared to flat wingtips. This is the greatest change in horizontal distance caused by any variable in all three experiments.

29. **C.** In Experiment 1, the increase in horizontal distance for all three airplanes with each subsequent trial can most appropriately be attributed to the student throwing each airplane with an increasingly greater initial force. The force exerted by the student contributes to the amount of thrust on the airplane.

30. **B.** In Table 14.4, wingtips bent up produced the greatest horizontal distance. In Table 14.5, no paperclips produced the greatest horizontal distance. No identifiable trend is present in the distance data in Table 14.3. Therefore, the combination of flat wings (Table 14.3), wingtips bent up (Table 14.4), and no paperclips (Table 14.5) can be expected to produce the airplane with the greatest horizontal distance.

31. **A.** As illustrated in Figure 14.3, gram-positive bacteria have a cell wall composed of a thick layer of peptidoglycan and no outer membrane surrounding it. Gram-negative bacteria have a much thinner layer of peptidoglycan, surrounded by an outer membrane consisting of a lipid bilayer.

32. **C.** As illustrated in Figure 14.3, both gram-positive and gram-negative cells have a periplasmic space located between the peptidoglycan layer and the cell membrane below.

33. **B.** The lipid bilayer that makes up the outer membrane of gram-negative cells consists of an outer lipopolysaccharide layer and an inner phospholipid layer. Porins are transport channels that exist within this lipid bilayer, but they do not extend into the peptidoglycan layer. The thick peptidoglycan layer of gram-positive cells has no porins. This suggests that peptidoglycan is more permeable than the lipopolysaccharide-phospholipid bilayer, because the peptidoglycan layer does not contain any special transport channels, and both cell types must have the ability to transport substances into and out of the cell.

34. **D.** As explained in the passage, ethyl alcohol is used as a decolorizer, not as a stain. Crystal violet is the primary stain, and safranine and fuchsin are two common counterstains, used in Gram staining.

35. **D.** At the end of the Gram staining technique, cells appear either purple or red under the microscope. Gram-positive cells appear purple as a result of retaining the crystal violet stain. Gram-negative cells appear red because they do not retain the crystal violet and are subsequently stained by the counterstain.

36. **C.** The purpose of adding iodine in the Gram staining technique is to form a complex with crystal violet that will become trapped inside gram-positive cells during the decolorization step. Application of the primary stain, crystal violet, must occur before iodine is added to allow this complex to form.

37. **D.** Since gram-negative cells appear colorless after the decolorization step washes the primary stain out, the addition of a counterstain allows these cells to be seen more easily under a microscope. As noted in the passage, the red counterstain is lighter colored than the purple primary stain, so the addition of the counterstain does not affect the appearance of gram-positive cells.

38. **A.** Ethyl alcohol acts as a decolorizer in the Gram staining technique. As described in the passage, the decolorization step degrades the outer membrane of gram-negative bacteria. Since this outer membrane consists of a lipid bilayer, it is most reasonable to assume that a chain of lipids will degrade in the presence of ethyl alcohol.

39. **A.** According to the dichotomous key in Table 14.6, *Streptococcus* bacteria are gram-positive. Gram-positive bacteria appear purple when exposed to Gram staining.

40. **A.** Step 1a directs the user to continue to step 2 for gram-positive cells. Step 1b directs the user to continue to step 3 for gram-negative cells. Since the descriptions used in both steps 2 and 3 are identical, it

can be assumed that rod-shaped and sphere-shaped bacteria species exist in both groups.

41. **B.** Two of the genera (*Staphylococcus* and *Streptococcus*) in Table 14.6 are identified as gram-positive. Gram-positive bacteria have a thick peptidoglycan layer.

42. **A.** By following Table 14.6 beginning at step 1, it can be determined that the genus *Pseudomonas* consists of bacteria that are gram-negative (step 1b), rod-shaped (step 3a), and do not ferment lactose (step 5b).

43. **D.** By working backward through Table 14.6, it can be determined that both *Pseudomonas* and *Enterobacter* are gram-negative (step 1b) and rod-shaped (step 3a). *Pseudomonas* is identified as not fermenting lactose in step 5b. *Enterobacter* is identified as fermenting lactose (step 5a) and using citric acid (step 6a).

44. **B.** Based on Table 14.6, the genus *Escherichia* has gram-negative cells, which should appear red after Gram staining because they absorb the counterstain instead of retaining the primary stain. This means that colorless gram-negative cells most likely indicate an error in the counterstaining step.

45. **A.** According to the information in Table 14.6, *Staphylococcus* and *Streptococcus* are both gram-positive bacteria. Since gram-positive bacteria are less resistant than gram-negative bacteria to antibiotic treatment, it would be most effective to treat infections caused by bacteria in these genera with penicillin.

Chapter 15: Test 2

46. **C.** According to the information in Table 15.1, European honeybee and jack jumper ant males are both haploid. The male swamp wallaby has one less chromosome than the female. Slime mold has no notation indicating a variability in chromosome numbers among individuals of the species.

47. **D.** The coyote ($2n = 78$ chromosomes) and dog ($2n = 78$) both belong to the genus *Canis*. The horse ($2n = 64$) and the donkey ($2n = 62$) both belong to the genus *Equus*. The Bengal fox ($2n = 60$ chromosomes) and red fox ($2n = 34$) both belong to the genus *Vulpes*. These pairs of species demonstrate that two members of the same genus may have the same chromosome count (coyote and dog) or very different chromosome counts (Bengal fox and red fox).

48. **B.** As the diploid number of chromosomes decreases, the complexity of the organism does not decrease,

as exemplified by a human having fewer chromosomes than a potato. Neither does the complexity of the organism increase, as exemplified by oats having fewer chromosomes than a human. Therefore, based on the information in Table 15.1, no significant correlation can be identified between the complexity of organisms and their diploid chromosome count.

49. **B.** The adder's-tongue fern has the greatest diploid number of chromosomes ($2n = 1,260$) in Table 15.1. A fern is a plant, which belongs to the kingdom Plantae.

50. **A.** The dog has 78 diploid chromosomes, while a human has 46. The silkworm, *Bombyx mori*, falls between these numbers with a total of 54.

51. **B.** The zebra fish and pineapple both have 50 diploid chromosomes. This means that total chromosomes are contained in the nucleus of each somatic cell of both organisms.

52. **D.** The data in Table 15.1 indicates that a wide variability of chromosome counts exists, even among related species. Because of this, the diploid chromosome count of a new species cannot be predicted easily without more information. Genetic testing such as karyotyping can be used to positively identify the number of chromosomes for each species.

53. **C.** Gametes contain the haploid (n) number of chromosomes. Table 15.1 identifies the diploid ($2n$) number of chromosomes that are present in an organism's somatic cells. The horse (*Equus ferus caballus*) has a diploid number of $2n = 64$. This means the haploid number in gametes would be $n = 32$.

54. **C.** Table 15.1 indicates that male European honeybees are haploid rather than diploid. This means a male has n chromosomes, while a female has $2n$ chromosomes. Since the diploid number of chromosomes is 32, $n = 16$. Therefore, females have 16 more total chromosomes than males.

55. **D.** The total number of chromosomes in a somatic cell is referred to as the diploid number. The diploid number is represented by the term $2n$, in which n represents the number of chromosomes in a gamete from the same organism. The number of chromosomes in a somatic cell is twice the number of chromosomes in a gamete.

56. **C.** As stated in the passage, the gametes of most species contain one complete set of chromosomes, and the somatic cells contain two complete sets. In polyploid species, the somatic cells contain more than two sets of chromosomes, but the gametes still contain half of the total number of chromosomes in a

somatic cell. This means a gamete will contain more than one complete set of chromosomes.

57. **A.** Table 15.1 indicates that alfalfa is a tetraploid species. The prefix *tetra* means "four." Therefore, as described in the passage, the somatic cells of a tetraploid species have four complete sets of chromosomes.

58. **B.** The monoploid number (x) identifies the number of chromosomes an organism has in one set. For the hexaploid oat species *Avena sativa*, $6x = 42$. This means $x = 7$, or the number of chromosomes present in one set is 7.

59. **A.** Table 15.1 indicates that the potato (*Solanum tuberosum*) is a tetraploid. Tetraploid organisms have four complete sets of chromosomes. As explained in the passage, the diploid number ($2n$) is always twice the haploid number (n). $2n$ always represents the total number of chromosomes in a somatic cell, regardless of whether the organism exhibits any type of polyploidy. Since a tetraploid has four complete sets of chromosomes, the total number of chromosomes ($2n$) must be divided by 4 to determine the monoploid number (x).

60. **B.** According to Scientist 1, increased temperatures will help some crops and harm others. The growth rate for many crops increases with temperature, which is beneficial to those crops and the agriculture industry. However, increased temperature suppresses the reproductive ability of some crops, which endangers their survival.

61. **D.** Based on the opinion of Scientist 1, a crop has its greatest yield close to its optimal growth temperature. Since average temperatures are predicted to rise as a result of climate change, plants with higher optimal growth temperatures are more likely to produce higher yields than those with lower optimal growth temperatures because they can better withstand the heat.

62. **D.** Scientist 2 discussed the potential for crop destruction due to an increase in the frequency of flooding. Scientist 1 did not discuss the effects of flooding or any other extreme weather events.

63. **C.** Scientist 2 discussed an increase in the production of weeds, pests, and fungi in response to the effects of climate change. Only Scientist 1 addressed the potential effect of climate change on seed production.

64. **A.** In Scientist 1's opinion, increases in average temperature and carbon dioxide levels will have positive effects on some types of crops and negative effects on others. Scientist 2 only discusses the negative effects of these increases.

65. **B.** Scientist 2 states that increased carbon dioxide levels will allow weeds, pests, and fungi to thrive. The increased presence of these organisms is predicted to impact crop yields negatively by competing with and damaging crops.

66. **B.** In Scientist 2's opinion, climate change will lead to an increase in agricultural pests. An observed increase in pesticide use would provide evidence to support this opinion.

67. **B.** Scientist 1 states that once the optimal growth temperature is surpassed, crop yields will decline. Though crops will still grow in the higher-than-optimal temperatures, the amount of growth will be reduced.

68. **D.** Both scientists agree that increasing average temperatures will be beneficial to some organisms, though they do not agree on the particular organisms that will benefit. Scientist 1 suggests that increasing average temperatures will increase the growth rate of many crops, whereas Scientist 2 suggests that they will increase the growth of weeds, pests, and fungi, which will inhibit the growth of crops.

69. **D.** Scientist 1 states that increased carbon dioxide levels will increase crop yields. It can be inferred that this change would be due to an increase in the rate at which crops carry out photosynthesis, since increased food production would lead to increased growth.

70. **A.** Scientist 2 discusses the northward spread of weeds and pests as being detrimental to northern crops. While pests will directly damage crops, weeds will compete with crops for resources such as soil nutrients and water.

71. **D.** According to Scientist 1, higher average temperatures and carbon dioxide levels will have direct, positive effects on many crops. This hypothesis can best be tested by gathering data on these two variables and the crop yields that result.

72. **A.** According to Scientist 2, increased temperatures and carbon dioxide levels will cause the ranges of more heat-tolerant southern species to expand northward. As southern species expand northward, the ranges of northern species will likely narrow due to the increase in competition and new pests.

73. **B.** Scientist 1 states that an increase in carbon dioxide causes crop yields to increase. However, once the optimal growth temperature for a crop is surpassed, crop yields will decline. Graph B best matches the scientist's description, with the maximum of Graph C representing the point at which the optimal growth temperature has been reached.

74. **B.** According to the photosynthesis equation, plants take in carbon from the environment in the form of carbon dioxide. This atmospheric carbon is used to produce organic carbon in the form of carbohydrates like glucose.

75. **D.** According to the photosynthesis equation, plants use sunlight to convert carbon dioxide and water into a useable form of carbon (glucose). The by-product of this process is oxygen, which is released back into the environment.

76. **B.** The passage states that each leaf was initially exposed to a light intensity of $300\,\mu E/m^2/s$ for a period of time to stimulate photosynthesis. According to Figure 15.5, this initial $300\,\mu E/m^2/s$ exposure began at approximately 5 minutes and ended at approximately 25 minutes, for a total duration of 20 minutes.

77. **A.** As shown in Figure 15.7, the air temperature increased continuously over the course of the study. This continuous increase can best be attributed to the increase in light intensity over the same time. It can be inferred that increasing the intensity output of a light source also increases the heat output.

78. **A.** The reactants of the photosynthesis equation are carbon dioxide and water. Figure 15.6 depicts the change in carbon dioxide concentration as recorded by sensors within the chamber over the course of the study.

79. **C.** According to the passage, students manipulated the light intensity within the chamber and observed the effects on carbon dioxide concentration. This means that light intensity, depicted in Figure 15.5, is the independent variable.

80. **D.** The lower the concentration measured within the chamber, the faster the leaf is absorbing carbon dioxide. This means that the lowest point on the graph in Figure 15.6, occurring at approximately 50 minutes, represents the highest absorption rate. According to Figure 15.5, the leaf is being exposed to a light intensity of $1,000\,\mu E/m^2/s$ at 50 minutes.

81. **B.** In Table 15.2, the mean carbon dioxide exchange rate was the highest for the sunflower plant as compare to the other three plant types. This means that sunflower leaves absorb carbon dioxide fastest. Since carbon dioxide and oxygen are exchanged in a 1:1 ratio, it can also be stated that sunflower leaves release oxygen fastest.

82. **C.** According to Table 15.2, rhoeo leaves showed the smallest standard deviation (1.3) across 10 trials of all four plant species studied. A low standard deviation indicates a low amount of variability across trials.

83. **C.** The passage states that carbon dioxide and oxygen are exchanged in a 1:1 ratio during photosynthesis. As the carbon dioxide concentration in the chamber decreases, the oxygen concentration increases in direct proportion. Therefore, the oxygen concentration graph, just like the light intensity graph in Figure 15.5, would be the inverse of the carbon dioxide concentration graph in Figure 15.6.

84. **B.** In Table 15.2, the mean carbon dioxide exchange rate for pothos leaves is 6.0 μmol/m^2/s. The means for both sunflower leaves (17.4 μmol/m^2/s) and water hyacinth leaves (14.3 μmol/m^2/s) are greater. A greater carbon dioxide exchange rate indicates a greater rate of photosynthesis.

85. **C.** Figures 15.5 and 15.6 indicate that light intensity and carbon dioxide concentration within the chamber show an inverse correlation. This means that light intensity directly correlates to carbon dioxide absorption and therefore photosynthesis rate.

86. **A.** In Table 15.2, the highest carbon dioxide exchange rate was recorded for the sunflower leaf (27 μmol/m^2/s) during Trial 3. A higher value indicates a faster exchange rate.

87. **A.** As indicated in Figures 15.5 and 15.6, a plant's rate of photosynthesis depends on the light intensity in its environment. Plants with a low maximum rate of photosynthesis have a low need for light, making them more tolerant to low-light environments. In Table 15.2, the mean carbon dioxide exchange rate was observed to be the lowest for rhoeo leaves, at 3.5 μE/m^2/s. A low exchange rate indicates a low rate of photosynthesis.

88. **D.** Figures 15.5 and 15.6 indicate carbon dioxide concentration within the chamber is lowest when light intensity is highest. This means that the maximum carbon dioxide exchange rates identified in Table 15.2 were most likely recorded at 50 minutes, when light intensity was at its maximum (1,000 μE/m^2/s) and carbon dioxide concentration was at its minimum (approximately 880 ppm).

Chapter 16: Test 3

89. **D.** Four possible ABO blood types (A, B, AB, and O) are listed in Table 16.1, and two possible Rh blood types (Rh+ or Rh−) are listed in Table 16.2. Each of the ABO blood types may be paired with either of the Rh blood types, resulting in eight possible medical blood types.

90. **B.** As seen in Table 16.1, each ABO blood type is named for the antigen(s) present on the red blood cells. Blood type A has A antigens, and so on. Type O is so named because it has no antigens.

91. **A.** According to the passage, a cell's antigens serve as a unique chemical signature that distinguishes it from other cell types. This allows the body to determine the identity of a wide variety of different cells.

92. **A.** As seen in Table 16.2, blood identified as Rh+ contains the Rh antigen but not the Rh antibodies.

93. **B.** Blood type is identified by the antigens present on the red blood cells. Since only B antigens are present, the blood type would be B−. The presence of anti-A and anti-Rh antibodies means that A and Rh antigens are absent.

94. **C.** Figure 16.1 indicates that 9% of the general population has type B+ blood and 2% has type B− blood, for a total of 11% of the general population with type B blood.

95. **D.** According to Figure 16.1, only 1% of the general population has the AB− blood type.

96. **A.** A higher percentage of individuals of Asian ethnicity have B+ blood (25%) than any other ethnicity. It can therefore be inferred that this blood type is more common in Asia than in the other three continents.

97. **C.** A antigens are present on the red blood cells of both type A and type AB blood. The sum of type A+ (33%), type A− (6%), type AB+ (4%), and type AB− (1%) is 44%.

98. **B.** In Table 16.3, 53% of Hispanic individuals, or a little over half, have O+ blood. The percentage of the general population that is Hispanic and has this blood type cannot be determined from the data provided.

99. **A.** Based on the data in Table 16.3, an individual of African-American ethnicity has an 18% chance of having B+ blood. This is greater than the 9% of the general population with the same blood type.

100. **C.** As illustrated in Table 16.1, AB blood contains A and B antigens but no antibodies. Since no antibodies are present, the antigens on the donated blood will not be attacked, leading to no immune reaction to the donated type A blood.

101. **B.** As illustrated in Tables 16.1 and 16.2, blood type O− has no antigens on its red blood cells. If no antigens are present, there is nothing to trigger antibodies to attack.

102. **C.** An individual can safely receive a transfusion of his or her own blood type because the donor blood contains the exact same antigens (A antigens in this case) as are already present, triggering no antibody attack. Any individual can also receive a transfusion of O– blood because it is the universal donor, containing no antigens at all.

103. **C.** According to Table 16.3, 1% of the Caucasian population has AB– blood. Figure 16.1 indicates that 1% of the general population also has this blood type.

104. **A.** According to the passage, a DNA ladder is loaded into the first well in the agarose gel. The DNA samples being studied are loaded in the subsequent wells.

105. **D.** In Figure 16.2, the cathode is shown at the top of the diagram and the anode is at the bottom. When the power supply is turned on, the resulting electric current causes the DNA samples loaded in the wells to travel away from the negative charge produced by the cathode and toward the positive charge of the anode.

106. **B.** A DNA ladder is a solution containing DNA fragments of known sizes. When an electrophoresis procedure is run, the migration of these fragments provides a reference by which to estimate the sizes of DNA fragments in the samples.

107. **A.** Since Table 16.4 identifies the voltage range as 0.25–7 V/cm, a voltage of 6 V/cm is relatively high. Table 16.4 indicates that a high voltage may cause smearing or poor resolution of large DNA fragments.

108. **C.** In Table 16.5, a 0.5% agarose concentration is recommended to resolve DNA fragments of 1–30 kb, or a 29 kb range. This range decreases incrementally as agarose concentration increases. A 1.5% concentration is recommended to resolve DNA fragments from 0.2–0.5 kb, which is only a 0.3 kb range.

109. **C.** Based on the information in Table 16.5, DNA fragments of 0.5–0.7 kb are relatively small. Table 16.4 indicates that a high agarose concentration provides a sharper resolution of small DNA fragments, and low voltage may cause fragments of less than 1 kb to diffuse in the gel. This means that a high agarose concentration (1.2%) and a high voltage (5 V/cm) would provide the best results for DNA fragments of this size. Table 16.5 indicates that the highest agarose concentration (1.5%) is only appropriate for fragments smaller than 0.5 kb.

110. **A.** According to the passage, large DNA fragments travel more slowly than small fragments. This means the largest DNA fragments will appear closest to the cathode, because they will have traveled the least distance from the wells.

111. **B.** The passage indicates that Allele 2 is larger than both Alleles 1 and 3. Therefore, Allele 2 will travel through the agarose gel more slowly than the other two.

112. **D.** According to the passage, a single band that appears darker is an indicator of two copies of the same allele. Individuals E and K both appear to have two copies of Allele 2, while N and O appear to have two copies of Allele 1.

113. **A.** Based on information in the passage, Allele 2 is the largest of the three alleles. Therefore, Allele 2 is indicated by the band that has traveled the least distance down the gel. The size of this band is approximately 3.0 kb.

114. **B.** The combination of Alleles 1 and 2 occurs most frequently in Figure 16.3, appearing in a total of six lanes (Lanes A, B, D, I, L, and M).

115. **D.** In Figure 16.3, all three alleles appear to be present in the sample in Lane J. The most reasonable explanation is that this lane contains DNA from more than one individual, since each individual can carry only two copies of one gene.

116. **C.** In Figure 16.3, all allele combinations (Alleles 1 and 1, 1 and 2, 1 and 3, etc.) are represented in at least one lane except the combination of two copies of Allele 3.

117. **C.** The three alleles in Figure 16.3 appear to be approximately 2–5 kb in size. The most appropriate agarose concentration for this size range is 1.0%. A higher concentration of agarose is more appropriate for DNA fragments that are smaller than these, and a lower concentration is more appropriate for larger DNA fragments.

118. **D.** According to Table 16.4, low agarose concentration and low voltage both cause longer run times (possibly over multiple days). Therefore, DNA fragments should migrate most slowly when agarose concentration and voltage are both at their minimum. This corresponds to an agarose concentration of 0.5% and a voltage of 0.25 V/cm.

119. **B.** A *stimulus* is a change in the environment, such as the sounding of a tone or the appearance of an image. A *response* is the individual's reaction to the stimulus. The experiment descriptions identify the

response time as the time between the sounds of a tone or the appearance of an image (stimulus) and the student pressing the spacebar (response).

120. **A.** In Experiment 1, the student pressed the spacebar in response to the sounding of a tone, so the sounding of the tone was the stimulus.

121. **D.** Both Experiments 2 and 3 tested response time to auditory and visual stimuli. In Experiment 2, three successive trials were performed using an auditory stimulus, and then three were performed using a visual stimulus. In Experiment 3, the type of stimulus alternated with each new trial. All other conditions were held constant between the two experiments.

122. **D.** According to Table 16.7, the response time to an auditory stimulus is consistently lower (faster) than the response time to a visual stimulus. A faster response time indicates that auditory processing occurs faster than visual processing, suggesting that the sense of hearing is more acute.

123. **D.** All three experiments used a stimulus duration of 400 ms for at least some trials. In Experiment 1, trials 4 through 6 used a 400 ms tone length. A 400 ms stimulus duration was used on all trials during Experiments 2 and 3.

124. **B.** The fastest reaction time was 142 ms. This occurred during Trial 5 of Experiment 1 as well as Trials 2 and 3 of Experiment 2. All three of these trials recorded response times to an auditory stimulus lasting a duration of 400 ms.

125. **A.** In Table 16.6, Trials 1 through 3 were conducted using a 200 ms tone length and Trials 4 through 6 used a 400 ms tone length. The average response times were approximately 10 ms faster for the trials using the longer tone.

126. **C.** In Tables 16.7 and 16.8, the response times for the auditory stimulus were consistently more than 40 ms faster than for the visual stimulus. It can be inferred that a faster response time is the result of a signal reaching the brain faster.

127. **A.** The average response times for auditory and visual stimuli both increased (got slower) as Experiment 3 progressed. The average response times in Table 16.8 are also higher than those for both stimuli in Table 16.7.

128. **A.** The response times recorded for auditory stimuli across all three experiments range from 142–158 ms. It is therefore reasonable to infer that the typical auditory response time range is 140–160 ms.

129. **C.** According to the description of Experiment 2, 6 total trials were conducted, and each trial consisted of 10 stimulus-response cycles. This means that a total of 60 responses to a stimulus were recorded during Experiment 2.

130. **C.** Both auditory and visual response times increased over the course of Experiment 3. Therefore, the graph for the data in Table 16.8 should consist of two lines, each with a small positive slope. Response time to the visual stimulus was consistently higher than to the auditory stimulus, so the visual line should be above the auditory line.

131. **B.** The student's new experimental design should be the same as in Experiment 1, but using a visual stimulus (image) instead of an auditory one (tone). The student can then test the difference in response time to an image shown for 200 ms versus an image shown for 400 ms.

132. **D.** The lowest auditory response time occurred during Trial 1 of Experiment 1. The actual response time was 158 ms.

133. **C.** In Tables 16.6 and 16.7, the response time for a particular stimulus decreased (got faster) over subsequent trials. In Table 16.8, the response time for a particular stimulus increased (got slower) as the type of stimulus alternated with each trial. This suggests that repetitive exposure to the same stimulus improves an individual's reaction time.

Chapter 17: Test 4

134. **B.** Organic molecules are found only in the bodies or products of living organisms. Carbohydrates, lipids, proteins, and nucleic acids are all produced by living organisms. Although living organisms are composed largely of water, water is inorganic because it is not produced by living organisms.

135. **D.** Both the primordial soup theory and the hydrothermal vents theory assume that organic molecules can be produced by reactions that cause the rearrangement of atoms in certain inorganic molecules. Scientists believe this to be an important step toward the existence of life on the earth.

136. **A.** In Figure 17.1, the heat source is located underneath the small sphere that simulates the water in the earth's oceans. According to the diagram, the ocean (small sphere) supplies water vapor for the reactions in the atmosphere (large sphere). The heat source facilitates the production of water vapor.

137. **A.** According to the passage, ammonia was believed to be a major inorganic component of the primitive atmosphere that contributed to the production of organic molecules.

138. **B.** In Figure 17.1, the small sphere simulates the ocean, which provides water vapor for the primitive atmosphere. The actual reaction that produces organic molecules occurs as the electrical current is passed through the large sphere that simulates the primitive atmosphere. The condenser then cools the gases in the atmosphere, allowing newly produced organic molecules to condense into solution and travel to the trap for sampling.

139. **D.** The passage states that the minimum and maximum temperatures around hydrothermal vents are 4°C and 300°C, and organic molecules are only stable within a narrow temperature window. An optimal temperature range of 4°C to 25°C meets both of these criteria.

140. **C.** Both theories identify water as playing an integral role in the development of organic compounds on Earth. The primordial soup theory identifies water as one of the four major components of the primitive atmosphere. The hydrothermal vents theory identifies deep ocean water as the site of organic compound formation.

141. **C.** The two theories disagree on the energy source used to fuel the reactions that originally produced organic compounds. The primordial soup theory identifies atmospheric lightning as the energy source, whereas the hydrothermal vents theory argues that the energy came from within the earth.

142. **D.** The primordial soup theory is based on the assumption that the primitive atmosphere was mainly composed of methane, ammonia, hydrogen, and water vapor. Helium is not believed to have made up a significant percentage of that atmosphere.

143. **C.** The presence of a constant electrical charge is a potential limitation of the Miller-Urey apparatus, because it causes experimental conditions to differ from the conditions scientists believe actually existed in the primitive atmosphere. The constant charge simulates a constant supply of lightning that scientists do not believe existed.

144. **C.** The hydrothermal vents theory identifies the location of organic molecule formation as the deep ocean. Hot gases and energy from inside the earth enter the deep ocean through hydrothermal vents. The theory suggests that organic molecules are then produced within the temperature gradient generated at hydrothermal vents.

145. **B.** The Miller-Urey experiment supports the primordial soup theory because it successfully produced organic compounds under the same conditions as scientists believed existed on primitive Earth. The experiment was specifically designed to investigate this theory and does not provide direct evidence to support or reject the hydrothermal vents theory.

146. **A.** Based on the passage, the constant release of hot gases into the cold deep ocean water produces a temperature gradient. This temperature gradient is believed to provide sufficient conditions for the production of organic molecules.

147. **B.** The primordial soup theory assumes that the compositions of the primitive and current atmospheres vary widely. This assumption led to the development of the Miller-Urey experiment, which produced various organic molecules from the compounds thought to be most abundant in the primitive atmosphere. The current atmosphere is composed mostly of nitrogen and oxygen.

148. **D.** The passage defines the normal boiling point as the temperature at which vapor pressure and standard atmospheric pressure are equal. The normal boiling point of a substance does not change.

149. **B.** The boiling point of a compound is always the temperature at which the liquid's vapor pressure is equal to atmospheric pressure. A change in atmospheric pressure results in a similar change in the vapor pressure required to induce boiling.

150. **B.** According to Figure 17.3, hexane will boil at 0°C when the vapor pressure is decreased to approximately 50 mmHg. The vapor pressures required to boil heptane and octane at 0°C are both less than 50 mmHg. The vapor pressure required to boil pentane at 0°C is approximately 200 mmHg.

151. **D.** In Figure 17.3, the normal boiling point for pentane is about 36°C. Increasing the temperature to 40°C requires an increase in vapor pressure as well. Thus, 850 mmHg is the best estimation for this vapor pressure.

152. **A.** The difference between normal boiling points for each consecutive pair of alkanes in Figure 17.3 is about 30°C. Adding 30°C to the boiling point of heptane (98.4°C) provides an approximate value of 128°C for octane's normal boiling point.

153. **A.** In Figure 17.4, the alkanes are near the alkenes and alkynes. These three functional groups exhibit

similar boiling point trends in the graphs, which happen to be the lowest of the functional groups included.

154. **C.** According to Figure 17.4, a 2-carbon alcohol has an approximate boiling point of 75°C. Figure 17.4 indicates that a 4-carbon ketone would have approximately the same boiling point.

155. **C.** The passage indicates that stronger bonds require higher temperatures to break. The alkanes, alkenes, and alkynes have the lowest boiling points in Figure 17.4. The lowest boiling points mean that the bonds (Van der Waals) in these functional groups are the easiest to break.

156. **A.** According to its molecular formula, caproic acid contains six carbon atoms. Figure 17.4 illustrates that a 6-carbon carboxylic acid will have a boiling point of approximately 200°C.

157. **B.** According to the passage, strong bonds require higher boiling points to break, while weak bonds require lower boiling points. Carboxylic acids have the highest boiling points (Figure 17.4) and therefore the strongest bonds (double hydrogen). Ordering the functional groups in Figure 17.4 from highest to lowest boiling points allows for the identification of bonds from strongest to weakest.

158. **D.** In Table 17.2, the molecular weights of each molecule are similar, but the boiling points are not. This indicates that molecular weight does not directly affect boiling point.

159. **A.** In Table 17.2, n-Butanol contains four carbon atoms and has a boiling point of 117°C. In Figure 17.4, a boiling point of 117°C most closely resembles the boiling point of a 4-carbon member of the alcohol group.

160. **C.** Based on the number of carbon atoms it contains (three) and its high boiling point (140°C), Figure 17.4 can be used to identify propanoic acid as a 3-carbon carboxylic acid. According to Table 17.1, carboxylic acids contain double hydrogen bonds.

161. **D.** Based on the data in Table 17.1 and Figure 17.4, double hydrogen bonds are the strongest, followed by single hydrogen bonds, dipole-dipole bonds, and Van der Waals bonds. At the same vapor pressure, stronger bonds require a higher temperature to break than weaker bonds. Since single hydrogen bonds are stronger than dipole-dipole bonds, single hydrogen bonds require a higher boiling point.

162. **B.** In both Figures 17.3 and 17.4, the boiling point increases as the number of carbon atoms increases within a specific functional group. This means the number of carbon atoms can be used to predict the relative boiling point for compounds containing a known number of carbon atoms in a known functional group. A common number of carbon atoms among compounds from different groups does not necessarily indicate similarities in boiling point.

163. **A.** A closed ecosystem is characterized by a lack of migration into and out of it. There are several possible causes, one of which is geographic isolation. The passage states that Shebay Park consists of a group of isolated islands. Since the islands are separated from the mainland, migration to and from this ecosystem is rare.

164. **B.** In Figure 17.5, the peccary population is shown to feed on four different types of plants. A consumer that feeds exclusively on plant matter is termed a *herbivore.*

165. **C.** In Figure 17.6, the peak in the jaguar population occurred around 1990. In this year, the population consisted of 50 individuals.

166. **A.** In Figure 17.6, the smallest value for the peccary population was 500 individuals. This occurred in roughly 2006.

167. **A.** According to Figure 17.6, the peccary population experienced many consecutive years of positive population growth beginning around 1990. Immediately preceding this growth period, the jaguar population was devastated by exposure to feline leukemia (1989). It can be inferred that the sharp decline in the jaguar population caused a decrease in predatory pressure on the peccary population, thereby allowing the latter population to increase.

168. **D.** Consumers in an ecosystem are identified according to how far removed they are from the ecosystem's producers (plants). Primary consumers are herbivores that feed only on plants. Secondary consumers feed on primary consumers. According to the food web in Figure 17.5, two secondary consumers exist in the ecosystem—the fox and the jaguar.

169. **D.** The food web in Figure 17.5 shows that the nutria and the duck share common food sources and a common predator with the peccary. These similarities indicate that the three populations occupy similar niches within the ecosystem.

170. **B.** In Figure 17.6, the sharp declines in the jaguar (1990) and peccary (2004) populations coincide with the occurrence of rare environmental events. The passage indicates that the 1990 decline in the

jaguar population can be attributed to the introduction of feline leukemia in 1989, and the 2004 decline in the peccary population can be attributed to severe winter conditions and a tick outbreak. Each of these events reduced the immediate ability of individuals to survive, resulting in a population size that was drastically reduced in a matter of two years.

171. **A.** The passage states that an outbreak of ticks occurred in 2004. This coincides with the severe reduction in peccary population size beginning that year, suggesting that the parasite outbreak contributed to the decrease in the population.

172. **D.** Several factors influencing the peccary population size are discussed in the passage, including interactions with other species and environmental conditions.

173. **B.** While most species in the food web (Figure 17.5) are directly linked to the peccary, the squirrel shares no direct connection with that population. Squirrels and peccaries have no common predators or food sources; therefore, the squirrel should be less affected by a change in the peccary population than other species in the food web.

Chapter 18: Test 5

174. **B.** An invasive species is both non-native to an ecosystem and harmful in some way. Non-native species that move into a new ecosystem will disrupt that ecosystem by competing with native species for resources and introducing new feeding relationships into the food web.

175. **C.** The passage indicates that water hyacinths are able to withstand fluctuations in pH, but it does not indicate that these plants induce changes in pH. Water hyacinths upset freshwater ecosystems in a number of ways, but not by altering pH.

176. **B.** In Table 18.1, the final weed combination studied was the combination of all four weed species. This same combination is not present in Table 18.2.

177. **A.** Plant density is identified in the description of Study 1 as the total number of water hyacinth plants within a sample area. A sample area was defined as 1 square meter.

178. **D.** The sample areas in which water hyacinth was found growing alone provide the control group for Study 1. These sample areas indicated water hyacinth growth when there was no competition from other weed species.

179. **C.** In Study 1, *Justicia* sp. had a slightly more negative impact on water hyacinth fresh weight than did *V. cupsidata*. *V. cupsidata* exhibited the most negative effect on all other growth parameters in Study 1.

180. **C.** In Table 18.1, the weed combination of *E. crassipes* and *Commelina* sp. exhibits the least difference from the control group (*E. crassipes* alone) out of all possible combinations. This means that *Commelina* sp. exerts the least competitive pressure on water hyacinth.

181. **D.** In Table 18.2, water hyacinths grown alone were shown to have an average height of 8.69 cm. When grown with *Commelina* sp. and *Justicia* sp. in a greenhouse, the average water hyacinth height was shown to increase to 8.8 cm and 8.88 cm, respectively. The increase in growth suggests a positive effect of these competitor species on water hyacinth height.

182. **A.** The number of leaves per plant for a water hyacinth grown alone was higher in Table 18.2 than in Table 18.1. The values for fresh weight and plant height were both much lower in Table 18.2 than in Table 18.1.

183. **A.** In the description of Study 1, total biomass was described as being calculated by multiplying plant density by fresh weight. Since plant density is a component of total biomass and was not recorded in Study 2, total biomass could not be calculated for this study.

184. **A.** In both studies, *V. cupsidata* was shown to decrease water hyacinth growth by all parameters, except for fresh weight in Study 1. These data support the claim that *V. cupsidata* has the most negative impact on water hyacinth growth.

185. **B.** In Table 18.2, all three competitor weeds were shown to reduce water hyacinth fresh weight, thus leading to lighter plants than when water hyacinth grew alone. For both plant height and leaves per plant, at least one competitor species was shown to increase water hyacinth growth.

186. **C.** In Study 2, scientists removed young weed plants from the Kagera River and grew them in a greenhouse. Within the greenhouse, the researchers had more control over the environmental conditions to which the plants were exposed, thus controlling any environmental factors (other than competitor species) that may influence water hyacinth growth.

187. **D.** In Table 18.1, the average fresh weight of water hyacinth growing in the presence of all three competitor species was 342 g. This value is approximately equal to the mean (average) water hyacinth

fresh weight of 368 g when growing in the presence of each competitor species individually.

188. **D.** Throughout both studies, *V. cupsidata* consistently showed the most negative effect on water hyacinth growth. This is true for all growth parameters except one (fresh weight in Study 1). *Commelina* sp. and *Justicia* sp. both showed mixed effects on water hyacinth growth, depending on the growth parameter observed and the study environment. Therefore, increasing the presence of *V. cupsidata* alone can be predicted to significantly reduce the water hyacinth population.

189. **D.** The passage provides the formula for gravitational potential energy as $PE_g = m \times g \times h$, in which m represents the object's mass, g represents acceleration due to gravity, and h represents the object's height above the ground. Acceleration due to gravity does not change on Earth. Therefore, g is a constant.

190. **A.** Based on the formula $PE_g = m \times g \times h$, increasing the value of h will cause a similar increase in the value of $PE_{(g)}$. This means the total gravitational potential energy of an object will double when the object's height is doubled.

191. **B.** As stated in the passage, the amount of potential energy at the beginning (point A) and end (point C) of the rollercoaster would be equal in a frictionless environment. This is explained by the law of conservation of energy, which states that energy cannot be lost or gained within a system. For the marble to have the same potential energy at points A and C, the rollercoaster must have the same drop height and hill height.

192. **C.** As stated in the description of Experiment 1, altering the drop height changed the marble's initial amount of gravitational potential energy because, according to the formula provided in the passage, an object's gravitational potential energy is dependent on the object's height.

193. **B.** The maximum drop height used in both experiments was 1.2 m. This drop height was tested in Trial 4 of Experiment 1 and held constant for Experiment 2.

194. **C.** In Table 18.3, drop height and hill height exhibit a direct relationship. As drop height increases, so does hill height. Figure 18.4 provides a visual representation of this direct relationship between the two variables.

195. **A.** Table 18.4 indicates that when drop height was held constant, a longer horizontal distance required a shorter hill height. This means that although each

marble began at the same height, marbles that traveled a longer track had more energy transformed to heat and sound through frictional dissipation. This increase in frictional dissipation left less kinetic energy available to propel the marble as far up the hill.

196. **D.** The smallest hill height recorded in Experiment 2 was 0.97 m. This height was recorded during Trial 3 as the result of a drop height of 1.2 m and a horizontal distance of 1.5 m.

197. **D.** In Experiment 1, drop height was the independent variable. Students varied the drop height to determine the effects on hill height. In Experiment 2, drop height was held constant to determine the effects of horizontal distance on hill height. Neither experiment measured drop height as the dependent variable.

198. **A.** To study the relationship between marble mass and hill height, students should hold drop height constant, with marble mass becoming the independent variable and hill height remaining the dependent variable. To accommodate this change in the data table, an additional column for marble mass should be added, just as the horizontal distance column was added in Table 18.4.

199. **A.** As stated in the description of Experiment 1, Point A indicates the starting height (or drop height) of the marble. Because of frictional dissipation, the marble has the greatest gravitational potential energy at Point A. Once the marble begins moving along the track, frictional dissipation begins transforming some of the marble's energy to heat and sound, leaving less energy available for the marble itself.

200. **B.** Changes in a dependent variable are measured to determine the effects of the independent variable. In both experiments, hill height was the dependent variable. Changes in hill height provided information on the effects of the independent variables on initial gravitational potential energy (Experiment 1) and frictional dissipation (Experiment 2).

201. **C.** Mechanical energy is the energy related to an object's motion and position, and it consists of the sum of an object's potential and kinetic energy. During the rollercoaster experiments, mechanical energy was transformed between potential and kinetic forms. Frictional dissipation also caused some mechanical energy to be transformed to thermal energy (heat) and sound. No transformation to chemical energy occurred.

202. **B.** In Table 18.4, hill height decreased as horizontal distance increased. Therefore, increasing the longest

horizontal distance in Trial 3 (1.5 m) to 1.75 m would further decrease the hill height.

203. **A.** According to Table 18.5, all organisms in the phylogenetic tree are members of the class Mammalia. This means that all of the organisms are mammals.

204. **C.** *Panthera pardus* is the scientific name for leopard. Table 18.5 identifies the leopard as belonging to the family Felidae.

205. **B.** All organisms listed in Table 18.5 share a common kingdom, phylum, class, and order. The organisms diverge into different taxa beginning with the family level.

206. **D.** Table 18.5 lists *Canis latrans* as the genus and species of the coyote.

207. **C.** In a phylogenetic tree, a species is most closely related to the species with which it shares the most recent common ancestor, or node. According to Figure 18.6, the European otter *(Lutra lutra)* shares the most recent common ancestor with *Taxidea taxus*.

208. **B.** In a phylogenetic tree, the number of common ancestors shared by two species is indicated by the number of nodes shared by those species. In Figure 18.6, *Panthera pardus* diverges from the other four species at the very first node, indicating that it shares only one common ancestor with the other four species.

209. **D.** The passage states that the length of the horizontal lines on a phylogenetic tree indicates the relative divergence time between species. *Canis latrans* and *Canis lupus* are connected to their most recent common ancestor by the shortest lines, indicating that these two species diverged most recently.

210. **A.** The passage identifies an extant species as one that is currently living. *Taxidea taxus*, listed along the right side of the phylogenetic tree in Figure 18.6, is currently living.

211. **B.** The seven-level classification system used in Table 18.5 classifies organisms using a hierarchical system that goes from broadest grouping (kingdom) to most specific (species). As shown in Table 18.5, organisms that share a certain taxonomic level also share the same higher taxonomic levels, but they may diverge in lower levels. This means that species belonging to the same order must also belong to the same phylum and kingdom, but they may belong to a different order.

212. **C.** The lynx belongs to the family Felidae. *Panthera pardus* also belongs to this family. Based on the phylogenetic tree in Figure 18.6, the lynx shares the most recent common ancestor with *Panthera pardus*.

213. **D.** The lynx belongs to a different family than the gray wolf, but the same taxa for order and above. This means that the lynx and gray wolf share four common taxonomic levels.

214. **B.** The five species in Table 18.5 belong to three different families, but they all belong to the same order (Carnivora). This means the most recent common ancestor shared by all five species was also a member of the Carnivora taxon.

215. **C.** A clade must include all extant taxa that have descended from a particular ancestral taxon. In Figure 18.6, *Canis latrans, Canis lupus,* and *Lutra lutra* do not constitute a complete clade because their most recent common ancestor is also the ancestor of *Taxidea taxus*.

216. **D.** According to Table 18.5, members of the family Mustelidae are also members of the order Carnivora. This is the same order to which the coyote belongs, since all species in Table 18.5 belong to this order. There is not enough information to determine to which member of Mustelidae in Table 18.5 the wolverine is more closely related.

217. **A.** According to Figure 18.6, the member of the family Felidae *(Panthera pardus)* diverged from the other four species first. The members of Mustelidae and Canidae are then shown to diverge from each other next. This means the Canidae taxon diverged from the Mustelidae taxon more recently than from the Felidae taxon.

Chapter 19: Test 6

218. **C.** The code for building a protein is stored in the cell's DNA. As with any protein, the first step in building a tropomyosin protein is transcribing the α-TM gene into mRNA. After RNA splicing, this mRNA transcript can be used to build the protein.

219. **A.** According to the passage, different mRNA transcripts can be produced from the same α-TM gene. Figure 19.1 shows seven different α-TM mRNA transcripts that scientists discovered were produced from the same α-TM gene.

220. **A.** The maximum number of exons present in an mRNA transcript is 10. Both types of striated muscle exhibit mRNA transcripts with 10 exons.

221. **D.** Exon 4 is present in all seven transcripts in Figure 19.1. This suggests that Exon 4 is a constitutive exon necessary for all tropomyosin proteins.

222. **B.** The mRNA transcript found in the brain contains six constitutive exons and one alternatively spliced exon. Exon 7 is present in the brain but not in all tissue types.

223. **C.** Exons 2 and 3 do not appear together in any of the seven mRNA transcripts in Figure 19.1. Exons 11 and 12 also do not appear together.

224. **D.** Since two samples of striated muscle are shown in Figure 19.1, it can be assumed that one sample is skeletal muscle and the other is cardiac muscle. Examining both mRNA transcripts shows that the sample labeled Striated muscle ends with Exon 11, while the sample labeled Striated muscle′ ends with Exon 12. No other differences exist between the two types.

225. **B.** According to Figure 19.2, the α-TM gene contains 12 total exons. Though the number of exons in the mRNA transcripts varies, the number of exons in the actual gene does not change.

226. **B.** According to Table 19.1, Exon 4 codes for amino acids 81–125. This is a total of 44 amino acids, which is the greatest number of amino acids coded by any single exon in the table.

227. **D.** According to Table 19.1, either Exon 10 or 12 codes for amino acids 258–284. The brain mRNA transcript contains neither Exon 10 or 12.

228. **A.** Table 19.1 shows that Exons 10 and 12 both code for amino acids 258–284. Though all other transcripts only contain one of the two exons, striated muscle′ contains both. This means that the striated muscle′ mRNA transcript contains two copies of the code for amino acids 258–284.

229. **B.** Based on Figure 19.1, the difference between a myoblast and a smooth muscle transcript involves Exons 2 and 3. Exon 3 is present in the myoblast transcript but is absent from the smooth muscle transcript, where it is replaced by Exon 2.

230. **C.** According to Table 19.1, Exon 11 codes for no amino acids. This suggests that Exon 11 must contain an untranslated region instead of an amino acid code.

231. **A.** In Figure 19.1, the first four mRNA transcripts are from different types of muscle (or muscle precursor) cells. The last three transcripts are from different types of nonmuscle cells. All four of the muscle cell transcripts contain either Exon 2 or Exon 3. None of the nonmuscle transcripts contain either of these exons. Therefore, it can be inferred that the extra function of tropomyosins in muscle cells could be related to the sequence of amino acids (amino acids 39–80) coded by Exons 2 and 3.

232. **D.** According to Figure 19.1, the hepatoma is the only tissue type from which Exon 7 is missing. This implies that a loss of Exon 7 may be correlated to tumor formation.

233. **C.** The passage identifies neonicotinoids as a class of pesticides thought to be harmful to honeybees.

234. **B.** Scientist 1 states that neonicotinoids have been shown to increase honeybees' susceptibility to disease and parasites. Though no direct link between neonicotinoids and honeybee population loss has been found, Scientist 1 believes neonicotinoids to be an indirect factor.

235. **A.** Scientist 1 lists almonds, apples, onions, and carrots as crops that rely almost exclusively on honeybees for pollination. Cherries are not mentioned.

236. **B.** Scientist 1 states that any measures with the potential to improve honeybee health, such as a neonicotinoid ban, should be attempted. Scientist 2 states that a neonicotinoid ban should not be attempted because neonicotinoids are not among the greatest threats to honeybee health, and efforts should instead be focused on the strongest known threats.

237. **A.** According to Scientist 1, reproductive rates of honeybee-dependent crops vary directly with the availability of honeybees. This would also apply to honeybee-dependent producers in the natural ecosystem. Figure 19.3 demonstrates a direct relationship between honeybee population size and producer reproductive rate. As honeybee population size increases, so does the producer reproductive rate.

238. **A.** Scientist 2 states that varroa mites and disease are the greatest known threats to honeybee health and suggests that efforts to improve that health should focus on these threats.

239. **D.** Scientist 2 identifies water that is scarce or of poor quality as an environmental stressor to honeybees. Scientist 1 does not mention water quality as a factor affecting honeybee health.

240. **C.** Scientist 1 states that honeybees are important to the overall ecosystem because plants at the base of the food web depend on pollination by honeybees.

This indicates that Scientist 1 believes transferring pollen between plants is honeybees' most important contribution to natural ecosystems.

241. **D.** Scientist 2 indicates that greater exposure to neonicotinoids does correlate slightly to a decrease in honeybee population size. Figure 19.10 demonstrates a weak negative correlation between pesticide exposure and honeybee population size. Though the data points do not form a tight line, a negative average slope is identifiable.

242. **C.** The passage states that the European Union recently instituted a two-year ban on neonicotinoids in an effort to improve the health of European honeybee populations. A doubling of European honeybee populations over the next five years would indicate that the neonicotinoid ban was effective in improving honeybee health. This supports the opinion of Scientist 1, who believes a neonicotinoid ban would be effective in the United States.

243. **B.** Both scientists discussed disease and parasites (varroa mites) as contributing to the decline of honeybee populations. Scientist 2 asserts that disease and parasites are the greatest threats to honeybee health. Scientist 1 asserts that any measures available to improve honeybee health should be taken. Therefore, it can be inferred that both scientists would support efforts to improve disease and parasite prevention.

244. **A.** Scientist 1 states that 23% of crops in the United States rely on honeybee pollination. This percentage accounts for approximately ¼ of the agriculture industry.

245. **C.** According to Scientist 2, a ban on neonicotinoids would not be effective in increasing honeybee populations because neonicotinoids are only weakly correlated to honeybee population declines. This weak correlation would lead honeybee populations to continue to decline during a neonicotinoid ban but at a slightly slower rate.

246. **D.** Scientist 2 identifies disease and varroa mites as the greatest threats to honeybee health. So it can be inferred that these biotic, or living, factors have the strongest effect on honeybee populations.

247. **A.** Most reef-building corals have a mutually beneficial symbiotic relationship with a microscopic unicellular algae called zooxanthellae that lives within the cells of the coral's stomach. The coral provides the algae with a protected environment, and the compounds necessary for photosynthesis.

248. **A.** As the concentration of CO_2 in the water increases, the pH decreases and the balance between bicarbonate and carbonate shifts increasingly toward bicarbonate as the ocean attempts to buffer the drop in pH by combining H+ with CO_3^{2-} to produce HCO^{3-}. As the carbonate ion concentration decreases, it becomes more difficult for the corals to extract the CO_3^{2-} from the seawater to build their skeletons. It is presently unknown how species vary in their ability to cope with the decrease in carbonate ion concentration in a process known as acclimation.

249. **C.** Ocean acidification, like global warming, is a predictable response to those human activities that increase the atmospheric concentration of carbon dioxide. The magnitude and rate of ocean acidification can be predicted with more confidence than the rise in temperature due to global warming, as they are less dependent on climate-system feedbacks.

250. **B.** Seasonal changes such as those in temperature and bioproductivity, including variations in photosynthesis and respiration, contribute to fluctuations in ocean pH. Coastal waters are more likely to be affected by the terrestrial system, such as runoff from rivers, leading to wider variations in ocean pH in these areas.

251. **C.** Crustaceans live below the saturation point and show a significant increase in calcification, unlike gastropods, corals, and calcareous algae.

252. **A.** The aragonite form of calcium carbonate is more soluble than calcite because the aragonite saturation horizon is always nearer the surface of the oceans than the calcite saturation horizon. Therefore, calcifying organisms that produce the calcite form of calcium carbonate (coccolithophores and foraminifera) may be less vulnerable to changes in ocean acidity than those that construct aragonite structures (corals and pteropods).

253. **B.** Figure 19.12 shows that bivalve fertility is also negatively impacted by acidification, with slowed development and decreased fertilization and larval survival.

254. **A.** As noted in Figure 19.12, the decline in coral calcification is noted as significant with an asterisk.

255. **C.** Calcareous algae is most affected, showing a significant decline in growth and photosynthesis, as well as a decrease in reproduction.

256. **C.** Most reef-building corals have a mutually beneficial, symbiotic relationship with the microscopic

unicellular algae called zooxanthellae. The coral provides the algae with a protected environment and the compounds necessary for photosynthesis.

257. **D.** The outer epidermis provides a layer of protection over the coral animal.

258. **D.** Coral eggs combining with sperm in sexual reproduction produces the most genetic diversity.

259. **A.** Coral bleaching occurs when the corals lose their color due to stress-induced expulsion of the symbiotic unicellular algae.

260. **A.** The best design would be to use two tanks filled with seawater and corals, adding carbon dioxide bubbles to only one tank. The tank with added carbon dioxide is the variable, while the other serves as the experimental control.

261. **B.** Any changes in the biological processes in the surface ocean waters also affect the deeper water. This is because organisms and habitats living at the lower levels of the oceans—far from sunlight—rely mainly on the products created by life in the surface waters. On a longer time scale, these organisms may also be vulnerable to acidification and changes in ocean chemistry as higher levels of carbon dioxide mix throughout the oceans.

Chapter 20: Test 7

262. **A.** Since the eye's lens is thicker in the middle, it is convex. Since distant objects are being viewed, we can assume that the object is more than two focal lengths away and forms an inverted, smaller image (row 1 in Table 20.1). This image is real because actual light rays are converging to a point after (to the right of) the lens.

263. **D.** According to the passage, real images are formed to the right of the lens. According to Table 20.1, all images formed to the right of the lens are inverted.

264. **A.** Since the object is located more than two focal lengths from the lens, the first row in Table 20.1 is applicable. A real image forms to the right of the lens and is described as inverted and smaller.

265. **C.** According to the passage, convex lenses take parallel rays and converge them to the focal point, which is one focal length from the center of the lens.

266. **A.** Since the slide is placed between one and two focal lengths from the lens, the image will be inverted and larger. Because it was placed in the projector upside down, the image on the screen will be upright.

267. **B.** Because the image is on the same side as the object, it is a virtual image in one of the two bottom rows of Table 20.1. Since the image is larger, it has to be the convex lens.

268. **B.** The only lens in Table 20.1 that produces a same-size image requires the object to be two focal lengths away from the lens (2 × 30 cm = 60 cm).

269. **C.** Since the image of the trees is still distant, the image location is on the same side as the object (to the left of the lens). According to Table 20.1, the only option for smaller images is a concave lens with an upright image.

270. **D.** Since the image is located between one and two focal lengths to the right of the lens, the lens must be convex. Table 20.1 indicates that the object is more than two focal lengths from the lens.

271. **C.** Since the lens is thicker in the middle, it is convex, and since the candle is within one focal length of the lens, it will form a virtual, upright, larger, image.

272. **B.** This piece of evidence involves the reduction of predators, which is Scientist A's primary view on the issue. All other choices represent evidence that would be presented by Scientist B regarding the lack of competition for resources from other herbivores.

273. **C.** Both scientists agree on the mechanism of the demise of the deer population; their opinions differ on how the population grew and on the data presented.

274. **C.** This statement focuses only on the predator-prey relationship, and Scientist B tends to downplay the effects of predator reduction in the description of the Kaibab Plateau.

275. **A.** Both scientists agree on the negative implications of interfering in ecosystems.

276. **D.** Scientist A focuses on food chain disruption, especially in regard to removing predators.

277. **D.** The lesson of this situation, according to Scientist A, is that predators are a necessary part of the ecosystem and removing them can have catastrophic results.

278. **B.** The scientists disagree on how the population increased (lack of predation versus lack of competition for resources), but the reason the population decreased catastrophically is clear—disease and starvation from overpopulation.

279. **D.** Scientist B believes that the reduction in competition for grasses caused the increase in the population.

280. **B.** While the other statements could potentially be true, this cautionary statement shows a link between the practice suggested for increasing the duck population and what happened on the Kaibab. Removing the midsized mammals (raccoons, foxes, and so forth) in this ecosystem could have a similar ripple effect that removing the large predators (such as coyotes) had on the Kaibab Plateau.

281. **B.** Although the two scientists differ in their reactions to the environmental mechanisms that led to the problem, they agree that a lesson should be learned from the Kaibab Plateau situation about human intervention in natural ecosystems.

282. **B.** To determine the effect of amplitude, tension must remain constant so it is a controlled variable.

283. **D.** In Figure 20.3, the high-tension/high-amplitude wave traveled approximately 1.10 m at the one-second mark. Therefore, it traveled 1.10 m/s.

284. **C.** The straight line indicates that it traveled an equal distance each tenth of a second as time went on, thus remaining at a constant speed.

285. **A.** When comparing the two high-amplitude lines, the steeper slope for the high-tension case shows that the wave traveled a greater distance each second than it did in the low-tension case.

286. **C.** Since the slopes of the two low-tension cases were almost identical but the amplitudes were different, one can conclude that amplitude has no significant effect on wave speed.

287. **A.** One can infer that loud sounds are big waves of large amplitude, but amplitude has no effect on wave speed.

288. **A.** The only time wave speed changed in Figure 20.3 was when the tension was increased, which effectively altered the characteristics of the medium. Thus one can infer that the speed of light will be altered by the material through which it travels.

289. **D.** Since the waves maintained a steady speed as they traveled, one can infer that a water wave will maintain constant speed.

290. **C.** The low-tension/low-amplitude wave went about 0.8 m in one second. Since its speed was constant, it should move six times that distance in six seconds, thus moving approximately 4.8 m.

291. **C.** Since wave speed is independent of the size of the wave (amplitude), it should take the same amount of time for the small wave to travel the same distance as the large wave.

292. **B.** Heptane is an alkane (circle marker) with a molar mass of 100 g/mol. In Figure 20.4, the corresponding dot has a boiling point just less than 100°C.

293. **B.** As the molar mass for both alkanes and alcohols increases, so does the boiling point. This is shown by the two linear trends with positive slopes in Figure 20.4.

294. **C.** Propanol is an alcohol, so it follows the trend of the green squares at the top of Figure 20.4. Extrapolating backward from a molar mass of about 74 g/mol to 60 g/mol would correspond to a 12°C to 14°C decrease in boiling points.

295. **C.** Since 150°C is higher than the boiling point of pentanol, the substance would already have boiled and become gaseous.

296. **A.** The addition of a hydroxyl group to any of the alcohols makes the boiling points higher than those of the alkanes that have similar molar masses. Look at pentane and butanol: these have similar molar masses, but butanol (which has a hydroxyl group) has a much higher boiling point.

297. **C.** This model has the six carbon groups and the hydroxyl group that makes it an alcohol. In Table 20.2, all substances ending in -ol are alcohols. The chemical hexane also has six carbon groups, so the base of the structure must have something to do with the hexa- prefix.

298. **B.** The model shows that each point on the skeletal structure indicates a carbon atom. The carbon on each end is filled with three hydrogen atoms and the carbons in the middle each have two hydrogen atoms attached. Eight lines mean 10 carbons: 8 inside ($8 \times 2 = 16$) and 3 on each end ($2 \times 3 = 6$) equals 22 hydrogen atoms ($16 + 6 = 22$).

299. **B.** To figure this out, extend the lower line on Figure 20.4 out to 142 g/mol. The boiling points of alkanes seem to increase about 60°C for an increase of 25 g/mol. A molar mass increase from 100 g/mol to 142 g/mol equates to about a 90°C increase in the boiling point, which is closest to 185°C.

Chapter 21: Test 8

300. **A.** Figure 21.1 best represents the relationship between the dependent and independent variables. Figure 21.2 is a bar graph (which is best used for categorical data) and does not have the correct data.

Figure 21.3 has the dependent and independent variables on the wrong axes and also does not represent the *x*-axis data in an appropriately scaled manner. Figure 21.4 does not correlate the correct data, as a downward curve should immediately be expected when looking at the results from the experiment.

301. **A.** This is the only question that could be addressed using only the data students have already collected.

302. **C.** No relationship was shown between the cost of sunglasses and the amount of UVB they blocked.

303. **C.** If each bottle of sunscreen held 10 oz, the costs would be $0.89, $0.49, $0.79, $1.59, and $1.09. SPF 4 can be eliminated because it is more expensive than SPF 8 and clearly blocks less UVB. SPFs 30 and 50 can also be eliminated because although they block more UVB than SPF 8, the higher cost (double and triple the cost per ounce) could not possibly offset the only marginal increase in protection.

304. **D.** It would be important for students to control the amount and thickness of the sunscreen to obtain consistent and reliable results. The other selections represent variables that cannot be controlled, such as sunscreen ingredients, or are not pertinent to this investigation.

305. **D.** This cannot be predicted because there is no clear relationship between the cost of the glasses and the amount of UVB blocked.

306. **A.** If the trend from Table 21.2 continues, the amount of UVB reaching the sensor will decrease slightly.

307. **B.** Students are testing the type of sunglasses. The experimental, or independent, variable is the item that is changed between each trial.

308. **A.** As the SPF increases past 30, only slight increases in the amount of UVB blocked occur.

309. **C.** This is the only question that can be answered using the existing equipment. Students can use a consistent SPF and vary the thickness to determine whether this affects what reaches the sensor.

310. **D.** This statement is false. The more water in the initial amounts, the *lower* the evaporation rates, although this is probably a result of the different surface areas exposed and not a function of the amount of water. The data for water alone does not warrant any conclusion here.

311. **B.** 80.0 mL – 3.0 mL = 77.0 mL.

312. **B.** Since rubbing alcohol had the highest evaporation rate, Student 1's hypothesis is supported.

The average evaporation rates for Student 2's data are approximately the same for the three liquids. Student 3's hypothesis is disproved because the data show that the greater the surface area, the greater the evaporation rate.

313. **D.** The data in Table 21.3 indicates that the amount evaporated is directly proportional to surface area. The average amount evaporated goes up approximately 9 mL for every 4 cm² of surface area exposed. Since the surface area is increased by a factor of 5, the amount evaporated will also (5 × 9 mL = 45 mL).

314. **A.** If you extrapolate the rubbing alcohol line for two additional weeks, it will reach zero at approximately 9 weeks of exposure.

315. **A.** The line for water drops 21 mL in seven weeks. That's an average evaporation rate of 3 mL of water each week.

316. **C.** The slope of the line for rubbing alcohol in Figure 21.5 is constant over the seven weeks. This indicates that the rate of evaporation is constant.

317. **C.** The data indicate that none of the vegetable oil evaporated. Therefore the graph would be a steady, flat line at 80 mL.

318. **A.** The variation between the trials for rubbing alcohol is greater for the experiments with bigger surface areas.

319. **D.** The initial amount of liquid was the same in each case for rubbing alcohol.

320. **D.** To answer this question, one can examine the last five rows of Table 21.4, where the radius and release height are constant, but the mass is changing. Notice that the speed remains constant.

321. **C.** When mass and radius are held fixed in the middle rows of Table 21.4, the kinetic energy is one tenth of the release height.

322. **A.** The middle rows on Table 21.4 have a fixed mass and radius but differing release heights. One can compare the effect of doubling the release height from 0.05 m to 0.10 m, or 0.10 m to 0.20 m, on gravitational energy to observe the doubling effect.

323. **D.** All the gravitational energy at the top of the swing transfers to kinetic energy at the bottom because the values are identical in Table 21.4.

324. **A.** According to the data in Table 21.4, when the mass doubles from 0.020 kg to 0.040 kg, the kinetic energy also doubles.

325. **C.** The middle rows in Table 21.4 are for a fixed pendulum design, and the speed increases by a factor of 1.4 J when the kinetic energy doubles.

326. **A.** The last five rows in Table 21.5 (where radius and release height are held constant) demonstrate that centripetal acceleration does not depend on mass.

327. **C.** The first five rows of Table 21.5 (where mass and release height are held constant) show that each time the radius doubles, the centripetal force values are cut in half.

328. **D.** By examining the middle rows in Table 21.4, where mass remains the same, when the speed doubles from 0.99 m/s to 1.98 m/s, the kinetic energy quadruples from 0.005 J to 0.020 J. Thus, kinetic energy is directly proportional to the square of the speed.

329. **B.** The last five rows of Table 21.5 apply to a pendulum with a 0.40-m arc and a release height of 0.25 m. The centripetal force increases by 0.123 N for each 0.010 kg of mass. Adding 0.123 N to the last row of Table 21.5 yields $0.613N + 0.123N = 0.736N$.

330. **B.** The target for the North Lake area is 25 μg/L. In all years of the study, the values of phosphorus measured in North Lake have exceeded that level.

331. **B.** According to Table 21.6, a phosphorus level between 12 μg/L and 24 μg/L would be classified as mesotrophic. The target for Bay Area 2 is 14 μg/L.

332. **C.** All of the areas except for South Lake were above their target phosphorus level in 2011. South Lake was at 48 μg/L with a goal of 54 μg/L or below.

333. **D.** South Lake is the only area that shows a downward trend in phosphorus levels starting in 2005.

334. **C.** In 2002, the South Lake phosphorus level was 38 μg/L. This falls in the category of eutrophic.

335. **D.** Bay Area 2 fell in the range of 12 μg/L to 24 μg/L for 19 years of the study.

336. **D.** Bay Area 1 fell in the range of 12 μg/L to 24 μg/L during 2011.

337. **A.** By subtracting the approximate value of the shortest bar from that of the highest bar in Figure 21.10, a range can be determined ($61 - 21 = 32$ μg/L).

338. **A.** Bay Area 1 had a range of only 5 μg/L ($13 - 8 = 5$ μg/L). It is important to pay attention to the scale in each figure, as each has a different unit scale on the y-axis. The ranges for each lake area can be found by subtracting the approximate value of the shortest bar from that of the highest bar in each figure.

339. **B.** According to the passage, the value must be at or *below* the target value of phosphorus to surpass the standard. By counting the bars at or below 10 μg/L in Figure 21.7, one can determine that the standard was met or surpassed for 10 years in Bay Area 1.

340. **B.** In 1993, Bay Area 1 had an approximate phosphorus concentration of 9 μg/L and North Lake had a concentration of 50 μg/L ($50 - 9 = 41$ μg/L).

341. **A.** In 2005, Bay Area 1 had the most similar phosphorus concentration to that of the neighboring lake.

342. **D.** To be classified as hypereutrophic, the phosphorus level of a lake needs to be higher than 96 μg/L. None of the lake areas exceeded that level during the 21-year study.

343. **C.** The North and South Lake areas most frequently fell into the range of 24 μg/L to 96 μg/L.

344. **B.** According to the passage, lakes classified as eutrophic have low levels of dissolved oxygen. In 2010, North Lake was the most eutrophic of all the areas studied and would therefore be expected to have the lowest dissolved oxygen level.

Chapter 22: Test 9

345. **A.** The independent variable is the variable the experimenter purposely changes. The types of metals were varied throughout this experiment, so this is the independent variable.

346. **B.** The control variable must remain constant for all trials. The type of metal cannot be controlled since it is varied for each experiment. Independent variables cannot be control variables.

347. **B.** Silver acts as the cathode in this reaction. From the passage, we know that metal ions (Ag^+) join the Ag strip as solid metal atoms. This diminishes the amount of metal ions in the jar. After repeated use, the silver ions will be attracted to the silver cathode, and the concentration of Ag^+ will decrease.

348. **C.** To get a positive voltage, the sum of the cathode and anode must be 0.63. This is only true if zinc is the anode with 0.76V and lead is the cathode at –0.13V.

349. **D.** The passage stated that metal from the anode strip dissolves into solution and metal from the solution is added to the cathode strip. Zinc metal was the anode in Experiment 2, so its atoms dissolved into zinc ions, decreasing the strip's mass.

Copper was the cathode, so the dissolved zinc ions attached themselves to the strip, increasing the strip's mass.

350. **A.** Figure 22.1 shows zinc as the anode and copper as the cathode. The anode table in Table 22.2 shows that zinc has a more positive voltage than copper. It can thus be inferred that aluminum would be the anode, because it also has a more positive voltage than copper.

351. **D.** The aluminum anode has a potential of 1.66 V, and the copper cathode has a potential of 0.34 V. Added together, this yields a sum of 2.00 V. Switching the anode and cathode would give a sum of –2.00 V, which is not a choice.

352. **C.** Each copper/zinc cell can produce 1.10 V. Using the equation $12 \div 1.10 = 10.9$ V, or between 10 and 11. Ten cells clearly do not produce quite enough voltage, so 11 cells are needed.

353. **A.** In Table 22.3, the voltage divided by the resistance predicts the current.

354. **D.** The passage states that power is the product of current and voltage, so $150 \text{ V} \times 3.0 \text{ A} = 450$ W.

355. **C.** For the 120 V rows in Table 22.3, when the resistance triples from 120 ohms to 360 ohms, the power drops from 120 W to 40 W, thus decreasing to one-third of its initial power.

356. **A.** For the 480-ohm rows in Table 22.3, when the voltage doubles from 120 V to 240 V, the current doubles from 0.25 A to 0.50 A.

357. **D.** According to Table 22.3, the 480-ohm bulb at 120 V has an energy usage of 108 kJ per hour. To find the energy needed, we use $108 \times 4 = 432$ kJ.

358. **B.** According to the data in Table 22.3, doubling the resistance from 120 ohms to 240 ohms decreases the power to one-half of 120 W. Tripling the resistance decreases the power to one-third of 120 W. Thus, power is inversely proportional to resistance (for a fixed voltage). When resistance is increased by a factor of 5 from 120 ohms to 600 ohms, the power must reduce to one-fifth of 120 W, or 24 W.

359. **A.** In Table 22.3, a basic circuit with a single 240-ohm bulb has a power output of 60 W when connected to a power supply of 120 V. According to Table 22.4, when identical bulbs are connected in parallel at 120 V, they also output 60 W. According to the passage, power is the amount of energy transferred each second.

360. **C.** According to Table 22.4, as the number of bulbs in a series circuit increases, the individual bulbs output less power.

361. **A.** According to Table 22.3, increasing the resistance of a single bulb in the circuit decreases the power output. Since the circuit's power output increases as bulbs are added in parallel in Table 22.4, one can infer that the resistance of the entire circuit decreases.

362. **B.** This statement is false because even if Bulb 2 breaks, there is still a series pathway for Bulbs 1 and 3 through the power supply.

363. **D.** According to Table 22.4, more bulbs being added to a parallel circuit results in more power output from the entire circuit.

364. **C.** The five bulbs that went out are wired in series with each other because when one went out, the others did as well. Since the other four bulbs remained lit, they must be on a separate circuit.

365. **A.** According to Table 22.4, the current decreases as bulbs are added in series. Table 22.3 shows that current decreases in the circuit when resistance increases. Thus, adding bulbs effectively increases the total circuit resistance.

366. **D.** According to Table 22.4, three 240-ohm bulbs wired in series to a 120-V power supply outputs a total of 20 W. That's 20 J of energy transferred each second, so in 10 seconds, there is a total of 200 J.

367. **C.** According to Table 22.4, each bulb wired in parallel requires 60 W, so for six bulbs, the equation is $6 \times 60 \text{ W} = 360$ W.

368. **B.** Experiment 1 looked at cathode rays that were attracted to a positively charged area. This suggests that the rays are negatively charged. Experiment 2 suggests that something inside the atom is sturdy or dense enough to reflect alpha particles.

369. **D.** If the mass-to-charge ratio of a particle is small, either the mass of the particle is small or the charge of the particle is large. From the ratio alone, it is impossible to know which factor creates the small ratio. Both (A) and (C) might be true, but (D) is the best conclusion because it notes both possible factors.

370. **C.** The neutron has some mass but is neutral, so it has no charge. An object with zero charge would have an undefined mass-to-charge ratio, no matter what the mass of the particle is.

371. **C.** Both experiments agree that atoms have subatomic particles. This conflicts with Democritus's view that atoms are indivisible.

372. **D.** Only 1 out of every 20,000 particles was deflected to a large degree, meaning that 19,999 out of every 20,000 particles went straight through the foil. This suggests that there is a tiny chunk of dense material in an atom, but the rest is empty space.

373. **D.** The gold foil was 8.6×10^{-8} m, or 0.000000086 m. One micrometer is 0.000001 m, but the gold foil is not as thick as 1 μm. The only reasonable answer is 0.086 μm because it shows that the gold foil is much thinner than 1 μm.

374. **A.** This statement is talking about cathode rays that have been proven to be negatively charged and very small.

375. **C.** This headline matches what the gold foil experiment concluded. An atom must have a dense particle in it to make the alpha particles bounce off the foil. However, this particle must be very small if only 1 out of 20,000 alpha particles bounced back.

376. **B.** In the capture theory, the moon was formed in another area of the solar system; therefore, it would likely have different rock compositions.

377. **C.** In the fission theory, the moon came directly from the earth and would therefore have the same rock composition. In the coaccretion theory, the moon and the earth formed side by side from the nebula and would therefore have very similar compositions.

378. **B.** The fact that Jupiter and Saturn both have captured moons makes it more likely that the earth could have captured a moon.

379. **A.** Fission = Daughter (the moon was "born" from the earth in this theory). Coaccretion = Sister (the moon and the earth formed side by side from the same "parent" material). Capture = Spouse (the moon was formed elsewhere and was "married" to the earth when captured by the earth's gravitational field).

380. **A.** This is a description of fission theory, the leading theory in the mid-1930s. This is most evident by the mention of the sun's gravity and the phrase "a bulge broke away with such momentum that it could not return to the body of Mother Earth."

381. **D.** If the moon was formed 4.5 billion years ago, it could not have broken away from the earth to form the Pacific Ocean basin.

382. **C.** In the capture theory, the moon formed in another part of the solar system; therefore, the earth's gravity would not have played a role in the formation of its crust.

383. **D.** The giant impact theory is the only theory to account for why the moon rocks partially, but not fully, match the rocks on the earth. In this theory, the collision with the Mars-sized object would have caused a mixing of materials from both.

384. **D.** Based on the information in the passage, it is evident that the giant impact theory is the most current theory of moon formation based on scientific evidence.

385. **C.** These two pieces of evidence best support the coaccretion theory, in which the earth and moon formed side by side.

386. **A.** All of the other pieces of evidence point toward a moon formed close to the earth, but this theory does not account for the similarity in the crust/mantle rock from both the moon and the earth.

Chapter 23: Test 10

387. **B.** The velocity in the first column of Table 23.1 always increases by 9.8 m/s each and every second.

388. **C.** According to Table 23.1, the distance fallen in the first second is 4.9 m. During the second second, the distance fallen is 19.6 − 4.9 = 14.7 m. The intervals only increase from there.

389. **B.** During the fourth second, the air drag force increases from 0.061 N to 0.080 N, an increase of 0.019 N.

390. **D.** Since the velocity goes up about 10 m/s each second, we can add 10 to 118 m/s (the speed 12 seconds into the fall) two more times to get 138 m/s at the 14-second clock reading.

391. **A.** The velocity shown for a ball falling with air increases at a lesser rate than the velocity of one falling without air (freefall).

392. **D.** The last column in Table 23.1 shows big changes each second initially, but by the end of the drop, the air drag does not change.

393. **D.** Figure 23.1 shows that the 30-g mass gains speed at a greater rate than the 10-g mass (both falling with air).

394. **B.** During the first two seconds in Figure 23.1, there is not much difference between the with-air and without-air data. Beyond two seconds, when the velocities are greater than 20 m/s, the data diverge significantly.

395. **C.** Figure 23.2 shows how the 0.5-cm ball's velocity increases at a greater rate than that of the 1.0-cm ball.

396. **D.** Figure 23.2 shows the 0.05-cm ball's velocity plateauing at about 62 m/s at 12 seconds into the fall.

397. **A.** In Figure 23.2, the line for both balls falling without air is identical.

398. **C.** In Figure 23.1, the 10-g ball reaches terminal velocity 6 seconds into the drop, whereas the 30-g ball reaches terminal velocity 12 seconds into the drop.

399. **B.** The belly-first twin hits more air just like the larger radius ball. By examining Figure 23.2, one can see that the larger radius ball reaches terminal velocity sooner than the smaller radius ball, and the belly-first twin will do the same.

400. **C.** According to Figure 23.1, both the 10-g ball and the 30-g ball have the same velocities when falling without air. Therefore, mass has no effect on freefall velocities and the balls will reach the ground at the same time.

401. **A.** According to Figure 23.1, the greater mass falls with greater velocity through the air and will get to the ground sooner.

402. **B.** Both figures and Table 23.1 show that dropped balls speed up steadily. There is no evidence that the steady gain in velocity will ever change.

403. **B.** The mass of sample can be found by taking the mass of the crucible + sample and subtracting the mass of the empty crucible (32.569 − 26.449 = 6.120 g).

404. **C.** Even though the sample was heated again, no additional water molecules were driven off between the third and fourth heatings; instead, only anhydrous $MgSO_4$ was left in the container.

405. **A.** *Percent mass* is the mass of the investigated quantity (mass of water) divided by the total mass. The ratio of these numbers describes the percent of water in the original solution.

406. **C.** The difference in the first two rows of Table 23.2 shows that approximately 6 g of the hydrated sample were used. The difference between the mass of the sample at the end and the mass of the sample before heating was approximately 3 g (of water driven off). This indicates the sample was around 50% water and 50% magnesium sulfate.

407. **A.** The percent mass of water would increase if some solid splattered out of the jar. When the mass of the sample was measured after the last heating,

it would be less than expected because some of the solid had sprayed out, but the student would (incorrectly) assume the lost mass to be solely water that had evaporated.

408. **C.** The mass of the sample increased during the additional 40 minutes. The number of $MgSO_4$ crystals could not increase, and any "expansion" in size would not change the mass. A change in temperature also does not change the mass. The only reasonable choice is that water molecules from the atmosphere were able to rehydrate the crystals.

409. **B.** The hydrate would still heat up and water would be driven off, but that water could not leave the crucible. If the crucible were opened, drops of water would be found on the sides, but the mass would not have changed because the water was not allowed to go into the atmosphere.

410. **B.** Both beakers contain 50 g of measured solid, but much of that mass would be water molecules in Beaker 2. The 50 g of solid in Beaker 1 contains all $MgSO_4$ and no water molecules. When dissolved, there would be a much higher concentration of Mg in Beaker 1.

411. **D.** Hyperion's 21.3-day orbit is closest to the moon's 27.3-day orbit.

412. **B.** Andrastea and Miranda have the same orbital radius, and they orbit planets with different mass. Thus, the effect of only one variable (central planet mass) may be analyzed.

413. **D.** The data for Saturn shows that larger radii correlate with greater periods. The moons of Jupiter and Uranus confirm that observation.

414. **A.** The data indicates that gravitational acceleration is directly proportional to the inverse radius squared. In other words, gravitational acceleration is inversely proportional to the square of the radius.

415. **D.** Larger radii correlate with smaller orbital speeds. Since 422 million meters is less than 181 million meters for Amalthea, than the correct answer must be significantly less than Amalthea's orbital speed of 26.5 km/s. Thus, 17 km/s is the only answer that fits that criterion.

416. **A.** Andrastea (orbiting Jupiter) has about 20 times the gravitational acceleration of Miranda (orbiting Uranus), but they have the same orbital radius. Jupiter has about 20 times the mass of Uranus, so gravitational acceleration appears to be directly proportional to planet mass. Using Figure 23.3, the greater slope for Jupiter compared with that of

Saturn confirms this observation, because Jupiter is about three times the mass of Saturn.

417. **C.** The passage indicates that speed was calculated by taking orbital circumference divided by period and that gravitational acceleration was calculated by the square of speed divided by orbital radius.

418. **C.** We divide Phoebe's period by that of the moon ($550 \div 27.3 = 20$).

419. **C.** According to Table 23.4, Helene travels 10.0 km/s. That means in 15 seconds, it will travel 150 km.

420. **D.** As noted earlier, since gravitational acceleration is directly proportional to planet mass, a light planet like Mars would have moons whose gravitational acceleration was much less than those of Jupiter or Saturn, so the line would be below that of the moons of Saturn.

421. **A.** The temperature changed 10°C during the first 6-minute interval. From 6 to 20 minutes, the temperature barely decreased. The temperature did decrease from 20 to 30 minutes, but only about half as rapidly.

422. **A.** If the thermometer was touching the bottom of the test tube, it may have recorded the temperature of the glass as well as the temperature of the sample. This would have caused the temperature to be higher. A reasonable thermometer reading would be 80°C if the tip of the thermometer was resting on hot glass and the rest of the thermometer was in the 55°C solution.

423. **D.** There are three separate parts to this cooling curve. The first and third parts are downward-slanting lines that indicate the temperature decreased in both parts. The middle part shows constant temperature, so the phase must have been changing.

424. **B.** The middle plateau shows the lauric acid cooled down but did not change temperature. This must indicate a phase change. Liquid to solid is the freezing point.

425. **A.** Since 25°C is well below the freezing/melting point of lauric acid, all material would be in the solid phase.

426. **C.** The temperature decreases about 1.5°C every 2 minutes after 20 minutes. At 30 minutes, the temperature is nearly 34°C. The temperature would still need to drop 14°C. This would take almost 20 more minutes.

427. **A.** The melting/freezing point does not depend on the amount of lauric acid. It may take more time to reach the melting point, but it would still occur around 43°C.

428. **C.** Since 50°C is higher than the melting point of lauric acid, the sample would never have crystallized into a solid. It would have remained a liquid throughout the experiment.

429. **B.** Since 25°C is between the melting and boiling point, all of the substance would be a liquid. This is equivalent to water at 25°C, which is between the melting point of ice and the boiling point of water.

430. **A.** If the water started at 55°C and was allowed to cool to 20°C, it would indeed decrease in temperature, but it would not go through melting or boiling. There would be no plateau areas in Figure 23.5, but the temperature would decrease.

Chapter 24: Test 11

431. **C.** Volume is a measurement of how much space something occupies. Sample 6 had a volume of 44.8 L, which was the largest volume of any sample.

432. **D.** Samples 1 and 3 have the same volume, which means they are the same size. Sample 3, however, has a mass of 10 g, whereas Sample 1 has a mass of only about 1 g.

433. **C.** Both samples are 22.4 L. Avogadro's law states that any two gasses at the same volume, temperature, and pressure will contain the same number of molecules.

434. **C.** An 11.2-L sample of oxygen gas would have a mass of 16.0 g. To calculate the mass for 22.4 L, one needs to double the volume, which would be twice the mass of Sample 7.

435. **B.** The neon balloon has a mass of 10.1 g, and 11.2 L of hydrogen gas has a mass of 1 g. One would need 10 times that much mass of hydrogen gas, or $10 \times 11.2 = 112.0$ L.

436. **D.** Avogadro's law states that equal volumes of gasses at the same pressure and temperature would have an equal number of molecules. All three samples have a volume of 11.2 L.

437. **B.** While 11.2 L of oxygen has a mass of 16 g, 22.4 L of helium has a mass of only 4 g. Therefore, 11.2 L of helium would have a mass of 2 g. Thus, a sample of oxygen gas is 8 times heavier than an equal-sized sample of helium gas.

438. **A.** If 11.2 L of oxygen has ½ mol of molecules and a mass of 16.0 g, then 1 mol of molecules would be twice the volume and twice the mass to equal 32.0 g.

439. **C.** Chlorophyll *a* and *b* have the lowest absorption in the 525 to 625 nm portion of the spectrum, which corresponds to the greatest reflection. Even without a knowledge of light principles, this can be determined through the process of elimination, since the other answers do not match the data in Figure 24.1.

440. **B.** The blue portion of the visible spectrum is between 450 and 495 nm.

441. **B.** A wavelength of 440 nm represents considerable absorption for all three pigments.

442. **A.** From Figure 24.1, it can be determined that red light has wavelengths greater than 620 nm. Chlorophyll *a* has the highest peak in the range of wavelengths greater than 620 nm.

443. **D.** Carotenoids absorb 50% of visible light at 450 nm, and chlorophyll *b* absorbs 80%, which means the carotenoids have ⅝ (62.5%, or approximately 60%) of the absorbing power at that wavelength.

444. **A.** The pigment with the highest absorption at 425 nm is chlorophyll *a*.

445. **B.** The highest peak for chlorophyll *b* in Figure 24.1 is at 450 nm.

446. **C.** Absorption and reflection are opposites, but one would not have to be familiar with the term or process of reflection/principles of color to determine that green light is reflected by chlorophyll *a* and *b*, making plants appear green. Figure 24.1 shows that (A) and (B) are false. (D) is the opposite of (C) and can be eliminated by looking at Figure 24.1, which shows higher absorption in the red portion of the spectrum than in the green.

447. **C.** The peaks of this pigment are the opposite of those of chlorophyll *a* and *b*, as it absorbs the most light in the green portion of the visible spectrum where the absorption of chlorophyll is the lowest.

448. **C.** Particles tend to move in straight lines. As the particles stream from the bulb in straight lines, they are blocked at angles by the card and form the large shadow on the screen.

449. **D.** The first three answers all deal with the reflection, refraction, and absorption of light waves and support Huygens's theory. Visualizing a photon as a bundle of energy is a particle-like concept.

450. **A.** The vacuum of space has no air, so how can a wave travel without matter to transfer the energy? Huygens's theory could not explain this, whereas Newton's particles could travel through the nothingness of space.

451. **A.** The bright regions on the screen can be explained by constructive interference and the dark areas by destructive interference. Interference is a wave phenomenon.

452. **D.** The fuzzy edge may be explained by the diffraction (spreading) of light around the sharp edge of the penny. The bright area at the middle of the shadow is the result of constructive interference of the light diffracting around the edge of the penny.

453. **C.** The semicircles are like water-wave ripples traveling through the air. This supports Huygens's wave theory.

454. **B.** Since the quote states that light does not consist of any "transport of matter" (arrows or particles), it is not consistent with Newton's particle theory of light. The emphasis of the spreading of light does not contradict Huygens's wave theory.

455. **A.** The photon as a basic unit of light can be visualized as a particle, and this is consistent with Newton's particle theory.

456. **D.** If light is a particle moving in a straight line, rotating the second filter should affect the intensity of the light.

457. **A.** This high absorbance in Figure 24.4 means lots of light is being absorbed. $NiSO_4$ has an absorbance of around 0.075 at 380 nm. This light is purple in color. Most of the purple light gets absorbed by the green nickel sulfate solution.

458. **B.** Low absorbance means little light is absorbed and lots of light passes through. The green $NiSO_{4(aq)}$ solution allows most of the green light from the spectrometer to pass through, but it absorbs most other colors.

459. **D.** As the concentration increases, the absorbance increases proportionally. The concentration of $NiSO_{4(aq)}$ is changed, and this changes the absorbance proportionally.

460. **C.** The absorbance of $NiSO_{4(aq)}$ increases about 0.90 for each increase of 0.08 mol/L. This is a proportional increase that can be used to predict the concentration of unknown solutions.

461. **C.** Figure 24.4 shows that $NiSO_4$ does not absorb much light at 490 nm. Since the absorbance is so low, the absorbance of each sample in Investigation 2 will be considerably lower than the absorbance found at 740 nm.

462. **B.** A solution of NaCl is a clear liquid, so it will not absorb any light. All colors of light will pass

straight through it. Absorbance depends on certain frequencies (colors) of light being absorbed.

463. **D.** Following the trend, a 0.48mol/L solution should have an absorbance of 0.542. However the fingerprint would cause more light to be absorbed, so the answer has to be greater than 0.542.

464. **A.** The chemical $NiSO_{4(aq)}$ has a unique spectral fingerprint that is shown in Figure 24.4. A more concentrated solution would absorb more light because more of the chemical would be present. The graph would be the same as the one in Figure 24.4, but the line would be higher, showing that each wavelength would have slightly more absorbance.

465. **B.** The data for Group 1 show *S. aureus* growing most rapidly and to the highest turbidity at 37°C.

466. **C.** At 600 minutes, the data reached their maximum value. Visualizing a graph of this data, one would see it level off at this point, corresponding to the stationary phase of growth.

467. **D.** pH is one of the variables that is controlled for Group 1 and is the variable being tested by Group 2.

468. **B.** Twenty-nine minutes most closely approximates the generation time. One can choose any two pieces of data up to 100 minutes where the absorbance value doubles (for example, 0.047 and 0.099) and determine the amount of time that has passed by subtracting the time readings (68 and 97 minutes, respectively). Even if other data points are selected (such as 0.035 and 0.070) or one chooses another method of approximation, (C) is the only answer that is reasonable.

469. **B.** The temperature of incubation is the experimental variable for Group 1, not one of the controls.

470. **D.** *S. aureus* has a faster growth rate at pH 5 than at pH 7, as evidenced by the more rapid increase in absorbance values in Table 24.5.

471. **B.** The information in the passage provides the distinction between acidity and alkalinity. At this high level of alkalinity, *S. aureus* bacteria cannot grow, as evidenced by the lack of increase in turbidity.

472. **C.** Group 1/Trial 3 and Group 2/Trial 3 were both performed under conditions of 37°C and pH 6.

473. **A.** It can be concluded from the growth data that 37°C and pH 6 represent the ideal growth conditions for *S. aureus*.

474. **A.** The graph will be a curve, as the data increases and then levels off between 10 and 24 hours.

475. **C.** This trial is the only one mentioned that occurred at 37°C and featured growth that was retarded but not completely inhibited by the conditions.

476. **A.** Time is the independent variable, as its presence determines the value of the other variables.

477. **C.** Comparing generation time at a standard temperature would be the most accurate way to determine the type of bacteria using spectrophotometry. Although (A) and (D) are true of *S. aureus*, they are likely true of many other bacteria as well and lack the specificity of a calculation such as generation time.

478. **B.** The population (as indicated by turbidity) remained relatively stable, which means that birth and death must be balanced.

Chapter 25: Test 12

479. **A.** The first ionization energy (900 kJ/mol) is defined as the amount of energy required to remove the outermost electron.

480. **D.** The ionization trends upward briefly but then drops severely between beryllium (Be) and boron (B). After that, the trend is generally toward higher ionization levels.

481. **D.** The formula refers to the fourth ionization energy of nitrogen as nitrogen is going from the +3 charge to the +4 charge.

482. **C.** The main difference between the outermost electron from helium and lithium is that the outermost electron from lithium is on the second shell. The second shell is farther away from the nucleus and therefore has less attraction to it.

483. **B.** The passage states that neutral atoms have the same number of protons and electrons. Carbon is listed at six protons, so the sixth ionization energy removes all of its electrons.

484. **A.** Oxygen is shown to have eight electrons. Oxygen is neutral when it has eight electrons (because it has eight protons), so the image shows the first ionization.

485. **B.** There is a large jump between the fifth and sixth ionization energies of nitrogen. This means it is much harder to remove the sixth electron than it is the fifth. The sixth electron must start in a closer shell to the nucleus, and the first five electrons must have been in an outer shell.

486. **B.** The last two ionization energies are always significantly larger than any of the others. This means the

last two electrons are very hard to remove because they are closest to the nucleus in the inside shell.

487. **B.** There is a large jump in relative ionization energies from the first to the second ionization energy. This means it is relatively easy to remove the first electron but much harder to remove the second electron because it occupies a closer shell.

488. **A.** Helium has fewer protons providing an attraction for the two negative electrons. Lithium has three positive protons in the nucleus pulling those two electrons with more force.

489. **C.** Each piece of helium has two electrons. To remove all of the electrons from helium, both electrons must be removed from 1 mol of particles. This requires the amount of energy equal to the sum of the first and second ionization energies (2,372 + 5,250 = 7,622 kJ).

490. **C.** The data for both brands was nearly identical while they operated within the effective range above 2.2 V.

491. **C.** Brand P sustained a voltage of 2.2 V or more for approximately 3.5 hours.

492. **B.** The data for the alkaline batteries are nearly identical, whereas the data for the heavy-duty batteries are quite different.

493. **D.** The uncertainty in the data set for the remote-control car is so significant that no valid conclusion

may be made about battery performance. Most likely, the method of testing the car was flawed.

494. **B.** The line on Figure 25.3 shows that Brand K's battery had a voltage of 3 V at about 0.25 hours and 2 V at about 2.25 hours. Therefore, 2.25 − 0.25 = 2.0 hours.

495. **B.** Brand D's average was (11.5 + 12.5 + 13.5) ÷ 3 = 12.5 hours. Brand E's average was (13.5 + 12.25 + 13.25) ÷ 3 = 13.0 hours. So 13.0 − 12.5 = 0.5 hours.

496. **C.** Below the 2.2-V line, the slope for Brand E is steeper than that for Brand P.

497. **B.** If the batteries had been used previously, then any experiment to test longevity would be invalid. Effects of temperature and manufacture date may have only a slight effect on the data. The selection of time intervals is arbitrary, although they must be small enough to discern performance.

498. **B.** Because the LED bulb lasts so long, one can conclude that it is a low-drain device.

499. **C.** According to Table 25.2, the LED times are about six times longer than the incandescent bulb times.

500. **A.** In two of the three trials, the incandescent bulb flashlight had the shortest times, and it had the shortest average time across all three tests. Therefore, it is most likely to be called a high-drain device.

PART V

POSTTEST

ACT PRACTICE TEST 1
Answer Sheet

ENGLISH

1 Ⓐ Ⓑ Ⓒ Ⓓ	21 Ⓐ Ⓑ Ⓒ Ⓓ	41 Ⓐ Ⓑ Ⓒ Ⓓ	61 Ⓐ Ⓑ Ⓒ Ⓓ
2 Ⓕ Ⓖ Ⓗ Ⓙ	22 Ⓕ Ⓖ Ⓗ Ⓙ	42 Ⓕ Ⓖ Ⓗ Ⓙ	62 Ⓕ Ⓖ Ⓗ Ⓙ
3 Ⓐ Ⓑ Ⓒ Ⓓ	23 Ⓐ Ⓑ Ⓒ Ⓓ	43 Ⓐ Ⓑ Ⓒ Ⓓ	63 Ⓐ Ⓑ Ⓒ Ⓓ
4 Ⓕ Ⓖ Ⓗ Ⓙ	24 Ⓕ Ⓖ Ⓗ Ⓙ	44 Ⓕ Ⓖ Ⓗ Ⓙ	64 Ⓕ Ⓖ Ⓗ Ⓙ
5 Ⓐ Ⓑ Ⓒ Ⓓ	25 Ⓐ Ⓑ Ⓒ Ⓓ	45 Ⓐ Ⓑ Ⓒ Ⓓ	65 Ⓐ Ⓑ Ⓒ Ⓓ
6 Ⓕ Ⓖ Ⓗ Ⓙ	26 Ⓕ Ⓖ Ⓗ Ⓙ	46 Ⓕ Ⓖ Ⓗ Ⓙ	66 Ⓕ Ⓖ Ⓗ Ⓙ
7 Ⓐ Ⓑ Ⓒ Ⓓ	27 Ⓐ Ⓑ Ⓒ Ⓓ	47 Ⓐ Ⓑ Ⓒ Ⓓ	67 Ⓐ Ⓑ Ⓒ Ⓓ
8 Ⓕ Ⓖ Ⓗ Ⓙ	28 Ⓕ Ⓖ Ⓗ Ⓙ	48 Ⓕ Ⓖ Ⓗ Ⓙ	68 Ⓕ Ⓖ Ⓗ Ⓙ
9 Ⓐ Ⓑ Ⓒ Ⓓ	29 Ⓐ Ⓑ Ⓒ Ⓓ	49 Ⓐ Ⓑ Ⓒ Ⓓ	69 Ⓐ Ⓑ Ⓒ Ⓓ
10 Ⓕ Ⓖ Ⓗ Ⓙ	30 Ⓕ Ⓖ Ⓗ Ⓙ	50 Ⓕ Ⓖ Ⓗ Ⓙ	70 Ⓕ Ⓖ Ⓗ Ⓙ
11 Ⓐ Ⓑ Ⓒ Ⓓ	31 Ⓐ Ⓑ Ⓒ Ⓓ	51 Ⓐ Ⓑ Ⓒ Ⓓ	71 Ⓐ Ⓑ Ⓒ Ⓓ
12 Ⓕ Ⓖ Ⓗ Ⓙ	32 Ⓕ Ⓖ Ⓗ Ⓙ	52 Ⓕ Ⓖ Ⓗ Ⓙ	72 Ⓕ Ⓖ Ⓗ Ⓙ
13 Ⓐ Ⓑ Ⓒ Ⓓ	33 Ⓐ Ⓑ Ⓒ Ⓓ	53 Ⓐ Ⓑ Ⓒ Ⓓ	73 Ⓐ Ⓑ Ⓒ Ⓓ
14 Ⓕ Ⓖ Ⓗ Ⓙ	34 Ⓕ Ⓖ Ⓗ Ⓙ	54 Ⓕ Ⓖ Ⓗ Ⓙ	74 Ⓕ Ⓖ Ⓗ Ⓙ
15 Ⓐ Ⓑ Ⓒ Ⓓ	35 Ⓐ Ⓑ Ⓒ Ⓓ	55 Ⓐ Ⓑ Ⓒ Ⓓ	75 Ⓐ Ⓑ Ⓒ Ⓓ
16 Ⓕ Ⓖ Ⓗ Ⓙ	36 Ⓕ Ⓖ Ⓗ Ⓙ	56 Ⓕ Ⓖ Ⓗ Ⓙ	
17 Ⓐ Ⓑ Ⓒ Ⓓ	37 Ⓐ Ⓑ Ⓒ Ⓓ	57 Ⓐ Ⓑ Ⓒ Ⓓ	
18 Ⓕ Ⓖ Ⓗ Ⓙ	38 Ⓕ Ⓖ Ⓗ Ⓙ	58 Ⓕ Ⓖ Ⓗ Ⓙ	
19 Ⓐ Ⓑ Ⓒ Ⓓ	39 Ⓐ Ⓑ Ⓒ Ⓓ	59 Ⓐ Ⓑ Ⓒ Ⓓ	
20 Ⓕ Ⓖ Ⓗ Ⓙ	40 Ⓕ Ⓖ Ⓗ Ⓙ	60 Ⓕ Ⓖ Ⓗ Ⓙ	

MATHEMATICS

1 Ⓐ Ⓑ Ⓒ Ⓓ Ⓔ	16 Ⓕ Ⓖ Ⓗ Ⓙ Ⓚ	31 Ⓐ Ⓑ Ⓒ Ⓓ Ⓔ	46 Ⓕ Ⓖ Ⓗ Ⓙ Ⓚ
2 Ⓕ Ⓖ Ⓗ Ⓙ Ⓚ	17 Ⓐ Ⓑ Ⓒ Ⓓ Ⓔ	32 Ⓕ Ⓖ Ⓗ Ⓙ Ⓚ	47 Ⓐ Ⓑ Ⓒ Ⓓ Ⓔ
3 Ⓐ Ⓑ Ⓒ Ⓓ Ⓔ	18 Ⓕ Ⓖ Ⓗ Ⓙ Ⓚ	33 Ⓐ Ⓑ Ⓒ Ⓓ Ⓔ	48 Ⓕ Ⓖ Ⓗ Ⓙ Ⓚ
4 Ⓕ Ⓖ Ⓗ Ⓙ Ⓚ	19 Ⓕ Ⓖ Ⓗ Ⓙ Ⓚ	34 Ⓕ Ⓖ Ⓗ Ⓙ Ⓚ	49 Ⓐ Ⓑ Ⓒ Ⓓ Ⓔ
5 Ⓐ Ⓑ Ⓒ Ⓓ Ⓔ	20 Ⓕ Ⓖ Ⓗ Ⓙ Ⓚ	35 Ⓐ Ⓑ Ⓒ Ⓓ Ⓔ	50 Ⓕ Ⓖ Ⓗ Ⓙ Ⓚ
6 Ⓕ Ⓖ Ⓗ Ⓙ Ⓚ	21 Ⓐ Ⓑ Ⓒ Ⓓ Ⓔ	36 Ⓕ Ⓖ Ⓗ Ⓙ Ⓚ	51 Ⓐ Ⓑ Ⓒ Ⓓ Ⓔ
7 Ⓐ Ⓑ Ⓒ Ⓓ Ⓔ	22 Ⓕ Ⓖ Ⓗ Ⓙ Ⓚ	37 Ⓐ Ⓑ Ⓒ Ⓓ Ⓔ	52 Ⓕ Ⓖ Ⓗ Ⓙ Ⓚ
8 Ⓕ Ⓖ Ⓗ Ⓙ Ⓚ	23 Ⓐ Ⓑ Ⓒ Ⓓ Ⓔ	38 Ⓕ Ⓖ Ⓗ Ⓙ Ⓚ	53 Ⓐ Ⓑ Ⓒ Ⓓ Ⓔ
9 Ⓐ Ⓑ Ⓒ Ⓓ Ⓔ	24 Ⓕ Ⓖ Ⓗ Ⓙ Ⓚ	39 Ⓐ Ⓑ Ⓒ Ⓓ Ⓔ	54 Ⓕ Ⓖ Ⓗ Ⓙ Ⓚ
10 Ⓕ Ⓖ Ⓗ Ⓙ Ⓚ	25 Ⓐ Ⓑ Ⓒ Ⓓ Ⓔ	40 Ⓕ Ⓖ Ⓗ Ⓙ Ⓚ	55 Ⓐ Ⓑ Ⓒ Ⓓ Ⓔ
11 Ⓐ Ⓑ Ⓒ Ⓓ Ⓔ	26 Ⓕ Ⓖ Ⓗ Ⓙ Ⓚ	41 Ⓐ Ⓑ Ⓒ Ⓓ Ⓔ	56 Ⓕ Ⓖ Ⓗ Ⓙ Ⓚ
12 Ⓕ Ⓖ Ⓗ Ⓙ Ⓚ	27 Ⓐ Ⓑ Ⓒ Ⓓ Ⓔ	42 Ⓕ Ⓖ Ⓗ Ⓙ Ⓚ	57 Ⓐ Ⓑ Ⓒ Ⓓ Ⓔ
13 Ⓐ Ⓑ Ⓒ Ⓓ Ⓔ	28 Ⓕ Ⓖ Ⓗ Ⓙ Ⓚ	43 Ⓐ Ⓑ Ⓒ Ⓓ Ⓔ	58 Ⓕ Ⓖ Ⓗ Ⓙ Ⓚ
14 Ⓕ Ⓖ Ⓗ Ⓙ Ⓚ	29 Ⓐ Ⓑ Ⓒ Ⓓ Ⓔ	44 Ⓕ Ⓖ Ⓗ Ⓙ Ⓚ	59 Ⓐ Ⓑ Ⓒ Ⓓ Ⓔ
15 Ⓐ Ⓑ Ⓒ Ⓓ Ⓔ	30 Ⓕ Ⓖ Ⓗ Ⓙ Ⓚ	45 Ⓐ Ⓑ Ⓒ Ⓓ Ⓔ	60 Ⓕ Ⓖ Ⓗ Ⓙ Ⓚ

READING

1 Ⓐ Ⓑ Ⓒ Ⓓ   11 Ⓐ Ⓑ Ⓒ Ⓓ   21 Ⓐ Ⓑ Ⓒ Ⓓ   31 Ⓐ Ⓑ Ⓒ Ⓓ
2 Ⓕ Ⓖ Ⓗ Ⓙ   12 Ⓕ Ⓖ Ⓗ Ⓙ   22 Ⓕ Ⓖ Ⓗ Ⓙ   32 Ⓕ Ⓖ Ⓗ Ⓙ
3 Ⓐ Ⓑ Ⓒ Ⓓ   13 Ⓐ Ⓑ Ⓒ Ⓓ   23 Ⓐ Ⓑ Ⓒ Ⓓ   33 Ⓐ Ⓑ Ⓒ Ⓓ
4 Ⓕ Ⓖ Ⓗ Ⓙ   14 Ⓕ Ⓖ Ⓗ Ⓙ   24 Ⓕ Ⓖ Ⓗ Ⓙ   34 Ⓕ Ⓖ Ⓗ Ⓙ
5 Ⓐ Ⓑ Ⓒ Ⓓ   15 Ⓐ Ⓑ Ⓒ Ⓓ   25 Ⓐ Ⓑ Ⓒ Ⓓ   35 Ⓐ Ⓑ Ⓒ Ⓓ
6 Ⓕ Ⓖ Ⓗ Ⓙ   16 Ⓕ Ⓖ Ⓗ Ⓙ   26 Ⓕ Ⓖ Ⓗ Ⓙ   36 Ⓕ Ⓖ Ⓗ Ⓙ
7 Ⓐ Ⓑ Ⓒ Ⓓ   17 Ⓐ Ⓑ Ⓒ Ⓓ   27 Ⓐ Ⓑ Ⓒ Ⓓ   37 Ⓐ Ⓑ Ⓒ Ⓓ
8 Ⓕ Ⓖ Ⓗ Ⓙ   18 Ⓕ Ⓖ Ⓗ Ⓙ   28 Ⓕ Ⓖ Ⓗ Ⓙ   38 Ⓕ Ⓖ Ⓗ Ⓙ
9 Ⓐ Ⓑ Ⓒ Ⓓ   19 Ⓐ Ⓑ Ⓒ Ⓓ   29 Ⓐ Ⓑ Ⓒ Ⓓ   39 Ⓐ Ⓑ Ⓒ Ⓓ
10 Ⓕ Ⓖ Ⓗ Ⓙ   20 Ⓕ Ⓖ Ⓗ Ⓙ   30 Ⓕ Ⓖ Ⓗ Ⓙ   40 Ⓕ Ⓖ Ⓗ Ⓙ

SCIENCE

1 Ⓐ Ⓑ Ⓒ Ⓓ   11 Ⓐ Ⓑ Ⓒ Ⓓ   21 Ⓐ Ⓑ Ⓒ Ⓓ   31 Ⓐ Ⓑ Ⓒ Ⓓ
2 Ⓕ Ⓖ Ⓗ Ⓙ   12 Ⓕ Ⓖ Ⓗ Ⓙ   22 Ⓕ Ⓖ Ⓗ Ⓙ   32 Ⓕ Ⓖ Ⓗ Ⓙ
3 Ⓐ Ⓑ Ⓒ Ⓓ   13 Ⓐ Ⓑ Ⓒ Ⓓ   23 Ⓐ Ⓑ Ⓒ Ⓓ   33 Ⓐ Ⓑ Ⓒ Ⓓ
4 Ⓕ Ⓖ Ⓗ Ⓙ   14 Ⓕ Ⓖ Ⓗ Ⓙ   24 Ⓕ Ⓖ Ⓗ Ⓙ   34 Ⓕ Ⓖ Ⓗ Ⓙ
5 Ⓐ Ⓑ Ⓒ Ⓓ   15 Ⓐ Ⓑ Ⓒ Ⓓ   25 Ⓐ Ⓑ Ⓒ Ⓓ   35 Ⓐ Ⓑ Ⓒ Ⓓ
6 Ⓕ Ⓖ Ⓗ Ⓙ   16 Ⓕ Ⓖ Ⓗ Ⓙ   26 Ⓕ Ⓖ Ⓗ Ⓙ   36 Ⓕ Ⓖ Ⓗ Ⓙ
7 Ⓐ Ⓑ Ⓒ Ⓓ   17 Ⓐ Ⓑ Ⓒ Ⓓ   27 Ⓐ Ⓑ Ⓒ Ⓓ   37 Ⓐ Ⓑ Ⓒ Ⓓ
8 Ⓕ Ⓖ Ⓗ Ⓙ   18 Ⓕ Ⓖ Ⓗ Ⓙ   28 Ⓕ Ⓖ Ⓗ Ⓙ   38 Ⓕ Ⓖ Ⓗ Ⓙ
9 Ⓐ Ⓑ Ⓒ Ⓓ   19 Ⓐ Ⓑ Ⓒ Ⓓ   29 Ⓐ Ⓑ Ⓒ Ⓓ   39 Ⓐ Ⓑ Ⓒ Ⓓ
10 Ⓕ Ⓖ Ⓗ Ⓙ   20 Ⓕ Ⓖ Ⓗ Ⓙ   30 Ⓕ Ⓖ Ⓗ Ⓙ   40 Ⓕ Ⓖ Ⓗ Ⓙ

RAW SCORES		SCALE SCORES		DATE TAKEN:
ENGLISH	_____	ENGLISH	_____	
MATHEMATICS	_____	MATHEMATICS	_____	ENGLISH/WRITING _____
READING	_____	READING	_____	
SCIENCE	_____	SCIENCE	_____	**COMPOSITE SCORE**

1 ■ ■ ■ ■ ■ ■ ■ ■ 1

ENGLISH TEST

45 Minutes – 75 Questions

DIRECTIONS: In the passages that follow, some words and phrases are underlined and numbered. In the answer column, you will find alternatives for the words and phrases that are underlined. Choose the alternative that you think is best, and fill in the corresponding bubble on your answer sheet. If you think that the original version is best, choose "NO CHANGE," which will always be either answer choice A or F. You will also find questions about a particular section of the passage, or about the entire passage. These questions will be identified either by an underlined portion or by a number in a box. Look for the answer that clearly expresses the idea, is consistent with the style and tone of the passage, and makes the correct use of standard written English. Read the passage through once before answering the questions. For some questions, you should read beyond the indicated portion before you answer.

PASSAGE I

A New Perspective

If you had asked me in high school if I planned to become a professor like my dad, my answer was
<u>1</u>

a <u>resounding</u>
<u>2</u>

"No!" I'd spent a long time resenting my dad's scholarly eccentricities, and I wasn't eager to follow his path. My dad's passion for sharing knowledge <u>approached such an extremity</u>
<u>3</u>

that it was embarrassing to be seen with him in public ☐4.
Dad taught French language and literature at the state university,

but he didn't leave his scholarly enthusiasm on campus. ☐5 For example, when he walked my siblings and me to school in the morning, he would encourage us to recite our French

1. **A.** NO CHANGE
   B. used to be
   C. is still
   D. would have been

2. If the author deleted the word *resounding* here, the primary effect would be:
   F. to reverse the meaning of the sentence.
   G. to imply that the author's desire not to follow her father's career path was less emphatic.
   H. to imply that the narrator had not given much thought to her answer.
   J. to set a more formal tone.

3. **A.** NO CHANGE
   B. was so interesting
   C. was understated to the extent
   D. was so unobtrusive

4. If the author wanted to introduce topics addressed later in the essay, she might end this sentence with the clause:
   F. but he made up for it with his riveting dinner conversations.
   G. even though he was very polite to strangers.
   H. but he tried to act normally when he was with more than one of his children.
   J. and tedious to spend time with him at home.

5. The preceding sentence best belongs:
   A. where it is now.
   B. before the second sentence in the paragraph.
   C. after the second sentence in the paragraph.
   D. before the first sentence in the paragraph.

GO ON TO THE NEXT PAGE.

1 ■ ■ ■ ■ ■ ■ ■ ■ **1**

vocabulary out loud irregardless
                        ___
                         6

of how many passersby could hear. Another time on another
                                  _____
                                            7
occasion, when we went sightseeing on a family vacation
_____
   7
in Rome, he chastised our tour guides for having their facts

wrong and tried to engage strangers in conversations about

the history of the Coliseum. My siblings and me pretended
                              _____
                                      8
not to know him.

☐9 Each of our family meals

was an opportunity for Dad to give a lecture. Anything at all
___
10
might send him into professor

mode, the pinecone centerpiece on the table will set him off
_____
   11
on a 30-minute monologue about the history of the pinecone

as a symbol of welcome; a simple asparagus side dish could

prompt him to recite all he knew about how medieval farmers

cultivate asparagus; a fleeting reference to horses could
_____
   12
provoke a long-winded

explanation of the Trojan horse. ☐13 My siblings and I spent

6. F. NO CHANGE
   G. regardless
   H. irrespective
   J. knowledgeable

7. To avoid redundancy, the author should:
   A. REPLACE the underlined words with "On another occasion,"
   B. REPLACE the underlined words with "Once on vacation,"
   C. OMIT the underlined words
   D. REPLACE the underlined words with "For example"

8. F. NO CHANGE
   G. They
   H. My siblings and I
   J. My siblings, and I

9. The best sentence to transition from the first paragraph to the second is:
   A. Dad loved to eat asparagus, even when he wasn't in Rome.
   B. The humiliation was endless.
   C. Unfortunately, we couldn't pretend to ignore Dad's enthusiasm at home.
   D. Tour guides turned out to be less forgiving than passersby.

10. F. NO CHANGE
    G. were
    H. would be
    J. being

11. A. NO CHANGE
    B. mode. The
    C. mode: the
    D. mode; the

12. F. NO CHANGE
    G. would cultivate
    H. cultivated
    J. had cultivated

13. The primary flaw in the preceding sentence is:
    A. the verb tense is inconsistent and not parallel.
    B. commas should be used in place of semicolons.
    C. the phrase about the history of medieval asparagus cultivation is irrelevant.
    D. each word after a semicolon should start with a capital letter.

GO ON TO THE NEXT PAGE.

1 ■ ■ ■ ■ ■ ■ ■ ■ **1**

our entire childhoods steeling myself against these unsolic-
                    ⎯⎯⎯⎯⎯⎯⎯⎯⎯⎯⎯⎯
                         14
ited lectures.

Eventually, I left home to go to college, where I met a lot of
students and teachers who were just as excited about learning
as my dad. During one visit home from college, my dad and
I got in a rowdy debate about our favorite authors. We were
talking with a liveliness that would have embarrassed or exas-
            ⎯⎯⎯⎯⎯⎯⎯⎯⎯
                 15
perated me when I was younger. I had come to realize that my
dad's eagerness to share his wealth of knowledge was the best
way he knew how to show his children he loved them. Now,
when asked if I would ever consider being a professor, my
"no" is not so resounding.

14. **F.** NO CHANGE
     G. childhood steeling myself
     H. childhood steeling ourselves
     J. childhoods steeling ourselves

15. **A.** NO CHANGE
     B. liveliness, which
     C. liveliness which
     D. liveliness, that

GO ON TO THE NEXT PAGE.

1 ■ ■ ■ ■ ■ ■ ■ ■ 1

PASSAGE II

Germany's Black Forest

The Black Forest, a large, forested mountain range, lies in
                                            16
the far southwest corner of Germany. Today it occupies about

2,320 square miles, but its current area is only a small

indication of its anterior sprawl. Loggers cleared a huge num-
                    17
ber of hardwood trees from the Black Forest in the eighteenth

century, planting instead pines and firs. Commercial
          18
deforestation and natural phenomenon, such as a huge

cyclone in 1999, have transformed the forest's topical flora,
                                    19

but many natural features endures. The region's major rivers,
                              20
deep lakes, and high mountain peaks were formed by giant

glaciers thousands of years ago, and these formations still

exist. 21

In the nineteenth century, the kingdom became well-
                              22
known for its master clockmakers, who produced beau-

tifully crafted and famously accurate mechanical clocks.

Accordingly, one branch of Black Forest Clockmakers pro-
23
duced the iconic cuckoo clocks, which came to the height of

their popularity in the 1850s. Later on, the Black Forest clocks
                              24
had become a mass-produced commodity. The industry lost

16. Given that all choices are true, which one best shows that
    the Black Forest is aptly named?
    F. NO CHANGE
    G. A region whose many inhabitants are known to be
       superstitious
    H. A forested mountain range that offered inspiration for
       many traditional fairy tales
    J. A region that was once so thick with trees that very
       little light penetrated through the canopy

17. A. NO CHANGE
    B. former
    C. ensuing
    D. later

18. F. NO CHANGE
    G. replacing it with
    H. replacing them with
    J. interspersing

19. A. NO CHANGE
    B. forests' topical flora,
    C. topical flora (of the forest),
    D. topical flora aspects within the forest,

20. F. NO CHANGE
    G. are enduring.
    H. have endured.
    J. ANY of the above options are correct.

21. If the author were to delete the words *major, deep,* and
    high, the sentence would primarily lose:
    A. a visual sense of what is being described.
    B. erroneous modifiers.
    C. a subtle contrast between these geological formations
       and the topical flora.
    D. an indirect acknowledgment of the size of the glaciers.

22. F. NO CHANGE
    G. country
    H. city
    J. region

23. A. NO CHANGE
    B. For example,
    C. OMIT the underlined portion.
    D. Inevitably,

24. Given that all choices are true, which option provides the
    reader with the most specific information:
    F. NO CHANGE
    G. Shortly after the height of their popularity,
    H. Before the turn of the century,
    J. By the 1870s,

GO ON TO THE NEXT PAGE.

1 ■ ■ ■ ■ ■ ■ ■ ■ 1

its prestige shortly after World War II. [25]

In modern times, the major industry in the Black Forest is international tourism. Local Germans spend a lot of time hiking the forest's long-distance footpaths. Another major attraction for tourists is the fairy tale landscape. The Black

Forest was the unofficial setting of many German fairy tales, including "Hansel and Gretel" and "Little Red Riding Hood." The mountainsides are still said to be haunted with werewolves, witches, and sorcerers. Still others are attracted by the delicious food native to the region. Of the many pastries that originated in the Black Forest region, the Black Forest Gateau, a chocolate layer cake—is by far the most popular.

Although the land and the inhabitants have changed through the years, the Black Forest region continues to produce the clocks, hiking, and culinary delights that bring fame to Germany.

25. At this point, the author is considering including the following sentence:

> Some of the handmade clocks from the Black Forest featured tiny, wooden figurines that moved every second or every hour.

Should the writer make this addition?

A . No, because it is only tangentially related to the theme of the essay.
B . Yes, it is an important detail that helps the reader visualize the clocks.
C . No, because it distracts the reader from the longevity of the clock-making industry.
D . Yes, but this sentence would make the most sense following the first sentence of the paragraph.

26. **F.** NO CHANGE
G. Hikers come from all over the world to travel the long-distance footpaths.
H. The footpaths in the Black Forest are really worth a gander.
J. Hikers on the long-distance footpaths are usually also tourists.

27. **A.** NO CHANGE
B. is
C. used to be
D. could be

28. **F.** NO CHANGE
G. werewolves witches, and sorcerers.
H. werewolves witches and sorcerers.
J. werewolves, witches and sorcerers.

29. **A.** NO CHANGE
B. Gateau ... a chocolate layer cake ... is
C. Gateau, a chocolate layer cake, is
D. Gateau; a chocolate layer cake; is

30. The phrase that best completes this passage is:
F. NO CHANGE
G. continues to play a major role in shaping Germany's identity.
H. is threatened by acid rain and other environmental pollutants, and it desperately needs our help.
J. is unlikely to diminish in size since so many people are now committed to protecting its beauty and preserving the culture it produces.

GO ON TO THE NEXT PAGE.

1 ■ ■ ■ ■ ■ ■ ■ ■ **1**

PASSAGE III

The Final Frontier

Space travel became <u>a reality from the science fiction</u>
in April 1961, when the Russian astronaut Yuri Gagarin
became the first man to orbit the Earth. The American craft,
Apollo 11, landed on the moon in 1969. Before this accom-
plishment, manned and unmanned satellites, <u>craft which</u>
circle the Earth without landing, were the

only means of exploring <u>"the final frontier."</u>

[34] Emboldened by multiple successful trips to the

<u>moon, (there were six *Apollo* landings between 1969 and
1972) space</u>

travelers quickly increased their <u>ambitions: within</u> a matter of
months, Mars became the new target of space exploration.

Mars is <u>farther from the Earth than the moon, and</u>
requires precise calculations and greater resources to reach.

The Soviet Union <u>launches</u> unmanned probes bound for
Mars in 1969, but none of these actually reached the surface
of the planet until 1971. Two crafts called *Mars 2* and *Mars 3*
reached the Martian surface. <u>Although</u> *Mars 2* was destroyed
in a crash landing, *Mars 3* made a soft landing and was able

---

31. **A.** NO CHANGE
    B. a reality, previously existing only in science fiction novels,
    C. something real brought from science fiction
    D. a reality

32. **F.** NO CHANGE
    G. craft that
    H. either F or G is correct
    J. craft, that

33. If the author were to delete the quotation marks in the underlined portion, the major result would be:
    A. the reader would not understand that the final frontier is an institutionalized concept understood by most people who know anything about space travel.
    B. the phrase would refer to the American West instead of outer space.
    C. the phrase would take on a colloquial tone.
    D. the phrase would become meaningless.

34. For the sake of the logic and coherence of the paragraph, the preceding sentence should be:
    F. placed at the beginning of the paragraph.
    G. placed where it is now, after the third sentence in the paragraph.
    H. placed at the end of the paragraph.
    J. This sentence should be omitted entirely.

35. **A.** NO CHANGE
    B. moon (there were six *Apollo* landings between 1969 and 1972), space
    C. moon, (there were six *Apollo* landings between 1969 and 1972), space
    D. moon (there were six *Apollo* landings between 1969 and 1972) space

36. **F.** NO CHANGE
    G. ambitions, and within
    H. ambitions. Within
    J. Any of the above is correct.

37. **A.** NO CHANGE
    B. farther to the Earth than the moon,
    C. farther to the Earth then the moon,
    D. farther from the Earth then the moon,

38. **F.** NO CHANGE
    G. launched
    H. would launch
    J. began launching

39. **A.** NO CHANGE
    B. Despite
    C. Granted,
    D. To the extent that

GO ON TO THE NEXT PAGE.

1 ■ ■ ■ ■ ■ ■ ■ ■ **1**

to transmit readings to Earth for 20 seconds before it stopped working. Together, the Soviet Union and United States have launched two dozen spacecraft toward Mars that have collected large amounts of data about the planet's chemical makeup and environment. Data which have fueled many debates about whether Mars could ever have supported life. While these debates rage on, a new group is preparing to establish human life on Mars in the very near future.

No human has ever landed on Mars, but a new group is hoping to do just that. Mars One is a Dutch nonprofit organization, founded in 2012 with the aim of establishing a permanent human colony on Mars by 2025. Mars One plans to select 24 applicants; train them for eight years before sending them on a one-way trip to Mars. As of 2014, more than 200,000 people from 140 countries had applied for the chance to be sent to colonize Mars. I think it's odd that people would voluntarily leave their families and friends for the rest of their lives. 44 Whether or not the Mars One effort is ever launched, the serious funding and organization, and public interest in the project demonstrate that the final frontier is still calling, and many people around the world are still answering that call.

40. If the author were to delete the underlined section, the sentence would primarily:
    F. lose information about how long the probes were supposed to function after landing.
    G. lose the information that the probes did not land smoothly.
    H. gain clarity by eliminating a redundancy.
    J. lose the information that *Mars 3* stopped working for reasons other than a crash landing.

41. A. NO CHANGE
    B. The data, which
    C. This data
    D. These data

42. For the sake of the logic and coherence of the paragraph, the preceding sentence should be:
    F. Moved to the very beginning of the first paragraph in the essay.
    G. Moved to the beginning of the second paragraph.
    H. Omitted entirely because it is redundant.
    J. Moved to follow the third sentence of the first paragraph.

43. A. NO CHANGE
    B. applicants and
    C. applicants, and
    D. applicants,

44. The preceding sentence should be omitted because:
    F. It contradicts an earlier statement.
    G. The use of first person is inappropriate given the tone of the rest of the essay.
    H. The reader probably does not care about the personal statement the author is making.
    J. The people colonizing Mars will be able to come back to Earth eventually.

45. A. NO CHANGE
    B. serious funding organization and public interest
    C. serious funding, organization, and public interest
    D. serious funding organization, and public interest

1 ■ ■ ■ ■ ■ ■ ■ ■ 1

PASSAGE IV

Sir Francis Bacon's Scientific Method

Sir Francis Bacon led an extraordinary career in late sixteenth- and early seventeenth-century England. He spent a majority of his years advancing through ranks of

lawyers and statesmen, but he is best known for his invention
                                        47
of the Baconian method, an experiment-driven approach to

scientific inquiry. Before the Baconian method became wide-

spread, exploration of the natural world was enshrouded by
                                        48

superstitious, religion, and metaphysical beliefs. The
                49
chemistry that Bacon first learned was really more like

alchemy that used poetic, esoteric language to describe the
50
interactions of metals and minerals. Science and the natural

world was invariably associated with mystical ceremonies
        51
and with the occult. Scientists did not find it problematic to

explain the physical world with nonphysical phenomenon in

seventeenth-century England. Though Bacon did.
                                        52

One of the leading schools in England, Bacon attended
                        53

Cambridge University in the mid-1570s. Cambridge was as
                            54

46. If the author were to delete the underlined portion, the paragraph would primarily lose:
    F. an extraneous prepositional phrase.
    G. important information that contextualizes the main character.
    H. generalized information that is repeated in detail later in the paragraph.
    J. the approximate date of Francis Bacon's birth.

47. A. NO CHANGE
    B. greater known
    C. wider known
    D. farthest known

48. F. NO CHANGE
    G. enshrined
    H. enclosed
    J. informed

49. A. NO CHANGE
    B. penitentiary
    C. religious
    D. religiosity

50. F. NO CHANGE
    G. alchemy, which used
    H. alchemy using
    J. alchemy, the use of which

51. A. NO CHANGE
    B. they were
    C. which was
    D. were

52. F. NO CHANGE
    G. England, but Bacon did.
    H. England; Bacon did.
    J. England like Bacon.

53. The underlined phrase only makes sense in the following position:
    A. after "University."
    B. at the beginning of the sentence, where it is now.
    C. after "Bacon."
    D. at the very end of the sentence.

54. F. NO CHANGE
    G. mid Fifteen-Seventies.
    H. mid-1570's.
    J. mid fifteen-seventies.

GO ON TO THE NEXT PAGE.

1 ■ ■ ■ ■ ■ ■ ■ ■ **1**

reputable in Bacon's time as it is today. [55] It was here that he began to question the traditional Aristotelian approach to

science, which he deemed "unfruitful". Disgusted with the Aristotelian method, he eventually left the school to develop his own method of inquiry, one that relied on objective experimentation. The goal of Bacon's method was to make new discoveries that would directly benefit human life. [57]

Bacon published a detailed description of his scientific

method in his book "Novum Organum," which translates

from Latin to "New Instrument." Founded on the same principles of our modern scientific method, in this text, he describes a technique: an indifference to preexisting principles that have not been objectively tested; the rejection of all variables that cannot be tested; and the repetition of experiments. Among Bacon's many other publications is *The New Atlantis*, a utopian novel depends upon an idealized society benefits from research conducted using the Baconian method. The ideas proposed in these books strongly influenced the research of scientists in the Royal Society and came to bear on the progressive scientific thinking of the Enlightenment period. Bacon died of pneumonia in 1626, which he contracted while performing an experiment to determine if meat could be kept fresh by freezing it.

55. The preceding sentence should be omitted because:
- **A.** it does not reference a specific time.
- **B.** its information is extraneous.
- **C.** it is a fragment.
- **D.** it presents information that may confuse the reader about why Bacon eventually left school.

56. F. NO CHANGE
- **G.** 'unfruitful.'
- **H.** 'unfruitful'.
- **J.** "unfruitful."

57. This paragraph could be made much stronger by:
- **A.** adding information about the history of Cambridge.
- **B.** deleting information about the reputation of Cambridge.
- **C.** adding information about the Aristotelian method.
- **D.** listing other subjects Bacon studied at Cambridge.

58. F. NO CHANGE
- **G.** 'Novum Organum'
- **H.** *Novum Organum,*
- **J.** (Novum Organum)

59. A. NO CHANGE
- **B.** He describes a technique in this text, founded on the same principles of our modern scientific method:
- **C.** Our modern scientific method is founded on the same principles as the technique he describes in this text:
- **D.** In this text, he describes a technique, which is founded on the same principles of our modern scientific method:

60. F. NO CHANGE
- **G.** in which
- **H.** in, which
- **J.** where

1 ■ ■ ■ ■ ■ ■ ■ ■ **1**

PASSAGE V

Adapted from *The Heart of the Sunset* by Rex Beach

Where it showed between the clumps of grass, the naked

earth was baked plaster hard. It burned like hot coal, and

in spite of a panting lizard here and there, or a dust-gray
<u>61</u>

jack-rabbit startled from its covert, nothing animate stirred

upon its face. A fitful breeze played among the mesquite
<u>62</u>

bushes. A buzzard poised high and motionless in the blinding

sky, long-tailed Mexican crows among the thorny branches
<u>63</u>

creaked and whistled, choked and rattled, snored and

grunted; <u>a dove surveyed the verdant landscape;</u> and out of
<u>64</u>

the sky, the metallic cries of insects clamored, <u>its source</u>
<u>65</u>

unknown.

But the country was of a deadly and a deceitful sameness,

devoid of landmarks and lacking well-defined water-courses.

Out of these unending acres, occasional knolls and low stony

hills lifted themselves <u>or</u> one came, now and then, to van-
<u>66</u>

tage-points where the eye leaped for great distances to

horizons far away. To the <u>womens</u> mind, these outlooks were
<u>67</u>

unutterably depressing, merely serving to reveal the vastness

of the desolation about her.

She felt dizzily for the canteen hanging on her shoulder,

only to find it dry; the galvanized mouthpiece burned her

fingers. With a little shock she remembered that she had done

this very thing several times before, and her forgetfulness

61. **A.** NO CHANGE
    B. accept for
    C. in lieu of
    D. except for

62. The underlined pronoun refers to:
    F. the earth
    G. the sun
    H. the narrator
    J. the rabbit

63. **A.** NO CHANGE
    B. sky.
    C. sky-
    D. sky;

64. Which option is most consistent with the other images in this passage?
    F. NO CHANGE
    G. a seagull searched the horizon,
    H. a dove mourned inconsolably,
    J. a hawk soared joyfully,

65. **A.** NO CHANGE
    B. they're
    C. their
    D. it's

66. **F.** NO CHANGE
    G. so that
    H. although
    J. but

67. **A.** NO CHANGE
    B. womens'
    C. womans
    D. woman's

GO ON TO THE NEXT PAGE.

1 ■ ■ ■ ■ ■ ■ ■ ■ 1

frightened her, since it seemed to show that her mind had
                                                68
been slightly unbalanced by the heat.

In all probability a man situated as she was <u>will speak</u>
                                                69

aloud, in an endeavor to steady himself; <u>but this woman did</u>
                                                                    70
<u>nothing of the sort.</u> Seating herself in the densest shade
       70

she could find <u>(it was really no shade at all),</u> she closed
                              71

her eyes and <u>relaxed, no</u> easy thing to do in such a stifling
                   72
temperature.

At length she opened her eyes again, only to find that she
could make out nothing familiar. Undoubtedly she was lost;
the water-hole might be anywhere. 73 She listened tensely,
and the very air seemed to listen with her; the leaves hushed
their faint whisperings; a nearby cactus held its fleshy ears

alert, while others more distant poised in the same <u>deaf</u>
                                                        74
attitude. It seemed to the woman that a thousand ears were
straining with hers. Her focus returned with the sound of the
whispering leaves, and suddenly she looked straight ahead,
remembering exactly in which direction her destination <u>lay.</u>
                                                          75

68. The pronoun *it* refers to:
   F. her dizziness.
   G. her chronic forgetfulness.
   H. the "little shock."
   J. the galvanized mouthpiece.

69. A. NO CHANGE
   B. would speak
   C. would have spoken
   D. would have spoke

70. F. NO CHANGE
   G. but this woman disdained men.
   H. but this woman was too forgetful to remember to speak.
   J. OMIT the underlined portion.

71. If the author were to delete the underlined phrase, the reader would primarily:
   A. lose an appreciation for how hot it was.
   B. believe there was more shade than there really was.
   C. be lulled into a false sense of security.
   D. erroneously believe that the woman had found shelter.

72. F. NO CHANGE
   G. relaxed. No
   H. relaxed, and no
   J. relaxed: no

73. The author is considering revising the preceding two sentences to be more concise. The best option to achieve this goal is:
   A. Omit the first sentence.
   B. Add the following after the second sentence: "It could be behind her, or maybe it was still miles ahead, or maybe it had dried up. She might have passed it already. She didn't know, and that frightened her."
   C. Replace with, "At length she opened her eyes again, but could see nothing familiar; she was lost."
   D. Replace with, "All was lost."

74. F. NO CHANGE
   G. harkening
   H. indifferent
   J. effusive

75. A. NO CHANGE
   B. laid.
   C. lain.
   D. lie.

END OF ENGLISH TEST.
STOP! IF YOU HAVE TIME LEFT OVER, CHECK YOUR WORK ON THIS SECTION ONLY.

MATHEMATICS TEST

60 Minutes – 60 Questions

DIRECTIONS: Solve each of the problems in the time allowed, and then fill in the corresponding bubble on your answer sheet. Do not spend too much time on any one problem; skip the more difficult problems and go back to them later. You may use a calculator on this test. For this test you should assume that figures are NOT necessarily drawn to scale, that all geometric figures lie in a plane, and that the word *line* is used to indicate a straight line.

DO YOUR FIGURING HERE.

1. The coefficient of lift (C_L) of a certain business jet depends on the angle of attack (α) according to the following equation:

$$C_L = 0.00050\,\alpha^2 + 0.020$$

where angle of attack is measured in degrees. What is the angle of attack that corresponds to a coefficient of lift of 0.030?

   A. 0.078 degrees
   B. 0.097 degrees
   C. 2.0 degrees
   D. 4.5 degrees
   E. 20 degrees

2. A company is deciding between two different car models as it updates its fleet of cars. The purchase price for model A is $30,000, and the price for model B is $35,000. However, model A has an average gas mileage of 27 miles per gallon while model B's is 36 miles per gallon. Each car in the fleet drives an average of 20,000 miles each year. If a gallon of gas costs $4, during which year of driving is the extra cost for model B made up by its superior gas mileage?

   F. Fourth year
   G. Fifth year
   H. Sixth year
   J. Seventh year
   K. Eighth year

3. What are the zeros of the following function?

$$f(x) = x^2 - 5x - 14$$

   A. 0, 0
   B. −7, 2
   C. 7, −2
   D. −1, 14
   E. −14, 1

GO ON TO THE NEXT PAGE.

2   **2**

4. The graph below shows the position of a truck moving on the highway throughout a six-hour trip.

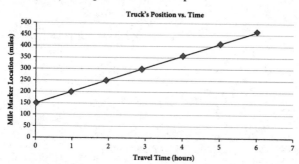

Which of the following equations best represents the relationship between the truck's mile marker location (M) and the travel time (T)?

F. $M = 50T + 150$
G. $T = 50M + 150$
H. $M = 100T - 50$
J. $M = 300T$
K. $T = 6M$

5. The giant sequoia tree known as "General Sherman" is the world's largest tree. If a child wraps 25 meters of rope around the trunk of a giant sequoia tree, what is the trunk's diameter (rounded to the nearest meter)?

A. 4 meters
B. 8 meters
C. 9 meters
D. 10 meters
E. 79 meters

6. What is the sum of angles a, b, and c in the parallelogram?

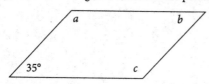

Note: Figure is not to scale.

F. 145°
G. 180°
H. 215°
J. 290°
K. 325°

7. What is the maximum value for y in the following function?

$$y = 5 \sin (2x) + 3$$

A. 2
B. 3
C. 5
D. 8
E. 13

GO ON TO THE NEXT PAGE.

2   **2**

DO YOUR FIGURING HERE.

8. Simplify the following expression:

$$\frac{2\,a^5 b^6 c}{6\,a^3 b^2}$$

   F. $\dfrac{a^8 b^8 c}{3}$

   G. $\dfrac{a^2 b^4 c}{3}$

   H. $\dfrac{11\,abc}{15\,ab}$

   J. $3\,a^2 b^4 c$

   K. $3\,a^8 b^8 c$

9. In 2013, there were 4 different colors of the Titanium-X pickup truck available. The automobile manufacturer built the following models:

   3,000 silver metallic models
   3,500 red pearl models
   4,000 twilight blue models
   4,200 midnight black models

   If you pass a Titanium-X car on the highway, what is the probability that it is a twilight blue color?

   A. 20%
   B. 23%
   C. 25%
   D. 27%
   E. 73%

10. What is the distance between points $(-1, 5)$ and $(3, 2)$ on a coordinate grid?

   F. 2
   G. 3
   H. 4
   J. 5
   K. 6

11. What is the value of angle x in the diagram?

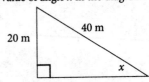

Note: Figure is not to scale.

   A. 20°
   B. 25°
   C. 30°
   D. 45°
   E. 60°

GO ON TO THE NEXT PAGE.

2   △ △ **2**

12. The shaded region displayed in the graph does not include the dashed line. Which of the following best represents all the shaded points?

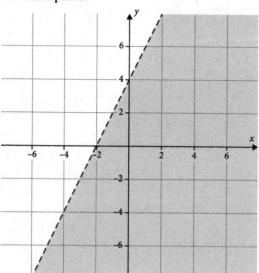

- **F.** $y = 2x + 4$
- **G.** $y \leq 2x + 4$
- **H.** $y < 4x + 2$
- **J.** $y \leq 2x + 4$
- **K.** $y < 2x + 4$

13. What value of x satisfies the following equation?

$$25x + 5 = 40x - 25$$

- **A.** -2
- **B.** 0
- **C.** 2
- **D.** 3
- **E.** 5

14. Evaluate the following function when $x = -1$ and $x = 2$ and determine the sum of the two results:

$$f(x) = 3 - x^2$$

- **F.** -3
- **G.** -2
- **H.** -1
- **J.** 1
- **K.** 3

GO ON TO THE NEXT PAGE.

2   △ △ △ **2**

15. The volume of a right circular cone is determined by the following formula:

$$V = \frac{1}{3}\pi r^2 h$$

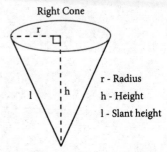

Right Cone

r - Radius
h - Height
l - Slant height

If the volume of a certain cone is 302 cm³ and the height is 8 cm, determine the slant height of the cone.

- **A.** 10 cm
- **B.** 36 cm
- **C.** 12 cm
- **D.** 24 cm
- **E.** 6 cm

16. Simplify the following expression:

$$\sqrt{25x^2 y^6}$$

- **F.** $25(xy)^{12}$
- **G.** $25xy^3$
- **H.** $5(xy)^6$
- **J.** $5(xy)^{12}$
- **K.** $5xy^3$

17. Using the following set of data, determine the mean, mode, and median, respectively.

$$19, 20, 22, 22, 32$$

- **A.** 22, 23, 22
- **B.** 23, 22, 22
- **C.** 19, 22, 29
- **D.** 115, 22, 22
- **E.** 19, 23, 23

18. What value(s) of x satisfies the following equation?

$$|2x - 1| = 9$$

- **F.** −4, 5
- **G.** −5, 4
- **H.** 8, −12
- **J.** 4
- **K.** 5

GO ON TO THE NEXT PAGE.

2   2

19. In the figure, segments $\overline{AC}$ and $\overline{CB}$ are perpendicular, and $\overline{AB}$ goes through the center of the circle. If the radius of the circle is 13 inches and $\overline{CB}$ is 10 inches long, what is the length of $\overline{AC}$?

DO YOUR FIGURING HERE.

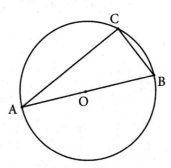

Note: Figure is not to scale.

A. 20 in.
B. 28 in.
C. 16 in.
D. 24 in.
E. 12 in.

20. What point on the coordinate plane is the midpoint of the line segment connecting the points (2, 1) and (10, 5)?

F. (3, 6)
G. (4, 10)
H. (6, 3)
J. (10, 4)
K. (4, 2)

21. Two matrices are multiplied below. Determine the value of x.

$$\begin{bmatrix} 2 & 3 \\ 1 & -1 \end{bmatrix} \begin{bmatrix} 2 \\ x \end{bmatrix} = \begin{bmatrix} 13 \\ -1 \end{bmatrix}$$

A. 2
B. 3
C. 6
D. −1
E. −2

22. After leaving a 20% tip, the total money Sadie spent at a restaurant was $42. Assuming there is no sales tax, what was the amount of Sadie's original bill?

F. $8.40
G. $33.60
H. $35.00
J. $38.50
K. $50.40

2   **2**

23. $\overline{BC}$ is parallel to $\overline{DE}$ in the figure. If $\angle DAE$ is 65° and $\angle AED$ is 30°, what is the value of angle x?

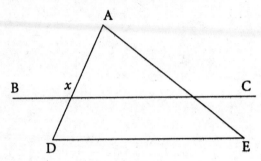

Note: Figure is not to scale.

A. 85°
B. 95°
C. 100°
D. 115°
E. 150°

24. What are the slope and y-intercept, respectively, for the following algebraic expression for the line $6x + 3y = 12$?

F. −6, 9
G. 9, −6
H. 4, −2
J. −2, 4
K. −6, 12

25. The bounce height of a tennis ball is directly proportional to its drop height. A new tennis ball is dropped from a height of 80 cm and bounces to a height of 50 cm. How high will this tennis ball bounce if it is dropped from a height of 120 cm?

A. 50 cm
B. 75 cm
C. 70 cm
D. 80 cm
E. 192 cm

26. The two identical rectangles in the figure each have a length, l, and a height, h. If they are arranged side by side as shown, what function below represents the perimeter, P, of the figure in the new arrangement?

F. $P = 2l + 2h$
G. $P = 4l + 4h$
H. $P = 4h^2\, l^2$
J. $P = 4l + 2h$
K. $P = 2h^2\, l^2$

2   **2**

27. What is the greatest common factor of 27, 54, and 243?

    A. 3
    B. 7
    C. 9
    D. 27
    E. 243

28. Which equation represents the curve shown in the figure?

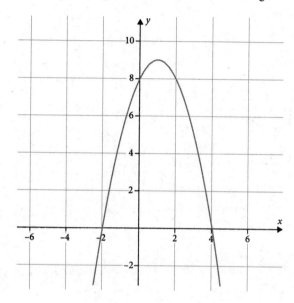

    F. $y = -x^2 + 6x - 8$
    G. $y = x^2 + 2x + 8$
    H. $y = x^2 - 6x + 8$
    J. $y = -2x + 8$
    K. $y = -x^2 + 2x + 8$

29. By definition, $i^2 = -1$. Solve the following expression for x:

$$\sqrt{(5x - 1)} = 6i$$

    A. −7
    B. −7.4
    C. 1.4
    D. 30
    E. Not possible to solve this expression

GO ON TO THE NEXT PAGE.

2　△　△　△　△　△　△　△　△　**2**

30. The area of the trapezoid is 78 in.² Find the height of the trapezoid.

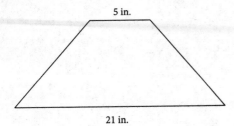

5 in.

21 in.

Note: Figure is not to scale.

   F. 6 in.
   G. 7.4 in.
   H. 10 in.
   J. 27 in.
   K. 24.7 in.

31. Simplify the following expression:

$$\frac{2\sin x}{-\cos x} + 3\sin^2 x + 3\cos^2 x$$

   A. $3 + 2\cot x$
   B. $9x^2 - 2\sin x$
   C. $-3 + 2\tan x$
   D. $3 - 2\tan x$
   E. $-2\sin x + 9x^2$

32. Which of the following equations represent a circle centered at $(-3, 6)$ that passes through the point $(-3, 9)$ on the standard (x, y) coordinate plane?

   F. $(x - 3)^2 + (y + 6)^2 = 9$
   G. $(x + 3)^2 + (y - 6)^2 = 9$
   H. $2x + y = 3$
   J. $-3x + 6y = 3$
   K. $x^2 + y^2 = 90$

33. Which function best represents the graph?

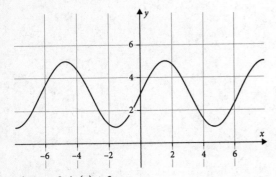

   A. $y = 3\sin(x) + 2$
   B. $y = 2\sin(x) + 3$
   C. $y = 3\cos(x) + 2$
   D. $y = 2\cos(x) + 3$
   E. $y = 3\tan(x) + 2$

DO YOUR FIGURING HERE.

GO ON TO THE NEXT PAGE.

2   **2**

34. What is one value of x that satisfies this equation?

$$(x^3)^{\frac{2}{3}} - 2x = 3$$

- **F.** 3
- **G.** 1
- **H.** 5
- **J.** 1.6
- **K.** −3

DO YOUR FIGURING HERE.

35. Which of the following numbers completes this sequence?

50, 40, 31, 23, 16, _____

- **A.** 9
- **B.** 10
- **C.** 11
- **D.** 12
- **E.** 13

36. The graph shows a line going through points A and B. Which of the following equations represents the line passing through point C that is parallel with line AB?

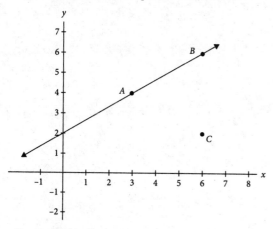

- **F.** $y = (2/3)x + 2$
- **G.** $y = (3/2)x + 2$
- **H.** $y = (2/3)x - 2$
- **J.** $y = 2x + (3/2)$
- **K.** $y = (3/2)x - 2$

37. Line BE is perpendicular to the hypotenuse of right triangle ACD as shown in the figure. What is the value of angle EBC?

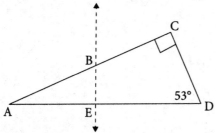

Note: Figure is not to scale.

- **A.** 37°
- **B.** 53°
- **C.** 127°
- **D.** 143°
- **E.** 180°

GO ON TO THE NEXT PAGE.

2   **2**

38. If $h(x) = x^{1/2} + x^2$ and $g(x) = 4x - 3$, then $g(h(4)) = ?$

   F. 12.6
   G. 21
   H. 21.6
   J. 69
   K. 72

39. Which of the following graphs best represents the relationship between the area of a circle and its radius?

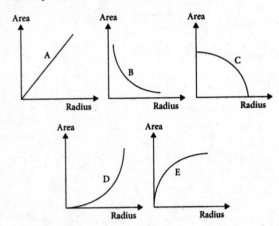

40. The volume of the cube is 27 in³. What is the length of the diagonal line AG?

   F. 3 in.
   G. 4.2 in.
   H. 5.2 in.
   J. 9 in.
   K. 8.9 in.

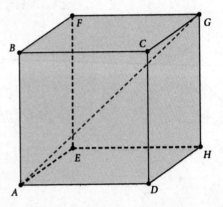

41. Two cars are traveling north on an interstate highway. Lexy's car enters the highway at mile marker 3 and is able to maintain a constant speed of 65 mph. At the same clock reading, Zach's car enters at mile marker 18 and maintains a constant speed of 60 mph. At what mile marker does Lexy catch up with Zach?

   A. 198-mile marker
   B. 14-mile marker
   C. 180-mile marker
   D. 195-mile marker
   E. Never

DO YOUR FIGURING HERE.

GO ON TO THE NEXT PAGE.

2   **2**

42. Which of the following expresses the number 0.000361 in scientific notation?

    F. 3.61×10^{-3}
    G. 3.61×10^{-4}
    H. 3.61×10^{4}
    J. 3.61×10^{3}
    K. 3.61×10^{6}

43. What is the value of $2 + 3 \times 6 - (10 - 8)^2$?

    A. -54
    B. -16
    C. 8
    D. 16
    E. 26

44. What is the complete solution to the following equation?

$$28 + 10x < 4 - 2x$$

    F. $x > -2$
    G. $x < -4$
    H. $x < 4$
    J. $x > 4$
    K. $x < -2$

45. What is the difference between 43 and the sum of the squares of -2, 1, and 6?

    A. 23
    B. 97
    C. 53
    D. 31
    E. 39

46. Malcolm collected a total of 37 rare nickels and dimes. The face value of this collection is $2.95. How many nickels are in Malcolm's coin collection?

    F. 22
    G. 17
    H. 25
    J. 15
    K. 20

47. Solve the following equation for x:

$$54! \, (x - 500) = 56!$$

    A. 2,580
    B. 3,580
    C. 501
    D. -499
    E. 611

48. What are all the values of x that satisfy the following equation?

$$\ln (x + 2) + \ln (x + 4) = \ln (3x + 12)$$

    F. 1 and -4
    G. 1
    H. -4
    J. -1 and 4
    K. 4

DO YOUR FIGURING HERE.

GO ON TO THE NEXT PAGE.

2   **2**

DO YOUR FIGURING HERE.

49. Given $f(x) = 3x^2 - 2$ with a domain between 2 and 8, determine the function's range, R.

   A. $10 < R < 190$
   B. $0.66 < R < 1.83$
   C. $4 < R < 22$
   D. $1.3 < R < 3.3$
   E. All real numbers

50. Which of the following functions has 3 zeros: $-2i$, 0, and $2i$?

   F. $f(x) = x^2 + 4$
   G. $f(x) = x^3 + 4x$
   H. $f(x) = x^2 - 4$
   J. $f(x) = x^3 - 4x$
   K. $f(x) = x^2 + 4x + 4$

51. If $\cos x = \dfrac{-\sqrt{2}}{2}$ and $\pi < x < 2\pi$, what is the value of x^2?

   A. $\dfrac{\pi^2}{4}$

   B. $\dfrac{3\pi}{4}$

   C. $\dfrac{9\pi^2}{16}$

   D. $\dfrac{25\pi^2}{16}$

   E. $\dfrac{5\pi}{4}$

52. Given the parallelogram ABCD shown in the diagram, which of the following statements could NOT be used as part of the proof that triangle ABD is congruent to triangle DCA?

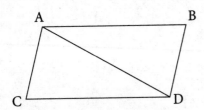

   F. Angle CDA is congruent to angle BAD.
   G. Segment AC is congruent to BD.
   H. Segment DA is congruent to DA by the reflexive property.
   J. Segment AB is congruent to CD.
   K. Angle ACD is congruent to angle BDA.

GO ON TO THE NEXT PAGE.

53. Which of the following is the equation for the conic section displayed in the graph?

DO YOUR FIGURING HERE.

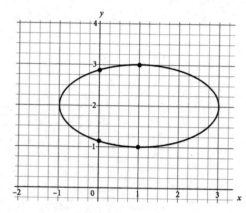

A. $\dfrac{(x-4)^2}{1} + \dfrac{(x-1)^2}{2} = 1$

B. $\dfrac{(x+1)^2}{4} + \dfrac{(x+2)^2}{1} = 1$

C. $\dfrac{(x-1)^2}{4} + \dfrac{(x-2)^2}{1} = 1$

D. $\dfrac{(x+4)^2}{1} + \dfrac{(x+2)^2}{2} = 1$

E. $(x+1)^2 + (y+2)^2 = 4$

54. The points $(-2, -1)$ and (x, y) define a line that is perpendicular to the line shown in the diagram. Select a possible point (x, y):

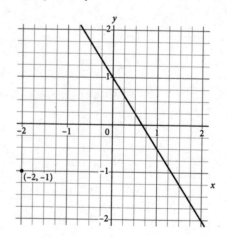

F. $(1, 1)$

G. $\left(-\dfrac{3}{2}, 1\right)$

H. $\left(\dfrac{2}{3}, \dfrac{1}{3}\right)$

J. $(2, 1)$

K. $(2, 2)$

GO ON TO THE NEXT PAGE.

2   **2**

55. Line A is parallel with line B as shown in the diagram. Given the angles x and y, which of the following is a valid expression for angle z in terms of angles x and y?

DO YOUR FIGURING HERE.

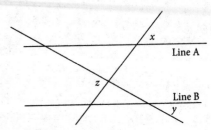

A. $z = 2x - y$
B. $z = 360 - 2x + y$
C. $z = 90 + x - y$
D. $z = 180 - (x + y)$
E. $z = x + y$

56. Evaluate the following expression when $x = 4$ and $y = 27$:

$$\frac{9xy}{18x^{-\frac{1}{2}}y^{\frac{1}{3}}}$$

F. 25.5
G. 36
H. 81
J. 243
K. 324

57. $g(x)$ is a transformation that moves $f(x)$ 2 units in the negative x-direction and 3 units in the positive y-direction in the standard coordinate plane. What is $g(x)$?

A. $g(x) = f(x - 2) - 3$
B. $g(x) = f(x + 2) + 3$
C. $g(x) = f(x + 3) - 2$
D. $g(x) = f(x - 3) + 2$
E. $g(x) = f(x - 2) + 3$

58. What 3-dimensional figure forms as the quadrilateral ABCD rotates about the y-axis?

F. right circular cylinder
G. rectangular prism
H. cone
J. parallelogram
K. cube

GO ON TO THE NEXT PAGE.

2 △ △ △ △ △ △ △ △ **2**

59. The length, L, of a rectangular field of grain is twice its width. Which of the following expresses the area of the field?

   A. $2L^2$
   B. $\dfrac{L^2}{4}$
   C. $\dfrac{L^2}{2}$
   D. $3L$
   E. $6L$

60. A particular satellite moves 27,000 kilometers per hour. How much time does it take the satellite to travel 3.24×10^5 km?

   F. 12 hours
   G. 8.3×10^8 hours
   H. 8.7×10^9 hours
   J. 1.2×10^{-2} hours
   K. 24 hours

DO YOUR FIGURING HERE.

END OF THE MATHEMATICS TEST.
STOP! IF YOU HAVE TIME LEFT OVER, CHECK YOUR WORK ON THIS SECTION ONLY.

3

3

READING TEST

35 Minutes – 40 Questions

DIRECTIONS: This test includes four passages, each followed by 10 questions. Read the passages and choose the best answer to each question. After you have selected your answer, fill in the corresponding bubble on your answer sheet. You should refer to the passages as often as necessary when answering the questions.

PASSAGE I

LITERARY NARRATIVE: *This passage is adapted from the novel* The Secret Garden, *by Frances Hodgson Burnett (© 1910, 1911, by The Phillips Publishing Co., 1911 Frances Hodgson Burnett)* http://www.gutenberg.org/files/113/113-h/113-h.htm#chap04

After Martha was gone Mary turned down the walk which led to the door in the shrubbery. She could not help thinking about the garden which no one had been into for ten years. She wondered what it would look like and
5 whether there were any flowers still alive in it. When she had passed through the shrubbery gate she found herself in great gardens, with wide lawns and winding walks with clipped borders. There were trees, and flower-beds, and evergreens clipped into strange shapes, and a large pool
10 with an old gray fountain in its midst. But the flower-beds were bare and wintry and the fountain was not playing. This was not the garden which was shut up. How could a garden be shut up? You could always walk into a garden.

She was just thinking this when she saw that, at the end
15 of the path she was following, there seemed to be a long wall, with ivy growing over it. She was not familiar enough with England to know that she was coming upon the kitchen-gardens where the vegetables and fruit were growing. She went toward the wall and found that there was a green door
20 in the ivy, and that it stood open. This was not the closed garden, evidently, and she could go into it.

She went through the door and found that it was a garden with walls all round it and that it was only one of several walled gardens which seemed to open into
25 one another. She saw another open green door, revealing bushes and pathways between beds containing winter vegetables. Fruit-trees were trained flat against the wall, and over some of the beds there were glass frames.

The place was bare and ugly enough, Mary thought, as
30 she stood and stared about her. It might be nicer in summer when things were green, but there was nothing pretty about it now.

Presently an old man with a spade over his shoulder walked through the door leading from the second garden.
35 He looked startled when he saw Mary, and then touched his cap. He had a surly old face, and did not seem at all pleased to see her—but then she was displeased with his garden and wore her "quite contrary" expression, and certainly did not seem at all pleased to see him.

40 Mary made no response. She went down the path and through the second green door. There, she found more walls and winter vegetables and glass frames, but in the second wall there was another green door and it was not open. Perhaps it led into the garden which no one had
45 seen for ten years. As she was not at all a timid child and always did what she wanted to do, Mary went to the green

door and turned the handle. She hoped the door would not open because she wanted to be sure she had found the mysterious garden—but it did open quite easily and
50 she walked through it and found herself in an orchard. There were walls all round it also and trees trained against them, and there were bare fruit-trees growing in the winter-browned grass—but there was no green door to be seen anywhere. Mary looked for it, and yet when she
55 had entered the upper end of the garden she had noticed that the wall did not seem to end with the orchard but to extend beyond it as if it enclosed a place at the other side. She could see the tops of trees above the wall, and when she stood still she saw a bird with a bright red breast sit-
60 ting on the topmost branch of one of them, and suddenly he burst into his winter song—almost as if he had caught sight of her and was calling to her.

She stopped and listened to him and somehow his cheerful, friendly little whistle gave her a pleased
65 feeling—even a disagreeable little girl may be lonely, and the big closed house and big bare moor and big bare gardens had made this one feel as if there was no one left in the world but herself. If she had been an affectionate child, who had been used to being loved, she would have broken
70 her heart, but even though she was "Mistress Mary Quite Contrary" she was desolate, and the bright-breasted little bird brought a look into her sour little face which was almost a smile. She listened to him until he flew away. He was not like an Indian bird and she liked him and won-
75 dered if she should ever see him again. Perhaps he lived in the mysterious garden and knew all about it.

1. According to the passage, for what reason did Mary first go into the gardens?
   A. To climb in the oddly shaped trees
   B. To find the door to a mysterious garden
   C. To play with the bird that had a cheerful song
   D. To help the old man who tended the gardens

2. It can be reasonable inferred from the passage that Mary could be characterized as being:
   F. vapid.
   G. indolent.
   H. genial.
   J. petulant.

3. Which of the following statements about the gardens best represents what Mary thought of them?
   A. They weren't very pretty but might look better in the summer.
   B. They made her feel lonely and homesick for India.
   C. They were full of strange plants and dead trees.
   D. They had far too many glass frames.

GO ON TO THE NEXT PAGE.

3 ████████████████████████████████ **3**

4. It can be reasonably inferred from the passage that the gardener felt which way when he saw Mary?

   F. Glad to see her
   G. Annoyed that she was there
   H. Disappointed that she didn't bring a shovel
   J. Sorry that she hadn't come sooner

5. According to the passage, which of these statements best expresses Mary's attitude?

   A. She was usually afraid of new and different things.
   B. She was anxious to find her way out of the garden.
   C. She preferred her own company.
   D. She generally did as she pleased.

6. The last paragraph establishes all of the following EXCEPT:

   F. Mary lives in a big house on the moor.
   G. the bird wasn't like any Mary had ever seen.
   H. the garden had ivy growing on its walls.
   J. Mary wasn't accustomed to affection.

7. Which of the following statements about what the old man did when he saw Mary in the garden is supported by the passage?

   A. He threw his spade over his shoulder and walked away.
   B. He took off his cap and wiped his face with it.
   C. He was surprised to see her and gave her a silent greeting.
   D. He told her he was displeased that she was in his garden and sent her on her way.

8. It can be reasonably inferred from the passage that listening to the bird made Mary wonder:

   F. if the bird knew where to find the secret garden.
   G. when she would be able to return to India.
   H. why no one was ever very affectionate to her.
   J. how long she would have to live in the big house on the moor.

9. According to the passage, which of the following did Mary find in the garden?

   A. A fountain
   B. A maze
   C. An apple tree
   D. A rose bed

10. It can reasonably be inferred from the passage that Mary felt which way about finding door after door in the garden?

   F. Indifferent
   G. Curious
   H. Uneasy
   J. Confused

GO ON TO THE NEXT PAGE.

3 ██ **3**

PASSAGE II
SOCIAL STUDIES:
http://www.touregypt.net/featurestories/sphinx1.htm
http://www.ancientegypt.co.uk/pyramids/about/
sphinx.html
http://www.aeraweb.org/projects/sphinx/
http://www.smithsonianmag.com/history/
uncovering-secrets-of-the-sphinx-5053442/?all
http://www.britannica.com/EBchecked/topic/594507/
Thutmose-IV

The Great Sphinx has long symbolized Ancient Egypt. It was carved some 4,500 years ago from a single, enormous mass of limestone in the sands of the Sahara desert near Giza, on the site of a horseshoe-shaped quarry that
5 provided the material for the monument. The statue, which is 66' tall and 240' long, has a human head on the body of a lion in repose, with its front paws outstretched. Traces of red pigment on the face suggest it was once painted, while traces of blue and yellow paint were found elsewhere on
10 the Sphinx. Because the Egyptians did not record history, the original name has been lost to the ages. The current name probably came into use about 2,000 years after it was built, borrowing the moniker from a figure in ancient Greek mythology.

15 Built for the Egyptian pharaoh Khafre between 2520 and 2494 BCE, the purpose of the Sphinx was to guard the entrance to the pyramid where he would eventually be buried after his death. One of the world's foremost experts in Egyptology, Dr. Mark Lehner, believes that the Sphinx was
20 not built by slaves as had long been thought, but rather by well-fed workers who dined on "prime beef" and who may have been on a rotating schedule in a type of a national service or some other form of obligation to the pharaoh, according to a 2010 article in *Smithsonian Magazine*.

25 Over the ages, the Sphinx underwent various repairs and transformations. For example, there was once a hole in the top of its head where a royal cobra headdress had been affixed. The hole has since been filled in by erosion caused by sand and wind over the millennia. Remnants of
30 the adornment have since been excavated by archaeologists. A more recent addition was the iconic braided beard, which was believed to have been added hundreds of years after the original construction took place. It fell off at some unknown point in time. It's believed that the nose may
35 have dropped off sometime during the 13th century CE.

Sand has long been both friend and foe of the Great Sphinx. For as much as sand contributed to the gradual but steady deterioration of the monolith, it also created a protective covering. As the Sphinx became buried, it was
40 shielded from the corrosive effects of wind-blown sand. It spent most of its life hidden from view. Roughly seven centuries after it was created, it had all but disappeared under the relentlessly drifting sands, until just the head was showing.

45 Then the Sphinx was rescued from oblivion. According to legend, while King Thutmose IV was still a prince, he had a prophetic dream around 1400 BCE. He had been out hunting when he sought out the shade of the Sphinx in which to take a nap. In the dream, the Sphinx called itself
50 Horemakhet, meaning "Horus-in-the-Horizon," which is the oldest extant name for the Sphinx. Horemakhet told Thutmose that if he cleared away the sand surrounding it, he would become the king of Egypt. Thutmose did as

he was told. He was rewarded by being named pharaoh,
55 despite the fact that he was not his father's first choice as to succeed him to the throne.

In order to commemorate the event, Thutmose had the tale engraved on a slab of pink granite called the Dream Stela and it was placed between the Sphinx's paws. King
60 Thutmose is credited with starting a Sphinx-worshipping cult, and its image began to show up in artwork, such as paintings and statues all over the country. The Sphinx became the symbolic embodiment of royalty as well as of the sun, which the Egyptians worshipped as a sacred god.
65 Thutmose is believed to be responsible for the first attempt to repair the Sphinx. Slabs of stone covering the dilapidated colossus date to his time as a ruler.

Over the millennia since it was hewn, there were three other known large-scale attempts during ancient times to
70 repair the Sphinx. The most recent of these spanned from 332 BCE to 642 CE.

By the time Napoleon Bonaparte beheld the Great Pyramid in Giza in 1798, one of the last existing wonders of the ancient world, the Sphinx was once again buried up
75 to its neck in sand. In 1817, 160 men were led by a Genoese Egyptologist named Capt. Giovanni Battista Caviglia in the first effort to reclaim the Sphinx from the sand in modern times. However, sand quickly filled in the excavated areas and the project was abandoned.

80 It wasn't until the late 1930s that the Sphinx was finally uncovered. Selim Hassan, an Egyptian archaeologist, accomplished what had not been done in more than 3,000 years. With the successful completion of this feat, Hassan paved the way for archaeologists to examine and study the
85 giant figure in the desert. Thanks to him, untold generations will have the opportunity to appreciate the marvel that is the Great Sphinx.

11. One of the author's main points about the history of the Great Sphinx is that:

A. it's the last of the existing wonders of the ancient world.
B. Napoleon Bonaparte was one of the first people in modern times to see it in its entirety.
C. being buried in sand saved it from obliteration.
D. no attempt to repair it was made until the second century BCE.

12. As it is used in line 51 in the fifth paragraph, what meaning does the word *extant* have?

F. Commonly used
G. Divinely given
H. Translation of
J. Still existing

13. The passage indicates that although it was long thought that slaves built the Great Sphinx, evidence has come to light that suggests the workers were actually:

A. athletes in training.
B. fulfilling a civic responsibility.
C. working off tax debts.
D. Roman artisans.

GO ON TO THE NEXT PAGE.

3 ▐███████████████████████████▌ **3**

14. Which sentence best summarizes the fourth paragraph?

   F. It's only been since modern times that the Sphinx couldn't be seen.
   G. Blowing sand eroded the Sphinx until there was very little of it left.
   H. Only the head of the Sphinx is left from the original monument.
   J. If the Sphinx hadn't been buried underneath the sand, it might not still exist.

15. Based on the passage, the primary reason the Great Sphinx was originally constructed was to:

   A. commemorate Thutmose becoming king.
   B. protect the tomb of Khafre.
   C. legitimize a new Sphinx-worshipping cult.
   D. glorify Egyptian civilization.

16. According to the passage, what was the Dream Stela?

   F. A part of the original Sphinx that was later excavated by archaeologists
   G. A memorialization of the pact between Thutmose and Horemakhet
   H. A sacred monument to the glory of Pharaoh Khafre's kingdom
   J. An engraved granite block used as the cornerstone of the Sphinx

17. The passage indicates that the Genoese Egyptologist Capt. Giovanni Battista Caviglia tried to excavate the Great Sphinx, but he had to abandon the project for which reason?

   A. It proved to be futile.
   B. He couldn't get enough men.
   C. Napoleon Bonaparte ordered him to stop.
   D. The Egyptian government only allowed Egyptian archaeologists to work on the Sphinx.

18. Based on the passage, for which reason was the original name of the Great Sphinx NOT known?

   F. Ancient Egyptians considered its name too sacred to use.
   G. Ancient Egyptians never gave it any particular name.
   H. Ancient Egyptians didn't write it down.
   J. Ancient Egyptians renamed the Sphinx so often that the name was forgotten.

19. According to the passage, the Sphinx originally had which feature?

   A. It was painted several different colors.
   B. It had a protective layer of pink granite slabs covering it.
   C. It had a headdress with an ankh on it.
   D. It had a carved stone cobra between its paws.

20. In a dream, Horemakhet told Thutmose that he would become the king if he:

   F. cleared the sand covering the Great Sphinx.
   G. started a cult devoted to the Great Sphinx.
   H. worshipped the Great Sphinx as a god.
   J. constructed the Great Sphinx as a tribute.

GO ON TO THE NEXT PAGE.

PASSAGE III
HUMANITIES:
http://webs.anokaramsey.edu/stankey/eng2230/docs2230/
romantic/romretbl.htm
http://www.macalester.edu/~hammarberg/russ251/
romreal.html
http://www.luc.edu/faculty/cschei1/teach/rrn.html
http://www.luc.edu/faculty/cschei1/teach/rrn2.html
http://public.wsu.edu/~campbelld/amlit/realism.htm
http://archive.csustan.edu/english/reuben/pal/chap3/
3intro.html
http://www.westga.edu/~mmcfar/worksheet%20on%20
American%20Realism.htm

Romanticism and realism were two different the-
matic approaches to literature in the nineteenth century. Although both schools of thought began in Europe,
American writers embraced both styles. Romanticism
5 lasted from approximately 1830 to 1865. Realism lasted
from 1860 until the second decade of the twentieth century. Each reflected larger social and political issues of the
time.

During the period in which literature had a roman-
10 tic theme, America was in a time of growth. Westward
expansion of the country, also known as manifest destiny,
helped fuel an optimistic outlook. Exploring and settling
the uncharted territories of the frontier fostered a feeling of
freedom. Science and conventional social institutions saw
15 much experimentation. Immigrants from foreign lands
brought new customs and different ways of thinking with
them.

The romantic period was characterized by emotions
and escapism. A "willing suspension of disbelief" was
20 often employed as stories of the improbable became popular. Tales tended to be highly imaginative and showed
the common man as a hero, such as in Herman Melville's
1851 novel *Moby-Dick*. Characters were often "larger
than life," such as Rip Van Winkle, a character in an 1819
25 short story of the same name by Washington Irving.
Subject matter often included such themes as the mysterious or the grotesque, as in Edgar Allan Poe's 1843 work,
The Tell-Tale Heart. Fanciful and imaginary settings were
often employed during the romantic period. Even when
30 real locations were used, they were portrayed in a mysterious or exotic light, for example, Transylvania or the
South Seas.

Plots in romantic literature were central to the story.
Generally, there was some sort of crisis that involved
35 romantic love, with emotions being valued over ratio-
nality. The idealism of self was also employed, as demonstrated by the penitence in Nathaniel Hawthorne's 1850
work, *The Scarlet Letter*. Honor and integrity beyond
what was possessed by the average person were common
40 themes. Stories were told on a grand scale that had no
bearing on most people's day-to-day reality. Happy endings were the norm.

The writing in this period was highly stylized. The language used was often deliberately flowery and literary in
45 tone. Exaggeration was a common component. Tales of the
improbable were prevalent. The author would sometimes
speak directly to the audience. Romanticized notions of
the past and the future were employed. In addition, characters were often on the unusual side. Such figures as ban-
50 dits or gypsies were popular. The characters in stories were
frequently endowed with striking characteristics or man-
nerisms, such as being especially tall or having a "glower-
ing intensity."

By the time realism became a literary convention,
55 starting around 1860 and lasting until roughly the turn
of the century, Americans had seen much change in the
world around them. For instance, the industrial revolution was a particularly polarizing event. Northern states
became industrialized while southern states continued to
60 be primarily agrarian. This schism would widen and divide
the country, eventually leading to the American Civil War
(1861–1865).

Perhaps due in part to the impending American Civil
War, literary works became focused on the mundane world.
65 In this way realism was the polar opposite of romanticism:
where romanticism could be characterized by hearts and
flowers, realism could be viewed in terms of hearths and
plows. Sentiment shifted to practical matters, and reason
overtook fancy. Writings of the time were concerned with
70 reality as it actually was for most people. The lives of ordinary people going about their day-to-day existence were a
typical theme of stories during this period. Tales involved
subjects that nearly everyone could relate to, such as farming or marriage. A happy ending was not guaranteed.

75 Settings were intended to reflect reality. Whether
it was rural life on a farm or life in the expanding and
increasingly industrialized cities, the setting in which the
story took place was familiar and relatable to most people. Writings were also becoming regional as "local color"
80 sought to capture traditions that people feared would be
lost in the increasingly modernized world of mass production and factories. An example of this regional type
of writing was *Life on the Mississippi*, written by Mark
Twain in 1896. In 1899 Kate Chopin wrote about the role
85 of women in society and marriage in *The Awakening*.
Later Upton Sinclair would write about the life of factory
workers in 1906 in *The Jungle*. With rise of the middle
class and an increase in the rate of literacy, people became
more interested in reading about the world around them
90 in order to better understand the societal changes that
were taking place.

The plots in stories written in the realist manner were
quite plausible. Events generally took place in the present
and were presented in a straightforward, chronological
95 manner. The style of writing during the realist period used
common vernacular, which reflected how everyday people
spoke. There was no attempt to make people sound any
smarter or more poetic than they were in real life, unlike
the flowery language of the romantic period. Characters
100 were based on average people. They looked average and
had average lives. Readers could relate to them because
they were just like their friends and neighbors. Where
romanticism made life appear much more interesting and
intriguing than was the experience of most people, realism
105 sought to celebrate the lives led by regular people.

William Dean Howells was one of the most important writers of realism, producing works about unvarnished
contemporary life, such as *Suburban Sketches* in 1871. He
wrote about ordinary people going about their everyday
110 business. Stephen Crane was also a noted realist author
who penned *Maggie: A Girl of the Streets*. Other notable
American writers of realism include Sarah Orne Jewitt,
Jack London, John Steinbeck, and Edith Wharton.

GO ON TO THE NEXT PAGE.

3　　　　　　　　　　　　　　　　　　　　**3**

21. Based on the passage, which of the following settings would be typical of a novel written in the romantic style?

   A. An old castle
   B. A factory
   C. A boarding house
   D. A university

22. The passage states that social and political issues of the time influenced the two different writing styles, with which event being influential to the rise of the realism period?

   F. Manifest Destiny
   G. The U.S. Civil War
   H. Immigration
   J. Scientific experimentation

23. As it is used in line 63 in the seventh paragraph, what does the word *impending* mean?

   A. Divisive
   B. Long ago
   C. Disruptive
   D. About to happen

24. Based on the passage, which of the following statements best represents the romantic style of writing?

   F. The writing style was flamboyant, the setting was familiar, and the characters were peculiar.
   G. The writing style was credible, the setting was fantastic, and the characters were commonplace.
   H. The writing style was ornate, the setting was mythical, and the characters were fanciful.
   J. The writing style was familiar, the setting was credible, and the characters were down-to-earth.

25. The passage states that writers during the realist period sought to portray life in which way?

   A. As mysterious and unknowable
   B. Making the future sound better than the present
   C. Reflecting the lives of everyday people
   D. Capturing the inner world of the imagination

26. The passage states that as the middle class rose, so did literacy rates, which led to more people being interested in reading for which of the following reasons?

   F. They wanted a sense of perspective on the shifting world around them.
   G. They didn't want to see their children struggle with illiteracy as they had.
   H. They wanted to get better jobs and improve their standard of living.
   J. They saw reading as a way to escape their dull, day-to-day lives.

27. Based on the passage, which of these characters would most likely be in a work in the realist style?

   A. A riverboat captain
   B. A South Seas cannibal
   C. A phantasm
   D. A princess

28. Based on the passage, which of the following words would best characterize the writings of the romantic period?

   F. Mundane
   G. Flamboyant
   H. Authentic
   J. Pedestrian

29. According to the passage, which of the following authors wrote in the realist style?

   A. Nathaniel Hawthorne
   B. Herman Melville
   C. Edgar Allan Poe
   D. Jack London

30. Based on the passage, what was the main stylistic difference between the romanticism period and the realism period?

   F. Romanticism sought to preserve fading traditions, with realism primarily focused on the future.
   G. Romanticism projected life as the author wanted it to be, while realism focused on life as it was.
   H. Romanticism was concerned about the here and now, while realists wanted to rewrite history in a better light.
   J. Romanticism primarily used commonplace language, but writings in the realism style used a much more embellished style of language.

GO ON TO THE NEXT PAGE.

3   **3**

PASSAGE IV
NATURAL SCIENCE:
Passage A Sources:
http://www.nasa.gov/audience/forstudents/k-4/stories/what-is-pluto-k4.html
http://news.nationalgeographic.com/news/2006/08/060824-pluto-planet.html
http://www.loc.gov/rr/scitech/mysteries/pluto.html

Passage A

Pluto is more than 3.6 billion miles away from Earth. It's smaller than the Earth's moon, and it has an average temperature of roughly 400 degrees below zero. Its orbit is elliptical, and it takes 248 years to travel around the sun. A
5 day on Pluto lasts for the equivalent of 6.5 Earth days.

In 2006 Pluto lost its status as a major planet. According to Marc Kuchner, a planetary scientist at NASA's Goddard Space Flight Center, astronomers didn't really have much of a choice. "It was either going to be eight planets or a
10 whole lotta planets. Nature sort of forced our hand."

When Eris was discovered in 2003, it triggered the debate about what should be considered a planet. Eris is even larger and farther away than Pluto. The International Astronomical Union (IAU) put together a diverse team
15 of science-minded professionals, ranging from planetary scientists to science writers, to form the Planet Definition Committee. It was their task to reach a consensus on what conditions a celestial body should meet in order to be considered a planet.

20 Under those new guidelines, the IAU decided that Pluto only met two of the three requirements needed to be considered a planet. Although Pluto orbited the sun, and had sufficient mass to be round in shape, it did not meet the third requirement, that it "had cleared the neigh-
25 borhood around its orbit." What that means is, if an object entered the orbit of a planet, then that object would either strike the planet or be flung away into another orbit.

Pluto was reclassified as a dwarf planet, which is a category of solar system objects unto itself. Astronomers argued
30 that if Pluto were a planet, then that would mean that its moon, Charon, would also have to be considered a planet and so would the giant asteroid Ceres. In all, there are five currently known dwarf planets: Ceres, Eris, Haumea, Makemake, and Pluto.

35 Neil deGrasse Tyson, an astrophysicist with the American Museum of Natural History and director of the Hayden Planetarium, noted in a 2008 *National Geographic* article that the word, *planet*, itself has, "lost all scientific value." He added that "we are in desperate
40 need for a lexicon to accommodate this new knowledge."

Also, due to Pluto's size and location in the solar system, astronomers decided that it should be considered a plutoid. A plutoid is a planet that exists in space beyond Neptune, takes more than 200 Earth years to make one
45 revolution around the sun, and has an elliptical orbit. Such objects are also called Trans-Neptunian Objects. Pluto is located in the Kuiper Belt, and there are thousands of objects there that are also small and icy, just like Pluto.

When Pluto was discovered by researchers at the
50 Lowell Observatory in 1930, it was named the ninth planet. However, as technology advanced, astronomers were able to peer far deeper into the cosmos. As they did so, many more objects were discovered. As knowledge grows
55 and evolves, so too must the way in which astronomers describe the universe.

Passage B Sources:
http://www.scientificamerican.com/article/new-planet-definition-enl/
http://www.space.com/43-pluto-the-ninth-planet-that-was-a-dwarf.html
http://www.space.com/5503-astronomers-argue-pluto-planet.html
http://news.nationalgeographic.com/news/2011/08/110824-pluto-dwarf-planet-definition-nasa-iau-space-science/?rptregcta=reg_free_np&rptregcampaign=20131016_rw_membership_n1p_us_se_c1#
http://news.nationalgeographic.com/news/2008/08/080815-pluto-planet.html

Passage B

Following its discovery in 1930, Pluto was named the ninth planet in our solar system. But in 2006 the International Astronomical Union (IAU) decided that it did not meet the new requirements for being a planet.
5 Even so some astronomers maintain that it should still be considered a planet.

Mark Sykes, director of the Planetary Science Institute, favors a 13-planet solar system. He was quoted in a 2010 *National Geographic* article, stating that "If a nonstellar
10 object is massive enough to be round and orbits a star, it ought to be a planet." This would fulfill two of the three qualifications that the IAU deemed to be characteristics of a planet.

Sykes's model of the solar system would include Pluto,
15 along with one of its moons, Charon. Nix and Hydra are Pluto's other two moons. The dwarf planets Eris and Makemake would be included along with Ceres, which would be the smallest planet. Ceres is the largest object found so far in the asteroid belt that exists between Jupiter
20 and Mars.

Shortly after the IAU announced the change in the criteria of what constitutes a planet, a 2006 article in *The Scientific American* noted that the new definition of what a planet is "would expand the solar system to Pluto and
25 beyond, encompassing 12 bodies in all." This model of the solar system would include dwarf planets Ceres and Eris, and Pluto-Charon would be a double planet, a first for the solar system. In addition, 12 other objects would qualify as planets.

30 In 2006 the IAU declared that Pluto was a dwarf planet. Then, in 2008, the committee decided that it was, in fact, a plutoid. This reclassification came as a surprise to other members of the IAU, including researchers who discovered objects, such as Eris, that might fall under this
35 classification.

However, some space scientists reject the authority of the IAU to make such decisions. Sykes noted in a 2008 interview for Space.com that the definitions of a planet as set forth by the IAU "may be convenient for some, but [its
40 ruling] does not reflect reality."

GO ON TO THE NEXT PAGE.

3   **3**

Steve Maran, a retired astronomer for NASA, believes that Pluto should be regarded a planet. "I think there is a strong sentiment among a modest number of astronomers and a great many laypersons that Pluto should be rein-
45 stated or that the IAU action on Pluto should be ignored."

In addition, as astronomers continue to make new finds the idea of what celestial objects should be called a planet is further muddled by the discovery of planets that don't orbit stars, called rogue planets, according to a 2011
50 article in *National Geographic*.

Questions 31–33 ask about Passage A.

---

31. According to the passage, which event began a discussion among astronomers regarding which conditions needed to be met in order for a celestial body to be considered a planet?

A. The annual meeting of the IAU
B. The discovery of Eris
C. The recognition of Pluto as a plutoid
D. The idea that the word *planet* has lost all meaning

32. What is the author's main point in the seventh paragraph of Passage A?

F. Pluto is only one of many plutoids in the Kuiper Belt.
G. Because Pluto is a Trans-Neptunian Object, it isn't really a part of the solar system.
H. Pluto takes too long to orbit the sun to be considered a plutoid.
J. Because Pluto has an elliptical orbit, it can't be called a planet.

33. According to the passage, if Pluto were to remain a planet, then:

A. Neptune would have to be reclassified as a plutoid.
B. the Kuiper Belt would become known as another galaxy.
C. four other celestial bodies would have to be recognized as planets.
D. the idea of what constituted a solar system would have to be redefined.

Questions 34–36 ask about Passage B.

---

34. It can be reasonable inferred from the passage that some space scientists feel that the reclassification of what determines if an object is a planet or not:

F. leads to a larger discussion of what exactly constitutes a solar system.
G. has no bearing on objects closer to Earth than Neptune.
H. could lead to there being more than 12 planets in the solar system.
J. calls into question the definition of a plutoid.

35. According to the passage, the IAU decided in 2006 that Pluto should be considered:

A. a plutoid.
B. a double planet.
C. a rogue planet.
D. a dwarf planet.

36. The third paragraph of Passage B indicates that Nix and Hydra:

F. should be considered the smallest planets.
G. are two of Pluto's moons.
H. are the largest asteroids in the Kuiper Belt.
J. are both larger than Charon.

Questions 37–40 ask about both passages.

---

37. Scientists on both sides of the debate about Pluto agree that it is all of the following EXCEPT:

A. a Trans-Neptunian Object.
B. a plutoid.
C. a double planet.
D. a dwarf planet.

38. Compared to Passage A, Passage B states that:

F. space scientists should call for the IAU to revisit the issue with more astronomers on the committee.
G. another committee comprised of only space scientists should debate the issue.
H. the IAU should have the final say on what is a planet.
J. the authority of the IAU should be refuted.

39. Scientists in both passages agree that:

A. a planet is round and orbits the sun.
B. a planet should have a mass equal to or greater than that of its own moon.
C. a planet doesn't have an elliptical orbit.
D. a planet in the Kuiper Belt isn't really a part of the solar system.

40. The main difference between Passage A and Passage B is that:

F. some space scientists aren't sure if Neptune is a planet.
G. some space scientists think there should be more than nine planets.
H. some space scientists want to use a new word instead of *planet*.
J. some space scientists don't like the whole concept of plutoids.

END OF THE READING TEST.
STOP! IF YOU HAVE TIME LEFT OVER, CHECK YOUR WORK ON THIS SECTION ONLY.

4 ○ ○ ○ ○ ○ ○ ○ ○ ○ **4**

SCIENCE REASONING TEST

35 minutes – 40 Questions

DIRECTIONS: This test includes seven passages, each followed by several questions. Read the passage and choose the best answer to each question. After you have selected your answer, fill in the corresponding bubble on your answer sheet. You should refer to the passages as often as necessary when answering the questions. You may NOT use a calculator on this test.

PASSAGE I

A group of physics students conducted a laboratory investigation to determine how the number and arrangement of lightbulbs in a circuit affect the amount of time needed to completely discharge a capacitor. The group gathered 2 "D-cell" 1.5-volt batteries, a 1.0 Farad capacitor, three small identical lightbulbs, and a variety of wires. During background research the students determined a capacitor consists of two metal plates separated by an insulating material.

Capacitors can be charged if they are connected to a voltage source such as a battery. A fully charged capacitor has a voltage difference between the two plates equal to the source to which it is connected. A charged capacitor can then be connected to an electrical circuit without a battery to move current around the circuit until the capacitor is discharged. Figure 1 shows a neutral capacitor being charged and then discharged.

Neutral Capacitor	Charged Capacitor	Discharged Capacitor
	+ + + + + + +	
	- - - - - - -	

Figure 1

To start the experiment the students hooked a neutral capacitor up to a charging circuit shown in Figure 2. The charging circuit contains the 1 Farad capacitor (C1), a lightbulb (R1), and the two batteries as a voltage source. The lightbulb was on when the charging circuit was connected but eventually dimmed and when out. When the lightbulb went out, the charging circuit was disconnected, and the voltage across the capacitor was measured with a voltmeter.

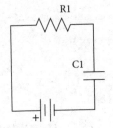

Figure 2

To test how the number and arrangement of lightbulbs affected the amount of time necessary to discharge the capacitor, several discharging circuits were created. The physics group connected the discharging circuit and used a stopwatch to measure the amount of time the lightbulbs were lit. Schematics of these circuits, along with data from the experiment, can be found in Table 1.

	Table 1		
Circuit	Schematic of Circuit	Time Needed to Discharge Capacitor(s)	Qualitative Notes
1	R1, C1	24.9 sec / 24.6 sec	**Circuit 1** Simple series One lightbulb Moderately Bright
2	R1, R2, C1	27.2 sec / 27.5 sec	**Circuit 2** Series circuit Two lightbulbs Dim
3	R1, R2, C1	12.4 sec / 12.2 sec	**Circuit 3** Parallel circuit Two lightbulbs Bright
4	R1, R2, R3, C1	29.8 sec / 29.8 sec	**Circuit 4** Series circuit Three lightbulbs Very dim
5	R1, R2, R3, C1	8.3 sec / 8.4 sec	**Circuit 5** Parallel circuit Three lightbulbs Very bright

GO ON TO THE NEXT PAGE.

4 ◯ ◯ ◯ ◯ ◯ ◯ ◯ ◯ ◯ **4**

1. Which of the following statements is an appropriate conclusion for this experiment?

   A. As the number of lightbulbs increases, the time required to discharge a capacitor also increases.
   B. The capacitor discharges more quickly through the parallel circuit compared to the series circuit.
   C. Doubling the amount of lightbulbs connected in series doubles the time required to discharge the capacitor.
   D. Adding an additional lightbulb in a parallel circuit reduces the amount of time required to discharge a capacitor by a factor of two.

2. At the completion of the experiment the student group set up the circuit found in trial 1 in an attempt to replicate their data. They recorded a time of 23.8 seconds to discharge the capacitor. Which of the following best describes that result?

   F. The students got better at measuring time required as the experiment went on.
   G. Each circuit is not exactly reproducible. Every measurement has some error associated with it and 22.8 seconds just demonstrates that error.
   H. Because of continued use the lightbulb, filaments are beginning to oxidize and obstruct the flow of current through the bulb.
   J. The batteries used to charge the capacitor have been used and do not produce the same voltage as at the start of the experiment.

3. In an additional experiment the circuit shown (*circuit 6*) was tested using the same procedure. Which time shows how long it would take a 1 Farad capacitor to discharge through circuit 6?

   A. 3.1 seconds
   B. 6.2 seconds
   C. 7.1 seconds
   D. 31.6 seconds

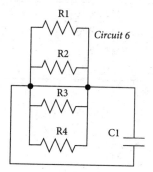

Figure 3

4. Which of the following equations best represents the relationship between the amount of lightbulbs wired in *series* and the time necessary to discharge the 1 Farad capacitor?

   F. Time = 2.5 sec/bulb × (number of bulbs) + 24.7 sec
   G. Time = 24.7 sec + number of bulbs

   H. $\text{Time} = \dfrac{24.7 \text{ seconds}}{\text{number of bulbs}}$

   J. $\text{Time} = \dfrac{24.7 \text{ seconds}}{\text{number of bulbs}^2}$

5. The student group used a voltmeter to determine the voltage across the capacitor right before and after discharging. The voltage reading before the bulbs were connected was 2.90 volts. After the lightbulb went out, the circuit was disconnected and the voltage read 0.54 volts. How could the students have minimized this error?

   A. The students could have discharged the capacitor for the same amount of time in each trial.
   B. The students could have added 2.1 seconds to each recorded time to account for the extra voltage.
   C. The students could have darkened the room to get a more accurate time for when the bulbs stopped being lit.
   D. The students could have used a voltmeter instead of the bulb appearance to measure when the capacitor is discharged.

6. One student in the group would like to measure the amount of time needed to discharge the capacitor through 24 lightbulbs hooked in parallel. According to the data in Figure 3, why might this NOT yield accurate results?

   F. The lightbulbs will be too dim to record a good measurement.
   G. That many bulbs pose a real risk of personal injury or electric shock.
   H. The time needed to discharge will be too small to accurately measure with a stopwatch.
   J. The circuit cannot power that many lightbulbs when charged from only two batteries.

GO ON TO THE NEXT PAGE.

4 ◯ ◯ ◯ ◯ ◯ ◯ ◯ ◯ 4

PASSAGE II

Since healthy streams are so vital to ecosystems, measuring stream quality is an important function of environmental scientists. Oxygen is one indicator of stream health, and it is measured in its dissolved form as dissolved oxygen (DO). The stream system gains oxygen from the atmosphere and from photosynthetic organisms. Respiration by aquatic organisms and decomposition by micro-organisms deplete available oxygen. Dissolved oxygen can also vary with physical factors, such as temperature, altitude, salinity, and stream structure. If dissolved oxygen levels decline, aquatic creatures may migrate, weaken, or die.

Table 1	
Level of Oxygen (mg/L)	Indicates
6–15	Healthy Stream
4–6	Stressed
2–4	Dangerously Low
0–2	Dead Area

While taking a sample of an indicator such as DO is helpful in stream quality monitoring, it is only a snapshot of the water at that moment. As a more stable indicator of health, scientists also like to measure the local macroinvertebrate population. During this testing, macroinvertebrates are collected from the stream and surveyed to determine which types are present and how frequently they occur. As the types of macroinvertebrates present have varying tolerances of pollution, these data can be used to determine the health of that portion of the stream.

Table 2 details some of the macroinvertebrates used to determine water quality.

Table 2 Invertebrates and Pollution Sensitivity/Tolerance					
Organism	Sensitivity	Score	Organism	Sensitivity	Score
Mayfly	Sensitive	3	Dobsonfly	Sensitive	3
Riffle Beetle	Sensitive	3	Aquatic Worm	Tolerant	1
Water Penny	Sensitive	3	Snail	Tolerant	1
Mosquito Larva	Tolerant	1	Dragonfly	Moderate	2
Clam	Moderate	2	Scud	Moderate	2
Mite	Moderate	2	Crayfish	Moderate	2
Midge	Tolerant	1	Damselfly	Moderate	2

Table 3 Water Quality as Indicated by Macroinvertebrates	
Water Quality Rating	Score
Excellent	>22
Good	17–22
Fair	11–16
Poor	<11

GO ON TO THE NEXT PAGE.

4 ◯ ◯ ◯ ◯ ◯ ◯ ◯ ◯ ◯ **4**

The dissolved oxygen data in Figure 1 was taken from two areas in a Boulder, Colorado, stream over several years.

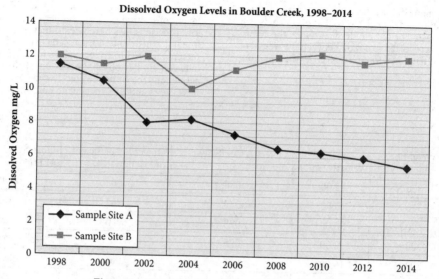

Figure 1   Dissolved Oxygen Data for Boulder Creek

7. Environmental scientists looking for a biological indicator of the health of a stream would be most concerned if the macroinvertebrate sampling showed a lack of:

   A. mayflies.
   B. dragonflies.
   C. aquatic worms.
   D. damselflies.

8. A sampling of macroinvertebrates at Sample Site A showed predominantly mosquito larvae, snails, and mites and an absence of riffle beetles. This would most likely indicate:

   F. the presence of pollution in the area.
   G. levels of pollution are decreasing.
   H. dissolved oxygen is currently high.
   J. increasing stream health.

9. A sampling of macroinvertebrates performed at Sample Site A in Boulder Creek yielded the following results: two riffle beetles, one crayfish, four damselflies, and one snail. The water quality by macroinvertebrate indicator would be:

   A. excellent.
   B. good.
   C. fair.
   D. poor.

10. Boulder Creek is a popular location for recreational fishing. In order to support fish reproduction, the water may not have less than 7.0 mg/L DO during the spawning season. According to the information in Figure 1, it was no longer possible for spawning to occur:

    F. at Sample Site B after 2002.
    G. at Sample Site A after 2002.
    H. at Sample Site B after 2007.
    J. at Sample Site A after 2007.

11. Which of the following statements could NOT be made about Sample Site B?

    A. Very little overall change in water quality occurred over the course of the study.
    B. Dissolved oxygen levels fell outside of the normal range for two years of the study.
    C. Sample Site B results are indicative of a healthy stream.
    D. A variety of macroinvertebrates could be supported by Sample Site B.

GO ON TO THE NEXT PAGE.

324

PASSAGE III

Physicists and engineers use the coefficient of friction (μ) to describe the amount of frictional force that occurs between an object and a surface. For flat and level surfaces, the coefficient of friction (μ) is reported as a ratio between the weight of an object (F_w) and its frictional force (F_f) given by the equation:

$$F_f = \mu \times F_w$$

The coefficient of friction is widely known to be high between rubber and dry concrete (μ = 0.75) and much lower between rubber and wet concrete (μ = 0.45). While the coefficient of friction between rubber and ice is known to be very low, precise values have been difficult to obtain due to experimental constraints. In a recent experiment a precise tribometer was used to collect values for the coefficient of friction between similar objects made out of three different types of rubber and ice while the object was moving at different velocities. The results of Experiment 1 are shown in Table 1.

Table 1					
Trial	Weight of Object (N)	Velocity (m/s)	Object A Coefficient of Friction (μ)	Object B Coefficient of Friction (μ)	Object C Coefficient of Friction (μ)
1	300 N	2.00	.080	.068	.106
2	300 N	5.00	.079	.067	.103
3	300 N	8.00	.078	.066	.099
4	300 N	12.00	.075	.063	.094
5	300 N	15.00	.074	.062	.091
6	300 N	16.00	.074	.061	.091
7	300 N	20.00	.073	.061	.086
8	300 N	25.00	.071	.059	.080

In a similar experiment, the coefficient of friction between a rubber object and ice was measured. The rubber object was made of the same material as Object A, but the weight of the object was varied. The results of the second experiment are shown in Figure 1.

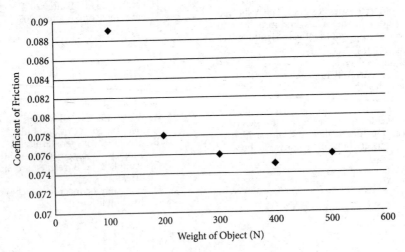

Figure 1

4 ○ ○ ○ ○ ○ ○ ○ ○ **4**

12. According to Table 1, which of the following best describes the role that the movement of an object has on the coefficient of friction between that object and ice?

    A. The velocity of the object has an insignificant or nonexistent influence on the coefficient of friction.

    B. As the velocity of an object increases, the coefficient of friction decreases slightly but steadily.

    C. Velocity affects the coefficient of friction at high velocities.

    D. The weight of an object has a greater impact on the coefficient of friction than the object's velocity.

13. Which of the following best describes the data represented in Figure 1?

    F. The frictional force on a rubber object decreases as the weight of that object increases.

    G. The coefficient of friction decreases as the weight increases.

    H. The weight placed on an object has a limited impact on the coefficient of friction.

    J. Weights above 300 N do not significantly change the coefficient of friction.

14. If all experiments were performed with a similar object and sheet of ice, with what velocity was the object moved in the second experiment?

    A. 1.0 m/s
    B. 8.0 m/s
    C. 11.0 m/s
    D. 22.0 m/s

15. Which rubber object would be expected to have the lowest coefficient of friction?

    F. A lightweight object moving at a high speed
    G. A lightweight object moving at a low speed
    H. A heavy object moving at a high speed
    J. A heavy object moving at a low speed

16. Which of the following hypotheses would be supported by the data from Experiment 2?

    A. Ice is slippery because objects push on the ice and melt the top layer.

    B. Ice is slippery because it is much smoother than other objects.

    C. Ice is slippery because materials cannot bond with the ice molecules.

    D. Ice is slippery because large object do not deform its surface.

17. A materials company is investigating new types of rubber to minimize stopping distances for trucks that drive in icy conditions. Which type of rubber would be the best choice?

    F. Object A
    G. Object B
    H. Object C
    J. All three surfaces would give similar stopping distances.

4 ◯ ◯ ◯ ◯ ◯ ◯ ◯ ◯ ◯ **4**

PASSAGE IV

Monosodium glutamate, or MSG, is a commonly used food additive used to enhance the flavor of low sodium, low-fat, and highly processed foods. MSG targets taste receptors for "umami," which is the fifth taste and characterized as savory, meaty, and rich. The chemical is found everywhere from fast-food meat entrées to canned soups and potato chips.

While glutamate is a naturally occurring amino acid in the body, controversy has been associated with the compound since the late 1960s when a physician first identified the MSG Symptom Complex. Commonly referred to as "Chinese Restaurant Syndrome," this complex includes variety of symptoms ranging from mild headaches to migraines, chest pain, flushing, and muscle weakness. Further studies on laboratory animals linked MSG to brain lesions and neuroendocrine disorders, particularly in the very young. In the early 1970s, baby food manufacturers voluntarily removed MSG from their products as a result of these studies.

Although MSG is generally recognized as safe by the U.S. Food and Drug Administration (FDA), many opponents feel that MSG should be avoided completely as an additive because of potentially negative effects. The following reflect the viewpoints of two different scientists on MSG.

Scientist A

MSG is a safe food additive. Studies on the effects of MSG are inconclusive and anecdotal. The chemical naturally occurs in foods as well as the human body and is harmless in normal amounts. There is no evidence that MSG crosses the blood-brain barrier and can cause neurological effects. Research proving that MSG is unsafe often lacks the characteristics of true double-blind studies or involves laboratory animals consuming abnormally large quantities. Although some individuals are sensitive to MSG, the rest of the general population has no reason avoid it.

Scientist B

Monosodium glutamate should be avoided as a food additive, as the short-term effects can be negative for those with sensitivity and the long-term effects on the general population have not been fully determined. Even foods high in natural glutamates should also be approached with caution. Glutamate is an important neurotransmitter in the human body, and consumption of excess free glutamate through food sources has the potential to interfere with the body's natural pathways. Studies have been conducted to link glutamate to conditions including asthma, Parkinson's disease, autism, and obesity.

18. Scientist A and scientist B tend to agree upon the statement that MSG:

    A. causes reactions in sensitive individuals.
    B. is a safe food additive.
    C. affects the brain.
    D. causes obesity.

19. Which statement would MOST likely be made by scientist B during an interview about monosodium glutamate?

    F. "Findings from the literature indicate that there is no consistent evidence to suggest that individuals may be uniquely sensitive to glutamate."
    G. "Processed Chinese food is higher in MSG than even American processed food. Between 1985 and 2000, overweight and obesity in China's children has increased an extremely alarming 28-fold."
    H. "Despite concerns raised by early reports, decades of research have failed to demonstrate a clear and consistent relationship between MSG ingestion and the development of these conditions."
    J. "There is no evidence that excessive consumption of MSG actually raises the blood levels of free glutamate."

20. Which of these statements would most likely be made exclusively by scientist A?

    A. Glutamate occurs naturally in the human body.
    B. Many foods contain high levels of natural glutamate.
    C. Glutamate is safe for consumption in normal amounts.
    D. Glutamate does not cross the blood-brain barrier.

21. Many of the studies that provide evidence for the safety of MSG as a food additive have been funded or conducted in whole or in part by members of the food industry. This would be of concern to scientist B because the studies would be more likely to include:

    F. insufficient data to form conclusions.
    G. bias on the part of the researcher.
    H. improper control of variables.
    J. an inadequate number of trials.

22. In Spain, MSG is referred to as E-621 and must be declared as a food additive on all packaging. In 2005, scientists at the Complutense University of Madrid discovered a 40 percent increase in appetite in rats that were fed MSG. Although the exact mechanisms for appetite increase are unknown, the results of this study:

    A. weaken the argument of scientist B.
    B. support the argument of scientist B.
    C. support the argument of scientist A.
    D. do not support or refute either argument.

GO ON TO THE NEXT PAGE.

4 ◯ ◯ ◯ ◯ ◯ ◯ ◯ ◯ ◯ 4

PASSAGE V

The relationship between how fast a steel ball is traveling when it leaves the edge of a table and how far that ball travels before it hits the ground is investigated using a ramp, table, and photogate in the apparatus shown in Figure 1.

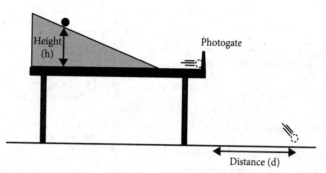

Figure 1

The ball is released from various heights (h) on the ramp and allowed to roll down the ramp and off the table. Right before leaving the table the ball passes through a photogate that measures how much time it takes for the ball to pass completely through a small laser beam. The speed of the ball is calculated by taking the diameter of the ball divided by the time measured by the photogate. Different metal balls are used in the experiment, but each has an identical diameter. The measured and calculated data from all experiments are shown in Table 1.

			Table 1		
Ball	Trial	Mass of ball (g)	Height of Drop (cm)	Velocity (cm/s)	Distance (cm)
A	1	20.0	5	98.8	44.6
	2	20.0	5	99.1	44.9
	3	20.0	10	139.8	63.1
	4	20.0	15	172.0	77.5
B	5	10.0	5	99.2	44.4
	6	10.0	10	141.0	62.8
	7	10.0	10	139.6	63.3
	8	10.0	15	171.1	76.9
C	9	30.0	5	98.7	44.7
	10	30.0	10	140.0	63.3
	11	30.0	15	171.5	77.5
	12	30.0	15	171.0	77.3

g = grams
cm = centimeters
s = seconds
cm/s = centimeters per second
Table height = 100 cm off the ground

GO ON TO THE NEXT PAGE.

4 ◯ ◯ ◯ ◯ ◯ ◯ ◯ ◯ **4**

23. If ball A had been released another time from a height of 20 cm, what distance would it have travelled until it hit the floor?

   A. 77.5 cm
   B. 89.5 cm
   C. 95.4 cm
   D. 92.3 cm/s

24. If all three balls were dropped simultaneously from a height of 20.0 cm, in what order would they reach the edge of the table?

   F. Ball A, ball B, ball C
   G. Ball C, ball B, ball A
   H. Ball B, ball A, ball C
   J. All would reach the edge at nearly the same time.

25. Which of the following conclusions best matches the data?

   A. More massive steel balls are able to travel farther off the side of a table.
   B. The height that a ball is released on a ramp is proportional to the velocity of that ball at the bottom of the ramp.
   C. The mass of a steel ball has no effect on the speed that ball will be travelling at the bottom of a ramp.
   D. The velocity and mass of a steel ball both have a positive correlation with the distance that ball travels before it hits the ground.

26. What would happen to the calculated velocity of each steel ball if the actual diameter of the ball was 2.2 cm but the students rounded this value and used 2 cm in their calculations?

   F. The calculated velocities would have been too large.
   G. The calculated velocities would have been too small.
   H. The calculated velocities would have remained unchanged.
   J. The measured distances would have been shorter.

27. A very heavy, 100-gram steel ball was used in an additional trial and released from a drop height of 15.0 cm. Which describes where it would hit the ground?

   A. 76.2 cm
   B. 77.4 cm
   C. 79.6 cm
   D. 98.9 cm

28. Which of the following modifications to the experiment would NOT increase the distance that the steel ball traveled before it hit the ground?

   F. Moving the photogate closer to the edge of the ramp
   G. Increasing the drop height to 20.0 cm
   H. Changing the table height from 100 cm to 150 cm
   J. Giving the steel ball an initial push instead of just releasing the ball

GO ON TO THE NEXT PAGE.

4 ◯ ◯ ◯ ◯ ◯ ◯ ◯ ◯ ◯ 4

PASSAGE VI

Cortisol is a hormone commonly associated with stress. The release of cortisol triggers the body to reserve available glucose for the brain, and in doing so diverts energy from less essential functions such as the immune system. Cortisol is released in a diurnal pattern, with levels peaking in the morning shortly after awakening and decreasing gradually throughout the day. The short-term advantage of cortisol secretion is an increased ability to respond to challenging situations. However, the long-term effects of elevated cortisol levels can be detrimental and have been linked to conditions such as abdominal weight gain and reduction in memory.

Scientists often use cortisol levels to quantify the stress humans experience from particular situations, or to test the effects of treatments and therapies on stress reduction. Each of the teams of scientists in the following experiments used salivary cortisol levels to test a stress response.

Experiment 1

The scientists performing Experiment 1 tested the effects of sleep deprivation on salivary cortisol levels. Sixty healthy young men ages 20–32 were divided into three test groups: normal sleep (8 hrs), partial sleep deprivation (4 hrs), and total sleep deprivation (0 hrs). Cortisol levels were tested at regular intervals for 24 hours before (Day 1) and 24 hours following (Day 2) the period of sleep deprivation. Table 1 shows a portion of the average cortisol levels gathered during the experiment.

Table 1 Cortisol Levels Before and After Sleep Deprivation				
Group	8 a.m. Day 1	8 p.m. Day 1	8 a.m. Day 2	8 p.m. Day 2
Normal Sleep	.49 µg/dL	.08 µg/dL	.48 µg/dL	.07 µg/dL
Partial Sleep Deprivation	.50 µg/dL	.10 µg/dL	.66 µg/dL	.14 µg/dL
Total Sleep Deprivation	.47 µg/dL	.09 µg/dL	.71 µg/dL	.16 µg/dL

Experiment 2

Scientists performing Experiment 2 tested the effects of yoga on salivary cortisol levels. The goal was to determine if the practice of daily yoga could impact the levels of cortisol in a person's body, potentially helping to reduce stress. Forty healthy males and 20 healthy females of varying ages were selected for the study. All subjects had no previous yoga experience and agreed to be tested over the course of 10 days.

On day one, cortisol levels were measured before and after a 50-minute "quiet period," without yoga. During the next nine days, the subjects participated in 50-minute yoga sessions each day at 11 a.m., with cortisol measured before and after the experiment on Day 2 only. On the tenth day, cortisol levels were measured before and after yoga.

The cortisol results are detailed in Table 2.

Table 2 Cortisol Levels Before and After Yoga				
	Males—Before	Males—After	Females—Before	Females—After
Day 1 (Quiet period)	.32 µg/dL	.18 µg/dL	.31 µg/dL	.15 µg/dL
Day 2 (Yoga)	.33 µg/dL	.10 µg/dL	.31 µg/dL	.11 µg/dL
Day 10 (Yoga)	.27 µg/dL	.09 µg/dL	.28 µg/dL	.10 µg/dL

29. In Experiment 1, the control group is represented by:

   F. normal sleep.
   G. partial sleep deprivation.
   H. total sleep deprivation.
   J. This experiment lacks a control group.

30. Using the information in the passage, what is the MOST likely explanation for the cortisol data in Experiment 2 when no yoga is performed?

   A. Men and women respond differently to rest periods.
   B. Cortisol decreases naturally as the day progresses.
   C. Cortisol peaks in the early afternoon.
   D. Resting causes a significant decrease in cortisol.

31. According to the findings of Experiment 1:

   F. there is a negative correlation between sleep deprivation and cortisol levels.
   G. there is a positive correlation between sleep deprivation and cortisol levels.
   H. there is no correlation between sleep deprivation and cortisol levels.
   J. cortisol levels naturally fluctuate and are not affected by sleep deprivation.

GO ON TO THE NEXT PAGE.

4 ◯ ◯ ◯ ◯ ◯ ◯ ◯ ◯ ◯ **4**

32. Which analysis of the data from Experiment 2 is most reasonable?

   A. Regular practice of yoga by males can reduce cortisol levels by 50 percent.

   B. Yoga increases overall cortisol in females by 33 percent.

   C. Regular practice of yoga increases cortisol by close to 50 percent in both males and females.

   D. Regular practice of yoga by females can reduce cortisol levels by 50 percent.

33. Which of the following is LEAST likely to represent a control that would have been used to ensure reliability of data in Experiment 2?

   F. The time of day that the tests were performed

   G. The particular yoga routine used

   H. The duration of the yoga practice

   J. The amount of saliva taken for the sample

34. According to the results of Experiment 1:

   A. sleep deprivation causes no change in the cortisol levels of the test subjects on the following day.

   B. sleep deprivation causes a decrease in cortisol the following day.

   C. the amount of sleep deprivation does not impact the stress response of individuals.

   D. the cortisol stress response increases in relationship with the amount of sleep deprivation.

GO ON TO THE NEXT PAGE.

PASSAGE VII

The rate of a chemical reaction can be defined as the amount of chemical created during a reaction divided by the amount of time it takes to create that chemical. A reaction rate depends on two major factors: the concentration of the reacting chemicals and the temperature of the reaction. Several other variables such as surface area, stirring rate, and the presence of a catalyst can also influence the rate of a reaction.

In order to determine what specific factors affect the rate at which triiodide ions (I_3^{-1}) are created, a chemist studies a particular reaction between iodide ions (I^{-1}), hydrogen peroxide (H_2O_2), and hydronium ions (H_3O^+) as shown:

$$3I^{1-} + H_2O_2 + 2H_3O^{1+} \rightarrow I_3^{1-} + 4H_2O$$

All reactants and products in this reaction are colorless. In order to see the creation of triiodide ions, the chemist adds starch because starch turns dark blue in the presence of the triiodide ion. In order to measure a reaction rate, the chemist adds a known constant amount of thiosulfate ions ($S_2O_3^{-2}$) to each reaction vessel. The thiosulfate ions react with triiodide ions before they can turn the starch black according to the following reaction:

$$2S_2O_3^{2-} + I_3^{1-} \rightarrow S_4O_6^{2-} + 3I^{1-}$$

Once all thiosulfate ions are consumed, the solution turns black and the rate of the reaction can be measured. The chemist carried out a series of experiments with the contents of each trial beaker; results are shown in Table 1. The amount of hydronium ion (H_3O^+) in each trial is traditionally measured in pH. A low pH value has a large concentration of H_3O^+ and higher pH values have a smaller concentration of H_3O^+.

Table 1					
Trial	Volume 0.05 M I^{-1} (mL)	Volume 0.01M H_2O_2 (mL)	Volume Distilled Water (mL)	Amount of $S_2O_3^{-2}$ (mol)	pH of Reaction (Measure of H_3O^+)	Time for Color Change (s)
1	10.0	20.0	20.0	5×10^{-5}	5	10.5
2	10.0	15.0	25.0	5×10^{-5}	5	18.6
3	10.0	11.0	29.0	5×10^{-5}	5	42.0
4	10.0	7.5	32.5	5×10^{-5}	5	74.8
5	8.0	20.0	22.0	5×10^{-5}	5	15.1
6	6.0	20.0	24.0	5×10^{-5}	5	22.5
7	4.0	20.0	26.0	5×10^{-5}	5	30.0
8	3.0	20.0	27.0	5×10^{-5}	5	44.9
9	10.0	20.0	20.0	5×10^{-5}	2	10.5
10	10.0	15.0	25.0	5×10^{-5}	2	18.5

mL = milliliters
mol = moles of molecules
s = seconds
*All trials take place in 100-mL beakers at 298 K.

35. According to the results in Table 1, which variable changed the Time for Color Change the most?

F. Concentration of hydrogen peroxide
G. Concentration of iodide ions
H. Hydronium ion concentration
J. Amount of thiosulfate ion present in the reaction

36. Which two trials can be used to decide if the concentration of hydronium ions had any effect on the reaction rate?

A. Trial 1 and trial 2
B. Trial 1 and trial 5
C. Trial 9 and trial 10
D. Trial 1 and trial 9

37. What is the function of the water in each reaction beaker?

F. Dissolve all reactants and maintain an aqueous environment
G. Maintain a constant volume across each trial
H. Indicate the presence of the triiodide ion
J. Allow for the effective timing of the reaction progress

38. Which trial shows the fastest rate of reaction?

A. Trial 1
B. Trial 4
C. Trial 5
D. Trial 8

GO ON TO THE NEXT PAGE.

4 ◯ ◯ ◯ ◯ ◯ ◯ ◯ ◯ ◯ **4**

39. What happens to the time necessary for the color change to occur when the concentration of hydrogen peroxide doubles?

   F. The time required doubles.
   G. The time required gets cut in half.
   H. The time required quadruples.
   J. The time required gets quartered.

40. How long would it take to achieve a color change if trial 10 was repeated with 1×10^{-4} moles of thiosulfate instead of 5×10^{-5} moles?

   A. 9.25 seconds
   B. 18.5 seconds
   C. 37.0 seconds
   D. 74.8 seconds

END OF THE SCIENCE REASONING TEST.
STOP! IF YOU HAVE TIME LEFT OVER, CHECK YOUR WORK ON THIS SECTION ONLY.

PART V ANSWERS AND EXPLANATIONS

English Test Explanations

PASSAGE I

1. **The best answer is D.** Because the sentence starts with *If*, it is a conditional sentence. The phrase *would have been* is also conditional. Both signify that no action took place. No one actually asked the author if she wanted to become a professor and therefore the question was never answered.

2. **The best answer is G.** By using the word *resounding* to modify the refusal of the possibility of becoming a professor like her father, the author is emphasizing emphatically how opposed she was to that career path. It also signals that the author had considered the possibility and dismissed it after having given thought to the possibility and deciding strongly against following in her father's footsteps.

3. **The best answer is A.** The author is trying to point out how far her father's passion for sharing his love of knowledge went. At the time, she felt it was extreme to the point of being embarrassing. She did not find his lectures interesting, as suggested by answer B. There is not anything understated or unobtrusive about her father's passion, as suggested by answers C and D.

4. **The best answer is J.** Because the author and her siblings did not appreciate the knowledge her father shared and mealtimes at their home were an occasion for him to launch into a half-hour monologue on any given subject matter, the author thought her father was tedious to spend time with at home. The author thought her father's monologues at dinner were long-winded and not at all *riveting*, as suggested by answer F. Also, strangers may not have found his unsolicited lectures about the Coliseum very polite, as suggested by answer G. Her father did not change his behavior whether he was with more than one child or not, as suggested by answer H. He lectured with passion at will.

5. **The best answer is A.** This sentence belongs where it is because it gives context to the reason why the author did not want to become a professor. Were the sentence earlier in the paragraph, it would distract from the reason why the author felt adamant about not becoming a professor. If it were later in the paragraph, the author's point would be weakened.

6. **The best answer is G.** Although *irregardless* is often used, it is a nonstandard word. *Regardless* means that her father did not care how many passersby heard his children reciting their French vocabulary as they walked to school.

7. **The best answer is A.** This phrase is the most appropriate because it refers to a set of events that took place rather than a solitary event that occurred while on vacation or something that happened only once.

8. **The best answer is H.** This wording is correct because *I* is the subjective singular first-person personal pronoun. This form is used when writing or speaking about oneself in an inside-looking-out perspective. The objective form *me* is used in an outside-looking-in perspective, as in, "Like me, my siblings pretended not to know him." There's no need for a comma, because it isn't a list of things and the two words *my siblings* are not a phrase.

9. **The best answer is C.** This sentence signals that the author will be discussing how her father behaved at home in this paragraph. Nothing in the second paragraph mentions anything about Rome, tour guides, or humiliation.

10. **The best answer is F.** The use of the singular past tense *was* agrees with the singular usage of *each*. This usage signifies that the opportunity for a lecture actually existed at each meal. The use of *were*, as suggested by answer G, would only work when referring to plural events, such as "All of our family meals were opportunities for Dad." The use of *would be*, as suggested by answer H, implies that there may have been an opportunity rather than conveying that it was inevitable.

11. **The best answer is C.** The colon is being used to signal that an explanation is about to follow.

12. **The best answer is H.** Since medieval farmers grew their asparagus at a past point in history, the past tense of the verb is used. The action was completed. The response *would cultivate* implies a sense of that action being possible but not having taken place, as suggested by answer G. The response of *had cultivated* would make the sentence mean that they did in so the past but no longer do. Since asparagus is still being cultivated, the response suggested by answer J is not correct.

13. **The best answer is A.** This sentence starts off using the future tense *will* to explain the author's father launching into professor mode. The author then lists the next two examples in the sentence using the conditional verb *could*. This usage implies that pinecones definitely sent the author's father into professor mode, while the asparagus side dish and the reference to horses had the potential to send him into professor mode, but did not necessarily do so.

14. **The best answer is J.** Because this sentence is talking about the author and her siblings, she refers to their collective childhoods in the plural. Since the author is including herself as one of the children, the plural *ourselves* is used.

15. **The best answer is A.** The word *that* is used instead of *which* because "that would have embarrassed me when I was younger" is a restrictive clause. A restrictive clause is one that may not be removed and leave the meaning of the sentence intact. The use of *which* would be a part of a nonrestrictive clause in which the information could be regarded as parenthetical and not necessary. This sentence does not require a comma, as suggested by answers B and D.

PASSAGE II

16. **The best answer is J.** Answer F does not speak to the question. Answer G is not correct, because the author does not state that the inhabitants are superstitious, only that "the mountainsides are still said to be haunted." The author also does not say that the mountains inspired the fairy tales, rather that the mountains are the "unofficial setting" of many of the tales, so answer H is not correct. Answer J is the best answer because the first paragraph discusses the "huge number of hardwood trees." From this information it may logically be inferred that the information in answer J is correct.

17. **The best answer is B.** The word *anterior* is a synonym of *former*. The prefix *ante-* refers to something that came before. *Ensuing* and *later* both refer to events that occurred after an action, which is not what the author meant.

18. **The best answer is H.** Because "a huge number of hardwood trees" is plural, the best choice would refer to replacing *them* rather than a solitary tree, which would be an *it*, as suggested by answer G. Because pine and fir trees replaced the hardwood trees, there was nothing with which the new trees could be interspersed, as suggested by answer J.

19. **The best answer is A.** This phrase refers to the plant life of a certain, singular forest. The second choice refers to the plant life in more than one forest. The other choices are unnecessarily wordy.

20. **The best answer is H.** This is the best answer because earlier in the sentence the author used *have transformed*. This answer maintains parallel structure within the sentence.

21. **The best answer is A.** The answer conveys the scale of these geographical features. The modifiers are

accurate and not erroneous, as suggested by answer B. The contrast between the geological formations is dramatic, not subtle as suggested by answer C. The essay states that the glaciers were giant, which is a direct acknowledgment of their size rather than an indirect acknowledgment, as suggested by answer D.

22. **The best answer is J.** This is the best answer because the Black Forest is a distinct geographical area within Germany. The Black Forest is neither a separate city nor a country. *Kingdom* is not accurate, because Germany has not had a ruling monarchy since 1918.

23. **The best answer is C.** The word *accordingly* makes no sense as it's used in this sentence. There was nothing inevitable about one branch of Black Forest Clockmakers producing cuckoo clocks, and the essay gives no reason why this would be a forgone conclusion. It was also not inevitable that they produced cuckoo clocks, as they could have just as easily built grandfather clocks or pocket watches.

24. **The best answer is J.** This answer states precisely when the cuckoo clock became mass produced. This answer also gives the reader the time frame of when the clocks peaked in popularity until the time when they were manufactured in a factory. The other answers are vague.

25. **The best answer is D.** This sentence would add to the description of the clocks as being beautifully crafted. In addition, most cuckoo clocks are known for their moving figures and this unique feature is a part of their popularity. The addition of the sentence may be tangential to the overall essay, as suggested by answer A, but it does give an important detail about the cuckoo clocks in this paragraph. Although the sentence does help the reader to visualize the clocks, as suggested by answer B, if it were added as the last sentence in the paragraph, it would read as if the figures were not added until after World War II. The longevity of the clock-making industry, in answer C, has nothing to do with the features of the clocks.

26. **The best answer is G.** Although many Germans may hike the footpaths, the paragraph is about tourism in the Black Forest. As international tourism is the major industry for the region, it is reasonable to draw the conclusion that the hikers visit from many other countries. However, these footpaths are not used predominantly by either Germans or tourists. While the footpaths are *worth a gander*, the focus of the paragraph is on the tourism industry and not the scenic nature of the footpaths.

27. **The best answer is B.** Because the Black Forest is still currently considered the "unofficial setting of many

German fairy tales," the present tense is used to convey this meaning. None of the other answers implies that this is the case.

28. **The best answer is F.** Commas are used to separate items in a list, such as the one in this paragraph. This list of three preternatural beings is properly punctuated with the use of a comma before *and*. Answers G and H list two creatures, witches that are also werewolves and sorcerers. Answer J is incorrect because it does not have a comma before *and*.

29. **The best answer is C.** When a group of words is used to define a preceding word, it is called an appositive. An appositive is punctuated by using commas at the beginning and the end of the phrase, as illustrated in the correct response. The punctuation in answer B is called an ellipsis and is used to show the omission of words in a direct quote, which is not the case in this sentence. Answer D uses semicolons improperly.

30. **The best answer is G.** The Black Forest region can be characterized by more than just the three features noted in the sentence in the essay. Because the region is closely associated with Germany as a whole, this sentence provides closure to the essay, which began with identifying where the region existed within the country. The points in answers H and J are not mentioned in the essay.

PASSAGE III

31. **The best answer is D.** The phrase *from the science fiction* is distracting and beside the point. The essay is about the reality of space travel and exploration. There is no need to mention science fiction, as it is not discussed later in the essay.

32. **The best answer is G.** The use of the word *which* signals that the phrase is nondefining. However, this phrase defines the meaning of unmanned satellites, so *that* is the proper word. A comma after *craft* is unnecessary.

33. **The best answer is A.** These words are in quotation marks to signal to the reader that it is a commonly used phrase and not to be taken in a literal sense.

34. **The best answer is G.** This sentence belongs where it is because it fits in with the developing time line of space travel. If it were placed in any of the other suggested positions, it would damage the sense of the paragraph.

35. **The best answer is B.** Because the information about successful trips to the moon is placed within parentheses, there is no need for a comma before the additional information. However, a comma is required after the parenthetical information because it functions as a part of a clause.

36. **The best answer is J.** The punctuation is proper as it stands. A colon can be used to signal that additional information explaining the preceding clause is to follow. When the colon is replaced by a comma and a conjunction is added, as in answer G, this is another way of joining the two independent clauses. Answer H is also correct because the two clauses in this sentence are independent of each other, so they can be split apart to stand on their own.

37. **The best answer is A.** The use of *farther to* as opposed to *farther from* completely changes the spatial relationship of Mars and the Earth. *Than* denotes a comparison. The word *then* is used to reference a point in time, rather than referring to a point in space.

38. **The best answer is J.** Because Russia started launching probes to Mars in 1969 but they weren't successful until 1971, it was an ongoing process. If the past tense is used, such as in answer G, the meaning of the sentence would be changed completely. It would then read as if the same probes that were launched in 1969 did not land on Mars until 1971. Answer H is also not correct, because it makes it sound as if the Russians were going to launch probes, but did not do so, when they actually did launch the probes.

39. **The best answer is A.** Just because *Mars 2* crashed, that had no bearing on the performance of *Mars 3*. The use of *despite* in answer B would make the sentence read as if *Mars 3* was launched in an act of defiance over the crash of *Mars 2*. Answer C would make the information that *Mars 2* crashed sound trivial. Answer D does not work, because there is no range or scope expressed in the sentence.

40. **The best answer is J.** This information lets the reader know that after landing *Mars 3* did work for a limited time. There was no mention of how long the probes were supposed to work. The essay states that one probe landed smoothly while the other crashed. The underlined section does not repeat information given previously in the essay, so there is no redundancy to be eliminated.

41. **The best answer is D.** This is the best answer because the word *data* is being used in the plural sense; the essay states that "large amounts" had been collected. The use of *which* at the beginning of the sentence makes the sentence read as if it were a clause.

42. **The best answer is H.** The second sentence states the same thing as the first, making it redundant.

43. **The best answer is B.** The use of *and* joins the two parts of the sentence into a coherent whole. There is no need for any punctuation after *applicants,* as suggested by answers C and D.

44. **The best answer is G.** The author has consistently used third person throughout the essay. Answers F and J are not supported by information in the essay. Answer H presumes that the reader does not care about the opinion of the author, which may or may not be the case.

45. **The best answer is C.** Commas are used to separate items in a list. A comma precedes the word *and* in a list.

PASSAGE IV

46. **The best answer is G.** This sentence should not be deleted, because it gives the reader a sense of perspective regarding when and where Sir Francis Bacon lived. The sentence is not a prepositional phrase, as suggested in answer F. This information is not repeated later in the paragraph, as suggested by answer H. The date of Francis Bacon's birth is not given in the essay, as suggested by answer J.

47. **The best answer is A.** Answer A is the best choice because it uses a phrase commonly employed to explain the reason for which someone or something is remembered. The other answers invite a comparison to something that does not exist in the sentence or anywhere else in the essay.

48. **The best answer is J.** Because religious and metaphysical beliefs influenced exploration of the natural world, ideas were shaped, or informed, by these beliefs. Answers G and H would not make sense in the sentence.

49. **The best answer is C.** As the sentence is written, *religion* is being used as a noun. The sentence requires an adjective that modifies *beliefs*. Although *penitentiary* is an adjective, *penitence* was not a factor in the exploration of the natural world. Answer D is a noun.

50. **The best answer is G.** The use of the comma after *alchemy* sets off a description of what alchemy is. The other answer choices are awkward.

51. **The best answer is D.** Science and the natural world are two things being discussed and together they are plural, thus the use of *were*. This also rules out answer C. Answer B creates an awkward, appositive-like structure.

52. **The best answer is G.** As the underlined text is written in the essay, the last three words are incorrectly punctuated as if they were a sentence. The correct punctuation joins the clause to the sentence following a necessary comma. In answer H, *Bacon did* does not constitute a main clause, so a semicolon may not be used to join it to the preceding sentence.

53. **The best answer is A.** Because the underlined phrase describes Cambridge University, it should follow directly after the mention of the school. As the sentence stands, the phrase appears to signal that Bacon was being described, which is also the effect of answer C. If the underlined phrase came at the end of the sentence, as suggested by answer D, the sentence would lose its meaningfulness.

54. **The best answer is F.** When writing out dates, any prefix is hyphenated. Numerals are used rather than writing out the words, as suggested by answers G and J. No apostrophe is needed when indicating a decade, as suggested by answer H.

55. **The best answer is B.** The essay is focused on Bacon and things as they were during his lifetime. To mention the current reputation of the college he attended is irrelevant.

56. **The best answer is J.** Double quotes are used when citing what someone said or felt to indicate such is the case. Any punctuation used should be enclosed within the double quotes.

57. **The best answer is C.** The point of the paragraph is that Bacon devised his own method of inquiry. By not describing what the Aristotelian method was and why Bacon was "disgusted" with it deprives the reader of valuable information. Neither adding nor deleting information about Cambridge advances the point of the paragraph, as suggested by answers A and B. Additional information about what Bacon studied at Cambridge, as suggested by answer D, is extraneous to the focus of the paragraph.

58. **The best answer is H.** Because *Novum Organum* is the title of a book, it should be italicized when included in the body of a written work.

59. **The best answer is D.** All of the other answers are unnecessarily awkward.

60. **The best answer is G.** There is no need for a comma before *which*. The novel is being discussed, rather than Atlantis the place, so *where*, as suggested in answer J, is incorrect.

PASSAGE V

61. **The best answer is D.** Answer B is a malapropism of the correct answer. Answer C makes no sense in the sentence.

62. **The best answer is F.** The underlined pronoun refers to the subject of the first sentence, which was the earth. The sun and the narrator were never mentioned, as suggested by answers G and H. The rabbit is part of a clause.

63. **The best answer is D.** Because the sentence contains a series of items that have commas within them,

the items are separated using semicolons. Answer A would create a fragment. A hyphen is not used to separate items in a list, as shown in answer C.

64. **The best answer is H.** Because the landscape was described as being "baked plaster hard," there was no verdant landscape for the dove to survey. It is also unlikely that it was near a body of water or any shore birds, such as the seagull. The tone of the paragraph does not indicate than any creature could be described as doing anything *joyfully*.

65. **The best answer is C.** The sentence could stay as written if only one insect were crying. Because there is more than one insect, the plural possessive form is correct. Answers B and D are contractions and do not denote possession.

66. **The best answer is G.** The correct answer gives the sentence the meaning that because the stony hills lifted themselves, the occasional vantage point was created. The word *or* does not belong in this sentence, because there is no choice to be made, as suggested by answer F. Answers H and J imply a negativity that does not exist.

67. **The best answer is D.** The correct answer is the proper punctuation when discussing the mind of one woman. Answer B would refer to the minds of several women. An apostrophe is used to show possession.

68. **The best answer is F.** This is the best answer because the author wants the reader to understand that dizziness from the heat made the woman feel unbalanced. Neither answer H nor answer J could make her feel that her mind was unbalanced. Answer G is incorrect because she had only recently become forgetful.

69. **The best answer is C.** This sentence discusses the theoretical actions a man might have taken had he been in the same situation as the woman. Answer B implies that a man had the prerogative to speak in the present, when the sentence is in past tense. Answer D is not grammatically correct.

70. **The best answer is F.** This sentence is acceptable as is because it contrasts what the woman did with what a man in her situation might have done. There was nothing in the essay to suggest that the woman did not like men, as suggested by answer G. The essay mentioned that the woman was forgetful about checking her canteen, but not in any other way, as suggested by answer H.

71. **The best answer is B.** The phrase *densest shade* implies a comparison with another place that was less shady. The underline phrase lets the reader know that the place with the most shade was actually not very shady. Without this phrase the reader would be led to believe that the woman was in a cool and comfortable place.

72. **The best answer is F.** The sentence is correctly punctuated as written, expressing that relaxing was difficult in the heat. Answer G would create a sentence fragment. Answer H is syntactically incorrect. Answer J uses improper punctuation.

73. **The best answer is C.** The best answer combines the pertinent elements in the first two sentences in a more concise fashion than the original two sentences. If the first sentence were omitted, as suggested by answer A, the reader would lose the sense that the woman had rested. Answer B focuses on the location of the water-hole, when the main point is that the woman is lost. Answer D does not give the reader any perspective to the woman's situation.

74. **The best answer is G.** If a cactus had ears that were alert, they would be harkening, or listening intently.

75. **The best answer is A.** The word *lay* refers to a place. Answer B is a past participle form of the verb *lay* and its usage would lend the meaning that the woman knew her destination at some point in the past, but no longer knew it. This is not the case, because in the essay she was "remembering exactly." Answer D refers to the physical act of reclining horizontally.

Mathematics Test Explanations

1. **The best answer is D.** Solve the equation algebraically:

$$C_L = 0.00050\,\alpha^2 + 0.020$$
$$C_L - 0.020 = 0.00050\,\alpha^2$$
$$(C_L - 0.020)/0.00050 = \alpha^2$$

Plug in 0.030 for C_L:

$$(0.030 - 0.020)/0.00050 = \alpha^2$$
$$20.0 = \alpha^2$$
$$4.5 \; degrees = \alpha^2$$

2. **The best answer is J.** Driving cost for first one year:

Car A = ($4/gallon) × (1 gallon/27 miles)
× (20,000 miles/year) = $2,963
Car B = ($4/gallon) × (1 gallon/36 miles)
× (20,000 miles/year) = $2,222

Car B saves $2,963 − $2,222 = $ 741 each year.

6 years of savings = $741 × 6 = $4,446
7 years of savings = $741 × 7 = $5,187

Therefore, during the seventh year, the $5,000 extra cost for model B is made up by model B's superior gas mileage.

3. **The best answer is C.** The zeros are the values of x that make $f(x) =$ zero.

$$f(x) = x^2 - 5x - 14$$
$$0 = (x - 7)(x + 2)$$
$$x = 7, x = -2$$

4. **The best answer is F.** The slope of the graph is $(y_2 - y_1)/(x_2 - x_1) = (400 - 150)$ miles$/(5 - 0)$ hours $= 50$ miles per hour. The y-intercept is 150 miles. Using the slope-intercept form: $y = mx + b$:

$$M = (50 \text{ mi/hr}) \, T + (150 \text{ mi})$$

5. **The best answer is B.**

Circumference = pi × diameter
Diameter = circumference/pi
Diameter = 25 meters/3.14159 = 8 meters

6. **The best answer is K.** The sum of all the interior angles in a quadrilateral is 360°.

$$a + b + c + 35° = 360°$$
$$a + b + c = 360° - 35° = 325°$$

7. **The best answer is D.** The maximum value for any sine function is 1. Therefore: $y_{max} = 5 \times (1) + 3 = 8$.

8. **The best answer is G.**

$$\frac{2a^5b^6c}{6a^3b^2} = \left(\frac{1}{3}\right) a^{(5-3)} \, b^{(6-2)} \, c = \frac{a^2b^4c}{3}$$

9. **The best answer is D.**

Blue probability = (Blue cars/total cars)
Blue probability = 4,000/(3,000 + 3,500 + 4,000 + 4,200)
Blue probability = 0.27
Blue probability = 27%

10. **The best answer is J.** The distance formula is:

$$d^2 = (x_2 - x_1)^2 + (y_2 - y_1)^2$$
$$d^2 = (3 - (-1))^2 + (2 - 5)^2$$
$$d^2 = (4)^2 + (-3)^2$$
$$d^2 = 25$$
$$d = 5$$

11. **The best answer is C.** In a right triangle, the sine of the angle x is the ratio of the side opposite the angle to the hypotenuse: $\sin(x) = 20/40 = 0.5$. (Note: If you're using a calculator, make sure you're in the degrees mode before taking the inverse sine.)

$$x = \sin^{-1}(0.5) = 30°$$

12. **The best answer is K.** The line has a slope of 2 rise units for every run unit. The y-intercept is $+4$. Using the slope-intercept form, the equation of the line is $y = 2x + 4$. The solution is all points in the shaded area that

are below (but not including the points on) the dashed line, so $y < 2x + 4$.

13. **The best answer is C.**

$$25x + 5 = 40x - 25$$

Subtract $25x$ from both sides: $5 = 15x - 25$.
Add 25 to both sides: $30 = 15x$.
Divide both sides by 15: $30/15 = x$.

$$x = 2$$

14. **The best answer is J.**

$$f(-1) = 3 - (-1)^2 = 2$$
$$f(2) = 3 - (2)^2 = -1$$
$$2 + (-1) = 1$$

15. **The best answer is A.** First find the radius of the cone:

$$V = \frac{1}{3}\pi r^2 h$$
$$\frac{3V}{\pi h} = r^2$$
$$\frac{3(302)}{\pi(8)} = r^2$$
$$36 = r^2$$
$$r = 6$$

Then use the Pythagorean Theorem to find the slant height l:

$$l^2 = r^2 + h^2$$
$$l^2 = 6^2 + 8^2 = 100$$
$$l = 10$$

16. **The best answer is K.** Break the radical down to the square root of $25 = 5$, the square root of $x^2 = x$, and the square root of $y^6 = y^3$. Answer $= 5xy^3$.

17. **The best answer is B.**

Mean = average = $(19 + 20 + 22 + 22 + 32)/5$
$= 23$
Mode = most common value = 22
Median = middle value = 22

18. **The best answer is F.** Since $(2x - 1)$ is in the absolute value, set it equal to ±9.

First solve: $2x - 1 = +9$ to get $x = 5$.
Second solve: $2x - 1 = -9$ to get $x = -4$.

19. **The best answer is D.** The hypotenuse of the triangle is the diameter, which is twice the radius = 26 inches. Using the Pythagorean Theorem, $AC =$ square root $(26^2 - 10^2) = 24$ inches.

20. **The best answer is H.** The midpoint x-coordinate is the average of the x values.

$$x = (2 + 10)/2 = 6$$

Likewise, $y = (1 + 5)/2 = 3$.
Therefore, the coordinate is (6, 3).

ANSWERS AND EXPLANATIONS

339

21. **The best answer is B.** The first equation is $4 + 3x = 13$ and the second equation is $2 - x = -1$; $x = 3$ satisfies both equations.

22. **The best answer is H.** Let $B =$ Original bill:

$$B + 0.20B = \$42$$
$$1.2B = \$42$$
$$B = \$42/1.2 = \$35.00$$

23. **The best answer is B.** Since all the angles in the larger triangle must add up to 180 degrees, angle ADE $= 180^0 - 30^0 - 65^0 = 85^0$. Line AD may be considered as a transversal through the two parallel lines; therefore, angle ADE is congruent to angle AxC $= 85$. Angle x is supplementary to AxC because the two angles form a line. Therefore, $x = 180^0 - 85^0 = 95^0$.

24. **The best answer is J.** First divide both sides by 3 to get $2x + y = 12$. Arrange the equation in slope intercept form: $y = -2x + 4$. Slope $= -2$, y-intercept $= 4$.

25. **The best answer is B.** Since bounce height (b) is directly proportional to drop height, the ratio of bounce-to-drop will stay constant: $50/80 = b/120$. Solving by cross-multiplying: $b = 75$ cm.

26. **The best answer is J.** The perimeter includes 4 sides of length l and 2 sides of length h: $P = 4l + 2h$.

27. **The best answer is D.** Factors of 27 are 1, 3, 9, and 27. Factors of 54 are 1, 2, 3, 6, 9, 18, 27, and 54. The factors of 243 are 1, 3, 9, 27, 81, and 243. The greatest factor that is common to all numbers is 27.

28. **The best answer is K.** The correct function must satisfy the point $(0, 8)$. This eliminates choice F. Choice J is the function of a line and not a quadratic and must be eliminated. When $x = -2$, the correct function must give zero for y. Choice K is the only choice left.

29. **The best answer is A.** Squaring both sides, $5x - 1 = 36i^2$.

Substituting -1 for i^2 gives:

$$5x - 1 = -36$$
$$x = -7$$

30. **The best answer is F.** The area of a trapezoid is found by multiplying the average of the parallel bases (13 inches) by the height, h:

$$13h = 78$$
$$h = 78/13 = 6 \text{ in.}$$

31. **The best answer is D.** There are two facts (identities) of trigonometry needed to simplify this expression:

$$\sin^2 x + \cos^2 x = 1 \text{ and } \frac{\sin x}{\cos x} = \tan x.$$

$$\frac{2\sin x}{-\cos x} + 3\sin^2 x + 3\cos^2 x = -2\left(\frac{\sin x}{\cos x}\right) + 3(\sin^2 x + \cos^2 x)$$
$$= -2\tan x + 3(1) = 3 - 2\tan x$$

32. **The best answer is G.** The standard equation of a circle is $(x - a)^2 + (y - b)^2 = r^2$ where a is the x-coordinate of the center, b is the y-coordinate of the center, and r is the radius. The only equation that centers the circle at $(-3, 6)$ is choice G. Additional note: Point $(-3, 9)$ is 3 units away from the center, and this corresponds with the radius, thus $r^2 = 9$.

33. **The best answer is B.** Fact: $\sin(0) = 0$ and $\cos(0) = 1$. $(0, 3)$ is a point on the graph, and function B is the only one that satisfies this point.

34. **The best answer is F.**

$$\left(x^3\right)^{\frac{2}{3}} = x^{3 \cdot \frac{2}{3}} = x^2$$
$$x^2 - 2x = 3$$
$$x^2 - 2x - 3 = 0$$
$$(x - 3)(x + 1) = 0$$
$$x = 3, x = -1$$

35. **The best answer is B.** Examine the difference between each adjacent number in the series:

$$50 - 40 = 10$$
$$40 - 31 = 9$$
$$31 - 23 = 8$$
$$23 - 16 = 7$$
$$16 - x = 6$$
$$x = 10$$

36. **The best answer is H.** The line parallel with line AB must have the same slope as line AB. The line rises 2 units and goes over 3 units from point A to point B, so the slope is 2/3. So answers F and H are the only options. Point C at $(6, 2)$ satisfies $y = (2/3)x - 2$.

37. **The best answer is C.** The angles in quadrilateral EBCD must add up to 360°, so angle EBC $= 360 - 53 - 90 - 90 = 127°$.

38. **The best answer is J.**

$$h(4) = 4^{\frac{1}{2}} + 4^2 = 18$$
$$g(h(4)) = g(18) = 4(18) - 3 = 69$$

39. **The best answer is D.** For a circle, area $=$ pi $\times r^2$. The curve in choice D shows the parabola that represents this function.

40. **The best answer is H.** Since each side (s) is congruent in a cube and the volume is $s^3 = 27$, $s = 3$. Diagonal AG is the hypotenuse of right triangle AGB.

$$BG = 3$$
$$AB = \sqrt{3^2 + 3^2} = 3\sqrt{2}$$

Using the Pythagorean Theorem, AG $= \sqrt{(3\sqrt{2})^2 + 3^2} = 5.2$.

41. **The best answer is A.** The following functions predict the Lexy's position (L) and Zach's position (Z) verses time (t):

$$L = 65t + 3$$
$$Z = 60t + 18$$

Set the functions equal to solve for the time that they reach the same position:

$$65t + 3 = 60t + 18$$
$$5t = 15$$
$$t = 15/5 = 3 \text{ hours}$$

Insert these numbers into both position functions to check the answer:

$$L = 65(3) + 3 = 198 \text{ miles}$$
$$Z = 60t + 18 = 198 \text{ miles}$$

42. **The best answer is G.** Multiplying by 10^{-4} moves the decimal four positions to the left.

43. **The best answer is D.** The order of operations is PEMDAS (parentheses, exponents, multiplication, division, addition, and subtraction).

$$2 + 3 \times 6 - (10 - 8)^2 = 2 + 3 \times 6 - (2)^2 = 2 + 3 \times 6 - 4 = 2 + 18 - 4 = 16$$

44. **The best answer is K.**

$$28 + 10x < 4 - 2x$$
$$12x < -24$$
$$x < -2$$

45. **The best answer is A.**

$$(-2)^2 + 1^2 + 6^2 = 41$$
$$4^3 = 4 \times 4 \times 4 = 64$$
$$64 - 41 = 23$$

46. **The best answer is J.** Let $n = \#$ of nickels and $d = \#$ of dimes.

$$0.05n + 0.10d = 2.95$$
$$n + d = 37$$

Solving these two equations simultaneously using your preferred method gives:

$$n = 15, d = 22$$

47. **The best answer is B.** The "!" after a number is called a "factorial," which is a command to take the given number times every integer less than it down to 1. When 56! is divided by 54!, all the numbers will cancel except 56 and 55:

$$(x - 500) = 55 \times 56$$
$$x - 500 = 3,080$$
$$x = 3,580$$

48. **The best answer is F.**

$$\ln (x + 2) + \ln (x + 4) = \ln (3x + 12)$$
$$\ln [(x + 2)(x + 4)] = \ln (3x + 12)$$
$$(x + 2)(x + 4) = (3x + 12)$$
$$x^2 + 6x + 8 = 3x + 12$$
$$x^2 + 3x + -4 = 0$$
$$(x + 4)(x - 1) = 0$$
$$x = -4, x = 1$$

49. **The best answer is A.**

$$f(2) = 3(2)^2 - 2 = 10$$
$$f(8) = 3(8)^2 - 2 = 190$$
$$10 < R < 190$$

50. **The best answer is G.** Recall that $i^2 = -1$. Choice G factors to $(x)(x^2 + 4) = x(x + 2i)(x - 2i)$.

51. **The best answer is D.** On the coordinate plane, quadrants 3 & 4 are in the range $\pi < x < 2\pi$. The cosine function is only negative in quadrant 3. The inverse cosine of $\frac{\sqrt{2}}{2}$ is $\frac{\pi}{4}$ and in the third quadrant, x is $\frac{5\pi}{4}$. Therefore, $x^2 = \left(\frac{5\pi}{4}\right)^2 = \frac{25\pi^2}{16}$.

52. **The best answer is K.** Statements F–J are all part of the proof. Statement K is patently false.

53. **The best answer is C.** The generic equation of an ellipse centered at (h, k) is:

$$\frac{(x - h)^2}{a^2} + \frac{(x - k)^2}{b^2} = 1$$

where $a = 2$ is the radius on the x-axis and $b = 1$ is the radius on the y-axis. Since the ellipse shown is centered at $(1, 2)$, the following equation applies:

$$\frac{(x - 1)^2}{4} + \frac{(x - 2)^2}{1} = 1$$

54. **The best answer is F.** The slope of the line given is $-3/2$, so the slope of a line perpendicular to that is $+2/3$. Going up 2 units and over 3 units from $(-2, -1)$ gives $[(-2 + 3), (-1 + 2)] = (1, 1)$.

55. **The best answer is E.** Focus on the small triangle at the bottom of the diagram. The angle on the bottom left of the triangle is congruent to x (alternate interior). The angle on the bottom right is congruent to y (vertical angles). Since all angles in the triangle add up to 180 degrees, the top angle in the triangle must measure $180 - x - y$. Angle z is supplementary to that top angle, so $z = 180 - (180 - x - y) = x + y$.

56. **The best answer is G.**

$$\frac{9(4)(27)}{18(4)^{-\frac{1}{2}}(27)^{\frac{1}{3}}} = \frac{9(4)(27)}{18\left(\frac{1}{2}\right)(3)} = 36$$

57. **The best answer is B.** $f(x + 2)$ shifts the function 2 units to the left. Adding 3 to that shifts $g(x)$ up by 3 units.

58. **The best answer is F.** Looking down the $+y$-axis, segment AB will make a circular disk as point B revolves around the y-axis. Thus the entire rectangle will form a right circular cylinder.

59. **The best answer is C.** Since $L = 2W$ can be written as $W = L/2$, the area can be found by taking $LW = L(L/2) = L^2/2$.

60. **The best answer is F.** Since distance = rate × time:

Time = distance/rate = $(3.24 \times 10^5 \text{ km})/(27,000 \text{ km/hr}) = 12$ hours

Reading Test Explanations

PASSAGE I

1. **The best answer is B.** When Mary first went into the gardens, her intention was to find "the garden which no one had been into for ten years." It wasn't until after she was in the gardens that she discovered the oddly shaped trees, the gardener, and the bird. She did not enter the garden expecting to find any of those things.

2. **The best answer is J.** Because Mary was described as wearing a "'quite contrary' expression," "always did what she wanted to do," and had a "sour little face," she is best described as being petulant or ill-tempered. Nowhere in the passage is she described as being stupid, lazy, or pleasant.

3. **The best answer is A.** This is the best answer because the passage states "It might be nicer in summer when things were green, but there was nothing pretty about it now."

4. **The best answer is G.** This is the best answer because the passage states that the gardener "did not seem at all pleased to see her." Answer F contradicts this statement. The gardener did not know she was coming, so he had no reason to expect that she would bring a shovel, or that she would come to the garden at all.

5. **The best answer is D.** This is the best answer because the passage states that Mary "always did what she wanted to do."

6. **The best answer is H.** The second paragraph contains the information that the garden had "a long wall, with ivy growing over it." The other three answers contain information found in the last paragraph.

7. **The best answer is C.** This is the best answer because the passage states "He looked startled when he saw Mary, and then touched his cap."

8. **The best answer is F.** This is the best answer because the passage states "Perhaps he lived in the mysterious garden and knew all about it." Nowhere in the passage does Mary wonder about going back to India or how long she will have to live in the big house. She also did not question the lack of affection in her life.

9. **The best answer is A.** This is the best answer because the first paragraph of the passage states that Mary found "a large pool with an old gray fountain in its midst." Although in the second paragraph she did find a garden where fruit was growing, there was no mention of what type of fruit. There was no maze nor rose bed mentioned anywhere in the passage.

10. **The best answer is G.** If answer F were correct, Mary would not have "hoped the door would not open because she wanted to be sure she had found the mysterious garden. . . ." Answer H is not the best answer because Mary "was not at all a timid child." Nowhere in the passage is Mary confused about all of the doors in the garden, rather she hoped to find the green door that would lead her to the hidden garden. Her sole purpose in entering the garden was to find "the garden which was shut up," so answer G is the best answer.

PASSAGE II

11. **The best answer is C.** This is the best answer because the fourth paragraph discusses the role sand had in preserving the Sphinx. The passage states "As the Sphinx became buried, it was shielded from the corrosive effects of wind-blown sand." Answer A is not correct because although the Sphinx is one of the existing wonders of the ancient world, it is not the only one. Answer B is not correct because when Bonaparte saw the Sphinx in 1798, the Sphinx was "buried up to its neck in sand." The Sphinx wasn't built until the third millennium BCE, so it didn't even exist in the second century BCE.

12. **The best answer is J.** This is the best answer because Horemakhet is the oldest known name for the Sphinx. Answers F and G are incorrect because the name came to Thutmose IV in a dream.

13. **The best answer is B.** The essay states that the Sphinx was built by workers who "may have been on a rotating schedule in a type of national service."

14. **The best answer is J.** This is the best answer because the paragraph states that "for as much as sand contributed to the gradual but steady deterioration on the monolith, it also created a protective covering." Answer F is not correct, because the Sphinx was buried in sand as far back as 1400 BCE. Answers G and H are not correct, because although sand did erode the Sphinx to an extent, the whole of the colossus still exists.

15. **The best answer is B.** The essay states that "the purpose of the Sphinx was to guard the entrance to the pyramid where he would eventually be buried after his death."

16. **The best answer is G.** This is the best answer because the essay states that "in order to commemorate the event, Thutmose had the tale engraved on a slab of pink granite called the Dream Stela. . . ."

17. **The best answer is A.** This is the best answer because the essay states that sand "quickly filled in the excavated areas." Even if there had been more men, as suggested in answer B, the sand still would have filled back in as soon as it was dug out.

18. **The best answer is H.** The essay states that "because Egyptians did not record history, the original name has been lost to the ages."

19. **The best answer is A.** The first paragraph of the essay notes that traces of red, blue, and yellow paint "suggest it was once painted." Answer B is not the best answer, because the essay does not state that the Sphinx had a protective layer of any sort. Answer D is not correct, because the Sphinx has "a slab of pink granite called the Dream Stela and it was placed between the Sphinx's paws."

20. **The best answer is F.** This is the best answer because the essay states that when King Thutmose IV was a prince, he had a dream in which the Sphinx "told Thutmose that if he cleared away the sand surrounding it, he would become the king of Egypt." It wasn't until after Thutmose IV became king that the Sphinx-worshipping cult came about, which was not a condition of his becoming king, as suggested in answer G. Neither of the remaining two answers were what Horemakhet told Thutmose to do in order to become king.

PASSAGE III

21. **The best answer is A.** This is the best answer because an old castle is much more likely to be considered a "fanciful" or "mysterious" setting, as was typical of the romantic style. The other three answers would be typical of a "familiar and relatable" setting used in the realistic style.

22. **The best answer is G.** The essay states that "due in part to the impending American Civil War, literary works became focused on the mundane world." This perspective was a characteristic of the realistic style. The other three answers are events that influenced the romantic period.

23. **The best answer is D.** Although the Civil War was divisive and disruptive and happened long ago, the Civil War had not yet happened when "realism became a literary convention starting around 1860."

24. **The best answer is H.** This is the best answer because answer J describes the realistic style of writing. Answers F and G combine elements of both the romantic and realistic styles.

25. **The best answer is C.** This is the best answer because the essay states that "realism sought to celebrate the lives led by regular people." The other three answers describe how life was portrayed in the romantic style.

26. **The best answer is F.** This is the best answer because the essay states that "people became more interested in reading about the world around them in order to better understand the societal changes that were taking place." None of the other answers are supported by material in the essay.

27. **The best answer is A.** A riverboat captain would have been considered an everyday figure in the lives of ordinary people during the time in which the realistic style flourished. The characters in the other three answers would have typically been used by writers in the romantic style.

28. **The best answer is G.** This is the best answer because traits of the romantic period included exaggeration and flowery language, which the answer describes. Answers F, H, and J describe traits found in the realist style of writing.

29. **The best answer is D.** The essay states that the other three authors wrote in the romantic style.

30. **The best answer is G.** This is the best answer because the remaining answers have the words *romanticism* and *realism* reversed.

PASSAGE IV

31. **The best answer is B.** The passage states that "when Eris was discovered in 2003, it triggered the debate about what should be considered a planet." There was no information in the essay that suggests the IAU met on an annual basis, so answer A is not supported. Pluto was not considered a plutoid until after Eris was discovered, as suggested in answer C. Astrophysicist Neil DeGrasse Tyson did not make his statement about how the word *planet* had "lost all scientific value" until five years after the discovery of Eris, as suggested by answer D.

32. **The best answer is F.** This is the only statement supported by information given in the seventh paragraph.

33. **The best answer is C.** The passage states "that if Pluto were a planet, then that would mean that its moon, Charon, would also have to be considered a planet and so would the giant asteroid Ceres" along with Eris.

34. **The best answer is H.** This is the best answer because it is the only one supported by material in the passage. The passage did not mention any debate concerning the solar system, as suggested by answer F. Answer G is also not correct, because the objects being debated as to whether or not they are planets exist farther out in space than Neptune. The definition of a plutoid was not being debated by scientists in this passage, as suggested by answer J.

35. **The best answer is D.** The passages states that "in 2006, the IAU declared that Pluto was a dwarf planet." Answer A is not correct because it wasn't until later, in 2008, that the IAU decided that Pluto was instead a plutoid. Answers B and C are not correct, because the IAU never considered Pluto to be either of the choices presented.

36. **The best answer is G.** The passage states that "Nix and Hydra are Pluto's other two moons," along with Charon. The paragraph makes no mention of Nix and Hydra being considered anything but moons, as suggested by answer F. Answer H is not correct, because the paragraph states that Ceres "is the largest object found so far in the asteroid belt." The paragraph does not state whether or not Nix and Hydra are larger than Charon, as answer J suggests.

37. **The best answer is C.** This is the best answer because only scientists who think Pluto should be a planet support the model that would include Pluto and its moon Charon as a double planet.

38. **The best answer is J.** In the sixth paragraph, passage B states that "some space scientists reject the authority of the IAU to make such decisions," regarding the definition of what constitutes a planet.

39. **The best answer is A.** This is the best answer because scientists on both side of the debate about whether or not Pluto is a planet agree that it meets these two criteria.

40. **The best answer is G.** This is the best answer because some space scientists, such as Mark Sykes, believe that "if a nonstellar object is massive enough to be round and orbits a star, it ought to be a planet." Answer F is not correct, because there was no information in either passage to suggest that there was any disagreement among scientists regarding Neptune's status as a planet. Answer H is not correct, because none of the scientists in either passage wanted to use a new word for *planet*. Answer J is not correct, because there is no information in the passage to suggest that space scientists had issues with the concept of plutoids.

Science Reasoning Test Explanations

1. **The best answer is B.** Notice how the parallel circuits all have discharge times less than the series circuits.

2. **The best answer is J.** All the pairs of trials were within 0.3 seconds of each other, and 22.8 seconds is significantly off from the trials of 24.9 and 24.6 seconds. Many circuits were tested throughout the different trials of experiment, so the most reasonable explanation is that the batteries were not charging the circuit as well, resulting in smaller discharge times.

3. **The best answer is B.** Compared to the basic circuit, 2 parallel resistors reduces the discharge time by one-half and 3 resistors by one-third. So the discharge time for 4 resistors should be approximately one-quarter of 24.7 seconds, or 6.2 seconds.

4. **The best answer is F.** Notice how the discharge time increases about 2.5 seconds each time a bulb is added.

5. **The best answer is D.** Since there was still a voltage on the capacitor, it must not have been completely discharged. Apparently, there is still current flowing even when the eye can't detect the light. To minimize this error, the students could have waited until the voltmeter reading approached zero volts.

6. **The best answer is H.** The discharge time would be 1/24th of the time for the simple series circuit. This would only be about one second of time and very difficult to measure precisely.

7. **The best answer is A.** According to Table 2, mayflies are very sensitive to pollution. A lack of mayflies points to the possibility of pollution in the stream.

8. **The best answer is F.** Riffle beetles are sensitive to pollution according to Table 2, so their absence indicates possible presence of pollution.

9. **The best answer is B.** Water Quality = Riffle Score × Count + Crayfish Score × Count + Damselflies Score × Count + Snail Score × Count = 17. According to Table 3, this is good.

10. **The best answer is J.** According to Figure 1, sample site A dips below the 7 mg/L DO mark around the year 2007.

11. **The best answer is B.** Sample Site B stays above the 7 mg/L DO mark for all the years tested, thus remaining in the normal range.

12. **The best answer is B.** Notice that for all three objects tested, the coefficient of friction decreases as the velocity increases.

13. **The best answer is J.** All the coefficients are close for large weights, but the small weight had a significantly larger coefficient.

14. **The best answer is C.** According to Figure 1, a weight of 300 N of rubber object A has a coefficient of 0.076. Table 1 indicates that a coefficient of 0.076 for object A occurs at a speed just under 12 m/s.

15. **The best answer is H.** According to Table 1, high velocities have the least coefficients. According to Figure 1, the heavier objects also have the least coefficients.

16. **The best answer is A.** The smaller coefficients for the heavier objects indicate that the ice has less friction and thus is slipperier, so it makes sense that the heavier objects might melt the ice.

17. **The best answer is H.** Object C has the greatest friction coefficients, and thus more frictional force to stop the car.

18. **The best answer is A.** Even scientist A, in the last paragraph, states that some individuals are sensitive to MSG.

19. **The best answer is G.** In the last sentence, scientist B indicates a link between obesity and MSG. Option G provides evidence to this fact.

20. **The best answer is C.** Scientist A's first statement in the viewpoint is completely consistent with option C. Scientist B cites studies that indicated MSG is NOT safe.

21. **The best answer is G.** Members of the food industry could be biased because they may produce foods with MSG flavoring and not have another chemical that they can economically substitute for it.

22. **The best answer is B.** Increased appetite in the lab rats supports scientist B's obesity argument.

23. **The best answer is B.** Option D may be in the range of the predicted answer, but the units are incorrect. Seeing the trend for ball A in the data table for distance, 89.5 cm is the closest to the trend.

24. **The best answer is J.** All three balls have approximately the same velocities when they reach edge of the table, so it makes sense that they will all reach the table at nearly the same time.

25. **The best answer is C.** Balls A, B, and C all have approximately the same velocities when they reach the edge of the table.

26. **The best answer is G.** Since the velocities through the photogate are calculated by taking the ball diameter divided by time, the smaller diameter would have systematically reduced all the velocity calculations. *Note: The measured times would be the same because the actual ball was not altered, and the distance traveled would also be the same.*

27. **The best answer is B.** The distance traveled is independent of mass, so the answer should be consistent with all the other 15-cm data points, thus 77.4 cm is the best answer.

28. **The best answer is F.** The photogate measures only the velocity and should not affect the distance that the ball travels.

29. **The best answer is F.** A control group shows what happens with no intervention, which is normal sleep.

30. **The best answer is B.** The passage states, "Cortisol is released in a diurnal pattern, with levels peaking in the morning shortly after awakening and decreasing gradually throughout the day."

31. **The best answer is G.** By Day 2 of sleep deprivation (both partial and full), the cortisol levels were significantly higher than the control group with normal sleep, thus showing a positive correlation between sleep deprivation and cortisol levels.

32. **The best answer is A.** Compared with cortisol values for males after the quiet period (0.18 units), the Day 2 and Day 10 values after yoga were approximately half as much (0.10 and 0.09 units).

33. **The best answer is J.** A minimum amount of saliva is probably needed for a valid test and will be part of the procedure, but the total amount does not

need to be carefully controlled, since the concentration of cortisol is measured in micrograms per milliliter.

34. **The best answer is D.** Clearly, the cortisol levels increased with sleep deprivation according to the data in Table 1.

35. **The best answer is F.** Trials 1–4 independently changed the concentration of hydrogen peroxide while holding the concentration of iodine ions constant, and the time for color change varied by more than 60 seconds, the largest variation in the table.

36. **The best answer is D.** Trial 1 and trial 9 have every variable the same except for pH, and the passage states, "the amount of hydronium ion in each trial is traditionally measured in pH."

37. **The best answer is G.** Notice that the amount of distilled water keeps the total volume of the fluids constant and is not part of either reaction.

38. **The best answer is A.** Trial 1 has the shortest time for color change, and reaction rate is defined as, "the amount of chemical created during a reaction divided by the amount of time it takes to create that chemical."

39. **The best answer is J.** The volume of hydrogen peroxide in trial 2 is double that of trial 4, with the amount of iodide ions remaining controlled. Trial 2's time (18.6 seconds) is approximately one-fourth trial 4's time (74.8).

40. **The best answer is C.** 1×10^{-4} is twice the amount of moles compared with 5×10^{-5}. With twice the amount of thiosulfate, it will take twice the amount of time for the color change to occur.